Lecture Notes in Computer Science 9955

Commenced Publication in 1973
Founding and Former Series Editors:
Gerhard Goos, Juris Hartmanis, and Jan van Leeuwen

More information about this series at http://www.springer.com/series/7410

Jiageng Chen · Vincenzo Piuri
Chunhua Su · Moti Yung (Eds.)

Network and System Security

10th International Conference, NSS 2016
Taipei, Taiwan, September 28–30, 2016
Proceedings

 Springer

Editors
Jiageng Chen
Central China Normal University
Wuhan
China

Chunhua Su
Osaka University
Osaka
Japan

Vincenzo Piuri
Università degli Studi di Milano
Crema (CR)
Italy

Moti Yung
Columbia University
New York, NY
USA

ISSN 0302-9743   ISSN 1611-3349 (electronic)
Lecture Notes in Computer Science
ISBN 978-3-319-46297-4   ISBN 978-3-319-46298-1 (eBook)
DOI 10.1007/978-3-319-46298-1

Library of Congress Control Number: 2016950742

LNCS Sublibrary: SL4 – Security and Cryptology

Printed on acid-free paper

This Springer imprint is published by Springer Nature
The registered company is Springer International Publishing AG
The registered company address is: Gewerbestrasse 11, 6330 Cham, Switzerland

Preface

This volume contains the papers presented at NSS 2016: The 10th International Conference on Network and System Security held during September 28–30, 2016, in Taipei, Taiwan. NSS 2016 was organized and supported by the Chinese Cryptology and Information Security Association (CCISA), Taiwan. Since its inauguration in 2007, NSS has become a highly successful series of annual international gatherings, for academic and industrial researchers and practitioners to exchange ideas in the area of network and system security. Previous editions of NSS were held in: New York, USA (2015); Xi'an, China (2014); Madrid, Spain (2013); Wu Yi Shan, China (2012); Milan, Italy (2011); Melbourne, Australia; (2010); Gold Coast, Australia (2009); Shanghai, China (2008); and Dalian, China (2007).

The conference received 105 submissions. Each submission was carefully reviewed by at least three committee members. The Program Committee decided to accept 31 full papers and four short papers. We would like to thank all authors who submitted their papers to NSS 2016, and the conference attendees for their interest and support, which made the conference possible. We further thank the Organizing Committee for their time and efforts; their support allowed us to focus on the paper selection process. We thank the Program Committee members and the external reviewers for their hard work in reviewing the submissions; the conference would not have been possible without their expert reviews.

We also thank the invited speakers for enriching the program with their presentations. We thank Prof. Yang Xiang, Chair of the NSS Steering Committee, for his advice throughout the conference preparation process. We also thank Prof. Yeh Kuo-Hui for the contributions to the local arrangements, which helped make this conference happen in Taipei. Last but not least, we thank EasyChair for making the entire process of the conference convenient.

We hope you find these proceedings educational and enjoyable!

September 2016

Jiageng Chen
Vincenzo Piuri
Chunhua Su
Moti Yung

Organization

Honorary Chairs

D.J. Guan	National Sun Yat-sen University, Taiwan
Yen-Nun Huang	Academia Sinica, Taiwan
Der-Tsai Lee	Academia Sinica, Taiwan

General Co-chairs

Chun-I Fan	National Sun Yat-sen University, Taiwan
Nai-Wei Lo	National Taiwan University of Science and Technology, Taiwan
Shiuhpyng (Winston) Shieh	National Chiao Tung University, Taiwan
Tzong-Chen Wu	National Taiwan University of Science and Technology, Taiwan

Program Co-chairs

Jiageng Chen	Central China Normal University, China
Vincenzo Piuri	University of Milan, Italy
Chunhua Su	Osaka University, Japan
Moti Yung	Columbia University, USA

Executive Co-chairs

Chen-Mou (Doug) Cheng	National Taiwan University, Taiwan
Wen-Chung Kuo	National Yunlin University of Science and Technology, Taiwan
Kuo-Hui Yeh	National Dong Hwa University, Taiwan

Publicity Co-chairs

Brij Gupta	National Institute of Technology, Kurukshetra, India
William Liu	Auckland University of Technology, New Zealand
Al-Sakib Khan Pathan	Southeast University, Bangladesh
Yu Wang	Deakin University, Australia

Program Committee

Joonsang Baek	Khalifa University of Science, Technology and Research, UAE
Rida Bazzi	Arizona State University, USA
Alex Biryukov	University of Luxembourg, Luxembourg
Pino Caballero-Gil	DEIOC, University of La Laguna, Spain
Marco Casassa-Mont	Hewlett Packard Labs, UK
David Chadwick	University of Kent, UK
Chia-Mei Chen	National Sun Yat-sen University, Taiwan
Jiageng Chen	Central China Normal University, China
Songqing Chen	George Mason University, USA
Chen-Mou Cheng	National Taiwan University, Taiwan
Hung-Yu Chien	National Chi Nan University, Taiwan
Kim-Kwang Raymond Choo	University of South Australia, Australia
Mauro Conti	University of Padua, Italy
He Debiao	Wuhan University, China
Roberto Di Pietro	Bell Labs, Italy
Ruggero Donida Labati	Università degli Studi di Milano, Italy
Jesús Díaz-Verdejo	University of Granada, Spain
Keita Emura	National Institute of Information and Communications Technology, Japan
José M. Fernandez	Ecole Polytechnique de Montreal, Canada
Alban Gabillon	University of Polynésie Française, France
Joaquin Garcia-Alfaro	Telecom SudParis, France
Matt Henricksen	Institute for Infocomm Research, Singapore
Shoichi Hirose	University of Fukui, Japan
Chien-Lung Hsu	Chang Gung University, Taiwan
Ren-Junn Huang	Tamkang University, Taiwan
Xinyi Huang	Fujian Normal University, China
James Joshi	University of Pittsburgh, USA
Wen-Shenq Juang	National Kaohsiung First University of Science and Technology, Taiwan
Shinsaku Kiyomoto	KDDI R&D Laboratories Inc., Japan
Ram Krishnan	University of Texas at San Antonio, USA
Chin-Laung Lei	National Taiwan University, Taiwan
Kaitai Liang	Aalto University, Finland
Joseph Liu	Monash University, Australia
Zhe Liu	University of Waterloo, Canada
Giovanni Livraga	Università degli Studi di Milano, Italy
Javier Lopez	University of Malaga, Spain
Di Ma	University of Michigan-Dearborn, USA
Chris Mitchell	Royal Holloway, University of London, UK
Jose Morales	Carnegie Mellon University – CERT, USA
Yi Mu	University of Wollongong, Australia

Kazumasa Omote	JAIST, Japan
Mathias Payer	Purdue University, USA
Günther Pernul	The University of Regensburg, Germany
Vincenzo Piuri	University of Milan, Italy
Michalis Polychronakis	Stony Brook University, USA
Indrajit Ray	Colorado State University, USA
Chester Rebeiro	IIT Madras, India
Na Ruan	Shanghai Jiaotong University, China
Sushmita Ruj	Indian Statistical Institute, India
Kouichi Sakurai	Kyushu University, Japan
Masakazu Soshi	Hiroshima City University, Japan
Anna Squicciarini	The Pennsylvania State University, USA
Chunhua Su	Osaka University, Japan
Hung-Min Sun	National Tsing Hua University, Taiwan
Shamik Sural	IIT, Kharagpur, India
Nils Ole Tippenhauer	Singapore University of Technology and Design, Singapore
Kuo-Yu Tsai	Chinese Culture University, Taiwan
Yuh-Min Tseng	National Changhua University of Education, Taiwan
Jaideep Vaidya	Rutgers University, USA
Chih-Hung Wang	National Chiayi University, Taiwan
Huaxiong Wang	Nanyang Technological University, Singapore
Zhe Xia	Wuhan University of Technology, China
Shouhuai Xu	University of Texas at San Antonio, USA
Toshihiro Yamauchi	Okayama University, Japan
Wun-She Yap	Universiti Tunku Abdul Rahman, Malaysia
Kuo-Hui Yeh	National Dong Hwa University, Taiwan
Moti Yung	Columbia University, USA
Haibo Zhang	University of Otago, New Zealand
Mingwu Zhang	Hubei University of Technology, China
Zonghua Zhang	Institute TELECOM/TELECOM Lille, France

Additional Reviewers

Al Khalil, Firas	Larangeira, Mario	Ueshige, Yoshifumi
Ben Jaballah, Wafa	Le Corre, Yann	Velichkov, Vesselin
Biryukov, Maria	Matsumoto, Shinichi	Wang, Janice
Boehm, Fabian	Nieto, Ana	Wang, Yilei
Chi, Cheng	Richthammer, Christian	Weber, Michael
Gochhayat, Sarada Prasad	Signorini, Matteo	Yong, Xie
Hao, Wang	Spolaor, Riccardo	Zhang, Yubo
Isawa, Ryoichi	Su, Ming	Zhao, Chuan
Jia, Xiaoying	Tran, Thao	Zhao, Fangming
Kunz, Michael	Tsuda, Yu	Zhu, Youwen
Lal, Chhagan	Udovenko, Aleksei	

Contents

Digital Signature

Privacy-Preserving Technologies

Network Security and Forensic

Searchable Encryption

Security Policy and Access Control

Security Protocols

Symmetric Key Cryptography

System Security

Web Security

Data Mining for Security Application (Short Paper)

Provable Security (Short Paper)

Security Protocol (Short Paper)

Invited Paper

While Mobile Encounters with Clouds

Man Ho Au[1], Kaitai Liang[2]([⊠]), Joseph K. Liu[3], and Rongxing Lu[4]

[1] Department of Computing, Hong Kong Polytechnic University,
Kowloon, Hong Kong
csallen@comp.polyu.edu.hk
[2] Department of Computer Science, Aalto University, Espoo, Finland
kaitai.liang@aalto.fi
[3] Faculty of Information Technology, Monash University, Melbourne, Australia
joseph.liu@monash.edu
[4] Faculty of Computer Science, University of New Brunswick,
Fredericton, NB, Canada
rlu1@unb.ca

Abstract. To date the considerable computation and storage power of clouds that have attracted great attention from mobile users and mobile service providers over the past few years. The convergence of mobile devices and clouds that leads to a brand new era of could-based mobile applications. It brings long-listed advantages for mobile users to get rid of the constraints of mobile devices (including limited mobile memory, data processing ability and battery). However, mobile clouds yield new security and privacy risks in open network setting. This survey paper attempts to introduce security risks on mobile clouds in the view point of applied cryptography.

1 Background

The report given by comScore [28] shows that the number of increasing usage of mobile devices (up to 1.9 billions) exceeds that of desktop (with nearly 1.7 billions) in 2015. Besides, the average time people spend on mobile apps. is increased by 21 % over the last year (2014) conducted by a Go-Globe survey [11]. Both data interpret a strong signal that an increasing number of people tend to spend more time in using their mobile devices compared to other unportable electronic devices. The massive usage of mobile devices lights up the booming of all kinds of mobile network applications, which can be available and downloaded from either Apple's iTunes or Google Play Store.

Although mobile devices connected to Internet can enjoy many network services and applications much like desktop, they, to a large extent, cannot fully provide excellent user experiences for their clients because of their "natural-born" constraints including limited memory, processing power and battery life. To help mobile devices to move beyond the restrictions, mobile research and industrial communities invent a new framework, *mobile cloud*, which is the convergence of mobile devices and clouds, such that device users are allowed to offload heavy

© Springer International Publishing AG 2016
J. Chen et al. (Eds.): NSS 2016, LNCS 9955, pp. 3–18, 2016.
DOI: 10.1007/978-3-319-46298-1_1

storage and computational cost to clouds to reduce the local resource and energy consumption.

There are long-list advantages of leveraging clouds in storage and computation with mobile devices. One of them is that mobile users can store and gain access to more data than the mobile is capable of holding. For instance, a tourist with mobile device does not need to spend lots of bandwidth in downloading a full local map with hotel, restaurant, sightseeing information, but simply reporting his location to cloud, with help of cloud-based mobile Global Positioning System (GPS) navigation. Take social media networking app as another example. While using Tinder (https://www.gotinder.com) to find friends around us, it is unnecessary for us to download all system users' information locally, but just upload our current locations. The outsource of mobile contents (e.g. personal photos) from local to clouds prevents information leakage incurred by mobile stolen or lost incidences. By using considerable computational power of clouds, mobile devices with limited computation resource can enable users to play 3D games, to run mobile commercial systems, and even to participate into mobile-learning platforms (e.g. Litmos (https://www.litmos.com)).

Lifting weight from mobile devices, mobile clouds, at the same time, yield security and privacy challenges. There are various challenges incurred by usage of mobile clouds, e.g., identity management and standardization. As we mention previously, a mobile device user can upload his/her personal photos to a cloud, which is trusted by the user. However, this may endanger the privacy of the user while the cloud server is intruded by malicious hackers. Even in more trustworthy commercial bank systems, the records of customers may be suffered from malicious leak as well. For example, the leaking iCould celebrity picture [29] and Barclays bank client records leak incidence [4] are recent wake-up call for cloud storage service.

In this survey, we stand at some practical behaviors of mobile device users to discuss the security risks in mobile clouds. Specifically, we mainly focus on the following clients' behaviors: identity authentication before connection, data encryption before uploading, data integrity check after data uploading, remote data search, share and computation.

2   Mobile Cloud - Bring Benefit to Us

2.1   For Mobile Users

In addition to traditional services (e.g. phone call), mobile service providers cloud can promote new and more convenience offers to their clients by using mobile cloud. Mobile learning is a novel merging service in which clients are allowed to take classes, finish homework and join real-time seminar via mobile devices. On-line learners can search what they want to learn in mobile cloud, and download unlimited but easy accessible resources from courses, on-line universities', and even public libraries.

Clinics, hospitals and heal care centers can be benefited from another mobile cloud service, mobile-health care. Getting rid of tedious paper works and wasting time in long queue waiting, patients can use mobile devices for doctor appointment booking. Moreover, new health sensor techniques can be employed into mobile devices, such that the health condition of patients can be immediately updated to hospital for better medical treatment track.

More and more Internet users prefer to launch commercial activities in their smart-phones. A blooming period for mobile commercial ear is approaching. Due to being equipped with powerful computational resources, mobile cloud is strong enough to support various commercial actions, such as money transfer, and bank payment.

Mobile cloud game service is also another potential commercial market. There are many new and popular game apps. promoted by Apple Store every year. Nevertheless, the visual/sound effect and complex game design of those apps. seriously consume smart-phone's battery and memory. With help of mobile cloud, the game engine and effect/upgrade packages can be completely offloaded to cloud and meanwhile, the cloud can be used to run large computational cost algorithms (e.g. graphic rendering).

Last but not least, mobile cloud also provides large-scale stream media store, large volume of social network data share, and location-based service for smart-phone users. Considerable storage space, unlimited computational power, and convenient interface, these extremely appealing advantages of mobile cloud, that light up a bright prospective for diverse mobile services.

2.2 For Academic Communities, Industries and Authorities

Mobile cloud does encourage visible and invisible opportunities for other entities including academic researchers, industries and authorities. The academic communities may be inspired to invent more lightweight and secure protocols/systems to lessen the workload of device users to mobile cloud. With the assistance of mobile cloud, industries and companies are able to provide more powerful data computing, more efficient data processing, and more considerable storage services for their clients, e.g., Portable Genomics (http://www.portablegenomics.com/#!home) offers convenient genome data analysis services to smart-phone users. The authorities, such as local transportation center, may leverage mobile cloud to monitor public events, e.g. mobile data traffic forecast.

Furthermore, the quick expansion of mobile cloud yields an opportunity of collaboration among mobile device users, mobile service providers, and local authorities. The collaboration of the three parties, definitely, contributes more correct, accurate and trustworthy outcomes compared to the only-one-side-working mode. Moreover, mobile device users need to worry about battery, memory and computation limitation no more with help of service provider/cloud server. For example, mobile data encryption and decryption could be partially offloaded to a cloud server, so that the users only are required a small piece of computation, and the rest of the computation is transfered to the server. The collaboration, however, should ensure that even the service provider colludes with some hackers, they cannot access to the users' data. Working together may be an effective way to tackle efficiency, privacy and security problems.

3 Mobile Cloud - Its Own Security Risks

Standing at the viewpoint of applied cryptography by the side of mobile cloud users, this paper investigates some security risks based on the following frequently users operations: (1) (login) authentication between client and mobile clouds; (2) outsource data from local mobile device to remote clouds, and data integrity check; (3) search and share client's remote data with others, and remote data computation. Meanwhile, the paper will show that existing tools do not fully satisfy the security requirements for mobile cloud users.

3.1 Authentication for Mobile Clients

While talking about authentication, we usually consider the single way of authentication, i.e. "client to cloud authentication mode" where the cloud server will only allows valid clients to access the cloud system if the clients pass the corresponding authentication check. This type of "proof of identity" is extremely necessary upon protecting cloud clients data privacy.

To date, there are various mobile-to-cloud authentication methods that have been proposed. They can be categorized into three branches: knowledge-based, possession-based and biometric-based authentications. Individually leveraging one of the approaches that may yield security concern. Using username and password for (knowledge-based) authentication [2] that is one of most convenience authentication mechanisms. Some of the existing systems are already built in the context of mobile devices. For example, Acar et al. [2] introduced a single password authentication in which a mobile device must be trusted. Specifically, the hash value $Hash(pw)$ of a user's password pw is used as a key to encrypt a randomly string K generated by a mobile user (i.e. $CT = Encrypt(Hash(pw), K)$), and the encryption is further stored in the mobile device; meanwhile, the user's ID and the string K are delivered to a cloud server. When trying to login the server, the user sends its ID to the server who returns a challenge $chal$. The user then taps password pw into the mobile, such that the mobile can recover $K = Decrypt(Hash(pw), CT)$ and compute a $MAC(K, chal)$ to the server. With knowledge of K and $chal$, the server can check the validity of the MAC value. To secure passwords, mobile clients usually use a long and complex enough combination, (e.g. using image as password [20]), or password manager apps. (e.g. SafeInCloud - https://www.safe-in-cloud.com/) to manage passwords.

Possession-based approach enables mobile client to leverage something his hold to execute identity authentication. Thus, we may choose to use secure USB token, one-time password [33], or embed a public key infrastructure (e.g. [35]) into mobile device, to strengthen the security of authentication. But this approach requires more computational cost and energy consumption, for example, key management could be a problem for mobile devices upon usage of public key infrastructure. Furthermore, the possessed device might be stolen by adversary or lost by careless owner, such that they may be misused.

Due to advance mobile technology, the biometric authentication [7] can be used to provide a unique and portable way for client identification via making use of client's bio-characteristics, such as voice, face, iris and fingerprint [31]. How to secretly store and process personal bio-information in authentication is a major privacy concern. Since one's biometric information is unique, if adversary obtains the information by hacking into the client's mobile device, it will bring serious harm to personal privacy.

To achieve stronger authentication security, multi-factor authentication systems (e.g. [27]) have been introduced in the mobile cloud scenario. Usually, more than one factor are implemented into mobile device in advance. The device and a cloud server will also share some secret information, such as $Hash(pw)$ or random string K. The authentication phase will take 2–3 factors' information into the we call "challenge-and-respond" interaction (Fig. 1). The multi-factor mechanism strengthens the difficulty of attacking login authentication in the sense that malicious adversary has to compromised all factors to result in a successful attack. Because of its high security guarantee, many companies has employed multiple factors for clients authentication, e.g., SafeNet (http://www.safenet-inc.com/), Microsoft Azure (http://azure.microsoft.com/en-us/) and rackspace (http://www.rackspace.com/).

Fig. 1. Unidirectional mobile to cloud authentication structure

Table 1. Comparison among different types of authentication

Category	Security	Client to cloud	Cloud to client	Factor update/revoke	Authentication delegation
Password	weak	✓	✗	✗	✗
Possession	weak	✓	✗	✗	✗
Biometric	weak	✓	✗	✗	✗
Multi-factor	strong	✓	✗	✗	✗

Nonetheless, the "most secure look" multi-factor authentication still suffers from thorny challenges incurred by factor update and revocation, delegation in authentication, and bidirectional authentication (see Table 1). The update and revocation of factor is needed while the factor is compromised by attackers. How to effectively and efficiently detect the compromise factor and further renew the factor in both cloud and client sides is a formidable task. An identity verification delegation is very common in daily life. For example, an on-line eBay user is redirected to a third-party payment platform. Here, the first login cloud service provider should take responsibility for the second platform authentication, so that no privacy information will be "curiously" collected by the latter, e.g., the client's transaction history. The authentication delegation may also happen in client side in the sense that a client A requires another client B to login a cloud system to use the data/service on behalf of A. Some naive solutions, such as requesting the server to modify access control list for B, may work. But allowing the server to know the delegation between A and B may lead to high risk of commercial secret leak in some business settings. Therefore, a privacy-preserving client-side authentication delegation is desirable. Last but not least, a bidirectional authentication system should be considered (i.e. client $\leftrightarrow$ cloud) due to unpredictable security risks in an open network. The growing number fishing and fake cloud services have been taking serious influence in mobile cloud security. Mobile clients must need a way to verify a cloud service provider before authorizing it further operation to the device.

In addition to the previously introduced cloud-based authentication mechanisms, there are some interesting systems in the literature, such as behavior-based authentication [13], single sign on [12] and mobile trusted module [21]. These systems, however, cannot address the above challenges as well.

3.2   Data Secrecy and Integrity

The confidentiality and integrity of the data outsource and stored in mobile cloud should be put at the top of priority list. Encryption technology seems to be an appropriate option that can be used to protect the on-device (local) data and the outsourced data. Effective and efficient data protection and integrity check techniques can deliver sense of trust and safety to mobile cloud users.

Traditional Encryption. We first consider the case that mobile device users prefer to install a cryptographic system in their devices. The traditional cryptographic encryption is classified into two branches - symmetric encryption and asymmetric encryption. Advanced Encryption Standard (AES) [1] and Data Encryption Standard (DES) [26] are the standard examples of the former, while public key based encryption (e.g. [17]), identity-based encryption (e.g. [8]), attribute-based encryption (e.g. [18]) and functional encryption (e.g. [30]) are considered as the latter. Symmetric encryption and its contemporary have respective pros and cons.

Compared to symmetric encryption, asymmetric technique provides fine-grained data share ability, for example, an encryption can be intended for a group of users (e.g., broadcast encryption). For example, in RSA, a mobile user, say Alice, may choose two distinct prime numbers p and q, computes $n = pq$

and $\phi(n) = (p - 1)(q - 1)$, and choose an integer e so that $gcd(e, \phi(n)) = 1$. Alice further chooses a d so that $d = e^{-1} mod \ \phi(n)$, publishes n and e as public key, and keeps d secretly as secret key. Any system user knowing a user Alice's public key (n, e) that can encrypt an integer m $(0 \leq m < n, gcd(m, n) = 1)$ as $C = m^e \ mod \ n$ to Alice, such that Alice can use her secret key d to recover the m as $m = C^d \ mod \ n$, where $n = pq$, $1 < e < \phi(n)$, $gcd(e, \phi(n)) = 1$ and $d = e^{-1} mod \ \phi(n)$.

This fine-grained property, however, yields huge computation, communication and storage complexity as opposed to symmetric encryption. Even RSA, the most efficient public key encryption, cannot outperform symmetric encryption in power consumption, and encryption/decryption speed (the benchmark can be referred to Crypto++) (see Table 2 for the comparison. We note that the data in Table 2 is collected from Crypto++ (https://www.cryptopp.com/) whereby AES is 128 bits, and RSA is 2048 bits. For RSA 2048-bit encryption, 0.16 Milliseconds/Operation is given. We assume that one operation roughly proceeds 1024-bit data. Thus, the encryption complexity is around 7.63 MiB/s. Similarly, we have the decryption complexity of RSA is approximately 0.020 MiB/s.

If mobile users are only with single purpose - outsourcing their own data to mobile cloud, they may choose to employ symmetric encryption technology to encrypt the data before uploading to the cloud.

Table 2. Comparison among DES, AES and RSA

	Key size (bit)	Round	Running time (MiB/Second)	Power consumption	Hard/Software implementation
DES	56	16	32	Low	Better in hardware
AES	128, 192, 256	10, 12, 14	139	Low	Fast
RSA	≥1024	1	0.763 (Encryption)	High	Inefficient
			0.020 (Decryption)		

Symmetric encryption looks like a very promising solution to guarantee data security. Nevertheless, a direct and critical problem incurred by using symmetric encryption in mobile devices that is key management. Mobile users need to store encryption/decryption key locally, such that they can re-gain access to their data in the future. If the clients only upload a few files with small size (e.g. 1 MB) to clouds, key management problem may be ignored. But if they outsource a great amount of image, audio, and video data with huge size (e.g. 2 GB), the key management problem is extremely apparent as the devices suffer from large-size key file storage consumption. A naive solution for the problem is to encrypt the key file and next upload the encrypted file to mobile clouds. Nevertheless, again, the clients are still required to store some keys locally. Once the devices are intruded by mobile attackers, the keys are compromised as well.

Symmetr and Asymmetric Method. To reduce local key storage cost, a mobile user may combine symmetric encryption with asymmetric encryption. Suppose SYE is a symmetric encryption with key generation algorithm $SYE.KeyGen$, encryption algorithm $SYE.Enc$, and decryption algorithm $SYE.Dec$; PKE is a traditional public encryption, key generation algorithm $PKE.KeyGen$, encryption algorithm $PKE.Enc$, and decryption algorithm $PKE.Dec$. The user may first generate a symmetric key $SYE.key$ for a file f to be encrypted, runs $C = SYE.Enc(SYE.key, f)$ and further encrypts the key $SYE.key$ as $V = PKE.Enc(PKE.pk, SYE.key)$, and finally uploads C and V to a mobile cloud, where public/secret key pair $(PKE.pk, PKE.sk) \leftarrow PKE.KeyGen$. After that, the user can reuse the same $PKE.pk$ to encrypt all the symmetric keys, next upload the encryptions to the cloud. Here all ciphertexts and their corresponding encrypted keys are stored in the cloud. The user is only required to locally store the $PKE.sk$. This hybrid method is more efficiency than managing a bunch of symmetric keys in local.

Mobile Data Encryption Apps. Mobile encryption apps. bring hope for lessening key management problem. Many mobile devices in various platforms (e.g. Apple iOS, Android, and Windows) enable users to encrypt personal data in a hard-cored way. Some data encryption apps. (e.g. boxcryptor) also are invented to allow users to encrypt mobile contents before uploading. The encryption for the platforms/apps mostly depends on password/PIN mode whereby the password/PIN is used to encrypt encryption/decryption key. The encrypted key may be stored in remote clouds as well based on user preference. We note that even a mobile hard-cored security system tries to protect user data, a malicious attacker may be able to find a way to extract personal data from mobile device [15].

Nonetheless, both hybrid and apps. modes leave computation, communication and trust problems to us. No matter which apps or platforms we use, we have to encrypt data in local devices beforehand. This is a barrier to fully leverage the computational power of mobile clouds. Moreover, encrypting large file will occupy local computation resource, increase battery consumption and meanwhile, large encrypted block might jam the bandwidth. At last, a potential security risk pops up from a fact that we have to fully trust the apps/platforms we use. Once the trusted facilities are crushed by attackers, our data secrecy is smashed.

Bypassing the usage of heavy cryptographic encryption tools, some lightweight academic research works (e.g. [14]) have been proposed to achieve high efficiency for mobile data encryption. For instance, an efficient image sharing system for mobile devices is introduced in [14], in which 90 % of the image transmission cost is eliminated at the mobile user side.

However, the lightweight solutions are only the first step for mobile data outsourcing. Much like the aforementioned encryption approaches, these academic works fail to support remote data integrity check. Without integrity check, taking the image sharing system as an example, we cannot guarantee that the shared images are 100 % identical to the original ones.

Remote Data Integrity. The integrity check of outsourced data is desirable while data owner loses the physical control of data. In traditional scenario, the check is fulfilled by simply using message digest technique (e.g. MD5 [6]). Suppose there are a file f and its digest $D = H(f)$, a data owner is able to retrieve an encrypted file $Enc_{key}(f)$ from a mobile cloud, next to recover f with key, and finally to compare $H(f)$ with the digest D (stored in mobile) to check if f is modified/tempered. Nevertheless, this technique requires data owner to possess a copy of the data (or its digest) which is stored locally. This brings storage hindrance for mobile device users.

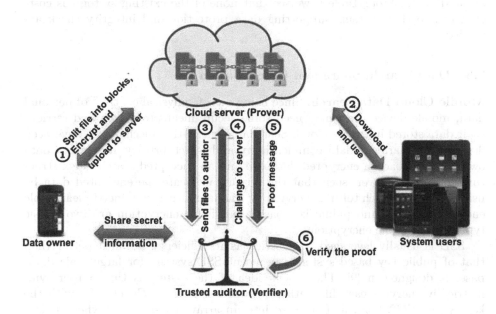

Fig. 2. Remote data auditing system with data protection

Remote data auditing offers data integrity check with help of a trusted (third party) auditor even the data is outsourced to clouds. It has three different models: provable data possession-based (PDP), proof of retrievability-based (POR) and proof of ownership-based (POW). A remote data auditing system with data protection is shown in Fig. 2. The PDP method only takes responsibility for preserving the integrity of outsourced data. Some existing PDP systems cannot guarantee data protection, e.g. [16], either are lack of data recovery functionality (i.e. the damaged data cannot be recovered) with linear complexity, e.g. [32] with $O(t)$ computation cost for client and the same complexity for communication, where t is the number of blocks to be changed; whilst the systems guarantee data recovery but leading to high (linearly) computation complexity for client (e.g. [5]). The recent POR solution, [10], is a type of cryptographic proof of knowledge, protecting privacy and providing data recovery strategy. But its computation and storage overheads (with $O(t log^2 n)$ computation complexity for client side, and $O(t^2 log^2 n)$ communication complexity) hinder its exploration into mobile applications, where n denotes the number of blocks of each file, respectively. Similarly, the latest POW method [34], single-instance data storage for removing data redundancy, yields huge computation complexity - $O(t)$ client computation and $O((m+t)n)$ communication cost, where m is the number of symbols of a block. Besides, it cannot recover correct data from broken ones.

On one hand, mobile device users are willing to offload computational complexity but also storage overhead to clouds. On the other hand, the users want to maintain the (periodically) data availability and integrity check for the "out of hand" data. From Table 3, we see that none of the existing systems is cost-effective, so that systems supporting data protection and integrity check are needed.

3.3 Data Search, Share and Computation

Mobile Cloud Data Search. Since being out of "physical control" of personal data, mobile device users may need some secure means to search and retrieve their data stored in mobile cloud. Searchable encryption mechanisms have been designed to guarantee data confidentiality and search privacy, in which a data owner will upload an encrypted database and an encrypted search index structure to a cloud server, such that the server can locate the encrypted data by using so-called search token generated by the data owner. Symmetric searchable encryption (SSE) and public key based searchable encryption are two classic types of searchable encryption.

SSE is usually leveraged in practice as its efficiency is much better than that of public key based systems. A recent SSE system, for large scale database, is designed in [9]. The crucial idea of the system is that a user symmetrically encrypts each file with a keyword w as $d \leftarrow Enc(K_2, I_i)$ with the key $K_2 \leftarrow F(K, 2||w)$, and stores d into an array A ($|A| = T$), where F is a pseudorandom function, and K is its seed. The user further partitions A into

Table 3. Summarization for data protection and integrity check

Systems	Data protection	Integrity check	High computation complexity for client	Data recovery
DES	✓	✗	✗	✗
AES	✓	✗	✗	✗
RSA	✓	✗	✗	✗
PDP	✓[a]	✓	✓	✗[b]
POR	✓	✓	✓	✓[c]
POW	✓	✓	✓	✗

[a] Some PDP cannot fully provide data protection.
[b] Most of PDP fail to provide data recovery.
[c] Most of POR support data recovery.

b blocks $(T' \leftarrow \lceil T/b \rceil)$ and computes the new indices as $l \leftarrow F(K_1, c)$ and $d' \leftarrow Enc(K_2, J_c)$, where $c \in [0, ..., T']$ and J_c is the c-th block of A, and $K_1 \leftarrow F(K, 1 \| w)$. The tuples (l, d') are stored in a list γ. For data search, given K_1 and K_2, the server first locates $d \leftarrow Get(\gamma, F(K_1, c))$ from γ, recovers $(i_1, ..., i_b) \leftarrow Dec(K_2, d)$, and finally computes $l_i \leftarrow Dec(K_2, A[i_j])$. The system is efficient as only pseudorandom function and symmetric encryption are used. However, users have to undertake high computation complexity for encrypting "the whole" database and its search index structure, but also to spend large communication cost in transferring the encrypted database and the index structure. This can be seen from the above details that a user has to build up a search index structure, and next compute each related file's encryption and pseudorandom value. Furthermore, the symmetric encryption and pseudorandom computation for l as well as encrypted files are linearly in the product of number of keyword and the related files. If there is a great amount of files in the database, say 10 GB, a mobile user has to take a long time to upload the encrypted database.

To offload the above burden to a third party, we have to assume that the party is fully trusted as a secret information of data search belonging to data owner will be shared with that party. This trusted assumption does not scale well in practice, since once the party is compromised by malicious attackers, the attackers can fully obtain the search ability. More recently, Li et al. [22] introduced a traffic and energy saving encrypted search system to remove the fully trust assumption and furthermore to protect data privacy. The system, unfortunately, cannot support expressive search query, such as range, and more complex formula query.

All aforementioned systems only provide "plain" text based search for mobile device users. In real-world applications, audio/video-based, and even bio-based search pattens are desirable. Designing privacy-preserving search with workload offloading (to cloud) without loss of search expressiveness is a challenging and unsolved problem.

Mobile Cloud Data Share. To securely share a file with others, a mobile device user may use traditional encryption (e.g. attribute-based encryption [24]). But the traditional encryption requires the user to be always on-line, and to consume considerable computation resource, communication cost and battery to fulfill a simple data sharing. Proxy re-encryption (PRE) has been invented to tackle the above efficiency problem in the sense that a user only generates a special key (other than a ciphertext, as the golden coin in Fig. 3) for cloud server, such that the server can convert the ciphertexts of the user into those for others. Alice is a delegator, while Bob is a delegatee; the golden coin is a re-encryption key for the ciphertext conversion.

The premise of PRE relies on the design of re-encryption algorithm that guarantees the server to run a "partial decryption" for an original ciphertext of a user for another, so that the data receiver can recover the message by its decryption key and meanwhile, the server knows nothing about the message. To achieve the secure re-encryption, the construction of a re-encryption key is somewhat tricky. For instance, given a ciphertext $(Z_1 = g^{xr}, Z_2 = e(g, g)^r \cdot m)$, a user A may construct a re-encryption key $g^{y/x}$ for the server, such that the server can compute $Z_3 = e(Z_1, g^{y/x})$ for another user Y who recovers m by computing $Z_2/Z_3^{1/y}$, where (g^x, x) and (g^y, y) are public/secret key pairs for X and Y. Recent PRE techniques enable users to perform fine-grained data share in the context of identity-based [23], attribute-base and even functional encryption.

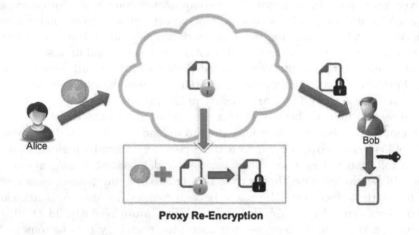

Proxy Re-Encryption

Fig. 3. Secure encrypted cloud-based data share - proxy re-encryption

Nevertheless, the simple usage of PRE yields a potential security risk in ciphertext conversion that no one knows if the conversion is correct. A direct solution is introduced in [25] in which an encryption receiver with appropriate decryption rights can check the validity of conversion. This post-check mode, actually, does not scale well in real world, as it is too late to detect the errors - after the encrypted data being downloaded, and meanwhile, only a valid decryptor can tell the errors upon accessing the encryption. A practical and publicly validity check method - before downloading data, is necessary here.

Another efficiency problem incurred by PRE is that a re-encryption key can only be used to handle the conversion of a "fixed" type of ciphertext format. For example, an identity-based encryption can be converted to another "identity-based" ciphertext, while an attribute-based ciphertext corresponds to a "attribute-based" one. Furthermore, for more fine-grained encryption, e.g., functional encryption, the construction of re-encryption key is heavy for mobile user, as it usually is linearly in either the size of policy or the size of attribute set. Here, users have to take great resource and energy cost in generating different re-encryption keys for the purpose of sharing various encrypted format data with others. One key for all types of encryption conversion, definitely, brings convenience for users that is extremely desire as well.

Mobile Cloud Data Computation. Homomorphic encryption technique is an effective approach for encrypted data computation whereby an untrusted party can compute the encrypted data in a "blind" way but outputting valid "encrypted" result. The party here knows nothing about the result but also underlying encrypted input. To date homomorphic encryption can support ciphertext additive property, multiplicative operation, or both of the operations. For multiplication, for example ElGamal, we have $Enc(m_1) \otimes Enc(m_2) = Enc(m_1 \cdot m_2)$; $Enc(m_1) \otimes Enc(m_2) = (g^{r_1}, m_1 h^{r_1})(g^{r_2}, m_2 h^{r_2}) = (g^{r_1+r_2}, (m_1 \cdot m_2)h^{r_1+r_2})$; for additive property, e.g., Paillier, we have $Enc(m_1) \otimes Enc(m_2) = Enc(m_1 + m_2)$. $Enc(m_1) \oplus Enc(m_2) = (g^{m_1}r_1^x)(g^{m_2}r_2^x) = g^{m_1+m_2}(r_1 r_2)^x$, where x is the modular, r_1, r_2 are random seeds, and m_1, m_2 are messages. Whereas the fully homomorphic encryption can provide both types of calculation - $Enc(m_1) \cdot Enc(m_2) = Enc(m_1 + m_2)$ and $Enc(m_1) \cdot Enc(m_2) = Enc(m_1 \cdot m_2)$. An advantage of homomorphic encryption is that the computation cost can be offloaded from users to clouds.

Although there exist some improved versions of homomorphic encryption over efficiency and properties, e.g., [3][1], there are some limitations when using homomorphic technologies in mobile cloud context. We note secure multi-party computation (MPC) systems can support cloud-based encrypted data computing as well in sense that a server intakes two respective encrypted values as input and outputs a "masked" result. However, those systems suffer from similar limitations as the homomorphic encryption does as follows. First of all, no current systems enable the encryption of arbitrary values in $\mathbb{R}$, i.e. real number. Although Chinese Remainder Theorem can be used to increase message space of systems to support large integer, it seems there is still a long way for homomorphic encryption to achieve real number encryption. In addition to huge ciphertext size cost for just a small dataset, there is no homomorphic system providing a native division operations. Mobile users have to download the corresponding encrypted data from clouds to decrypt-then-calculate the division on their owns. Moreover, if the homomorphic computation outputs a "long" encrypted result, such as a set of "masked" biometric data, the devices will suffer from huge computation and communication cost for download-then-decrypt operation. Last but not least, the existing homomorphic encryption systems fail to support search functionality, so that a cloud may take the whole encrypted database as input for calculation. We note that [19] introduces more security tools for mobile cloud computing. Due to limited space, we refer the readers to that paper for more technical details.

In addition to aforementioned limitations, the single ability providing in searchable encryption (searchability), homomorphic encryption/MPC (secure computation) and PRE (secure data share) cannot fully satisfy the multiple functionalities need of mobile device users (see Table 4). A naive "all-in-one" solution is to trivially combine a searchable encryption, a homomorphic encryption/MPC and a PRE into one system. Nevertheless, it is unknown that if the building blocks are compatible with each other and furthermore, and the combination is effective and secure.

---

[1] This paper limits the computation to small number of AND gates with shallow depth, and the multiplications are in GF(2).

Table 4. Functionalities summarization

Systems	Share	Search	Computation
Searchable encryption	✗	✓	✗
Homomorphic encryption/MPC	✗	✗	✓
PRE	✓	✗	✗

4   Conclusions

In investigating the security riks of mobile cloud, our goal is to inspire academic and industrial communities to tackle all the problems involved. We also would like to light in the hopes that mobile cloud service providers, mobile device users and local authorities will be more conscious of the challenges and embrace the opportunities to work together to create a brighter future for the mobile cloud applications.

Acknowledgments. K. Liang is supported by privacy-aware retrieval and modelling of genomic data (No. 13283250), the Academy of Finland.

References

1. Announcing the Advanced Encryption Standard (AES). Federal Information Processing Standards Publication 197. United States National Institute of Standards and Technology (NIST), 26 November 2001. Accessed 2 Oct 2012
2. Acar, T., Belenkiy, M., Küpçü, A.: Single password authentication. Comput. Netw. **57**(13), 2597–2614 (2013)
3. Albrecht, M.R., Rechberger, C., Schneider, T., Tiessen, T., Zohner, M.: Ciphers for MPC and FHE. In: Oswald, E., Fischlin, M. (eds.) EUROCRYPT 2015. LNCS, vol. 9056, pp. 430–454. Springer, Heidelberg (2015)
4. Ashford, W.: Barclays bank leaks thousands of customer records. http://www.computerweekly.com/news/2240214060/barclays-under-scrutiny-after-leak-of-27000-customer-records
5. Ateniese, G., Burns, R.C., Curtmola, R., Herring, J., Khan, O., Kissner, L., Peterson, Z.N.J., Song, D.: Remote data checking using provable data possession. ACM Trans. Inf. Syst. Secur. **14**(1), 12 (2011)
6. Berson, Thomas, A.: Differential cryptanalysis mod 2^{32} with applications to MD5. In: Rueppel, Rainer A. (ed.) EUROCRYPT 1992. LNCS, pp. 71–80. Springer, Heidelberg (1993). doi:10.1007/3-540-47555-9_6
7. Bhattasali, T., Saeed, K., Chaki, N., Chaki, R.: A survey of security and privacy issues for biometrics based remote authentication in cloud. In: Saeed, K., Snášel, V. (eds.) CISIM 2014. LNCS, vol. 8838, pp. 112–121. Springer, Heidelberg (2014)
8. Boneh, D., Boyen, X.: Efficient selective-ID secure identity-based encryption without random oracles. In: Cachin, C., Camenisch, J.L. (eds.) EUROCRYPT 2004. LNCS, vol. 3027, pp. 223–238. Springer, Heidelberg (2004)

9. Cash, D., Jaeger, J., Jarecki, S., Jutla, C.S., Krawczyk, H., Rosu, M.-C., Steiner, M.: Dynamic searchable encryption in very-large databases: data structures and implementation. In: 21st Annual Network and Distributed System Security Symposium, NDSS 2014, San Diego, California, USA, 23–26 February 2014. The Internet Society (2014)

10. Cash, D., Küpçü, A., Wichs, D.: Dynamic proofs of retrievability via oblivious RAM. In: Johansson, T., Nguyen, P.Q. (eds.) EUROCRYPT 2013. LNCS, vol. 7881, pp. 279–295. Springer, Heidelberg (2013)

11. Chaffey, D.: Mobile marketing statistics compilation. http://www.smartinsights.com/mobile-marketing/mobile-marketing-analytics/mobile-marketing-statistics

12. Chen, J., Guihua, W., Shen, L.L., Ji, Z.: Differentiated security levels for personal identifiable information in identity management system. Expert Syst. Appl. **38**(11), 14156–14162 (2011)

13. Chow, R., Jakobsson, M., Masuoka, R., Molina, J., Niu, Y., Shi, E., Song, Z.: Authentication in the clouds: a framework and its application to mobile users. In: Perrig, A., Sion, R. (eds.) Proceedings of the 2nd ACM Cloud Computing Security Workshop, CCSW 2010, Chicago, IL, USA, 8 October 2010, pp. 1–6. ACM (2010)

14. Cui, H., Yuan, X., Wang, C.: Harnessing encrypted data in cloud for secure and efficient image sharing from mobile devices. In: 2015 IEEE Conference on Computer Communications, INFOCOM 2015, Kowloon, Hong Kong, 26 April – 1 May 2015, pp. 2659–2667. IEEE (2015)

15. Do, Q., Martini, B., Choo, K.-K.R.: Exfiltrating data from android devices. Comput. Secur. **48**, 74–91 (2015)

16. Erway, C.C., Küpçü, A., Papamanthou, C., Tamassia, R.: Dynamic provable data possession. ACM Trans. Inf. Syst. Secur. **17**(4), 15 (2015)

17. El Gamal, T.: A public key cryptosystem and a signature scheme based on discrete logarithms. IEEE Trans. Inf. Theory **31**(4), 469–472 (1985)

18. Goyal, V., Pandey, O., Sahai, A., Waters, B.: Attribute-based encryption for fine-grained access control of encrypted data. In: Juels, A., Wright, R.N., De Capitani di Vimercati, S. (eds.) ACM Conference on Computer and Communications Security, pp. 89–98. ACM (2006)

19. Khan, A.N., Mat Kiah, M.L., Khan, S.U., Madani, S.A.: Towards secure mobile cloud computing a survey. Future Gener. Comput. Syst. **29**(5), 1278–1299 (2013)

20. Khan, W.Z., Aalsalem, M.Y., Xiang, Y.: A graphical password based system for small mobile devices. CoRR, abs/1110.3844 (2011)

21. Kim, M., Hongil, J., Kim, Y., Park, J., Park, Y.: Design and implementation of mobile trusted module for trusted mobile computing. IEEE Trans. Consum. Electron. **56**(1), 134–140 (2010)

22. Li, J., Ma, R., Guan, H.: TEES: an efficient search scheme over encrypted data on mobile cloud. IEEE Trans. Cloud Comput. **1**, 1 (2015)

23. Liang, K., Susilo, W., Liu, J.K.: Privacy-preserving ciphertext multi-sharing control for big data storage. IEEE Trans. Inf. Forensics Secur. **10**(8), 1578–1589 (2015)

24. Liu, J.K., Au, M.H., Susilo, W., Liang, K., Lu, R., Srinivasan, B.: Secure sharing and searching for real-time video data in mobile cloud. IEEE Netw. **29**(2), 46–50 (2015)

25. Ohata, S., Kawai, Y., Matsuda, T., Hanaoka, G., Matsuura, K.: Re-encryption verifiability: how to detect malicious activities of a proxy in proxy re-encryption. In: Nyberg, K. (ed.) CT-RSA 2015. LNCS, vol. 9048, pp. 410–428. Springer, Heidelberg (2015)

26. Paar, C., Pelzl, J.: The data encryption standard (DES) and alternatives. Understanding Cryptography, pp. 55–86. Springer, Germany (2000)

27. Pointcheval, D., Zimmer, S.: Multi-factor authenticated key exchange. In: Bellovin, S.M., Gennaro, R., Keromytis, A.D., Yung, M. (eds.) ACNS 2008. LNCS, vol. 5037, pp. 277–295. Springer, Heidelberg (2008)

28. Rudolph, S.: Mobile apps usage statistics and trends. http://www.business2 community.com/infographics/mobile-apps-usage-statistics-trends-infographic-01248837

29. BBC Technology. FBI investigates 'cloud' celebrity picture leaks. http://www.bbc.com/news/technology-29011850

30. Waters, B.: Functional encryption for regular languages. In: Safavi-Naini, R., Canetti, R. (eds.) CRYPTO 2012. LNCS, vol. 7417, pp. 218–235. Springer, Heidelberg (2012)

31. Xi, K., Ahmad, T., Han, F., Jiankun, H.: A fingerprint based bio-cryptographic security protocol designed for client/server authentication in mobile computing environment. Secur. Commun. Netw. 4(5), 487–499 (2011)

32. Yang, K., Jia, X.: An efficient and secure dynamic auditing protocol for data storage in cloud computing. IEEE Trans. Parallel Distrib. Syst. 24(9), 1717–1726 (2013)

33. Yassin, A.A., Jin, H., Ibrahim, A., Qiang, W., Zou, D.: Cloud authentication based on anonymous one-time password. In: Han, Y.-H., Park, D.-S., Jia, W., Yeo, S.-S. (eds.) Ubiquitous Information Technologies and Applications. Lecture Notes in Electrical Engineering, vol. 214, pp. 423–431. Springer, Netherlands (2013)

34. Zheng, Q., Shouhuai, X.: Secure and efficient proof of storage with deduplication. In: Bertino, E., Sandhu, R.S. (eds.) Second ACM Conference on Data and Application Security and Privacy, CODASPY 2012, San Antonio, TX, USA, 7–9 February 2012, pp. 1–12. ACM (2012)

35. Zissis, D., Lekkas, D.: Addressing cloud computing security issues. Future Gener. Comput. Syst. 28(3), 583–592 (2012)

Authentication Mechanism

Multi-device Anonymous Authentication

Kamil Kluczniak[1]($\boxtimes$), Jianfeng Wang[2], Xiaofeng Chen[2],
and Mirosław Kutyłowski[1]

[1] Department of Computer Science, Wrocław University of Science and Technology,
Wrocław, Poland
{kamil.kluczniak,miroslaw.kutylowski}@pwr.edu.pl
[2] State Key Laboratory of Integrated Service Networks (ISN),
Xidian University, Xi'an, China
wjf01@163.com, xfchen@xidian.edu.cn

Abstract. Recently, a few pragmatic and privacy protecting systems for
authentication in multiple systems have been designed. The most prominent examples are Restricted Identification and Pseudonymous Signature
schemes designed by the German Federal Office for Information Security
for German personal identity cards. The main properties are that a user
can authenticate himself with a single private key (stored on a smart-
card), but nevertheless the user's IDs in different systems are unlinkable.

We develop a solution which enables a user to achieve the above mentioned goals while using more than one personal device, each holding a
single secret key, but different for each device – as for security reasons
no secret key is allowed to leave a secure device. Our solution is privacy
preserving: it will remain hidden for the service system which device is
used. Nevertheless, if a device gets stolen, lost or compromised, the user
can revoke it (leaving his other devices intact).

In particular, in this way we create a strong authentication framework
for cloud users, where the cloud does not learn indirectly personal data.
In the standard solutions there is no way to avoid leaking information
that, for instance, the user is in his office and authenticates via his desktop computer.

Our solution is based on a novel cryptographic primitive, called
Pseudonymous Public Key Group Signature.

Keywords: Signature schemes · Privacy · Pseudonyms · Group
signature

1 Introduction

So far most authentication systems for web services or cloud servers where
designed having in mind a single user or a group of users and a single service

This research was supported by National Research Center grant PRELUDIUM
8 number 02NP/0016/15 (decision number 2014/15/N/ST6/04655) and Polish-
Chinese cooperation venture of Xidian University and Wrocław University of Science
and Technology on Secure Data Outsourcing in Cloud Computing.

J. Chen et al. (Eds.): NSS 2016, LNCS 9955, pp. 21–36, 2016.
DOI: 10.1007/978-3-319-46298-1_2

provider. Today such systems become increasingly popular and the number of systems used per user is rapidly growing. If authentication is taken seriously (not based just on a login and a password), then for each service we get an independent authentication environment that requires generating and distribution of the secret keys for the users. Such a framework has serious disadvantages: the necessity of managing secret/public keys among certain parties, constant updates of user secret keys and maintaining large and costly PKI infrastructures.

In this paper, we develop a framework which aims to provide a cryptographically sound authentication scheme to a dynamically growing set of services, which preserves privacy for groups of users and does not require expensive, time and resource consuming infrastructures as well as key management procedures.

Application Scenario. In order to be more specific, we consider an application scenario of Multiple Mobile Devices and Authentication for Web Services, called below *domains*: We assume that:

- a user registers to a given domain only once,
- the user may register himself in many different domains, but he should use the same device or set of devices for interaction with these domains,
- a given user is in possession of a few devices that may be used interchangeably (mobiles devices, desktop computers, etc.),
- the user should not be bothered to register these devices in each single domain in order to use them, ...
- ... but must be able to revoke each of the devices in a case of theft, key leakage, etc.

For usability reasons, we assume that a user registers once in a domain by providing his public key for this domain. Moreover, no party except for the user and the service domain should be involved. (We do not consider how the user is initially authenticated – he may appear in person, authenticate himself via a payment, authenticate himself with a personal identity card or by other means.)

After registration, without any updates or interaction with any party, the participant should be able to delegate the right to run authentication protocol on behalf of the user and sign digitally challenges in order to authenticate the user.

Privacy and Unlinkability Issues. One of the major threats in a multi-system environment is that the authentication means from one domain can be misused for getting unlawful access into user's accounts in another domain. For password based systems this is a severe threat as the users tend to use the same password in multiple places. Many recent examples are known where compromise of one system resulted in compromising users' accounts in another systems.

Apart from unlawful access, it might be necessary to protect the information that a given physical person is a user in a domain. Therefore after the phase of registration the user's identity should be anonymized. Moreover, the pseudonyms in different domains should be unlinkable, even when the data from authentication sessions are at hand. In this case a potential data leakage is not threatening the principles of personal data protection.

Group Signatures. Group signatures as defined in [1] or [2] are signature schemes in which a *group manager* admits the users to the group. Each of the group members may sign data anonymously on behalf of the group. Only an entity called an *opener* may *"open"* a signature and derive the signer's real identity. Informally, a group signature scheme has to fulfil the following properties:

anonymity: it is infeasible to establish the signer of a message. To be more specific, it is infeasible to link the signature to a single user, i.e. having two signatures one cannot even say whether they originate from one signer or from two different signers.

unframeability: it is infeasible, even for a coalition of malicious group members, to forge a signature which would open to the identity of a group member not belonging to the coalition.

traceability: it is infeasible to produce a signature which would open to an identity not added to the group by the group manager.

Group signatures is a well studied cryptographic primitive. There are many variants of them, with security proofs based either on the random oracle model (e.g. [3]), or on the standard model (e.g. [4]). Many variants of group signatures have been developed, like Verifier Local Group Signatures [5], Traceable Signatures [6], Hierarchical [7], Attribute [8] and Identity Based Group Signatures [9].

Ad Hoc Solution Based on Group Signatures. At a first look, group signature schemes address our practical problem pretty well. The user plays the role of the group manager for group signatures, while his devices play the role of group members (admitted by the manager). Note that this constructions gives some functionalities for free:

- the user can delegate his rights to authenticate on behalf of him to any number of his devices – indeed, the number of group members is typically unlimited,
- the devices are indistinguishable from the point of view of the verifier – this is the basic feature of group signatures,
- in case of a misbehavior, the user may open a signature and find which device has created it.

Unfortunately, there are also some drawbacks that have to be addressed. The main problem is that we have to create separate and unlinkable authentication means for different domains. Creating a new independent group for each domain separately would solve this problem, however this would require installing separate keys for each domain on each single device. For practical reasons this is not really acceptable.

Unfortunately, existing group signature schemes have been designed having in mind single groups or a hierarchy of groups with central authorities. In particular, existing schemes assume that a group of such a hierarchy is identified by a public key determined by the scheme setup. This makes such schemes unsuitable for our application. Our aim is therefore to design a group signature scheme in which group public keys may be derived spontaneously from a domain specific bit string (e.g. www.some-service.com), a secret key of the group manager, and with no involvement of PKI infrastructures and/or trusted authorities.

Moreover, group public keys or, as we will call it, *domain pseudonyms* must be unlinkable, what means that having two or more domain pseudonyms from distinct domains it is infeasible to tell whether the pseudonyms correspond to a group manager.

Such an anonymity notion is known from Domain Pseudonymous Signature schemes (see e.g. [10]), (see e.g. Direct Anonymous Attestation [11]) and Anonymous Credential Systems (see e.g. [12]). What is important, creating new public keys by a group manager does not require from group members to update their secret keys or any other information and they might automatically sign data corresponding to the new public key.

Contribution and Paper Overview. Our main technical contribution is a new concept of group signatures, where group public keys are domain pseudonyms which may be derived spontaneously. The particular setting is tailored for the above mention application of delegating authentication chores to multiple devices of a user.

In Sect. 3 We give a formal definition for our new primitive. This is followed in Sect. 4 by a relatively efficient construction based on pairings. We give also some intuition about its security properties and formulate corresponding theorems. The proofs of these theorems are based on the random oracle model assumption, which is dictated mainly by efficiency and practical needs of the construction. In Sect. 4.3 we provide some additional remarks and we show how to apply our scheme to solve our practical problem.

2 Preliminaries

Bilinear Groups. Let $\mathbb{G}_1$, $\mathbb{G}_2$ and $\mathbb{G}_T$ be cyclic groups of a prime order p, generated by $g_1 \in \mathbb{G}_1$ and $g_2 \in \mathbb{G}_2$. In our scheme we make use of bilinear maps $e : \mathbb{G}_1 \times \mathbb{G}_2 \to \mathbb{G}_T$, which are:

- *bilinear*: for $a, b \in \mathbb{Z}_p$, we have $e(g_1^a, g_2^b) = e(g_1, g_2)^{a \cdot b}$,
- *non-degenerate*: the element $e(g_1, g_2) \in \mathbb{G}_T$ is a generator of $\mathbb{G}_T$.

Additionally, we require that e and all group operations are efficiently computable.

Throughout the paper we will use Type-3 pairing according to the classification from [13]. We call a pairing of Type-3, if $\mathbb{G}_1 \neq \mathbb{G}_2$ and no efficiently computable homomorphism between $\mathbb{G}_1$ and $\mathbb{G}_2$ is known.

Security Assumptions.

Definition 1 (Discrete Logarithm Problem (DLP)). *Let $\mathbb{G}$ be a cyclic group of prime order p with a generator $g \in \mathbb{G}$. An algorithm A has advantage ϵ in solving the DLP if*

$$\Pr[A(g, g^\alpha) \to \alpha] \geq \epsilon,$$

where the probability is taken over the random choice of the generator $g \in \mathbb{G}$, the random choice of $\alpha \in \mathbb{Z}_p$, and the random bits of A.

We say that the (t, ϵ)-DL assumption holds in $\mathbb{G}$ if no time t algorithm has advantage ϵ in solving DLP in $\mathbb{G}$.

Definition 2 (Decisional Diffie-Hellman Problem (DDH)). *Let $\mathbb{G}$ be a cyclic group of order p with a generator $g \in \mathbb{G}$. An algorithm A has advantage ϵ in solving the DDH problem if*

$$|\Pr[A(g^\alpha, g^\beta, g^{\alpha \cdot \beta}) \to 1] - \Pr[A(g^\alpha, g^\beta, g^\gamma) \to 1]| \geq \epsilon,$$

where the probability is taken over the random choice of $g \in \mathbb{G}$, the random choice of $(\alpha, \beta, \gamma) \in \mathbb{Z}_p^3$, and the random bits of A.

We say that the (t, ϵ)-DDH assumption holds in $\mathbb{G}$, if no time t algorithm has advantage at least ϵ in solving the DDH problem in $\mathbb{G}$.

Definition 3 (Symmetric eXternal Diffie-Hellman assumption (SXDH)). *Let $\mathbb{G}_1$, $\mathbb{G}_2$ be cyclic groups of a prime order and $e : \mathbb{G}_1 \times \mathbb{G}_2 \to \mathbb{G}_T$ be a bilinear map. The SXDH assumption says that the DDH assumption holds in both $\mathbb{G}_1$ and $\mathbb{G}_2$.*

Definition 4 (Bilinear Decisional Diffie-Hellman Assumption). *Let $\mathbb{G}$ be a cyclic group of a prime order and $e : \mathbb{G} \times \mathbb{G} \to \mathbb{G}_T$ be a bilinear map. An algorithm A as advantage ϵ in solving the BDDH problem if*

$$|\Pr[A(g^\alpha, g^\beta, g^\gamma, e(g, g)^{\alpha \cdot \beta \cdot \gamma}) \to 1] - \Pr[A(g^\alpha, g^\beta, g^\gamma, e(g, g)^\delta) \to 1]| \geq \epsilon,$$

where the probability is taken over the random choice of $g \in \mathbb{G}$, the random choice of $(\alpha, \beta, \gamma, \delta) \in \mathbb{Z}_p^3$, and the random bits of A.

We say that the (t, ϵ)-BDDH assumption holds in $\mathbb{G}$, if no time t algorithm has advantage at least ϵ in solving the BDDH problem in $\mathbb{G}$.

Definition 5 (Collusion attack algorithm with q traitors (q-CAA)). *Let $\mathbb{G}_1$ and $\mathbb{G}_2$ be groups of a prime order p and generated by $g_1 \in \mathbb{G}_1$ and $g_2 \in \mathbb{G}_2$. Let $e : \mathbb{G}_1 \times \mathbb{G}_2 \to \mathbb{G}_T$ be a bilinear map which maps into a target group $\mathbb{G}_T$.*

An algorithm A has advantage ϵ in solving the q-CAA problem, if

$$\Pr\left[\begin{matrix} A(g_1, g_1^z, (m_1, g_1^{\frac{1}{z+m_1}}), \ldots, (m_q, g_1^{\frac{1}{z+m_q}}), \\ g_2, g_2^z) \to (m, g_1^{\frac{1}{z+m}}) \wedge m \notin \{m_1, \ldots, m_q\} \end{matrix} \right] \geq \epsilon,$$

where the probability is taken over the random choice of $(g_1, g_2) \in \mathbb{G}_1 \times \mathbb{G}_2$, the random choice of $z \in \mathbb{Z}_p$, the random choice of $(m_1, \ldots, m_q) \in \mathbb{Z}_p^q$, and the random bits of A.

We say that (q, t, ϵ)-CAA assumption holds in $(\mathbb{G}_1, \mathbb{G}_2)$, if no time t algorithm has advantage at least ϵ in solving the q-CAA problem in $(\mathbb{G}_1, \mathbb{G}_2)$.

3 Formal Model of Pseudonymous Public Key Group Signature

A Pseudonymous Public Key Group Signature scheme consists of the following procedures:

Setup(1^λ): On input a security parameter λ, it outputs global parameters *param*.

CreateUser(*param*): On input the global parameters *param*, it creates and outputs the user's master secret key mSK.

ComputePseudonym(*param*, mSK, dom): On input the global parameters *param*, the master secret key mSK and a domain name dom, it returns a pseudonym nym within domain dom for the user holding mSK.

AddDevice(*param*, mSK, i): On input the global parameters *param*, the master secret key mSK and a device identifier i, this procedure returns a device secret key uSK_i.

CreateRevocationToken(*param*, mSK, dom, i, j): On input the global parameters *param*, user index i and his secret key mSK, the domain name dom and a device identifier j, this procedure computes and outputs a device revocation token $uRT_{i,j,\text{dom}}$ within the domain dom.

Sign(*param*, uSK, dom, m): On input the global parameters *param*, a device secret key uSK, a domain name dom and a message m, it returns a signature σ on the message m. (Note that we do not require that the pseudonym nym is used.)

Verify(*param*, nym, dom, σ, m, uRT): On input the global parameters *param*, a pseudonym nym with regards to a domain name dom, a signature σ on a message m, and a revocation token uRT, this algorithm returns 1 (accept), or 0 (reject).

Below we discuss the required properties of Pseudonymous Public Key Group Signature.

Correctness. A Pseudonymous Public Key Group Signature is correct, if for every $\lambda \in \mathbb{N}$, $param \leftarrow$ Setup(1^λ), domain name dom $\in \{0,1\}^*$, and message $m \in \{0,1\}^*$, if

$$mSK_i \leftarrow \text{CreateUser}(param)$$
$$uSK_{i,j} \leftarrow \text{AddDevice}(param, mSK_i, j)$$
$$nym \leftarrow \text{ComputePseudonym}(param, mSK_i, \text{dom})$$
$$uRT_{i,j,\text{dom}^*} \leftarrow \text{CreateRevocationToken}(param, mSK_i, \text{dom}^*, j)$$
$$\sigma \leftarrow \text{Sign}(param, uSK_{i,j}, \text{dom}, m)$$

then

$$\text{Verify}(param, nym, \text{dom}, \sigma, m, R) = 1 \quad \text{for} \quad R \neq uRT_{i,j,\text{dom}^*}$$
$$\text{Verify}(param, nym, \text{dom}, \sigma, m, uRT_{i,j,\text{dom}^*}) = 0.$$

In order to define the remaining properties we use the following notation: $\mathcal{U}_{SET}$ stands for the list of users and their secret keys, $\mathcal{D}_{SET}$ contains triples

(i, j, uSK), where i denotes a user index, j is a device index and uSK is its secret key, $\mathcal{CD}$ is a list pointing to corrupted devices and $\mathcal{S}$ is a list of signature query records. Then we define the following oracles used by the adversary during the security games:

$\mathcal{O}_{\mathsf{CreateUser}}$: On input i, if there exists an entry $(i, .)$ in $\mathcal{U}_{SET}$, the oracle aborts. Otherwise the oracle runs $mSK_i \leftarrow \mathsf{CreateUser}(param)$ and adds the pair (i, mSK_i) to $\mathcal{U}_{SET}$.

$\mathcal{O}_{\mathsf{GetNym}}$: On input dom and i, the oracle finds the secret key mSK_i in $\mathcal{U}_{SET}$ corresponding to i. If no such entry exists, then the oracle aborts. Otherwise the oracle computes $nym_{i,\mathsf{dom}} \leftarrow \mathsf{ComputePseudonym}(param, mSK_i, \mathsf{dom})$ and returns $nym_{i,\mathsf{dom}}$.

$\mathcal{O}_{\mathsf{AddDevice}}$: On input a user index i and a device identifier j, the oracle finds an entry $(i, mSK_i) \in \mathcal{U}_{SET}$ and checks that $(i, j, \cdot) \notin \mathcal{D}_{SET}$. If $(i, j, \cdot) \notin \mathcal{D}_{SET}$, then the oracle aborts. Then $uSK_{i,j} \leftarrow \mathsf{AddDevice}(param, mSK_i, j)$ and the oracle adds the tuple $(i, j, uSK_{i,j})$ to $\mathcal{D}_{SET}$.

$\mathcal{O}_{\mathsf{AddCorruptedDevice}}$: On input a user identifier i and a device identifier j, the oracle finds $(i, mSK_i) \in \mathcal{U}_{SET}$ and checks that $(i, j, \cdot) \notin \mathcal{D}_{SET}$ (if this is not the case, then the oracle aborts). Otherwise the oracle runs $uSK_{i,j} \leftarrow \mathsf{AddDevice}(param, mSK, j)$, adds the tuple $(i, j, uSK_{i,j})$ to $\mathcal{D}_{SET}$ and $\mathcal{CD}$, and outputs $uSK_{i,j}$.

$\mathcal{O}_{\mathsf{GetRT}}$: On input a user identifier i and his master key mSK_i, a device identifier j and a domain name dom, the oracle checks that $(i, j, \cdot) \in \mathcal{D}_{SET}$, (if this is not the case, then the oracle aborts). Then the oracle computes $uRT_{i,j,\mathsf{dom}} \leftarrow \mathsf{CreateRevocationToken}(param, mSK_i, \mathsf{dom}, j)$ and returns $uRT_{i,j,\mathsf{dom}}$.

$\mathcal{O}_{\mathsf{Sign}}$: On input a user identifier i, a device identifier j, a domain name dom and a message m, the oracle finds the corresponding secret key $uSK_{i,j}$ in $\mathcal{D}_{SET}$, (if such an entry does not exist, then the oracle aborts). Otherwise, the oracle runs $\sigma \leftarrow \mathsf{Sign}(param, uSK_{i,j}, \mathsf{dom}, m)$, adds $(\sigma, m, \mathsf{dom}, j, i)$ to $\mathcal{S}$ and returns σ.

$\mathcal{O}_{\mathsf{CorruptDevice}}$: On input a user identifier i and a device identifier j, the oracle finds the secret key $uSK_{i,j}$ in $\mathcal{D}_{SET}$ corresponding to i and j. (If such an entry does not exist, then the oracle aborts.) Then the oracle returns $uSK_{i,j}$ and adds (i, j) to $\mathcal{CD}$.

Unforgeability. This property says that no coalition of malicious devices of a user can forge a signature on behalf of a device not belonging to the coalition. We define the unforgeability property by the following experiment:

Experiment $\mathsf{UNF}_{\mathsf{A}}^{S}(\lambda)$:

- $(param) \leftarrow \mathsf{Setup}(1^\lambda)$.
- $\mathcal{O} \leftarrow \{\mathcal{O}_{\mathsf{CreateUser}}, \mathcal{O}_{\mathsf{GetNym}}, \mathcal{O}_{\mathsf{AddDevice}}, \mathcal{O}_{\mathsf{GetRT}}, \mathcal{O}_{\mathsf{Sign}}, \mathcal{O}_{\mathsf{CorruptUser}}\}$.
- $(\sigma^*, m^*, \mathsf{dom}^*, nym^*) \leftarrow \mathsf{A}^{\mathcal{O}}(param)$.

- If
  - $\mathsf{Verify}(param, nym^*, \mathbf{dom}^*, \sigma^*, m^*, \perp) = 1$ and
  - There exists $(i, mSK_i) \in \mathcal{U}_{SET}$, $(i, j, \cdot) \in \mathcal{D}_{SET}$ such that
    $nym^* = \mathsf{ComputePseudonym}(param, mSK_i, \mathbf{dom}^*)$,
    $uRT_{i,j,\mathbf{dom}^*} \leftarrow \mathsf{CreateRevocationToken}(param, mSK_i, \mathbf{dom}^*, j)$
    $\mathsf{Verify}(param, nym^*, \mathbf{dom}^*, \sigma^*, m^*, uRT_{i,j,\mathbf{dom}^*}) = 0$
    $(i, j) \notin \mathcal{CD}$ and $(\sigma^*, m^*, \mathbf{dom}^*, j, i) \notin \mathcal{S}$,
  then the challenger returns 1.
- Otherwise the challenger returns 0.

Definition 6. *A Pseudonymous Public Key Group Signature S is (t, ϵ)-unforgeable if $\Pr[UNF_{\mathsf{A}}^S(\lambda) = 1] \leq \epsilon$ for any adversary A running in time t.*

Seclusiveness. Seclusiveness means that it is infeasible to produce a signature on behalf of the user and that does not correspond to any device of the user. In other words, it is infeasible to create a signature that corresponds to none of the revocation tokens. Seclusiveness is formally defined by the following experiment.

Experiment $SEC_{\mathsf{A}}^S(\lambda)$:

- $(param) \leftarrow \mathsf{Setup}(1^\lambda)$.
- $\mathcal{O} \leftarrow \{\mathcal{O}_{\mathsf{CreateUser}}, \mathcal{O}_{\mathsf{GetNym}}, \mathcal{O}_{\mathsf{AddCorruptedDevice}}, \mathcal{O}_{\mathsf{GetRT}}\}$.
- $(\sigma^*, m^*, \mathbf{dom}^*, nym^*) \leftarrow \mathsf{A}^{\mathcal{O}}(param)$.
- If
  - $\mathsf{Verify}(param, nym^*, \mathbf{dom}^*, \sigma^*, m^*, \perp) = 1$ and
  - there exists $(i, mSK_i) \in \mathcal{U}_{SET}$ such that
    $nym^* = \mathsf{ComputePseudonym}(param, mSK_i, \mathbf{dom}^*)$
    and for all j such that $(i, j, \cdot) \in \mathcal{D}_{SET}$:
    $uRT_{i,j,\mathbf{dom}^*} \leftarrow \mathsf{CreateRevocationToken}(param, mSK_i, \mathbf{dom}^*, j)$
    $\mathsf{Verify}(param, nym^*, \mathbf{dom}^*, \sigma^*, m^*, uRT_{i,j,\mathbf{dom}^*}) = 1$
  the challenger returns 1.
- Otherwise the challenger returns 0.

Definition 7. *We say that a Pseudonymous Public Key Group Signature S is (t, ϵ)-seclusive, if $\Pr[SEC_{\mathsf{A}}^S(\lambda) = 1] \leq \epsilon$ for any adversary A running in time t.*

Anonymity. We require that it is infeasible to correlate two signatures of the same device (unless its revocation token is used). For the anonymity experiment we define an additional oracle:

$\mathcal{O}_{\mathsf{Challenge}}$: This oracle takes as input a bit b, a user index i^*, a domain name $\mathbf{dom}^*$, two device indexes j_0^*, j_1^* and a message m^*. If

- $(i^*, \cdot) \notin \mathcal{U}_{SET}$ or $j_0^* = j_1^*$, or

- $(i^*, j_0^*, \cdot) \notin \mathcal{D}_{SET}$ or $(i^*, j_1^*, \cdot) \notin \mathcal{D}_{SET}$, or
- $(i^*, j_0^*) \in \mathcal{CD}$ or $(i^*, j_1^*) \in \mathcal{CD}$, or
- the $\mathcal{O}_{\mathsf{GetRT}}$ oracle was called on input $(i^*, j_0^*, \mathsf{dom}^*)$ or $(i^*, j_1^*, \mathsf{dom}^*)$,

then the oracle returns $\perp$ and aborts. Otherwise, the oracle computes $\sigma \leftarrow$ $\mathsf{Sign}(param, uSK_{i^*,j_b^*}, \mathsf{dom}^*, m^*)$ and returns σ.

After calling the $\mathcal{O}_{\mathsf{Challenge}}$ oracle, the adversary cannot call the $\mathcal{O}_{\mathsf{GetRT}}$ on input $(i^*, j_0^*, \mathsf{dom}^*)$ or $(i^*, j_1^*, \mathsf{dom}^*)$, and the $\mathcal{O}_{\mathsf{CorruptUser}}$ on input (i^*, j_0^*) or (i^*, j_1^*).

Experiment $\mathsf{Anon}_\mathcal{A}^S$:

- $(param) \leftarrow \mathsf{Setup}(1^\lambda)$.
- choose $b \in \{0, 1\}$ at random,
- $\mathcal{O} \leftarrow \{\mathcal{O}_{\mathsf{CreateUser}}, \quad \mathcal{O}_{\mathsf{GetNym}}, \quad \mathcal{O}_{\mathsf{AddDevice}}, \quad \mathcal{O}_{\mathsf{GetRT}}, \quad \mathcal{O}_{\mathsf{Sign}}, \quad \mathcal{O}_{\mathsf{CorruptUser}},$ $\mathcal{O}_{\mathsf{Challenge}}(b, \cdot, \cdot, \cdot, \cdot)\}$.
- $\hat{b} \leftarrow \mathsf{A}^\mathcal{O}(param)$.
- If $\hat{b} = b$, then output 1, otherwise output 0.

Definition 8. *A Pseudonymous Public Key Group Signature S is (t, ϵ)-anonymous if $|\Pr[\mathsf{Anon}_\mathsf{A}^S(\lambda) = 1] - \frac{1}{2}| \leq \epsilon$ for any adversary A running in time t.*

Domain Unlinkability. Informally, domain unlinkability means that it is infeasible to correlate two domain pseudonyms with a single user. We will give a simulation based definition for the domain unlinkability property.

First we need to define the following data structures: $\mathcal{D}$ denotes a set of domain names, $\mathcal{U}_{SET}^I$ is the set of user indexes, $\mathcal{K}$ denotes an associative map which maps a pair $(\mathsf{dom}, i) \in \{0,1\}^* \times \mathbb{N}$ into a master secret key from the secret key space $\mathcal{USK}$. Then we define an associative map $\mathcal{UK}$ which maps a tuple $(\mathsf{dom}, i, j) \in \{0,1\}^* \times \mathbb{N}^2$ into a device secret key.

Then we define the following oracles which implement the ideal functionality, where the keys of the user for different domains are independent (note that for Pseudonymous Public Key Group Signature they are the same):

$\mathcal{O}_{\mathsf{CreateUser}}^{Ideal}$: The query requests to create a secret key for the i-th user. If $i \notin \{1, \ldots, n\}$ or $i \in \mathcal{U}_{SET}^I$, then the oracle aborts. Otherwise, the oracle adds i to $\mathcal{U}_{SET}^I$ and for each $\mathsf{dom} \in \mathcal{D}$, the oracle chooses a secret key $mSK_{i,\mathsf{dom}}$ at random from $\mathcal{USK}$ and sets $\mathcal{K}[(i, \mathsf{dom})] \leftarrow mSK_{i,\mathsf{dom}}$.

$\mathcal{O}_{\mathsf{AddDevice}}^{Ideal}$: The query requests to create the j-th device for user i. For each $\mathsf{dom} \in \mathcal{D}$ the oracle obtains $mSK_{i,\mathsf{dom}} \leftarrow \mathcal{K}[(i, \mathsf{dom})]$ and runs $uSK_{\mathsf{dom},i,j} \leftarrow \mathsf{AddDevice}(param, mSK_{\mathsf{dom},i}, j)$, and sets $\mathcal{UK}[(\mathsf{dom}, i, j)] \leftarrow uSK_{\mathsf{dom},i,j}$.

$\mathcal{O}_{\mathsf{GetNym}}^{Ideal}$: The query requests the pseudonym of the i-th user with regards to a domain name dom. If $i \notin \mathcal{U}_{SET}^I$, then the oracle aborts. If $\mathcal{K}[(i, \mathsf{dom})]$ is undefined, then the oracle chooses a secret key $mSK_{i,\mathsf{dom}} \in \mathcal{USK}$ at random and sets $\mathcal{K}[(i, \mathsf{dom})] \leftarrow mSK_{i,\mathsf{dom}}$. Then the oracle runs $nym_{i,\mathsf{dom}} \leftarrow$ ComputePseudonym$(params, mSK_{i,\mathsf{dom}}, \mathsf{dom})$ and outputs $nym_{i,\mathsf{dom}}$.

$\mathcal{O}_{\mathsf{GetRT}}^{Ideal}$: The query requests a revocation token for the j-th device of user i with regards to a domain name dom. If $i \notin \mathcal{U}_{SET}^I$, then the oracle aborts. If $\mathcal{UK}[(\mathsf{dom}, i, j)]$ is undefined, then the oracle runs the procedure $uSK_{\mathsf{dom},i,j} \leftarrow$ AddDevice$(param, mSK_{\mathsf{dom},i}, j)$, and sets $\mathcal{UK}[(\mathsf{dom}, i, j)] \leftarrow uSK_{\mathsf{dom},i,j}$. Then the oracle runs $uRT_{i,j,\mathsf{dom}} \leftarrow$ CreateRevocationToken$(param, mSK_{\mathsf{dom},i}, \mathsf{dom}, j)$ and outputs $uRT_{i,j,\mathsf{dom}}$.

$\mathcal{O}_{\mathsf{Sign}}^{Ideal}$: The query requests to sign a message m by the j-th device of user i with regards to a domain name dom. If $i \notin \mathcal{U}_{SET}^I$, then the oracle aborts and returns $\bot$. If $\mathcal{UK}[(\mathsf{dom}, i, j)]$ is undefined, then the oracle runs $uSK_{\mathsf{dom},i,j} \leftarrow$ AddDevice$(param, mSK_{\mathsf{dom},i}, j)$, and sets $\mathcal{UK}[(\mathsf{dom}, i, j)] \leftarrow uSK_{\mathsf{dom},i,j}$. Finally, the oracle runs $\sigma \leftarrow$ Sign$(param, uSK_{\mathsf{dom},i,j}, \mathsf{dom}, m)$ and returns σ.

Definition 9. *We say that a Pseudonymous Public Key Group Signature S is (t, ϵ)-domain unlinkable if for any adversary A running in time t we have*

$$| \Pr[(param) \leftarrow \mathit{Setup}(1^\lambda); A^{\mathcal{O}_{Real}}(param)] -$$
$$\Pr[(param) \leftarrow \mathit{Setup}(1^\lambda); A^{\mathcal{O}_{Ideal}}(param)]| \leq \epsilon,$$

where $\mathcal{O}_{Real} = \{\mathcal{O}_{CreateUser}, \mathcal{O}_{AddDevice}, \mathcal{O}_{GetNym}, \mathcal{O}_{GetRT}, \mathcal{O}_{Sign}\}$ *and* $\mathcal{O}_{Ideal} = \{\mathcal{O}_{CreateUser}^{Ideal}, \mathcal{O}_{AddDevice}^{Ideal}, \mathcal{O}_{GetNym}^{Ideal}, \mathcal{O}_{GetRT}^{Ideal}, \mathcal{O}_{Sign}^{Ideal}\}$.

4   Efficient Construction

4.1   Scheme Specification

In this section we describe our implementation of a Pseudonymous Public Key Group Signature.

The idea behind the construction is as follows. First a user chooses a secret key for the Boneh-Boyen signature scheme [14], i.e. $z \in \mathbb{Z}_p$ chosen at random. This key is then used to compute "pseudonymized" public keys as $nym \leftarrow H_0(\mathsf{dom})^z$, where H_0 is a hash function and dom is a domain name. The same key is then used to issue Boneh-Boyen signatures $A_j \leftarrow g_1^{1/(z+u_j)}$ on a secret key $u_j \in \mathbb{Z}_p$ of his device j. Note that according to our security definition from Sect. 3, the user generates all secret keys for his devices and we do not define a Join/Issue procedure to ensure exculpability[1]. We intentionally defined our group signature scheme in this way due to specific use case.

Now, a device j holding a "certified" secret key (u_j, A_j), computes a signature of knowledge which is based on a Σ-protocol and turned into a signature scheme using the Fiat-Shamir paradigm. Informally, the signature carries a proof

---

[1] The exculpability property is known from dynamic group signatures [2] and assures that even the group manager cannot forge signatures on behalf of a user.

that the signer knows a secret key with a certificate which verifies correctly with a "pseudonymized" public key nym. The tricky part of our construction is that the signer does not know the "pseudonymized" public key to which his certificate verifies. The only information which allows to sign with regards to a pseudonymized public key is the basis of the public key, i.e. $\hat{g}_2 \leftarrow H_0(\mathsf{dom})$.

Bellow, we describe our scheme more formally.

Setup(1^λ):
1. Choose groups $\mathbb{G}_1$, $\mathbb{G}_2$ of a prime order p, a bilinear map $e : \mathbb{G}_1 \times \mathbb{G}_2 \to \mathbb{G}_T$, and choose a generator $g_1 \xleftarrow{R} \mathbb{G}_1$ at random.
2. Define a hash function H_0 which maps into $\mathbb{G}_2$ and a hash function H which maps into $\mathbb{Z}_p$.
3. Output the global parameters $param = (p, \mathbb{G}_1, \mathbb{G}_2, e, g_1, H_0, H)$.

CreateUser($param$):
1. Choose $z \in \mathbb{Z}_p$ at random and output $mSK \leftarrow z$.

ComputePseudonym($param, mSK, \mathsf{dom}$):
1. Compute $\hat{g}_2 \leftarrow H_0(\mathsf{dom})$ and output $nym \leftarrow \hat{g}_2^{\,z}$.

AddDevice($param, mSK, i$):
1. Choose $u_i \in \mathbb{Z}_p$ at random[2].
2. Compute $A_i = g_1^{1/(u_i+z)}$, return $uSK[i] \leftarrow (A_i, u_i)$ and store u_i for future use.

CreateRevocationToken($param, mSK, \mathsf{dom}, i$):
1. Retrieve the user secret key u_i, compute $\hat{g}_2 \leftarrow H_0(\mathsf{dom})$ and return $uRT \leftarrow \hat{g}_2^{\,u_i}$.

Sign($param, uSK, \mathsf{dom}, m$):
1. Compute $\hat{g}_2 \leftarrow H_0(\mathsf{dom})$.
2. Choose $(r_1, r_2) \in \mathbb{Z}_p^2$ at random and compute $R_1 \leftarrow A_i^{r_1}$, $R_2 \leftarrow g_1^{r_2}$ and $R_3 \leftarrow e(R_2, \hat{g}_2)^{u_i}$.
3. Compute the following signature of knowledge:

$$S \leftarrow SoK\{(\alpha, \beta, \gamma) : R_1 = g_1^{\beta/(z+\alpha)} \wedge R_2 = g_1^\gamma \wedge R_3 = e(g_1, \hat{g}_2)^{\alpha \cdot \gamma}\}(m)$$

(a) Choose $t_1, t_2, t_3 \in \mathbb{Z}_p$ at random and compute

$$T_1 \leftarrow e(A_i, \hat{g}_2)^{-t_1 \cdot r_1} \cdot e(g_1, \hat{g}_2)^{t_2} , \quad T_2 \leftarrow g_1^{t_3} \quad and \quad T_3 \leftarrow e(R_2, \hat{g}_2)^{t_1}.$$

(b) Compute the challenge $c = H(param, m, \mathsf{dom}, T_1, T_2, T_3)$.
(c) Compute $s_1 \leftarrow t_1 + c \cdot u_i$, $s_2 \leftarrow t_2 + c \cdot r_1$ and $s_3 \leftarrow t_3 + c \cdot r_2$.
(d) Set $S = (c, s_1, s_2, s_3)$
4. Output the signature $\sigma = (S, R_1, R_2, R_3)$.

Verify($param, nym, \mathsf{dom}, \sigma, m, uRT$):
1. Compute $\hat{g}_2 \leftarrow H_0(\mathsf{dom})$.
2. Parse the signature as $\sigma = (S, R_1, R_2, R_3)$, where $S = (c, s_1, s_2, s_3)$.

---

[2] This value may be derived in a deterministic way, e.g. $u_i \leftarrow H(z, i)$.

3. Restore the values

$$\tilde{T}_1 = e(R_1, nym)^{-c} \cdot e(R_1, \hat{g}_2)^{-s_1} \cdot e(g_1, \hat{g}_2)^{s_2}$$
$$\tilde{T}_2 = g_1^{s_3} \cdot R_2^{-c}$$
$$\tilde{T}_3 = e(R_2, \hat{g}_2)^{s_1} \cdot R_3^{-c}$$

4. If $c \neq \mathsf{H}(param, m, \mathsf{dom}, \tilde{T}_1, \tilde{T}_2, \tilde{T}_3)$, then return 0 (reject).
5. If $e(R_2, uRT) = R_3$, then return 0 (reject).
6. Return 1 (accept).

Theorem 1. *Pseudonymous Public Key Group Signature is correct.*

Proof. The proof is simply due the inspection of the following equations:

$$\tilde{T}_1 = e(R_1, nym)^{-c} \cdot e(R_1, \hat{g}_2)^{-s_1} \cdot e(g_1, \hat{g}_2)^{s_2} =$$
$$\left(e(R_1, \hat{g}_2)^{-t_1} \cdot e(g_1, \hat{g}_2)^{t_2} \right) \cdot e(R_1, nym)^{-c} \cdot e(R_1, \hat{g}_2^{-c \cdot u_i}) \cdot e(g_1^{c \cdot r_1}, \hat{g}_2) =$$
$$T_1 \cdot e(A_i^{r_1}, \hat{g}_2^{-c \cdot z} \cdot \hat{g}_2^{-c \cdot u_i}) \cdot e(g_1^{c \cdot r_1}, \hat{g}_2) = T_1 \cdot e(g_1, \hat{g}_2)^{-r_1 \cdot c} \cdot e(g_1, \hat{g}_2)^{r_1 \cdot c} = T_1$$
$$\tilde{T}_2 = g_1^{s_3} \cdot R_2^{-c} = g_1^{t_3} \cdot g_1^{c \cdot r_2} \cdot g_1^{-c \cdot r_2} = T_2$$
$$\tilde{T}_3 = e(R_2, \hat{g}_2)^{s_1} \cdot R_3^{-c} = e(R_1, \hat{g}_2)^{t_1} \cdot e(g_1, \hat{g}_2)^{r_2 \cdot c \cdot u_i} \cdot e(g_1, \hat{g}_2)^{-r_2 \cdot c \cdot u_i} = T_3$$

For the revocation procedure, let $uRT \leftarrow \hat{g}_2^{u_i}$ be a revocation token. Then we have $e(R_2, uRT) = e(g_1^{r_2}, \hat{g}_2^{u_i}) = R_3$.

4.2 Security Analysis

Due to space limitation we give only an intuition behind the security proofs. A detailed formal analysis is postponed to the full version of the paper.

Zero-Knowledge and Witness Extraction. Our construction is based on a known technique of using a Σ-protocol converted into a signature scheme via the Fiat-Shamir heuristic. For such a construction we may show that, in the random oracle model, there is a witness extractor (so the protocol is a proof of knowledge) and a simulator (so the protocol is zero-knowledge). Using the witness extractor, from a forged signature for a pseudonym nym within domain dom, we may extract values $\tilde{u}, \tilde{r}_1, \tilde{r}_2$ and $\tilde{A}$, such that $g_1^{\tilde{r}_2} = R_2$, $e(R_2, \mathsf{H}_0(\mathsf{dom}))^{\tilde{u}} = R_3$ and $e(g_1, \mathsf{H}_0(\mathsf{dom})) = e(\tilde{A}, \mathsf{H}_0(\mathsf{dom})^{\tilde{u}} \cdot nym)$. Using the simulator we may generate a correct signature having only $g_1, \hat{g}_2, nym$ and a revocation token $\mathsf{H}_0(\mathsf{dom})^{\tilde{u}}$.

Lemma 1. *The protocol has an extractor.*

Proof. Suppose we can rewind the Prover to the moment when he is given the challenge c. The Prover will send R_1, R_2, R_3, T_1, T_2 and T_3 and respond with the challenge c and s_1, s_2 and s_3. Then we rewind to the step when the Prover obtains c and send a different challenge $c' \neq c$. The Prover will answer with s_1',

s_2' and s_3' satisfying the verification equations. Let $\Delta s_i = (s_i - s_i')$ for $i = 1, 2, 3$ and $\Delta c = (c - c')$. From the equality

$$T_1 = e(R_1, nym)^{-c} \cdot e(R_1, \hat{g}_2)^{-s_1} \cdot e(g_1, \hat{g}_2)^{s_2} = e(R_1, nym)^{-c'} \cdot e(R_1, \hat{g}_2)^{-s_1'} \cdot e(g_1, \hat{g}_2)^{s_2'}$$

we have that

$$e(R_1, \hat{g}_2)^{-\Delta s_1} \cdot e(g_1, \hat{g}_2)^{\Delta s_2} = e(R_1, nym)^{\Delta c}$$
$$e(R_1, \hat{g}_2)^{-\Delta s_1/\Delta c} \cdot e(g_1, \hat{g}_2)^{\Delta s_2/\Delta c} = e(R_1, nym)$$
$$e(g_1, \hat{g}_2)^{\Delta s_2/\Delta c} = e(R, \hat{g}_2^{\Delta s_1/\Delta c} \cdot nym)$$
$$e(g_1, \hat{g}_2) = e(R_1^{(\Delta s_2/\Delta c)^{-1}}, \hat{g}_2^{\Delta s_1/\Delta c} \cdot nym)$$

Then from $T_2 = g_1^{s_3} \cdot R_2^{-c} = g_1^{s_3'} \cdot R_2^{-c'}$ we have

$$g_1^{\Delta s_3} = R_2^{\Delta c}$$
$$g_1^{\Delta s_3/\Delta c} = R_2$$

So, we may compute $\tilde{u} = \Delta s_1/\Delta c$, and $\tilde{r}_1 = \Delta s_2/\Delta c$, $\tilde{r}_2 = \Delta s_3/\Delta c$ and $\tilde{A} = R^{\tilde{r}_1^{-1}}$ such that $g_1^{\tilde{r}_2} = R_2$ and $e(g_1, \hat{g}_2) = e(\tilde{A}, \hat{g}_2^{\tilde{u}} \cdot nym)$.

Finally, from $T_3 = e(R_2, \hat{g}_2)^{s_1} \cdot R_3^{-c} = e(R_2, \hat{g}_2)^{s_1'} \cdot R_3^{-c'}$ we have

$$e(R_2, \hat{g}_2)^{\Delta s_1} = e(R_3, \hat{g}_2)^{\Delta c}$$
$$e(g_1, \hat{g}_2)^{\tilde{r}_2 \cdot \tilde{u}} = R_3.$$

Lemma 2. *The protocol is Zero-Knowledge.*

Proof. Given the common input $(\mathbb{G}_1, \mathbb{G}_2, e, g_1, \hat{g}_2, nym)$, where $\hat{g}_2 = \mathsf{H}_0(dom)$ and $nym = \hat{g}_2^z$ for some $z \in \mathbb{Z}_p$, the simulator works as follows. Choose $R_3 \xleftarrow{\mathcal{R}} \mathbb{G}_1$ and $R_2 \xleftarrow{\mathcal{R}} \mathbb{G}_1$. Note that now the value of A_i is fixed by the choice of R_3 and R_2. In order to highlight this we may denote $R_2 = g_1^{r_2}$ and $R_3 = e(R_2, \hat{g}_2)^{u_i}$ for some $u_i \in \mathbb{Z}_p$, hence we have $A = g_1^{1/(u_i+z)}$. Choose $R_1 \xleftarrow{\mathcal{R}} \mathbb{G}_1$ at random. See that $R_1 = A^{r_1/(u+z)}$ for some r_1, thus the values R_1, R_2, R_3 are distributed as in a real protocol. Now, the simulator chooses $(c, s_1, s_2, s_3) \xleftarrow{\mathcal{R}} \mathbb{Z}_p^4$ and computes

$$T_1 \leftarrow e(R_1, nym)^{-c} \cdot e(R_1, \hat{g}_2)^{-s_1} \cdot e(g_1, \hat{g}_2)^{s_2},$$
$$T_2 \leftarrow g_1^{s_3} \cdot R_2^{-c} \quad \text{and} \quad T_3 \leftarrow e(R_2, \hat{g}_2)^{s_1} \cdot R_3^{-c}.$$

Obviously, T_1, T_2 and T_3 along with the values c, s_1, s_2, s_3 satisfy the verification equations. Moreover, R_1, R_2, R_3, c, s_1, s_2, s_3 are uniformly distributed as in the real executions, so the simulation is perfect.

Theorem 2. *If DLP is (ϵ', t')-hard in $\mathbb{G}_2$, then the Pseudonymous Public Key Group Signature is (ϵ, t)-unforgeable, where $\epsilon \approx q_U \cdot n \cdot \sqrt{q_{\mathsf{H}}(\epsilon' + 1/p)}$ and $t \approx t'$, and n, q_U and q_{H} are the upper bounds on the number of invocations of, respectively, $\mathcal{O}_{CreateUser}$, $\mathcal{O}_{AddDevice}$ and hash queries.*

The unforgeability property relies on the DLP problem. Here we put a DL problem instance $\Lambda \in \mathbb{G}_2$ into the revocation tokens of a chosen device. We may program the random oracle to output $g_2^{r_{\text{dom}}} \leftarrow \mathsf{H}_0(\mathsf{dom})$, and then we may compute the revocation tokens as $uRT \leftarrow \Lambda^{r_{\text{dom}}}$. If the adversary successfully forges a signature for that device, we use the extractor and extract the discrete logarithm $\alpha = \log_{g_2}(\Lambda)$.

Theorem 3. *If q-CAA is (ϵ', t')-hard in $\mathbb{G}_1$, then the Pseudonymous Public Key Group Signature is (ϵ, t)-seclusive, where $\epsilon \approx n \cdot \sqrt{q_{\mathsf{H}}(\epsilon' + 1/p)}$, $t \approx t'$, and n, q and q_{H} are the upper bounds on the number of, respectively, $\mathcal{O}_{CreateUser}$, $\mathcal{O}_{AddDevice}$ and hash queries.*

Seclusiveness follows from the fact that device secret keys are CAA instances, i.e. they consist of pairs $(u, g_1^{1/(u+z)}) \in \mathbb{Z}_p \times \mathbb{G}_1$. If an adversary would forge a signature, then from the extractor we may obtain a pair $(\tilde{u}, \tilde{A})$. If the forged signature cannot be revoked, then from the revocation equation $e(R_2, \hat{g}_2^{u_i}) \neq R_3$ follows that $\tilde{u} \neq u_i$ for each device secret key u_i issued by the user holding z. Thus $(\tilde{u}, \tilde{A})$, is the solution to the CAA problem instance.

Theorem 4. *If BDDH is (ϵ', t')-hard in $\mathbb{G}_1, \mathbb{G}_2$, then the Pseudonymous Public Key Group Signature is (ϵ, t)-anonymous, where $\epsilon \approx \frac{\epsilon'^2}{n \cdot q_{\mathsf{H}} \cdot q_U^2}$, $t \approx t'$, and n, q_U and q_{H} are upper bounds on the number of, respectively, $\mathcal{O}_{CreateUser}$, $\mathcal{O}_{AddDevice}$ and hash queries.*

In order to proof anonymity, we describe a sequence of games. We will start with a game where the challenge signature is returned by the device j_0^* (bit $b = 0$). Then in each game we change the protocol execution so that the adversary has only a negligible chance of noticing these changes. Finally, we will end up in a game where the challenge signature is computed for user j_1^* (bit $b = 1$).

The strategy of changing the protocol is as follows. First we need to simulate the signatures for all devices. Then, for the j_0^*-th device, under the BDDH assumption, we choose these values independently at random. Next, instead of choosing R_1, R_2, R_3 independently we compute these values as for device j_1^*. Below, we shed some light on the step of changing the values of R_1, R_2, R_3 into random values.

Let (g_2^a, g_2^b, g_1^c) be a BDDH problem instance and let dom^* denote the domain from the challenge oracle. In all domains $\mathsf{dom} \neq \mathsf{dom}^*$ we choose r_{dom} at random, program the hash oracle to output $g_2^{r_{\text{dom}}} \leftarrow \mathsf{H}_0(\mathsf{dom})$ and we compute $uRT \leftarrow (g_2^a)^{r_{\text{dom}}}$ and $R_3 \leftarrow e(g_1^{r_{\text{dom}}}, g_2^a)^{r_2}$ for device j_0^*. In domain dom^*, we program the hash oracle to return $g_2^b \leftarrow \mathsf{H}_0(\mathsf{dom}^*)$. Then, we choose $r_2 \xleftarrow{\mathcal{R}} \mathbb{Z}_p$ at random, compute $R_2 \leftarrow g_1^{c \cdot r_2}$ and $R_3 \leftarrow e(g_1, g_2)^{abc \cdot r_2}$ (the current game) or R_3 is chosen at random (the next game). Note that if an adversary would distinguish whether $R_3 = e(g_1, g_2)^{abc \cdot r_2}$ or R_3 is random, then it would break the BDDH assumption.

Theorem 5. *If SXDH is (ϵ', t')-hard in $\mathbb{G}_1$, then the Pseudonymous Public Key Group Signature is (ϵ, t)-domain unlinkable, where $\epsilon \approx \epsilon' \cdot q_{\mathsf{H}}(q_U + n)$, $t \approx t'$, and n, q_U and q_{H} are the upper bounds on the number of, respectively, $\mathcal{O}_{CreateUser}$, $\mathcal{O}_{AddDevice}$ and hash queries.*

Domain unlinkability follows from the fact that we may simulate the signatures for each device and that in each domain we have a distinct base $\hat{g}_2 \leftarrow H_0(\text{dom})$. Note that the device revocation tokens are computed as $uRT_{i,j,\text{dom}} = \hat{g}_2{}^{u_j}$ for a device secret key $u_j \in \mathbb{Z}_p$. In a given domain we may choose $uRT_{i,j,\text{dom}}$ at random. It is easy to see that if an adversary would recognize this change, he would serve as a distinguisher for the SXDH problem. In the proof, we need to choose revocation tokens of all devices in all domains at random. Finally, we may use the same reasoning to choose pseudonyms $nym = H_0(\text{dom})$ at random in each domain, finally ending up in an ideal system as defined in Sect. 3.

4.3 Additional Procedures and Scheme Variants

Here we describe briefly some additional procedures and variations of our scheme, which may be useful for certain practical situations.

First, note that the signing device needs only to know his private key consisting of an SDH pair $(u, g_1^{1/(z+u)})$ and nothing else, in order to create a signature. In particular, the signing device does not need to know the public key, aka the pseudonym, with which the signature will later be verified. Moreover, it seems that the signing device alone is not even able to compute the pseudonym by itself. However, in some cases it may be desirable that the signing device can compute a pseudonym, what in our case may be $nym' - e(Z, \hat{g}_2)$, assuming the user also issues the value $Z = g_1^z$. Such nym' may serve as a temporal pseudonym, until the owner of the device confirms this pseudonym by proving his knowledge of the secret key $z \in \mathbb{Z}_p$.

Proving the knowledge of the master key may be required as a part of user registration. This may be simply done by designing a Σ-protocol [15] which will prove the knowledge of $\log_{g_1}(nym)$. Such standard protocol may be transformed into a zero-knowledge proof of knowledge protocol or into its non-interactive version in the random oracle model.

5   Conclusions

Beyond the concrete application case of delegating the rights by a user to multiple own devices, we have introduced a novel notion for group signature schemes. It expands the functionality of group signatures by adding the feature that group public keys may be pseudonyms derived ad hoc.

We have introduced a security framework for our scheme supporting strong privacy protection on one hand, and revocation capabilities on the other hand.

Finally, we have designed a scheme based on bilinear groups which implements such a system. Even if it uses bilinear groups and pairings, it is relatively simple and implementable on relatively weak devices. Note that the user's root of trust may be a relatively weak device, since no procedure executed by it requires computation of pairings. They are needed for signature creation (this can be done by smart phones) and verification (on strong servers).

References

1. Bellare, M., Micciancio, D., Warinschi, B.: Foundations of group signatures: formal definitions, simplified requirements, and a construction based on general assumptions. In: Biham, E. (ed.) EUROCRYPT 2003. LNCS, vol. 2656, pp. 614–629. Springer, Heidelberg (2003). doi:10.1007/3-540-39200-9_38
2. Bellare, M., Shi, H., Zhang, C.: Foundations of group signatures: the case of dynamic groups. In: Menezes, A. (ed.) CT-RSA 2005. LNCS, vol. 3376, pp. 136–153. Springer, Heidelberg (2005)
3. Boneh, D., Boyen, X., Shacham, H.: Short group signatures. In: Franklin, M. (ed.) CRYPTO 2004. LNCS, vol. 3152, pp. 41–55. Springer, Heidelberg (2004)
4. Boyen, X., Waters, B.: Full-domain subgroup hiding and constant-size group signatures. In: Okamoto, T., Wang, X. (eds.) PKC 2007. LNCS, vol. 4450, pp. 1–15. Springer, Heidelberg (2007)
5. Boneh, D., Shacham, H.: Group signatures with verifier-local revocation. In: Proceedings of the 11th ACM Conference on Computer and Communications Security, CCS 2004, pp. 168–177. ACM, New York (2004)
6. Kiayias, A., Tsiounis, Y., Yung, M.: Traceable signatures. In: Cachin, C., Camenisch, J.L. (eds.) EUROCRYPT 2004. LNCS, vol. 3027, pp. 571–589. Springer, Heidelberg (2004)
7. Trolin, M., Wikström, D.: Hierarchical group signatures. In: Caires, L., Italiano, G.F., Monteiro, L., Palamidessi, C., Yung, M. (eds.) ICALP 2005. LNCS, vol. 3580, pp. 446–458. Springer, Heidelberg (2005)
8. Ali, S.T., Amberker, B.B.: Dynamic attribute based group signature with attribute anonymity and tracing in the standard model. In: Gierlichs, B., Guilley, S., Mukhopadhyay, D. (eds.) SPACE 2013. LNCS, vol. 8204, pp. 147–171. Springer, Heidelberg (2013)
9. Han, S., Wang, J., Liu, W.: An efficient identity-based group signature scheme over elliptic curves. In: Freire, M.M., Chemouil, P., Lorenz, P., Gravey, A. (eds.) ECUMN 2004. LNCS, vol. 3262, pp. 417–429. Springer, Heidelberg (2004)
10. Bringer, J., Chabanne, H., Lescuyer, R., Patey, A.: Efficient and strongly secure dynamic domain-specific pseudonymous signatures for ID documents. In: Christin, N., Safavi-Naini, R. (eds.) FC 2014. LNCS, vol. 8437, pp. 252–269. Springer, Heidelberg (2014)
11. Brickell, E., Camenisch, J., Chen, L.: Direct anonymous attestation. In: Proceedings of the 11th ACM Conference on Computer and Communications Security, CCS 2004, pp. 132–145. ACM, New York (2004)
12. Camenisch, J., Mödersheim, S., Sommer, D.: A formal model of identity mixer. In: Kowalewski, S., Roveri, M. (eds.) FMICS 2010. LNCS, vol. 6371, pp. 198–214. Springer, Heidelberg (2010)
13. Galbraith, S.D., Paterson, K.G., Smart, N.P.: Pairings for cryptographers. Discrete Appl. Math. **156**(16), 3113–3121 (2008)
14. Boneh, D., Boyen, X.: Short signatures without random oracles and the sdh assumption in bilinear groups. J. Cryptol. **21**(2), 149–177 (2008)
15. Damgård, I.: On Σ-protocols. Lecture notes for CPT, v. 2

A Mobile Device-Based Antishoulder-Surfing Identity Authentication Mechanism

Jia-Ning Luo[1(✉)], Ming-Hour Yang[2], and Cho-Luen Tsai[1]

[1] Department of Information and Telecommunications Engineering,
Ming Chuan University, Taoyuan, Taiwan
deer@mail.mcu.edu.tw
[2] Department of Information and Computer Engineering,
Chung Yuan Christian University, Taoyuan, Taiwan
mhyang@cycu.edu.tw

Abstract. Text-based passwords are unable to prevent shoulder-surfing attacks. In this paper, a new authentication mechanism was introduced to send out misleading information to attackers when the former entered its text-based passwords; the latter was unable to decipher the true passwords by simply recording or looking at them. The misleading information was the pressure values (i.e., pressures exerted by the users) measured by pressure sensors embedded under the smartphone touchscreens. The systems detected each pressure value entered by the users and determined whether it was to be saved (i.e., as a true password) or omitted (i.e., as misleading information). Regarding this authentication method, because attackers were unable to know the users' pressure values, they were unable to differentiate between true and misleading information and thus had no way of knowing the users' actual passwords. In the end, our authentication mechanism improved the deficiency of current text-based passwords and enhanced system security.

Keywords: Shoulder-surfing attacks · Graphical password

1 Introduction

Shoulder-surfing attacks signify the practice of spying on the user of a device to obtain his/her passwords. Methods to protect users from shoulder-surfing attacks have been proposed in numerous studies: (1) Virtual password. Users obtain their password via calculations made using mathematical functions [6]. (2) Virtual keyboard. Users are asked to enter their password in advance. Text on the keyboard is then removed during authentication, preventing attackers from seeing the text [8]. (3) Graphical password. This type of method uses a graphical interface as its verification tool, in which buttons are employed to move icons to the authentication area or range [3–5,9]. (4) Second channel. A second channel is added to general authentication methods to eliminate shoulder-surfing attacks. Examples include telling users a verification code via earphones connected to their mobile phones and asking the users to enter the said verification code [1,2,7].

© Springer International Publishing AG 2016
J. Chen et al. (Eds.): NSS 2016, LNCS 9955, pp. 37–46, 2016.
DOI: 10.1007/978-3-319-46298-1_3

In this study, we introduced a password system that eliminated shoulder-surfing and recording attacks. In general, users show one of two behavioral patterns (i.e., honest or deceptive) when inputting information. For example, the former involves the users operating touchscreens in a habitual manner, whereas the latter involves the users operating the touchscreens in a manner that differs from their habits. Our system was able to identify users' behavioral patterns and separate the two input types into different categories while providing the same user interface, which enabled us to mislead our attackers.

In this study, a pressure sensor was installed on smartphone touchscreens to obtain the pressure value when users pressed on the touchscreens. Next, the users' behavioral patterns were determined by analyzing pressure value changes when the users input information. The results were incorporated into an existing authentication system to improve security. This method was effective because attackers were unable to steal the users' behavioral patterns (i.e., pressure values) by using shoulder-surfing attacks or recording attacks.

The method introduced in this study elevated a system's defense capability against shoulder-surfing attacks, effectively deterred recording attacks, and reduced a system's false positive rate. The goals of this study are to enhance system security while providing users with a quick and convenient authentication process.

2   An Antishoulder-Surfing Attack-Based Identity Authentication System for Mobile Devices

In this section, we introduce an antishoulder-surfing attack-based identity authentication system suitable for touchscreen-based smartphones. The said system was incorporated into Android screen pattern locks, in which pressure exerted by users' fingers on the smartphone touchscreens was used as the basis for authentication. The method by which the users' pressure values were recorded is then explained. This method effectively prevented attackers from learning about users' true input values by looking at the users' passwords and did not require verification codes be sent via secure channels. Table 1 lists the notations.

2.1   New Methods for Defending Shoulder-Surfing Attacks

In this study, we introduced a new method in which pressure values input by users (measured by using touchscreen pressure sensors) were used as auxiliary inputs in addition to passwords. Shoulder-surfing attackers were thus unable to learn about the said values. Concerning the unit used by the smartphone pressure sensors to measure pressure values, it was hPa.

Smartphone touchscreens were employed as the users input interface. Because the amount of pressure exerted by the users' fingers when operating the touchscreens differed between letters/numbers/symbols, our method recorded the corresponding times and pressure values for each letter/number/symbol input by the users. Our recording method was divided into five stages and are described

Table 1. Notations

w_i	x, y coordinates, pressure, and time of the data input by users;
	$w_i = (x_i, y_i, g_i, \Delta t)$
W	Input sequence starting from the time when the user first touched the screen to the time he/she released his/her finger from the screen;
	$W_i = \{w_1, w_2, w_3, ..., w_n\}$
F	Set of input sequences; $F = \{W_1, W_2, W_3, ..., W_m\}$
$Map()$	Mesh number converted from x and y coordinates
v_i	Mesh number converted from the coordinates;
	$v_i = Map(w_i) = (Mx_i, My_i, g_i, \Delta t)$
V	Set of mesh numbers $V_i = \{v_1, v_2, v_3, ..., v_n\}$
G	Set of Vs; $G = \{V_1, V_2, V_3, ..., V_m\}$
v'	Mean pressure value obtained by first removing repeated mesh numbers and then taking the average of the pressure values
V'	Set of $v's$ (repeated mesh numbers removed); $V_i' = \{v_1', v_2', v_3', ..., v_p'\}$
G'	Set of $V's$; $G' = \{V_1', V_2', V_3', ..., V_q'\}$
t_{u_i}	Pressure threshold of user u_i
V''	Set of $V's$ greater than the threshold value; $V_i'' = \{V_1'', V_2'', V_3'', ..., V_q''\}$
G''	Set of $V''s$

as follows: (1) Record user's input; (2) Convert coordinates to mesh numbers; (3) Combine continuous and identical mesh numbers; (4) Differentiate between pressures exerted (i.e., light and heavy pressure values); and (5) Convert data into authentication system outputs.

When a user drew a continuous line on the touchscreen (as shown on the left in Fig. 1, segments with a pressure value greater than the threshold value of t were represented in red and a subsequent line was generated by our system, as shown on the right in Fig. 1.

Stage 1: Record User's Input. The x, y coordinates, pressure, and time of a series of lines drawn by a user are represented as follows:

$$w_i = (x_i, y_i, g_i, \Delta t)$$
$$W_i = \{w_1, w_2, w_3, ..., w_n\}$$
$$F = \{W_1, W_2, W_3, ..., W_m\}$$

In which a line drawn by a user when he/she touched the screen and released his/her finger from the screen (one time) was set as the first input. F represents the series of lines drawn by the user. W_i was a set of inputs in sequence, whereas g_i and Δt were the corresponding pressure value and time, respectively.

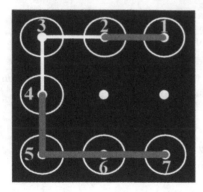
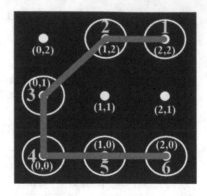

Fig. 1. Continuous line drawn by user and subsequent line generated by the system (Color figure online)

Stage 2: Convert Coordinates to Mesh Numbers. Coordinate w_i was converted into a mesh number v_i in the authentication system, as shown below:

$$v_i = Map(w_i) = (Mx_i, My_i, g_i, \Delta t)$$
$$V_i = \{v_1, v_2, v_3, ..., v_n\}$$
$$G = \{\{V_1, V_2, V_3, ..., V_m\}\}$$

Using the x and y coordinates of w_i, the mesh in which w_i was located could be calculated. The size of the mesh was related to the authentication method used and determined by the authentication system. Assuming that the x and y coordinates of w_i were $(4, 5)$ and that mesh size was $3 * 3$ (as shown in Fig. 2, the mesh number of x and y would be 1 (i.e., $4/3 = 1$) and 1 (i.e., $5/3 = 1$), respectively. Therefore, w_i would be located in mesh number $(1, 1)$.

Stage 3: Combine Continuous and Identical Mesh Numbers. Continuous and identical mesh numbers were combined and the average pressure value was calculated. When the mesh number of v_i equaled v_j, the mean pressure value was substituted into v_i and v_j was deleted.

$$g_i = \frac{g_i \cdot \Delta t + g_i \cdot \Delta t}{2 \cdot \Delta t}$$

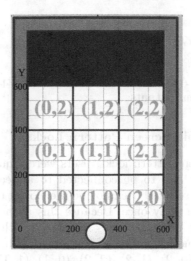

Fig. 2. Coordinates and mesh

This produced $V_i' = \{V_1', V_2', V_3', ..., V_q'\}$ and $G' = \{V_1', V_2', V_3', ..., V_q'\}$.

---

input : V
output: V'

1 $i \leftarrow 1$;
2 **while** $i <= |V_i|$ **do**
3      $j \leftarrow i$;
4   **while** $j <= |V_i|$ **do**
5         $j \leftarrow j + 1$;
6   **if** $(Mx_i = Mx_j)\&(My_i = My_j)$ **then**
7            $g_i = \frac{g_i \cdot \Delta t_i + g_j \cdot \Delta t_j}{2 \cdot \Delta t_i}$
8   **end**
9   **else**
10   continue ;
11   **end**
12   **end**
13     $V_i' = V_i' \cup \{v_i\}$;
14     $i \leftarrow j$;
15 **end**

Algorithm 1. Mesh-combining algorithm

Stage 4: Differentiate Between Pressures Exerted (i.e., Light and Heavy). Each input (i.e., V_i') was separated into light or heavy pressure according to the threshold value t_{u_i}; different threshold values were set for different users. Only the heavy pressure values (i.e., V_i'') were retained and all the V_i''s were grouped to form Set G''.

$$V_i'' = \{v_i'|g_i > t_{u_i}\}$$
$$G'' = \{\{V_1'', V_2'', V_3'', ..., V_q''\}\}$$

Stage 5: Convert into Authentication System Output. G'' was converted into authentication system outputs.

2.2 Improved Android Screen Pattern Locks

To unlock Android screen pattern locks, users were required to choose four of the nine dots (each dot had to be connected to at least one other dot), as shown in Fig. 3; the dots selected need not be the closest to subsequent dots and each dot could be chosen only once. Because this authentication method was prone to shoulder-surfing attacks, it was integrated with the method proposed in this study. First, the mesh numbers of the nine dots from left to right, top to bottom were defined as (0, 2), (1, 2), (2, 2), (0, 1), (1, 1), (2, 1), (0, 0), (1, 0), and (2, 0).

Stage 1: Record User's Input. In addition to the coordinates drawn by the user, the pressure values of the coordinates were obtained. The lock pattern selected by the user is shown in Fig. 3. Because Android screen pattern lock allowed only one input, the user's input (i.e., F) contained only one set (i.e., W_1).

$$W_1 = \{w_1, w_2, w_3, ..., w_n\}$$
$$F = \{W_1\}$$

Stage 2: Convert Coordinates to Mesh Numbers. All the coordinates of W_1 (i.e., w_is) were converted into mesh numbers (i.e., v_i s) to produce Set V_1, which contained all the mesh numbers.

$$v_i = Map(w_i) = (Mx_i, My_i, g_i, \Delta t)$$
$$V_1 = \{v_1, v_2, v_3, ..., v_n\} = \{(0, 2, 0.21, \Delta t_1), (1, 2, 0.18, \Delta t_2),$$
$$(1, 2, 0.18, \Delta t_3), (2, 2, 0.1, \Delta t_4), (2, 1, 0.12, \Delta t_5), (2, 1, 0.12, \Delta t_6),$$
$$(2, 0, 0.19, \Delta t_7), (1, 0, 0.2, \Delta t_8), (1, 0, 0.2, \Delta t_9)\}$$
$$G = \{V_1\} = \{\{(0, 2, 0.21, \Delta t_1), (1, 2, 0.18, \Delta t_2),$$
$$(1, 2, 0.18, \Delta t_3), (2, 2, 0.1, \Delta t_4), (2, 1, 0.12, \Delta t_5), (2, 1, 0.12, \Delta t_6),$$
$$(2, 0, 0.19, \Delta t_7), (1, 0, 0.2, \Delta t_8), (1, 0, 0.2, \Delta t_9)\}\}$$

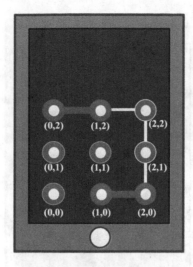

Fig. 3. Android pattern lock interface

Stage 3: Combine Continuous and Identical Mesh Numbers. Continuous and identical mesh numbers were combined, producing the following result:

$$v_i = Map(w_i) = (Mx_i, My_i, g_i, \Delta t)$$
$$V_1' = \{v_1', v_2', v_3', ..., v_p'\} = \{(0, 2, 0.21, \Delta t_1), (1, 2, 0.18, \Delta t_2),$$
$$(2, 2, 0.1, \Delta t_3), (2, 1, 0.12, \Delta t_4), (2, 0, 0.19, \Delta t_5), (1, 0, 0.2, \Delta t_6)\}$$
$$G = \{V_1'\} = \{\{v_1', v_2', v_3', ..., v_p'\} = \{(0, 2, 0.21, \Delta t_1), (1, 2, 0.18, \Delta t_2),$$
$$(2, 2, 0.1, \Delta t_3), (2, 1, 0.12, \Delta t_4), (2, 0, 0.19, \Delta t_5), (1, 0, 0.2, \Delta t_6)\}\}$$

Stage 4: Differentiate Between Pressures Exerted (i.e., Light and Heavy). Mesh numbers of light pressure values were removed and heavy pressure values retained according to the threshold value t_{u_1} ($t_{u_1} = 0.15$ hPa) to form V_1'', which was incorporated into G''.

$$V_1'' = \{v_i' \| g_i > t_{u_i}\} = \{v_i' \| g_i > 0.15\}$$
$$= \{(0, 2, 0.21, \Delta t_1), (1, 2, 0.18, \Delta t_2), (2, 0, 0.19, \Delta t_5), (1, 0, 0.2, \Delta t_6)\}$$
$$G'' = \{V_1''\} = \{\{(0, 2, 0.21, \Delta t_1), (1, 2, 0.18, \Delta t_2), (2, 0, 0.19, \Delta t_5), (1, 0, 0.2, \Delta t_6)\}\}$$

Stage 5: Convert into Authentication System Output. Mesh numbers with heavy pressure values were retained and connected to produce the following result (Fig. 4), which differed from the pattern observed by the attacker.

The results showed that despite the attacker seeing the authentication pattern entered by the user, such a pattern differed from the actual pattern

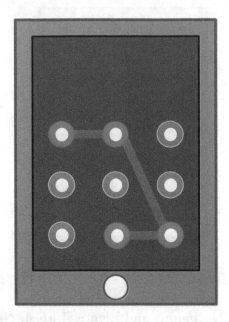

Fig. 4. Authentication pattern generated by the system

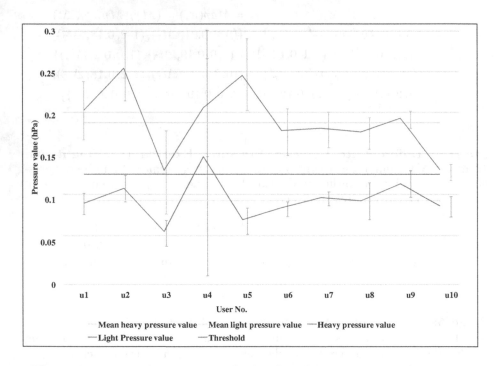

Fig. 5. Comparisons between 10 randomly selected pressures exerted by 10 users

generated by the system. This confirms that our method can be applied to Android pattern locks to prevent shoulder-surfing attacks.

3   Experiment and Analysis

Because pressure values differed between users and that pressure threshold set for each user differed, instances in which the user considered a pressure value to be light but the system assessed it to be heavy may occur. Therefore, this study analyzed and investigated the threshold value t_{u_1}.

A total of 10 pressures exerted by 10 users (total: 100 pressure values) were randomly selected and the average pressure value for each user was taken (as shown in Fig. 5). According to the figure, the pressure values differed significantly between different users, in which light pressure values fell at approximately 0.0987 ± 0.05 (hPa) and heavy pressure values fell at approximately 0.1909 ± 0.07 (hPa). In fact, pressure values that were considered light for some users were heavy for others, signifying considerable differences in light and heavy pressure values between users. Therefore, different threshold value ranges were set for different users.

4   Conclusion

In this study, pressure values (i.e., pressures exerted by users) were measured using pressure sensors embedded under smartphone touchscreens. Such pressure values were combined with identity authentication methods currently employed by smartphones to protect users from shoulder-surfing attacks. Because attackers are unable to differentiate between true and misleading information, the said authentication system can effectively defend users from shoulder-surfing attacks.

The method introduced in this study can be used by any touchscreen-based authentication system operated by fingers. The method protects users from leaking their text-based passwords and Android screen pattern locks when they are shoulder surfed by attackers, elevating their information security. In addition, attackers are unable to decipher the true passwords even if they have successfully observed the complete passwords.

Acknowledgements. This research was supported by the Ministry of Science and Technology, Taiwan under grant no. MOST 104-2221-E-103-009 and MOST 105-2221-E-130-005.

References

1. Bianchi, A., Oakley, I., Kostakos, V., Kwon, D.S.: The phone lock: audio and haptic shoulder-surfing resistant PIN entry methods for mobile devices. In: Proceedings of the Fifth International Conference on Tangible, Embedded, and Embodied Interaction, pp. 197–200 (2011)

2. Chakraborty, N., Mondal, S.: SLASS: secure login against shoulder surfing. In: Recent Trends in Computer Networks and Distributed Systems Security, pp. 346–357 (2014)
3. Chen, Y.L., Ku, W.C., Yeh, Y.C., Liao, D.M.: A simple text-based shoulder surfing resistant graphical password scheme. In: Proceedings of the 2013 IEEE International Symposium on Next-Generation Electronics (ISNE), pp. 161–164 (2013)
4. Kim, S.H., Kim, J.W., Kim, S.Y., Cho, H.G.: A new shoulder-surfing resistant password for mobile environments. In: Proceedings of the 5th International Conference on Ubiquitous Information Management and Communication, Article no. 27 (2011)
5. Lee, M.K.: Security notions and advanced method for human shoulder-surfing resistant pin-entry. IEEE Trans. Inf. Forensics Secur. 9(4), 695–708 (2014)
6. Lei, M., Xiao, Y., Vrbsky, S.V., Li, C.C., Liu, L.: A virtual password scheme to protect passwords. In: Proceedings of the IEEE International Conference on Communications (ICC 2008), pp. 1536–1540 (2008)
7. Perkovi, T., agalj, M., Raki, N: SSSL: shoulder surfing safe login. In: Profeedings of the 17th International Conference on Software, Telecommunications and Computer Networks (SoftCOM 2009), pp. 270–275 (2009)
8. Rajarajan, S., Maheswari, K., Hemapriya, R., Sriharilakshmi, S.: Shoulder surfing resistant virtual keyboard for internet banking. World Appl. Sci. J. 31(7), 1297–1304 (2014)
9. Yi, H., Piao, Y., Yi, J.H.: Touch logger resistant mobile authentication scheme using multimodal sensors. In: Jeong, H.Y., Obaidat, M.S., Yen, N.Y., Park, J.J. (eds.) Advances in Computer Science and its Applications. LNEE, pp. 19–26. Springer, Heidelberg (2014)

Mutual Authentication with Anonymity for Roaming Service with Smart Cards in Wireless Communications

Chang-Shiun Liu[1], Li Xu[2], Limei Lin[2], Min-Chi Tseng[1], Shih-Ya Lin[1], and Hung-Min Sun[1(✉)]

[1] Department of Computer Science, National Tsing Hua University, Hsinchu, Taiwan
hmsun@cs.nthu.edu.tw
[2] Fujian Provincial Key Laboratory of Network Security and Cryptology, School of Mathematics and Computer Science, Fujian Normal University, Fuzhou, Fujian, China

Abstract. Most of the mutual authentication protocols with user anonymity proposed for providing secure roaming service through wireless communications are based on smart cards and have to establish public key cryptosystems in advance. To solve this, Guo et al. firstly proposed an efficient mutual authentication protocol with user anonymity using smart card for wireless communications. Unfortunately, we will demonstrate their scheme requires high modular exponential operations for security issues, and does not allow users to change passwords freely. Based on modular square root, we propose an efficient remote user authentication protocol with smart cards for wireless communications. Compared with others, our protocol is more suitable for mobile devices and smart-card users.

Keywords: Anonymity · Roaming service · Chaotic map · Modular square root

1 Introduction

Global mobility network (GLOMONET) provides global roaming service permitting mobile users MU to access the services provided by the home agent in a foreign network. When a MU roams to a foreign network managed by a foreign agent FA, it performs authentication with FA, under the assistant of his home agent HA in the home network. Hence, a remote user authentication scheme over wireless networking has raised security concerns among MUs and service providers. Newly, many authentication protocols for GLOMONET were proposed [5,9,12]. In 2011, He et al. developed a strong user authentication scheme with smart card for wireless communications [2]. Furthermore, most previous schemes proposed for wireless networks utilized modular exponential computing and scalar multiplication on elliptic curves to ensure their security [2,5,9,12]. In 2013, based on Chebyshev chaotic maps [11], Guo et al. proposed mutual

© Springer International Publishing AG 2016
J. Chen et al. (Eds.): NSS 2016, LNCS 9955, pp. 47–61, 2016.
DOI: 10.1007/978-3-319-46298-1_4

authentication key agreement protocol using smart card for wireless communications [1], which avoids time-consuming modular exponential computing and scalar multiplication on elliptic curve cryptosystem in authentication processes. They claimed their protocol is able to provide user anonymity even though the adversary could extract the data stored in the smart card [1]. However, we will show that Guo et al.'s scheme is suffered from the impersonation attack by using information extracted from his own smart card, and does not allow changing password freely for *MU*.

Based on quadratic residue [4,6,8] and one-way hash function, we propose a new efficient authentication protocol with user anonymity for wireless communications. Performance analysis shows our proposed mechanism is much better compared with other protocols [1,2,5,9]. Without any modular exponentiation, scalar multiplication on elliptic curves, and symmetric encryption/decryption for *MU*, the proposed protocol is especially suitable for mobile devices or smart cards.

In next section, we discuss the security requirements for wireless communications. In Sect. 3, we introduce the modular square root technique and review Guo et al.'s scheme. The proposed scheme is presented in Sect. 4. In Sect. 5, the security and performance analysis of the proposed scheme are stated. In Sect. 6, we conclude the paper.

2 Background

In wireless networks, *MU* can access the services provided by *HA* in a *FA* and establish mutual authentication with the corresponding *FA*. Generally, to design a strong user authentication scheme in wireless networks should satisfy:

(1) Anonymity of users identity (2) Low communication cost and computation complexity (3) Confidentiality of the session key (4) User friendly (5) Password table: No password tables stored in *FA* or *HA* to avoid leak-of-verifier attacks. (6) Update password securely and freely (7) Mutual authentication (8) Security: Although attackers can obtain the secret information stored in the smart card, they cannot retrieve the right system secret. (9) Forward and backward secrecy: Even if the intruder obtains the current session key, the secrecy of previous or future session keys is not affected. (10) Fairness in key agreement: The session key contains equal contributions from both parties.

Recently, many user authentication schemes with smart card have been proposed for roaming services [1,2,9]. However, most are vulnerable to masquerade attack, insider attack, password-guessing attack, and could not provide mutual authentication [2,9]. To overcome these security issues, we propose a mutual authentication with anonymity for roaming service with smart cards in wireless communication.

3   Related Works

3.1   Preliminary

The modular square root (MSR) technique [4,6,8] is built on the quadratic residues and its property.

Let t be any integer and $n \in N$. Suppose the greatest common divisor of t and n is 1 ($\gcd(t, n) = 1$). Then t is called a quadratic residue modulo n if the congruence $x^2 = t(\bmod n)$ is soluble. The solutions are called MSR of quadratic residue t modulo n.

Euler's Criterion: When $p = 3(\bmod 4)$ and t is a quadratic residue modulo p, there is a simple formula to compute square roots of quadratic residue t modulo p as follows:

$$r_{1,2} = \pm t^{\frac{p+1}{4}} (\bmod p). \tag{1}$$

Based on Euler's Criterion:

Property 1. Let $n = p \cdot q$ and $\gcd(t, n) = 1$, where p and q are two distinct odd primes and $p = q = 3(\bmod 4)$. Then t is a quadratic residue modulo n if and only if $t^{\frac{p-1}{2}} = 1(\bmod p)$ and $t^{\frac{q-1}{2}} = 1(\bmod q)$.

Under the assumption of Property 1, based on Eq. (1) and the Chinese remainder theorem, these four modular square roots $r_{1,2,3,4}$ of a quadratic residue a modulo n can be computed as follows:

$$r_{1,2} = \alpha \cdot q \cdot q^* \pm \beta \cdot p \cdot p^* (\bmod n) \tag{2}$$

$$r_{3,4} = -\alpha \cdot q \cdot q^* \pm \beta \cdot p \cdot p^* (\bmod n) \tag{3}$$

where $\alpha = t^{\frac{p+1}{4}} (\bmod p)$, $\beta = t^{\frac{q+1}{4}} (\bmod q)$, $p^* = p^{-1}(\bmod q)$, and $q^* = q^{-1}(\bmod p)$. Since $\gcd(p, q) = 1$, both p^* and q^* can be determined based on the extended Euclidean algorithm.

The security of MSR is based on the difficulty of extracting modular square roots of a quadratic residue modulo n ($n = p \cdot q$) when p and q are unknown. It is computationally infeasible to factorize n if p and q are large enough.

3.2   Review of Guo et al.'s Protocol

Basic key-agreement protocol of Guo et al.'s is based on the Chebyshev chaotic map, similar to the Diffie-Hellman key-agreement protocol [7,10]. A session key can be established between two communication entities, A and B.

(1) User A and B choose a random number $x \in (-1, 1)$ together.
(2) A selects a random larger integer r and computes $X = T_r(x)$, and sends X to B.
(3) B randomly selects a larger integer s and computes $Y = T_s(x)$, and sends Y to A.

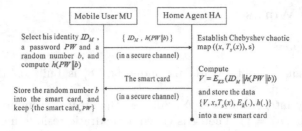

Fig. 1. Registration phase of Guo et al.'s protocol

(4) A and B could compute the common secret key $k = T_r(Y) = T_s(X) = T_{rs}(x)$.

Since $T_r(T_s(x)) = T_s(T_r(x)) = T_{rs}(x)$, A and B could construct the common secret key for the secure communication. To enhance the security, Zhang proved that property holds for Chebyshev polynomials defined on interval $(-\infty, \infty)$ [11]. In Guo et al.'s scheme, they use the enhanced Chebyshev polynomials: $T_n(x) = 2xT_{n-1}(x) - T_{n-2}(x) \bmod N$, where $n \geq 2$, $x \in Z_N$, and N is a large prime number. And it is obvious that $T_r(T_s(x)) = T_s(T_r(x)) = T_{rs}(x)$.

Guo et al.'s protocol consists of three phases:

(1) Registration phase:
In this phase, HA must choose a public key cryptosystem based on the Chebyshev chaotic map; the corresponding public key is $(x; T_s(x))$, and his private key is s. When a MU wants to register to HA, MU chooses his identity ID_M and password PW, selects a random number b and submits ID_M and $h(PW \| b)$ to HA for registration over a secure channel. HA computes $V = E_{KS}(ID_M \| h(PW \| b))$, where KS is a secret key kept by HA, and issues a smart card to MU over a secure channel containing V, x, $T_s(x)$, $E_K(.)$ and a one-way hash function $h(\_)$. When MU receives the smart card, he stores b into the smart card. Finally, the smart card contains $\{b, V, x, T_s(x), E_K(.), h(.)\}$ (Fig. 1).

(2) Mutual authentication and session key agreement phase:
When MU visits a new foreign network, if he wants to access several services or establish a session with FA, MU and FA must perform mutual authentication and agree on a session key. Similar to Xu et al.'s protocol [12], HA pre-shares a distinct symmetric key KHF with FA. As shown in Fig. 2, the following steps are performed in this phase.

- Step 1. MU inserts his smart card into a card reader and inputs his identity ID_M and password PW. Then, the device selects a random number u and computes $KMH = T_u(T_s(x))$ and $R = E_{KMH}(h_{pw} \| V \| T_{MU})$, where $h_{pw} = (ID_M \| h(PW \| b))$ and T_{MU} is the current timestamp. Then, MU sends an authentication request message $m_1 = \{ID_H, R, T_u(x), T_{MU}\}$ to FA, where ID_H is the identity of the HA.

- Step 2. FA checks whether the timestamp T_{MU} is valid. If it is, FA selects a random number v and computes $T_v(x)$. Then, FA computes $M = E_{KFH}(T_{MU} \| T_{FA} \| T_u (x) \| R \| T_v (x))$, where T_{FA} is the current timestamp, and sends the message $m_2 = \{M\}$ to HA.
- Step 3. HA decrypts M with KHF to recover $T_{MU} \| T_{FA} \| T_u (x) \| R \| T_v (x)$. First, HA checks the timestamp T_{FA} with current time. If it is valid, HA computes $KMH = T_s(T_u(x))$ with his private key s. Then, HA decrypts R with KMH to recover h_{pw}, V, and T_{MU}. HA checks whether the T_{MU} is equal to the previous one that was decrypted from M. If they are correct, HA decrypts V by using his secret key KS to obtain ID'_M and $h'(PW \| b)$. Finally, HA computes $h'_{pw} = h(ID'_M \| h'(PW \| b))$ and compares the computed value of h'_{pw} with the recovered value of h_{pw}. If they are equal, HA knows MU is authorized.
- Step 4. HA computes $Q = E_{KHF}(T_{MU} \| T_{FA} \| T_u(x) \| T_v (x))$ and $P = E_{KMH}(T_{MU} \| T_u(x) \| T_v (x) \| ID_F)$, and sends the message $m_3 = \{Q, P\}$ to FA, where ID_F is the identity of the FA.
- Step 5. FA decrypts Q with KHF to obtain T_{FA}, T_{MU}, $T_u(x)$, and $T_v(x)$. If the recovered T_{FA} is equal to the original choice, FA confirms that MU is authenticated by HA. Then, FA forwards P to MU.
- Step 6. MU decrypts P to recover T_{MU}, $T_u(x)$, $T_v(x)$, and ID_F. If the recovered T_{MU} is equal to the previous one and ID_F is the assigned FA, MU believes that the message P is computed from HA. Then, FA is authenticated.
- Step 7. Finally, MU and FA compute their common session key $k = h(T_u T_v(x)) = h(T_v T_u(x))$.

(3) Password change phase:

To change his password, MU inserts his smart card into a card reader and performs the following steps:

- Step 1. MU inserts his smart card into a card reader and inputs his identity ID_M and his old password PW and requests to change the password. Then MU submits his new password PW^*.
- Step 2. The smart card selects a random number u' and computes $V' = E_{KMH}(ID_M \| h(PW \| b))$, where $KMH = T_{u'}(T_s(x))$. Next, the device sends the authentication request message $\{u', V', V\}$ to the corresponding HA.

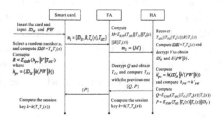

Fig. 2. The authentication and key agreement phase of Guo et al.'s protocol

- Step 3. HA computes the session key $KMH = T_s(T_{u'}(x))$, and decrypts $V' = E_{KMH}(ID_M \| h(PW \| b))$ to obtain ID_M and the information $h(PW \| b)$. Then, HA compares whether $V = E_{KS}(ID_M \| h(PW \| b))$. If it holds, HA computes $V^* = E_{KS}(ID_M \| h(PW^* \| b))$ and replaces V with V^*.

3.3   Weakness of Guo et al.'s Protocol

Guo et al. is based on Chebyshev chaotic maps. In the Chebyshev polynomials: $T_n(x) = 2xT_{n-1}(x) - T_{n-2}(x) \bmod N$, where $n \geq 2$, $T_0(x) = 1$, $T_1(x) = x$, $x \in (-\infty, \infty)$, and N is a larger prime number. It is obvious that if given x and s, it is easy to compute $T_s(x) = y$; however, given y, it is very difficult to find the exact parameters x and s such that $y = T_s(x)$. There are many pairs x and s such that $y = T_s(x)$. The probability of obtaining the exact x and s are equivalent to performing an exhaustive search on $y = T_s(x)$. On the other hand, from the recurrent relation $T_n(x) = 2xT_{n-1}(x) - T_{n-2}(x) \bmod N$, given y and x, it is computationally tractable to obtain s such that $y = T_s(x)$ when s is not large enough.

Guo et al. claimed their scheme is efficient since no time-consuming modular exponential computing and scalar multiplication on elliptic curve cryptosystem are involved in the authentication processes. However, in the registration phase of Guo et al.'s protocol [1], the mobile user MU's smart card contains $\{b, V, x, T_s(x), E_K(.), h(.)\}$, where $V = E_{KS}(ID_M \| h(PW \| b))$ and KS is a secret key kept by HA. Now, suppose the adversary (someone U_a) could extract the data x and $T_s(x)$ which stored in $U_a's$ smart card, with the communication information of authentication request message $m_1 = \{ID_H, R, T_u(x), T_{MU}\}$, U_a could be able to find u from the given values x and $T_u(x)$ when u is not large enough. Similarly, with the communication message $m_1 = \{ID_H, R, T_u(x), T_{MU}\}$, U_a could compute $KMH = T_u(T_s(x))$ and decrypt $R = E_{KMH}(h_{pw} \| V \| T_{MU})$ with the key KMH when u is not large enough. Thus, U_a could obtain h_{pw} and V; then impersonates the mobile user MU for passing the authentication phase in the future. Hence, U_a could attack and access the system. In this situation, Guo et al.'s protocol could not provide secure mutual authentication and key-agreement protocol for roaming service.

With the key KMH, U_a could decrypt the transmitted information $P = E_{KMH}(T_{MU} \| T_u(x) \| T_v(x) \| ID_F)$ to obtain $T_v(x)$. In this situation, from the messages $T_u(x)$ and $T_v(x)$, U_a could compute $T_{v'}(T_u(x))$ and $T_{u'}(T_v(x))$ by means of the recurrent relation $T_n(x) = 2xT_{n-1}(x) - T_{n-2}(x)$. If u and v are not large enough like the Diffie-Hellman key-agreement protocol [3], U_a could be computationally tractable to derive the common session key $k = h(T_uT_v(x)) = h(T_vT_u(x))$ for MU and FA. Therefore, Guo et al.'s protocol also relies on the hard problem of high-degree polynomials when the smart card's data x and $T_s(x)$ are extracted. Their scheme still required high modular exponential operations for the security. Also, MU cannot freely update his password without HA joining this password change phase.

4 The Proposed Scheme

In the initialization, HA chooses two distinct large primes p_1 and q_1 such that $p_1 = q_1 = 3 \pmod 4$ and computes the product $n_1 = p_1 \times q_1$. Next, HA selects its secret key d. Then, it publishes n_1 and $h(\cdot)$ but keeps d, p_1, and q_1 secret, where $h(\cdot)$ is a secure one-way hash function with fixed-length output. Similarly, FA selects two distinct large primes p_2 and q_2 such that $p_2 = q_2 = 3 \pmod 4$ and computes the product $n_2 = p_2 \times q_2$. And FA publishes n_2. In addition, K_{FH} is a pre-shared secret key between FA and HA. Our scheme consists of three phases:

(1) Registration phase:
When MU wants to access the systems, he selects a password PW_M and a random number b_M and computes $h(PW_M \| b_M)$, where "$\|$" is string concatenation operator. Next, MU submits his identity ID_M and $h(PW_M \| b_M)$ to HA for registration.

- Step 1. HA computes $u = (h(ID_M \| d))^2 \bmod n_1$, $C = h(u \| ID_M)$, and $v = u \oplus h(PW_M \| b_M)$.
- Step 2. Then HA issues a smart card containing $\{n_1, h(\cdot), v, C\}$, and sends it to MU through a secure channel.
- Step 3. MU stores the random number b_M into the smart card.

(2) Mutual authentication phase:
In this phase, MU and FA perform the mutual authentication as follows:

- Step 1. When MU enters a foreign network managed by FA, MU inserts his smart card into the smart card reader and inputs his ID_M and PW_M. Then, the device calculates $u^* = v \oplus h(PW_M \| b_M)$ and $C^* = h(u^* \| ID_M)$, and checks whether $C^* = C$. If it is not equal, the device terminates this login request for a period of time. Otherwise, the device selects two random numbers n_a and n_b, then computes $CID = (ID_M \oplus n_a)$, $A = (ID_H \| n_a)^2 \bmod n_1$, $B = (ID_F \| n_b)^2 \bmod n_2$, and $R_1 = h(u^* \| n_a \| B \| T_M)$, where T_M is the current timestamp of the device. Then, it sends the information $m_1 = \{A, CID, B, R_1, ID_H, T_M\}$ to FA, where ID_H and ID_F are the identity number of HA and FA, respectively.
- Step 2. Upon receiving $m_1 = \{A, CID, B, R_1, ID_H, T_M\}$, FA first checks whether the timestamp T_M is valid. If it is valid, FA randomly chooses n_F and computes $S_1 = h(K_{FH} \| A \| CID \| B \| R_1 \| n_F \| ID_F \| T_M \| T_F)$, then forwards the information $m_2 = \{A, CID, B, R_1, n_F, ID_F, S_1, T_M, T_F\}$ to HA, where K_{FH} is a pre-shared secret key between HA and FA and T_F is the current timestamp of FA.
- Step 3. After receiving m_2, HA checks the current timestamp T_F with the current time. If it holds, HA computes $S_1^* = h(K_{FH} \| A \| CID \| B \| R_1 \| n_F \| ID_F \| T_M \| T_F)$ and checks whether $S_1^* = S_1$ or not. If so, HA can obtain the nonce n_a from MSR of $A = (ID_H \| n_a)^2 \bmod n_1$ with the knowledge of ID_H, and computes $ID_M^* = CID \oplus n_a^*$, $u^* = (h(ID_M^* \| d))^2 \bmod n_1$, and $R_1^* = h(u^* \| n_a \| B \| T_M)$ with its secret key d.

Next, HA verifies whether $R_1^* = R_1$ holds. If it holds, HA calculates $R_2 = h(u^* \| n_a \| ID_F \| n_F \| T_M)$ and $S_2 = h(K_{FH} \| n_F \| B \| R_2 \| T_M \| T_F)$, then sends the message $m_3 = \{R_2, S_2\}$ to FA. Otherwise, HA terminates this request for a period of time.

- Step 4. Upon receiving $m_3 = \{R_2, S_2\}$, FA computes $S_2^* = h(K_{FH} \| n_F \| B \| R_2 \| T_M \| T_F)$ with K_{FH}. Then, FA checks whether the equation $S_2^* = S_2$ holds. If it holds, FA believes that MU is authorized. Then, FA can derive the nonce n_b from MSR of $B = (ID_F \| n_b)^2 \bmod n_2$ with the knowledge of identity number ID_F. Next, FA computes the session key $K = h(n_b \| n_F)$ and $Q = h(K \| n_F)$ then delivers the message $m_4 = \{ID_F, n_F, R_2, Q\}$ to MU.

- Step 5. After receiving $m_4 = \{ID_F, n_F, R_2, Q\}$, MU computes $R_2^* = h(u * \| n_a \| ID_F \| n_F \| T_M)$ and verifies whether the equation $R_2^* = R_2$ holds. If it holds, MU believes that FA is authenticated, and computes the session key $K = h(n_b \| n_F)$ and $Q^* = h(K \| n_F)$. Then, MU verifies whether the equation $Q^* = Q$ holds. If it holds, then K is a common session key for securing communications with FA. Otherwise, MU stops the request.

Through the above steps, both MU and FA can use this common session key K for the secure communication. Here, K, n_a, n_b and n_F are only used once. The above mutual authentication process is illustrated in Fig. 3.

(3) Updated password phase:
In our method, if MU wants to arbitrarily update his password PW_M, he does not need to register with HA.

Fig. 3. The proposed protocol of mutual authentication phase

- Step 1. MU inserts the smart card into the smart card reader and then inputs his ID_M and old PW_M. Next, the device computes $u = v \oplus h(PW_M \| b_M)$ and $C^* = h(u \| ID_M)$, then checks whether $C^* = C$. If it holds, MU chooses a new password $PW_M{}'$ and performs Step 2; otherwise, the device terminates the login request for a period of time.
- Step 2. Compute $v' = v \oplus h(PW_M \| b_M) \oplus h(PW'_M \| b_M)$.
- Step 3. Replace v with v' on the memory of the smart card. It is accepted because

$$v' = v \oplus h(PW_M \| b_M) \oplus h(PW'_M \| b_M)$$
$$= u \oplus h(PW_M \| b_M) \oplus h(PW_M \| b_M)$$
$$\oplus h(PW'_M \| b_M)$$
$$= u \oplus h(PW'_M \| b_M).$$

5   Discussion

First, we will review some security terms needed for our security analysis.

Definition 1. The difficulty of the integer factoring problem is: suppose $n = p \times q$, it is computationally infeasible to factorize n when p and q are large enough.

Definition 2. A secure hash function, $h()$: $x \to y$, is a one-way function, if given x, it is easy to compute $h(x) = y$; however, given y, it is hard to compute $h^{-1}(y) = x$.

5.1   Security Analysis

In this section, the security and functionality of the proposed scheme are shown:

(1) Security of the system secret
In our protocol, only HA contains the system secrets d. For a MU, even if he extracts the data $v = u \oplus h(PW_M \| b_M)$ and b_M from his smart card, then derives $u = v \oplus h(PW_M \| b_M)$ with his password PW_M, where $u = (h(ID_M \| d))^2 \bmod n_1$, MU still needs to solve the factoring problem so as to find the system secret d. Generally, the length of d is about 512–1024 bits. The probability of obtaining the exact d is equivalent to performing an exhaustive search on $u = (h(ID_M \| d))^2 \bmod n_1$. Therefore, it is very difficult for someone to impersonate HA if not knowing d.

(2) Replay attack
In replay attack, U_a may pretend to be MU by replaying $m_1 = \{A, CID, B, R_1, ID_H, T_M\}$ to FA; and FA forwards $m_2 = \{A, CID, B, R_1, n_F, ID_F, S_1, T_M, T_F\}$ to HA, where K_{FH} is a pre-shared symmetric key between HA and FA and T_F is the current timestamp. However, HA

could find the attack through checking the validity of $S_1 = h(K_{FH} \| A \| CID \| B \| R_1 \| n_F \| ID_F \| T_M \| T_F)$ with the current timestamps T_F and T_M. Similarly, U_a may intercept the messages $m_3 = \{R_2, S_2\}$ and $m_4 = \{ID_F, n_F, R_2, Q\}$, and reply m_3 and m_4 to FA and MU, respectively. MU could find the attack through checking the validity of $R_2 = h(u \| n_a \| ID_F \| n_F \| T_M)$ with the timestamp T_M. FA could also find the reply attack through verifying the validity of $S_2 = h(K_{FH} \| n_F \| B \| R_2 \| T_M \| T_F)$ with the timestamp T_F. It will only lead to false verification for FA and MU in Steps 4 and 5 of the proposed mutual authentication phase.

(3) The user anonymity property

In the mutual authentication phase, with $m_1 = \{A, CID, B, R_1, ID_H, T_M\}$, it is very hard for U_a to derive MU's ID_M from CID and A, where n_a is a fresh random value, $CID = (ID_M \oplus n_a)$, and $A = (ID_H \| n_a)^2 \bmod n_1$. The security of n_a is based on the difficulty of extracting MSR of a quadratic residue modulo n_1. And not knowing primes p_1 and q_1 ($n_1 = p_1 \times q_1$), U_a cannot trace the same user's ID_M and the nonce n_a from the value of $A = (ID_H \| n_a)^2 \bmod n_1$ and $CID = (ID_M \oplus n_a)$. The random number n_a is used one time. Hence, the proposed protocol could resist leaking the logging of user's identity if the authentication messages are eavesdropped.

(4) On-line and off-line password guessing attacks

Now suppose the malicious user has the smart card-loss of some MU. From the above proposed scheme, the malicious user uses this smart card and inputs ID'_M and guessing the password PW'_M to perform the mutual authentication with FA and HA. According to Step1 of mutual authentication phase, the device calculates $u' = v \oplus h(PW'_M \| b_M)$ and $C' = h(u' \| ID'_M)$, then checks whether $C' = C$. If it is not equal, the device terminates this login request for a period of time. Hence, the on-line password guessing attack will not be arisen by the proposed method. A failed guess could be detected and logged by the device.

Moreover, the proposed scheme could achieve the user anonymity property. Even if U_a could eavesdrop all transmitted messages and extract the data $\{n_1, h(\cdot), v, C, b_M\}$ which stored in MU's smart card, where $v = u \oplus h(PW_M \| b_M)$, $C = h(u \| ID_M)$, and $u = (h(ID_M \| d))^2 \bmod n_1$. It is computationally intractable to obtain the same user's identity ID_M and the nonce n_a from all transmitted messages of $A = (ID_H \| n_a)^2 \bmod n_1$ and $CID = (ID_M \oplus n_a)$. Therefore, without the right identity ID_M and the password PW_M of MU, it is very hard for U_a to perform the off-line password guessing attack even if the attacker could obtain the secret information stored in the smart card.

(5) Security of the password

From the proposed mutual authentication protocol, for MU, we can find the authentication message $m_1 = \{A, CID, B, R_1, ID_H, T_M\}$ only contains $CID = (ID_M \oplus n_a)$, $A = (ID_H \| n_a)^2 \bmod n_1$, $B = (ID_F \| n_b)^2 \bmod n_2$, and $R_1 = h(u \| n_a \| B \| T_M)$, where T_M is the current timestamp of the device. These values do not contain any information about the user's password PW_M. This protects the system from off-line password dictionary searching from the interactive authentication messages.

(6) The impersonation attack

With $m_1 = \{A, CID, B, R_1, ID_H, T_M\}$, U_a cannot easily derive the exact ID_M and the nonce n_a from $A = (ID_H \| n_a)^2 \bmod n_1$ and $CID = (ID_M \oplus n_a)$. It is protected under the difficulty of the integer factoring problem. The probability of obtaining the exact ID_M and n_a is equivalent to performing an exhaustive search on $A = (ID_H \| n_a)^2 \bmod n_1$ and $CID = (ID_M \oplus n_a)$. Without the exact ID_M and n_a, it is computationally intractable for U_a to impersonate the valid MU. In addition, without the information $u = (h(ID_M \| d))^2 \bmod n_1$ of MU, U_a could not calculate the validity of $R_1 = h(u \| n_a \| B \| T_M)$ for passing the proposed mutual authentication phase. On the other hand, suppose malicious user has the smart card of some MU, not knowing the user's password PW_M and ID_M, it is very difficult for someone to impersonate MU.

Similarly, not knowing the secret key K_{FH}, it is difficult for the masked agents to compute exact $S_1 = h(K_{FH} \| A \| CID \| B \| R_1 \| n_F \| ID_F \| T_M \| T_F)$ and $S_2 = h(K_{FH} \| n_F \| B \| R_2 \| T_M \| T_F)$, where K_{FH} is a pre-shared symmetric key between FA and HA. Getting that far will only lead to false verification for FA and HA in Steps 3 and 4 of the proposed mutual authentication phase.

(7) The insider attack

In the registration of our method, MU sends the hash value $h(PW_M \| b_M)$ instead of the password PW_M to the server side or HA, where b_M is a random number generated by MU. The privileged insider HA cannot easily get the password.

(8) Forward and backward secrecy

After a successful mutual authentication, the session key $K = h(n_b \| n_F)$ is created for MU and FA. From the transmission information $m_1 = \{A, CID, B, R_1, ID_H, T_M\}$, U_a cannot easily obtain the exact nonce n_b from $B = (ID_F \| n_b)^2 \bmod n_2$. It depends on the difficulty of solving MSR. Therefore, it is computationally infeasible for U_a to derive the session key K from B. Even if an intruder obtains the current session key K, it is not easy for him to obtain the current value n_b from K, since it is protected under the one-way hash function $h(\cdot)$. The probability of obtaining the exact n_b is equivalent to performing an exhaustive search on n_b. It is not helpful to find the system secret d. Moreover, the nonce n_b and n_F are used once. Therefore, the intruder cannot derive private messages from the past. For K is used for one time only, even if the intruder obtains the current session key K, it is no use for him to obtain the past communication or future transactions.

(9) User friendliness

In our scheme, MU can freely choose his identity ID_M and password PW_M, then submits his identity ID_M and $h(PW_M \| b_M)$ to HA for registration. When MU wants to change his password, he performs the steps in updated password phase.

(10) No password/verification table

In the registration phase, HA computes $C = h(u\|ID_M)$, and $v = u \oplus h(PW_M\|b_M)$ and stores C and v into the smart card, where C contains the identity of MU and v contains the corresponding password. When MU inserts his smart card, the device can determine whether MU is legitimate with the assistance of the information C and v.

(11) Fairness in key agreement

In our protocol, both MU and FA can compute the session key $K = h(n_b\|n_F)$.

(12) Mutual authentication

In the proposed protocol, the goal of mutual authentication is to ensure MU, FA, and HA are legitimate and to establish the session key between MU and FA for further communications.

(1) Mutual authentication between MU and HA:

In Step 3 of the mutual authentication phase, because $A = (ID_H\|n_a)^2 \bmod n_1$, only HA can derive the nonce n_a with the knowledge of ID_H, and computes $ID_M^* = CID \oplus n_a^*$, $u* = (h(ID_M^*\|d))^2 \bmod n_1$, and $R_1^* = h(u * \|n_a\|B\|T_M)$ with its secret key d. Next, HA verifies whether $R_1^* = R_1$ holds. If it holds, HA believes MU is authorized. Similarly, in Step 5, upon receiving the message R_2 from FA, MU can compute $R_2^* = h(u * \|n_a\|ID_F\|n_F\|T_M)$ and verifies whether $R_2^* = R_2$. If so, HA can be authenticated by MU.

(2) Mutual authentication between FA and HA:

In Step 2 of the mutual authentication phase, FA computes $S_1 = h(K_{FH}\|A\|CID\|B\|R_1\|n_F\|ID_F\|T_M\|T_F)$, where K_{FH} is shared between FA and HA. In Step 3, HA computes $S_1^* = h(K_{FH}\|A\|CID\|B\|R_1\|n_F\|ID_F\|T_M\|T_F)$ and checks whether $S_1^* = S_1$. If so, he ensures the message is from FA. In Step 4, FA computes $S_2^* = h(K_{FH}\|n_F\|B\|R_2\|T_M\|T_F)$ with K_{FH} then checks whether the equation $S_2^* = S_2$ holds. If so, he ensures the message is from HA.

(3) Mutual authentication between MU and FA:

In Step 4 of the mutual authentication phase, FA can ensure MU is authenticated by HA. Therefore, FA believes MU is a legitimate user and forwards R_2 to MU. In Step 5, MU computes $R_2^* = h(u * \|n_a\|ID_F\|n_F\|T_M)$ and verifies whether the equation $R_2^* = R_2$ holds. If so, MU believes FA is legitimate. In addition, MU can compute the session key $K = h(n_b\|n_F)$ and $Q* = h(K\|n_F)$. Then MU can reconfirm FA by verifying whether the equation $Q* = Q$ holds.

Finally, we compare the functionality of the proposed scheme with Guo et al. [1], He et al. [2], Xu et al. [9], and Lee et al. [5].

5.2   Performance Comparison

Guo et al. proposed a new chaotic maps-based mutual authentication and key-agreement protocol for wireless communications. Their scheme avoids modular

Table 1. Security and functionality comparisons between our proposed mechanism and other related protocols

Schemes	Ours	[1]	[2]	[9]	[5]
Mutual authentication	Yes	Yes	Yes	Yes	Yes
User friendliness	Yes	Yes	Yes	Yes	No
No password /verification table	Yes	Yes	Yes	Yes	Yes
Fairness in key agreement	Yes	Yes	No	Yes	No
User identity anonymity	Yes	Yes	No	Yes	No
Withstanding the insider attack	Yes	Yes	Yes	No	No
Withstanding the smart card-loss case	Yes	No	Yes	Yes	Yes
Withstanding the replay attack	Yes	Yes	Yes	Yes	Yes
Confidentiality of the session key	Yes	Yes	No	No	No

exponential computing or scalar multiplication on elliptic curve that used in traditional authenticated key agreement protocols using smart cards, which is more efficient than previously proposed schemes. Therefore, we only compare the proposed scheme with Guo et al.'s protocol. Compared to the modular exponentiation computation such as MSR or Diffie-Hellman key agreement, the one-way hash function offer faster computation. Besides, the modular multiplication computation is more efficient than one-way hash function; a MSR computation in z_n needs same amount of computation time as a modular exponentiation operation; and one-way hash function is more efficient than symmetric encryption or decryption [6,8]. For efficiency, we define related notations to analyze computational complexity. The notation S means time complexity of symmetric encryption or decryption, T denotes time complexity of Chebyshev polynomial computation, R represents time complexity of MSR, M is time complexity of modular multiplication computation, C stands for time complexity of scalar multiplication on elliptic curve, E expresses time complexity of modulus exponential operation, and H symbolizes time complexity of executing adopted one-way hash function in one's scheme. Note that times for computing modular addition and exclusive-or are ignored, since they are much smaller than S, T, R, M, C, E and H (Table 1).

In Table 2, the proposed scheme requires $6H$ (hash functions) and $2M$ (modular multiplication computations) for MU; $1R$ (MSR computation) and $4H$ for FA; and $1R$, $5H$, and $1M$ for HA. Obviously, our scheme has better performance than Guo et al.'s for MU. Moreover, Guo et al.'s authentication protocol for roaming service in the global mobility network is still vulnerable when the smart card's data x and $T_s(x)$ are extracted. Therefore, the Chebyshev polynomial computation (T) is still required high modular exponential operations for the security. In this situation, our scheme could offer more efficiency than Guo et al.'s scheme in both of FA and HA.

Table 2. The comparisons of computation performance for MU, FA, and HA between our proposed mechanism and protocols of Guo et al. [1], He et al. [2], Xu et al. [9], and Lee et al. [5]

Schemes	Ours	[1]	[2]	[9]	[5]
MU	$6H + 2M$	$3H + 3T + 1S$	$10H + 2S$	$1H + 2E + 3S$	$2H + 2S$
FA	$4H + 1R$	$1H + 2T + 2S$	$5H + 1S + 3C$	$2S$	$1S$
HA	$5H + 1R + 1M$	$1H + 1T + 4S$	$5H + 2S + 3C$	$1E + 6S$	$3H + 1S$

6 Conclusion

In this paper, we proposed an efficient remote user authentication protocol with smart cards for wireless communications based on MSR. The proposed method could resist attacks even when the information stored in the smart card is disclosed. Our scheme provides following functions: (1) no password table is required for designated servers (2) users can freely choose their passwords (3) users can update their passwords without server or home agent joining (4) user anonymity property is provided (5) supplies mutual authentication for mobile user, foreign agent, and home agent (6) session key is generated by user and remote foreign agent for each session. The computational costs of our scheme are low. Thus, our scheme is more suitable for mobile clients and smart-card users.

References

1. Guo, C., Chang, C.C., Sun, C.Y.: Chaotic maps-based mutual authentication and key agreement using smart cards for wireless communications. J. Inf. Hiding Multimedia Sig. Process. 4(2), 99–109 (2013)
2. He, D., Ma, M., Zhang, Y., Chen, C., Jiajun, B.: A strong user authentication scheme with smart cards for wireless communications. Comput. Commun. 34(3), 367–374 (2011)
3. Campello de Souzac, R.M., Limaa, J.B., Panariob, D.: Public-key encryption based on chebyshev polynomials over gf(q). Inf. Process. Lett. 111, 51–56 (2010)
4. Jebek, E.: Integer factoring and modular square roots. J. Comput. Syst. Sci. 82, 380–394 (2016)
5. Lee, C.C., Hwang, M.S., Liao, I.E.: Security enhancement on a new authentication scheme with anonymity for wireless environments. IEEE Trans. Ind. Electron. 53(5), 1683–1687 (2006)
6. Rabin, M.O.: Digitalized signatures and public-key functions as intractable as factorization. Technical report, Cambridge, MA, USA (1979)
7. Wang, X., Zhao, J.: An improved key agreement protocol based on chaos. Commun. Nonlinear Sci. Numer. Simul. 15(12), 4052–4057 (2010)
8. Williams, H.C.: A modification of the rsa public-key encryption procedure (corresp.). IEEE Trans. Inf. Theory 26(6), 726–729 (1980)
9. Jing, X., Zhu, W.T., Feng, D.G.: An efficient mutual authentication and key agreement protocol preserving user anonymity in mobile networks. Comput. Commun. 34(3), 319–325 (2011)

10. Yoon, E.J., Jeon, I.S.: An efficient and secure diffie-hellman key agreement protocol based on chebyshev chaotic map. Commun. Nonlinear Sci. Numer. Simul. **16**(6), 2383–2389 (2011)
11. Zhang, L.: Cryptanalysis of the public key encryption based on multiple chaotic systems. Chaos, Solitons Fractals **37**(3), 669–674 (2008)
12. Zhou, T., Jing, X.: Provable secure authentication protocol with anonymity for roaming service in global mobility networks. Comput. Netw. **55**(1), 205–213 (2011)

Cloud Computing Security

Efficient Fine-Grained Access Control for Secure Personal Health Records in Cloud Computing

Kai He[1,2], Jian Weng[1,3(✉)], Joseph K. Liu[2], Wanlei Zhou[4], and Jia-Nan Liu[1]

[1] Department of Computer Science, Jinan University, Guangzhou, China
hekai1214@yahoo.com, cryptjweng@gmail.com
[2] Faculty of Information Technology, Monash University, Melbourne, Australia
[3] Guangdong Provincial Big Data Collaborative Innovation Center,
Shenzhen University, Shenzhen, China
[4] School of Information Technology, Deakin University,
Melbourne, Australia

Abstract. In this paper, we propose an efficient fine-grained access control system for secure Personal Health Records (PHRs) in cloud computing. In this system, the patients have fine-grained access control for their health records. The underlying primitive of this system is a newly designed identity-based conditional proxy re-encryption scheme with chosen-ciphertext security, which is the first of its kind that achieves the highest security level. It is also highly efficient. The public parameters size and also, the private key and ciphertext size are constant and our experimental results indicate that the computational cost does not rely on the message size.

Keywords: Personal health records · Cloud computing · Fine-grained access control · Chosen-ciphertext security

1 Introduction

A personal health record (PHR) is a comprehensive electronic version of a patient's lifelong health information, which is managed by the patient himself at any time and at any location as long as there exists a networked device. It brings out great convenience for the patients to maintain their personal health records (PHRs). Especially for the emergency care, the doctors need to know the histories of the patient's health as soon as possible. Additionally, it greatly reduces the health-care cost and improves the treatment quality and efficiency.

Cloud computing owns large-scale storage space and huge computing power, which brings great benefits to many large organizations and individual users. Now it is widely adopted by all walks of life. In medical treatment, in order to save storage costs, the patients outsource their PHRs (as shown in Fig. 1) to the cloud server. However, in a way, it directly makes the patients lost control for their PHRs. Additionally, not merely the semi-trust cloud server can smoothly view the patients' PHRs, even in some cases, their PHRs may be utilized as an

© Springer International Publishing AG 2016
J. Chen et al. (Eds.): NSS 2016, LNCS 9955, pp. 65–79, 2016.
DOI: 10.1007/978-3-319-46298-1_5

unauthorized secondary use or a commercial use. Thus, it is necessary to resolve the problem of the access control and the security for the PHRs of the patients in the cloud server [8, 9].

Usually, to guard against the security risks, it is essential for each patient to encrypt his/her PHRs ahead uploading their PHRs to the cloud server. Nevertheless, once the PHRs are encrypted, all the authorized users (e.g., family members, friends, doctors, and health care providers) are hard to access the patients' PHRs. Therefore, it is essential to construct a secure PHRs system with fine-grained access control.

Fig. 1. Personal health information sources

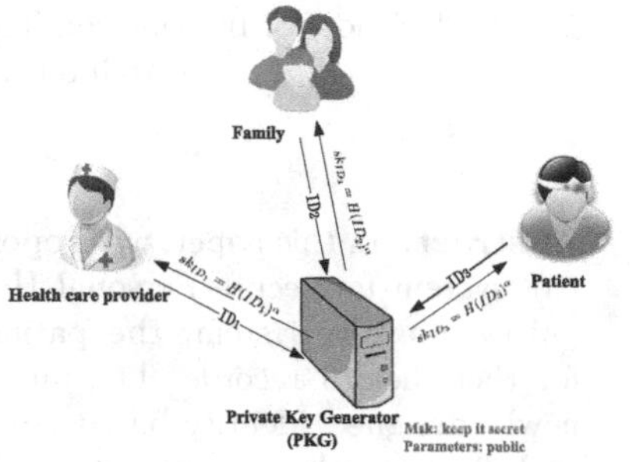

Fig. 2. PKG generates the users' private keys

In order to achieve the access control for the encrypted PHRs, in the early secure PHRs system [27], the patients encrypt their health records using a symmetric encryption scheme, where the encryption key is the same as the decryption key. In this case, if the patients want to share their PHRs which is encrypted under the symmetric scheme to the other users, they need to generate a secret key and distribute the secret key through a secure channel. However, this is a troublesome problem. With the development of cryptography, the appearance of the public key encryption [7] had cancelled the key distribution, since it uses a public key which is public to encrypt a message and a private key which is secretly kept by the owner to decrypt the encrypted message. But while the patient shares his PHRs which are encrypted under his public key to the other users, first the patient needs to download the encrypted PHRs (the ciphertext) from the cloud server. Then he decrypts the ciphertext with his private key to obtain the message. Next he encrypts the message under the user's public key and uploads the user's ciphertext to the cloud server. Obviously, it needs huge computation cost and communication load.

Attribute-based encryption (ABE) [25] is a special public-key encryption, in which both the private key and the ciphertext are related with the attributes. It has been at large used to design some access control systems [10, 13, 17, 24, 29, 30, 35, 37]. Currently, there exists some systems with fine-grained access control for the patients' PHRs by employing ABE as a primitive. Here we discuss some of the state-of-the-art ones [14, 18, 28].

In 2009, Ibraimi et al. [14] applied a variant of ABE scheme to manage the patients' PHRs, which took into consideration the authorized users belong to either a social domain or a professional domain. In 2010, Li et al. [18] proposed a patient-centric secure PHRs system with fine-grained access control in multi-owner settings. In their system, the authors divided the users into a public domain and a personal domain. In order to reduce the complexity of the key management, they utilized a multi-authority ABE scheme [3] to manage the access control of the users in a public domain and employed signal-authority ABE scheme [10] to manage the access control of the users in the personal domain. In 2013, they extended their construction to a multiple data owner scenario [19]. Meanwhile, they provided a formal security proof for their construction and evaluated the performance of their construction. In 2014, Wang et al. [28] proposed a cloud-based PHRs system by adopting the ABE scheme for the users in the public domain and an anonymous multi-receiver identity-based encryption scheme for the users in the personal domain. However, the computational cost of the ABE schemes is very high, as it increases with the access structure complexity and requires a large amount of pairing computations. Especially for the complexity of the key management for the patients and the users. This may a main obstacle to put into use the ABE scheme as a primitive in building a PHRs system.

To obtain an efficient fine-grained access control for secure PHRs in cloud computing, Leng et al. [16] and Huang et al. [12] respectively proposed an efficient conditional proxy re-encryption (CPRE) scheme [1, 4, 6, 11, 15, 22, 23, 26, 31–34, 36], in which a semi-trust proxy can transform the patients' PHRs which is encrypted under the patient's public key to the same PHRs which is encrypted under another user's public key. In this case, the semi-trust proxy does not know the patient's PHRs. However, the two schemes are just in the public key environment, where it requires a third party (Certificate Authority) to certify the authenticity of the users' public keys. And even the two schemes do not provide the security proofs. Although there exists two CPRE schemes in the identity-based environment [20, 21] and the authors claimed that their schemes are chosen-ciphertext secure under the standard model. Nevertheless, in the two schemes, we find that some ciphertext components cannot be verified before running the transformed algorithm, so that it is hard to achieve chosen-ciphertext security in the proxy re-encryption setting.

Therefore, we present a cost-efficient and chosen-ciphertext secure condition proxy re-encryption scheme in the identity-based environment, which directly develops a secure PHRs system with fine-grained access control function in cloud computing.

1.1 Contributions

We propose a highly efficient and secure fine-grained access control system for PHRs in cloud computing. The underlying primitive of the system is a new identity-based conditional proxy re-encrypted scheme. It has the following nice features. First, it is in an identity-based setting, in which an arbitrary string can be the user's public key, provided that the string can uniquely identify the user, such as passport number and email address. Second, this scheme is the first of its kind to reach the highest security level under a standard assumption: adaptive chosen-ciphertext security. Third, the scheme is very efficient and the result of experiment demonstrates that the computational cost is independent on the plaintext size.

1.2 Organization

The remainder of the paper is organized as follows. In Sect. 2, we present some fundamental notations and cryptographic definitions. In Sect. 3, we present the framework of the PHRs system in cloud computing, describe the algorithm of the underlying scheme and give a secure analysis for the scheme. In Sect. 4, we simulate the performance of all the algorithms of the underlying scheme. Finally, we present the conclusion in Sect. 5.

2 Preliminaries

2.1 Bilinear Map

$\mathbb{G}$ and $\mathbb{G}_T$ are two multiplicative cyclic groups with prime order p. The bilinear map $e : \mathbb{G} \times \mathbb{G} \to \mathbb{G}_T$ has three properties:

- **Bilinearity:** $e(u^a, v^b) = e(u, v)^{ab}$ for all $u, v \in \mathbb{G}$ and $\forall a, b \in \mathbb{Z}_p$.
- **Non-degeneracy:** $e(g, g) \neq 1_\mathbb{G}$, where g is a generator of $\mathbb{G}$.
- **Computability:** There exists a probabilistic algorithm to compute $e(u, v)$ for $\forall u, v \in \mathbb{G}$.

2.2 Decisional Bilinear Diffie-Hellman (BDH) Assumption

The decisional BDH assumption in a bilinear group $(p, \mathbb{G}, \mathbb{G}_T, e)$ is shown as follows: A challenger takes as input (g, g^a, g^b, g^c, Z) for the unknown $a, b, c \leftarrow_R \mathbb{Z}_p$. A probabilistic polynomial time (PPT) adversary decides $Z = e(g, g)^{abc}$ or Z is a random value. The advantage for the PPT adversary $\mathcal{A}$ to solve the decisional BDH assumption is defined:

$$Adv_{\mathcal{A}}^{\mathrm{DBDH}} = |\Pr[\mathcal{A}(g, g^a, g^b, g^c, e(g, g)^{abc}) = 1] - \Pr[\mathcal{A}(g, g^a, g^b, g^c, Z) = 1]|.$$

If the advantage is negligible, the DBDH assumption holds in the bilinear map $(p, \mathbb{G}, \mathbb{G}_T, e)$.

2.3 Identity-Based Conditional Proxy Re-encrypt (IBCPRE)

We review the definition and the security notion for the IBCPRE scheme [5,32]. An IBCPRE scheme includes the following seven algorithms:

- **Setup**(1^λ): Given a security parameter 1^λ, it outputs the public parameters *params* and a master secret key *msk*.
- **Extract**(msk, ID): Given the master secret key *msk* and an identity ID, it generates a private key sk_{ID}.
- **ReKeyGen**(sk_{ID_i}, ID_j, w): Given a private key sk_{ID_i}, an identity ID_j, and a condition w, it generates a re-encryption key $rk_{w|ID_i \rightarrow ID_j}$ from ID_i to ID_j associated with w.
- **Enc**($params, ID_i, w, m$): Given the public parameters *params*, an identity ID_i, a condition w and a plaintext $m \in \mathcal{M}$, it generates an initial ciphertext $CT_{(ID_i,w)}$ under an identity ID_i associated with w.
- **ReEnc**($rk_{w|ID_i \rightarrow ID_j}, ID_j, CT_{(ID_i,w)}$):   Given   a   re-encryption   key $rk_{w|ID_i \rightarrow ID_j}$, an identity ID_j, and an initial ciphertext $CT_{(ID_i,w)}$, it generates a transformed ciphertext $CT_{(ID_j,w)}$.
- **Dec$_2$**($sk_{ID_i}, CT_{(ID_i,w)}$): Given a private key sk_{ID_i} and an initial ciphertext $CT_{(ID_i,w)}$, it returns a plaintext m or an invalid symbol $\perp$.
- **Dec$_1$**($sk_{ID_j}, CT_{(ID_j,w)}$): Given a private key sk_{ID_j} and a transformed ciphertext $CT_{(ID_j,w)}$, it returns a plaintext m or an invalid symbol $\perp$.

Consistency: For any $m \in \mathcal{M}$, sk_{ID_i} and sk_{ID_j} are generated from Extract algorithm, it holds that $\mathsf{Dec_2}(sk_{ID_i}, CT_{(ID_i,w)}) = m$ and $\mathsf{Dec_1}(sk_{ID_j},$ ReEnc(ReKeyGen(sk_{ID_i}, ID_j, w), $ID_j, CT_{(ID_i,w)})) = m$.

Next, we give the security definition for the IBCPRE scheme in the sense of indistinguishability under chosen-ciphertext attacks (IND-CCA), which is described by the following game between a challenger $\mathcal{C}$ and an adversary $\mathcal{A}$. Adversary $\mathcal{A}$ is able to obtain a series of queries. In spite of this, adversary $\mathcal{A}$ cannot distinguish which message is encrypted from the challenge ciphertext.

- **Setup:** Challenger $\mathcal{C}$ runs (*params, msk*)←Setup(1^λ), then it sends *params* to $\mathcal{A}$ and keeps *msk* itself.
- **Phase 1:** Adversary $\mathcal{A}$ adaptively issues a polynomial number of queries:
  - *Extraction query* $\langle ID_i \rangle$: Challenger $\mathcal{C}$ runs Extract(msk, ID_i) to obtain a private key sk_{ID_i} and returns it to adversary $\mathcal{A}$.
  - *Re-encryption key query* $\langle ID_i, ID_j, w \rangle$: Challenger $\mathcal{C}$ first gets the private key $sk_{ID_i} \leftarrow$ Extract (msk, ID_i) and runs $rk_{w|ID_i \rightarrow ID_j} \leftarrow$ ReKeyGen(sk_{ID_i}, ID_j, w). Then it returns $rk_{w|ID_i \rightarrow ID_j}$ to adversary $\mathcal{A}$.
  - *Re-encryption query* $\langle ID_i, ID_j, CT_{(ID_i,w)} \rangle$: Challenger $\mathcal{C}$ first gets the re-encryption key $rk_{w|ID_i \rightarrow ID_j} \leftarrow$ ReKeyGen(sk_{ID_i}, ID_j, w) and runs $CT_{(ID_j,w)} \leftarrow$ ReEnc $(rk_{w|ID_i \rightarrow ID_j}, ID_j, CT_{(ID_i,w)})$. Then it returns $CT_{(ID_j,w)}$ to adversary $\mathcal{A}$.
  - *Decryption query* $\langle ID, CT_{(ID,w)} \rangle$: Challenger $\mathcal{C}$ first gets the private key $sk_{ID} \leftarrow$ Extract(msk, ID) and runs the decryption algorithm to get the the result $\mathsf{Dec}(sk_{ID}, CT_{(ID,w)})$. Then it returns the result to adversary $\mathcal{A}$.

– **Challenge:** Adversary $\mathcal{A}$ outputs a target identity ID^*, a target condition w^* and two distinct plaintexts $m_0, m_1 \in \mathcal{M}$, where $|m_0| = |m_1|$. Challenger $\mathcal{C}$ picks $\beta \in_R \{0,1\}$ and returns $CT^*_{(ID^*, w^*)} = \mathsf{Enc}\,(params, ID^*, w^*, m_\beta)$ to adversary $\mathcal{A}$.

– **Phase 2:** Adversary $\mathcal{A}$ keeps on issuing the queries as in Phase 1, challenger $\mathcal{C}$ responds the queries as in Phase 1. But the difference is that Phase 2 needs to satisfy the following conditions:
  - Adversary $\mathcal{A}$ cannot issue the *Extraction query* on ID^*.
  - Adversary $\mathcal{A}$ cannot issue the *Decryption query* on neither $\langle ID^*, CT^*_{(ID^*, w^*)} \rangle$ nor $\langle ID_j, \mathsf{ReEnc}(rk_{w^*|ID^* \to ID_j}, ID_j, CT^*_{(ID^*, w^*)}) \rangle$.
  - If adversary $\mathcal{A}$ gets sk_{ID_j} on ID_j, it cannot issue *Re-encryption query* on $\langle ID^*, ID_j, CT^*_{(ID^*, w^*)} \rangle$ and the *Re-encryption key query* on $\langle ID^*, ID_j, w^* \rangle$.

– **Guess:** Adversary $\mathcal{A}$ makes a guess $\beta' \in \{0,1\}$ and wins the game if $\beta' = \beta$.

We define the adversary's advantage in the above game as $Adv_{\mathcal{A}}^{\text{IND-IBCPRE-CCA}} = |\Pr[\beta' = \beta] - 1/2|$.

Definition 1 *(IND-IBCPRE-CCA Security). We say that an IBCPRE scheme is IND-CCA secure, if for any PPT adversary $\mathcal{A}$, the advantage in the above security game is negligible, that is $Adv_{\mathcal{A}}^{\text{IND-IBCPRE-CCA}} \leq \epsilon$.*

3   A Fine-Grained Access Control System for Secure PHRs in Cloud Computing

In this section, we first introduce the framework of the fine-grained access control system for PHRs in cloud computing. Then we present the underlying scheme of the system. Finally, we give the security analysis for the scheme.

3.1   System Framework

We describe the framework on how to realize the fine-grained access control for secure PHRs in cloud computing, which is shown in Fig. 3. The core process is included the following steps.

1. Encrypt and upload: If a patient has a PHRs database, he encrypts each PHRs M with a related condition W under his identity ID_A and then uploads them to the cloud server.
2. Transform: When a data user wants to access the patient's PHRs, the patient generates a re-encryption key to the the data user ID_B under a condition W and uploads it to the cloud server. Then the cloud server transforms only the patient's encrypted PHRs with the same condition W as in the re-encryption key to the encrypted PHRs under the data user's identity ID_B. The concrete process is showed in Fig. 4 and the algorithm is presented in the next subsection.
3. Download and decrypt: The data user downloads the transformed PHRs ciphertext and decrypts it by using his private key to obtain the patient's PHRs.

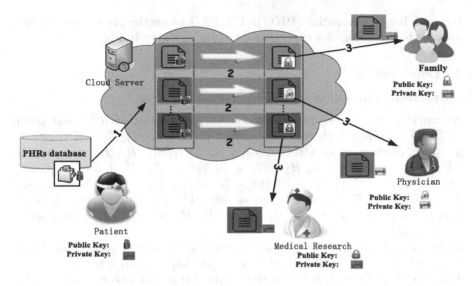

Fig. 3. Fine-grained access control for secure PHRs in clouds

The framework mainly involves four entities. A brief description of the entities is given below.

- **Patient:** The patient (data owner) stores his PHRs in cloud server and has fine-grained access control his PHRs.
- **Data User:** The data user wants to share the patients' PHRs. (eg. the patients' family members and friends, medical researches or health-care providers).
- **Cloud Server:** The cloud server owns huge space to store the encrypted PHRs and the re-encryption keys and enormous computing power to transform the encrypted PHRs from the data owner to the data user as shown in Fig. 4. It is a semi-trust cloud server, so it might be concern about the privacy information (eg. PHRs) and try to get some secret information.

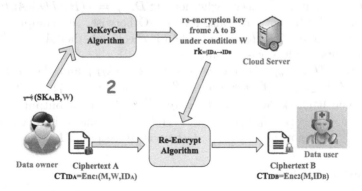

Fig. 4. Cloud server transforms ciphertext A to ciphertext B

- **Private Key Generator (PKG):** The PKG issues the private key to each user in the fine-grained access control system as shown in Fig. 2.

3.2 Construction

The construction consists of the following seven algorithms.

- **Setup(1^λ):** Given a security parameter 1^λ, it first outputs a bilinear group $(p, \mathbb{G}, \mathbb{G}_T, e)$. Then it chooses a generator $g \in_R \mathbb{G}$, $\alpha \in_R \mathbb{Z}_p$ and computes $g_1 = g^\alpha$. Next, it chooses six hash functions H_1, H_2, H_3, H_4, H_5 and H_6, where $H_1 : \{0,1\}^* \to \mathbb{G}$, $H_2 : \mathbb{G}_T \times \{0,1\}^n \to \mathbb{Z}_p$, $H_3 : \mathbb{G}_T \to \{0,1\}^n$, $H_4 : \{0,1\}^* \times \mathbb{G} \times \mathbb{G}_T \times \{0,1\}^n \times \mathbb{G} \to \mathbb{G}$, $H_5 : \{0,1\}^* \to \mathbb{G}$ and $H_6 : \{0,1\}^n \to \mathbb{G}$, where n is related with 1^λ. The public parameters are $params = ((p, \mathbb{G}, \mathbb{G}_T, e), g, g_1, H_1, H_2, H_3, H_4, H_5, H_6)$ and the master secret key is $msk = \alpha$.
- **Extract(msk, ID):** Given the master secret key msk and an identity ID, it computes $Q_{ID} = H_1(ID)$ and sets the private key as $sk_{ID} = Q_{ID}^\alpha$.
- **Enc($params, ID_i, w, M$):** Given the public parameter $params$, an identity ID_i, a condition w and a message M from the message space $\mathcal{M}$, it picks $\delta \in_R \mathbb{G}_T$ and sets $r = H_2(\delta||M)$, $A = g^r$, $B = \delta \cdot e(g_1, H_1(ID_i))^r$, $C = H_3(\delta) \oplus M$, $D = H_5(ID_i||w)^r$, $S = H_4(ID_i||A||B||C||D)^r$. Then it outputs an initial ciphertext $CT_{(ID_i,w)} = (A, B, C, D, S, w)$.
- **ReKeyGen(sk_{ID_i}, ID_j, w):** Given the private key sk_{ID_i}, an identity ID_j and a condition w, it first picks $\theta \in_R \mathcal{M}$, $\delta' \in_R \mathbb{G}_T$ and sets $r' = H_2(\delta'||\theta)$, $rk_1 = g^{r'}$, $rk_2 = \delta' \cdot e(g_1, H_1(ID_j))^{r'}$, $rk_3 = H_3(\delta') \oplus \theta$. Then, it picks $s \in_R \mathbb{Z}_p$ and sets $RK_1 = sk_{ID_i} \cdot H_5(ID_i||w)^s \cdot H_6(\theta)$, $RK_2 = g^s$. Fianlly, it outputs the re-encryption key $rk_{w|ID_i \to ID_j} = (rk_1, rk_2, rk_3, RK_1, RK_2)$.
- **ReEnc($rk_{w|ID_i \to ID_j}, ID_j, CT_{(ID_i,w)}$):** Given the re-encryption key, the identity ID_j and the initial ciphertext $CT_{(ID_i,w)}$, it first checks whether $e(SD, g) = e(H_4(ID_i||A||B||C||D)H_5(ID_i||w), A)$. If not, it outputs $\perp$. Otherwise it computes $B' = B \cdot e(D, RK_2)/e(A, RK_1) = \delta/e(A, H_6(\theta))$. Then it outputs the transformed ciphertext $CT_{(ID_j,w)} = (A, B', C, rk_1, rk_2, rk_3)$.
- **Dec$_2$($sk_{ID_i}, CT_{(ID_i,w)}$):** Given the private key sk_{ID_i} and the initial ciphertext $CT_{(ID_i,w)}$, it first checks whether $e(SD, g) = e(H_4(ID_i||A||B||C||D)H_5(ID_i||w), A)$. If not, it outputs $\perp$. Otherwise, it computes $\delta = B/e(A, sk_{ID_i})$ and $M = H_3(\delta) \oplus C$. Then it checks whether $A = g^{H_2(\delta||M)}$. If not, it outputs $\perp$. Otherwise it outputs M.
- **Dec$_1$($sk_{ID_j}, CT_{(ID_j,w)}$):** Given the private key sk_{ID_j} and the transformed ciphertext $CT_{(ID_j,w)}$, it first computes $\delta' = rk_2/e(rk_1, sk_{ID_j})$ and $\theta = H_3(\delta') \oplus rk_3$. Then it checks whether $rk_1 = g^{H_2(\delta'||\theta)}$, if not, it outputs $\perp$; else it computes $\delta = B' \cdot e(A, H_6(\theta))$ and $M = H_3(\delta) \oplus C$. Finally, it checks whether $A = g^{H_2(\delta||M)}$. If not, it outputs $\perp$. Otherwise it outputs M.

3.3 Security Analysis

In the following, we prove that our construction is IND-IBCPRE-CCA secure in the random oracle model.

Theorem 1. *Suppose that the decisional BDH assumption holds in a bilinear group (p, G, G_T, e). Then the above IBCPRE scheme is IND-CCA secure in the random oracle model.*

Concretely, if adversary $\mathcal{A}$ with a non-negligible advantage against the above IBCPRE scheme, then there exists a challenger $\mathcal{C}$ to solve the DBDH assumption with a non-negligible advantage.

Proof. Suppose that adversary $\mathcal{A}$ has non-negligible advantage to attack the above IBCPRE scheme. We can build a PPT challenger $\mathcal{C}$ that makes use of $\mathcal{A}$ to solve the DBDH problem. Challenger $\mathcal{C}$ is given a DBDH instance (g, g^a, g^b, g^c, Z) with unknown $a, b, c \in \mathbb{Z}_p$, challenger $\mathcal{C}$'s aim is to decide $Z = e(g, g)^{abc}$ or Z is a random value. Challenger $\mathcal{C}$ works by interacting with $\mathcal{A}$ in the above security game as follows:

- **Setup:** Adversary $\mathcal{A}$ is given the public parameters $params = ((p, \mathbb{G}, \mathbb{G}_T, e), g, g_1, H_1, H_2, H_3, H_4, H_5, H_6)$, where $g_1 = g^a$ and $H_1, H_2, H_3, H_3, H_4, H_5, H_6$ are random oracles managed by challenger $\mathcal{C}$. The master secret key a is unknown to challenger $\mathcal{C}$.
- **Phase 1:** Adversary $\mathcal{A}$ adaptively asks the following queries:
  Hash Oracle Queries. Adversary $\mathcal{A}$ freely queries H_i with $i \in \{1, 2, 3, 4, 5, 6\}$. Challenger $\mathcal{C}$ maintains six hash tables H_i-list with $i \in \{1, 2, 3, 4, 5, 6\}$. At the beginning, the tables are empty. Challenger $\mathcal{C}$ replies the queries as follows:
  - $Hash_1$ Query (ID_j): If ID_j is on the H_1-list in the form of $\langle ID_j, Q_j, q_j, \varpi_j \rangle$, challenger $\mathcal{C}$ returns the predefined value Q_j. Otherwise, it chooses $q_j \in_R \mathbb{Z}_p$ and generates a random $\varpi_j \in \{0, 1\}$. If $\varpi_j = 0$, challenger $\mathcal{C}$ computes $Q_j = g^{q_j}$; else it computes $Q_j = g^{bq_j}$ and adds $\langle ID_j, Q_j, q_j, \varpi_j \rangle$ into the H_1-list, and then it returns Q_j.
  - $Hash_2$ Query $(\delta \| M)$: If $(\delta \| M)$ is on the H_2-list in the form of $\langle \delta \| M, r, g^r \rangle$, return r. Otherwise, challenger $\mathcal{C}$ selects $r \in_R Z_p^*$ and adds $\langle \delta \| M, r, g^r \rangle$ into the H_2-list, then it returns r.
  - $Hash_3$ Query $(\delta \in \mathbb{G}_T)$: If δ is on the H_3-list in the form of $\langle \delta, X \rangle$, challenger $\mathcal{C}$ returns X. Otherwise, it chooses $X \in_R \{0, 1\}^n$ and adds $\langle \delta, X \rangle$ into the H_3-list, then it returns X.
  - $Hash_4$ Query $(ID_j \| A \| B \| C \| D)$: If $\langle ID_j \| A \| B \| C \| D \rangle$ is on the H_4-list in the form of $\langle ID_j \| A \| B \| C \| D, T_j, t_j \rangle$, challenger $\mathcal{C}$ returns the value T_j. Otherwise, it chooses $t_j \in_R \mathbb{Z}_p$, computes $T_j = g^{t_j}$ and adds $\langle ID_j \| A \| B \| C \| D, T_j, t_j \rangle$ into the H_4-list, and then $\mathcal{C}$ returns T_j.
  - $Hash_5$ Query (ID_j, w_j): If $\langle ID_j, w_j \rangle$ is on the H_5-list in the form of $\langle ID_j \| w_j, \widehat{Q_j}, \widehat{q_j}, \widehat{\varpi_j} \rangle$, challenger $\mathcal{C}$ returns the value $\widehat{Q_j}$; Otherwise, it picks $\widehat{q_j} \in_R \mathbb{Z}_p$ and $\widehat{\varpi_j} \in_R \{0, 1\}$. If $\widehat{\varpi_j} = 0$, challenger $\mathcal{C}$ computes $Q_j = g^{\widehat{q_j}}$; else it computes $Q_j = g^{b\widehat{q_j}}$. Challenger $\mathcal{C}$ adds $\langle ID_j \| w_j, \widehat{Q_j}, \widehat{q_j}, \widehat{\varpi_j} \rangle$ into the H_5-list, and then it responds with $\widehat{Q_j}$.
  - $Hash_6$ Query $(\theta \in \{0, 1\}^n)$: If θ is on the H_6-list in the form of $\langle \theta, Y \rangle$, challenger $\mathcal{C}$ returns the value Y; Otherwise, it chooses $Y \in_R \mathbb{G}$ and adds $\langle \theta, Y \rangle$ into the H_6-list, and then challenger $\mathcal{C}$ returns Y.

Extraction query (ID_j): Challenger $\mathcal{C}$ recovers the tuple $\langle ID_j, Q_j, q_j, \varpi_j \rangle$ from the H_1-list. If $\varpi_j = 1$, challenger $\mathcal{C}$ outputs $\bot$ and aborts; Otherwise, challenger $\mathcal{C}$ returns $sk_{ID_j} = g_1^{q_j}$ to adversary $\mathcal{A}$. (Note that $sk_{ID_j} = g_1^{q_j} = g^{aq_j} = Q_j^a = H_1(ID_j)^\alpha$, so that this is a proper private key for the identity ID_j).

Re-encryption key query (ID_i, ID_j, w): Challenger $\mathcal{C}$ first picks $\delta' \in_R \mathbb{G}_T$, $\theta \in_R \{0,1\}^n$ and recovers $\langle ID_i, Q_i, q_i, \varpi_i \rangle$ and $\langle ID_j, Q_j, q_j, \varpi_j \rangle$ from the H_1-list and $\langle \delta' || \theta, r', g^{r'} \rangle$ from the H_2-list, $\langle \delta', X \rangle$ from the H_3-list, $\langle ID_i || w_i, \widehat{Q_i}, \widehat{q_i}, \widehat{\varpi_i} \rangle$ from the H_5-list and $\langle \theta, Y \rangle$ from the H_6-list. Lets $rk_1 = g^{r'}$, $rk_2 = \delta' \cdot e(g_1, Q_j)^{r'}$, $rk_3 = X \oplus \theta$. Then challenger $\mathcal{C}$ constructs RK_1, RK_2 as follows:

- If $\varpi_i = 0$, challenger $\mathcal{C}$ picks $s \in_R \mathbb{Z}_p$ and lets $RK_1 = g_1^{q_i} \cdot \widehat{Q_i}^s \cdot Y$, $RK_2 = g^s$.
- If $\varpi_i = 1$ and $\widehat{\varpi_i} = 1$: challenger $\mathcal{C}$ sets $RK_1 = g^{b\widehat{q_i}s'} \cdot Y$, $RK_2 = g_1^{-q_i/\widehat{q_i}} g^{s'}$, where $s = -aq_i/\widehat{q_i} + s'$.
- If $\varpi_i = 1$ and $\widehat{\varpi_i} = 0$: challenger $\mathcal{C}$ outputs $\bot$ and aborts.

Finally, challenger $\mathcal{C}$ returns the re-encryption key $rk_{w|ID_i \to ID_j} = (rk_1, rk_2, rk_3, RK_1, RK_2)$ to adversary $\mathcal{A}$.

Re-encryption query $(ID_i, ID_j, CT_{(ID_i, w)})$: Their exists the following cases to generate the re-encrypted ciphertext:

- If $\varpi_i = 1$ and $\widehat{\varpi_i} = 0$, challenger $\mathcal{C}$ first parses the ciphertext $CT_{(ID_i, w)}$ as (A, B, C, D, S, w) and checks whether $e(SD, g) = e(H_4(ID_i || A || B || C || D) H_5(ID_i || w), A)$. If not, it returns $\bot$. Otherwise, challenger $\mathcal{C}$ checks whether there exists a tuple $\langle \delta || M, r, g^r \rangle$ from the H_2-list such that $A = g^r$. If no, it returns $\bot$. Otherwise, $\mathcal{C}$ recovers the tuple $\langle ID_j, Q_j, q_j, \varpi_j \rangle$ from the H_1-list and $\langle \delta', X \rangle$ from the H_3-list, and then it picks $\theta \in_R \{0,1\}^n$, $\delta' \in_R \mathbb{G}_T$ and sets $r' = H_2(\delta' || \theta)$, $rk_1 = g^{r'}$, $rk_2 = \delta' \cdot e(g_1, Q_j)^{r'}$, $rk_3 = X \oplus \theta$. Next, $\mathcal{C}$ recovers the tuple $\langle \theta, Y \rangle$ from the H_6-list and sets $B' = \delta/e(A, Y)$. Finally, $\mathcal{C}$ outputs the transformed ciphertext $CT_{(ID_j, w)} = (A, B', C, rk_1, rk_2, rk_3)$ to adversary $\mathcal{A}$.

- Otherwise, challenger $\mathcal{C}$ first queries the re-encryption key to get $rk_{w|ID_i \to ID_j}$, and then it runs the ReEnc $(rk_{w|ID_i \to ID_j}, ID_j, CT_{(ID_i, w)})$ algorithm to obtain the transformed ciphertext $CT_{(ID_j, w)}$. Finally challenger $\mathcal{C}$ returns the transformed ciphertext $CT_{(ID_j, w)}$ to adversary $\mathcal{A}$.

Decryption query $(ID, CT_{(ID, w)})$: Challenger $\mathcal{C}$ checks whether $CT_{(ID, w)}$ is an initial or a transformed ciphertext.

- For an initial ciphertext, challenger $\mathcal{C}$ first extracts $CT_{(ID, w)}$ as (A, B, C, D, S, w). Then challenger $\mathcal{C}$ recovers a tuple $\langle ID, Q, q, \varpi \rangle$ from the H_1-list. If $\varpi = 0$ (meaning $sk_{ID} = g_1^q$), challenger $\mathcal{C}$ decrypts the ciphertext $CT_{(ID, w)}$ using sk_{ID}; Otherwise, challenger $\mathcal{C}$ first checks whether $e(SD, g) = e(H_4(ID || A || B || C || D) H_5(ID || w), A)$ holds. If no, it returns $\bot$; else challenger $\mathcal{C}$ searches the tuple $\langle \delta || M, r, g^r \rangle$ from the H_2-list such that $A = g^r$. If it cannot find such tuple, it returns $\bot$; else searches whether there exists a tuple $\langle \delta, X \rangle$ from the H_3-list, a tuple $\langle ID || w, \widehat{Q}, \widehat{q}, \widehat{\varpi} \rangle$ from the H_5-list and a tuple $\langle ID||A||B||C||D, T, t \rangle$ from the H_4-list, such that $M \oplus X = C$, $\widehat{Q}^r = D$ and $T^r = S$. If not, it returns $\perp$; Otherwise, challenger $\mathcal{C}$ returns M to adversary $\mathcal{A}$.

- For a transformed ciphertext, challenger $\mathcal{C}$ first parses $CT_{(ID,w)}$ as $(A, B', C, rk_1, rk_2, rk_3)$. Then challenger $\mathcal{C}$ recovers tuple $\langle ID, Q, q, \varpi \rangle$ from the H_1-list. If $\varpi = 0$ (meaning $sk_{ID} = g_1^q$), challenger $\mathcal{C}$ decrypts the ciphertext $CT_{(ID,w)}$ using sk_{ID}; Otherwise, challenger $\mathcal{C}$ searches whether there exists a tuple $\langle \delta'||\theta, r', g^{r'} \rangle$ from the H_2-list such that $rk_1 = g^{r'}$. If not, it returns $\perp$; else searches whether there exists a tuple $\langle \delta', X \rangle$ from the H_3-list and a tuple $\langle ID, Q, q, \varpi \rangle$ from the H_1-list such that $\theta \oplus X = C$ and $\delta' \cdot e(g_1, Q)^{r'} = rk_2$. If not, it returns $\perp$; Otherwise, challenger $\mathcal{C}$ recovers $\langle \theta, Y \rangle$ from the H_6-list, and it computes $\delta = B' \cdot e(A, Y)$ and $M = H_3(\delta) \oplus C$. Finally, challenger $\mathcal{C}$ returns M to adversary $\mathcal{A}$.

- **Challenge:** Adversary $\mathcal{A}$ outputs an identity ID^*, a condition w^* and two different plaintexts M_0, M_1, where $|M_0| = |M_1|$. Challenger $\mathcal{C}$ recovers the tuple $\langle ID^*, Q^*, q^*, \varpi^* \rangle$ from the H_1-list and a tuple $\langle ID^*||w^*, \widehat{Q^*}, \widehat{q^*}, \widehat{\varpi^*} \rangle$ from the H_5-list. If $\varpi^* = 0$ or $\widehat{\varpi^*} = 1$, challenger $\mathcal{C}$ outputs $\perp$ and aborts; else challenger $\mathcal{C}$ first picks $\beta \in_R \{0,1\}$, $\delta^* \in_R \mathbb{G}_T$, $X^* \in_R \{0,1\}^n$, and then it inserts the tuple $\langle \delta^*, X^* \rangle$ into the H_3-list and the tuple $\langle \delta^*, M_\beta, \cdot, g^c \rangle$ into the H_2-list. Next challenger $\mathcal{C}$ sets $A^* = g^c$, $B^* = \delta^* \cdot T^{q^*}$, $C^* = X^* \oplus M_\beta, D^* = g^{c\widehat{q^*}}$ and selects $t^* \in_R \mathbb{Z}_p$, and then it inserts the tuple $\langle ID^*||A^*||B^*||C^*||D^*, g^{t^*}, t^* \rangle$ into the H_4-list, and sets $S^* = g^{ct^*}$. Finally, challenger $\mathcal{C}$ sends the challenge ciphertext $CT^*_{(ID^*, w^*)} = (A^*, B^*, C^*, D^*, S^*)$ to adversary $\mathcal{A}$.

- **Phase 2:** Adversary $\mathcal{A}$ continues to adaptively issue queries as in Phase 1. But it needs to satisfy the conditions which are described the above security model.

- **Guess:** Adversary $\mathcal{A}$ outputs a guess $\beta' \in \{0,1\}$.

4   Performance Evaluation

In this section, we simulate the experiment of the underlying primitive of the fine-grained access control system for the secure PHRs in cloud computiong, that is the the above identity-based conditional proxy re-encryption (IBCPRE) construction. The results of the experiments are shown in Fig. 5. To simulate all the experiments, all the programs were implemented on a Win7 PC with Inter(R) Core(TM) i5-3470 CPU @ 3.20 GHz processor and 4G DDR3-RAM. In software, we use the jPBC library [2] and the JDK 1.7 to implement the underlying primitive (IBCPRE). In order to achieve the practical function, we choose an elliptic cure group with 160-bit pairing type-A.

In our experiments, we first set the size of the message to be many different values respectively. Then for each value, we evaluated the running time of the Enc algorithm, the ReEnc algorithm, the Dec_1 algorithm and the Dec_2 algorithm, which are shown in Fig. 5. Meanwhile, we have tested the average running time of the ReKeyGen algorithm as shown in Fig. 5. It is easy to find that the running time of the Enc algorithm, the ReEnc algorithm, the Dec_1 algorithm and the Dec_2 algorithm is almost constant, which means that the running time of these algorithms are independent of the message size. The encryption time is more than the time of the ReEnc algorithm and the two decryption algorithm. But it is still very efficient. Its average running time is just 125 ms, which is no matter how large the message. The average running time of the ReEnc algorithm, the Dec_1 algorithm and the Dec_2 are 54 ms, 64 ms and 63 ms respectively. We also evaluate the performance of the ReKeyGen algorithm. We run the ReKeyGen

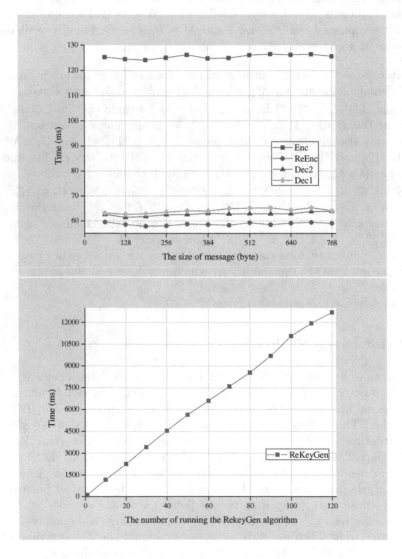

Fig. 5. The running time of all algorithms in our construction

algorithm 120 times and get the average time is about 108 ms. It is also very efficient.

5 Conclusion

In this paper, we propose an identity-based conditional proxy re-encryption encryption scheme with adaptive chosen-ciphertext security, which is the highest security level of its kind under the standard (DBDH) assumption. The scheme is very efficient. It is almost constant regardless of the size of the plaintext. Based on our scheme, we design a fine-grained access control system for secure PHRs in cloud computing. We believe that this system meets the practical requirements.

Acknowledgments. This work was supported by National Science Foundation of China (Grant Nos. 61272413, 61133014, 61272415 and 61472165), Research Fund for the Doctoral Program of Higher Education of China (Grant No. 20134401110011), the 2016 special fund for Applied Science & Technology Development and Transformation of Major Scientific and Technological Achievements, the fund for Zhuhai City Predominant Disciplines, and the Open Project Program of the Guangdong Provincial Big Data Collaborative Innovation Center.

References

1. Canetti, R., Hohenberger, S.: Chosen-ciphertext secure proxy re-encryption. In: Proceedings of the 2007 ACM Conference on Computer and Communications Security, CCS 2007, Alexandria, Virginia, USA, 28–31 October 2007, pp. 185–194 (2007)
2. De Caro, A., Iovino, V.: jPBC: Java pairing based cryptography. In: Proceedings of the 16th IEEE Symposium on Computers andCommunications, ISCC 2011, Kerkyra, Corfu, Greece, 28 June – 1 July 2011, pp. 850–855 (2011)
3. Chase, M., Chow, S.S.M.: Improving privacy and security in multi-authority attribute-based encryption. In: Proceedings of the 2009 ACM Conference on Computer and Communications Security, CCS 2009, Chicago, Illinois, USA, 9–13 November 2009, pp. 121–130 (2009)
4. Chow, S.S.M., Weng, J., Yang, Y., Deng, R.H.: Efficient unidirectional proxy re-encryption. In: Bernstein, D.J., Lange, T. (eds.) AFRICACRYPT 2010. LNCS, vol. 6055, pp. 316–332. Springer, Heidelberg (2010). doi:10.1007/978-3-642-12678-9_19
5. Chu, C.-K., Weng, J., Chow, S.S.M., Zhou, J., Deng, R.H.: Conditional proxy broadcast re-encryption. In: Boyd, C., González Nieto, J. (eds.) ACISP 2009. LNCS, vol. 5594, pp. 327–342. Springer, Heidelberg (2009). doi:10.1007/978-3-642-02620-1_23
6. Deng, R.H., Weng, J., Liu, S., Chen, K.: Chosen-ciphertext secure proxy re-encryption without pairings. In: Franklin, M.K., Hui, L.C.K., Wong, D.S. (eds.) CANS 2008. LNCS, vol. 5339, pp. 1–17. Springer, Heidelberg (2008). doi:10.1007/978-3-540-89641-8_1
7. Diffie, W., Hellman, M.E.: New directions in cryptography. IEEE Trans. Inf. Theor. **22**(6), 644–654 (1976)
8. Fernandes, D.A.B., Soares, L.F.B., Gomes, J.V.P., Freire, M.M., Inácio, P.R.M.: Security issues in cloud environments: a survey. Int. J. Inf. Sec. **13**(2), 113–170 (2014)

9. Gouglidis, A., Mavridis, I., Vincent, C.H.: Security policy verification for multi-domains in cloud systems. Int. J. Inf. Sec. **13**(2), 97–111 (2014)

10. Goyal, V., Pandey, O., Sahai, A., Waters, B.: Attribute-based encryption for fine-grained access control of encrypted data. In: Proceedings of the 13th ACM Conference on Computer and Communications Security, CCS 2006, Alexandria, VA, USA, 30 October – 3 November 2006, pp. 89–98 (2006)

11. Hanaoka, G., Kawai, Y., Kunihiro, N., Matsuda, T., Weng, J., Zhang, R., Zhao, Y.: Generic construction of chosen ciphertext secure proxy re-encryption. In: Dunkelman, O. (ed.) CT-RSA 2012. LNCS, vol. 7178, pp. 349–364. Springer, Heidelberg (2012). doi:10.1007/978-3-642-27954-6_22

12. Huang, K.-H., Chang, E.-C., Wang, S.-J.: A patient-centric access control scheme for personal health records in the cloud. In: 2013 Fourth International Conference on Networking and Distributed Computing (ICNDC), pp. 85–88, December 2013

13. Hur, J., Noh, D.K.: Attribute-based access control with efficient revocation in data outsourcing systems. IEEE Trans. Parallel Distrib. Syst. **22**(7), 1214–1221 (2011)

14. Ibraimi, L., Asim, M., Petkovic, M.: Secure management of personal health records by applying attribute-based encryption. In: 2009 6th International Workshop on Wearable Micro and Nano Technologies for Personalized Health (pHealth), pp. 71–74, June 2009

15. Isshiki, T., Nguyen, M.H., Tanaka, K.: Proxy re-encryption in a stronger security model extended from CT-RSA2012. In: Dawson, E. (ed.) CT-RSA 2013. LNCS, vol. 7779, pp. 277–292. Springer, Heidelberg (2013). doi:10.1007/978-3-642-36095-4_18

16. Leng, C., Huiqun, Y., Wang, J., Huang, J.: Securing personal health records in the cloud by enforcing sticky policies. TELKOMNIKA Indonesian J. Electr. Eng. **11**(4), 2200–2208 (2013)

17. Li, J., Chen, X., Li, J., Jia, C., Ma, J., Lou, W.: Fine-grained access control system based on outsourced attribute-based encryption. In: Crampton, J., Jajodia, S., Mayes, K. (eds.) ESORICS 2013. LNCS, vol. 8134, pp. 592–609. Springer, Heidelberg (2013). doi:10.1007/978-3-642-40203-6_33

18. Li, M., Yu, S., Ren, K., Lou, W.: Securing personal health records in cloud computing: patient-centric and fine-grained data access control in multi-owner settings. In: Jajodia, S., Zhou, J. (eds.) SecureComm 2010. LNICST, vol. 50, pp. 89–106. Springer, Heidelberg (2010). doi:10.1007/978-3-642-16161-2_6

19. Li, M., Shucheng, Y., Zheng, Y., Ren, K., Lou, W.: Scalable and secure sharing of personal health records in cloud computing using attribute-based encryption. IEEE Trans. Parallel Distrib. Syst. **24**(1), 131–143 (2013)

20. Liang, K., Chu, C.-K., Tan, X., Wong, D.S., Tang, C., Zhou, J.: Chosen-ciphertext secure multi-hop identity-based conditional proxy re-encryption with constant-size ciphertexts. Theor. Comput. Sci. **539**, 87–105 (2014)

21. Liang, K., Liu, Z., Tan, X., Wong, D.S., Tang, C.: A CCA-secure identity-based conditional proxy re-encryption without random oracles. In: Kwon, T., Lee, M.-K., Kwon, D. (eds.) ICISC 2012. LNCS, vol. 7839, pp. 231–246. Springer, Heidelberg (2013). doi:10.1007/978-3-642-37682-5_17

22. Libert, B., Vergnaud, D.: Unidirectional chosen-ciphertext secure proxy re-encryption. In: Cramer, R. (ed.) PKC 2008. LNCS, vol. 4939, pp. 360–379. Springer, Heidelberg (2008). doi:10.1007/978-3-540-78440-1_21

23. Matsuda, T., Nishimaki, R., Tanaka, K.: CCA proxy re-encryption without bilinear maps in the standard model. In: Nguyen, P.Q., Pointcheval, D. (eds.) PKC 2010. LNCS, vol. 6056, pp. 261–278. Springer, Heidelberg (2010). doi:10.1007/978-3-642-13013-7_16

24. Narayan, S., Gagné, M., Safavi-Naini, R.: Privacy preserving EHR system using attribute-based infrastructure. In: Proceedings of the 2nd ACM Cloud Computing Security Workshop, CCSW 2010, Chicago, IL, USA, 8 October 2010, pp. 47–52 (2010)
25. Sahai, A., Waters, B.: Fuzzy identity-based encryption. In: Cramer, R. (ed.) EURO-CRYPT 2005. LNCS, vol. 3494, pp. 457–473. Springer, Heidelberg (2005). doi:10.1007/11426639_27
26. Shao, J., Wei, G., Ling, Y., Xie, M.: Identity-based conditional proxy re-encryption. In: Proceedings of IEEE International Conference onCommunications, ICC 2011, Kyoto, Japan, 5–9 June 2011, pp. 1–5 (2011)
27. Smith, E., Eloff, H.P.: Security in health-care information systemscurrent trends. Int. J. Med. Inform. **54**(1), 39–54 (1999)
28. Wang, C.-J., Xu, X.-L., Shi, D.-Y., Lin, W.-L.: An efficient cloud-based personal health records system using attribute-based encryption and anonymous multi-receiver identity-based encryption. In: 2014 Ninth International Conference on P2P, Parallel, Grid, Cloud and Internet Computing, Guangdong, China, 8–10 November 2014, pp. 74–81 (2014)
29. Wang, S., Liang, K., Liu, J.K., Chen, J., Jianping, Y., Xie, W.: Attribute-based data sharing scheme revisited in cloud computing. IEEE Trans. Inf. Forensics Secur. **11**(8), 1661–1673 (2016)
30. Wang, S., Zhou, J., Liu, J.K., Jianping, Y., Chen, J., Xie, W.: An efficient file hierarchy attribute-based encryption scheme in cloud computing. IEEE Trans. Inf. Forensics Secur. **11**(6), 1265–1277 (2016)
31. Weng, J., Chen, M.-R., Yang, Y., Deng, R.H., Chen, K., Bao, F.: CCA-secure uni-directional proxy re-encryption in the adaptive corruption model without random oracles. Sci. China Inf. Sci. **53**(3), 593–606 (2010)
32. Weng, J., Deng, R.H., Ding, X., Chu, C-K., Lai, J.: Conditional proxy re-encryption secure against chosen-ciphertext attack. In: Proceedings of the 2009 ACM Symposium on Information, Computer and Communications Security, ASIACCS 2009, Sydney, Australia, 10–12 March 2009, pp. 322–332 (2009)
33. Weng, J., Yang, Y., Tang, Q., Deng, R.H., Bao, F.: Efficient conditional proxy re-encryption with chosen-ciphertext security. In: Samarati, P., Yung, M., Martinelli, F., Ardagna, C.A. (eds.) ISC 2009. LNCS, vol. 5735, pp. 151–166. Springer, Heidelberg (2009). doi:10.1007/978-3-642-04474-8_13
34. Weng, J., Zhao, Y., Hanaoka, G.: On the security of a bidirectional proxy re-encryption scheme from PKC 2010. In: Catalano, D., Fazio, N., Gennaro, R., Nicolosi, A. (eds.) PKC 2011. LNCS, vol. 6571, pp. 284–295. Springer, Heidelberg (2011). doi:10.1007/978-3-642-19379-8_18
35. Yang, K., Jia, X., Ren, K.: Attribute-based fine-grained access control with efficient revocation in cloud storage systems. In: 8th ACM Symposium on Information, Computer and Communications Security, ASIA CCS 2013, Hangzhou, China, 08–10 May 2013, pp. 523–528 (2013)
36. Yang, Y., Lu, H., Weng, J., Zhang, Y., Sakurai, K.: Fine-grained conditional proxy re-encryption and application. In: Chow, S.S.M., Liu, J.K., Hui, L.C.K., Yiu, S.M. (eds.) ProvSec 2014. LNCS, vol. 8782, pp. 206–222. Springer, Heidelberg (2014). doi:10.1007/978-3-319-12475-9_15
37. Yu, S., Wang, C., Ren, K., Lou, W.: Achieving secure, scalable, and fine-grained data access control incloud computing. In: 29th IEEE International Conference on Computer Communications, Joint Conference of the IEEE Computer and Communications Societies, INFOCOM 2010, San Diego, CA, USA, 15–19 March 2010, pp. 534–542 (2010)

An Energy-Efficient Task Scheduling Heuristic Algorithm Without Virtual Machine Migration in Real-Time Cloud Environments

Yi Zhang[1](✉), Liuhua Chen[2], Haiying Shen[2], and Xiaohui Cheng[1]

[1] School of Information and Engineering, Guilin University of Technology,
Guangxi 541004, China
zywait@glut.edu.cn

[2] School of Electrical and Computer Engineering, Clemson University,
Clemson 29631, SC, USA
liuhuachen@clemson.edu

Abstract. Reducing energy consumption has become an important task in cloud datacenters. Many existing scheduling approaches in cloud datacenters try to consolidate virtual machines (VMs) to the minimum number of physical machines (PMs) and hence minimize the energy consumption. VM live migration technique is used to dynamically consolidate VMs to as few PMs as possible; however, it introduces high migration overhead. Furthermore, the cost factor is usually not taken into account by existing approaches, which will lead to high payment cost for cloud users. In this paper, we aim to achieve energy reduction for cloud providers and payment saving for cloud users, and at the same time, without introducing VM migration overhead and without compromising deadline guarantees for user tasks. Motivated by the fact that some of the tasks have relatively loose deadlines, we can further reduce energy consumption by proactively postponing the tasks without waking up new PMs. In this paper, we propose a heuristic task scheduling algorithm called Energy and Deadline Aware with Non-Migration Scheduling (EDA-NMS) algorithm. EDA-NMS exploits the looseness of task deadlines and tries to postpone the execution of the tasks that have loose deadlines in order to avoid waking up new PMs. When determining the VM instant types, EDA-NMS selects the instant types that are just sufficient to guarantee task deadline to reduce user payment cost. The results of extensive experiments show that our algorithm performs better than other existing algorithms on achieving energy efficiency without introducing VM migration overhead and without compromising deadline guarantees.

Keywords: Virtualized cloud · Real-time task · Scheduling · Criticality · Energy-aware

1 Introduction

Cloud computing is one of the fastest evolving paradigm in the domain of computer science. Cloud serves as powerful computing platforms for a wide range

© Springer International Publishing AG 2016
J. Chen et al. (Eds.): NSS 2016, LNCS 9955, pp. 80–97, 2016.
DOI: 10.1007/978-3-319-46298-1_6

of applications, such as meteorological prediction, genomic analysis, real-time complex physics simulations, monitoring watershed parameters through software services, and biological and environmental assistance [15]. Consequently, tens of thousands of hosts in a cloud datacenter consume enormous amount of energy. Therefore, reducing energy consumption has become an important task when deploying and operating cloud datacenters. In a virtual cloud computing environment, a set of submitted tasks from different users are scheduled on a set of virtual machines (VMs), and the task scheduling has become a critical issue for achieving energy efficiency. Previous energy-aware scheduling approaches [6, 12, 16, 20, 22] try to consolidate VMs to the minimum number of physical machines (PMs) to minimize the energy consumption, which however introduces high migration overhead. Figure 1(a) illustrates how existing task scheduling algorithms use VM migrations to further save energy. Suppose we are scheduling three tasks to the VMs in a datacenter. The first-in-first-out (FIFO) scheduling algorithm will create a VM for each task consequently. As each PM has two VM slots, the scheduling will end up with using two PMs as show in the figure. As task 2 is short, it will finish soon. After that, two tasks (e.g., task 1 and task 3) occupy two PMs. In order to reduce energy consumption, VM 3 can be migrated to PM 1 so that PM 2 can be shut down. A primary fraction of computing applications in cloud datacenters are real-time tasks [6], which have timing requirements on the response results. The arrival times of these tasks are dynamic and the predictions of their execution duration can also be difficult and sometimes impossible [3]. Users usually prefer that their task execution must be finished within a given deadline constraint. Motivated by the fact that some of the tasks have relatively loose deadlines, we can further reduce energy consumption by proactively postponing the tasks without waking up new PMs. Also, we no longer need VM migration to reduce energy consumption, thus the VM migration overhead is reduced. Figure 1(b) illustrates how arranging task with respect to their deadlines can help in eliminating VM migrations. Take the same scheduling problem as an example. As task 2 is short, we expect that it will finish executing soon. On the other hand, as task 3 does not have a stringent deadline, we can proactively postpone its execution. We schedule task 3 to VM 2 in PM 1. In this case, we no longer need the VM migration in Fig. 1(a) when VM 2 finishes execution.

In this paper, we propose a heuristic task scheduling algorithm called Energy and Deadline Aware with Non-Migration Scheduling (EDA-NMS) algorithm. EDA-NMS aims to provide a solution for achieving energy reduction for cloud providers without compromising deadline guarantees for user tasks. EDA-NMS exploits the looseness of task deadlines and tries to postpone the execution of the tasks with loose deadlines in order to avoid waking up new PMs.

In order to maximally satisfy user requests with different priorities, the proposed approach also introduces the concept of real-time criticality to accelerate the scheduling of priority tasks with stringent deadline constraints. Criticality is a different dimension than hard or soft characterization of a task, which is a measure of the cost of a failure(the higher the cost of failure, the more critical the

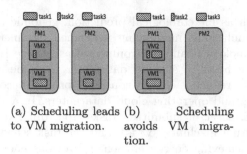

(a) Scheduling leads (b)   Scheduling
to VM migration.   avoids VM migration.

Fig. 1. Task scheduling examples.

task) [13]. If two tasks have the same deadline, the task with higher criticality should be scheduled first. When determining the VM instant types, EDA-NMS selects the instant types that are just sufficient to guarantee task deadline to reduce user payment cost. EDA-NMS gives higher priority to guaranteeing task deadlines than reducing energy consumption.

The key contributions of this paper are as follows:

- We propose an energy-saving EDA-NMS algorithm that reduces the number of running PMs and avoids VM migration by exploiting the looseness of task deadlines without compromising task schedulability (i.e., the condition of being schedulable) and throughput.
- We conduct extensive simulation-based experiments to evaluate and analyze the performance of the proposed task scheduling algorithm. The results show that the proposed heuristic task scheduling algorithm not only reduces energy consumption, but also improves the completion time of real-time tasks.

2   Related Work

A significant amount of research efforts has been devoted to investigating the task scheduling in the cloud systems over last decade. Qiu *et al.* [16] studied the problem of assigning computing units to each task in a system to achieve energy savings at a minimum cost. Hosseinimotlagh *et al.* [12] proposed a VM scheduling algorithm based on the unsurpassed utilization level, which achieves optimal energy consumption while meeting a given QoS. It focuses on increasing the acceptance rate of arrival tasks but ignores the type of workloads running in VMs which affects the QoS guarantee of scheduling algorithm. Besides these works, most existing cloud schedulers, such as FIFO scheduling in Hadoop MapReduce [9], Fair scheduler in Facebook [7] and Capacity scheduler in Yahoo [21] schedule tasks based on worst-case execution time while ignoring dynamically changing cloud computing environments. As a result, they fail to fully utilize the resource. In other word, those approaches assume that cloud computing environments are deterministic and pre-computed schedule decisions will be statically followed during schedule execution. Unlike those approaches, we leverage interval numbers to capture the dynamically changing cloud resource parameters to improve resource utilization.

Several scheduling works also address the problem of ensuring user deadlines as defined in Service Level Agreements (SLAs). Chen et al. [6] proposed a real-time scheduling strategy that allows executing only one task at any time instant on each VM. When the number of tasks increases, it needs vast VMs instants that will produce a lot of static energy consumption. Zhu et al. [22] presented a rolling-horizon optimization policy, which reduces energy consumption in virtualized data centers by supporting VM migration and VM placement optimization. These works reduce static energy consumption by migrating VMs between PMs. However, these works ignore the incurring VM migration overhead on the servers as well as the network infrastructure of the cloud. In contrast to previous researches, we propose the heuristic task scheduling algorithm to reduce static energy consumption. The total energy consumption consists of two parts: dynamic energy consumption and static energy consumption. The static energy consumption is the energy consumed by a host during idle time. The dynamic energy consumption is the extra energy consumed by a host when it is busy. As static energy consumption is dominant, our work focuses on reducing static energy consumption (i.e., reducing the number of active PMs). The proposed heuristic achieve reduce energy by selecting different types of VM instances with varying computing capacities for the tasks (i.e., we are actually adjusting execution speeds of real-time tasks, and consolidating these tasks into fewer number VMs, hence fewer number of PMs). As a result, it does not need to migrate VMs from an under-loaded host (PM) to other hosts (PMs). Furthermore, it also provides guarantees for the real-time tasks deadlines.

There are also some works that focus on the energy consumption model. The DVFS-enabled scheduling algorithms offers the minimum amounts of required CPU utilization to each task, and hence reduces the dynamic energy consumption as much as possible [5,18]. He et al. [10] developed a new energy-efficient adaptive scheduling algorithm (EASA) that can adaptively adjust supply voltages according to the system workload for dynamic energy efficiency. Most of previous research works like DVFS-enabled scheduling, focus on reducing the dynamic energy consumption as low as possible. However, the static power will last for a long time even for executing a low-speed task [11].

3   Model and System Architecture

In this section, we introduce the scheduling system architecture and three mathematical models: (i) the finishing time of a task, (ii) the laxity of a task, and (iii) the energy consumption of local a provider. These models will be used in our scheduling algorithm. Specifically, the scheduling system architecture is a VM based system, where VMs are launched for processing the submitted tasks and torn down when the tasks are finished. The system also dynamically turns on/off physical machines, and maintains the CPU utilization of the physical machines at the optimal level based on the number of VMs to reduce energy consumption.

(i) The finishing time of a task is calculated based on the length/size of the task and the computing capability of the VM to which the task is going to be assigned. It is used to estimate whether the task can be scheduled to a certain VM under deadline constrain.

(ii) The laxity of a task is calculated based on the task finishing time and its deadline. It is a measure of how urgent the task is. It is used for sorting the tasks in the scheduling queue.

(iii) The energy consumption is calculated based on the CPU utilizations of physical machines. Based on the estimated energy consumption, our algorithm dynamically turns on/off physical machines to reduce energy consumption.

4 Model and System Architecture

4.1 System Architecture

Figure 2 illustrates the compositional scheduling architecture used for the virtual cloud system.

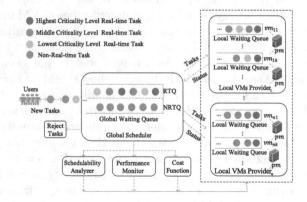

Fig. 2. Compositional scheduling architecture.

The scheduling architecture consists of two critical parts (the global scheduler and local VM providers) and three sub-components (performance monitor, schedulability analyzer and cost function), as shown in Fig. 2.

– The performance monitor observes the current workload in the system, checks the system status information such as currently allocated VMs, collects actual tasks processing time and arrival pattern information.

– The schedulability analyzer maintains and updates the configuration parameters which record tasks' deadlines and arrival time information provided by performance monitor. Also, the schedulability analyzer takes tasks from users and generates VMs startup plan from configuration parameters for different users.

– The cost function sub-component calculates the computing expense of executing tasks in the public cloud using price model offered by Amazon's Elastic Compute Cloud (EC2), based on the size of tasks and the computing price for renting a VM resource [3].

Cloud service providers (CSPs), who own large datacenters and server clusters, are incentivized by profits that they accrue by charging the end users for the service access [8]. CSPs provide services to end users through local VM providers. Each local VM provider is responsible for allocating cloud resource to the tasks of an individual user. One local VM provider offers one user massive computing power, needed storage and different services based on an SLA. Several neighboring local VM providers may form the CSPs with network connections. CSPs consist of a set of local VM providers: $LP = \{lp_1, lp_2, ..., lp_n\}$.

Each lp_j manages a set of PMs: $PM^j = \{pm_1^j, pm_2^j, ..., pm_k^j\}, k = 0, 1, ..., |PM^j|$. A PM can host one or more VMs. For each local VM provider lp_j, it manages a set of PMs which contains a set of VMs: $VM^j = \{VM_1^j, VM_2^j, ..., VM_k^j\}, k = 1, ..., |PM^j|$. VM_k^j is a set of VMs in pm_k^j that belongs to lp_j, and $VM_k^j = \{vm_{k1}^j, vm_{k2}^j, ..., vm_{kr}^j\}, r = 1, ..., |VM_k^j|$. vm_{kr}^j is the rth VM on PM pm_k^j that belongs to lp_j. The resource demands of a set VM^j cannot exceed the resource capacity of PM^j which belongs to lp_j.

To satisfy tasks diversity, multiple task queues are employed in global scheduler. Thus, the real-time tasks are assigned to global real-time waiting queues (RTQ), and non-real-time tasks are assigned to global non-real-time queue (NRTQ). In RTQ, all the real-time tasks are sorted by their laxity values in an ascending order, whenever a new real-time task arrives. The task with the smallest laxity which means a level of urgency is first considered for execution in scheduling. The motivation of sorting the tasks in RTQ based on their laxities is that tasks with tight deadlines are processed earlier than others in order to avoid SLA violations.

Definition 1. *The laxity ζ_i of real-time task τ_{ikr}^j belong to vm_{kr}^j means a level of urgency, and it is given as [6]:*

$$\zeta_{ikr}^j = d_i^u - (et_{ikr}^j)^+ - t_c, \tag{1}$$

where d_i^u is the deadline of task τ_i^u, $(et_{ikr}^j)^+$ represents the maximal execution time of task τ_i^u executing on vm_{kr}^j and t_c is the current time.

If some tasks have the same laxity value, then these tasks are sorted by their criticalities again. The tasks with higher criticality should be scheduled first. In NRTQ, the non-real-time tasks are sorted by their arrival times. The task with an earlier arrival time is scheduled first. Only when the RTQ is empty, the global scheduler schedules the tasks in NRTQ.

The local VM provider is bound to a specific user, so its VM instances can promote user context preservation, security and privacy. In other words, any VM instance of a local VM provider is dedicated to a single user until the instance is shut down when it approaches multiples of full hour operation (i.e., keep the instance busy doing work until the charging time interval is due) and no tasks are running on it. For example, since the instance is charged based on the unit of hour, we shut down the VM only when it is idle and reaching multiples of full hour operation. One local VM provider lp_j^u manages and monitors all pending and ready VM instances belong to one user u.

4.2   Task Model and Characteristics

The information provided by the task is the input to our scheduling algorithm. We introduce the task model and its characteristics in this section.

The tasks are submitted by individual users. We denote the set of tasks belonging to a separate user u as $T^u = \{\tau_1^u, \tau_2^u, ..., \tau_m^u\}$. The tasks considered in this paper can be divided into two types: real-time and non-real-time trivially parallel tasks which are independent and aperiodic. Each task requires to be executed in one VM instance type and cannot be partitioned to multiple computing nodes. Each task τ_i^u is characterized by a 4-tuple of parameters: $\tau_i^u = (at_i^u, \tilde{l}_i^u, d_i^u, k_i^u)$, where

- at_i^u is the arrival time for task τ_i^u.
- $\tilde{l}_i^u$ is the length/size of task t_i^u, which is the number of instructions (i.e., millions instructions, MI). Note that the length of a task is uncertain before scheduling, but its lower bound $(l_i^u)^-$ and upper bound $(l_i^u)^+$ can be gained [2,6]. As in [6,17], we regard $\tilde{l}_i^u$ as an interval number.
- d_i^u is the deadline of τ_i^u. Note that $d_i^u \geq at_i^u$. In this paper, the deadlines serve as the performance requirements specified by the users.
- $k_i^u \in \{K_1, K_2, K_3\}$ denotes the criticality of the task τ_i^u.
  The set of criticality is a designation of the level of assurance against failure needed for a system component [4]. In this paper, we use three generic criticality levels. K_1 is the lowest criticality level, K_3 is the highest criticality level. The task with higher criticality level indicates that it is more important and usually requires urgent response.

4.3   VM Instances

VMs are categorized into G distinct instance types: $it_1, it_2, ..., it_G$, and a VM of instance type it_g denotes as vm^g. VM is configured to have a number of slots for executing tasks. For a given VM vm_{kr}^j, it is characterized by its $\widetilde{cap}_{vm_{kr}^j}$ and τ_{ikr}^j, where $\widetilde{cap}_{vm_{kr}^j}$ denotes the CPU capacity represented by the number of instructions per second (MIPS), and τ_{ikr}^j is an indicator denoting that the task τ_i^u belong to vm_{kr}^j, respectively. Each user only specifies the types of VMs that are needed, but not the quantity of each requested VM type [8].

VM instance acquisition requests can be made at any time, but it may take startup time denoted as σ for newly requested pending instance to be ready to use. Based on the previous research [14], σ could take around 600 s from the arrival time of an instance acquisition request to the time when the VM is ready to use. The overhead is paid by the user although a task cannot be executed on the VM during the time when the VM is starting up. Because cloud VM instances are currently billed by instance hours (rather than the exact user consumption time), the scheduling and scaling (i.e., whether wake up extra PMs) decisions should avoid partial instance-hour waste. Therefore, a reasonable policy is that whenever an instance is started, it is better to be shut down when the VM usage approaches full hour operation (i.e., keep the instance busy doing work until the charging time interval is due) [14].

As mentioned before, clouds now normally offer various instance types for users to choose, instead of offering one suit-for-all instance type. Correspond to Amazon EC2 instance type with the only exception that all the VMs are single-core, our experiments model multiple VM instance types of a cloud with different performance and varying costs as shown in following Table 1. The it_1 and it_2 are compute and memory optimized instance types which are most suitable for CPU and memory intensive applications respectively, like image processing, database systems and memory caching applications. The it_3 is a general instance type which provides the balance between compute and memory. General type instances are suitable for all general purpose applications. A computing intensive task can run faster on high-CPU VM instance than on high-memory VM instance. Choosing cost-effective instance types can both guarantee task deadlines and save user payment cost [14].

4.4 Task Finishing Time Estimation

The CPU capacity allocated to a task in a VM is measured in MIPS (million instructions per second) $\widetilde{cap}_{vm^j_{kr}}$, which arbitrarily varies over time. We do not know its actual value, but its lower and upper bounds can be obtained before scheduling [6]. As a result, the real execution time $\widetilde{et}^j_{ikr}$ cannot be exactly determined before scheduling. We utilize the interval number described in [6,17] to determine these uncertain parameters as follows.

$$\widetilde{cap}_{vm^j_{kr}} = [cap^-_{vm^j_{kr}}, cap^+_{vm^j_{kr}}], \tag{2}$$

Table 1. Characteristics of types of VMs used

Type name	Description	Max MIPS	Cost	Startup lag
it_1	High-CPU	2500	\$0.68/hour	$\sigma = 720\,$s
it_2	High-Memory	2000	\$0.50/hour	$\sigma = 720\,$s
it_3	General type	1000	\$0.085/hour	$\sigma = 600\,$s

where $cap^-_{vm^j_{kr}}$ and $cap^+_{vm^j_{kr}}$ are the computing capacity lower and upper bound of the VMs with minimal and maximal CPU performance.

$$\tilde{et}^j_{ikr} = \frac{\tilde{l}^u_i}{\overline{cap}_{vm^j_{kr}}} = \left[\frac{(l^u_i)^-}{cap^+_{vm^j_{kr}}}, \frac{(l^u_i)^+}{cap^-_{vm^j_{kr}}}\right]. \tag{3}$$

$$\tilde{ft}^j_{ikr} = \tilde{st}^j_{ikr} + \tilde{et}^j_{ikr}, \tag{4}$$

where $\tilde{st}^j_{ikr}$ is the estimated start time of task τ^j_{ikr}, and $\tilde{ft}^j_{ikr}$ denotes the finish time of task τ^j_{ikr}.

$$\tilde{st}^j_{ikr} = max\{(ft^j_{ikr})^b, at^u_i\}, \tag{5}$$

where $(ft^j_{ikr})^b$ is the finish time of previously allocated task before τ^u_i executing on vm^j_{kr}.

4.5   Energy Consumption

CPU resource utilization. We first discuss the CPU resource utilization of the VMs and PMs, which are related to the energy consumption. The CSPs may offer different types of VM instances, which are suitable for different types of workloads. lp_j is associated with an integer array Q^j of G members: $q^j_1, q^j_2, ..., q^j_G$, where q^x_g indicates that number of type g VMs (vm^g) are hosted on the PMs set PM^j that belongs to lp_j. Since Q^j is dynamic, it may change over time due to VM terminations and reconfigurations. We denote it as $Q^j(t)$ at time t. lp_j contains a finite amount of computing resources C^j_{cpu} coming from PM^j. The CPU resource utilization of lp_j at time t is denoted as $U^j(t)$, and the CPU resource requirement of vm^g is denoted as R^g_{cpu}.

$$U^j(t) = \frac{\sum\limits_{g=1}^{G} Q^j_g(t) \cdot R^g_{cpu}}{C^j_{cpu}} \times 100\% \tag{6}$$

$$= \frac{\sum\limits_{k=1}^{|PM^j|} U^j_k(t)}{|PM^j|}, \tag{7}$$

where $U^j_k(t)$ is the CPU resource utilization of one PMs pm^j_k belongs to lp_j at time t.

The energy consumption (E) at a datacenter is defined as a total amount of power (P) consumed over a period of time (T) while performing the work [19].

$$E = P \cdot T. \tag{8}$$

The total energy consumption of pm^j_k is denoted as TE^j_k. In CMOS chips, the total energy-consuming contains two main parts, one is the static energy consuming SE_k^j and the other is dynamic energy consuming DE_k^j. The SE_k^j is the energy consumed during the idle time of pm_k^j. From [12], we can define SE_k^j as:

Static energy consumption. The SE_k^j is the energy consumed during the idle time of pm_k^j. From [12], we can define SE_k^j as:

$$SE_k^j = \begin{cases} \gamma \cdot ME_k^j, & \text{when } U_k^j > 0, \\ 0, U_k^j & \text{otherwise.} \end{cases} \tag{9}$$

where ME_k^j is the energy consumed when a PM works with its maximum utilization, γ is a constant ratio of the static energy consumption SE_k^j to the maximum energy consumption ME_k^j of pm_k^j ($0 < \gamma < 1$).

$$ME_k^j = P_{k\,max}^j \cdot t_{max}, \tag{10}$$

where $P_{k\,max}^j$ is the power consumed when a PM works with its maximum utilization, and t_{max} is the time in which a PM works at its maximum computing power to finish a certain amount of tasks.

This ratio γ depends on the physical characteristics of the PM, and it is constant during the time that a host is switched on.

Dynamic energy consumption. The relationship between dynamic energy consumption DE_k^j and $U_j(t)$ is much more complex. From [11], we can know that several models proposed for the dynamic energy consumption DE_k^j in the literature which are functions of the utilization of a PM. The dynamic energy consumption DE_k^j and the total energy consumption TE_k^j of pm_k^j to execute tasks can be defined as:

$$DE_k^j = (ME_k^j - SE_k^j) \cdot U_k^j. \tag{11}$$

$$TE_k^j = SE_k^j + DE_k^j \tag{12}$$

$$= [\gamma + (1 - \gamma) \cdot U_k^{j\,2}] \frac{P_{k\,max}^j \cdot t_{max}}{U_k^j}. \tag{13}$$

Equation (13) explains that CPU resource utilization U_k^j is the only adjustable parameter that has an impact on total energy consumption TE_k^j.

In the following, we will show that the static energy consumption dominates the total energy consumption. In Fig. 3, we assume the $\gamma = \{0, 0.2, 0.4, 0.8\}$, it means that the static energy consumption SE_k^j takes 0 %, 20 %, 40 %, 80 % of the maximum energy ME_k^j. We compare the total energy consumption TE_k^j under different static energy consumption by ignoring the exact value of $P_{k\,max}^j$. Figure 3 shows that the pm_k^j consumes a noticeable amount of static energy for a long-life computing. Therefore, the static energy plays a profound role in the total energy consumption, and sometimes it comprises up to 70 % of total energy consumption [11]. When the value of γ is larger, the static energy consumption is

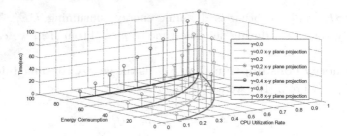

Fig. 3. Total energy consumption with various values of γ.

more than those with smaller γ. From the projection curves on x-y plane under various γ values, we can see that the increasing speeds of energy consumption are different. The smaller γ has faster increasing speed of energy consumption. This explains that most of total energy consumption is dynamic energy consumption when the γ is smaller.

Only alleviating the dynamic energy consumption cannot reduce the total energy consumption significantly as long as there is high static energy consumption. Previous research works focus on consolidating VMs to alleviate the static energy consumption. However, the migration process imposes a high overhead depending on the network infrastructure. In addition, the source local VM provider spends more computing power during the live migration transient interval which might result in SLA violations. In order to handle this problem, we propose a task scheduling strategy that launches as few VMs (hence few PMs) as possible to guarantee most of tasks' deadlines and to enhance the CPU utilization level to minimize the static energy consumption.

5   Scheduling Strategy with Deadline Guarantee

Our energy-aware scheduling strategy focuses on how to finish all the submitted tasks before user specified deadlines with as few VM instance hours as possible.

Definition 2. *The computing cost of running a task τ_i^u on provider lp_j with instance VM type $it_i \in \{it_1, it_2, it_3\}$ is defined as $C_{task}(\tau_i^u, lp_j, it_i)$.*

$$C_{task}(\tau_i^u, lp_j, it_i) = (\lceil \frac{\widetilde{l_i^u}}{\widetilde{cap}_{vm_{jk}}} \rceil \cdot C_{it_i}), \tag{14}$$

where $\lceil \frac{\widetilde{l_i^u}}{\widetilde{cap}_{vm_{jk}}} \rceil$ means that the execution time is rounded up to the nearest discrete time unit (i.e. 1 h) of lp_j's billing interval for cost calculations, C_{it_i} denotes as the cost of running the VM instance vm_{kr}^j of type it_i on lp_j for one time unit. When the deadline of task τ_i^u is not met, the computing cost is ∞.

Our scheduling policy first schedules the task τ_i^u within deadline constraint on the local waiting queue of the cheapest (low hourly-cost) VM instance type among all the live instances. A task τ_i^u will be removed from the cheapest VM instance type queue to more expensive (high hourly-cost) VM instance type queue from the all available instance types, when the current state of vm_{kr}^j is not able to finish task τ_i^u before its deadline. Even when there is no workload, a cloud application will always maintain at least one running VM instance. When one VM instance vm_{jk} is approaching full hour operation, we need to decide whether to shut down the machine or not. The detail pseudocode of our EDA-NMS algorithm is showed in Algorithm 1.

Algorithm 1. Pseudocode of EDA-NMS algorithm

1: $RTQ \leftarrow NULL$;
2: $NRTQ \leftarrow NULL$;
3: **for** each new task τ_i^u **do**
4:   **if** $d_i^u != NULL$ **then**
5:     $RTQ \leftarrow \tau_i^u$;
6:   **else**
7:     $NRTQ \leftarrow \tau_i^u$;
8:   **end if**
9:   **while** $RTQ != NULL$ **do**
10:     sort all the tasks in RTQ by laxity in ascending order;
11:     **if** more than two tasks have the same ζ_i **then**
12:       sort all the tasks with same ζ_i by criticality k_i^u in descending order;
13:     **end if**
14:     $\tau_i^u \leftarrow$ get the task at the head in RTQ;
15:     the global scheduler assigns task τ_i^u to specific lp_j belonging to one user;
16:     move τ_i^u to the tail of local waiting queue on most cost-efficient vm_{kr}^j;
17:     execute LRTS algorithm (Algorithm 2);
18:   **end while**
19:   **while** $RTQ == NULL$ && $NRTQ != NULL$ **do**
20:     $\tau_i^u \leftarrow$ get the task at the head in NRTQ;
21:     the global scheduler assigns task τ_i^u to specific lp_j belonging to one user;
22:     move τ_i^u to the tail of local waiting queue on most cost-efficient vm_{kr}^j;
23:     **for** each task in local waiting queue on vm_{kr}^j **do**
24:       execute τ_i^u;
25:     **end for**
26:   **end while**
27: **end for**

The pseudocode of local real-time scheduling (LRTS) algorithm is shown in Algorithm 2.

Algorithm 2. Pseudocode of LRTS algorithm

1: $\tau_i^u \leftarrow$ get the task at the head in local waiting queue on vm_{kr}^j;
2: calculate the start time $\widetilde{st}_{ikr}^j$, execution time $\widetilde{et}_{ikr}^j$ and finish time $\widetilde{ft}_{ikr}^j$ of τ_i^u;
3: **while** $\widetilde{ft}_{ijk}^u > d_i^u$ **do**
4:     Find next cost-efficient $vm_{kr'}^j$;
5: **end while**
6: **if** can find one vm_{kr}^j on lp_j make $\widetilde{ft}_{ijk}^u \leq d_i^u$ **then**
7:     **while** $\tau_i^u! = NULL$ **do**
8:         execute τ_i^u;
9:         $\tau_i^u \leftarrow$ get the task at the head in local waiting queue on vm_{kr}^j;
10:    **end while**
11: **else**
12:    reject τ_i^u
13: **end if**

---

6 Performance Evaluation

6.1 Environment Setup

To demonstrate the performance improvements gained by our EDA-NMS algorithm, we quantitatively compare it with a existing algorithms PRS using the CloudSim simulator [6]. We compare the user payment cost and the completion time of real-time tasks of running cloud applications. In the simulation framework, we can also control the input parameters, such as workload patterns and task deadlines. The detailed parameters are given as follows:

- The simulation environment consists of a datacenter with 10000 hosts, where each host is modeled to have a single CPU core (with CPU performance 3000 MIPS, 3500 MIPS and 4500 MIPS), 4 GB of RAM memory, and 1 TB of storage [1,6].
- We employ the interval number to control a task's deadline, which can be calculated as:

$$d_i^u = at_i^u + \frac{U\left[(l_i^u)^-, (l_i^u)^+\right]}{cap_{vm_{kr}^j}^+} + U[0, 500]\, s, \tag{15}$$

where $U[0, 500]\, s$ denotes a variable that subjects to uniformly distributed from 0 s to 500 s, and it determines whether the deadline of a task is loose or not.
- We randomly generated the task's length: $\widetilde{l}_i^u = [5000, 100000]$ MIs in a uniform distribution.
- The arrival of tasks follows Poisson distribution at the arrival rate of $Poisson(\lambda), \lambda = 4$ per unit of time, it means the arrival interval between two consecutive tasks obey the negative exponential distribution with parameter $Exp(1/\lambda)$.

6.2 Performance Under Changing Workloads

In these experiments, we focus on two types of workload. The single type work-load experiment for compute-intensive tasks whose main bottleneck is CPU's computing power. In the mix type workload evaluation, we simulated three types of tasks, including mix, computing intensive and I/O intensive. The processing time parameters of single type and mix type workload experiment on different types VM instance are summarized in Table 2.

Table 2. Mix type workload unit execution time

	Mix	Computing intensive	I/O intensive
General	50 s/MI	50 s/MI	50 s/MI
High-CPU	25 s/MI	15 s/MI	50 s/MI
High-Memory	25 s/MI	50 s/MI	15 s/MI

Three task trace groups are generated for the experiments, each includes 1000, 5000 and 10000 tasks and the number of real-time tasks, non-real-time tasks and reject tasks produced by the experiment results is summarized in Table 3.

Table 3. Some running results of single type workload/mix type workload

	Number of real-time tasks	Number of non-real-time tasks	Reject number of real-time tasks
EDA-NMS(1000 tasks)	584/587	416/413	0/0
PRS(1000 tasks)	587/581	413/419	0/0
EDA-NMS(5000 tasks)	2915/2912	2085/2088	0/0
PRS(5000 tasks)	2910/2913	2090/2087	1/0
EDA-NMS(10000 tasks)	5838/5835	4162/4165	5/2
PRS(10000 tasks)	5828/5832	4172/4168	6/2

To investigate the duration of the real-time tasks executions, we use the cumulative distribution function (CDF) of the response time lags (i.e., deadline - finish time) of the tasks. From the experiment result of Fig. 4, we can see the EDA-NMS and PRS scheduling algorithms' performance under these two types of workload conditions. EDA-NMS outperforms PRS in terms that it achieves bigger tasks response lag than PRS, it means that the completion time of the real-time tasks executed by EDA-NMS is shorter than PRS under different types of workloads.

By analysing the situation of the rejected tasks, we can know the system stability under EDA-NMS and PRS. The reject tasks of EDA-NMS consist of

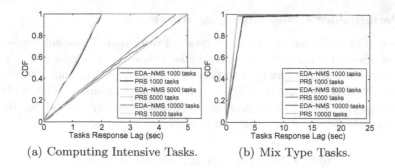

(a) Computing Intensive Tasks.   (b) Mix Type Tasks.

Fig. 4. Tasks response time lag.

7 tasks with middle criticality, and the reject tasks of PRS consist of 8 tasks including 3 ones with highest criticality, 4 ones with middle criticality and 2 ones with lowest criticality. The task with different criticality which misses the deadline has different influence on the system stability. So we can find that there are fewer rejected tasks with higher criticality of our EDA-NMS than PRS. It means that our EDA-NMS has better system stability than PRS.

6.3 Cost Efficient Comparison

By changing the task number from 1000 to 10000, we first use the average execution cost of real-time tasks to compare the performance of these two scheduling policies (EDA-NMS, PRS). The experiment results in Fig. 5 show that our EDA-NMS has lower average execution cost in both two computing intensive and mix type workload cases.

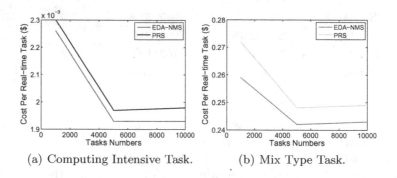

(a) Computing Intensive Task.   (b) Mix Type Task.

Fig. 5. Average cost per real-time task comparison.

We then compare the total cost of these two scheduling policies (EDA-NMS, PRS) with three different types of VM instances as shown in Table 1. From the comparison results of total cost are illustrated in Table 4, we can see that the

Table 4. Mix workload cost

No	Number of tasks	VM types	Total cost($)	Static energy consumption
Choice 1	10000	General, General	9.95×10^3 (58 % higher)	Standard
Choice 2	10000	General, High-Memory	7.74×10^3 (23 % higher)	Standard
Choice 3	10000	General, High-CPU	7.4×10^3 (17 % higher)	Standard
Optimal	10000	General, High-CPU, High-Memory	6.3×10^3	1.5 standard

choice 1, choice 2 and choice 3 incur 58 %, 23 % and 17 % more cost than the optimal solution separately. Our choice 3 is closest to the optimal cost, and it outperforms other two choices. Although the optimal solution can obtain the lowest cost, its statics energy consumption is 1.5 times of other three choices. Because the future workload cannot be known in advance, so the optimal cost can't be obtained in real life. Hence, our choice 3 is cost and energy efficient solution.

7   Conclusion

In this paper, EDA-NMS exploits the looseness of task deadlines and tries to postpone the execution of the tasks that have loose deadlines in order to avoid waking up new PMs. It incrementally provides cloud resources to the tasks based on the user specified deadlines, the estimated completion times of the tasks, and the resource utilization levels of the hosts. The results of extensive experiments show that our approach perform better than other existing approaches on achieving energy efficiency without introducing VM migration overhead and without compromising deadline guarantees. In the future, we are going to implement EDA-NMS in a real testbed and evaluate its performance.

Acknowledgments. The work on this paper has been supported by Scientific and Technological Research Program for Guangxi Educational Commission grants ♯2013YB113, Guangxi Universities key Laboratory Fund of Embedded Technology and Intelligent Information Processing.

References

1. Beloglazov, A., Buyya, R.: Optimal online deterministic algorithms and adaptive heuristics for energy and performance efficient dynamic consolidation of virtual machines in cloud data centers. Concurrency Comput. Pract. Experience **24**(13), 1397–1420 (2012)
2. Berral, J.L., Gavalda, R., Torres, J.: Adaptive scheduling on power-aware managed data-centers using machine learning. In: Proceedings of the 2011 IEEE/ACM 12th International Conference on Grid Computing. pp. 66–73. IEEE Computer Society (2011)
3. Van den Bossche, R., Vanmechelen, K., Broeckhove, J.: Cost-optimal scheduling in hybrid IaaS clouds for deadline constrained workloads. In: Proceedings of CLOUD, pp. 228–235. IEEE (2010)
4. Burns, A., Davis, R.: Mixed criticality systems-a review. Department of Computer Science, University of York, Technical report (2013)
5. Calheiros, R.N., Buyya, R.: Energy-efficient scheduling of urgent bag-of-tasks applications in clouds through DVFS. In: Proceedings of CloudCom, pp. 342–349. IEEE (2014)
6. Chen, H., Zhu, X., Guo, H., Zhu, J., Qin, X., Wu, J.: Towards energy-efficient scheduling for real-time tasks under uncertain cloud computing environment. J. Syst. Softw. **99**, 20–35 (2015)
7. Facebook. https://www.facebook.com/
8. Gao, Y., Wang, Y., Gupta, S.K., Pedram, M.: An energy and deadline aware resource provisioning, scheduling and optimization framework for cloud systems. In: Proceedings of the Ninth IEEE/ACM/IFIP International Conference on Hardware/Software Codesign and System Synthesis, p. 31. IEEE Press (2013)
9. Hadoop MapReduce. https://hadoop.apache.org/docs/r1.2.1/fair_scheduler.html
10. He, C., Zhu, X., Guo, H., Qiu, D., Jiang, J.: Rolling-horizon scheduling for energy constrained distributed real-time embedded systems. J. Syst. Softw. **85**(4), 780–794 (2012)
11. Hosseinimotlagh, S., Khunjush, F.: Migration-less energy-aware task scheduling policies in cloud environments. In: Proceedings of WAINA, pp. 391–397. IEEE (2014)
12. Hosseinimotlagh, S., Khunjush, F., Samadzadeh, R.: Seats: smart energy-aware task scheduling in real-time cloud computing. J. Supercomput. **71**(1), 45–66 (2015)
13. Mall, R.: Real-Time Systems: Theory and Practice. Pearson Education, India (2009)
14. Mao, M., Li, J., Humphrey, M.: Cloud auto-scaling with deadline and budget constraints. In: Proceedings of GRID, pp. 41–48. IEEE (2010)
15. Pop, F., Dobre, C., Cristea, V., Bessis, N., Xhafa, F., Barolli, L.: Deadline scheduling for aperiodic tasks in inter-cloud environments: a new approach to resource management. J. Supercomput. **71**(5), 1754–1765 (2015)
16. Qiu, M., Sha, E.H.M.: Cost minimization while satisfying hard/soft timing constraints for heterogeneous embedded systems. ACM Trans. Des. Autom. Electron. Syst. (TODAES) **14**(2), 25 (2009)
17. Sengupta, A., Pal, T.K.: Fuzzy preference ordering of intervals. In: Sengupta, A., Pal, T.K. (eds.) Fuzzy Preference Ordering of Interval Numbers in Decision Problems. STUDFUZZ, vol. 238, pp. 59–89. Springer, Heidelberg (2009)
18. Tang, Z., Qi, L., Cheng, Z., Li, K., Khan, S.U., Li, K.: An energy-efficient task scheduling algorithm in DVFS-enabled cloud environment. J. Grid Comput. 1–20 (2015)

19. Veni, T., Bhanu, S.: A survey on dynamic energy management at virtualization level in cloud data centers. Comput. Sci. Inf. Technol. **3**, 107–117 (2013)
20. Wang, W.J., Chang, Y.S., Lo, W.T., Lee, Y.K.: Adaptive scheduling for parallel tasks with QoS satisfaction for hybrid cloud environments. J. Supercomput. **66**(2), 783–811 (2013)
21. Yahoo. https://www.yahoo.com/
22. Zhu, X., Yang, L.T., Chen, H., Wang, J., Yin, S., Liu, X.: Real-time tasks oriented energy-aware scheduling in virtualized clouds. TOCC **2**(2), 168–180 (2014)

An Infrastructure-Based Framework for the Alleviation of JavaScript Worms from OSN in Mobile Cloud Platforms

Shashank Gupta and Brij B. Gupta[✉]

Department of Computer Engineering, National Institute of Technology
Kurukshetra, Haryana, India
gupta.brij@gmail.com

Abstract. This paper presents an infrastructure-based mobile cloud computing framework that obstructs the execution of JavaScript (JS) worms injected from the untrustworthy remote servers. The execution of such worms triggers the Cross-Site Scripting (XSS) attack on the mobile cloud-based Online Social Network (OSN). The framework executes in two steps. Initially, it extracts the Uniform Resource Identifier (URI) links embedded in the HTTP response for extracting the untrusted JS links/code. Secondly, our framework generates the Document Object Model (DOM) tree corresponding to each extracted HTTP response. This tree is explored for the script nodes and extracts the embedded JS code. Now, both these extracted set of JS code will be explored for the detection of similar code. Such similar code will simply point towards the untrusted JavaScript code that will be utilized by an attacker to exploit the vulnerabilities of XSS attack on the OSN. The prototype of our framework was developed in Java and integrated the functionality of its components on the virtual machines of mobile cloud platforms. The experimental testing and performance evaluation of our work was carried out on the open source OSN websites that are integrated in the virtual cloud servers. Evaluation results revealed that our framework is capable enough to detect the untrusted JS worms with very high precision rate, fewer rates of false positives and acceptable performance overhead.

Keywords: Mobile cloud computing · Cloud security · JavaScript worms · Cross-Site Scripting (XSS) attacks · Online Social Network (OSN)

1 Introduction

In order to fulfill the needs of growing smartphone users and essential constraints related to smartphone, mobile cloud computing evolved from cloud computing [16]. However, mobile cloud computing has raised numerous issues related to the privacy and security of the smart phone users. This is generally due to the fact that the sensitive credentials of such users are kept in the domain of public cloud that is managed by untrustworthy commercial service providers. In the modern era of mobile cloud computing, mobile cloud security has turned out to be an utmost key challenge that has appealed numerous efforts related to research and development in the recent times. The smart phone users access the facilities of OSN through the infrastructures of mobile

© Springer International Publishing AG 2016
J. Chen et al. (Eds.): NSS 2016, LNCS 9955, pp. 98–109, 2016.
DOI: 10.1007/978-3-319-46298-1_7

cloud. However, it is clearly known that the cloud settings are installed on the backbone of Internet [9]. Therefore, numerous Web application vulnerabilities in the conventional Internet infrastructures also exist in the backgrounds of mobile cloud-based environments.

The most prominent attack found on OSN sites is the Cross Site Scripting (XSS) attack [1–5]. XSS worms have turned out to be a plague for the mobile cloud-based OSN. Such worms steal the sensitive credentials of the active users by injecting the malicious JS worms in the form of some posts on such web applications [6–8]. Input sanitization is considered to be the most effective mechanism for alleviating and mitigating the effect of JS worms from the mobile cloud-based OSN on the virtual machines of cloud platforms. Numerous defensive methodologies had been proposed for thwarting the effect of JS worms or XSS attacks from such platforms [23]. Livshits et al. [10] proposed an automated technique of sanitizer placement by statically analyzing the stream of infected data in the program. Path Cutter [12] generally jams the transmission path of XSS worms by restricting the DOM access to several different views at the web browser and hampers the illicit HTTP web requests to the web server. Saner [11] is a tool that combines static and dynamic analysis practices to detect the defective sanitization techniques that can be evaded by a malicious attacker. The main objective of this tool is to analyze the working of sanitization procedures to report the web application vulnerabilities like XSS attack. XSSFilt [13] is a Firefox extension-based XSS filter that uses approximate string matching rather than exact string matching algorithm. XSS-Auditor [14] is integrated as an extension on the Google Chrome Web browser that circumvents the browser quirks problem via interposing at the Java-Script engine interface. It can detect the exploitation of JS worms that occur in web pages which are generated dynamically due to client-side script execution.

1.1 Existing Performance Issues

The main issue with these existing JS worm defensive techniques is that they cannot easily integrate in the existing virtual machines of mobile cloud platforms. Integration of their functionality demands major alterations in the source code of their prototypes. On the other hand, most of these existing techniques rely on exact JavaScript string matching. They cannot detect the partial injection of JS worms. In addition to this, these methodologies perform the sanitization of JavaScript worms in a context-insensitive manner. Sanitization of malicious variables of JS code without determining their context is considered to be an ineffective sanitization mechanism for alleviating the effect of JS worms.

1.2 Key Contributions

Based on such severe performance issues, this article presents a mobile cloud-based JS worm defensive framework that detects and alleviates the propagation of such worms from the cloud-based OSN. The framework intercepts each HTTP request from the smart phone user and detects the untrusted/malicious JavaScript code and performs the context-aware sanitization on the suspicious variables embedded in such code. Such sort of sanitization guarantees the complete alleviation of JS worms from the platforms of mobile cloud-based OSN. The experimental testing of our framework was done on real world OSN-based web applications that are integrated on the virtual machines of mobile cloud platforms. The next section discusses our mobile cloud-based framework in detail. The remainder of the paper is structured as follows: Sect. 2 illustrates our mobile cloud-based JS defensive framework. Implementation and experimental evaluation is presented in Sect. 3. Finally, Sect. 4 concludes our work and discusses the future work.

2 Proposed Framework

This article presents an infrastructure-based mobile cloud framework that obstructs the dissemination of JS worms from the contemporary platforms of OSN. Such worms are injected by an attacker to exploit the vulnerabilities of XSS attack on OSN. The novelty of our mobile cloud computing-based framework lies in the fact that it not only detects the propagation of JS worms but also completely alleviates the effect of such worms from OSN.

2.1 Abstract View

This sub-section discusses the abstract overview of our framework. Figure 1 highlights the abstract overview of our mobile cloud–based framework. Smartphone devices will access the Internet on the wireless network with the help of installed Base Transceiver Stations (BTS). Users of smartphone will transmit the HTTP request to the OSN web server deployed in the cloud platforms. The HTTP response generated by the OSN server will be transmitted to the virtual cloud JS worm detection server. This cloud-based JS worm detection server not only detects the propagation of JS worms but also determines the context of the malicious variables embedded in such worms. Accordingly, it alleviates the effect of such worms by performing the context-aware sanitization on these malicious variables. Finally, safe sanitized HTTP response is transferred to the smart phone user.

2.2 Detailed Illustration

The key goal of our infrastructure-based mobile cloud JS worm defensive framework is to compare the set of extracted JS code embedded in both URI links and DOM tree. Any similarity found in both the extracted set of JS code will simply point towards the location of JS worm. In addition, our framework defines the context of malicious variables embedded in such JS code and accordingly performs the context-aware sanitization on them. This sort of context-sensitive sanitization will guarantee the complete alleviation of JS worms from the OSN platforms deployed in the cloud-based mobile platforms. Figure 2 highlights the detailed design view of our mobile cloud-based framework.

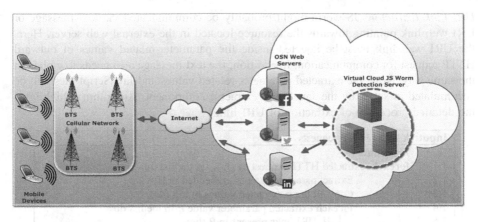

Fig. 1. Abstract overview of mobile cloud-based framework

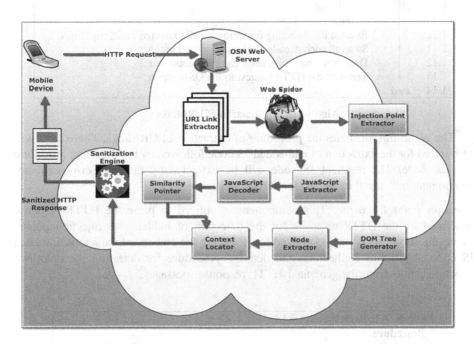

Fig. 2. Detailed design view of our framework

2.3   Key Modules

The modules of our framework are deployed on the virtual machines of mobile cloud servers. This sub-section discusses the detailed working of some of the key components utilized in our mobile cloud computing-based framework.

URI Link Extractor: JS worm might probably be communicated via text message or URI web link pointing towards the resource located in the external web server. Here, the URI web link must be injected inside the parameter-related values of outward HTTP request for communication. In addition, the text message also needs to embed in the same way. Now, the extracted parameter-related values and JavaScript files will be accumulated in set A by the JavaScript extractor component. Algorithm 1 highlights the detailed procedure of extraction of URI links.

Input: A list of HTTP requests	
	Procedure
1.1	**foreach** extracted HTTP request as H_{REQ} in the list **do**
1.2	Extract parameter values embedded in H;
1.3	Copy all these extracted values in log file;
1.4	**foreach** extracted parameter value P in the list **do**
1.5	**if** URI links present in P **then**
1.6	Transmit external HTTP request to remote servers;
1.7	Extract the JavaScript links embedded in URI;
1.8	**end**
1.9	**end**
1.10	Execute the decoding operation on all extracted JavaScript links;
1.11	Store all such decoded values in repository 'A';
1.12	Deactivate the sanitization engine component ;
1.13	Transmit the HTTP request to the OSN server;
1.14	**end**

Algorithm 1. Extraction of URI links

The algorithm illustrates the procedure of extraction of URI links. These links will be referred for the extraction of embedded JS code followed by the decoding procedure of such code. The resultant JS code will be extracted by the JavaScript extractor component and stored in set 'A' for further reference.

Injection Point Extractor: This component is utilized to parse the HTTP response generated by the HTTP response for the detection of hidden user injection points. These injection points will be utilized for detecting the embedded malicious/untrusted JS code. Algorithm 2 illustrates the detailed procedure for detecting the unknown injection points from the generated HTTP response messages.

Input: A list of retrieved URLs	
Procedure	
2.1	Generate the value of a variable φ by invoking **randGen()**;
2.2	**for** $i = 1 \Rightarrow \varphi$
2.3	**foreach** extracted web page as W_P **do**
2.4	Crawl the web page W_P by using web spider;
2.5	Explore the malicious context of W_P;
2.6	Determine the URL address of crawled web pages;
2.7	Extract the injection points embedded in W_P;
2.8	**end**
2.9	**end**

Algorithm 2. Extraction of unknown injection points

The HTML parser also causes the formation of script and text vertices in document tree. However, text vertices are of no interest to us. XSS-Immune transmits the JavaScript vertices to the Get/Post parameter detector and JavaScript component.

DOM Tree Generator: This component is utilized for generating the Document Object Model (DOM) representation of HTTP response messages. This representation of HTTP response is generally seen as a tree comprising of JavaScript and text vertices. Such nodes will be explored for the extraction of hidden JS code embedded in the unknown injection points of OSN-based web applications.

Node Extractor: The key goal of this module is to extract the JS vertices embedded in the DOM tree. Although, there are diverse categories of vertices available in the DOM tree, but the vertices, which are of concern to us are the JS vertices. Such vertices will be utilized for the extraction of JS code. Here the set of JavaScript code retrieved is transmitted to the JavaScript extractor component and stored in set 'B'.

JavaScript Extractor: This module will store the two sets of JavaScript code in set 'A' and 'B'. The set 'A' JavaScript code was extracted from the extracted URI links embedded in the HTTP response message. On the other hand, the set 'B' JavaScript code was extracted from the DOM tree. These two sets of JavaScript code will be compared for the similar code. Any similarity found in these two sets will simply indicate the presence of JS worms.

JavaScript Decoder: Keeping in view, that the malware of JS worm in both the sets 'A' and 'B' possibly be encrypted, we execute a recursive decoding technique before executing our similarity pointer component.

Similarity Pointer: This component is used to match the extracted code from set A and B for detecting the presence of similar untrusted/malicious JavaScript code. The similar code states the probable propagation activities of JS worm. Algorithm 3 illustrates the algorithm for detection of similar untrusted/malicious JavaScript code embedded in the HTTP request and response messages.

	Input: A series of HTTP response messages
	Procedure
3.1	**foreach** extracted HTTP response as H_{RES} in the list **do**
3.2	Parse the contents of URL;
3.3	Generate the HTML Web page by document generator;
3.4	**foreach** retrieved web page as W_P **do**
3.5	Perform the parsing on W_P by web spider;
3.6	Generate the DOM tree of W_P;
3.7	Traverse all the nodes of DOM tree;
3.8	**if** node is a JavaScript node **then**
3.9	Extract the GET/POST parameter values;
3.10	Execute the decoding operation on all such values;
3.11	Store all such values in repository 'B';
3.12	**if** (A = = B) **then**
3.13	Find out the context of malicious variables;
3.14	Inject the sanitization primitives on such variables;
3.15	Transmit the safe sanitized HTML document to the OSN web browser;
3.16	**end**
3.17	**end**
3.18	**else** node is a text node **then**
3.19	Extract the H_{RES};
3.20	Transmit H_{RES} to the web browser;
3.21	**end**
3.22	**end**
3.23	**end**

Algorithm 3. Detection of JavaScript worm

The algorithm not only illustrates the procedure of detection of JavaScript worm, it also explains the procedure to determine the context of malicious variables present in such worms. Accordingly, it performs the sanitization on such variables for completely alleviating the effect of JS worms. Algorithm 4 illustrates the detailed procedure of sanitization of JS worms.

Context Locator: The goal of this component is to identify the context for each type of untrusted variable of JavaScript worms corresponding to each untrusted input. It will represent the context in which untrusted JavaScript input is embedded and sanitizers are selected accordingly.

Sanitization Engine: Sanitization is a process of validating the untrusted user input to ensure that they are in correct format as perceived by the Web application. Context-aware sanitization applies sanitizer on each untrusted variable in an automated manner (i.e. dynamic content like JavaScript) according to the context in which they are used. There may be different contexts present in an HTML document like element tag, attribute value, style sheet, script, anchors, href, etc. These all contexts may be used by an attacker to launch the XSS attack. This component will determine the different possible contexts of extracted similar JavaScript code and accordingly performs the sanitization on such code. Algorithm 4 highlights the sanitization of similar untrusted/malicious JavaScript code.

Input: A list of decoded JavaScript Code/Links	
Procedure	
4.1	**foreach** extracted XSS attack vector as X_V **do**
4.2	Determine the untrusted/malicious JavaScript variables;
4.3	Find out the context of such variables;
4.4	Store the context of these variables in set 'C_V';
4.5	**foreach** extracted sanitizer primitive as S_P **do**
4.6	Define the context of S_P;
4.7	Store the context of S_P in set C_S;
4.8	**if** ($C_V == C_S$) **then**
4.9	Sanitize the malicious variables that belongs to context C_V;
4.10	Inject the sanitized variables in the H_{RES};
4.11	**end**
4.12	**end**
4.13	**end**
4.14	Deactivate all the modules in the framework;
4.15	return modified sanitized HTML document to the web browser;

Algorithm 4. Sanitization of JS worms

Here, note that the Algorithm 4 sanitizes the malicious variables of JavaScript code in a context-aware manner. The context of both the sanitizer primitive and malicious JavaScript variable will be found out. The sanitization of a JavaScript variable will be performed only if the context of sanitization primitive and the associated malicious JavaScript variable are same.

3 Implementation and Experimental Evaluation

We had developed a prototype of our mobile cloud-based JavaScript worm defensive framework in Java via introducing the Java Development Kit and integrate this framework in the virtual machine of cloud-based OSN server. The experiment background is simulated with the help of a normal desktop system, comprising 1.6 GHz AMD processor, 2 GB DDR RAM and Windows 7 operating system. The JS worm detection capability of our framework was evaluated on a tested suite of two open source OSN websites deployed in virtual machines of cloud platforms. Table 1 highlights the detailed configuration of these OSN-based web applications. We deploy these web applications on an XAMPP web server with MySQL server as the backend database. In addition, we verified the performance of our cloud-based framework against XSS cheat sheet repository [17–20], which includes the list of old and new XSS attack vectors. Very few XSS attack vectors were able to bypass our mobile cloud-based framework. We have injected the 120 JS attack vectors in the possible injection points of above two OSN-based web applications. Figures 3 and 4 highlights the statistics of results of two web applications based on some key factors like Quantity (#) of JS worms injected, Quantity (#) of True Positives (TP), Quantity (#) of True Negatives (TN), Quantity (#) of False Positives (FP) and Quantity (#) of False Negatives (FN). It is clearly reflected that the less number of false positives and false negatives are observed in Joomla as compared to Drupal.

Table 1. Details of configuration of OSN-based web applications

OSN-based web application	Lines of code	XSS vulnerabilities	Version
Joomla [21]	227351	CVE-2013-5738	3.2.0
Drupal [22]	43835	CVE-2012-0826	7.23

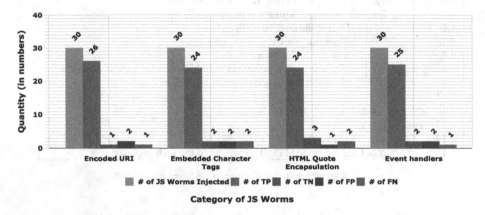

Fig. 3. Observed results of our mobile cloud-based framework on Joomla

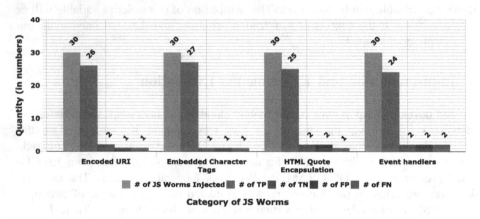

Fig. 4. Observed results of our mobile cloud-based framework on Drupal

The next sub-sections discuss the performance analysis of our framework and comparison of our work compared to existing defensive methodologies.

3.1 Performance Assessment

A well-known statistical method (i.e. F-Measure) is applied on the observed results of two OSN-based web applications for evaluating the performance of our mobile cloud-based framework. The analysis conducted reveal that the proposed framework produces better results as compared to existing state-of-art techniques. To perform binary classification, precision and recall are the parameters used for evaluations. And their harmonic mean is F-measure. Here we calculate the precision, recall and finally F-Measure of observed experimental results of our proposed mobile cloud-based framework. The analysis conducted reveals that the framework exhibits high performance as the observed value of F-Measures in all the platforms of OSN web applications is greater than 0.9. Therefore, the proposed framework exhibits 90–100 % success rate in the two OSN-based web applications. Table 2 highlights the detailed performance analysis of mobile cloud-based JS worm defensive framework on two OSN-based web applications.

$$Precision = \frac{True\ postitive\ (TP)}{True\ postitive\ (TP) + False\ postitive\ (FP)}$$

$$Recall = \frac{True\ postitive\ (TP)}{True\ postitive\ (TP) + False\ negative\ (FN)}$$

$$F\text{-}Measure = \frac{2(TP)}{2(TP) + FP + FN}$$

Table 2. Results of performance analysis of proposed framework

OSN-based web application	# of TP	# of FP	# of FN	Precision	Recall	F-Measure
Joomla	99	7	6	0.933	0.942	0.938
Drupal	102	6	5	0.944	0.953	0.949

3.2 Comparison-Based Assessment

This sub-section discusses the comparison of our proposed work with the other recent existing JS worm defensive methodologies. Table 3 compares the existing sanitization-based state-of-art techniques with our work based on seven identified metrics: Analyzing Mechanism (AM), Browser-Side Modifications Required (BSMR), Browsing of Source Code Required (BSCR), Context-Aware Sanitization Provision (CASP), Partial JS Worm Detection Support (PJWDS), Level of Precision (LOP) and False Positive Rate (FPR). It is clearly reflected from the Table 3 that most of the existing defensive frameworks do not perform context-aware sanitization in a complete manner. On the other hand, most of the existing defensive methodologies suffer from non-acceptable rate of false negatives and false positives. In addition, most of the existing techniques do not detect the partial injection of JavaScript worms. However, our proposed mobile cloud-based JS worm defensive methodology is entirely based on the detection of hidden injection points of JS attack worms and performs the sanitization of such worms in a context-aware manner.

The key difference between these sanitization based techniques and our framework is that the previous defensive solutions perform the sanitization mechanisms on all

Table 3. Summary of comparison of our mobile cloud-based JS worm defensive framework with existing work

Techniques metrics	Balzarotti et al. [11]	Livshits et al. [10]	Cao [12]	ScriptGard [15]	XSSFilt [13]	XSS auditor [14]	Our work
AM	Passive	Passive	Active	Passive	Passive	Passive	Active
BSMR	No	No	Yes	Yes	Yes	Yes	No
BSCR	Yes	Yes	Yes	Yes	Yes	Yes	Yes
CASP	Partial	Partial	Absent	Partial	Partial	Partial	Full
PJWDS	No	No	No	No	Yes	No	Yes
LOP	Low	Low	Low	Low	Low	Average	High
FPR	Low	Average	Low	Average	Low	Low	High

possible attack vectors. Hence, such solutions increase the complexity of injecting the sanitizers in the source code of web applications and as result, produces a high runtime overhead. However, our framework needs not to sanitize the whole string of JS attack worm, as our technique executes on the principle of partial detection of JavaScript worms. This uniqueness indicates the novelty of our work as compared to other existing approaches.

4   Conclusion and Future Work

This article presents a mobile cloud-based JavaScript worm defensive framework that mitigates the propagation of such worms from the mobile cloud-based OSN. The framework extracts the JS code embedded in URI links and DOM tree. These two locations of JS code will be compared for the similar code. Any similarity observed will simply point towards the presence of JS worm in the HTTP response generated for the smart phone user. Finally, the context of malicious/untrusted variables embedded in such worms will be found out and accordingly performs the context-sensitive sanitization on them. The evaluation of our work was carried out on the tested platforms of OSN-based web applications, whose functionality was integrated in the virtual machines of mobile cloud platforms. The results of performance analysis revealed that our work was capable enough to detect the JS worms with low false positive rate, false negative rate and incurs acceptable runtime overhead during the execution of context-sensitive sanitization procedure. We will also try to evaluate the JS worm detection capability of our framework on some more contemporary platforms of mobile cloud-based OSN as a part of our further work.

References

1. Gupta, S., Gupta, B.B.: JS-SAN: defense mechanism for HTML5-based web applications against JavaScript code injection vulnerabilities. Secur. Commun. Netw. **9**(11), 1477–1495 (2016)

2. Gupta, S., Gupta, B.B.: BDS: browser dependent XSS sanitizer. In: Book on Cloud-Based Databases with Biometric Applications. IGI-Global's Advances in Information Security, Privacy, and Ethics (AISPE) Series, pp. 174–191. IGI-Global, Hershey (2014)

3. Gupta, B.B., et al.: Cross-Site Scripting (XSS) abuse and defense: exploitation on several testing bed environments and its defense. J. Inf. Priv. Secur. **11**(2), 118–136 (2015)

4. Grossman, J., Hansen, R., Petkov, P.D., Rager, A., Fogie, S.: XSS attacks: cross-site scripting exploits and defense. Syngress, Burlington (2007). http://www.sciencedirect.com/science/book/9781597491549. ISBN 9781597491549

5. Gupta, S., Gupta, B.B.: Cross-Site Scripting (XSS) attacks and defense mechanisms: classification and state-of-the-art. Int. J. Syst. Assur. Eng. Manag. 1–19 (2015)

6. Gupta, S., Gupta, B.B.: PHP-sensor: a prototype method to discover workflow violation and XSS vulnerabilities in PHP web applications. In: Proceedings of the 12th ACM International Conference on Computing Frontiers. ACM (2015)

7. Hydara, I., et al.: Current state of research on Cross-Site Scripting (XSS)–a systematic literature review. Inf. Softw. Technol. **58**, 170–186 (2015)

8. Gupta, S., Gupta, B.B.: XSS-SAFE: a server-side approach to detect and mitigate Cross-Site Scripting (XSS) attacks in JavaScript code. Arab. J. Sci. Eng. **41**(3), 897–920 (2015)

9. Almorsy, M., Grundy, J., Mueller, I.: An analysis of the cloud computing security problem. In: The Proceedings of the 2010 Asia Pacific Cloud Workshop, Colocated with APSEC 2010, Australia (2010)

10. Hooimeijer, P., Livshits, B., Molnar, D., Saxena, P., Veanes, M.: Fast and precise sanitizer analysis with BEK. In: Proceedings of the 20th USENIX Conference on Security, p. 1. USENIX Association (2011)

11. Balzarotti, D., Cova, M., Felmetsger, V., Jovanovic, N., Kirda, E., Kruegel, C., Vigna, G.: Saner: composing static and dynamic analysis to validate sanitization in web applications. In: IEEE Symposium on Security and Privacy, SP 2008, pp. 387–401. IEEE, Oakland (2008)

12. Cao, Y., Yegneswaran, V., Porras, P.A., Che, Y.: PathCutter: severing the self-propagation path of XSS JavaScript worms in social web networks. In: NDSS (2012)

13. Pelizzi, R., Sekar, R.: Protection, usability and improvements in reflected XSS filters. In: ASIACCS, p. 5 (2012)

14. Bates, D., Barth, A., Jackson, C.: Regular expressions considered harmful in client-side XSS filters. In: Proceedings of the 19th International Conference on World Wide Web, pp. 91–100. ACM (2010)

15. Saxena, P., Molnar, D., Livshits, B.: SCRIPTGARD: automatic context-sensitive sanitization for large-scale legacy web applications. In: Proceedings of the 18th ACM Conference on Computer and Communications Security, pp. 601–614. ACM (2011)

16. Dinh, H.T., Lee, C., Niyato, D., Wang, P.: A survey of mobile cloud computing: architecture, applications, and approaches. Wireless Commun. Mobile Comput. **13**(18), 1587–1611 (2013)

17. HTML5 Security Cheat Sheet. http://html5sec.org/

18. XSS vectors. http://xss2.technomancie.net/vectors/

19. Technical Attack Sheet for Cross Site Penetration Tests. http://www.vulnerability-lab.com/resources/documents/531.txt

20. @XSS Vector Twitter Account. https://twitter.com/XSSVector

21. Joomla social networking site. https://www.joomla.org/download.html

22. Drupal social networking site. https://www.drupal.org/download

23. Gupta, S., Gupta, B.B.: XSS-secure as a service for the platforms of online social network-based multimedia web applications in cloud. Multimedia Tools Appl. 1–33 (2016)

Data Mining for Security Application

Ld-CNNs: A Deep Learning System for Structured Text Categorization Based on LDA in Content Security

Jinshuo Liu, Yabo Xu[✉], Juan Deng, Lina Wang, and Lanxin Zhang

Computer School of Wuhan University, Wuhan, Hubei, China
{liujinshuo,yaboxu,dengjuan,lnawang,lanxinzhang}@whu.edu.cn

Abstract. Text categorization is a foundational task in many NLP applications. Traditional text classifiers often rely on hand engineering features, and recently Convolutional Neural Networks (CNNs) with word vectors have achieved remarkably better performance than traditional methods [15, 20]. In this paper, we combined prior knowledge into deep learning method for structured text categorization. In our model, we apply word embedding to capture both semantic and syntactic information of words, and apply different convolutional neural networks to capture advanced features of different parts of the structured text. Since different text parts perform different impact on the text categorization result, a linear SVM kernel is then applied to decide the final categorization result. Moreover, in order to enhance discriminativeness of the word, we employ latent topic models to assign topics for each word in the text corpus, and learn topical word embeddings based on both words and their topics. We conduct experiments on several datasets. The experimental results show that our model outperforms typical text categorization models, especially when the text in the dataset have a similar structure.

Keywords: Text categorization · Structured text · Neural network · Content security

1 Introduction

Text categorization is an essential component in many applications, especially in content security. In order to ensure the Internet security, the network administrators often need to filter large amounts of text, such as news, blogs, posts, etc. This work takes much time and manual power. Therefore, text categorization has attracted considerable attention from many researchers.

A key problem in text categorization is feature selection. Most traditional methods design features based on the bag-of-words (BoW) model, where unigrams, bigrams, n-grams or some exquisitely designed patterns are typically selected as features. Due to the lack of discriminativeness of the Bow based features, some methods, such as pLSA [3], LDA [12], are applied to extract more discriminative features. However, the contextual information or word order in texts is ignored in traditional feature selection method. This leads to the dissatisfaction for capturing the semantics of the words, and heavily affects the categorization accuracy.

© Springer International Publishing AG 2016
J. Chen et al. (Eds.): NSS 2016, LNCS 9955, pp. 113–125, 2016.
DOI: 10.1007/978-3-319-46298-1_8

Recently, word embedding and deep neural network have achieved remarkably strong performance on many NLP tasks, they have brought new inspiration to various NLP applications. Word embedding, also known as word representation, can be pre-trained from large corpus and captures both semantic and syntactic information of words [19]. With the help of word embedding, some deep-learning-based methods are proposed to capture the semantic representation of texts, and have achieved good results on text categorization [21]. However, these methods ignore the text structure information, which can heavily affect the categorization result. For example, for most people who using different languages, they prefer containing the most important words into the title when they write an article, such as news, blogs, and so on. And in most instances, one always wants to summarize the text content at the last paragraph. This is the reason why we can get what happened from only the title or the previous part of news. From this point of view, combining the prior text structure knowledge into deep learning method can achieve better performance on text categorization. Moreover, due to homonymy and polysemy, we cannot assume each word preserves a single vector, which is a downside of most word embedding methods. Enhancing the discriminativeness of the word in different topics will help the categorization process.

In this paper, we develop a deep learning system for structured text categorization in content security. Our security system needs to filter vast amount of texts for public opinion monitoring, and these texts, consistent with news, blogs, posts etc., have almost same structure in the same data source. Following the idea above, we proposed a novel method for structured text categorization. Firstly, we employ the widely used latent Dirichlet allocation (LDA) [12] to obtain text topics, and perform collapsed Gibbs sampling [9] to assign latent topics for each word. This can be seen as a process of coarse-grained categorization of the texts. After that, each word will be discriminated into a specific topic. Then, we design ld-WE model to learn word vectors under different topics. Secondly, we design deep neural network architectures based on CNNs for the categorization of different text parts. The topical word vectors pre-trained in the first step are employed as the network input here. In this way, each part of the text will generate a single feature vector. Unlike CNN, Ld-CNNs doesn't perform *softmax* function on the generated feature vectors, but apply a linear SVM kernel on them to get a new single vector, which has the same size with the generated feature vectors. The main contribution of this step is that, different weights are assigned to different parts of the text for categorization result, so the text structure information can be employed to enhance the categorization accuracy. Last but not least, *softmax* function will be performed on the new feature vector, and categorization result is finally got through it. Figure 1 provides a simple schematic to illustrate the model architecture just described. We perform experiments that demonstrate the effectiveness of Ld-CNN for text categorization on three datasets: Sogou Lab Data, which contains over 10,000 Chinese news documents; Reuters-21578, which is consistent with over 1,000 English news documents labeled into 80 categories; The last one is the dataset collected by our content security system, which contains over 10,000 Chinese news documents of over 50 categories. Ld-CNNs outperforms most text classification models for these two datasets.

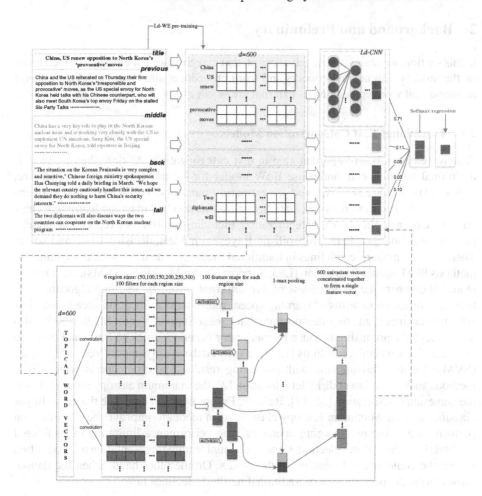

Fig. 1. The framework of Ld-CNNs. Here we depict three filter region size: 3, 4 and 5, each of which has 100 filters. Every filter performs convolution on the *text matrix* and generates feature maps. Then 1-*max* pooling is performed over each map. The *text matrix* is consistent with the generated topical word vectors by Ld-WE model. Thus a univariate feature vector is generated from all maps, and then is concatenated to form a feature vector for SVM regression. Finally categorization result is got from the *softmax* function on the new generated vector.

This work is organized as follows. In Sect. 2, we describe the background and preliminaries of this work. In Sect. 3, we describe the architecture of the proposed Ld-CNNs model, and the proposed topical word embedding model Ld-WE. Section 4 details our experimental setup and results. Finally, in Sect. 5 we present our final re-marks.

2 Background and Preliminary

In this section, we review recent advances on text categorization methods. We then focus on the models with neural networks and word embedding since our model uses neural networks and word embedding as external knowledge.

2.1 Traditional Text Categorization Models

Feature selection is an important step in text categorization. As described in Sect. 1, traditional methods commonly use BoW model for feature extraction. Furthermore, pLSA, LDA etc. are also explored for extracting more discriminative features. Based on these feature selection model, statistical classification and machine learning techniques have been applied to text categorization, including multivariate regression models, nearest neighbor classifiers, probabilistic Bayesian models, decision trees, and so on. There are two main research lines in traditional methods. The first one is discriminative methods like Logistic Regression (LR), Support Vector Machines (SVMs), etc. Dumais et al. [5] compare the effectiveness of five different automatic learning algorithms for text categorization in terms of learning speed, real-time classification speed, and classification accuracy, and they demonstrate that Linear Support Vector Machines (SVMs) are particularly promising because they are very accurate, quick to train, and quick to evaluate. More recently, Joachims [13] has explored the use of Support Vector Machines (SVMs) for text classification with promising results. The other one is probabilistic methods such as the latent dirichlet allocation [2], the maximum entropy model [7], and the Bayesian classification [10, 11]. Besides, Fragos et al. [7] combine the naive Bayes classifier and the Maximum Entropy classification model to improve the classification performance, using two merging operators. The performance limitation of traditional methods is on the feature selection, since traditional feature representation methods often ignore the contextual information of the words. On the other hand, when the dataset grows large, the performance of traditional methods declines fast.

2.2 Text Categorization with Neural Networks

Recently, the pre-trained word embedding and deep neural networks have developed rapidly, drawing more and more attentions from many researchers. David et al. firstly introduced word embedding in 1988 [4], and it has been successfully applied in many NLP tasks. With the help of word embedding, some deep-learning-based methods are proposed to capture the semantic representation of texts and have achieved good performance.

Compared to traditional text categorization methods, neural networks with word embedding can greatly alleviate the data sparsity problem. Besides, it has already been demonstrated that distributed representations for symbols combined with neural network can surpass standard n-gram models in many tasks [1]. Socher et al. [22, 23] proposed the Recursive Neural Network (RecursiveNN) for constructing sentence representation to classify text. The RecursiveNN exhibits a time complexity of at least $O(n^2)$, where n is the length of the text. It would consume too much time when the model meets a long document. Another deep learning architecture for text categorization is Recurrent Neural Network (RecurrentNN), whose time complexity is O(n). Since it can store the semantics of all the previous text in a fixed hidden layer, contextual information can be better captured through model. However, the RecurrentNN is a biased model, making it maybe not suitable for capturing the semantics of a whole document.

The last model, which is introduced to tackle the bias problem, is the Convolutional Neural Network (CNN). With the pooling layer, CNN can fairly determine discriminative phrases in a text. Kalchbrenner [14] apply CNN for text classification, and propose dynamic k-*max* pooling strategy. Siwei et al. [21] proposed a Recurrent Convolutional Neural Network (RCNN) for text categorization. They firstly apply a bi-directional recurrent structure, and then employ a max-pooling layer that automatically judges which features play key roles in text classification. However, it's controversial to use pooling tactics for key component capturing, since text structure plays an important role in classifying result, which cannot be captured by pooling strategy. Besides the three models described above, Goyal [8] proposed a method that combines Naive Bayesian text classification technique and neural networks for text categorization, however, the text structure information is ignored by these models, and thus the categorization accuracy still has great improving space.

3 Our Model

As its name suggests, the proposed Ld-CNNs model is built upon the Convolutional Neural Network (CNN). Ld-CNNs firstly uses the proposed Ld-WE model for topical word embedding pre-training. Then Ld-CNNs explores text structure information to train CNN-based classifier for each text parts, and generates a single vector for each part. Then a linear SVM kernel, but not *softmax* function, is applied on these vectors to affect the result through structure information. After the new vector is generated by SVM, *softmax* function is performed on it to get the final categorization result. Figure 1 shows the framework of our model. The input of the model is a document D, consistent with words w_1, $w_2 \dots w_n$. The output of the model contains class elements. In this paper, $p(k|D, \theta)$ is denoted as the probability of the document being class k, where θ is the parameters of our model.

3.1 Topical Word Representation Learning

Due to homonymy and polysemy, it's problematic to denote each word as a single vector. In our model, Ld-WE method is proposed to enhance discriminativeness of word vectors generated by common word embedding methods. Ld-WE learns word embeddings not only based on words and their topics, but also on their positions in text structure.

Skip-Gram is a famous and popular framework for learning word vectors [19]. This model aims to predict context words given a target word in a sliding window. Given a word sequence $D = \{w_1, \dots, w_m\}$, maximizing the following average log probability is the objective of Skip-Gram:

$$\mathcal{L}(\mathrm{D}) = \frac{1}{M} \sum_{i=1}^{M} \sum_{-k \leq c \leq k, c \neq 0} \log Pr\big(\omega_{i+c}|\omega_i\big) \tag{1}$$

In Eq. (1) k is the context size of a target word. Skip-Gram formulates the probability $Pr\big(\omega_c|\omega_i\big)$ using a *softmax* function as follows:

$$Pr\big(\omega_c|\omega_i\big) = \exp(\omega_c * \omega_i) / \sum_{\omega_i \in W} \exp(\omega_c * \omega_i) \tag{2}$$

In Eq. (2) ω_c and ω_i are respectively the vector representation of target word ω_i and context word ω_c, and W is the word vocabulary. Hierarchical softmax and negative sampling are often used when learning Skip-Gram in order to make it more efficient.

Ld-WE firstly uses LDA to iteratively assign latent topics for each word token, then different with Skip-gram, Ld-WE aims to learn vector representations for words and topics separately and simultaneously. The objective of Ld-WE is defined to maximize the following average log probability:

$$\mathcal{L}(\mathrm{D}) = \frac{1}{M} \sum_{i=1}^{M} \sum_{C} \log Pr\big(\omega_{i+c}|\omega_i\big) + \log Pr\big(\omega_{i+c}|z_i\big) + \log Pr\big(\omega_{i+c}|s_i\big) \tag{3}$$

In Eq. (3) set C means $-k \leq c \leq k, c \neq 0$, same as in Eq. (2). Compared to Skip-Gram which only using the target word ω_i to predict context words, Ld-WE also uses both the topic z_i of target word and the structure position s_i to predict context words. The basic idea of Ld-WE is to regard each topic as a pseudo word that appears in all positions of words assigned with this topic, and regard each text structure index as a auxiliary pseudo word that appears in all positions of words assigned with this text structure index. Hence, the vector of a topic will represent the collective semantics of words under this topic, and the vector of a text structure index will represent the collective semantics of words in this structure part.

In Ld-WE, the topical word embedding of a word w in topic z and text structure part s is got by concatenating the embedding of w, z and s, i.e., $w^z = w \oplus z \oplus s$, where $\oplus$ is the concatenation operation, and the length of w^z is triple of w or z or s.

Learning Ld-WE models follow the similar optimization scheme as that of Skip-Gram used in [19]. Stochastic gradient descent (SGD) is used for the optimization of Ld-WE, and gradients are calculated using the backpropagation algorithm. For parameter initialization, we first learn word embeddings using Skip-Gram. Afterwards, we initialize each topic vector with the average over all words assigned to this topics, and initialize each text structure part vector with the average over all words emerged in this text part. Then Ld-WE learns topic embeddings while keeping word embeddings and structure embeddings unchanged, and learns structure embeddings while keeping word embeddings and topic embeddings unchanged.

The idea of the design and implementation of Ld-WE is inspired from the TWE-1 model in [18]. Liu et al. proposed three topical word embedding models: TWE-1, TWE-2 and TWE-3. They conducted experiments to evaluate their TWE models and found that TWE-1 outperform state-of-the-art word embedding models for contextual word similarity and text classification. Inspired from this, we use the similar model objective as TWE-1, and add text structure information into our model Ld-WE to enhance discriminativeness of words. This is proved to be effective by our experiments, which will be described de-tailed in the next section.

3.2 Ld-CNNs Architecture

The architecture of Ld-CNNs is shown as Fig. 1. Ld-CNNs is consistent with several CNN-based neural net-works according to the text structure information. Then top-level feature vectors are generated from these networks which encoding salient features of each text structure part. Then a linear SVM kernel is applied on these vectors to generate the final top-level feature vector, which is more effective by exploring the text structure information. Afterwards, the final top-level feature vector is then fed through a *softmax* function to generate the final classification. By jointly embedding the topical word vectors generated by Ld-WE into Ld-CNNs, the categorization accuracy has been further improved.

The input of Ld-CNNs is the tokenized text which we then convert to a *text matrix*, the rows of which are the topical word vectors by Ld-WE for each token. Note that the *text matrix* is divided into several structure part matrixes ac-cording to the text structure information, each of which will be fed into the corresponding CNN-based neural net-work, i.e., Ld-CNN. Thus one input text will be processed by several neural networks for capturing the different semantics of different structure parts. Different Ld-CNN shares different model parameters, which makes sense since different text parts have different features such as writing habits, common-used words, and so on.

We then describe the architecture of the network for structure parts in this paper. We denote the dimensionality of the generated topical word vectors by d. If the length of the given structure part (i.e., token count) is s, then the dimensionality of the part matrix is $s \times d$. In this way, the part matrix can be treated as an 'image', and convolution operation can be performed on it via linear filters. Intuitively, since rows represent discrete words, it's reasonable to use filters whose width is equal to the dimensionality of the word vectors. Then the height of the filter can vary as different region sizes. From this point on, the height of the filter will be referred as the region size of the filter in this paper.

Suppose that there is a filter parameterized by the weight vector $w \in R^{h \times d}$ with region size h; w will contain h $\bullet$ d parameters to be estimated. In this paper we denote the part matrix by $A \in R^{s \times d}$, and use $A[i : j]$ to represent the submatrix of A from row i to row j. The output of the convolution operation is obtained by iteratively applying the filter on submatrices of A:

$$o_i = \omega \cdot A[i{:}i + h - 1] \tag{4}$$

In Eq. (4) i $= 1, \dots, s - h + 1$, and $\cdot$ is the dot production between the submatrix and the filter. Thus the length of the output o is $s - h + 1$. In order to induce the feature map $c \in R^{s-h+1}$ for the filter, we include a bias term b $\in R$ and an activation function f to each o_i as follows:

$$c_i = f(o_i + b) \tag{5}$$

In Ld-CNNs multiple filters for the same region size is used to learn complementary features from the same regions, and we also specify multiple kinds of filters with different region size, or 'heights'.

After all the feature maps are generated by Ld-CNN, a pooling function is applied to each feature map to reduce the dimension and the number of the parameters to be estimated. In this study, 1-*max* pooling function is elected as the pooling strategy [24]. Together, the outputs generated from each filter map can be concatenated into a top-level feature vector. Compared to standard CNN, the vector is not fed through a softmax function for final classification directly here, but is preserved for linear SVM regression. When all the top-level vectors of each Ld-CNN are generated, they are then input into the traditional linear SVM model. The linear SVM model can assign weights to these generated top-level vectors, to generate the final top-level vector. That means, the text structure information is integrated into our model through this linear regression in this step. This step is also called the feature fusion in our model.

This final top-level vector is then fed through a softmax function to generate the final categorization. At this *softmax* layer, a 'dropout strategy' is applied as means of regularization, which we choose as the l2 norm constraint. During training, the objective to be minimized is the categorical crossentropy loss, and the parameters to be estimated include: the weight vectors of the filters, the bias term in the activation function, the weight vector of the linear SVM model, and the weight vector of the softmax function.

After all the operations above are finished, the text categorization result is finally got from the output of the softmax function at the last layer.

4   Experiments and Analysis

In this section, we evaluate the Ld-CNNs on several datasets. Then we present some experimental results of Ld-CNNs based on different model settings, and compare the model result with other text categorization methods under the same experimental settings. We also describe the efficiency of Ld-CNNs at the tail of this section.

4.1   Datasets

We use two common-used datasets on text categorization and one dataset which is from our public opinion monitoring system. The brief introduction of these datasets is as follows:

- **Sogou Lab Data:** dataset collected by Sougou Lab, which can be got from https://www.sogou.com/labs/. It is from over 130 million original pages on the Internet and contains over 10,000 Chinese news documents.
- **Reuters-21578:** This dataset contains over 1,000 English news documents labeled into 80 categories. The documents in the Reuters-21578 collection appeared on the Reuters newswire in 1987.

- **LdCS Data:** This dataset is consistent of the documents from our public opinion monitoring system. It contains over 10,000 Chinese news documents of over 50 categories.

We report some information of these datasets in Table 1. For more details on these datasets, please refer to the official websites of them (The last one can be accessed through author's email).

Table 1. Some statistical information on the experimental datasets

Dataset	Documents	Categories	Size
Sogou lab data	10000	60	1 TB
Reuters-21578	1000	80	28.0 M
LdCS data	10000	50	142.1 M

4.2 Experiment Settings

Before the conduct of the experiments, experimental settings need to be determined. We describe the experimental settings from three aspects: datasets preprocess, parameter settings of Ld-WE and hyper-parameter settings of Ld-CNNs.

- **Datasets Preprocess.** We preprocess the dataset as follows. For Chinese documents, which are in Sougou and LdCS datasets in this paper, we use ICTCLAS[1] to segment the words. While for English documents, i.e. the documents in Reuters dataset, the Standford Tokenizer[2] is applied on them to obtain the tokens. For the Sougou and Reuters datasets, there is pre-defined training, development and testing separation for each dataset. For LdCS dataset, we split 20 % of the training set into a development and keep the remaining 80 % as the real training set. We select the Macro-F1 measure followed by the state-of-the-art work as the evaluation metric of the LdCS dataset, and choose accuracy as the metric for the other two datasets.
- **Parameter Settings of Ld-WE.** We adopt different knowledge base for the initialization of the word vectors pre-trained by Ld-WE. For Chinese documents, we use Sougou dataset to initialize the word embeddings in this paper based on Skip-Gram. At the same time, Wikipedia, the largest online knowledge base, is selected for English documents with the same Skip-Gram model. After the initializaiton is finished, Ld-WE is applied to get the discriminative topical word vectors in this study. We set the pre-defined topic number as 20 and the dimensionality of the word embeddings as 600. The text structure is denoted as the following five parts in a text in this paper, which are title part, previous part, middle part, back part and tail part. The structure index of these parts is from 1 to 5.
- **Hyper-parameter Settings of Ld-CNNs.** We use the development sets to tune the hyper-parameters of the Ld-CNN in this paper. Many different combinations of hyper-parameters can give similarly good results. We spend more time tuning the

---

[1] http://ictclas.nlpir.org/.

[2] nlp.stanford.edu/software/tokenizer.shtml.

learning rate than tuning other parameters, since it's the hyper-parameter which has the largest impact on the prediction performance. The hyper-parameter settings depend on the dataset being used somehow. In this paper we choose the same parameters for the three datasets, which are listed as follows: the number of the convolution filters in Ld-CNN is set to 6 and the number of convolutional feature maps is 100. We choose ReLU function as our activation strategy and 1-*max* pooling as our pooling method. The L2 regularization term is set to 1e-4, dropout is applied to the penultimate level with $p = 0.5$. As Fig. 1 shows, there is only one hidden layer in each Ld-CNN. Moreover, we set the learning rate of the stochastic gradient descent (SGD) α as 0.01.

4.3 Results and Analysis

The experimental results are shown in Table 2. We compare our model with several common-used text classification methods and the state-of-the-art models for each dataset. The compared models are listed as follows:

Table 2. Test results for the datasets. The top, middle, and bottom parts are the baselines, the state-of-the-art results and the results of our model, respectively. The test results are tested through the corresponding codes.

Model	Sogou lab data	Reuters-21578	LdCS data
LR + BoW	89.61	89.72	75.35
LR + Bigram	90.14	89.86	76.44
SVM + BoW	90.08	90.27	83.23
SVM + Bigram	90.13	91.03	81.08
ClassifyLDA-EM [12]	90.14	91.25	84.24
Character-Level CNN [28]	90.13	92.27	83.48
RecursiveNN [22]	92.74	91.28	83.57
RCNN [21]	93.41	93.35	86.17
CNN + Word2Vec	91.21	90.29	86.31
CNN + Ld-WE	93.79	92.98	88.73
Ld-CNNs	**94.48**	**94.13**	**92.73**

LR/SVM + Bag of Words/Bigrams. There are several strong baselines for text classification proposed by Wang and Manning in [24]. These baselines mainly choose unigram or bigrams as feature selecting method, and use logistic regression (LR) and SVM as classifiers. The weight of each feature is the term weight.

LDA-Based Methods. LDA-based approaches achieve good results in terms of capturing the semantics of texts in several classification tasks. ClassifyLDA-EM [12] is selected as the method for comparison.

Character-Level NN. Inspired from the big advance of convolutional neural networks (CNN) for image processing, some researchers propose to treat the character as pixel and the text as image, and then apply the CNN model on NLP applications and get good results [28]. We compare this method on our task in this paper.

RecursiveNN-Based Methods. We select two recursive-based methods for comparison with the proposed model: The Recursive Neural Network (RecursiveNN) [22] and The Recurrent Convolutional Neural Network (RCNN) [21].

We also conduct the experiments under different experimental settings on the dataset LdCS. The results are shown in Fig. 2. From the experimental results we can see:

- The neural network approaches outperform the traditional methods for all three datasets. It's proved that neural network based approach can effective compose the semantic representation of texts. Compared to the traditional methods, which may suffer from the data sparsity problem on BoW model, neural networks can capture more contextual information of features.
- For the first two common-used datasets, Sougou and Reuters, the categorization result is better than the dataset LdCS. This indicates that the text categorization in content security has special points. Thus more features should be employed into the classification model to enhance the accuracy of text categorization in content security. By using text structure information, the model makes a big advance on this task.
- We select a standard convolutional neural network for comparison, using CNN + word2vec and CNN + Ld-WE as compared model on text classification tasks. From the comparison we can see that both Ld-WE and Ld-CNN contribute to the performance of our model. It turns out that the combination of several CNN-based architecture networks for classification task is effective, and text structure information plays an important role in text categorization in content security.
- From Fig. 2 we can see the impacts of different experimental setting factors on the task results, such the selection of activation function, the region number, the fusion

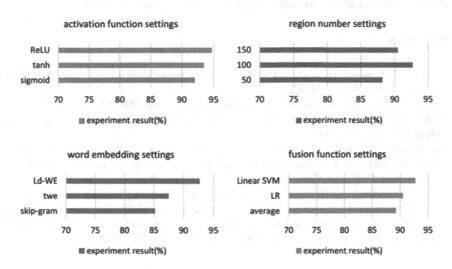

Fig. 2. The experiment results under different experimental settings on LdCS dataset.

function (i.e. the linear SVM kernel, or other regression function in this model) etc. It demonstrates that the ReLU activation function gets the best results among the selected activation functions, and Ld-WE embedding method has a better performance than other embedding strategies.

- Last but not least, from these experimental results we need to know that besides the text structure information, there are also other features that can be employed to enhance the categorization result for content security, which will be further studied in our future work.

5   Conclusion

In this paper, we propose a text categorization model named Ld-CNNs, whose aim is to enhance the accuracy of the structured text categorization in content security. The contribution of our model is that it employs the text structure information and word topics for effective text classification. The model uses the topical word embedding generated by the proposed Ld-WE embedding method to denote the *text matrixes* as model input, and for each structure part of the text, Ld-CNN is designed for encoding the top-level salient semantic feature vector for the part. Then a linear SVM kernel is applied on the generated top-level feature vectors to get the final new vector, which integrates the text structure weights into the final layer. Afterwards, the *softmax* function is performed on the final vector to get the final categorization result. We evaluate our Ld-CNNs model by conducting several experiments. The experimental results show that our model gets good result on text classification tasks, and outperform state-of-the-art text categorization models especially when the texts are structured in content security.

Acknowledgments. The authors would like to thank the anonymous reviewers for the constructive comments. This work was sponsored by the National Natural Science Foundation of China (No. 61303214 and No. 61303025, project approval number: U1536204).

References

1. Bengio, Y., Schwenk, H., Senécal, J.S., et al.: A neural probabilistic language model. J. Mach. Learn. Res. **3**(6), 1137–1155 (2003)
2. Blei, D.M., Ng, A.Y., Jordan, M.I.: Latent dirichlet allocation. JMLR **3**, 993–1022 (2003)
3. Cai, L., Hofmann, T.: Text categorization by boosting automatically extracted concepts. In: SIGIR, pp. 182–189 (2003)
4. Rumelhart, D.E., Hinton, G.E., Williams, R.J.: Learning representations by backpropagating errors. In: Anderson, J.A., Rosenfeld, E. (eds.) Neurocomputing: Foundations of Research, pp. 696–699. MIT Press, Cambridge (1988)
5. Dumais, S., Platt, J., Heckerman, D., Sahami, M.: Inductive learning algorithms and representations for text categorization. In: Proceedings of the Seventh International Conference on Information and Knowledge Management, pp. 148–155. ACM Press (1998)
6. Elman, J.L.: Finding struture in time. Cogn. Sci. **14**(90), 179–211 (1990)

7. Fragos, K., Maistros, I., Skourlas, C.: A X2-weighted maximum entropy model for text classification. In: Proceedings of 2nd International Conference on Natural Language Understanding and Cognitive Science, Miami, Florida, pp. 22–23 (2005)
8. Goyal, R.D.: Knowledge based neural network for text classification. In: IEEE International Conference on Granular Computing, p. 542 (2007)
9. Griffiths, T.L., Steyvers, M.: Finding scientific topics. PNAS **101**, 5228–5235 (2004)
10. Grossman, D., Domingos, P.: Learning Bayesian network classifiers by maximizing conditional likelihood. In: Proceedings of the Twenty-First International Conference on Machine Learning, pp. 361–368. ACM Press (2005)
11. Hamad, A.: Weighted naive Bayesian classifier. In: IEEE/ACS International Conference, on Computer Systems and Applications, AICCSA apos 2007, vol. 1(1), pp. 437–441 (2007)
12. Hingmire, S., Chougule, S., Palshikar, G.K., Chakraborti, S.: Document classification by topic labeling. In: SIGIR, pp. 877–880 (2013)
13. Joachims, T.: Text categorization with support vector machines: learning with many relevant features. In: Nédellec, C., Rouveirol, C. (eds.) ECML 1998. LNCS, vol. 1398. Springer, Heidelberg (1998)
14. Kalchbrenner, N., Grefenstette, E., Blunsom, P.: A convolutional neural network for modelling sentences. Eprint Arxiv, p. 1 (2014)
15. Kim, Y.: Convolutional neural networks for sentence classification. Eprint Arxiv (2014)
16. Le, Q.V., Mikolov, T.: Distributed representations of sentences and documents. Eprint Arxiv, vol. 4, pp. 1188–1196 (2014)
17. Liu, P., Qiu, X., Huang, X.: Learning context-sensitive word embeddings with neural tensor skip-gram model. In: International Conference on Artificial Intelligence. AAAI Press (2015)
18. Liu, Y., Liu, Z., Chua, T.S., et al.: Topical word embeddings. In: Twenty-Ninth AAAI Conference on Artificial Intelligence. AAAI Press (2015)
19. Mikolov, T., Yih, W.-T., Zweig, G.: Linguistic regularities in continuous space word representations. In: NAACL-HLT, pp. 746–751 (2013)
20. Johnson, R., Zhang, T.: Effective use of word order for text categorization with convolutional neural networks. arXiv preprint arXiv:1412.1058 (2014)
21. Lai, S., Xu, L., Liu, K., Zhao, J.: Recurrent convolutional neural networks for text classification. In: Proceeding of the Twenty-Ninth AAAI Conference on Artificial Intelligence, pp. 2267–2273 (2014)
22. Socher, R., Pennington, J., Huang, E.H., Ng, A.Y., Manning, C.D.: Semi-supervised recursive autoen-coders for predicting sentiment distributions. In: EMNLP, pp. 151–161 (2011)
23. Socher, R., Perelygin, A., Wu, J.Y., Chuang, J., Manning, C.D., Ng, A.Y., Potts, C.: Recursive deep models for semantic compositionality over a sentiment treebank. In: EMNLP, pp. 1631–1642 (2013)
24. Wang, S., Manning, C.D.: Baselines and bigrams: simple, good sentiment and topic classification. In: Meeting of the Association for Computational Linguistics: Short Papers, pp. 90–94 (2012)
25. Boureau, Y.-L., Ponce, J., LeCun, Y.: A theoretical analysis of feature pooling in visual recognition. In: International Conference on Machine Learning, p. 459 (2010)
26. Kim, Y.: Convolutional neural networks for sentence classification. arXiv preprint arXiv: 1408.5882 (2014)
27. Zeng, L., Li, Z.: Text classification based on paragraph distributed representation and extreme learning machine. In: Tan, Y., Shi, Y., Buarque, F., Gelbukh, A., Das, S., Engelbrecht, A. (eds.) ICSI-CCI 2015. LNCS, vol. 9141, pp. 81–88. Springer, Heidelberg (2015)
28. Zhang, X., Zhao, J., Lecun, Y.: Character-level convolutional networks for text classification. In: Neural Information Processing Systems (2015)

Realtime DDoS Detection in SIP Ecosystems: Machine Learning Tools of the Trade

Zisis Tsiatsikas[1]($\boxtimes$), Dimitris Geneiatakis[2], Georgios Kambourakis[1], and Stefanos Gritzalis[1]

[1] Department of Information and Communication Systems Engineering, University of the Aegean, Karlovassi, Greece
tzisis@aegean.gr
[2] Electrical and Computer Engineering Department, Aristotle University of Thessaloniki, 541 24 Thessaloniki, Greece

Abstract. Over the last decade, VoIP services and more especially the SIP-based ones, have gained much attention due to the low-cost and simple models they offer. Nevertheless, their inherently insecure design make them prone to a plethora of attacks. This work concentrates on the detection of resource consumption attacks targeting SIP ecosystems. While this topic has been addressed in the literature to a great extent, only a handful of works examine the potential of Machine Learning (ML) techniques to detect DoS and even fewer do so in realtime. Spurred by this fact, the work at hand assesses the potential of 5 different ML-driven methods in nipping SIP-powered DDoS attacks in the bud. Our experiments involving 17 realistically simulated (D)DoS scenarios of varied attack volume in terms of calls/sec and user population, suggest that some of the classifiers show promising detection accuracy even in low-rate DDoS incidents. We also show that the performance of ML-based detection in terms of classification time overhead does not exceed 3.5 ms in average with a mean standard deviation of 7.7 ms.

Keywords: VoIP · SIP · DoS · DDoS · Machine learning · Evaluation

1 Introduction

Throughout the last decade, Voice over IP (VoIP) services are gaining increasing attention due to the multiple advantages they offer in comparison to those provided by Public Switched Telephone Network (PSTN). Based on current market reports, VoIP is blooming and its market share is estimated to reach 130$ billion until 2020 [1]. On the other hand, as VoIP services rely on the open Internet, providers need to ensure availability levels similar to PSTN. This means that among other well-documented threats [2–5], they need to cope with resource consumtion attacks namely Denial os Service (DoS) as well as their distributed form (DDoS) that cause service disruptions and sometimes even complete outages. This is of high importance especially for critical voice services *e.g.*, emergency numbers. This threat is further aggravated as the current predominant

© Springer International Publishing AG 2016
J. Chen et al. (Eds.): NSS 2016, LNCS 9955, pp. 126–139, 2016.
DOI: 10.1007/978-3-319-46298-1_9

VoIP signaling protocol, namely Session Initiation Protocol (SIP), can be easily exploited by an attacker. This is mainly due to SIP text nature that allows the aggressor to straightforwardly craft and send large volumes of SIP requests toward its victim with the aim of paralyzing it. The perpetrator is also able to exercise more clever attacks, including low and slow ones [6] in order to consume a considerable amount of VoIP server's resources and network bandwidth, and thus degrade the quality of the service.

To cope with this threat, several SIP-oriented Intrusion Detection and prevention Systems (IDS) have been presented in the literature so far. Focusing on proposals to defend against DoS in these environments, one can identify simple statistical schemes as those given in [7,8]. In this category of solutions detection relies on different network statistics, including incoming traffic rate, and uses a predefined threshold above which the received traffic is classified as malicious. It is obvious though that such a solution cannot protect effectively SIP services against low-rate DoS attacks, as it is cumbersome to constantly adapt itself, say, by recalculating the underlying threshold to reflect the ongoing characteristics of the attack.

Further, most of the existing solutions do not consider SIP different inherent features and characteristics which can be exploited by an attacker to launch DoS, while the majority of them are privacy-invasive. A comprehensive analysis of existing protection solutions against DoS in SIP can be found in [9]. Therefore, as the aggressors become more sophisticated, there is a need for advanced (D)DoS detection methods that are able to automatically adjust their behavior to the attack traffic patterns. A way to achieve this is to use well-established classifiers from the Machine Learning (ML) toolbox.

Our Contribution: The paper at hand assesses the potential of using techniques borrowed from the ML realm to detect (D)DoS incidents in SIP services. In contrast to our previous work [10], the evaluation of the various classifiers is done in realtime in the SIP proxy. Our experiments involve 5 different well-known classifiers and a large variety of attack scenarios ranging from simple DoS to slow and high-rate DDoS. The evaluation is done in terms of both detection accuracy and processing time. The results show that the introduced overhead in the SIP server is negligible, while the average detection accuracy for the best-performing algorithms fluctuates between ≈89 % and 92 % depending on the scenario.

The remainder of the paper is organized as follows. The next section provides an overview of SIP architecture and briefly analyses the threat model. Section 3 describes the methodology and steps followed throughout our experiments. Section 4 presents the results. Section 5 overviews the related work. The last section concludes and provides directions to future work.

2   SIP Architecture and Threat Model

SIP is a text-based protocol with syntax similar to that of HTTP. As shown in Fig. 1, a SIP message (request in this case) consists of two basic parts. The upper one corresponds to the message headers and carries information in regards to the

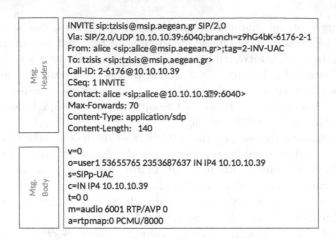

Msg. Headers

```
INVITE sip:tzisis@msip.aegean.gr SIP/2.0
Via: SIP/2.0/UDP 10.10.10.39:6040;branch=z9hG4bK-6176-2-1
From: alice <sip:alice@msip.aegean.gr>;tag=2-INV-UAC
To: tzisis <sip:tzisis@msip.aegean.gr>
Call-ID: 2-6176@10.10.10.39
CSeq: 1 INVITE
Contact: alice <sip:alice@10.10.10.3⊠9:6040>
Max-Forwards: 70
Content-Type: application/sdp
Content-Length:  140
```

Msg. Body

```
v=0
o=user1 53655765 2353687637 IN IP4 10.10.10.39
s=SIPp-UAC
c=IN IP4 10.10.10.39
t=0 0
m=audio 6001 RTP/AVP 0
a=rtpmap:0 PCMU/8000
```

Fig. 1. A typical SIP invite request

sender (caller) and the recipient (callee) of the message. The lower part is known as the message body and carries the media details. Communication resources in SIP are assigned a SIP Uniform Resource Identifier (URI), e.g., with reference to the first line of Fig. 1, sip:tzisis@msip.aegean.gr. Every SIP message is processed by the appropriate SIP component. A basic SIP infrastructure consists of:

- **SIP User Agent (UA)** - Represents the end points of the SIP protocol, that is, the User Agent Client (UAC) and the User Agent Server (UAS) which are able to initiate or terminate a session using a SIP software or hardware client.
- **SIP Proxy Server** - An intermediate entity which plays the role of the client and the server at the same time. Its task is to route all the packets being sent and received by the users participating in a SIP session. Note that one or more SIP proxies may exist between any two UAs.
- **Registrar** - Handles the authentication and register requests initiated by the UAs. For this reason, this entity stores the user's credentials and UA location information.

For a detailed analysis of SIP architecture the interested reader can consult the corresponding RFC [11].

So far, a plethora of attacks against SIP-based services have been identified in the literature. These include eavesdropping, flooding, SQL injection, manipulation of SIP messages, and so on [2–5,12]. In this work, we concentrate on resource consumption attacks caused by malicious entities who send a surge of SIP messages against their target, that is, a SIP server or UA. From an attacker's viewpoint, this category of assaults are considered quite straightforward mostly because of the text-based nature of the protocol, the lack of built-in countermeasures, and the existence of open source publicly available attack tools [13]. On the other hand, the impact of such an attack on the target is considerable and may vary from loss of service to entire network paralysis. From a VoIP provider viewpoint, this may result in many dissatisfied customers and loss of profit.

Having in mind all the above, in the following we formulate an attacker-centric threat model. Specifically, we assume that the perpetrator is able to fabricate a SIP message by simply spoofing its headers. The most appropriate SIP requests to achieve such a goal are Invite, Register, and Options [11]. The attacker spoofs certain headers of the message (Via, From, To, Call-ID, Contact) to create a flooding effect towards the victim and obfuscate the forensic signal of the attack. For instance, if the attacker knows the URI of a certain user, is then able to mount a high-rate DoS attack with Invite requests to choke the user's softphone. An indicative example of a device that is prone to such a vulnerability is Cisco SIP Phone 3905 [14]. An alternative attack strategy aims at paralysing critical components of SIP infrastructure, including SIP Proxy or Registrar.

In this paper we only consider the manipulation of Invite messages. However, as already pointed out, the same outcome can be achieved with other types of SIP requests.

3   Detection Engine

This section elaborates on the architecture of the proposed IDS, which as observed from Fig. 2, is composed of 3 modules. The first module is occupied with the extraction of the required classification features from the headers of the incoming SIP messages. The selected features are forwarded to an anonymisation module, and finally are fed to the classification engine. After a training phase, the latter module can be configured to operate in realtime using the ML algorithm of choice. The subsequent sections elaborate on each of the aforementioned IDS modules.

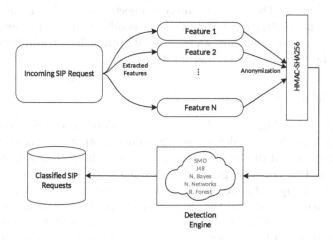

Fig. 2. Detection engine architecture

3.1   Feature Extraction and Anonymization of Data

As already mentioned, the feature extraction module operating on the SIP server examines the incoming SIP traffic for any request, say, Invite, Register. Next, the request is parsed to isolate the headers of interest, namely, <Via>, <From>, <To>, <Contact> and <Call-ID>. The extracted headers are anomymised with the help of HMAC-SHA256. The latter aims at preserving end-user privacy in cases where the detection task is outsourced to a third party. Also, it has the dual benefit of preserving the entropy of the original headers and making deanonymization as hard as reversing the HMAC-SHA256. The anonymized features along with its frequency of appearance are stored in a hash table data structure.

As described in Algorithm 1, every time a new (different) feature is extracted from an incoming SIP request a new record is inserted in the hash table with its corresponding value equals to 1. In case an already existing key is insterted in the table the corresponding frequency value is increased by 1. This procedure continues until the number of messages reaches a certain predefined Message Window M_w. For the needs of our experiments we picked arbitrarily a M_w equal to 1,000. Therefore, the detection engine starts the classification process from message 1001. That is, the hash values of the headers of this message will update the corresponding cells of the hash table and the resulting numbers will be fed to the classifier. This process is done in a message-by-message manner for every SIP request arriving after the 1000th.

Obviously, the value of M_w parameter is sure to affect the detection accuracy. Therefore, this parameter should be adjusted by the service provider itself, say, according to the average call rates. Nevertheless, to our knowledge, there is no foolproof approach to formally define this parameter, mainly because it is eminently contextual. That is, it is closely connected to the local characteristics of the service and underlying network. As a result, similar to other anomaly-based approaches, one can follow an error-trial approach to equilibrate between the M_w parameter and the false alarm rate.

3.2   Training and Operation

Similar to any other ML-powered approach, the detection engine requires the training of the classifier in order to be able to detect anomalies in the incoming traffic. This means that during service initialization, the classifier of choice must be trained based on some pregenerated training data. The creation of such a training dataset is up to the service provider because it mainly depends on the particular services it offers and the characteristics of the underlying network. In our case, the training file is produced using the "offline software module" given in [15]. More specifically, for generating the appropriate training file used by the SIP proxy at its initialization phase, we first execute a basic scenario and capture the SIP traffic in a log file. After that, this file is analysed with the previously mentioned module for the sake of generating a new training file ready to be fed to the SIP Proxy. Also, a renewal and/or amendment of the training

---

Algorithm 1. Extraction of classification features

    Input: Incoming SIP messages
    Output: Classification result
1 SIPHeaders[N] ← ExtractSipHeader(SIP Request);
2 **for** *(i=1; i ≤ N; i++)* **do**
3   HashedHeader[i] ← HMAC(SIPHeaders[i]);
4   **if** *(InsertToHashTable(HashedHeaders[i]) ≠ NULL)* **then**
5   GetValueofHashTable(HashedHeader[i])++;
6   **else**
7   InsertToHashTable(HashedHeaders[i]);
8   SetValueInHashTable(HashedHeader[i]) ← 1;
9   **end**
10 **end**
11 classificationResult ← classify(#HashedHeaders [1],... ,#HashedHeaders[N]);
12 **if** *(Mw = 1,000)* **then**
13   TotalMessages ← TotalMessages + M_w;
14   Re-Initialize(HashTable);
15 **end**

---

set is required as soon the network and/or service operating conditions change. In this paper, we opt not to address the two aforementioned issues which are left for future work.

Nevertheless, it should be stressed that the training data must contain both legitimate and attack traffic. This is necessary because in order for the classifier to build a realistic traffic model, the training data must contain classes of both attack and normal traffic. As soon as the training phase is completed, the detection engine starts on the SIP server as a realtime service.

3.3 Implementation

The realtime detection service has been implemented as a plug-in module of the well-known SIP proxy Kamailio [16]. Specifically, the module [15] is written in C programming language and is capable of processing any incoming SIP request as described in the previous subsection.

The feature extraction module stores temporarily the processed data to a hash table, while classification relies on Weka [17] a well-known framework for ML analysis. Given that Weka provides a Java interface, we use Java Native Interface (JNI) [18] to make possible the integration between the feature extraction and classification module. In this way, one can easily configure the employment of the appropriate classifier depending on the requirements at hand.

The implementation has been tested for possible memory leaks following an error-trial approach and monitoring the Linux OS memory consumption under various scenarios. This is because JNI implementation should be protected against potential out-of-memory conditions [19]. As pointed out in Sect. 1, our implementation is freely available [15] for further development and experimentation.

4 Results

This section details on the testbed used and presents the results in terms of both false alarms and processing overhead on the SIP server.

4.1 Test-Bed Setup

As illustrated in Fig. 3, we employed a virtualised testbed running over an i7 processor at 2.2 GHz. Three Virtual Machines (VMs) were created, each one equiped with 6 GB of RAM. These VMs respectively host the SIP proxy, the UAs, and the attack traffic generator. We created distinct patterns of legitimate, single source DoS and DDoS traffic using *sipp v.3.2* [20], *sipsak* [21], and SIPp-DD [22] tools respectively.

As observed from Table 1, twenty two disparate scenarios were created in total to replicate different (D)DoS incidents. Seven basic scenarios were used for training, while the others represent an attack incident. For all the scenarios, an exponential inter-arrival time distribution ($\lambda = 100$) is followed to produce the legitimate traffic. Note that this kind of distribution inherently presents the "lack-of-memory" property. Specifically, this property considers that the probability of a future event (call arrival) is the same regardless of the previous events that took place in a series of time frames. In our case, this is analogous to the traffic used for assessing VoIP systems' performance [23].

Furthermore, a range of different call rates has been used in the cases of DoS and DDoS, with the aim of simulating various call rates which may approximate the traffic patterns of a real VoIP provider. For example, as observed in Table 1, the call rate for SN6.1 is given as 20–120, where the first number indicates the call rate of the attack, and the second designates the call rate of the legitimate traffic both occurring in parallel. Keep in mind that for DDoS scenarios about half of the registered users were generating the normal traffic, while the other half were acting maliciously.

4.2 Detection Accuracy

In the context of our experiments, we employed 5 well-known classifiers, namely SMO, Naive Bayes, Neural Networks, Decision Trees (J48), and Random Forest. This particular choice has been done because these classifiers present a better detection accuracy when it comes to numerical data [24]. The detection accuracy of each classifier in terms of False Positives (FP) and False Negatives (FN) is estimated and the results are included in Table 2. Also, to ease the reading of the table, the mean, minimum, maximum FN and FP values per classifier and collectively per attack type (DoS/DDoS) are depicted in Fig. 4. From this figure it can be seen that FN metric fluctuates between 0.9 % and 23.7 % for DoS scenarios having an average of 14 %, while the corresponding values for DDoS are 2 %, 62 %, and 16 %.

Focusing on Table 2 and on its lines containing the average values of FN metric, one can conclude that SMO produces the worst results and therefore

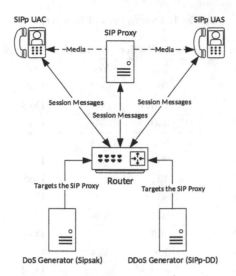

Fig. 3. Deployed testbed for (D)DoS simulations

should be avoided. The same observation applies to Random Forest but only for DoS scenarios. J48 on the other hand scores an average FN of 11.8 % but largely fails in terms of FP (interestingly, the FP metric is almost non-existent for all the algorithms but J48). It can be safely argued that the most reliable classifier across all scenarios and for both FN and FP metrics seems to be Naive Bayes followed by Random Forest. In any case, the FN percentages scored by both the aforementioned algorithms especially for DoS scenarios are not favorable for any real-world IDS. Putting aside SMO and Neural Networks, the rest of the classifiers produce an average FN lesser than 8.5 % for DDoS scenarios only. It can be therefore estimated that ML-driven detection shows greater potential in detecting more sophisticated attacks of this kind.

Having a complete view of the results, we consider that further experimentation is needed to obtain a better approximation of the power of ML-driven (D)DoS detection in SIP realms. In this direction, a future work could concentrate on testing more classifiers and tuning the Mw parameter based on the specific needs of the VoIP service provider.

4.3   Performance

Putting aside its effectiveness, the other decisive factor for any IDS is that of performance in terms of service time. This section elaborates on the per message (SIP request) processing time introduced by the realtime detection engine on the SIP server. It is to be noted that all the time measurements included in this section correspond to a worst case scenario as the SIP proxy for all the tests was configured with one serving thread.

Table 1. Description of scenarios

Scen	Num. of users	Calls/Sec	Train scen	Type of attack
SN1	30	2	Yes	-
SN1.1	30	50	-	DoS
SN1.2	30	175	-	DoS
SN1.3	30	350	-	DoS
SN2	30	5	Yes	-
SN2.1	30	20	-	DoS
SN2.2	30	40	-	DoS
SN2.3	30	80	-	DoS
SN3	30	20	Yes	-
SN3.1	30	266	-	DoS
SN4	30	120	Yes	-
SN4.1	30	800	-	DoS
SN5	50	120	Yes	-
SN5.1	50	400	-	DoS
SN5.2	50	1200	-	DoS
SN6	60	20	Yes	DDoS
SN6.1	60	20–120	-	low-rate DDoS
SN6.2	60	120-20	-	high-rate DDoS
SN7	500	100	Yes	DDoS
SN7.1	500	10–200	-	low-rate DDoS
SN7.2	500	100-40	-	high-rate DDoS
SN7.3	500	30–50	-	low-rate DDoS

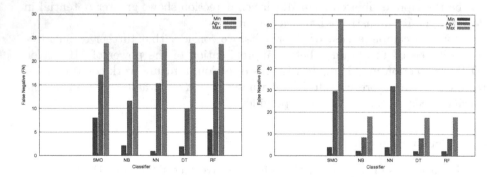

Fig. 4. DoS (left) and DDoS (right) minimum, maximum and average FN percentage values per classifer.

Figure 5 illustrates a random snapshot of the processing time introduced by our architecture, while Table 3 includes the average, max, min, and

Table 2. Summary of results for all the scenarios (The best performer per scenario in terms of FN is in bold).

SN	Traffic (Calls)		SMO		Naive Bayes		Neural networks		Decision trees (J48)		Random forest	
	Total rec	Attack rec	FP	FN	FP	FN	FP	FN	FP	FN	FP	FN
			%	%	%	%	%	%	%	%	%	%
SN1.1	2.4k	1.2k	0	23.7	0	23.7	0	**23.6**	35.1	23.7	0	**23.6**
SN1.2	2.5k	1.3k	0	22.9	0	**22.8**	0	22.9	33.7	**22.8**	0	23
SN1.3	2.7k	1.5k	0	**21.8**	0	21.8	0	**21.8**	32	22	0	**21.8**
SN2.1	2.7k	1.2k	0	21	0	7.3	0	14	36.9	**6.3**	36.3	19.6
SN2.2	2.7k	1.2k	0	16.1	0	7.3	0	28	29.9	**7.1**	0	9.9
SN2.3	3k	1.3k	0	12.4	0	**5.5**	0	24.8	44.1	14.7	0	27.3
SN3.1	5k	2.3k	0	19.8	0	**6.9**	0	9.1	47.1	7.2	0	20
SN4.1	8k	1.5k	0	8	0	8.9	0	4.7	75.1	**1.9**	0	15.7
SN5.1	7k	1k	0	11.7	0	9.2	0	**0.9**	0	11.2	0	5.5
SN5.2	9k	2.6k	0	12.3	0	2.1	0	2.2	59.9	**2**	0	12.3
Avg.	—	—	0	16.97	0	11.55	0	15.2	39.38	11.8	3.63	17.8
SN6.1	12k	6.6k	0	3.8	0	3.8	0	3.8	0	**3.4**	0	3.7
SN6.2	4.5k	2k	0	18.2	0	17.9	13.7	28.5	0	**17.4**	0	17.7
SN7.1	10.5k	3.3k	0	31.1	0	2.1	0	31.2	0	**2**	0	2.1
SN7.2	7k	2.2k	0	32	0	10.7	0	32.8	0	**10.5**	0	10.6
SN7.3	9k	6k	0	62.6	0	7	0	62.8	0	6.6	0	**5.1**
Avg.	—	—	0	29.5	0	8.3	2.74	31.8	0	7.98	0	7.84

standard deviation processing times per classifier for all the 15 attack scenarios. As observed from the Table, the average processing time remains under 4 ms, while it is easily seen that all classifiers follow a similar tendency. As the SIP proxy is configured in single-thread mode it can be safely argued that the induced overhead is negligible. The maximum values of, say, 300 ms contained in both Fig. 5 and Table 3 are unique or very scarce and are due to the activation of single-thread mode at SIP proxy side and the traffic pattern of the examined scenario. For instance, while in SN1.2 the normal traffic rate is 2 calls/sec, in SN7.1 is 200 calls/sec, resulting to an increment in the classifier's, average processing time.

Table 3. Summary of classification time overhead for all the scenarios (ms)

Classifier	Min	Max	Avg	St. dev
SMO	0.08	123.78	3.37	7.73
Naive Bayes	0.15	171.13	3.48	7.76
Neural networks	0.10	129.20	3.42	7.74
Decision trees (J48)	0.08	388.01	3.28	7.91
Random forest	0.08	91.74	3.56	7.72

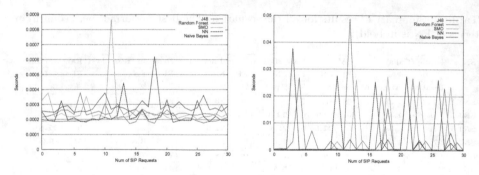

Fig. 5. A random snapshot of the time overhead for scenario SN-1-2 (left) and SN-7-1 (right)

5   Related Work

Until now, a handful of works in the literature discuss the suitability of methods borrowed from the ML community to detect DoS attacks in VoIP realms and particularly in SIP. In the following, we elaborate on each of them starting from those that are designed to work offline.

The authors in [10] provide an offline assessment of 5 different ML classifiers in detecting DoS and DDoS attacks in SIP. This was done by examining the recorded SIP audit trails in a forensic-like manner. Their results obtained under a variety of attack scenarios indicate that ML-powered methods achieve better results when compared to those scored by legacy statistical schemes [25,26]. They also highlight on the fact that some classifiers do achieve satisfactory results even in the case of low-rate flooding attacks. For instance, according to the authors, the Neural Networks classifier succeeds a FP rate of 5.2% and zero FN. Another offline proposal for detecting anomalies in SIP messages is given in [27]. Particularly, among others, the authors employ the Decision Tree (J48) classifier with the aim of exposing Invite and Register flooding incidents. To do so, they rely on classification features taken from three SIP message headers, namely <Method>, <To> and <From>. For DoS attacks, they report a detection accuracy of approximately equal to 99.7%.

The work in [28] also reports on the effectiveness of ML methods to cope with flooding incidents in SIP ecosystems. In this case, the authors focus on the first line of 13 different SIP requests and 6 different responses. The authors examine several classifiers, including Evolving Radial Basis Function, Fuzzy AdaBoost Genetic Classifier System, and others. They report sufficing results ranging from 0% to 1% for FP metric and 0% to 97.7% for FN. On the downside, the authors do not consider DDoS, and their experiments were conducted on an artificially created dataset where the simulated attack messages were injected to the normal traffic.

Three realtime detection schemes against Spam over Internet Telephony (SPIT) and flooding attacks are given in [29–31]. The first one deals with the detection of both SPIT and typical flooding attacks carried out via SIP messages. The detection mechanism proposed by the authors capitalizes on 38 distinct classification features and makes use of SVM classifier. The authors report a detection accuracy spanning from 0 % to 98.2 % depending on the flooding rate. The work in [30] proposes a mechanism that assembles vectors of certain features contained in SIP messages and subsequently feeds it to Naive Bayes and J48 classifiers. More specifically, the spatial features used in this work pertain to the IP address contained in the <From> header and the call ratio of Invite requests. As in their previous work [28], the authors synthetically inject attack messages to the normal SIP traffic in order to estimate the detection accuracy of their proposal. They mention false alarm rates ranging from 0 % to 0.7 % and 0 % to 25 % for FP and FN metrics respectively. The third work [31] offers an online IDS to combat DoS attacks. The authors argue that their system presents a 99 % accuracy, presenting a detection time overhead equal to $152\,\mu$. Nevertheless, they neither consider DDoS attacks nor different attack rates in their analysis.

From the above discussion, it becomes apparent that so far the related work on the topic presents two major shortcomings which are dealt by the work at hand:

1. It does not consider more sophisticated attacks scenarios like DDoS and low-rate DoS, which naturally are more difficult to detect and defeat. The works in [10,30] do take into consideration the aforementioned category of assaults but either the reported results are only concerned with offline detection or they solely address elementary DoS attacks.
2. No work occupied with realtime detection comprehensively reports on the overhead that the various classifiers induce to the system in terms of classification time. However, this is crucial for deciding if a particular detection method is suitable or not.

6   Conclusions

This work examines the applicability of several well-known ML techniques in detecting (D)DoS in SIP-based services. We implemented a Kamailio software module to achieve attack detection in realtime and tested both the detection accuracy and processing overhead of each classifier under 15 different attack scenarios representing DoS and DDoS incidents. All the algorithms but one achieve desirable detection accuracy in terms of FP, but only mediocre accuracy (for a real-life IDS product) when FN is considered. Therefore, further experimentation is needed to better appreciate this potential. From a processing overhead viewpoint, it can be safely argued that realtime operation is feasible as the induced time penalty is negligible even if the SIP server operates in single-thread mode.

It is worthy to note that the legitimate users' calling rate, the number of users included in every scenario, and the value of the M_w are sure to affect the false alarm rates. This happens because the selected features rely on the occurrences of the examined headers of interest, and thus are directly connected to the number of users and the M_w. That is, the greater the number of users the lesser the occurrences per message header. This fact indicates that one should lower the size of M_w as the population of users augments and vice versa. To this end, one can obtain the best results with an error-trial approach, calibrating the M_w proportionally to the population of users and the calling rate as the case may be.

Acknowledgements. This paper is part of the 5179 (SCYPE) research project, implemented within the context of the Greek Ministry of Development-General Secretariat of Research and Technology funded program Excellence II/Aristeia II, co-financed by the European Union/European Social Fund - Operational program Education and Life-long Learning and National funds.

References

1. Mohr, C.: Report: global voip services market to reach 137 billion by 2020, November 2014. http://www.tmcnet.com/channels/hosted-softswitch/articles/393593-report-global-voip-services-market-reach-137-billion.htm
2. Geneiatakis, D., Kambourakis, G., Lambrinoudakis, C., Dagiuklas, T., Gritzalis, S.: SIP message tampering: the SQL code injection attack. In: Proceedings of 13th International Conference on Software, Telecommunications and Computer Networks (SoftCOM 2005), Split, Croatia (2005)
3. Geneiatakis, D., Dagiuklas, T., Kambourakis, G., Lambrinoudakis, C., Gritzalis, S., Ehlert, K., Sisalem, D.: Survey of security vulnerabilities in session initiation protocol. IEEE Commun. Surv. Tutorials **8**(3), 68–81 (2006)
4. Geneiatakis, D., Kambourakis, G., Lambrinoudakis, C., Dagiuklas, T., Gritzalis, S.: A framework for protecting a SIP-based infrastructure against malformed message attacks. Commun. Netw. **51**(10), 2580–2593 (2007). Elsevier
5. Kambourakis, G., Kolias, C., Gritzalis, S., Park, J.H.: DoS attacks exploiting signaling in UMTS and IMS. Comput. Commun. **34**(3), 226–235 (2011). http://www.sciencedirect.com/science/article/pii/S014036641000085X
6. Shtern, M., Sandel, R., Litoiu, M., Bachalo, C., Theodorou, V.: Towards mitigation of low and slow application DDoS attacks. In: 2014 IEEE International Conference on Cloud Engineering (IC2E), pp. 604–609, March 2014
7. Ehlert, S., Zhang, G., Geneiatakis, D., Kambourakis, G., Dagiuklas, T., Markl, J., Sisalem, D.: Two layer denial of service prevention on SIP VoIP infrastructures. Comput. Commun. **31**(10), 2443–2456 (2008)
8. Tsiatsikas, Z., Geneiatakis, D., Kambourakis, G., Keromytis, A.D.: An efficient and easily deployable method for dealing with DoS in SIP services. Comput. Commun. **57**, 50–63 (2015)
9. Ehlert, S., Geneiatakis, D., Magedanz, T.: Survey of network security systems to counter SIP-based denial-of-service attacks. Comput. Secur. **29**(2), 225–243 (2010)
10. Tsiatsikas, Z., Fakis, A., Papamartzivanos, D., Geneiatakis, D., Kambourakis, G., Kolias, C.: Battling against DDoS in SIP - is machine learning-based detection an effective weapon? In: Proceedings of the 12th International Conference on Security and Cryptography, pp. 301–308 (2015)

11. Rosenberg, J., Schulzrinne, H., Camarillo, G., Johnston, A., Peterson, J., Sparks, R., Handley, M., Schooler, E.: SIP: session initiation protocol. Internet Requests for Comments, June 2002. http://www.rfc-editor.org/rfc/rfc3261.txt
12. Keromytis, A.D.: A comprehensive survey of voice over IP security research. IEEE Commun. Surv. Tutorials **14**(2), 514–537 (2012)
13. SIPVicious. (2016) Sipvicious. http://blog.sipvicious.org/
14. C.S. Advisory Cisco SIP Phone 3905 resource limitation denial of service vulnerability (2015). https://tools.cisco.com/security/center/content/CiscoSecurityAdvisory/cisco-sa-20151202-sip
15. Tsiatsikas, Z., Geneiatakis, D., Kambourakis, G.: Research project scype: Software modules. https://scype.samos.aegean.gr/tzisis/scype_5179_software/
16. Kamailio The Open Source SIP Server (2014). http://www.kamailio.org/w/
17. Hall, M., Frank, E., Holmes, G., Pfahringer, B., Reutemann, P., Witten, I.H.: The Weka data mining software: an update. SIGKDD Explor. Newsl. **11**(1), 10–18 (2009)
18. Gordon, R.: Essential JNI: Java Native Interface. Prentice-Hall Inc, Upper Saddle River (1998)
19. Oracle: Crashing JVM (2016). http://docs.oracle.com/cd/E15289_01/doc.40/e15059/crash.htm#i1010768
20. SIPp, Free open source test tool/traffic generator for the sip protocol. http://sipp.sourceforge.net/index.html
21. Ohlmeier, N.: SIP swiss army knife. http://sipsak.org/
22. Stanek, J., Kencl, L.: SIPp-DD: SIP DDoS flood-attack simulation tool. In: 2011 Proceedings of 20th International Conference on Computer Communications and Networks (ICCCN), pp. 1–7, July 2011
23. Krishnamurthy, R., Rouskas, G.: Evaluation of SIP proxy server performance: packet-level measurements and queuing model. In: 2013 IEEE International Conference on Communications (ICC), pp. 2326–2330, June 2013
24. Witten, I.H., Frank, E., Hall, M.A.: Data mining: practical machine learning tools and techniques. 3rd edn. Morgan Kaufmann, Burlington (2011). http://www.sciencedirect.com/science/book/9780123748560
25. Shannon, C.E.: A mathematical theory of communication. SIGMOBILE Mob. Comput. Commun. Rev. **5**(1), 3–55 (2001)
26. Nikulin, M.: Hellinger distance. Encyclopeadia of Mathematics (2001)
27. Bouzida, Y., Mangin, C.: A framework for detecting anomalies in VoIP networks. In: Third International Conference on Availability, Reliability and Security, ARES 2008, pp. 204–211. IEEE (2008)
28. Akbar, M.A., Farooq, M.: Application of evolutionary algorithms in detection of SIP based flooding attacks. In: Proceedings of the 11th Annual Conference on Genetic and Evolutionary Computation, pp. 1419–1426. ACM (2009)
29. Nassar, M., State, R., Festor, O.: Monitoring SIP traffic using support vector machines. In: Lippmann, R., Kirda, E., Trachtenberg, A. (eds.) RAID 2008. LNCS, vol. 5230, pp. 311–330. Springer, Heidelberg (2008)
30. Akbar, M.A., Farooq, M.: Securing SIP-based VoIP infrastructure against flooding attacks and spam over IP telephony. Knowl. Inf. Syst. **38**(2), 491–510 (2014)
31. Rafique, M.Z., Khan, Z.S., Khan, M.K., Alghatbar, K.: Securing IP-multimedia subsystem (IMS) against anomalous message exploits by using machine learning algorithms. In: 2011 Eighth International Conference on Information Technology: New Generations (ITNG), pp. 559–563. IEEE (2011)

Digital Signature

Two-in-One Oblivious Signatures Secure in the Random Oracle Model

Raylin Tso[✉]

Department of Computer Science, National Chengchi University,
No.64, Sec.2, ZhiNan Rd., Taipei City 11605, Taiwan
raylin@cs.nccu.edu.tw

Abstract. An oblivious signature is a kind of digital signature providing privacy protection for the signature requester. According to the pioneer work introduced by Chen in 1994, it is defined in two different types; an oblivious signature with n messages and, an oblivious signature with n keys. In an oblivious signature with n messages, it allows a signature requester to get a signature on 1-out-of-n messages while during the signing process, the signer cannot find out which one of the n messages has been signed. In an oblivious signature with n keys, it allows a signature requester to get a signature signed by 1-out-of-n signers while during the signing process, no one except the requester can know who has really signed the message. In 2008, Tso et al. gave formal definitions on the models of oblivious signatures and gave an example on the construction of oblivious signatures based on the Schnorr signature. In this paper, we follow Tso et al.'s work but combine the two functionalities into one scheme. We called it *Two-in-one oblivious signature*. In out scheme, a signature requester can ask 1-out-of-n_1 signers to sign 1-out-of-n_2 messages. At the end of our protocol, no one (including the n_1 possible-signers) knows who has really signed the message as well as which one of the n_2 message has been signed. The scheme is useful in many applications such as e-cash, e-voting and e-auction etc. We will give a formal model on our scheme and give a rigorous security proof based on the random oracle model.

Keywords: 1-out-of-n signature · Oblivious signature · Oblivious transfer · Privacy protection · Schnorr signature

1 Introduction

Nowadays, as the increasing awareness of personal privacy, privacy protection has become one of the most important features for designing a secure cryptographic protocol. For example, privacy preserving smart metering [1,7,14] which allows users to perform and prove the correctness of computations, without disclosing any fine grained consumption. Privacy preserving data outsourcing [12] which can outsource the sensitive data in an encrypted form without disclosing the real data. And many other privacy preserving schemes in data mining [10,22],

© Springer International Publishing AG 2016
J. Chen et al. (Eds.): NSS 2016, LNCS 9955, pp. 143–155, 2016.
DOI: 10.1007/978-3-319-46298-1_10

or in the e-health environments [23–25]. Moreover, in the applications of on-line shopping, on-line banking, Internet-voting or e-auction etc., consumers or users may worry about how their personal information will be used. Using an on-line shopping as an example. Users can download the free trial version of software, mobile Apps, musics or video from the Internet. To access the full version, users have to pay for authorization. An authorization on a software may be a digital signature on the software signed by the corresponding issuer. However, to avoid the abuse of the shopping and/or the browsing habits, the user may hope that he/she can get the authorization (i.e., a digital signature) from the issuer without disclosing his/her consumption habits. That is, to get a signature without showing who will really sign the message as well as which message will be signed on from signers perspective. In this case, oblivious signatures [5,18] will be a good method to satisfy the users requirement.

Oblivious signatures, which first introduced by Chen in 1994, was aimed to solve the privacy-protection problem relating to the activities on the Internet. In his pioneer work, an oblivious signature is defined in two types; an oblivious signature with n keys and, an oblivious signature with n messages. The two types of signatures are used in two different scenarios.

The oblivious signature with n keys is an interactive and multiparty protocol which consists of n signers (or simply a singer with n different keys) and a signature requester R. By executing the protocol, R interacts with the n signers to request a signature on a message m. At the end of the protocol, R got a signature on m signed by one of the n signers. The main feature of this scheme is:

1. R can get one and only one signature on the message m, and the signer (or the signing key from the n keys) is pre-determined by R before the execution of the protocol.
2. During the signing process, all the n signers have no idea on who has really signed the message m. But it is assured by the protocol that one and only one signer among the n possible signers will sign the message m.
3. When necessary, R can show that he has got a signature (on the message m) from one of the n signers (or one of the n keys from the same signer) without revealing with which special one.

On the other hand, the oblivious signature with n messages is an interactive protocol which consists of a signer S, a signature requester R and n messages $\{m_1, m_2, \cdots, m_n\}$. The n messages can either be determined by S or R as long as both party agreed on signing one of these n messages. By executing the protocol, R interacts with S and finally gets a signature signed by S on one of the n messages. The main feature of this scheme is:

1. R can get one and only one signature signed by S on one of the n messages, $\{m_1, m_2, \cdots, m_n\}$. The message to be signed is predetermined by R before the execution of the protocol.
2. During the signing process, the signer S has no idea on which one among the n messages has been signed by him. But it is assured by the protocol that only one among the n messages will be signed.

3. When necessary, R can show that he has got a signature on one of the n messages without revealing which special one.

Oblivious signatures with n keys can be considered as a complement of ring signatures [15,20,21] or group signatures [6,11]. The difference is that a ring signature as well as a group signature is aimed to protect the anonymity of a signer, but an oblivious signature with n keys is to protect the choice a signature requester made (i.e., who among the n possible signers will really sign the message). On the other hand, oblivious signatures with n messages can be considered as an improvement of blind signatures [2,4]. A blind signature, as introduced by Chaum [4], allows a user to get a message signed by a signer without revealing *any information* about the message to the signer. Since a signer's view is perfectly shut off from the resulting signatures, it is a risk from a signer's perspective to sign such a blinded message. However, in an oblivious signature with n messages, although a signer still cannot control over the message to be signed, he can see or control the message pool in advance and know that a message he will sign is picked from the pool. In other words, if a signer is willing to sign any one of the message from the pool, then he can perform the protocol and be convinced that no message outside the message pool will be signed.

Following Chen's work, Tso et al. in 2008 redefined the model of an oblivious signature in formal. One important change is that the property of *ambiguous verification* is neglected in Tso et al.'s model. Ambiguous verification means that, when necessary, the signature requester can show that he has got a signature with one the n keys (or messages) without revealing with which special one. Tso mentioned that the ambiguous verification property can be easy achieved on any three move type signature schemes [8] by the technique of *universal ring signature* [19]. Consequently, it should not be considered an a unique feature of oblivious signatures. Instead, it is an extended feature for all three-move type signatures.

Motivation and Contributions. Oblivious signatures have many useful applications. For oblivious signatures with n keys, It can be used in the case of accessing sensitive databases controlled by different administrators (or simply one administrator with different access keys). In this case, an authorization or a permit, which is a signature signed by the corresponding administrator is required. Using an oblivious signature scheme we can guarantee that a user can get the permit (i.e., the signature) for accessing only one of n databases without revealing which one. On the other hand, oblivious signatures with n messages is useful in the case of internet shopping. Users can download the free trial version of software, mobile Apps, musics or video from the Internet. To access the full version, users have to pay for authorization. An authorization on a software may be a digital signature on the software signed by the corresponding issuer. By using oblivious signatures, the user can choose n software and get one and only one signed by the issuer without revealing which one. Some researchers have also found its functionality in e-voting scheme [17].

However, for the case if the message as well as the identity of the real signer are both sensitive from a signature requester's perspective, then there is no scheme suitable for this case. For this reason, in this paper, we redefine the formal model again. We follow Tso et al.'s work and combine the two functionalities of oblivious signatures into one scheme. We called it *Two-in-one oblivious signature*. In out scheme, a signature requester can ask 1 out of n_1 signers to sign 1 out of n_2 messages. At the end of our protocol, no one (including the n_1 possible-signers) knows who has really signed the message as well as which one of the n_2 messages has been signed. If $n_1 = 1$, then it is the original oblivious signature with n_2 messages. On the other hand, if $n_2 = 1$, then it is the original oblivious signature with n_1 keys. We extend it functionality so that it can be used in more applications, such as e-cash, e-voting and e-auction etc. We will also give a formal model and construction on our scheme and give a rigorous security proof in the random oracle model.

Paper Organization. The rest of the paper is organized as follows. Section 2 is Preliminaries. Section 3 gives the formal model of the new oblivious signature scheme. In Sect. 4, we describe the detailed construction of our two-in-one oblivious signatures. The rigorous security proofs are also provided in this section. Finally, the conclusion is given in Sect. 5.

2   Preliminaries

This section gives some cryptographic primitives and definitions required for our construction.

2.1   Complexity Assumption and Forking Lemma

Definition 1 (Discrete Logarithm (DL) Problem). Let G be a finite group of prime order $q \geq 2^\lambda$ where λ is a security parameter. Let also g be a generator of G with order q. The DL problem is to output k of $\delta = g^k \mod q$ when given $g, q, \delta \in G$.

The success probability that an algorithm $\mathcal{F}$ has in solving the DL problem in G is $Succ_{\mathcal{F}}^{DL} = \Pr[\mathcal{F}(g, \delta) = k : \delta = g^k]$, where the probability is over the random choice of g, δ in G^2 and the random bits consumed by $\mathcal{F}$.

The Discrete Logarithm (DL) assumption is that $Succ_{\mathcal{F}}^{DL}$ is negligible for any polynomial-time algorithm $\mathcal{F}$ (for the security parameter κ). As one of the fundamental complexity assumptions, DL assumption has been widely used in the security analysis of cryptographic protocols.

Definition 2 (Forking Lemma [13]). Let $(\mathcal{K}, \mathcal{S}, \mathcal{V})$ be a digital signature scheme with security parameter 1^k, with a signature of the form $(m, \sigma_1, h, \sigma_2)$, where $h = \mathcal{H}(m, \sigma_1)$ and σ_2 depends on σ_1 and h only. Let $\mathcal{A}$ be a probabilistic polynomial time Turing machine whose input only consists of public data and which can ask $q_h > 0$ queries to the random oracle. Assume that, within time bound T, $\mathcal{A}$ produces, with probability $\epsilon \geq 7q_h/2^k$, a valid signature $(m, \sigma_1, h, \sigma_2)$. Then, a replay of the attacker $\mathcal{A}$, where interactions with the signer are simulated, outputs two valid signature $(m, \sigma_1, h, \sigma_2)$, and $(m, \sigma_1, h', \sigma_2')$ such that $h \neq h'$, within time $T' \leq 84480\, T q_h/\epsilon$.

2.2 Schnorr Signatures Revisited

Our oblivious signature is based on Schnorr signature [16], so we revisit it in this subsection. A Schnorr signature is a digital signature which consists of three algorithms; key generation algorithm (**KGen**), Signing algorithm (**Sign**) and Verification algorithm **Verify**.

Kgen: Given a security parameter 1^ℓ, this algorithm outputs the public key $pk = (p, q, g, \mathsf{H}, y)$ and the corresponding private key $x \in_R \mathbb{Z}_q^*$ of a signer, where

- p, q: two large primes such that $q|(p-1)$.
- g: an element of $\mathbb{Z}_p^*$ of order q.
- $\mathsf{H} : \{0,1\}^* \to \mathbb{Z}_q^*$: a cryptographic one way hash function.
- $y = g^x \bmod p$.

Sign: Given $pk = (p, q, g, \mathsf{H}, y)$, a message $m \in \{0,1\}^*$ and the corresponding private key x, this algorithm generates a Schnorr signature $\sigma = (r, s)$ on m, where

- $k \in_R \mathbb{Z}_q^*$.
- $r = \mathsf{H}(m, g^k \bmod p)$.
- $s = k - x \cdot r \bmod q$.

Verify: Given pk, a message m and a signature $\sigma = (r, s)$, this verification algorithm outputs "1" if $r = \mathsf{H}(m, y^r g^s \bmod p)$, which means the signature has been correctly verified. Otherwise, it outputs "0" which means the signature is incorrect.

3   Definitions of Two-in-One Oblivious Signature

We extend the formal model of an oblivious signature scheme defined by Tso et al. in [18]. In more detail, we combined their two models in one. Our new model allows a signature requester to receive a signature signed by one out of the predetermined n_1 signers (or simply a signer with n_1 different keys) and signed on one out of the predetermined n_2 messages. Our oblivious signature scheme (abbreviated to $\mathcal{OS}_1^{(n_1, n_2)}$) with n_1 signers and n_2 messages involves three types of entities: a signature requester $\mathcal{R}$, n_1 possible signers $\mathcal{S}_i, 1 \leq i \leq n_1$ and a verifier $\mathcal{V}$.

- **A signature requester $\mathcal{R}$:** for any input of n_1 possible signers $\mathcal{S}_i, 1 \leq i \leq n_1$ and n_2 messages, $m_1, \cdots, m_n$, $\mathcal{R}$ can choose any one of these n_2 messages to get signed by any one of the n_1 signers $\mathcal{S}_i, 1 \leq i \leq n_1$.
- **Oblivious signers $\mathcal{S}_i, 1 \leq i \leq n_1$:** each signer $\mathcal{S}_i, 1 \leq i \leq n_1$ performs as a real signer to sign the message chosen by $\mathcal{R}$, but he is not able to learn who among the n_1 signers is the real signer and which one of the n_2 messages has actually been signed.
- **A verifier $\mathcal{V}$:** $\mathcal{R}$ converts the oblivious signature into a generic signature σ and transmits σ to $\mathcal{V}$. $\mathcal{V}$ is able to verify the validity of the signature without any secrete information.

Definition 3. An $\mathcal{OS}_1^{(n_1,n_2)}$ scheme consists of four algorithms:

1. **System Setting**: A probabilistic polynomial-time algorithm (denoted by **SSet**. This algorithm is run by a trusted third party (TTP, also regarded as a trusted manager of the system). On input a security parameter 1^k, TTP runs the System-Setting algorithm to generate the system-wide public parameters *params* of the scheme.
2. **Key Generation**: A probabilistic polynomial-time algorithm (denoted by **KGen**). This algorithm is run by each signer $\mathcal{S}_i, 1 \leq i \leq n$, of the scheme in separate who takes the system parameters *params* as input and the output is the private/public key-pair (sk_i, pk_i) of the signer $\mathcal{S}_i, 1 \leq i \leq n$.
3. **Signature Generation**: An interactive polynomial-time algorithm (denoted by **Sign**) among a signature requester $\mathcal{R}$ and n_1 signers. It takes the system parameters *params*, n_1 signing keys $sk_i, 1 \leq i \leq n_1$, and n_2 message $m_j, 1 \leq j \leq n_2$, as input, and outputs a standard and publicly verifiable Schnorr signature σ.
4. **Signature Verification**: A deterministic polynomial-time algorithm (denoted by **Ver**) which takes a public key pk and a message/signature pair (m, σ) as input, and outputs 1 or 0 to accept or reject the signature.

Notice that when $n_1 = 1$, it is the type I oblivious signatures defined in [18], i.e., oblivious signature with different messages. Moreover, when $n_2 = 1$, it is the type II oblivious signatures defined in [18], i.e., oblivious signature with different keys. The two models cannot be combined in [18] but we successfully modified it into one model.

3.1   Security Requirements

We now define the securities required for our oblivious signatures $OS_1^{(n_1,n_2)}$. The securities defined in this section follows those defined in [18,19] with slight modifications. For an $\mathcal{OS}_1^{(n_1,n_2)}$ scheme, the securities requirements that must be considered are *correctness, unforgeability, ambiguity in selected signer* and *ambiguity in selected message*.

In the coming definitions, $negl(\lambda)$ denotes any function which grows slower than $\frac{1}{\lambda^c}$ for sufficiently large λ and some constant c.

Definition 4 (Correctness). If $\mathcal{S}_i, 1 \leq i \leq n_1$, and $\mathcal{R}$ follow the signature generation protocol properly and, at the end of the protocol, a signature σ has been generated, then, with probability at least $1 - negl(\lambda)$, $\mathcal{V}$ will accept the signature with probability at least $1 - negl(\lambda)$. In other words, σ satisfies $\mathbf{Ver}(\sigma, params, pk_i, m_j) = 1$ for some $i, 1 \leq i \leq n_1$, and $j, 1 \leq j \leq n_2$.

The signature σ on messages m_j is said valid with regard to $(params, pk_i)$ if it leads any verifier $\mathcal{V}$ to accept.

Except the completeness of the protocol, other requirements are defined separately for a signature requester $\mathcal{R}$ and for possible signers $\mathcal{S}_i, 1 \leq i \leq n_1$.

The security requirement for signers is the unforgeability of signatures and the security requirements for requester is the ambiguity in selected signers and the ambiguity in selected messages. The security for signers is protected in the sense of computational security and the security for a requester is protected in the sense of unconditional security.

To define the security for signers, we modify the definition of [18] and introduce the following game.

Definition 5 (Game A). Let $\mathcal{R}^*$ be a probabilistic polynomial time forging algorithm. $\mathcal{R}^*$ executes the part of a signature requester and tries to forge a new signature σ^* on a message m^*.

1. $(params) \leftarrow \mathbf{SSet}(1^k)$,
2. $\{(pk_1, sk_1), \cdots, (pk_{n_1}, sk_{n_1})\} \leftarrow \mathbf{KGen}(params, \mathcal{S}_1, \cdots, \mathcal{S}_{n_1})$,
3. $\mathcal{R}^*(params, pk_1, \cdots, pk_{n_1}, \mathcal{M})$ engages in the signature generation algorithm with $\mathcal{S}_1, \cdots, \mathcal{S}_{n_1}$ for any message-set $\mathcal{M}$ where $|\mathcal{M}| = n_2$. The message set $\mathcal{M}$, a message $m_j \in \mathcal{M}$ which will be signed and a real signer $\mathcal{S}_i \in \{\mathcal{S}_1, \cdots, \mathcal{S}_{n_1}\}$ to sign m_j can be adaptively chosen by $\mathcal{R}$. This step including the selection of the message set $\mathcal{M}$ can be executed in polynomially many number of times where $\mathcal{R}^*$ can decide in an adaptive fashion when to stop. In the end of each execution, $\mathcal{R}^*$ obtains a valid signature $\sigma_{i,j}$ on the message $m_j \in \mathcal{M}$ signed by $\mathcal{S}_i \in \{\mathcal{S}_1, \cdots, \mathcal{S}_{n_1}\}$. Let t denote the number of executions, and $\{\sigma_1, \cdots, \sigma_t\}$ denote the signatures obtained by $\mathcal{R}^*$ at this stage.
4. $\mathcal{R}^*$ outputs a new signature σ^* on a message m^* and claims it to be signed by $\mathcal{S}^* \in \{\mathcal{S}_1, \cdots, \mathcal{S}_{n_1}\}$ with $\mathcal{S}^*$'s public key pk^*. In addition, $\sigma^* \notin \{\sigma_1, \cdots, \sigma_t\}$.

Definition 6 (Security for Signers: Unforgeability). An oblivious signature scheme $\mathcal{OS}_1^{(n_1, n_2)}$ provides the security for signers if, for any probabilistic polynomial-time forging algorithm $\mathcal{R}^*$ that plays the above game, we have

$$Pr\left(\mathbf{Ver}(\sigma^*, params, m^*, pk^* \in \{pk_1, \cdots, pk_{n_1}\}) = 1\right) < negl(\lambda).$$

The security for signers is actually the same as the notion of Existential Unforgeability against Adaptive Chosen Message Attack (EUF-ACMA) [9] for any standard publicly verifiable signature scheme.

The security for recipients is defined through Game B.

Definition 7 (Game B). Let $\mathcal{S}^*$ be an attacking algorithm with unlimited computation power which executes the part of one of the possible signers and $\mathcal{R}$ be an honest requester that follows the signature generation algorithm. W.L.O.G, let $\mathcal{S}^* \in \{\mathcal{S}_a, \mathcal{S}_b\}$ and m_0, m_1 be two messages randomly picked by $\mathcal{S}^*$. Let $u \in_R \{a, b\}$ and $v \in_R \{0, 1\}$ which are kept secret from $\mathcal{S}^*$. The purpose of $\mathcal{S}^*$ is to predict u and /or v via the execution of the following game.

1. $(params) \leftarrow \mathbf{SSet}(1^k)$,
2. $\{(pk_a, sk_a), (pk_b, sk_b)\} \leftarrow \mathbf{KGen}(params, \mathcal{S}_a, \mathcal{S}_b)$,
3. $\mathcal{S}^*$ with knowledges of (pk_a, sk_a) and (pk_b, sk_b) engages in the signature generation algorithm with $\mathcal{R}(params, pk_u, m_v), u \in_R \{a, b\}$ and $v \in_R \{0, 1\}$,

4. S^* outputs $u' \in \{a, b\}$ and $v' \in \{0, 1\}$ according to the view from steps 1, 2, and 3 (i.e., S^* is not allowed to view the output of R at the end of the signature generation protocol).

We say that the attacking algorithm S^* wins the game if $u' = u$ and/or $v' = b$.

Definition 8 (Security for Recipients Against Signers: Ambiguity in Selected Messages and/or in Selected Signers). An oblivious signature scheme provides unconditional security for recipients against signers if, for any attacking algorithm S^* executing the signer's part, S^* wins in Game B with probability at most $1/2 + negl(\lambda)$.

Intuitively, the security for recipients against signers means that it is *unconditionally* infeasible for any attacker S^* to find out who is the real signer (or which key has been used to signed the message during the signature generation process) and /or which one of the messages is chosen by the signature requester R, during the execution of the signature generation process.

4   Proposed Schemes

In this section, we propose our two-in-one oblivious signatures $OS_1^{(n_1, n_2)}$ with n_1 signers (or a signer with n_1 keys) $\{S_1, \cdots, S_{n_1}\}$ and n_2 messages, $\{m_1, \cdots, m_{n_2}\}$. At the end of the protocol, one of the n_2 message, say m_l, will be signed by one of the n_1 signer, say S_t. m_l and S_t are selected and predetermined by the signature requester.

System Setting: On input a security parameter 1^λ, a Trusted Third Party (i.e., system administrator) runs the System-Setup algorithm **SSet**. The following output forms the public parameters of the scheme.

- p, q: two large primes such that $q|(p-1)$,
- g: an element of $\mathbb{Z}_p^*$ of order q.
- $\mathcal{H} : \{0, 1\}^* \rightarrow \mathbb{Z}_q^*$: a secure one-way hash function.

Key Generation: Each $S_i, 1 \le i \le n_1$ picks a random number $x_i \in \mathbb{Z}_q^*$ and computes $y_i \leftarrow g^{x_i} \bmod p$. x_i is kept secret as her private key and y_i is public as her public key.

Signature Generation: Assume that a signature requester R would like to get a signature $\sigma_{(t,l)}$ on a message $m_l \in \{m_1, \cdots, m_{n_2}\}$ which is obliviously signed by $S_t \in \{S_1, \cdots, S_{n_1}\}$, then R executes the following protocol with all possible signers $S_i, 1 \le i \le n_1$:

Step 1 R starts the protocol by picking a random number $r \in \mathbb{Z}_q^*$, then computes $c = g^r y_t^l \bmod p$ where y_t is the public key of the target signer (i.e., S_t). R then sends c together with the n_2 messages $\{m_1, \cdots, m_{n_2}\}$ listed in a fixed order to the signer S. Here l is the value of the subscript of m_l, which is the target message intended to be signed.

Step 2 After receiving c and the ordered message set $\{m_1, \cdots, m_{n_2}\}$, each possible signer $\mathcal{S}_i, 1 \leq i \leq n_1$ does the following steps, independently:

For $j = 1, \cdots, n_2$, $\mathcal{S}_i$ picks a random number $k_{(i,j)} \in_R \mathbb{Z}_q^*$ and computes:

- $K_{(i,j)} \leftarrow g^{k_{(i,j)}} \bmod p$,
- $\hat{e}_{(i,j)} \leftarrow \mathcal{H}(m_j, K_{(i,j)}c/(gy_i)^j \bmod p)$, and
- $\hat{s}_{(i,j)} \leftarrow k_{(i,j)} - x_i\hat{e}_{(i,j)} \bmod q$.

Each $\mathcal{S}_i, 1 \leq i \leq n_1$ then sends $(\hat{e}_{(i,j)}, \hat{s}_{(i,j)}), 1 \leq j \leq n_2$, back to $\mathcal{R}$.

Step 3 For $1 \leq i \leq n_1$, and $1 \leq j \leq n_2$, $\mathcal{R}$ computes $\delta_{(i,j)} \leftarrow g^{(r-j)}y_t^l y_i^{-j} \bmod p$ and accepts the oblivious signature if and only if

$$\hat{e}_{(i,j)} = \mathcal{H}(m_j, g^{\hat{s}_{(i,j)}} y_i^{\hat{e}_{(i,j)}} \delta_{(i,j)} \bmod p) \quad 1 \leq i \leq n_1, \quad 1 \leq j \leq n_2.$$

Step 4 To convert the oblivious signature into a generic (Schnorr) signature, $\mathcal{R}$ computes:

- $e \leftarrow \hat{e}_{(t,l)}$, and
- $s \leftarrow r - l + \hat{s}_{(t,l)} \bmod q$,

The signature on m_l signed by $\mathcal{S}_t$ is $\sigma_{(t,l)} \leftarrow (e, s)$.

Signature Verification: Any verifier $\mathcal{V}$ accepts the signature $\sigma_{(t,l)}$ as a valid signature on m_l if and only if

$$e = \mathcal{H}(m_l, g^s y_t^e \bmod p)$$

4.1 Security

In this section, we follow the security proofs of [18] and show the security of the proposed scheme. We first show the correctness of the scheme. Correctness means any signature signed follow the procedure of the signature generation process will always pass the signature verification process.

Correctness. The output signature $\sigma_{(i,j)} = (e, s)$ is a standard Schnorr signature, its correctness follows that of the Standard Schnorr signature and is trivial. We need only to show that $\hat{e}_{(i,j)} = \mathcal{H}(m_j, g^{\hat{s}_{(i,j)}} y_i^{\hat{e}_{(i,j)}} \delta_{(i,j)} \bmod p)$ for all i, j, where $1 \leq i \leq n_1$, $1 \leq j \leq n_2$.

It is correct since

$$\mathcal{H}(m_j, g^{\hat{s}_{(i,j)}} y_i^{\hat{e}_{(i,j)}} \delta_{(i,j)} \bmod p)$$
$$= \mathcal{H}(m_j, g^{k_{(i,j)} - x_i\hat{e}_{(i,j)}} y_i^{\hat{e}_{(i,j)}} g^{(r-j)} y_t^l y_i^{-j} \bmod p)$$
$$= \mathcal{H}(m_j, g^{k_{(i,j)} - x_i\hat{e}_{(i,j)}} g^{x_i\hat{e}_{(i,j)}} g^{(r-j)} y_t^l y_i^{-j} \bmod p)$$
$$= \mathcal{H}(m_j, g^{k_{(i,j)}} g^{(r-j)} y_t^l y_i^{-j} \bmod p)$$
$$= \mathcal{H}(m_j, K_{(i,j)} g^r y_t^l/(gy_i)^j \bmod p)$$
$$= \mathcal{H}(m_j, K_{(i,j)} c/(gy_i)^j \bmod p)$$
$$= \hat{e}_{(i,j)}. \qquad \square$$

Also notice that when $i = t$ and $j = l$, then y_t will be deleted so

$$\mathcal{H}(m_j, K_{(i,j)}g^{(r-j)}y_t^l y_i^{-j} \bmod p) = \mathcal{H}(m_l, K_{(t,l)}g^{(r-l)} \bmod p).$$

That is the reason why we need $s \leftarrow r - l + \hat{s}_{(t,l)} \bmod q$ at the end of Step 4 during the signature generation.

We than proof the security requirement for signers. That is, the unforgeability of the oblivious signature.

Unforgeability. If there exists an adaptively chosen message attacker $\mathcal{B}$ which wins Game A (see Definition 5) with an advantage ϵ within a time T, then there exists an algorithm $\mathcal{A}$ which can solve the DL problem with the same advantage within a time bound $T' \leq 84480 q_h T / \epsilon$, where q_h is the number of hash queries.

Proof: $\mathcal{A}$ is given a DL problem (p, q, g, y) where p, q are two large primes such that $q | (p - 1)$, and g, y are two elements of $\mathbb{Z}_p^*$ of the same order q. The purpose of $\mathcal{A}$ is to find $x = \log_g^y$, which is the solution to the DL problem.

In order to solve the problem, $\mathcal{A}$ utilizes $\mathcal{B}$ as a black-box. To get the black-box $\mathcal{B}$ run properly, $\mathcal{A}$ simulates the environments of the proposed $\mathcal{OS}_1^{(n_1, n_2)}$ scheme. In the following proof, we regard the hash function $\mathcal{H}$ as a random oracle. On the other hand, in the following proof, we assume that $\mathcal{B}$ is well-behaved in the sense that it always queries the random oracle $\mathcal{H}$ on the message m^* that it outputs as its forgery. According to [3], we know that it is trivial to modify any adversary-algorithm $\mathcal{B}$ to have this property.

W.L.O.G, assume there are n_1 possible signers $\{\mathcal{S}_1, \cdots, \mathcal{S}_{n_1}\}$. To simulate the environment of the scheme, $\mathcal{A}$ sets $(p, q, g, \mathcal{H})$ as the system-wide parameters where $\mathcal{H}$ is the random oracle controlled by $\mathcal{A}$. In addition, $\mathcal{A}$ picks n_1 random numbers $\{h_1, h_2, \cdots, h_{n_1}\}$ where each $h_i \in_R \mathbb{Z}_q^*$. $\mathcal{A}$ then computes $y_i = y^{h_i} \bmod p, 1 \leq i \leq n_{n_1}$ and sets $y_i, 1 \leq i \leq n_1$ as the public key of the possible signers $\mathcal{S}_i, 1 \leq i \leq n_1$. At the end of the system setting stage, $\mathcal{A}$ gives $(p, q, g, y_1, y_2, \cdots, y_{n_1})$ to $\mathcal{B}$ and allows $\mathcal{B}$ to run via Game A.

In this game, $\mathcal{B}$ takes part as a signature requester. $\mathcal{B}$ starts by sending $c_j = g^{r_j} y_i^{l_j}$ corresponding with a message set $\mathcal{M}_j = \{m_{j_1}, \cdots, m_{j_{n_2}}\}$ to $\mathcal{A}$ in order to get a signature on m_{l_j} signed by $\mathcal{S}_i$ in an oblivious way. For $\mathcal{S}_i$, its signing key should be $\log_g^{y_i}$ which is not known to the simulator $\mathcal{A}$. To respond to this query, for each request sent from $\mathcal{B}$, $\mathcal{A}$ does the following steps:

- For c_j, $\mathcal{A}$ picks $n_1 \times n_2$ random numbers $k_{(u,v)} \in_R \mathbb{Z}_q^*$ and
  - computes $K_{(u,v)} = g^{k_{(u,v)}} \bmod p$,
  - picks $\hat{s}_{(u,v)} \in_R \mathbb{Z}_q^*$,
  - sets $\hat{e}_{(u,v)} \leftarrow \mathcal{H}(m_v, K_{(u,v)} c_i / (g y_u)^v \bmod p)$.
- $\mathcal{A}$ returns $(\hat{e}_{(u,v)}, \hat{s}_{(u,v)}), 1 \leq u \leq n_1, 1 \leq v \leq n_2$, to $\mathcal{B}$ and records $(\mathcal{M}_i, c_i, K_{(u,v)}, \hat{e}_{(u,v)}, \hat{s}_{(u,v)}, 1 \leq u \leq n_1, 1 \leq v \leq n_2)$ to a Sign-List which is assumed to be initially empty.

The above execution can be executed at most t times. After the execution, $\mathcal{B}$ outputs its forgery $\sigma^* = (e^*, s^*)$ on a message m^*. Assume σ^* is a valid forgery on m^* signed by $\mathcal{S}^* \in \{\mathcal{S}_1, \cdots, \mathcal{S}_{n_1}\}$ and $\mathcal{B}$ wins Game A. According to the protocol, we have

$$e^* = \mathcal{H}(m^*, y^{*e^*} g^{s^*} \bmod p).$$

Since $\mathcal{B}$ is assumed to be well-behaved, we have $e^* = \mathcal{H}(m_v, K_{(u,v)}c_i/(gy_u)^v \bmod p) = \hat{e}_{(u,v)}$ for some $\hat{e}_{(u,v)}$ and $y^* = y^u, m^* = m_v$ which are recorded on the Sign-List.

According to the Forking Lemma [13]. By replaying the game with the same random tape but different choices of oracle $\mathcal{H}$, at the end of the second run, we obtain another valid forgery $(m^*, e^{*'}, s^{*'})$ on the same message m^* signed by the same signer $\mathcal{S}^*$. W.L.O.G, assume $\mathcal{S}^* = \mathcal{S}^a$ with public key $Y_a = y^{h_a} = g^{xh_a} \bmod p$. Since $s^* = k_{(a,v)} + r_j - l_v + x_a e^*$ and $s^{*'} = k_{(a,v)} + r_j - l_v + x_a e^{*'}$ for the same $k_{(a,v)} + r_j - l_v$ (according to the Forking Lemma), we obtain $x_a = xh_a = (s^* - s^{*'})(e^* - e^{*'})^{-1} \bmod q$. So, $\log_g^y = x = (s^* - s^{*'})(e^* - e^{*'})^{-1}h_a^{-1} \bmod q$. This is the solution to the DL problem. The advantage of $\mathcal{A}$ is the same as the advantage of $\mathcal{B}$ and the total running time T' of $\mathcal{A}$ is equal to the running time of the Forking Lemma [13] which is bound by $84480q_h T/\epsilon$. Here q_h is the number of hash queries in the game.   □

Theorem 1. The proposed scheme provides perfect security for recipients. In other words, the proposed scheme provides unconditional security on the ambiguity of the selected message as well as the selected signer.

Proof: It is sufficient to show that an attacker $\mathcal{F}$, taking parts as a signer, wins Game B with probability exactly the same as random guessing of $u \in \{a, b\}$ and $v \in \{0, 1\}$.

Assume $\mathcal{M} = \{m_1, \cdots, m_{n_2}\}$ and $c = g^r y_t^l \bmod p$, $t \in \{1, \cdots, n_1\}$, $l \in \{1, \cdots, n_2\}$, where c is chosen by the recipient $\mathcal{R}$. It is easy to see that for any such c, there exists an $r_{(i,j)} \in \mathbb{Z}_q$ such that

$$
\begin{aligned}
c &= g^r y_t^l &&\bmod p \\
&= g^{r(1,1)}y_1^1 = \cdots = g^{r(1,j)}y_1^j = \cdots = g^{r(1,n_2)}y_1^{n_2} &&\bmod p \\
&\qquad\qquad\qquad\qquad \vdots \\
&= g^{r(i,1)}y_i^1 = \cdots = g^{r(i,j)}y_i^j = \cdots = g^{r(i,n_2)}y_i^{n_2} &&\bmod p \\
&\qquad\qquad\qquad\qquad \vdots \\
&= g^{r(n_1,1)}y_{n_1}^1 = \cdots = g^{r(n_1,j)}y_{n_1}^j = \cdots = g^{r(n_1,n_2)}y_{n_1}^{n_2} &&\bmod p
\end{aligned}
$$

Consequently, we conclude that $\mathcal{F}$ wins Game B with probability exactly the same as random guessing of $u \in \{a, b\}$ and $v \in \{0, 1\}$. This ends the proof.   □

5   Conclusion

In 1994, Chen defined two types of oblivious signatures; an oblivious signature with n messages and, an oblivious signature with n keys. In 2008, Tso et al. gave formal definitions on the models of oblivious signatures and gave an example on the construction of oblivious signatures based on the Schnorr signature. In this paper, we combine the two functionalities into one scheme. We called it *Two-in-one oblivious signature*. In out scheme, a signature requester can ask 1-out-of-n_1 signers to sign 1-out-of-n_2 messages. At the end of our protocol, no one (including the n_1 possible-signers) knows who has really signed the message as well as which one of the n_2 message has been signed. The scheme is useful in many applications such as e-cash, e-voting and e-auction etc. We defined a formal model on our scheme and give a rigorous security proof based on the random oracle model.

Acknowledgement. This research was supported by the Ministry of Science of Technology, Taiwan, under the grants MOST 105-2221-E-004-001-MY3, MOST 104-2218-E-001-002 and by Taiwan Information Security Center (TWISC), Academia Sinica.

References

1. Birman, K., Jelasity, M., Kleinberg, R., Tremel, E.: Building a secure and privacy-preserving smart grid. ACM SIGOPS Oper. Syst. Rev. **49**(1), 131–136 (2015)
2. Baldimtsi, F., Lysyanskaya, A.: On the security of one-witness blind signature schemes. In: Sako, K., Sarkar, P. (eds.) ASIACRYPT 2013, Part II. LNCS, vol. 8270, pp. 82–99. Springer, Heidelberg (2013)
3. Boneh, D., Lynn, B., Shacham, H.: Short signatures from the Weil pairing. In: Boyd, C. (ed.) ASIACRYPT 2001. LNCS, vol. 2248, pp. 514–532. Springer, Heidelberg (2001)
4. Chaum, D.: Blind signatures for untraceable payments. Advances in Cryptology -CRYPTO 1982, pp. 199–203. Springer, Heidelberg (1983)
5. Chen, L.: Oblivious signatures. In: Gollmann, D. (ed.) ESORICS 1994. LNCS, vol. 875, pp. 161–172. Springer, Heidelberg (1994)
6. Chaum, D., van Heyst, E.: Group signatures. In: Davies, D.W. (ed.) EUROCRYPT 1991. LNCS, vol. 547, pp. 257–265. Springer, Heidelberg (1991)
7. Diao, F., Zhang, F., Cheng, X.: A privacy-preserving smart metering scheme using linkable anonymous credential. IEEE Trans. Smart Grid **6**(1), 461–467 (2015)
8. Fiat, A., Shamir, A.: How to prove yourself: a randomized protocol for signing contracts. In: Odlyzko, A.M. (ed.) CRYPTO 1986. LNCS, vol. 263, pp. 186–194. Springer, Heidelberg (1987)
9. Goldwasser, S., Micali, S., Rivest, R.: A digital signature scheme secure against adaptively chosen message attacks. SIAM J. Comput. **17**(2), 281–308 (1988)
10. Kaliski, Jr. B.S.: Privacy preserving data querying. U.S. Patent No. 20,160,085,987. 24. March 2016
11. Laguillaumie, F., Langlois, A., Libert, B., Stehlé, D.: Lattice-based group signatures with logarithmic signature size. In: Sako, K., Sarkar, P. (eds.) ASIACRYPT 2013, Part II. LNCS, vol. 8270, pp. 41–61. Springer, Heidelberg (2013)
12. Pasupuleti, S., Ramalingam, S., Buyya, R.: An efficient and secure privacy-preserving approach for outsourced data of resource constrained mobile devices in cloud computing. J. Netw. Comput. Appl. **64**, 12–22 (2016)
13. Pointcheval, D., Stern, J.: Security arguments for digital signatures and blind signatures. J. Cryptol. **13**(3), 361–396 (2000)
14. Rial, A., Danezis, G.: Privacy-preserving smart metering. In: Proceedings of the 10th Annual ACM Workshop on Privacy in the Electronic Society, pp. 49–60 (2011)

15. Rivest, R.L., Shamir, A., Tauman, Y.: How to leak a secret. In: Boyd, C. (ed.) ASIACRYPT 2001. LNCS, vol. 2248, pp. 552–565. Springer, Heidelberg (2001)
16. Schnorr, C.P.: Efficient signature generation by smart cards. J. Cryptol. **4**(3), 161–174 (1991)
17. Song, C., Yin, X., Liu, Y.: A practical electronic voting protocol based upon oblivious signature scheme, In: Proceedings of 2008 International Conference on Computational Intelligence and Security, pp. 381–384. IEEE (2008)
18. Tso, R., Okamoto, T., Okamoto, E.: 1-out-of-n oblivious signatures. In: Chen, L., Mu, Y., Susilo, W. (eds.) ISPEC 2008. LNCS, vol. 4991, pp. 45–55. Springer, Heidelberg (2008)
19. Tso, R.: A new way to generate a ring: universal ring signature. Comput. Math. Appl. **65**(9), 1350–1359 (2013)
20. Wang, J., Sun, B.: Ring signature schemes from lattice basis delegation. In: Qing, S., Susilo, W., Wang, G., Liu, D. (eds.) ICICS 2011. LNCS, vol. 7043, pp. 15–28. Springer, Heidelberg (2011)
21. Wang, H., Wu, Q., Qin, B., Zhang, F., Domingo-Ferrer, J.: A provably secure ring signature scheme with bounded leakage resilience. In: Huang, X., Zhou, J. (eds.) ISPEC 2014. LNCS, vol. 8434, pp. 388–402. Springer, Heidelberg (2014)
22. Yi, X., Rao, F.Y., Bertino, E., Bouguettaya, A.: Privacy-preserving association rule mining in cloud computing. In: Proceedings of the 10th ACM Symposium on Information, Computer and Communications Security, pp. 439–450 (2015)
23. Yang, J.J., Li, J.Q., Niu, Y.: A hybrid solution for privacy preserving medical data sharing in the cloud environment. Future Gen. Comput. Syst. **43**, 74–86 (2015)
24. Zhou, J., Lin, X., Dong, X., Cao, Z.: PSMPA: patient self-controllable and multi-level privacy-preserving cooperative authentication in distributed m-Healthcare cloud computing system. IEEE Trans. Parallel Distrib. Syst. **26**(6), 1693–1703 (2015)
25. Zhou, J., Cao, Z., Dong, X., Xiong, N., Vasilakos, A.V.: 4S: a secure and privacy-preserving key management scheme for cloud-assisted wireless body area network in m-healthcare social networks. Inf. Sci. **314**, 255–276 (2015)

A New Transitive Signature Scheme

Chao Lin[1], Fei Zhu[1], Wei Wu[1(✉)], Kaitai Liang[2],
and Kim-Kwang Raymond Choo[3,4]

[1] Fujian Provincial Key Laboratory of Network Security and Cryptology,
School of Mathematics and Computer Science, Fujian Normal University,
Fuzhou 350007, China
weiwu81@gmail.com
[2] Department of Computer Science, Aalto University, Espoo, Finland
[3] Department of Information Systems and Cyber Security,
University of Texas at San Antonio, San Antonio, USA
[4] School of Information Technology & Mathematical Sciences,
University of South Australia, Adelaide, Australia

Abstract. We present a novel design for stateless transitive signature (TS) for undirected graph to authenticate dynamically growing graph data. Our construction is built on the widely studied ZSS signature technology [19] with bilinear mapping, and using general cryptographic hash functions (e.g., SHA-512 and MD6). Compared with the existing stateless TS schemes for undirected graph in the literature, our scheme is more efficient. The scheme is also proven transitively unforgeable against adaptive chosen-message attack under the M2SDH assumption in the random oracle model.

Keywords: M2SDH · Transitive signature · Transitively unforgeability

1 Introduction

Transitive signature has attracted significant attention from both researcher and practitioners because of its practical functionality in offering authenticated mechanism for dynamically growing graph data [2]. As a case study, we consider the authenticity of a graph data system as a set of administrative domains, i.e., data represented by (undirected) graphs. We let the vertices i, j in the graph represent two distinct computers. We say that they are in the same administrative domain if and only if the edge (i, j) exists. In a transitive signature scheme, given the transitive signatures of the edge (i, j) and the edge (j, k), one is able to obtain a valid signature of the edge (i, k) without any interaction with the original signer (of the two signatures). In addition, the security of transitive signature schemes guarantees that even being able to adaptively request all valid transitive signatures of graph G, the signature forger cannot forge the signature of a new vertex or other edge outside the transitive closure of G in polynomial-time (i.e. achieving transitively unforgeability). We refer the interested reader to Sect. 3 for the formal security notion. Transitive signature technology has a number of

© Springer International Publishing AG 2016
J. Chen et al. (Eds.): NSS 2016, LNCS 9955, pp. 156–167, 2016.
DOI: 10.1007/978-3-319-46298-1_11

practical advantages. For example, it can reduce the amount of edge signatures and the corresponding computational complexity (when the signature objects are in a transitive graph).

Related Work. Micali and Rivest [12] introduced the seminal notion of transitive signatures in 2002. They proposed two schemes: one is proven transitively unforgeable against adaptive chosen message attacks under discrete logarithm assumption, and the other is merely proven transitively unforgeable against non-adaptive chosen message attacks under RSA assumption. Later, Bellare and Neven constructed several schemes, which are proved under some complexity assumptions (e.g., the factoring problem, the one-more discrete logarithm problem and the gap Diffie-Hellman groups), in the standard model. Another contribution of [2] is to propose the hash-based variants of their schemes so as to eliminate the need of node certificates. That decreases the computation cost of the original systems but with a price that the security is only proved in the random oracle model. Moreover, these variants mainly depend on the design of a special type of hash function (e.g., an admissible encoding function called Map-ToPoint) that is hard to be practically built. Although there have been many attempts on building the hash algorithm in the literature, all the constructions are probabilistic and generally inefficient. There is no a stateless transitive signature scheme for undirected graph without using any special hash function. This becomes our motivation of this work. We note that there also exist other transitive signature schemes, in which most of them are all for undirected graph only [8,11,15,16].

As mentioned in [1], a directed transitive signature scheme (DTS) considers a directed graph as a military command system, where vertices denote objects, and a directed edge (u, v) from u to v denotes that v is subordinate to u. Obviously, if v is subordinate to u and w is subordinate to v, w is subordinate to u. However, it is exactly an open problem of designing directed transitive signatures by Micali and Rivest [1], for which Hohenberger [14] showed that DTS may be very hard to construct because the signing algorithm in such schemes forms a special Abelian trapdoor group with infeasible inversion, whose construction remains unknown.

All existing directed transitive signature schemes have been proposed on a special directed graph, i.e., directed tree. In 2006, Yi [18] proposed a DTS scheme, which is proven transitively unforgeable in the standard model under the RSA inversion assumption. Neven in [13] presented a DTS by intaking any standard signatures, which is only supporting for directed tree. The scheme can be proven transitively unforgeable if the underlying standard signature scheme is unforgeable. Moreover, the proposed scheme [13] does not rely on any RSA-related problems but enjoys less computation cost and shorter signature length (considering the worst case) compared to that of Yi. In 2011, Camacho and Hevia [7] introduced a practical DTS using a new variant of collision resistance hash function with common-prefix proofs (CRHwCPP), which is also for directed tree only but with the best efficiency.

1.1 Our Contributions

The present paper introduces a new stateless transitive signature scheme for undirected graph. Our signing algorithm does not need to preserve the status information for each signed node in the graph. Besides, the security of our novel scheme is based on assuming the M2SDH problem is hard. Compared with the stateless schemes in [2], our proposed scheme is with less computational time for using only general hash functions, such as MD6 or SHA-512, instead of the special hash functions (introduced by [2]). Furthermore, our scheme is proven existentially unforgeable under the M2SDH assumption in the random oracle model.

1.2 Organization

The remainder of our paper is organized as follows. Section 2 provides some preliminaries. The formal system definition and security notion of TS are reviewed in Sect. 3. Section 4 recalls Bellare and Neven's Constructions. Section 5 introduces our SDHUTS scheme but also presents its security and performance analysis. We make conclusion in Sect. 6.

2 Preliminaries

This section introduces the preliminaries that will be used in our construction.

2.1 Notations

The notation $\mathbb{N} = \{1, 2, \ldots N\}$ denotes the set of positive integers from 1 to N, and $x \xleftarrow{R} \mathbb{S}$ denotes that x is chosen randomly and uniformly from the set $\mathbb{S}$. We call a function $f : \mathbb{N} \to \mathbb{R}$ is negligible if for each $m > 0$, there exists n_0 for all $n > n_0 : f(n) < 1/n^m$. If an algorithm is probabilistic and its running time is polynomial, we call it a $\mathcal{PPT}$ algorithm.

2.2 Graphs

All graphs we consider in this paper are all undirected. Denote $G = (V, E)$ as an undirected graph, where V denotes a finite set of vertices and $E \subseteq V \times V$ denotes a finite set of edges. The transitive closure $\widetilde{G} = (\widetilde{V}, \widetilde{E})$ of a graph $G = (V, E)$ is defined to have $\widetilde{V} = V$ and to have an edge $(i, j) \in \widetilde{E}$ when and only when there is a path between i and j in G. The transitive reduction of G is denoted as $G^* = (V^*, E^*)$, where $V^* = V$ and G has the minimum subset of edges with the same transitive closure as G.

2.3   Bilinear Mapping

This section reviews some notions about Bilinear Mapping [4–6,9].

Denote $\mathbb{G}_1$ as a cyclic multiplicative group, whose order is a prime p, generated by g_1. And $\mathbb{G}_2$ is denoted as a cyclic multiplicative group, which has the same order with $\mathbb{G}_1$. We denote $e : \mathbb{G}_1 \times \mathbb{G}_1 \to \mathbb{G}_2$ as a bilinear mapping with three properties as follows:

1. **Bilinear:** $\forall g, h \in \mathbb{G}_1$ and $a, b \in \mathbb{Z}_p$, $e(g^a, h^b) = e(g, h)^{ab}$.
2. **Non-degenerate:** $\exists g_1, h_1 \in \mathbb{G}_1$ such that $e(g_1, h_1) \neq 1$.
3. **Computable:** $\forall g_1, h_1 \in \mathbb{G}_1$, $e(g_1, h_1)$ can be computed efficiently.

What the above properties imply are: for any $g, h_1, h_2 \in \mathbb{G}_1$, $e(g, h_1 h_2) = e(g, h_1) \cdot e(g, h_2)$; $\forall g, h \in \mathbb{G}_1, e(g, h) = e(h, g)$. In our definitions, if $\mathbb{G}_1$ is generated by g_1, then $\mathbb{G}_2$ is generated by $e(g_1, g_1)$.

2.4   Complexity Assumptions

We denote $\mathbb{G}$ as a cyclic group generated by g, whose order is a prime p.

q-Strong Diffie-Hellman Problem. We define the q-SDH problem in $\mathbb{G}$ as follows: Given a $\mathcal{PPT}$ adversary $\mathcal{A}$ a $(q + 1)$-tuple $(g, g^x, g^{x^2}, \ldots, g^{x^q})$ as input, outputs a pair $(a, g^{\frac{1}{x+a}})$ where $a \in \mathbb{Z}_p^*$ and solves q-SDH with a non-negligible probability ϵ in $\mathbb{G}$ if

$$Pr[\mathcal{A}(g, g^x, g^{(x^2)}, \ldots, g^{(x^q)}) = (a, g^{\frac{1}{x+a}})] \geq \epsilon,$$

The q-SDH assumption is that there is not a $\mathcal{PPT}$ algorithm exist to solve the q-SDH problem with ϵ. We refer the readers to [3,10,17,19] to get more details.

Modified q-Strong Diffie-Hellman Poblem. We define the MqSDH problem in $\mathbb{G}$ as follows: Given a $\mathcal{PPT}$ adversary $\mathcal{A}$ a $(q + 1)$-tuple $(g, g^x, g^{x^2}, \ldots, g^{x^q})$ as input, outputs a triple $(a, b, g^{\frac{1}{x+a} - \frac{1}{x+b}})$ where $a, b \in \mathbb{Z}_p^*$ and has a non-negligible probability ϵ in solving MqSDH in $\mathbb{G}$ if

$$Pr[\mathcal{A}(g, g^x, g^{(x^2)}, \ldots, g^{(x^q)}) = (a, b, g^{\frac{1}{x+a} - \frac{1}{x+b}})] \geq \epsilon,$$

The MqSDH assumption is that there is not a $\mathcal{PPT}$ algorithm exist to solve the MqSDH problem with ϵ.

Modified 2-Strong Diffie-Hellman Problem. We define the M2SDH problem in $\mathbb{G}$ as follows: Given a $\mathcal{PPT}$ adversary $\mathcal{A}$ a triple (g, g^x, g^{x^2}) as input, has access to an modified q-SDH-inversion oracle $\mathcal{O}^{\mathsf{INV}}(\cdot, \cdot)$ that given $(a, b) \in \mathbb{Z}_p^*$ returns $g^{\frac{1}{x+a} - \frac{1}{x+b}}$, and has a non-negligible probability ϵ in solving M2SDH in $\mathbb{G}$ if

$$Pr[\mathcal{A}(g, g^x, g^{x^2}) = (a^*, b^*, g^{\frac{1}{x+a^*} - \frac{1}{x+b^*}})] \geq \epsilon, \text{ where}$$

1. (a^*, b^*) is not one of its previous oracle queries.
2. There does not exist a $c \in \mathbb{Z}_p^*$ that $(a^*, c), (c, b^*)$ are in its previous oracle queries.

3. There does not exist any $c_i \in \mathbb{Z}_p^* (i = 1, 2, \ldots)$ that $(a^*, c_1), (c_1, c_2), \ldots, (c_i, c_{i+1}), (c_{i+1}, b^*)$ are in its previous oracle queries.

The M2SDH assumption is that there is not a $\mathcal{PPT}$ algorithm exist to solve the M2DH problem with ϵ.

3   Transitive Signatures

This section reviews the definition of Transitive Signatures (TS). A transitive signature scheme is defined by four algorithms: TS = (TKG, TSign, TVf, Comp).

- $(tpk, tsk) \leftarrow$ TKG(1^k): The Transitive Key Generation algorithm (TKG) takes as input the security parameter 1^k, and outputs a pair (tpk, tsk) as the signer's public/private key-pair.
- $\sigma_{ij} \leftarrow$ TSign(tsk, i, j): The Transitive Signing algorithm (TSign) takes as input the private key tsk and nodes $i, j \in V$, and outputs a signature on edge (i, j) relative to tsk. TSign may maintain state between invocations in some stateful schemes.
- $\{0, 1\} \leftarrow$ TVf(tpk, σ_{ij}, i, j): The deterministic Transitive Verification algorithm (TVf) takes as input tpk, nodes i, j and a candidate signature σ_{ij} on edge (i, j), and outputs either 1 or 0. If the output is 1, σ_{ij} is a valid signature on edge (i, j).
- $\{\sigma_{ik}, \perp\} \leftarrow$ Comp($tpk, \sigma_{ij}, \sigma_{jk}, i, j, k$): The deterministic Composition algorithm (Comp) takes as input nodes $i, j, k \in V$ and edge signatures on σ_{ij}, σ_{jk}, and outputs a composed signature σ_{ik} of edge $(i, k) \in E$ if both σ_{ij} and σ_{jk} are valid; otherwise, it outputs $\perp$ to indicate failure.

Consistence of TS Schemes. Apart from the above, we also require two consistency properties in TS.

1. TVf Consistency of TSign: signatures generated by TSign must be accepted as valid by TVf.
2. TVf Consistency of Comp: signatures generated by Comp must be accepted as valid by TVf.

3.1   Unforgeability

This section recalls the security notion of [1]. Let a $\mathcal{PPT}$ algorithm $\mathcal{F}$ (called a tu-cma forger) be an adaptive chosen-message forger against a transitive signature scheme TS = (TKG, TSign, TVf, Comp). Here we define the unforgeability through the game between $\mathcal{F}$ and a challenger $\mathcal{C}$ as follows:

- Setup: $\mathcal{C}$ runs TKG with the input 1^k to obtain a public/private key-pair (tpk, tsk). Then $\mathcal{C}$ sends tpk to the forger $\mathcal{F}$.
- TSign queries: $\mathcal{F}$ is able to query the signature σ_{ij} on edge (i, j) that can be adaptively chosen by him. In reply to $\mathcal{F}$, $\mathcal{C}$ runs TSign to get the edge signature σ_{ij} and returns σ_{ij} to $\mathcal{F}$.

Here we denote E' as the set consists of all edges (i, j) queried by $\mathcal{F}$ to TSign oracle, and denote V' as the set consists of all nodes in E'. Finally, $\mathcal{F}$ forges a signature σ^* on edge (i^*, j^*) with the given public key tpk by $\mathcal{C}$. $\mathcal{F}$ wins the game if:

1. $\mathsf{TVf}(tpk, \sigma^*, i^*, j^*) = 1$.
2. $(i^*, j^*) \notin \widetilde{G'}$, where $\widetilde{G'} = (V', \widetilde{E'})$ is the transitive closure of graph $G' = (V', E')$.

The advantage of an adaptive chosen-message forger $\mathcal{F}$ with public key winning the game is denoted as $\mathsf{Adv}_{\mathcal{F},\mathrm{TS}}^{tu-cma}$. A TS scheme is transitively unforgeable against adaptive chosen-message attacks if $\mathsf{Adv}_{\mathcal{F},\mathrm{TS}}^{tu-cma}$ is negligible for any forger $\mathcal{F}$ with the polynomial running time.

3.2 Privacy

As mentioned in [12], in a transitive signature scheme, a valid composed signature should be indistinguishable from a valid original signature on the same edge, which means that composition algorithm can work even if the given signatures were obtained via composition algorithm.

4 Bellare and Neven's Constructions

This section recalls Bellare and Neven's constructions in [2], all of which are constructed without the need of node certificates. Although these stateless schemes are more efficient than the stateful ones in [2], they are all based on a special type of hash function (MapToPoint) which is hard to be practically built for now. Three stateless schemes (RSATS-2, FactTS-2 and GapTS-2) were proposed in [2], here we only take the RSATS-2 as an example. For more details of other schemes, the interested reader can refer to [2].

The RSATS-2 proposed by Bellare and Neven [2] eliminates node certificates and the basic edge signature for an edge (i, j) is a triple (h_i, h_j, δ_{ij}), where $h_i = H(i), h_j = H(j), H : \mathbb{N} \to \mathbb{Z}_N^*$ is a random function and $\delta_{ij} = (h_i h_j^{-1})^d$, where $(N, e, d) \leftarrow K_{rsa}(1^k)$, K_{rsa} is a RSA key generator and k is a security parameter. Composition of two signatures (h_i, h_j, δ_{ij}) and (h_j, h_k, δ_{jk}) is done by computing $\delta_{ik} \leftarrow \delta_{ij} \cdot \delta_{jk}$ and returning the triple (h_i, h_k, δ_{ik}). Note that node certificates are eliminated in RSATS-2, but node certificates σ_i and σ_j are required in RSATS-1 [2] and the basic edge signature for (i, j) is a tuple $(L_i, \sigma_i, L_j, \sigma_j, \delta_{ij})$. One can find that RSATS-2 is more efficient than RSATS-1, especially when the number of nodes is with an exponential increase. The problem is how to avoid using the special hash function and construct practical stateless schemes.

5 Our Construction

This section describes the proposed Transitive Signature (TS) scheme with the corresponding correctness, security and performance analysis.

5.1 Concrete Scheme

In this work, we design a new stateless (i.e., the signing algorithm does not need to keep state information for queried nodes in the graph) transitive signature scheme (called SDHUTS) for undirected graph, which is securely proved under the M2SDH assumption. Different from the approaches of [2], we make use of general cryptographic hashing such as MD6 or SHA-512 instead of special hash functions in [2]. The reason why we choose MD6 and SHA-512 is that they are practical to build and more secure than MD5 and SHA-1.

Our scheme is described as follows. System parameters involved in our scheme are $\{\mathbb{G}_1, \mathbb{G}_2, e, p, g, H\}$, where $H : \{0,1\}^* \to \{0,1\}^\lambda$ is a cryptographic hash function, g is a generator of $\mathbb{G}_1$ and $|p| \geq \lambda \geq 160$.

- TKG: Choose $x \xleftarrow{R} \mathbb{Z}_p^*$, and compute $y = g^x \in \mathbb{G}_1$ and $Y = y^x \in \mathbb{G}_1$. The public key is (g, y, Y) and the private key is x.
- TSign: Given a private key x and nodes $i, j \in \mathbb{N}$, the algorithm computes $\sigma_{ij} = g^{\frac{1}{h_i+x} - \frac{1}{h_j+x}}$, where $h_i = H(i), h_j = H(j)$. In general, we assume that $i < j$. If the above case does not happen, one can swap i and j. It returns the signature σ_{ij} on edge (i, j).
- TVf: Given a public key (g, y, Y), nodes $i, j \subset \mathbb{N}$ and a candidate signature σ_{ij}, the algorithm computes $h_i = H(i)$ and $h_j = H(j)$, and accepts when and only when $e(g^{h_i h_j} y^{h_i + h_j} Y, \sigma_{ij}) = e(g^{h_j - h_i}, g)$.
- Comp: Given two candidate signatures σ_{ij} on (i, j) and σ_{jk} on (j, k), if $\mathsf{TVf}(pk, i, j, \sigma_{ij}) = 0$ or $\mathsf{TVf}(pk, j, k, \sigma_{jk}) = 0$, the algorithm returns $\perp$ as an indication of failure. Otherwise, the algorithm returns $\sigma_{ik} = \sigma_{ij} \cdot \sigma_{jk}$ as the composed signature on edge (i, k). In general, we also assume that $i < j < k$. If the above case does not happen, one can swap these two signatures.

5.2 Correctness

Consistence of SDHUTS. Here, we show two consistency properties in our SDHUTS.

1. TVf Consistency of TSign: If $\sigma_{ij} = \mathsf{TSign}(tsk, i, j) = g^{\frac{1}{h_i+x} - \frac{1}{h_j+x}}$, where $h_i = H(i), h_j = H(j)$, then

$$e(g^{h_i h_j} y^{h_i + h_j} Y, \sigma_{ij}) = e(g^{h_i h_j + x(h_i + h_j) + x^2}, g^{\frac{1}{h_i+x} - \frac{1}{h_j+x}})$$
$$= e(g^{(h_i+x)(h_j+x)}, g^{\frac{1}{h_i+x}}) \cdot e(g^{(h_i+x)(h_j+x)}, g^{\frac{1}{h_j+x}})^{-1}$$
$$= e(g^{(h_j+x)}, g) \cdot e(g^{-(h_i+x)}, g) = e(g^{h_j - h_i}, g).$$

Therefore $\mathsf{TVf}(tpk, \mathsf{TSign}(tsk, i, j), i, j) = 1$.

2. TVf Consistency of Comp: If $\sigma_{ik} = \sigma_{ij} \cdot \sigma_{jk} = g^{\frac{1}{h_i+x} - \frac{1}{h_j+x}} \cdot g^{\frac{1}{h_j+x} - \frac{1}{h_k+x}} = g^{\frac{1}{h_i+x} - \frac{1}{h_k+x}}$, where $h_i = H(i), h_j = H(j), h_k = H(k)$, then

$$e(g^{h_i h_k} y^{h_i+h_k} Y, \sigma_{ik}) = e(g^{h_i h_k + x(h_i+h_k) + x^2}, g^{\frac{1}{h_i+x} - \frac{1}{h_k+x}})$$
$$= e(g^{(h_i+x)(h_k+x)}, g^{\frac{1}{h_i+x}}) \cdot e(g^{(h_i+x)(h_k+x)}, g^{\frac{1}{h_k+x}})^{-1}$$
$$= e(g^{(h_k+x)}, g) \cdot e(g^{-(h_i+x)}, g) = e(g^{h_k - h_i}, g).$$

Therefore $\mathsf{TVf}(tpk, \mathsf{Comp}(tpk, \sigma_{ij}, \sigma_{jk}, i, j, k), i, k) = 1$.

5.3   Security Analysis

We present the security results of our SDHUTS with the following two theorems and give formal proofs in this section.

Theorem 1 (Unforgeability of SDHUTS). *If the t'-M2SDH assumption is hard, then our proposed SDHUTS is transitively unforgeable against a (t, q_H, q_S) adaptive chosen message forger $\mathcal{F}$ in the random-oracle model.*

Proof. Suppose that there is a $\mathcal{PPT}$ forger $\mathcal{F}$ who is able to break the unforgeability of our proposed SDHUTS with a non-negligible advantage $\mathsf{Adv}^{tu-cma}_{\mathcal{F},SDHUTS}(k)$. We consider a $\mathcal{PPT}$ M2SDH adversary $\mathcal{A}$ that $\forall k \in \mathbb{N}$,

$$\mathsf{Adv}^{M2SDH}_{\mathcal{A}}(k) \geq \mathsf{Adv}^{tu-cma}_{\mathcal{F},SDHUTS}(k).$$

Given a random instance $(g, g^x, g^{x^2}) \in \mathbb{G}_1$, $\mathcal{A}$ can also gain access to an modified q-SDH-inversion oracle $\mathcal{O}^{INV}(\cdot, \cdot)$ of the M2SDH problem, where $\mathbb{G}_1$ is generated by g, for some x selected randomly from $\mathbb{Z}_p^*$. Algorithm $\mathcal{A}$'s aim is to output a triple $(a^*, b^*, g^{\frac{1}{x+a^*} - \frac{1}{x+b^*}})$ $(a^*, b^* \in \mathbb{Z}_p^*)$, without querying (a^*, b^*) itself, or $(a^*, c), (c, b^*)$ (for some $c \in \mathbb{Z}_p^*$), or $(a^*, c_1), (c_1, c_2), \ldots, (c_i, c_{i+1}), (c_{i+1}, b^*)$ (for some $c_i \in \mathbb{Z}_p^*, i = 1, 2, \ldots$) to the modified q-SDH-inversion oracle. Denote V' as the set consists of all queried vertices. Denote $\triangle : V' \times V' \rightarrow G'$ as a function storing all queried edge signatures. Algorithm $\mathcal{A}$ does the following by interacting with forger $\mathcal{F}$:

- Setup: $\mathcal{A}$ sets $y = g^x$ and $Y = g^{x^2}$, then sends (g, y, Y) to $\mathcal{F}$. From the perspective of the forger $\mathcal{F}$ all the distributions are identical to the real construction.
- Hash queries: $\mathcal{A}$ maintains a table to record queried hash values that represents H. When $\mathcal{F}$ queries $H(i)$, $\mathcal{A}$ proceeds as follows:
  1. If i is not in V' then $V' \leftarrow V' \cup i$; $H(i) \xleftarrow{R} \mathbb{Z}_p^*$; $\Delta(i, i) \leftarrow 1$
  2. Return $H(i)$ to $\mathcal{F}$
- TSign queries: Suppose $\mathcal{F}$ asks for a signature on edge (i, j) chosen by himself. In reply, $\mathcal{A}$ must generate a valid signature σ_{ij}. Here, $\mathcal{A}$ utilizes the modified q-SDH-inversion oracle to compute the edge signature. Note that $\mathcal{A}$ calls the inversion oracle only when he cannot compute the requested signature through composing previously signed edges. Therefore $\mathcal{A}$ does the following:

1. If $i > j$ then swap (i, j)
2. If $i \notin V'$ then $V' \leftarrow V' \cup i$; $H(i) \overset{R}{\leftarrow} \mathbb{Z}_p^*$; $\Delta(i, i) \leftarrow 1$
3. If $j \notin V'$ then $V' \leftarrow V' \cup j$; $H(j) \overset{R}{\leftarrow} \mathbb{Z}_p^*$; $\Delta(j, j) \leftarrow 1$
4. If $\Delta(i, j)$ is not defined then
5. $\Delta(i, j) \leftarrow \mathcal{O}^{\mathsf{INV}}(H(i), H(j))$
6. $\Delta(j, i) \leftarrow \Delta(i, j)^{-1}$
7. For all $v \in V' \setminus \{i, j\}$ do
8. If $\Delta(v, i)$ is defined then
9. $\Delta(v, j) \leftarrow \Delta(v, i) \cdot \Delta(i, j)$
10. $\Delta(j, v) \leftarrow \Delta(v, j)^{-1}$
11. If $\Delta(v, j)$ is defined then
12. $\Delta(v, i) \leftarrow \Delta(v, j) \cdot \Delta(j, i)$
13. $\Delta(i, v) \leftarrow \Delta(v, i)^{-1}$
14. $\sigma_{ij} \leftarrow \Delta(i, j)$
15. Return σ_{ij} to $\mathcal{F}$

Eventually, $\mathcal{F}$ returns a forgery signature σ^* on edge (i^*, j^*). In general, if $i^* > j^*$, then one can swap i^* and j^*. Denote $G' = (V', E')$ as the graph involved in the signatures queried by $\mathcal{F}$, and denote $\widetilde{G'} = (V', \widetilde{E'})$ as the transitive closure of G'. We can suppose that the hash oracle on i^* and j^* has been queried by $\mathcal{F}$, meaning that $i^*, j^* \in V'$; otherwise $\mathcal{A}$ is able to query the hash oracle itself after $\mathcal{F}$ outputs the forgery. σ^* is said to be a valid forgery, if the forgery satisfies the following:

1. $\mathsf{TVf}(tpk, \sigma^*, i^*, j^*) = 1$, that is: $\sigma^* = g^{\frac{1}{x+H(i^*)} - \frac{1}{x+H(j^*)}}$.
2. $(i^*, j^*) \notin \widetilde{G'}$, that is: σ^* cannot be computed simply and directly by composing previously signed edges in $\widetilde{G'}$.

Therefore, $\mathcal{A}$ outputs a solution $(H(i^*), H(j^*), \sigma^*)$ to $\mathcal{A}$'s challenge.

$\mathcal{F}$ is unable to distinguish $\mathcal{A}$'s simulation from the real scheme on account of simulating the hash function as a random-oracle in our proof. And $\mathcal{A}$'s running time is $t' = t$. Next, we discuss the probability of $\mathcal{A}$ not aborting. Obviously, $\mathcal{A}$ will not abort during Hash, TSign queries, therefore we have

$$\mathsf{Adv}_{\mathcal{A}}^{\mathrm{M2SDH}}(k) \geq \mathsf{Adv}_{\mathcal{F}, \mathrm{SDHUTS}}^{tu-cma}(k).$$

This completes the proof of Theorem 1.

Theorem 2 (Privacy of SDHUTS). *If the composition algorithm of SDHUTS is invoked on valid signatures, then it returns the same signature as the signer would have produced.*

Proof. Denote i, j, k as distinct nodes, where $i < j < k$. Suppose $\sigma_{ij} = g^{\frac{1}{h_i+x} - \frac{1}{h_j+x}}$ is a valid signature on edge (i, j) relative to (y, Y), where $h_i = H(i)$, $h_j = H(j)$, $y = g^x$ and $Y = g^{x^2}$. Suppose σ_{jk} is also a valid signature on edge (j, k) relative to (y, Y), where $h_j = H(j)$, $h_k = H(k)$. Take σ_{ij}, σ_{jk} as inputs, the composition algorithm of SDHUTS is defined to return σ_{ik} where

$$\sigma_{ik} = \sigma_{ij} \cdot \sigma_{jk} = g^{\frac{1}{h_i+x} - \frac{1}{h_j+x}} \cdot g^{\frac{1}{h_j+x} - \frac{1}{h_k+x}} = g^{\frac{1}{h_i+x} - \frac{1}{h_k+x}}.$$

Therefore, the composed signature in SDHUTS scheme is the same as the signature could have been produced by the original signer, and the proposed SDHUTS scheme satisfies the privacy of transitive signatures. This completes the proof of Theorem 2.

5.4 Comparison and Performance Analysis

In this section, we firstly compare the proposed scheme with some stateless schemes in [2] in terms of the computation cost. We denote $\mathbb{G}$ as the group of prime order p, and N as a modulus product of two big primes are utilized in the RSA and some schemes based integer factoring. Denote S_{ddh} as the decision Diffie-Hellman algorithm in $\widetilde{\mathbb{G}}$, where $\widetilde{\mathbb{G}}$ is a gap Diffie-Hellman group. Let $\mathsf{P_m}$ be the point scalar-multiplication in $\mathbb{G}$, $\mathsf{P_a}$ be the point addition in $\mathbb{G}$, $\mathsf{P_{Inv}}$ be the inversion in $\mathbb{Z}_p^*$ and $\mathsf{P_{MTP}}$ be the MapToPoint hash operation. Abbreviations are used as follows: "Exp." represents a modular exponentiation in $\mathbb{G}$; "RSA Enc." represents an RSA encryption; "RSA Dec." represents an RSA decryption; "Sq.r." represents a square root modulo N performed given the prime factors of N; and "Ops." represents the number of bit operations. Table 1 summarizes the comparison without considering the general hash operation.

Table 1. The comparison between our scheme and the stateless schemes in [2]

Scheme	Signing cost	Verification cost	Composition cost	Signature size
RSATS-2	$2\mathsf{P_{MTP}}+1\mathsf{P_{Inv}}+1\mathsf{P_m}+1$RSA Dec.	$2\mathsf{P_{MTP}}+1\mathsf{P_{Inv}}+1\mathsf{P_m}+1$RSA Enc.	$O(|N|^2)$ Ops	1 point in $\mathbb{Z}_N^*$
FactTS-2	$2\mathsf{P_{MTP}}+1\mathsf{P_{Inv}}+1\mathsf{P_m}+2$Sq.r. in $\mathbb{Z}_N^*$	$2\mathsf{P_{MTP}}+1\mathsf{P_{Inv}}+1\mathsf{P_m}+O(|N|^2)$ Ops.	$O(|N|^2)$ Ops	1 point in $\mathbb{Z}_N^*$
GapTS-2	$2\mathsf{P_{MTP}}+1\mathsf{P_{Inv}}+1\mathsf{P_m}+1$Exp. in $\widetilde{\mathbb{G}}$	$2\mathsf{P_{MTP}}+1\mathsf{P_{Inv}}+1\mathsf{P_m}+1S_{ddh}$	$O(|N|^2)$ Ops	1 point in $\widetilde{\mathbb{G}}$
SDHUTS	$2\mathsf{P_{Inv}}+3\mathsf{P_a}+1$Exp. in $\widetilde{\mathbb{G}}$	$3\mathsf{P_m}+2\mathsf{P_a}+1S_{ddh}$	$O(|N|^2)$ Ops	1 point in $\widetilde{\mathbb{G}}$

As mentioned in [19], one MapToPoint hash operation is more costly than one inversion operation in $\mathbb{Z}_q^*$. One can find that the signing and verification cost of SDHUTS are dramatically decreased (compared to those in Table 1), which provides a more efficient stateless and undirected transitive scheme.

We further show the time cost of sub algorithms of our proposed SDHUTS scheme. Here, we leverage the pairing-based library (version 0.5.12)[1] for our simulation. The composition algorithm in our scheme is one multiply computation, which is so simple that testing the composition operation cost can be ignored. Table 2 shows the tested information in our simulation, while Table 3 illustrates the time cost in our simulation. Tables 1 and 3 present that both signing and verification algorithms in our scheme are more efficient than the previous stateless and undirected transitive signature schemes.

---
[1] http://crypto.stanford.edu/pbc/.

Table 2. Simulation testbed

Operating system	Ubuntu 10.10
CPU	Intel Pentium Processor T4400
Memory	2.00 GB RAM
Hard disk	250 GB/5400 rpm
Program language	C

Table 3. Time cost (in s)

Algorithm	TKG	TSign	TVf
Max time	0.035832	0.018031	0.075022
Min time	0.012003	0.00551	0.056353
Average time	0.0252703	0.0104151	0.0639796

6 Conclusion

We proposed a novel stateless transitive signature scheme for undirected graph. Our scheme is the most efficient one among all the existing stateless transitive signature schemes. Furthermore, we proved the security of our scheme in the random oracle model assuming the M2SDH problem is hard.

Acknowledgement. This work is supported by National Natural Science Foundation of China (61472083, 61402110), Program for New Century Excellent Talents in Fujian University (JA14067), Distinguished Young Scholars Fund of Fujian (2016J06013) and Fujian Normal University Innovative Research Team (IRTL1207). K. Liang is supported by privacy-aware retrieval and modelling of genomic data (No. 13283250), the Academy of Finland.

References

1. Bellare, M., Neven, G.: Transitive signatures based on factoring and RSA. In: Zheng, Y. (ed.) ASIACRYPT 2002. LNCS, pp. 397–414. Springer, Heidelberg (2002). doi:10.1007/3-540-36178-2_25
2. Bellare, M., Neven, G.: Transitive signatures: new schemes and proofs. IEEE Trans. Inf. Theor. **51**(6), 2133–2151 (2005). doi:10.1007/3-540-36178-2_25
3. Boneh, D., Boyen, X.: Short signatures without random oracles. IACR CryptologyePrint Archive 2004, 171 (2004). http://eprint.iacr.org/2004/171
4. Boneh, D., Gentry, C., Lynn, B., Shacham, H.: Aggregate and verifiably encrypted signatures from bilinear maps. In: Biham, E. (ed.) EUROCRYPT 2003. LNCS, vol. 2656, pp. 416–432. Springer, Heidelberg (2003). doi:10.1007/3-540-39200-9_26
5. Boyen, X., Waters, B.: Compact group signatures without random oracles. In: Vaudenay, S. (ed.) EUROCRYPT 2006. LNCS, vol. 4004, pp. 427–444. Springer, Heidelberg (2006). doi:10.1007/11761679_26

6. Boyen, X., Waters, B.: Full-domain subgroup hiding and constant-size group signatures. In: Okamoto, T., Wang, X. (eds.) PKC 2007. LNCS, vol. 4450. Springer, Heidelberg (2007). doi:10.1007/978-3-540-71677-8_1
7. Camacho, P., Hevia, A.: Short transitive signatures for directed trees. IACR Cryptology ePrint Archive 2011, 438 (2011). http://eprint.iacr.org/2011/438
8. Gong, Z., Huang, Z., Qiu, W., Chen, K.: Transitive signature scheme from LFSR. J. Inf. Sci. Eng. **26**(1), 131–143 (2010)
9. Groth, J., Sahai, A.: Efficient non-interactive proof systems for bilinear groups. Electronic Colloquium on Computational Complexity (ECCC), 14(053) (2007). http://eccc.hpi-web.de/eccc-reports/2007/TR07-053/index.html
10. Liang, X., Cao, Z., Shao, J., Lin, H.: Short group signature without random. In: Qing, S., Imai, H., Wang, G. (eds.) ICICS 2007. LNCS, vol. 4861, pp. 69–82. Springer, Heidelberg (2007). doi:10.1007/978-3-540-77048-0_6
11. Ma, C., Wu, P., Gu, G.: A new method for the design of stateless transitive signature schemes. In: Shen, H.T., Li, J., Li, M., Ni, J., Wang, W. (eds.) APWeb 2006. LNCS, pp. 897–904. Springer, Heidelberg (2006). doi:10.1007/11610496_124
12. Micali, S., Rivest, R.L.: Transitive Signature Schemes. In: Preneel, B. (ed.) CT-RSA 2002. LNCS, vol. 2271, pp. 236–243. Springer, Heidelberg (2002). doi:10.1007/3-540-45760-7_16
13. Neven, G.: A simple transitive signature scheme for directed trees. Theor. Comput. Sci. **396**(1–3), 277–282 (2008). doi:10.1016/j.tcs.2008.01.042
14. Rivest, R.L., Hohenberger, S.R.: The cryptographic impact of groups with infeasible inversion. Masters thesis, MIT (2003)
15. Shahandashti, S.F., Salmasizadeh, M., Mohajeri, J.: A provably secure short transitive signature scheme from bilinear group pairs. In: Blundo, C., Cimato, S. (eds.) SCN 2004. LNCS, vol. 3352, pp. 60–76. Springer, Heidelberg (2004)
16. Wang, L., Cao, Z., Zheng, S., Huang, X., Yang, Y.: Transitive signatures from braid groups. In: Srinathan, K., Rangan, C.P., Yung, M. (eds.) INDOCRYPT 2007. LNCS, vol. 4859, pp. 183–196. Springer, Heidelberg (2007). doi:10.1007/978-3-540-77026-8_14
17. Wei, V.K.: Tight reductions among strong Di e-Hellman assumptions. IACR Cryptology ePrint Archive 2005, 57 (2005). http://eprint.iacr.org/2005/057
18. Yi, X.: Directed transitive signature scheme. In: Abe, M. (ed.) CT-RSA 2007. LNCS, vol. 4377, pp. 129–144. Springer, Heidelberg (2007). doi:10.1007/11967668_9
19. Zhang, F., Safavi-Naini, R., Susilo, W.: An efficient signature scheme from bilinear pairings and its applications. In: Bao, F., Deng, R., Zhou, J. (eds.) PKC 2004. LNCS, vol. 2947, pp. 277–290. Springer, Heidelberg (2004). doi:10.1007/978-3-540-24632-9_20

Privacy-Preserving Technologies

Privacy-Preserving Profile Matching Protocol Considering Conditions

Yosuke Ishikuro and Kazumasa Omote[✉]

JAIST, Asahidai 1-1, Nomi, Ishikawa 923-1292, Japan
{s1410007,omote}@jaist.ac.jp

Abstract. A social matching service has recently become popular. These services help a user to search friends having common preference or interest. On the other hand, users use their personal information for matching in social matching services, and thus the privacy-preserving profile matching protocols have been well studied. However, although there are various privacy-preserving profile matching protocols, they may cause unwilling matching. In order to solve this problem, it is necessary to achieve a fine-grained matching mechanism considering conditions.

In this paper, we propose a privacy-preserving profile matching protocol embedded with homomorphic encryption considering conditions: matching is established only when the conditions are satisfied. Our protocol reduces computational cost of user's device by using the map-to-prime technique and setting an honest-but-curious server. Furthermore, even if a server is attacked, user's secret key or personal data does not leak since our protocol is designed for a server without such confidential data.

Keywords: Privacy · Profile matching · Homomorphic encryption · Mobile social networks

1 Introduction

With the proliferation of mobile devices such as smart phones and tablets, a social network is becoming an inseparable part of our life. A social matching service has recently become popular. These services help users to search friends having common preference or interest. Users can make new social connections or friends based on matching of their personal profiles. However, a social matching service deals with user's personal profile which includes sensitive information such as name, age, location and preference. Thus, we should protect user's privacy. The service provider needs to reassure users by properly managing personal data and hence it is necessary to prevent leaking personal data. It is also required to safely manage user's personal data for improving quality of service.

A lot of privacy-preserving profile matching protocols have been studied for preventing the leakage of private information in recent years. So, in these protocols, matching is processed using encrypted user's profile. For example, a user

© Springer International Publishing AG 2016
J. Chen et al. (Eds.): NSS 2016, LNCS 9955, pp. 171–183, 2016.
DOI: 10.1007/978-3-319-46298-1_12

A answers some questions to construct her/his profile and then encrypts her/his answers. A's profile is compared with another profile of user B with encrypted. After that, A and B obtain the matching result by decrypting.

Thanks to such cryptographic technology, even if their profiles include sensitive information, a malicious user or a server cannot learn about it except for the matching result. However, the existing privacy-preserving profile matching protocols have a drawback of unwilling matching. In the existing protocols, if two users have at least one common preference or interest, then they output the result "matching is established". Namely, even if a user B has one profile item that another user A cannot accept, the matching between A and B may unwillingly established. For example, we assume that A wants to match to another user who likes baseball but A does not want to match to a smoker. If B likes baseball but B is a smoker, the existing protocols reluctantly output the result "matching is established" based on the attribute "baseball", although A does not fundamentally want to match to B. This result may disappoint A.

In this paper, we propose a privacy-preserving profile matching protocol embedded with homomorphic encryption considering conditions: matching is established only when the conditions are satisfied. As a result, our protocol can prevent the unwilling matching, which occurs in the existing protocols, by setting the conditions. If A wants to match to only a non-smoker, A sets the condition of "non-smoker" against another user. Even if both A and B like "baseball", they are not matched because B is smoker, that is, B does not satisfy the condition of A. Our protocol reduces computational cost of user's device by using the map-to-prime technique and setting an honest-but-curious server. Furthermore, even if a server is attacked, user's secret key or personal data does not leak since our protocol is designed for a server without such confidential data. We assume that every entity has honest-but-curious setting and that secure channel is used among A, B and S. A and B do not directly communicate in order to preserve the fairness and to reduce computational cost on users' devices.

The remainder of the paper is structured as follows: In Sect. 2, we discuss some related works of a privacy-preserving profile matching protocol. Section 3 includes preliminaries. In Sect. 4, we present the privacy-preserving profile matching system. Section 5 gives our proposed protocol in detail. In Sect. 6, performance evaluation is discussed. Finally, Sect. 7 concludes the paper.

2   Related Works

In 2004, PSI protocol using Oblivious Polynomial Evaluation (OPE) was proposed for the first time by Freedman et al. [2]. Then, Kim et al. [4] reduced computational cost of user's device by using the map-to-prime technique instead solution of the polynomial in OPE. Many existing matching protocols need to generate one ciphertext for one question about user profiles, and this means that the large amount of computational cost of encryption is required if the number of questions increases. The map-to-prime technique makes it possible to embed more than one profile inside one ciphertext and hence makes it possible to decrease the computational cost of encryption. We can mainly classify the existing schemes into two types: (1) enhancing the privacy and (2) enhancing the matching function.

Enhancing the privacy restricts the output contents of matching results. Abbas et al. [1] proposes cardinality matching which outputs only the number of matched elements without revealing the matched elements. In [6,7], the private attributes are certified by a trusted third party and these prevent honest-but-curious and malicious users from learning profile information of honest user by choosing their set arbitrarily. In [5,8,9], privacy is enhanced by restricting the information obtained from the matching result as the privacy level rises. For example in [9], in level 1 users can learn the matched elements and their level of interest. In level 2 it outputs the matched elements between users. In level 3 users can learn only if they matched without learning the matched elements.

Enhancing the matching function achieves more detailed matching of user's profiles. Zhu et al. [10] proposes the conditional matching protocol which is established only when the number of matched elements is equivalent to the number a user requires. However, the condition setting of this protocol is not realistic. He et al. [3] proposes more detailed matching protocol in which users can set weights to their profile. Thapam et al. [8] proposes the practical matching protocol which achieves a communication closer to real life, by using not only users' own information but also information of their friends. As explained above, although various matching protocols have been proposed, the fine-grained matching considering user's conditions has not been achieved yet.

3 Preliminaries

3.1 Requirements

Fain-grained profile matching:
The existing matching protocols have a drawback of unwilling match. Even if a user has some profiles that anther user is unacceptable, they may reluctantly match each other as described in Sect. 1. In order to solve this problem, the fine-grained profile matching protocol considering conditions is required.

Safety management of personal information:
Since user's profile includes personal information, it is required to store user's profile to keep a secret. Also, it is required that a server does not have private keys of users or a server and that it does not use them on itself. If a server does not have secret information, the safety management of a server becomes easy.

Reduction of computational cost:
Many existing matching protocols need to generate one ciphertext for one question of profiles, and this means that the large amount of computational cost of encryption is required if the number of questions increases. In order to solve this problem, one ciphertext for multiple profiles is required. This can reduce the computational cost and memory consumption.

3.2 Paillier Encryption

The protocol proposed in this paper is based on Paillier's homomorphic encryption. In the following, we summarize Paillier crypto system.

Key Generation:
The trusted third party chooses two large prime numbers p and q randomly such that $\gcd(pq, (p-1)(q-1)) = 1$ and compute $n = pq$ and $g = (1 + \alpha n)\beta^n \bmod n^2$ and $\lambda = \mathrm{lcm}(p-1, q-1)$, where $\gcd()$ and $\mathrm{lcm}()$ are the functions that computes the greatest common divisor and the least common multiple, respectively. Furthermore, it computes $\mu = (L(g^\lambda \bmod n^2))^{-1} \bmod n$, where $L(u) = (u-1)/n$. The Paillier public and private keys are (n, g) and λ, respectively.

Encryption:
Let $M \in \mathbb{Z}_n$ be a message to be encrypted and $r \in \mathbb{Z}_{n^2}^*$ be a random number. The ciphertext could be given by

$$E(M) = g^M r^n \bmod n^2 \tag{1}$$

Decryption:
Given a ciphertext $c = E(M)$, the corresponding plaintext can be derived as

$$\frac{L(c^\lambda \bmod n^2)}{L(g^\lambda \bmod n^2)} \bmod n = M \tag{2}$$

Homomorphic:
Given $m_1, m_2, r_1, r_2 \in \mathbb{Z}_N$, it satisfies the following homomorphic property:

$$E(m_1) \cdot E(m_2) = E(m_1 + m_2) \tag{3}$$

3.3 Adversary Model

We consider an internal attacker that is a malicious user or server. We assume that the adversary model is honest-but-curious setting. Honest-but-curious users or server follow the protocol but they are curious to learn about user's interest. Additionally, we do not consider the collusion among users and server. This model is required to satisfy correctness and privacy as follows.

- Correctness.
  If two users output the matching result of each profile correctly, this protocol has correctness.
- Privacy.
  If nothing is known about each user's profile which is not existed in the matching result, this protocol has privacy.

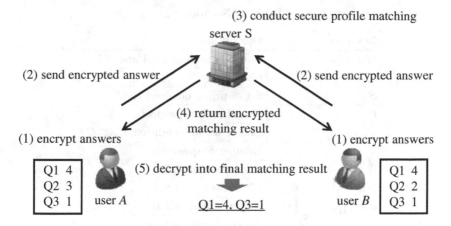

Fig. 1. Privacy-preserving profile matching system.

4   Privacy-Preserving Profile Matching System

A privacy-preserving matching system is that each user answers some questions about user's profile and then obtain only the matching result with another user. If users A and B are matched in some questions, they obtain only the matched items each other. Figure 1 shows an overview of privacy-preserving profile matching system. The basic procedure is as follows.

1. A and B encrypt their own answer about their profiles.
2. A and B send their encrypted answer to a server S.
3. S conducts the secure profile matching with keeping personal information secret.
4. S returns the encrypted matching result to A and B.
5. A and B respectively decrypt the matching result received from S and then they can obtain the final matching result.

In Fig. 1, the final matching result is Q1 = 4 and Q3 = 1 since A's answers of question 1 and 3 are the same as B. Note that the answer of question 2 is kept secret since the question 2 is not matched between A and B.

We assume that A, B and S are the honest-but-curious entities. In other words, S, A and B are curious to learn about a user's interest but honestly follow the protocol. In addition, we do not assume the collision among A, B and S and assume a secure channel between the server and users.

5   Our Protocol

In the existing protocols, even if a user B has preference or interest that another user A cannot accept, the matching between A and B may unwillingly established. In order to solve this problem, we propose a privacy-preserving profile

Table 1. Notation.

Notation	Description
pk_A, pk_B	Public keys of users A and B
C	Choice set
S	Set of prime numbers to C
t	Size of each prime in C
C_c	Choice set for condition, $C_c \subset C$
γ	Number of questions
$X_A = \{a_1, \ldots, a_\gamma\}$	A's answer, $a_i \in S$
$X_B = \{b_1, \ldots, b_\gamma\}$	B's answer, $b_i \in S$
$a = \prod_{i=1}^{\gamma}, b = \prod_{i=1}^{\gamma}$	Answers of A and B
a_c	B's condition for user A
b_c	A's condition for user B
$r_{aa}, r_{ab}, r_{ba}, r_{bb}$	Random numbers
X_{AB}, X_{BA}	Matching results of A and B

matching protocol embedded with homomorphic encryption considering conditions: matching is established only when the conditions are satisfied. Our protocol uses the map-to-prime technique to reduce the computational cost of user's device. Our protocol also has conditions that each user sets to achieve the fine-grained matching. We assume that the secure channel is used among A, B and S and that A and B do not directly communicate in order to preserve the fairness and to reduce computational cost on users' devices.

5.1   Notation

Table 1 shows the notation of our protocol. C is a set of choices contained in one ciphertext. Our protocol deals with single answer only from multiple-choice question. S is the set of prime numbers corresponding to C. Users A and B select prime numbers corresponding to their own answers as $X_A = \{a_1, ..., a_\gamma\} \in S$ and $X_B = \{b_1, ...b_\gamma\} \in S$, respectively. User's answer is represented by product of prime numbers. More precisely, the answers of A and B are denoted by $a = \prod_{i=1}^{\gamma} a_i$ and $b = \prod_{i=1}^{\gamma} b_i$, respectively. Each user chooses a condition from $C_c \subset C$. The conditions of A and B are denoted by $b_c \in S$ and $a_c \in S$, respectively. If A does not satisfy B's condition a_c or B does not satisfy A's condition b_c, then the matching result is not output. Only if both A and B satisfy conditions each other, the matching is certainly established as usual.

5.2   Protocol Detail

We explain about the procedure that A obtains the matching result since users A and B are in a symmetric position. Figure 2 shows our privacy-preserving profile

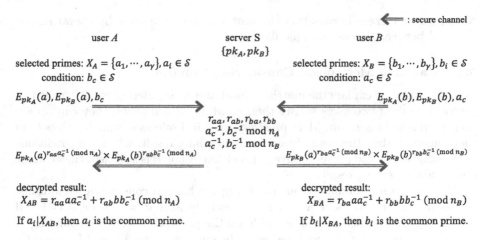

Fig. 2. Privacy-preserving profile matching protocol considering conditions between two users.

matching protocol considering conditions between two users. We need only one ciphertext for plural questions of profiles owing to the map-to-prime technique. Note that two or more ciphertext is required when $t\gamma > |n_A|$. The protocol detail is shown in Fig. 2.

1. S chooses a set $\mathcal{S}$ corresponding to a set C for the map-to-prime technique.
2. A and B respectively generate their own public key pk_A and pk_B and send them to S.
3. A receives pk_B from S. A computes $E_{pk_A}(a)$ and $E_{pk_B}(a)$ by encrypting her/his own answer, and then selects the condition b_c from C_c. A sends $E_{pk_A}(a)$, $E_{pk_B}(a)$ and b_c to S. B processes in a similar way.
4. S generates four random numbers r_{aa}, r_{ab}, r_{ba} and r_{bb} where $|r_{aa}| = |r_{ab}| = |n_A| - t\gamma + t - 1$ and $|r_{ba}| = |r_{bb}| = |n_B| - t\gamma + t - 1$. These random numbers are used to pad message space. S obtains the prime number corresponding to each condition received from A and B. Then, S computes the inverse elements of b_c and a_c on n_A and n_B, i.e., $b_c^{-1}(\text{mod } n_A)$, $a_c^{-1}(\text{mod } n_A)$, $b_c^{-1}(\text{mod } n_B)$ and $a_c^{-1}(\text{mod } n_B)$. Finally, S computes the following Eq. (4) and returns it to A.

$$E_{pk_A}(a)^{r_{aa}a_c^{-1} \ (\text{mod } n_A)} \times E_{pk_A}(b)^{r_{ab}b_c^{-1} \ (\text{mod } n_A)}$$
$$= E_{pk_A}(r_{aa}a_c^{-1} + r_{ab}b_c^{-1}) \tag{4}$$
$$= E_{pk_A}(X_{AB}),$$

where $X_{AB} = r_{aa}a_c^{-1} + r_{ab}b_c^{-1}$.
5. A decrypts $E_{pk_A}(X_{AB})$ to obtain X_{AB}.
6. A verifies the matching result, that is, A conducts $a_i | X_{AB}$ ($i = 1, ..., \gamma$). If it is true, a_i is the common prime between A and B, otherwise, a_i is not common. If A and B satisfy their conditions each other, both users can obtain the matching result. Otherwise, neither A nor B can obtain any matching result.

Note that we can easily construct the protocol among m users by operating our protocol between two users in parallel.

5.3   Matching Mechanism Considering Conditions

In this section, we explain the matching mechanism considering conditions in our protocol. Only if two users satisfy their conditions each other, they can obtain their final matching result. More precisely, only if A selects a_c and B selects b_c in their answers, then they can obtain their matching result, when the conditions of A and B are b_c and a_c, respectively. If neither A nor B is satisfied, they cannot obtain any matching result.

We explain an example of our matching mechanism considering conditions. We assume that two users A and B respectively have $a = xdh$ ($x \in C_c$) and $b = yeh$ ($y \in C_c$), where x, y, d, e and h are the prime numbers corresponding to answers. Additionally, A and B respectively select $a_c = x \in C_c$ and $b_c = y \in C_c$ as a condition. In this case, since A and B respectively have a_c and b_c in their answers (i.e., they satisfy their conditions each other.), they can obtain the matching result except for conditions a_c and b_c. Users can derive h as their common prime number as follows.

$$
\begin{aligned}
E_{pk_A}(a)^{r_{aa}a_c^{-1} \pmod{n_A}} &\times E_{pk_A}(b)^{r_{ab}b_c^{-1} \pmod{n_A}} \\
&= E_{pk_A}(r_{aa}xdhx^{-1} + r_{ab}yehy^{-1}) \\
&= E_{pk_A}(r_{aa}dh + r_{ab}eh) \\
&= E_{pk_A}(h(r_{aa}d + r_{ab}e))
\end{aligned}
\tag{5}
$$

The most important point of this computation is the cancel process of conditions. In Eq. (5), the inverse elements x^{-1} and y^{-1} are canceled by the primes $a_c = x$ and $b_c = y$ for conditions, respectively. From this computation, A and B can know that h is matched between them. If the inverse element of condition is not canceled, the matching result is randomized and hence two users cannot obtain any result.

On the other hand, when the conditions of A and B are respectively $b_c = z \in C_c$ and $a_c = x \in C_c$, the computation by S for a user A is as follows.

$$
\begin{aligned}
E_{pk_A}(a)^{r_{aa}a_c^{-1} \pmod{n_A}} &\times E_{pk_A}(b)^{r_{ab}b_c^{-1} \pmod{n_A}} \\
&= E_{pk_A}(r_{aa}xdhx^{-1} + r_{ab}yehz^{-1}) \\
&= E_{pk_A}(r_{aa}dh^{-1} + r_{ab}yehz^{-1}) \\
&= E_{pk_A}(\text{random})
\end{aligned}
\tag{6}
$$

In this case, the inverse element of A's condition z is not canceled since B does not select z. As a result, an overflow occurs with a high probability on message space n_A and thus users cannot obtain the common prime number. Unless the conditions are satisfied, the matching result becomes random.

We can regard our protocol as two-step matching by setting the conditions. At the first step our protocol conducts the matching of conditions, and also at the second step it conducts the matching of the profiles.

Table 2. Comparison of efficiency.

	Computation	Communication
KLC'11 [4]	$\mathcal{O}(|C|)$	$\mathcal{O}(|C|)$
TLSL'14 [8]	$\mathcal{O}(|C|^2)$	$\mathcal{O}(|C|)$
ZZSY'12 [9]	$\mathcal{O}(|C|)$	$\mathcal{O}(|C|)$
Our protocol	$\mathcal{O}(|C|)$	$\mathcal{O}(|C|)$

6   Evaluation

6.1   Security Analysis

In an honest-but-curious model, we have only to prove correctness and privacy as follows.

Theorem 1 (Correctness). *Our protocol outputs a matching result correctly.*

Proof. When we assume $x \in X_A \cap X_B$, both a and b are divided by x and hence both $X_{AB} = r_{aa}aa_c^{-1} + r_{ab}bb_c^{-1}$ (mod n_A) and $X_{BA} = r_{ba}aa_c^{-1} + r_{bb}bb_c^{-1}$ (mod n_B) are also divided by x. As a result, each user knows that x is a common answer. On the other hand, when we assume $x \notin X_A \cap X_B$, we can consider two cases: (1) x is included in X_A or X_B, and (2) x is included in neither X_A nor X_B. However, in both cases, x is accidentally existed as a common prime in $X_A \cap X_B$ with a probability of P (see P in Subsect. 6.3). Therefore, our protocol can guarantee the correctness with a failure probability of P.   □

We show the following lemma of indeterminate equation.

Lemma 1. *If $gcd(a, b) = 1$, then solution (x, y) of $ax + by = 1$ is existed certainly.*

We will not prove Lemma 1 since this is a famous theorem of indeterminate equation. Using this Lemma, we show that our protocol has privacy as follows.

Theorem 2 (Privacy). *An attacker cannot obtain any information about answers of honest user except for common elements between users.*

Proof. We assume that A is an honest user and another user B is an honest-but-curious attacker. B wishes to know A's answer. B can obtain b, $E_{pk_A}(b)$, $E_{pk_B}(b)$ and $X_{BA} = r_{ba}aa_c^{-1} + r_{bb}bb_c^{-1}$ (mod n_B) in the protocol. In order to know the result of A's selection, B needs to know the prime number selected by only A from $X_{BA} = r_{ba}aa_c^{-1} + r_{bb}bb_c^{-1} = \pi(r_{ba}a'a_c^{-1} + r_{bb}b'b_c^{-1})$ (mod n_B), where $a = \pi a'$ and $b = \pi b'$. Note that π is the common prime(s) between A and B. Since B knows X_{BA}, b' and π, B needs a' from following Eq. (7).

$$r_{ba}a' + r_{bb}b' = X_{BA}/\pi \tag{7}$$

$gcd(a', b') = 1$ holds since the common prime number is not existed in a' and b'. Even if a' has any value in Eq. (7), both r_{ba} and r_{bb} certainly exists from Lemma 1. As a result, it is difficult for an attacker to compute a'.   □

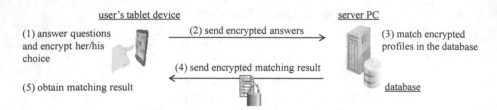

Fig. 3. Flow of our demonstration.

6.2 Efficiency

We evaluate computational/communication complexities of our protocol on user's tablet device and a server PC. We also evaluate the computation process time of our implemented system.

Complexity of Computation and Communication. Users send and receive two ciphertexts in our protocol. The communication complexity of ciphertext, which each user sends and receives, is $4|C|$. Therefore, the communication complexity of our proposed protocol is denoted as $\mathcal{O}(|C|)$.

We evaluate the computational complexity with the number of modulo exponentiation. In Paillier crypto system, it is required two modulo exponentiations in encryption and one modulo exponentiation in decryption. In our protocol, the number of each user's modulo exponentiation is $5|C|$ since it needs two encryptions and one decryption. Therefore, the computational complexity of our protocol is denoted as $\mathcal{O}(|C|)$.

Table 2 shows the comparison the efficiency of the existing schemes and our protocol. We employ the existing schemes that users can know which elements are matched, which is similar to our proposed protocol. The result show that our protocol has lower computational/communication complexities.

Implementation Evaluation. We implemented our proposed protocol in JAVA and evaluated it on a laptop with Intel Core i5 (1.4 GHz) and 8 GB RAM and a tablet device NEXUS 7 with Qualcomm Snapdragon S4 Pro (1.5 GHz) and 2 GB RAM. We evaluated the running time of our protocol on a laptop as a server and a tablet as a user's mobile device. Figure 3 shows the environment of our implementation evaluation. A user constructs her/his own profile by answering some questions. Figure 4 shows the answer window of our implemented application on the tablet device.

We evaluated the running time of two encryptions, one decryption and the verification of matching on a table device, and the matching process on the server PC. Table 3 shows ten times average of running time in each processing.

Table 3. Running time in each processing (10 times average).

Tablet			Server PC
Encryptions (two times)	Decryption (one time)	Matching verification	Matching processing
165 ms	51.3 ms	7.92 ms	30.6 ms

Fig. 4. The answer window of our application on the tablet device NEXUS 7.

6.3 Probability of Failure Matching

We note that our protocol does not deterministically output the matching result. For example, in spite of $x \notin X_A \cap X_B, x \in \mathcal{S}$, if x becomes accidentally the common prime number of A and B, then the matching result becomes wrong. Therefore, it is important that the failure probability is negligible. P is the failure probability that a common t-bit prime number in $X_A \cap X_B$ may be accidentally included in $\mathcal{S}$ as follows.

$$P = 1 - \left(1 - \frac{1}{2^t}\right)^{|\mathcal{S}|} \tag{8}$$

We assume that the message space of E is 1024 bits, i.e., $|n_A| = |n_B| = 1024$. Since the message space is fixed, t and C have the relation of tradeoff. As long

Table 4. The probability of failure matching when t and $|C|$ are changed.

t	$|C|$	P
25	34	5.07×10^{-6}
26	33	2.46×10^{-6}
27	31	1.15×10^{-6}
28	30	5.59×10^{-7}
29	29	2.70×10^{-7}
30	28	1.30×10^{-7}
31	27	6.29×10^{-8}

as the probability of failure matching is less than 2^{-20} ($\simeq 10^{-7}$), we assume that the correctness is guaranteed. Table 4 shows the probability of failure matching when t and $|C|$ are changed. In order to satisfy the above condition (i.e., less than 10^{-7}), we set $t = 28$ bits prime numbers and $|C| = 30$ from Table 4. In this implementation, a user selects a single answer from five items assigned to each question.

7   Conclusion

We have proposed a privacy-preserving profile matching protocol considering conditions. In the existing protocols, the unwilling matching may occur, that is, a user may match to another unacceptable user. In our protocol, matching is established only when the conditions are satisfied, and hence our protocol can prevent such unwilling matching, which occurs in the existing protocols, by setting conditions. Additionally, we have reduced computational cost and memory consumption by using the map-to-prime technique and an honest-but-curious server. As a future work, we try to enhance the privacy such as condition hiding and configuration of privacy level, which restrict the matching result.

Acknowledgements. This work was partly supported by Grant-in-Aid for Scientific Research (C) (16K00183).

References

1. Abbas, F., Rajput, U., Hussain, R., Eun, H., Oh, H.: A trustless broker based protocol to discover friends in proximity-based mobile social networks. In: Rhee, K.-H., Yi, J.H. (eds.) WISA 2014. LNCS, vol. 8909, pp. 216–227. Springer, Heidelberg (2015). doi:10.1007/978-3-319-15087-1_17
2. Freedman, M.J., Nissim, K., Pinkas, B.: Efficient private matching and set intersection. In: Cachin, C., Camenisch, J.L. (eds.) EUROCRYPT 2004. LNCS, vol. 3027, pp. 1–19. Springer, Heidelberg (2004). doi:10.1007/978-3-540-24676-3_1
3. He, D., Cao, Z., Dong, X., Shen, J.: User self-controllable profile matching for privacy-preserving mobile social networks. IEEE ICCS **2014**, 248–252 (2014)
4. Kim, M., Lee, H.T., Cheon, J.H.: Mutual private set intersection with linear complexity. In: Jung, S., Yung, M. (eds.) WISA 2011. LNCS, vol. 7115, pp. 219–231. Springer, Heidelberg (2012). doi:10.1007/978-3-642-27890-7_18
5. Li, M., Yu, S., Cao, N., Lou, W.: Privacy-preserving distributed profile matching in proximity-based mobile social networks. IEEE Trans. Wirel. Commun. **12**(5), 2024–2033 (2013)
6. Sarpong, S., Xu, C., Zhang, X.: An authenticated privacy-preserving attribute matchmaking protocol for mobile social networks. Int. J. Netw. Secur. **17**(3), 357–364 (2015)
7. Sarpong, S., Xu, C., Zhang, X.: PPAM: privacy-preserving attributes matchmaking protocol for mobile social networks secure against malicious users. Int. J. Netw. Secur. **18**(4), 625–632 (2016)
8. Thapam, A., Li, M., Salinas, S., Li, P.: Asymmetric social proximity based private matching protocols for online social networks. IEEE Trans. Parallel Distrib. Syst. **26**(6), 1547–1559 (2014)

9. Zhang, R., Zhang, Y., Sun, J.S., Yan, G.: Fine-grained private matching for proximity-based mobile social networking. IEEE INFOCOM **2012**, 1–9 (2012)
10. Zhu, H., Du, S., Li, M., Gao, Z.: Fairness-aware and privacy-preserving friend matching protocol in mobile social networks. IEEE Trans. Emerg. Top. Comput. **1**(1), 192–200 (2013)

Privacy Preserving Credit Systems

Sherman S.M. Chow, Russell W.F. Lai, Xiuhua Wang, and Yongjun Zhao[✉]

Department of Information Engineering,
The Chinese University of Hong Kong,
Sha Tin, N.T., Hong Kong
{sherman,wflai,wx015,zy113}@ie.cuhk.edu.hk

Abstract. Credit card system has proven itself to be a convenient way for individuals to complete transactions. Despite its great benefits, credit card system also brings in great privacy risks to users. The card issuing bank knows the details of all transactions made by every user, including transaction date, amount, and merchant. These contain sensitive information of the users which may reveal their whereabouts, preferences, daily routines, etc. In this paper, we build privacy preserving credit card systems that hide the expenses of individual users from the bank, while preserving most of the features provided by the current credit card system at the same time.

Keywords: Accountable privacy · Credit card · e-cash · Online banking · Group signatures

1 Introduction

Customers and merchants have enjoyed the benefits of plastic money for decades, in the form of credit cards and debit cards for examples. Plastic money saves the customers from the trouble of carrying large amount of money every day. One or two thin plastic cards suffice to settle most transactions. Payment can also be made in exact amount without any changes in the form of heavy metal coins. On the other hand, merchants do not need to worry about keeping the cash in a safe place or rush depositing them into their bank accounts in person, since all payments from their customers directly go to the bank. To encourage the use of credit card, bank and merchants often hold joint promotions so that customers can enjoy extra discounts if they choose to pay by cards. With such great benefit and convenience, credit/debit cards related transactions are immensely popular, ever increasingly. According to the Word Payments Report 2015 [13] from Capgemini and Royal Bank of Scotland, the growth rates in transactions using debit cards and credit cards are 11.5 % and 9.6 % respectively.

The conveniences come with the price of user privacy. In a credit card system, the bank will usually generate a monthly transaction record which lists clearly how much the customer has spent. Thus the bank knows the details of every single transaction, including the transaction date and amount, the parties

© Springer International Publishing AG 2016
J. Chen et al. (Eds.): NSS 2016, LNCS 9955, pp. 184–199, 2016.
DOI: 10.1007/978-3-319-46298-1_13

involved, etc. The bank can infer a lot of sensitive information about the customers, such as their favorite restaurants or travel plan in the near future. The
bank might make use of such information to build a full profile of the customer,
and later profit from it, e.g., by selling it to someone else.

Cryptographic e-cash [14] was invented to support transaction privacy in electronic payment systems. The typical workflow of an e-cash system is as follows.
Users withdraw coins from a bank, and then use those coins to settle payments
with the merchants. Merchants will deposit coins back to their bank accounts at
some later time. The privacy requirements mandate that the bank cannot infer
any information about who was the original owner of the coin just deposited by
the merchant. Transferable e-cash systems [8,17,23,24] allow a coin to circulate
within the system, while the traditional e-cash systems only allow a coin to be
spent once. Achieving anonymity in transferable e-cash systems [5,12,25] turns
out to be trickier than in traditional systems.

Nevertheless, e-cash systems are similar to debit card systems in nature, in
the sense that a user can never spend more than what s/he can pay for. Credit
card systems, however, grant users flexibility of purchasing goods which they
otherwise cannot afford at the moment. A natural question to ask is therefore
whether there exists electronic yet anonymous counterpart of credit card systems. At the first glance the answer to this question is obviously no. Credit
card system inherently requires recording transaction amounts so that the bank
can check in real time whether the user has exhausted his/her credit limit. The
bank will also need to know the total transaction amount to charge the user.
Anonymity offered by e-cash system seems to be contradicting to these functional
requirements of credit card systems.

This paper aims to tackle these seemingly inherently contradicting requirements of credit-based payment systems and e-cash systems. Our aim is to protect
the privacy of user even for the total amount s/he has spent over a time period,
yet the bank can still get enough pay-back from the users. Moreover, we aim to
retain as much functionalities of credit-based payment systems as possible, like
overdue interest charge, credit limit update, monthly payment settlement, etc.
This problem has not received much attention. As we will explain shortly, there
is no existing work that can deal with this problem completely.

1.1 Related Work

Most early electronic payment systems are centralized, with notable exceptions
of Karma+ [15] and Bitcoin [22], yet they do not preserve user privacy. Payment mechanisms with some degrees of privacy have already been considered
in the literature. Asokan et al. gave a detailed introduction about the state-of-
the-art electronic payment systems [3] by that time. Earlier works [6,19] only
protected credit card information from third parties or merchants, but not from
the bank. Low et al. introduced a credit card system which can provide card-
holder anonymity even towards the bank [21], but their scheme assumes many
trusted parties, and offers only a subset of functionalities in typical credit card
systems (e.g., no expense report or error correction service). Androulaki and

Bellovin [2] identified a set of properties of anonymous credit card systems, including privacy, deployability, unforgeability, and non-transferability. Moreover, the systems should provide expense report service, error correction service, loss recovery service, and special interest rate offers. Note that their privacy level is per-transaction. The bank has knowledge of the total expenditure of individual users in each time period.

1.2   Our Results

We propose two privacy-preserving credit systems, which hide the expenses of individual users from the bank. Our systems satisfy the traditional security requirements of e-cash, such as identification of double-spending, as well as other requirements specific to credit systems. Namely, our systems allow flexible control of the interest rates and credit limits of individual users, and protect against mischarges and undercharges.

Our first system is relatively lightweight, as it is constructed from traditional (non-transferable) e-cash systems [14] and (dynamic) group signatures [7]. The efficiency comes with a mild limitation of having all users share the same payment due date. Our second system makes use of anonymous transferable e-cash [5, 25] systems and (non-interactive) zero-knowledge proofs [9,18], and is able to overcome the above limitation.

1.3   Paper Organization

The rest of this paper is organized as follows: Sect. 2 develops the necessary notations, and introduces the basic building blocks of our system, including group signature, (transferable) e-cash system, and zero-knowledge proof system. We then describe the system model in Sect. 3, and present two different constructions of privacy preserving credit system in Sect. 4.

2   Preliminary

2.1   Dynamic Group Signature

A dynamic group signature scheme [7] involves a trusted party for initial public parameter generation, two authorities (issuer and opener) with a number of potential users, who may join the group dynamically, each with a unique identity $i \in \mathbb{N}$. Another name for users is signers since they sign on behalf of the group. Anyone can be a verifier of a signature, or the proof that a signature is attributed to a certain signer. For our application, we present a simplified definition where the group manager acts as both the issuer and the opener.

We additional require a claim algorithm which may not be a standard one in a typical (dynamic) group signature scheme. The claim algorithm enables a signer to later claim the authorship of an issued signature [1].

Definition 1. *A dynamic group signature scheme consists of the following* PPT *algorithms:*

- $(\mathsf{gpk}, \mathsf{ik}, \mathsf{ok}) \leftarrow \mathsf{GKg}(1^\lambda)$: The group manager generates the group public key gpk, the issuer key ik, and the opener key ok in the setup phase.
- $(\mathsf{upk}_i, \mathsf{usk}_i) \leftarrow (\mathsf{Join}_\mathcal{I}(\mathsf{ik}), \mathsf{Join}_\mathcal{U}(\mathsf{gpk}))$: A user i joins the group by engaging in a joining protocol with the issuer. If successful, the user and the issuer register the public key upk_i on the registration table **reg**, while the user obtains a secret signing key usk_i.
- $\sigma \leftarrow \mathsf{GSig}(\mathsf{usk}_i, m)$: User i can produce a signature σ on message $m \in \{0, 1\}^*$ using the signing key usk_i.
- $(\mathsf{accept}/\mathsf{reject}) \leftarrow \mathsf{GVf}(\mathsf{gpk}, m, \sigma)$: A verifier can verify a signature σ on a message m with the group public key gpk.
- $(i, \tau) \leftarrow \mathsf{Open}(\mathsf{ok}, \{\mathsf{upk}\}, m, \sigma)$: The opener has access to the registration table **reg**. Using the opener key ok, the opener can obtain an opening of a valid signature σ on message m pointing to a user i, with a proof τ of the correctness of the opening.
- $(\mathsf{accept}/\mathsf{reject}) \leftarrow \mathsf{Judge}(\mathsf{gpk}, \mathsf{upk}_i, m, \sigma, \tau)$: A judge can verify a proof τ of the correctness of an opening i of a valid signature σ on message m.

One can construct a dynamic group signature scheme from any accountable ring signature scheme [10, 20].

A dynamic group signature scheme should satisfy correctness (of signing and opening) and the following security properties:

Anonymity. A coalition of all parties except the opener cannot distinguish which of the two signers of its choice has signed a target message of its choice.

Traceability. If the issuer is honest, then it is infeasible to produce a signature whose opening does not point to any registered member.

Non-frameability. A coalition of all parties except an honest user cannot produce a signature which opens to that honest user.

2.2 Electronic Cash System

An (offline) electronic cash system [11] involves three usual kinds of players: the user, the bank, and the merchant.

Definition 2. *An electronic cash system consists of the following eight probabilistic algorithms:*

- $\mathsf{Pgen}(1^\lambda)$ on input the security parameter 1^λ outputs the system parameters pp, which is a default input to the remaining algorithms.
- There are two key generation algorithms, $\mathsf{KGen}_\mathcal{B}()$ and $\mathsf{KGen}_\mathcal{U}()$. $(\mathsf{pk}_\mathcal{B}, \mathsf{sk}_\mathcal{B}, \mathsf{L}) \leftarrow \mathsf{KGen}_\mathcal{B}(\mathsf{pp})$ and $(\mathsf{pk}_\mathcal{U}, \mathsf{sk}_\mathcal{U}) \leftarrow \mathsf{KGen}_\mathcal{U}(\mathsf{pp})$ generate the key pairs for the bank $\mathcal{B}$ and the user $\mathcal{U}$ respectively. The $\mathsf{KGen}_\mathcal{B}()$ algorithm additionally initializes the list of deposited coins L to be an empty list.

- Withdraw($\mathcal{U}(\mathsf{pk}_\mathcal{B}, \mathsf{sk}_\mathcal{U}, n), \mathcal{B}(\mathsf{pk}_\mathcal{U}, \mathsf{sk}_\mathcal{B}, n)$): This is a protocol for the user $\mathcal{U}$ to withdraw a *wallet* W of n coins from the bank $\mathcal{B}$. In other words, W is the user output. This bank maintains a database DB of $\mathsf{pk}_\mathcal{U}$. If this protocol fails, say due to the wrong inputs of either party, both outputs will become an error message instead.
- Spend($\mathcal{U}(W, \mathsf{sk}_\mathcal{U}, \mathsf{pk}_\mathcal{M}, \mathsf{pk}_\mathcal{B}), \mathcal{M}(\mathsf{sk}_\mathcal{M}, \mathsf{pk}_\mathcal{B})$): This is a protocol for user $\mathcal{U}$ to transfer one of the coins from his wallet W to merchant $\mathcal{M}$. Both parties obtain a serial number s of the coin, and a proof π of validity of the coin. The user additionally outputs an updated wallet W'.
- Deposit($\mathcal{M}(\mathsf{sk}_\mathcal{M}, s, \pi, \mathsf{pk}_\mathcal{B}), \mathcal{B}(\mathsf{pk}_\mathcal{M}, \mathsf{sk}_\mathcal{B}, \mathsf{L})$): This is the protocol for a merchant $\mathcal{M}$ to deposit a coin (s, π) into the account at the bank $\mathcal{B}$. Whenever an honest merchant obtained (s, π) by running the Spend protocol with any user, it is guaranteed that this coin will be accepted by the bank. Bank adds the coin (s, π) to its list L of spent coins. The merchant side gets an empty string, or a message denoting error if it occurs.
- $(\mathsf{pk}_\mathcal{U}, \Pi_G) \leftarrow$ Identify($\mathsf{pp}, s, \pi_1, \pi_2$): This algorithm identifies double-spenders using a serial number s and two proofs of validity of this coin π_1 and π_2, possibly submitted by malicious merchants. It outputs a public key $\mathsf{pk}_\mathcal{U}$ and a proof Π_G. If the merchants who had submitted π_1 and π_2 are not malicious, then the proof serves as the evidence that the public key $\mathsf{pk}_\mathcal{U}$ is the registered public key of a user who has double-spent coin s.
- (accept/reject) $\leftarrow$ VfGuilt($\mathsf{pp}, s, \mathsf{pk}_\mathcal{U}, \Pi_G$): This algorithm allows anyone to verify proof $\mathsf{pk}_\mathcal{U}$ that the user with public key $\mathsf{pk}_\mathcal{U}$ is guilty of double-spending coin s. If the proofs verify, it outputs accept; reject otherwise.

The above formulation is known as a compact e-cash system [11] since the size of a wallet is a constant with respect to the number of coins it holds. Similar idea has been utilized to build traceable signature schemes [16] which form an extended notion of group signature. There are other e-cash schemes which aim to minimize the bandwidth required by the spending protocol [4]. Below we describe the security properties of an electronic cash system.

Correctness. If the Withdraw protocol is run by an honest user and an honest bank, then the user will not output an error message, as well as the bank. If the Spend protocol is run by an honest user with an honest merchant, then the merchant accepts the coin.

Balance. No coalition of users and merchants can ever spend more coins than they withdraw from the bank.

Identification of Double-Spenders. This property guarantees that, with high probability, double-spender can be identified by the Identify algorithm. Specifically, Identify outputs a key $pk_\mathcal{U}$ and proof Π_G such that VfGuilt accepts.

Anonymity of Users. From the privacy point of view, the property ensures that the bank, even when cooperating with any coalition of malicious users and merchants, cannot learn anything about the spending of a user other than what is available as "side-channel" information from the environment.

Exculpability. Exculpability ensures that a malicious bank cannot frame an innocent user for double-spending. There are two levels of exculpability. *Weak exculpability* means that an honest user cannot be accused of double-spending his coins. *Strong exculpability* relaxes the restriction that the user must be honest. In other words, the protection is extended to user who could have double-spent some coins. Strong exculpability prevents a user who double-spent some coins from being accused of additional coins that he did not double-spend before.

2.3   Transferable Electronic Cash System

In a transferable e-cash system [5], there are two types of parties: the bank $\mathcal{B}$ and users $\mathcal{U}_i$. Merchants can also be regarded as users. Since the syntax is largely similar to those of the basic e-cash system, we only highlight the major difference below. For brevity, we simply use $\mathsf{sk}_\mathcal{B}$ to denote the secret key of the bank $\mathcal{B}$, but do not differentiate between its components for withdrawal and deposit respectively.

Definition 3. *A transferable e-cash scheme is an e-cash system with the following differences (cf., Definition 2).*

- There is an additional registration protocol executed between the bank and the user: $\mathsf{Registration}(\mathcal{B}(\mathsf{sk}_\mathcal{B}, \mathsf{pk}_\mathcal{U}), \mathcal{U}(\mathsf{sk}_\mathcal{U}, \mathsf{pk}_\mathcal{B}))$. At the end, the user receives a certificate $cert_\mathcal{U}$, which will be part of the input in the following Spend and Deposit protocols. If error occurred, both parties output $\bot$.
- The spend protocol $\mathsf{Spend}(\mathcal{U}_1(c, \mathsf{sk}_{\mathcal{U}_1}, cert_{\mathcal{U}_1}, \mathsf{pk}_\mathcal{B}), \mathcal{U}_2(\mathsf{sk}_{\mathcal{U}_2}, \mathsf{pk}_\mathcal{B}))$ is executed between a spending user $\mathcal{U}_1$, and $\mathcal{U}_2$ who receives the coin c from $\mathcal{U}_1$. (There is no merchant here.) At the end of the protocol, $\mathcal{U}_1$ either marks the coin c as spent, or outputs $\bot$ if error occurred. $\mathcal{U}_2$ either outputs a coin c' or $\bot$.
- The $\mathsf{Deposit}()$ and $\mathsf{Identify}()$ protocols are merged into a single one: $\mathsf{Deposit}(\mathcal{U}(c, \mathsf{sk}_\mathcal{U}, cert_\mathcal{U}, \mathsf{pk}_\mathcal{B}), \mathcal{B}(\mathsf{sk}_\mathcal{B}, \mathsf{pk}_\mathcal{U}, \mathsf{L}))$. This is the protocol for a user $\mathcal{U}$ to deposit a coin c at the bank. It consists of three sub-routines.
  1. Firstly, CheckCoin checks whether the coin c is consistent, and if not outputs $\bot$.
  2. If c passes CheckCoin, the bank runs CheckDS, which outputs the serial number s of the deposited coin. The bank checks whether L already contains an entry for s. If not, $\mathcal{B}$ adds s to L, credits the account of $\mathcal{U}$ and updated L.
  3. If the coin was double-spent, the subroutine DetectDS is run on the two coins and outputs $(\mathsf{pk}_\mathcal{U}, \Pi_G)$, where $\mathsf{pk}_\mathcal{U}$ is the public key of the accused user, and Π_G is a proof that the registered user who owns $\mathsf{pk}_\mathcal{U}$ double-spent the coin. Π_G should reveal nothing about the coin itself.

Now we describe the security properties of the transferable e-cash system. Again, we highlight the major difference from those of a normal e-cash system.

Correctness and *Unforgeability*. These two notions resemble the **Correctness** and **Balance** properties respectively in e-cash system except that merchants are treated as normal users in the context of transferable e-cash system.

Identification of Double-Spenders and *Exculpability*. These two properties are the same as those in a normal e-cash system.

Anonymity. Anonymity in transferable e-cash system is more complex than non-transferable ones, because the coins can be transferred back and forth multiple times. Early works [5,8,12] defined three incomparable anonymity notions.

- *Observe-then-receive full anonymity* means the adversary, controlling the bank, cannot link a coin it receives as an adversarial user or as the bank to a previously (passively) observed transfer between honest users.
- *Spend-then-observe full anonymity* ensures that the adversary, controlling the bank, cannot link a (passively) observed coin transferred between two honest users to a coin it has already owned as a "legitimate" user.
- *Spend-then-receive full anonymity* means that when the bank is honest, the adversary cannot recognize a coin it previously owned when it receives the same coin again. *Spend-then-receive** ensures that although the adversary, when controlling the bank, can tell whenever it receives a coin it owned before, it should not be able to learn anything about the identities of the users that owned the coin in between.

2.4   Non-interactive Zero-Knowledge

A non-interactive zero-knowledge (NIZK) proof system [9] for an NP language $\mathcal{L}$ allows a prover to produce a proof π that an instance x is a member of $\mathcal{L}$ without revealing the witness.

An NIZK proof system should satisfy completeness, soundness, and zero-knowledge. Completeness states that the proofs produced by an honest prover should always be accepted. Soundness requires that even a malicious computationally unbounded prover cannot falsely convince an honest verifier that a non-instance x is in the language. Zero-knowledge requires that there exists an efficient simulator which simulates valid proofs of instances without knowing the corresponding witnesses.

3   System Model

In real-world credit card systems, there are multiple entities besides the customer and the merchant behind a transaction. For simplicity, we consolidate all those entities as the bank. Our goal is to construct a privacy-preserving credit system which involves a bank, a group of users, and a group of merchants. To be concrete, we first characterize the expected functionalities, and security and privacy properties.

3.1 Functionalities

A privacy-preserving credit system consists of a tuple of efficient algorithms and protocols, executed by the bank, the users, and the merchants. Merchants can be seen as a subset of the users. The syntax is as follows:

- **Setup Phase:**
    - $pp \leftarrow Pgen(1^\lambda)$, $(pk_\mathcal{B}, sk_\mathcal{B}, BB, DB) \leftarrow KGen_\mathcal{B}(pp)$, $(pk_\mathcal{M}, sk_\mathcal{M}) \leftarrow KGen_\mathcal{M}(pp)$, $(pk_\mathcal{U}, sk_\mathcal{U}) \leftarrow KGen_\mathcal{U}(pp)$: The bank, the users, and the merchants run their respective *key generation* algorithms based on the public parameter pp generated by a trusted third party. The bank also maintains a public bulletin board readable by all entities anonymously, and a database DB which is kept private by the bank.
    - $(DB', \kappa) \leftarrow (Join_\mathcal{B}(sk_\mathcal{B}, DB, \ell), Join_\mathcal{U}(sk_\mathcal{U}, \ell))$: A user *joins* the system by engaging in a joining protocol with the bank. If successful, the bank will issue a credit card κ to the user, and then update its database to DB'. The credit limit of individual user ℓ is determined by external mechanisms.
- **Transaction Phase:**
    - $(r, (\kappa', r)) \leftarrow (Auth_\mathcal{M}(sk_\mathcal{M}, n), Auth_\mathcal{U}(sk_\mathcal{U}, \kappa, n))$: A user *authorizes* payment to a merchant by engaging in an authorization protocol. The payment is successful if the user possesses enough credits in κ. In that case, the credit count of the user is reduced by n. Both the user and the merchant obtain a receipt r of the transaction.
    - $(BB', \perp) \leftarrow (Batch_\mathcal{B}(sk_\mathcal{B}, BB), Batch_\mathcal{M}(sk_\mathcal{M}, R))$: The merchant collecting a set of receipts receives payment by engaging in a *batching* protocol with the bank. If successful, the bank updates the public bulletin board from BB to BB'.

        As in an e-cash system, the bank can use the Identify() algorithm to detect double-spending events when multiple merchants batch their receipts to the bank.
    - $(BB', (\kappa', R')) \leftarrow (Repay_\mathcal{B}(sk_\mathcal{B}, BB, n), Repay_\mathcal{U}(sk_\mathcal{U}, \kappa, R, n))$: The user can *repay* the debt in advance by engaging in a repaying protocol with the bank. If successful, the user gets an updated credit card κ' with the credit count is increased by n, and the bank updates the public bulletin board.
    - $st \leftarrow Track(sk_\mathcal{U}, BB, r)$: In a trackable scheme, the user can *track* a previous transaction from the public bulletin board maintained by the bank.
- **Settlement Phase:**
    - $(\perp, \kappa') \leftarrow (Settle_\mathcal{B}(sk_\mathcal{B}, \rho, \ell, \ell'), Settle_\mathcal{U}(sk_\mathcal{U}, \kappa, \ell, \ell'))$: On payment due date of a user, the user and the bank engage in a *settlement* protocol in which the bank charges the user interest ρ for the amount of credits the user failed to repay, and issues a new set of credits to the user. According to the payment repaid and the interest rate, the original credit

limit ℓ can be updated to a new one ℓ' in the updated credit card κ'. The interest rate and the credit limit of the user (which determines the number of credits issued) are again determined by external mechanisms.

Note that there is maximal flexibility in setting the credit limits and interest rates as they are determined by external mechanisms arbitrarily.

3.2 Security

Security properties of a privacy-preserving credit system are similar their counterparts in an e-cash system. Besides the properties which directly carry over, including identification and tracing of double-spenders, anonymity of users (during transaction), and exculpability, we further require the following additional properties.

Balance. Similar to e-cash systems, the bank wishes to ensure that no coalition of users can ever spend more than their collective credit limit.

Hiding Spending Pattern. The only information about the users' expenditure known by the bank is the total amount spent by each group of users with the same payment due date.

Anonymous Tracking of Transactions. Users can track their previous transactions from the public bulletin board. On the other hand, no coalition of users can infer information about other users not in the coalition from the public bulletin board.

Undercharge Resistance. In between payment due dates, either the user repays more than or equal to the amount of credit spent in transactions, or the bank can compute the exact amount the user owes the bank and apply interest. In particular, no coalition of users can spend more than the collective amount they repay on their respective payment due date without being charged for the interest determined externally.

Mischarge Resistance. It is infeasible for the bank and any coalition of merchants to accuse a user for not fully repaying the debt, and thereby charging unreasonable interest.

4 Constructing Credit Systems

We provide two constructions of privacy-preserving credit systems, both are built on top of an anonymous e-cash system. The intuition is to use coins in the e-cash system as credits. In other words, the user in the credit system is issued a wallet. The number of coins contained in it is equal to the credit limit of the user. To pay using the credit system, the user simply transfers some of the coins to the merchant, who can later deposit the coins back to the bank and settle the transaction.

Problem arises when the user repays the debt. One straightforward solution is to have the user purchase coins from the bank, which are then added to the wallet. On the payment due date, the user proves in zero-knowledge that the number of coins in the wallet is greater than the credit limit. Notice that this requires the anonymous e-cash system to be transferable. This forms the basis of our second construction.

Existing anonymous transferable e-cash systems are not that efficient when compared with non-transferable ones in general. Our first construction instead uses an anonymous (non-transferable) e-cash system with a dynamic group signature. A payment now consists of a number of coins and the same number of group signatures. While the former are deposited to the bank as described above, the latter are posted by the bank in a public bulletin board. To repay the debt, the user claims the authorship of the group signatures on the board. On the payment due date, the bank simply opens all the unclaimed signatures, and charges the corresponding users interests. Finally, the bank issues new e-cash wallets to all the users.

To hide the expenses of each user, we expect the user to repay the debt in small chunks over anonymous communication channel, and transfer physical currency to the bank anonymously. In this way, the payments by different users are indistinguishable in the view of the bank, who thus only knows the aggregated expenses of all users.

4.1 From Group Signatures and E-Cash Systems

We first construct a lightweight credit system using group signatures and e-cash systems. In this lightweight construction, all users have the same payment due date. The bank in the e-cash system also plays the roles of group manager and opener in the group signature scheme.

Setup Phase.

- $pp \leftarrow Pgen(1^\lambda)$: The bank or a trusted third party runs $pp \leftarrow ECash.Pgen(1^\lambda)$ to generate the public parameter.
- $(pk_\mathcal{B}, sk_\mathcal{B}, BB, DB) \leftarrow KGen_\mathcal{B}(pp)$: The bank in the credit system generates key pairs $(pk_\mathcal{B}, sk_\mathcal{B}, L) \leftarrow ECash.KGen_\mathcal{B}(pp)$ for the bank in the e-cash system, as well as the issuing and opening key pairs $(gpk, ik, ok) \leftarrow GSig.GKg(1^\lambda)$ for the group signature scheme. It initializes an empty set of signatures $\Sigma := \phi$ and sets the public bulletin board to $BB \leftarrow (\Sigma, L)$. It also initializes an empty database $DB := \phi$.
- $(pk_\mathcal{M}, sk_\mathcal{M}) \leftarrow KGen_\mathcal{M}(pp)$, $(pk_\mathcal{U}, sk_\mathcal{U}) \leftarrow KGen_\mathcal{U}(pp)$: The merchants and the users of the credit system act as the users of the e-cash system, who generate their key pairs via $(pk_\mathcal{U}, sk_\mathcal{U}) \leftarrow ECash.KGen_\mathcal{U}(pp)$.
- $(DB', \kappa) \leftarrow (Join_\mathcal{B}(sk_\mathcal{B}, DB, \ell), Join_\mathcal{U}(sk_\mathcal{U}, \ell))$: To join the system, the bank enrolls the user into the group by the group joining protocol

$(\text{upk}_i, \text{usk}_i) \leftarrow \text{GSig.}(\text{Join}_{\mathcal{I}}(\text{ik}), \text{Join}_{\mathcal{U}}(\text{gpk}))$, and issues an e-cash wallet with the amount of coins equal to the credit limit ℓ of the user by $(W, \text{pk}_{\mathcal{U}}) \leftarrow \text{ECash.Withdraw}(\mathcal{U}(\text{pk}_{\mathcal{B}}, \text{sk}_{\mathcal{U}}, \ell), \mathcal{B}(\text{pk}_{\mathcal{U}}, \text{sk}_{\mathcal{B}}, \ell))$. Upon termination of the protocol, the bank inserts the entry $(\text{pk}_{\mathcal{U}}, \text{upk}_i)$ to the database DB, and the user obtains the credit card $\kappa := (\text{usk}_i, W)$.

Transaction Phase.

- $(R, (\kappa', R)) \leftarrow (\text{Auth}_{\mathcal{M}}(\text{sk}_{\mathcal{M}}, n), \text{Auth}_{\mathcal{U}}(\text{sk}_{\mathcal{U}}, \kappa, n))$: To pay an amount n when there are sufficient credits, the user transfers n coins in the e-cash system to the merchant by engaging in the spend protocol $\text{Spend}(\mathcal{U}(W, \text{sk}_{\mathcal{U}}, \text{pk}_{\mathcal{M}}, \text{pk}_{\mathcal{B}}), \mathcal{M}(\text{sk}_{\mathcal{M}}, \text{pk}_{\mathcal{B}}))$ n times. The output of this protocol is a set of serial numbers S and a set of proofs Π asserting the validity of the coins. The user then issues n group signatures signing the pair of each serial number and validity proof. Denote the set of group signatures by Σ. The tuples $r = (S, \Pi, \Sigma)$ act as the receipts of the transaction.
- $(\text{BB}', \perp) \leftarrow (\text{Batch}_{\mathcal{B}}(\text{sk}_{\mathcal{B}}, \text{BB}), \text{Batch}_{\mathcal{M}}(\text{sk}_{\mathcal{M}}, R))$: At the end of the day, the merchant batches the receipts by depositing the coins back to the bank using the deposit protocol $\text{Deposit}(\mathcal{M}(\text{sk}_{\mathcal{M}}, S, \Pi, \text{pk}_{\mathcal{B}}), \mathcal{B}(\text{pk}_{\mathcal{M}}, \text{sk}_{\mathcal{B}}, L))$, while showing a batch of signatures $\Sigma' = \{\sigma \leftarrow \text{GSig}(\text{usk}_i, (s, \pi))\}$ signing the serial number and the proof of validity of the coin deposited. The bank verifies all received signatures. If valid, it appends the signatures $\Sigma' = \{\sigma\}$ to the set Σ and appends (S, Π) to L.
- $\text{st} \leftarrow \text{Track}(\text{sk}_{\mathcal{U}}, \text{BB}, r)$: Once the signatures are posted in the set Σ, the users can track their previous transaction recorded in the receipt $r = (S, \Pi, \Sigma)$ by looking for their previously issued group signatures Σ on the board.
- The bank can also run the identification and tracing algorithms of the e-cash system to catch double-spenders.
- $(\text{BB}', (\kappa', R')) \leftarrow (\text{Repay}_{\mathcal{B}}(\text{sk}_{\mathcal{B}}, \text{BB}, n), \text{Repay}_{\mathcal{U}}(\text{sk}_{\mathcal{U}}, \kappa, R, n))$: To preserve privacy, the user repays the outstanding fees in small chunks of n. To do so, the user claims n signatures listed in Σ corresponding to some of the previous transactions, and pays the amount n anonymously by an external mechanism (e.g., physically). After a signature has been claimed, the user removes the corresponding receipt from R, and the bank removes the signatures from the set Σ.

Settlement Phase.

- $(\perp, \kappa') \leftarrow (\text{Settle}_{\mathcal{B}}(\text{sk}_{\mathcal{B}}, \rho, \ell, \ell'), \text{Settle}_{\mathcal{U}}(\text{sk}_{\mathcal{U}}, \kappa, \ell, \ell'))$: On the payment due date, the bank opens all the unclaimed signatures σ in Σ corresponding to the spent coins $\{(s, \pi)\}$ via $(i, \tau) \leftarrow \text{Open}(\text{ok}, \{\text{upk}\}, (s, \pi), \sigma)$ to trace the users who have not paid off the debt. It then charges those users interests. Finally, the bank re-issues e-cash wallets to the users with the amount of coins equal to their (potentially updated) credit limits as in the join protocol.

4.2   From Anonymous Transferable E-Cash Systems

Next, we describe a construction from anonymous transferable e-cash. Each user in this credit system may have different payment due dates.

Setup Phase.

- pp ← Pgen(1^λ): The bank or a trusted third party runs pp ← ECash.Pgen(1^λ) to generate the public parameter.
- ($pk_\mathcal{B}$, $sk_\mathcal{B}$, BB, DB) ← $KGen_\mathcal{B}$(pp): The bank in the credit system generates key pairs ($pk_\mathcal{B}$, $sk_\mathcal{B}$, L) ← ECash.$KGen_\mathcal{B}$(pp) via the underlying e-cash system. It sets the public bulletin board to BB := L.
- ($pk_\mathcal{U}$, $sk_\mathcal{U}$) ← $KGen_\mathcal{U}$(pp): The merchants and the users of the credit system act as the users of the e-cash system, who generate their key pairs via ($pk_\mathcal{U}$, $sk_\mathcal{U}$) ← ECash.$KGen_\mathcal{U}$(pp).
- (DB′, κ) ← ($Join_\mathcal{B}$($sk_\mathcal{B}$, DB, ℓ), $Join_\mathcal{U}$($sk_\mathcal{U}$, ℓ)): To join the system, the bank enrolls the user into the group by issuing an e-cash wallet with the amount of coins equal to the credit limit ℓ of the user by (W, $pk_\mathcal{U}$) ← ECash.Withdraw($\mathcal{U}$($pk_\mathcal{B}$, $sk_\mathcal{U}$, ℓ), $\mathcal{B}$($pk_\mathcal{U}$, $sk_\mathcal{B}$, ℓ)). Upon termination of the protocol, the bank inserts the entry $pk_\mathcal{U}$ to the database DB, and the user obtains the credit card $\kappa := W$.

Transaction Phase.

- (R, (κ', R)) ← ($Auth_\mathcal{M}$($sk_\mathcal{M}$, n), $Auth_\mathcal{U}$($sk_\mathcal{U}$, κ, n)): To pay an amount n when there are sufficient credits, the user transfers n coins in the e-cash system to the merchant by engaging in the spend protocol Spend($\mathcal{U}$(c, $sk_\mathcal{U}$, $cert_\mathcal{U}$, $pk_\mathcal{B}$), $\mathcal{M}$($sk_\mathcal{M}$, $pk_\mathcal{B}$)) n times. The output of the merchant is n coins, which also act as the receipts of the transaction.
- (BB′, $\perp$) ← ($Batch_\mathcal{B}$($sk_\mathcal{B}$, BB), $Batch_\mathcal{M}$($sk_\mathcal{M}$, R)): At the end of the day, the merchant batches the receipts by depositing the coins back to the bank using the deposit protocol Deposit($\mathcal{M}$(c, $sk_\mathcal{M}$, $cert_\mathcal{M}$, $pk_\mathcal{B}$), $\mathcal{B}$($sk_\mathcal{B}$, $pk_\mathcal{M}$, L)). Any double-spenders will be identified in this process, and the list L will be updated accordingly.

  Unlike the previous construction, the information post by the bank on the public bulletin board is unlinkable by the users due to the anonymity of the e-cash system, which unfortunately makes this construction untraceable.
- (BB′, (κ', R')) ← ($Repay_\mathcal{B}$($sk_\mathcal{B}$, BB, n), $Repay_\mathcal{U}$($sk_\mathcal{U}$, κ, R, n)): To preserve privacy, the user repays the outstanding fees in small chunks of n. To do so, the bank creates a new dummy merchant by generating a new key pair ($pk_\mathcal{M}$, $sk_\mathcal{M}$) ← ECash.$KGen_\mathcal{U}$(pp), and withdrawing a new wallet with n coins by (W, $pk_\mathcal{M}$) ← ECash.Withdraw($\mathcal{U}$($pk_\mathcal{B}$, $sk_\mathcal{M}$, n), $\mathcal{B}$($pk_\mathcal{M}$, $sk_\mathcal{B}$, n)). It then transfers all the coins from the dummy user to the requesting user by engaging in the spend protocol Spend($\mathcal{U}$(c, $sk_\mathcal{U}$, $cert_\mathcal{U}$, $pk_\mathcal{B}$), $\mathcal{M}$($sk_\mathcal{M}$, $pk_\mathcal{B}$)) for n times, after accepted payment via an external mechanism.

Settlement Phase.

- $(\perp, \kappa')\ \leftarrow\ (\mathsf{Settle}_\mathcal{B}(\mathsf{sk}_\mathcal{B}, \rho, \ell, \ell'), \mathsf{Settle}_\mathcal{U}(\mathsf{sk}_\mathcal{U}, \kappa, \ell, \ell'))$: On the payment due date, there are only two cases: (1) The number of coins n in the wallet stored in the credit card κ is more than or equal to its original credit limit ℓ; (2) The number of coins n in the wallet is less than its credit limit. In the first case, the user can choose to prove in zero-knowledge that the wallet contains enough coins. Otherwise, the user deposits all of the coins in the wallet to the bank via the deposit protocol $\mathsf{Deposit}(\mathcal{U}(c, \mathsf{sk}_\mathcal{U}, cert_\mathcal{U}, \mathsf{pk}_\mathcal{B}), \mathcal{B}(\mathsf{sk}_\mathcal{B}, \mathsf{pk}_\mathcal{U}, \mathsf{L}))$. The bank thus charges the user interest based on the interest rate ρ and the amount deposited, and issues a new wallet to the user as the new credit card κ', possibly with a new limit ℓ'.

4.3   Security Analysis

From Group Signature and E-Cash Systems. If there is an adversary who can break the balance property of our system, it can also break the balance property of the e-cash system.

For hiding spending pattern, the bank would not open any signatures if all the users have honestly paid all their debt. The only information about the expenditure of user known by the bank is the total amount spent by all users, since they are assigned the same payment due date.

For anonymous tracking of transactions, the public bulletin board just contains a collection of signatures which are generated by different users in the group. As long as the underlying dynamic group signature scheme is anonymous, our system can ensure the anonymity when users track their transactions.

For undercharge resistance, once all users finished claiming their signatures on the due date, the left unclaimed signatures on the bulletin board will be opened by the bank to trace the users who have not settled the debt. Due to the traceability of the dynamic group signature scheme, users who still have debt will be traced out and the bank can apply external mechanisms on these users.

If there exists an adversary who can break the mischarge resistance of our system, this adversary must be able to produce a signature together with a judge-accepted proof. Therefore, the non-frameability of the dynamic group signature scheme is broken.

From Anonymous Transferable E-Cash Systems. If a coalition of users can spend more than their collective credit limit, at least one of them can spend more coins than the number of coins which was withdrawn. Thus, from any adversary breaking the property of balance, we can construct an adversary breaking the unforgeability of the transferable e-cash system.

We claim that the bank in our system only knows the total amount spent by each group of users who are assigned to the same payment due date. This means when the bank receives a coin, it does not know who paid this coin. Suppose our system is insecure against this property, namely the bank can recognize the payer who receives a coin. then by a direct reduction we can construct an adversary who can break the *spend-and receive** property of the transferable e-cash system.

Our system provides undercharge resistance. On the payment due date, if the user proves in zero-knowledge that the wallet contains more coins than its credit limit, it must be the case that the user has already paid off all the debt. Otherwise, one can construct an adversary against the soundness of the proof system. Another case of undercharge is when the user deposit more coins than owned to the bank. We can separate this case into two sub-cases. In the first sub-case, the user generates some fake coins and deposits these fake coins to the bank. This however breaks unforgeability of transferable e-cash system. In the second sub-case, the user deposits a coin twice. This breaks the security of the transferable e-cash system since it fails to achieve identification of double-spenders.

For mischarge resistance, we have to consider two cases. The first case is that the bank and any coalition of merchants can accuse a user for not fully repaying the debt by arguing that some of the paid coins are invalid. When the user is honest and all the coins are transferable throughout the system, it means these invalid coins are spent by some users who can break the balance property of our system. Thus this case will not happen. The second case is that the bank and merchants accuse the user of double-spending. Due to the exculpability of the transferable e-cash system, this case will not happen as well.

5   Conclusion

In this paper, we study privacy preserving credit systems, for protecting the transaction privacy of credit card users from the banks. We present two different constructions such that neither the transaction amount nor the identity of participants in the transaction is known by the bank. The major building blocks are dynamic group signature scheme and anonymous transferable e-cash system respectively. Our system preserves most of the desirable features in a typical credit card system, such as personalized credit limit, interest rate control, etc.

Acknowledgments. Sherman Chow is supported by the Early Career Award and the Early Career Scheme (CUHK 439713), and General Research Funds (CUHK 14201914) of the Research Grants Council, University Grant Committee of Hong Kong.

References

1. Abe, M., Chow, S.S.M., Haralambiev, K., Ohkubo, M.: Double-trapdoor anonymous tags for traceable signatures. Int. J. Inf. Secur. **12**(1), 19–31 (2013)
2. Androulaki, E., Bellovin, S.M.: An anonymous credit card system. In: Proceedings of 6th Inernational Conference on Trust, Privacy and Security in Digital Business, TrustBus 2009, Linz, Austria, 3–4 September 2009, pp. 42–51 (2009)
3. Asokan, N., Janson, P.A., Steiner, M., Waidner, M.: State of the art in electronic payment systems. Adv. Comput. **53**, 425–449 (2000)

4. Au, M.H., Chow, S.S.M., Susilo, W.: Short e-cash. In: Maitra, S., Veni Madhavan, C.E., Venkatesan, R. (eds.) INDOCRYPT 2005. LNCS, vol. 3797, pp. 332–346. Springer, Heidelberg (2005). doi:10.1007/11596219_27

5. Baldimtsi, F., Chase, M., Fuchsbauer, G., Kohlweiss, M.: Anonymous transferable e-cash. In: Katz, J. (ed.) PKC 2015. LNCS, vol. 9020, pp. 101–124. Springer, Heidelberg (2015). doi:10.1007/978-3-662-46447-2_5

6. Bellare, M., Garay, J.A., Hauser, R.C., Herzberg, A., Krawczyk, H., Steiner, M., Tsudik, G., Van Herreweghen, E., Waidner, M.: Design, implementation, and deployment of the iKP secure electronic payment system. IEEE J. Sel. Areas Commun. 18(4), 611–627 (2000)

7. Bellare, M., Shi, H., Zhang, C.: Foundations of group signatures: the case of dynamic groups. In: Menezes, A. (ed.) CT-RSA 2005. LNCS, vol. 3376, pp. 136–153. Springer, Heidelberg (2005). doi:10.1007/978-3-540-30574-3_11

8. Blazy, O., Canard, S., Fuchsbauer, G., Gouget, A., Sibert, H., Traoré, J.: Achieving optimal anonymity in transferable e-cash with a judge. In: Nitaj, A., Pointcheval, D. (eds.) AFRICACRYPT 2011. LNCS, vol. 6737, pp. 206–223. Springer, Heidelberg (2011). doi:10.1007/978-3-642-21969-6_13

9. Blum, M., Feldman, P., Micali, S.: Non-interactive zero-knowledge and its applications (extended abstract). In: 20th ACM STOC, Chicago, Illinois, USA, 2–4 May 1988, pp. 103–112. ACM Press (1988)

10. Bootle, J., Cerulli, A., Chaidos, P., Ghadafi, E., Groth, J., Petit, C.: Short accountable ring signatures based on DDH. In: Pernul, G., Ryan, P.Y.A., Weippl, E. (eds.) ESORICS 2015. LNCS, vol. 9326, pp. 243–265. Springer, Heidelberg (2015). doi:10.1007/978-3-319-24174-6_13

11. Camenisch, J., Hohenberger, S., Lysyanskaya, A.: Compact e-cash. In: Cramer, R. (ed.) EUROCRYPT 2005. LNCS, vol. 3494, pp. 302–321. Springer, Heidelberg (2005). doi:10.1007/11426639_18

12. Canard, S., Gouget, A.: Anonymity in transferable e-cash. In: Manulis, M., Sadeghi, A.-R., Schneider, S. (eds.) ACNS 2008. LNCS, vol. 5037, pp. 207–223. Springer, Heidelberg (2008). doi:10.1007/978-3-540-68914-0_13

13. Capgemini, Royal Bank of Scotland. World payments report (2015). https://www.fr.capgemini-consulting.com/resource-file-access/resource/pdf/world_payments_report_2015_vfinal.pdf. Accessed 18 July 2016

14. Chaum, D.: Blind signatures for untraceable payments. In: Chaum, D., Rivest, R.L., Sherman, A.T. (eds.), CRYPTO 1982, Santa Barbara, CA, USA, pp. 199–203. Plenum Press, New York (1982)

15. Chow, S.S.M.: Running on karma – P2P reputation and currency systems. In: Bao, F., Ling, S., Okamoto, T., Wang, H., Xing, C. (eds.) CANS 2007. LNCS, vol. 4856, pp. 146–158. Springer, Heidelberg (2007). doi:10.1007/978-3-540-76969-9_10

16. Chow, S.S.M.: Real traceable signatures. In: Knudsen, L.R., Wu, H. (eds.) SAC 2009. LNCS, vol. 5867, pp. 92–107. Springer, Heidelberg (2009). doi:10.1007/978-3-642-05445-7_6

17. Fuchsbauer, G., Pointcheval, D., Vergnaud, D.: Transferable constant-size fair e-cash. In: Reiter, M., Naccache, D. (eds.) CANS 2009. LNCS, vol. 5888, pp. 226–247. Springer, Heidelberg (2009). doi:10.1007/978-3-642-10433-6_15

18. Goldwasser, S., Micali, S., Rackoff, C.: The knowledge complexity of interactive proof systems. SIAM J. Comput. 18(1), 186–208 (1989)

19. Krawczyk, H.: Blinding of credit card numbers in the SET protocol. In: Hirschfeld, R. (ed.) FC 1999. LNCS, vol. 1648, pp. 17–28. Springer, Heidelberg (1999). doi:10.1007/3-540-48390-X_2

20. Lai, R.W.F., Zhang, T., Chow, S.S.M., Schröder, D.: Efficient sanitizable signatures without random oracles. In: Proceedings of Computer Security - ESORICS 2016–21st European Symposium on Research in Computer Security, Heraklion, Crete, Greece, 28–30 September 2016 (2016, to appear)
21. Low, S.H., Paul, S., Maxemchuk, N.F.: Anonymous credit cards. In: Proceedings of the 2nd ACM Conference on Computer and Communications Security, CCS 1994, Fairfax, Virginia, USA, 2–4 November 1994, pp. 108–117 (1994)
22. Nakamoto, S.: Bitcoin: a peer-to-peer electronic cash system (2008)
23. Okamoto, T., Ohta, K.: Disposable zero-knowledge authentications and their applications to untraceable electronic cash. In: Brassard, G. (ed.) CRYPTO 1989. LNCS, vol. 435. Springer, Heidelberg (1990)
24. Okamoto, T., Ohta, K.: Universal electronic cash. In: Feigenbaum, J. (ed.) CRYPTO 1991. LNCS, vol. 576, pp. 324–337. Springer, Heidelberg (1992). doi:10.1007/3-540-46766-1_27
25. Tewari, H., Hughes, A.: Fully anonymous transferable ecash. IACR Cryptology ePrint Archive 2016:107 (2016)

Evading System-Calls Based Intrusion Detection Systems

Ishai Rosenberg[1(✉)] and Ehud Gudes[1,2]

[1] The Open University of Israel, Raanana, Israel
`ishai.msc@gmail.com`
[2] Ben-Gurion University, Beer-Sheva, Israel

Abstract. Machine-learning augments today's IDS capability to cope with unknown malware. However, if an attacker gains partial knowledge about the IDS's classifier, he can create a modified version of his malware, which can evade detection. In this article we present an IDS based on various classifiers using system calls executed by the inspected code as features. We then present a camouflage algorithm that is used to modify malicious code to be classified as benign, while preserving the code's functionality, for decision tree and random forest classifiers. We also present transformations to the classifier's input, to prevent this camouflage - and a modified camouflage algorithm that overcomes those transformations. Our research shows that it is not enough to provide a decision tree based classifier with a large training set to counter malware. One must also be aware of the possibility that the classifier would be fooled by a camouflage algorithm, and try to counter such an attempt with techniques such as input transformation or training set updates.

Keywords: Malware detection · Malware obfuscation · Decision trees · Behavior analysis · Camouflage algorithm · Machine learning

1 Introduction

Past intrusion detection systems (IDS) generally used two methods of malware detection: (1) Signature-based detection, i.e., searching for known patterns of data within the executable code. A malware, however, can modify itself to prevent a signature match, for example by using encryption. Thus, this method can be used to identify only known malware. (2) Heuristic-based detection is composed of generic signatures, including wild-cards, which can identify a malware family. This method can identify only variants of known malware.

Machine-learning can be used in-order to extend the IDS capabilities to classify software unseen before as malicious or benign by using static or dynamic features. However, our research shows that malware code can be transformed to render machine learning classifiers almost useless, without losing the original functionality of the modified code. We call such a generic transformation, based on the classifier type and the features used, a *camouflage algorithm*.

© Springer International Publishing AG 2016
J. Chen et al. (Eds.): NSS 2016, LNCS 9955, pp. 200–216, 2016.
DOI: 10.1007/978-3-319-46298-1_14

In this paper, we present a camouflage algorithm for decision tree and random forest based classifiers whose input features are sequences of system calls executed by the code at run-time. Our research has three main contributions:

1. Developing an automatic algorithm to decide which system calls to add to a malware code to make this code being classified as benign by our IDS, without losing its functionality. We then alleviate the assumption of full knowledge of the classifier by the attacker, showing that partial training set information might be enough.
2. Evaluating the algorithm against a large subset of malware samples, while previous work evaluated specific examples only.
3. Investigating possible transformations of the IDS input in-order to counter the camouflage algorithm - as-well-as a modified camouflage algorithm to evade those transformations.

While the above contributions are shown for specific classifier types (decision tree and random forest) and for specific features as input (system calls sequences), we believe the ideas are more general, and can be applied also to different classifiers with different features. The rest of the paper is structured as follows: Sect. 2 discusses the related work. Section 3 presents the problem definition and the evaluation criteria for the camouflage algorithm. Section 4 describes the IDS in detail and Sect. 5 discusses the camouflage algorithm implementation. Section 6 presents the experimental evaluation and Sect. 7 concludes the paper and outlines future research.

2 Background and Related Work

2.1 Machine Learning Binary Classifiers

The use of system calls to detect abnormal software behavior was shown in [4,15]. System call pairs (n-grams of size 2) from test traces were compared against those in the normal profile. Any system call pair not present in the normal profile is called a mismatch. If the number of system calls with mismatches within their window in any given time frame exceeded a certain threshold, an intrusion was reported.

Various machine learning classifiers, such as decision trees, SVM, boosted trees, Bayesian Networks and Artificial Neural Networks have been compared to find the most accurate classification algorithm; with varying results (e.g.: [3] chose decision trees, [8] chose boosted decision trees, etc.). The different results were affected, e.g., by the training set and the type of the feature set used.

There are two ways to extract the classifier features. They can be extracted statically (i.e., without running the inspected code), e.g.: byte-sequence (n-gram) in the inspected code [8]. The features can also be extracted dynamically (i.e., by running the inspected code), including: CPU overhead, time to execute, memory and disk consumption [12] or executed system calls sequences, either consecutive [15] or not [14]. A survey of system calls monitors and the attacks against them was conducted in [5], stating that in-spite of their disadvantages, they are commonly used by IDS machine learning classifiers.

While using static analysis has a performance advantage, it has a main disadvantage: Since the code isn't being run, it might not reveal its "true features". For example, if one looks for byte-sequence (or signatures) in the inspected code [8], one might not be able to catch polymorphic malware, in which those signatures are either encrypted or packed and decrypted only during run-time, by a specific bootstrap code. Other limitations of static analysis and techniques to counter it appear in [11]. Obviously, a malware can still try to hide if some other application (the IDS) is monitoring its features dynamically. However, in the end, in-order to operate its malicious functionality, a malware must reveal its true features during run-time.

Since a dynamic analysis IDS must run the inspected code, it might harm the hosting computer. In-order to prevent that, it's common to run the code in a sandbox; a controlled environment, which isolates between the malicious code to the rest of the system, preventing damage to the latter. This isolation can be done: (1) At the application-level, meaning that the malicious code is running on the same operating system as the rest of the system, but its system calls affect only a quarantined area of the system, e.g., Sandboxie[1]. (2) At the operating system level (e.g., VMWare Workstation), meaning the operating system is isolated but the processor is the same. (3) At the processor level, meaning all machine instruction are generated by an emulator like Qemu (e.g. TTAnalyze). While an emulator-based sand-boxing technique might be harder to detect, it can be done, e.g., using timing attacks due-to the emulator performance degradation, as shown in [13]. Therefore, we have used the VM sandbox mechanism to implement our IDS.

2.2   The Camouflage Algorithms

Modification of the input to a decision-tree classifier based on static analysis features (binary n-grams) was presented in [7]. A simulation of the IDS classifier of the installed anti-virus program was constructed by submitting a collection of malicious and benign binaries to the classifier via a COM (Component Object Model) interface, which runs the installed anti-virus on a file path argument and returns the classifier's decision for this file. Then, a feature-set similar to the attacker's code that would be classified as benign was found manually in the simulated decision tree. Finally, the authors appended the feature bytes to positions ignored by the system loader in the attacker's code, manually transforming its feature set to the benign one. In contrast, we encountered a dynamic analysis classifier, which is harder to fool [11].

Suggested ways to modify system call sequences were presented in [18]. It deals with *mimicry attacks*, where an attacker is able to code a malicious exploit that mimics the system calls trace of benign code, thus evading detection. [18] presents several methods: (1) Make benign system calls generate

---

[1] http://www.sandboxie.com/.

malicious behavior by modifying the system calls parameters. This works since most IDSs ignore the system call parameters. (2) Adding semantic *no-ops* - system calls with no effect, or whose effect is irrelevant, e.g.: opening a non-existent file. The authors showed that almost every system call can be no-op-ed and thus the attacker can add any needed no-op system call to achieve a benign system call sequence. (3) Equivalent attacks – Using a different system call sequence to achieve the same (malicious) effect.

In our work, we also use the second technique, since it's the most flexible. Using it, we can add no-op system calls that would modify the decision path of the inspected code in the decision tree, as desired. Main differences: (1) We have created an automatic algorithm and tested it on a large group of malware to verify that it can be applied to any malware, not only specific samples. (2) We verified that the modified malicious code functions properly and evade by executing it after its camouflage. (3) We refer to partial knowledge of the attacker. The authors mentioned several other limitations of their technique in [5] due-to the usage of code injection, which don't apply to our paper. One may claim that the IDS should consider only successful system calls to counter this method. However, every system call in a benign code may return either successfully or not, depending on the system's state and therefore may cause such IDS to falsely classify this code.

A similar method to ours was presented in [10]. The authors used system calls dependence graph (SCDG) with graph edit distance and Jaccard index as clustering parameters of different malware variants and used several SCDG transformations on the malware source code to "move" it to a different cluster. Our approach is different in the following ways: (1) Our classification method is different, and handles cases which are not covered by their clustering mechanism. (2) [10] showed a transformation that can cause similar malware variants to be classified at a different cluster - but not that it can cause a malware to be classified (or clustered) as a benign program, as shown in this paper. (3) Their transformations are limited to certain APIs only - and would not be effective for malware code that doesn't have them.

[16] presented an algorithm for automated mimicry attack on FSA (or overlapping graph) classifier using system call n-grams. However, this algorithm limits the malware code that can be camouflaged using it, to one that can be assembled from benign trace n-grams.

In [1,2], attacker-generated samples were added to the training set of the classifier, in-order for it to subvert the classification of malware code to benign, due-to its similarity to the added samples. However, it requires the attacker to have access to the classifier's DB, which is secured. In contrast, our method, which does not modify the classifier, is more feasible to implement.

3   Problem Description

We deal with two separated issues: (1) Classification of the inspected code, which was not encountered before, by the IDS as benign or malicious, using its system calls sequences. (2) Developing an algorithm to transform the inspected code, in-order to change the classification of the inspected code by the IDS from malicious to benign, without losing its functionality. The general problem can be defined formally as follows:

Given the traced sequence of system calls as the array *sys_call*, where the cell: *sys_call[i]* is the i-th system call being executed by the inspected code (*sys_call[1]* is the first system call executed by the code).

Define the IDS classifier as:

classify(benign_training_set, malic_training_set, inspected_code_sys_calls), where *inspected_code_sys_calls* is the inspected code's system calls array, *benign_training_set* is a set of system calls arrays used to train the classifier with a known benign classification and *malic_training_set* is a set of system calls arrays used to train the classifier with a known malicious classification. *classify()* returns the classification of the inspected code: either benign or malicious.

Given that an inspected code generates the array: *malic_inspected_code_sys_calls*, define the camouflage algorithm as a transformation on this array, resulting with the array: *C(malic_inspected_code_sys_calls)*. The success of the camouflage algorithm is defined as follows: Given that:

classify(benign_training_set, malic_training_set, malic_inspected_code_sys_calls) = malicious, the camouflage algorithm result is:

classify(benign_training_set, malic_training_set, C(malic_inspected_code_sys_calls)) = benign and:

malic_behavior(C(malic_inspected_code_sys_calls)) = *malic_behaviour (malic_inspected_code_sys_calls)*.

While in Sect. 6.3 we would show that partial knowledge of the training set is enough to generate a probabilistic camouflage, we initially assume that the attacker has access to the IDS and to the decision tree model it is based upon. Such knowledge can be gained by reverse engineering the IDS on the attacker's computer, without the need to gain access to the attacked system - just to have access to IDS. As shown in [7], an IDS decision tree can be recovered this way by exploiting public interfaces of an IDS and building the decision tree by feeding it with many samples and examining their classifications. Reconstruction attacks such as the one described in [6] for a C4.5 decision tree could also be used for this purpose. This assumption, that the IDS classifier, can be reconstructed, is common in several papers on this subject (e.g.: [1,2,5,10,16,18], etc.), as-well-as in cryptography (Kerckhoffs's principle). We further assume the attacker knows the system calls trace that would be produced by the malware on the inspected system. While the system calls trace might be affected by, e.g., files' existence and environment variables' values on the target system, it is highly unlikely, since the IDS should be generic enough to work effectively on all the clients' systems, making system-dependent flows rare.

The effectiveness of our IDS is determined by two factors (P is the probability):

1. We would like to minimize the false negative rate of the IDS, i.e. to minimize P(*classify(benign_training_set, malic_training_set, malic_inspected_code_sys_calls)* = benign).
2. We would like to minimize the false positive rate of the IDS, i.e. to minimize P(*classify(benign_training_set, malic_training_set, benign_inspected_code_sys_calls)* = malicious).

The overall effectiveness of the camouflage algorithm will be measured by the increased number of false negatives, i.e. we would like that:

P(*classify(benign_training_set, malic_training_set, C(malic_inspected_code_sys_calls))* = benign)$\geq$
P(*classify(benign_training_set, malic_training_set, malic_inspected_code_sys_calls)* = benign).

Therefore, the effectiveness of the camouflage algorithm is defined as the difference between the two probabilities (which are computed by the respective frequencies). The higher the difference between those frequencies, the more effective is the camouflage algorithm.

One way to fight the camouflage algorithm is to apply transformations on the input sequences of system calls and apply the classifier on the transformed sequences. The assumption is that the transformed sequences would reduce the effectiveness of the camouflage algorithm. We define a transformation of the system calls trace of the inspected code as *T(malic inspected code_sys_calls)*. We define the transformation *T* to be *effective* iff:

1. It would not reduce the malware detection rate, i.e.:
P(*classify(T(benign_training_set), T(malic_training_set), T(malic_inspected_code_sys_calls))* = malicious) $\geq$ P(*classify(benign_training_set, malic_training_set, malic_inspected_code_sys_calls)* = malicious)
2. It would not reduce the benign software detection rate, i.e.:
P(*classify(T(benign_training_set), T(malic_training_set), T(benign_inspected_code_sys_calls))* = benign) $\geq$ P(*classify(benign_training_set, malic_training_set, benign_inspected_code_sys_calls)* = benign)
3. It would reduce the camouflage algorithm effectiveness:
P(*classify(benign_training_set, malic_training_set, C(malic_inspected_code_sys_calls))* = benign) $\geq$ P(*classify(T(benign_training_set), T(malic_training_set), T(C(malic_inspected_code_sys_calls)))* = benign).

In the next two sections we describe in detail the IDS and camouflage algorithm implementations.

4   IDS Implementation

In-order to implement a dynamic analysis IDS that would sandbox the inspected code effects, we have used VMWare Workstation, where changes made by a malicious code can be reverted. We used a Windows XP[2] SP3 OS without an internet connection (to prevent the possibility of infecting other machines). The inspected executables were run for a period of 10 s (and then forcefully terminated), which resulted in about 10,000 recorded system calls per executable on average (the maximum number recorded per executable was about 60,000)[3].

The system calls recorder we have used for Windows records the Nt* system-calls. The usage of this low layer of system calls was done in-order to prevent malware from bypassing Win32API (e.g. *CreateFile()*) recording by calling those lower-level, Nt* APIs (e.g. *NtCreateFile()*). We have recorded 445 different system calls, such-as *NtClose()*, etc.

We have implemented the classifier using scikit-learn[4]. We selected the CART decision tree algorithm, similar to C4.5 (J48) decision tree, which was already proven to be a superior algorithm for malware classification [3].

The training set for the binary classifier contains malicious and benign executables. The malicious executables were taken from VX Heaven[5]. They were selected from the'Win32 Virus' type. Focusing on this specific mode of action of the malicious code reduce the chance of infection of other computers caused by using, e.g., worm samples. The number of malicious and benign samples in the set was similar (521 malicious samples and 661 benign samples) to prevent a bias towards classification with the same value as the majority of the training samples.

As features for the decision tree we used the position and the type of the system call, e.g.: *sys_call[3]* = *NtCreateFile*. Thus, the number of available feature values was very large (about 850,000). Therefore, we performed a feature selection of the 10,000 (best) features with the highest values for the χ^2 (chi-square) statistic of the training set, and created the decision tree based only on the selected features. This choice was made to ease the explanation of our algorithm in the next section. In Sect. 6.2 we would use more robust features and show that our algorithm works in this case either.

5   The Camouflage Algorithm Implementation

The goal of the camouflage algorithm is to modify the sequence of system calls of the inspected code in a way that would cause the classifier to change its classification decision from malicious to benign without harming its functionality.

---

[2] We used Windows XP and not newer versions, in-order to allow computer viri that use exploits found on this OS but patched afterward to run on our IDS either, thus detecting both new and old (but still used) malware.

[3] Tracing only the first seconds of a program execution might not detect certain malware types, like "logic bombs" that commence their malicious behavior only after the program has been running some time. However, this can be mitigated both by classifying the suspension mechanism as malicious or by tracing the code operation throughout the program execution life-time, not just when the program starts.

[4] http://scikit-learn.org/.

[5] http://vxheaven.org/.

This is done by finding a benign decision path (i.e., a path that starts from the tree root and ends in a leaf with benign classification) in the decision tree with the minimal edit distance [9] from the decision path of the malware (or the minimal Levenshtein distance between the paths' string representations). Then we add (not remove or modify, to prevent harming the malware functionality) system calls to change the decision path of the modified malware code to that of the benign path. Selecting the minimal edit distance means less malware code modifications.

In-order to modify the system calls sequence without affecting the code's functionality, we add the required system calls with invalid parameters. This can be done for most system calls with arguments. Others can be called and ignored. For example: opening a (non-existent) file, reading (0 bytes) from a file, closing an (invalid) handle, etc. One may claim that the IDS should consider only successful system calls. However, it is difficult for it to determine whether a system call is invoked with invalid parameters just to fool it, since even system calls of legitimate programs are sometimes being called with arguments that seem to be invalid, e.g., non-exiting registry key. In addition, IDSs that verify the arguments tend to be much slower (4–10 times slower, as mentioned in [17]).

In the basic version of our classifier, an internal node in the decision tree contains a decision condition of the form: $system\_call[i] =? system\_call\_type[k]$. Assume without loss of generality that if the answer is yes (i.e., $system\_call[i] = system\_call\_type[k]$), the branch is to the right (R child), and if the answer is no, the branch is to the left (L child). An example of a decision tree is presented in Fig. 1. In this decision tree, if the malware code trace contains: $\{sys\_call[1]=NtQueryInformationFile,\ sys\_call[2]=NtOpenFile,\ sys\_call[3]=NtAddAtom,\ sys\_call[4]=NtWriteFile\}$ (decision path: $M'=RRRR$, classified as a malicious) and if the algorithm will insert as the fourth system call a system call with a type different than $NtWriteFile$, the classifier will declare this malware code as benign, since the decision path would change from M' to $P1$.

While there is no guarantee that the algorithm would converge (step 3 in Algorithm 1 exists in-order to prevent an infinite loop by switching back and forth between the same paths), it did converge successfully for all the tested samples, as shown in Sect. 6. The reason for this is the rationale behind the decision tree based on system calls: The behavior of malware (and thus the system calls sequences used by it) is inherently different from that of benign software. Because-of that, and since the decision tree is trying to reduce the entropy of its nodes, the malicious and benign software do not spread uniformly at the leaf nodes of the decision tree but tend to be clustered at certain areas. Our path modifications direct the decision path to the desired cluster.

The general algorithm is depicted in Algorithm 1. Before explaining the details of the algorithm, let's discuss the possible edit operations when modifying a malware decision path. We will demonstrate the edit operations using the decision tree depicted in Fig. 1:

1. *Substitution*: There can be two types of substitutions: Sub_L - a substitution $L{\rightarrow}R$ (e.g., from $P=RRRL$ to $P'=RRRR$) and Sub_R - a substitution $R{\rightarrow}L$ (e.g., from $M=RRL$ to $P3=LRL$ in Fig. 1).
2. *Addition: Add_R* - an addition of R (e.g., from $M=RRL$ to $P1=RRRL$ in Fig. 1) or Add_L - an addition of L (e.g., from $P=RRL$ to $P'=LRRL$).
3. *Deletion: Del_L* - A deletion of L (e.g., from $P=LRL$ to $P'=RL$) or Del_R - a deletion of R (e.g., from $P=RRL$ to $P'=RL$).

Since the only allowed modification is an insertion of a dummy system call, the algorithm handles the above 6 edit operations as follows:

- If the edit_op is Sub_L, or Add_R, or Del_L: Given that the condition (in the parent node of the modified\added node) is: *sys_call[i]* =? *sys_call_type[k]*, add *sys_call[i]=sys_call_type[k]*. Note that the equivalent of Del_L is Sub_L followed by a tree re-evaluation, since this is the only edit op allowing you to remove the L without actually deleting a system call, which might harm the code's functionality.
- If the edit_op is Sub_R, or Add_L or Del_R: Given that the condition: *sys_call[i]* =? *sys_call_type[k]*, add *sys_call[i]=sys_call_type[m]* s.t. $m \mathrel{!=} k$. The above note about deletion applies here too.

After each edit operation, the malware trace changes: The dummy system call addition might have affected every condition on the tree in the form of: *sys_call[j]* =? *sys_call_type[k]* s.t. $j \geq i$. Therefore, we need to re-evaluate the entire decision path and find again the benign paths which are closest to it. Step 2(a) exists in-order to minimize the effects of the current edit operation on the path after re-evaluating it. The system calls insertion would ideally be done automatically, e.g., by usage of tools such-as *LLVM*, as done in [10], However, as mentioned by the authors, such tools are currently lack support for dealing with the Windows CRT and Platform SDK API calls, which are used by most Windows malware. Thus we assume that the attacker would manually insert the system calls, added by the camouflage algorithm, to the malware source code. This is demonstrated for the "Beetle" virus, in the next section.

Example 1. We demonstrate Algorithm 1 using the decision tree in Fig. 1:
   Given the malware code:
   {sys_call[1]=NtQueryInformationFile, sys_call[2] = NtOpenFile, sys_call[3]= NtWriteFile, sys_call[4]=NtClose},
   Its path in the IDS's decision tree is: $M=RRL$ (=Right-Right-Left), and the benign paths in the decision tree are: $P1=RRRL$, $P2=LLL$ and $P3=LRL$, the edit distances are $d(M, P1)=1$, $d(M, P2)=2$, $d(M, P3)=1$. The tuples to check are: $\{(M, P1), (M, P2), (M, P3)\}$. We have two paths with a minimal edit distance: *edit_sequence(M, P1)={Add_R (at position 3)}* and *edit_sequence(M, P3) = {Sub_R(at position 1)}*. The condition for-which we need to add R *in P1* is: *system_call[3] = NtAddAtom*. Thus: $i=3$. The condition for-which the edit operation applies in *P3* is: *system_call[2] = NtOpenFile*. Thus: $i=2$. Therefore, we start from *P1* and not from *P3*, since its index is larger.

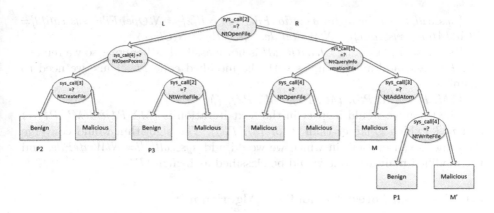

Fig. 1. A system calls based decision tree

Algorithm 1. System-Calls Based Decision Tree's Camouflage Algorithm

---

1. Given the decision tree of the IDS and a specific malware trace (i.e. its sequence of system calls as recorded) with the decision tree's path M, find all the IDS's decision tree's benign paths, *P1..Pm*, and create a list l of m tuples to check: *l={(M, P1)..(M, Pm)}*. Set *path_count[M] = 0*

2. For each tuple *(dec_path, Pj)* in l, find the minimum edit distance between *dec_path* and *Pj*, *d(dec_path, Pj)*. Select the tuple with the minimal such edit distance and find the minimal sequence of edit operations needed to change *dec_path* to *Pj*, ordered from the root of the tree to the leaf\classification node (i.e. by position in the decision path). If l is empty: Report failure.

   (a) If there is more than a single path with the same minimal edit distance, look at the first edit operation in each such path. Assuming the condition is of the form: *system_call[i] =? system_call_type[k]*, select the path that maximizes *i*.

3. Set *path_count[des_path] += 1*. If *path_count[des_path]≥max_decision_path_count* : Remove all tuples that contain *dec_path* from l and go to step 2.

4. Assuming the benign path to fit is *Pj*, modify the malware code based on the first edit operation in the edit sequence, as was explained above:

   (a) If the edit_op is *Sub_L*, *Add_R*, or *Del_L* then: Add *sys_call[i]=sys_call_type[k]*. Else: Add *sys_call[i]=sys_call_type[m]* s.t. *m != k*.

5. *system_call[i..n]* from before the modification now become *system_call[i+1..n+1]*. Re-evaluate the new system calls sequence and generate a new decision path *M'*.

6. If M' ends with a benign leaf: Report success. Else: Remove *(dec_path, Pj) from l*, and add all the tuples with the modified malware code *{ (M', P1)..(M', Pm)}* to l. Set *path_count[M'] = 0*

7. Go to step 2.

In-order to modify *M* to *P1*, we add: *sys_call[3] = NtAddAtom(NULL, 0, NULL)* (the edit_op is *Add_R*). Notice that we add the system call with invalid parameters. The new malware code is:

{*sys_call[1]=NtQueryInformationFile, sys_call[2] = NtOpenFile, sys_call[3]= NtAddAtom, sys_call[4]= NtWriteFile, sys_call[5]=NtClose*}.

Its decision path is $M'=RRRR$. M' is not classified as benign – so we remove (M, P1), and add all the tuples with the modified code M'. Thus, we need to examine:

{{(M, P2), (M, P3), (M', P1), (M', P2), (M', P3)}}.

The tuple we would inspect in the next iteration is (M', P1): d(M', P1)=1 and i=4 (which is larger than 2 for (M, P3)). The algorithm would converge after the next iteration, in which we would add sys_call[4]!= NtWriteFile, and the modified malware code would be classified as benign (P1).

5.1   Random Forest Camouflage Algorithm

In Sect. 6.2, the classifier with the best performance was random forest. Since a random forest is actually a collection of decision trees, if we extend the same assumptions made in Sect. 3, that-is: we know all the trees in the random forest, we can create a camouflage algorithm for random forest.

The rationale of the algorithm is simple: Since all decision trees in the random forest actually represents parts of the same code flow, we can modify each of them in turn, using Algorithm 1, and keep using the modified system calls trace, until we can fool the majority of them, thus fooling the entire random forest.

6   Experimental Evaluation

In-order to test the detection rate of our IDS, we used benign files collection from the Program Files folder of Windows XP SP3 and from our collection of third party benign programs and malware of Win32 Virus type, from VX Heaven's collection. The test set contained about 650 benign programs and 500 malware, which were different from the ones used to train the IDS in Sect. 4. The malware detection rate and the benign detection rate (as computed by the definitions specified in Sect. 3), were 84.3 % and 88.9 % respectively, as shown in the first line of Table 2.

In-order to test our camouflage algorithm, we have selected all the malware samples from our test set, which were correctly classified (i.e., as malicious) by our IDS (436 samples). We applied the camouflage algorithm on them: *None* of the camouflaged system calls sequences of those samples were identified by our IDS (effectiveness of 100 %, by the definition in Sect. 3).

We have applied the random forest camouflage algorithm on all the malware code that were detected by the random forest: 445 different samples. While there is no guarantee that the algorithm would converge, all modified section traces were classified as benign by our IDS, i.e., camouflage algorithm effectiveness of 100 %. This is due-to the same rationale mentioned in Sect. 5.

To test a complete "end-to-end" application of our system in real-life, we used the source code of the virus "Beetle"[6]. We compiled the source code and

---

[6] The description and the source code of this virus are available at: http://vxheaven.org/lib/vpe01.html.

ran it through our IDS. The virus system calls trace was classified correctly as malicious by our IDS. After using our camouflage algorithm, we received the modified system calls sequence, classified as benign by our IDS. We manually matched the system calls in this sequence to the virus original source code, and applied the same modifications to it - and then recompiled the modified version. The modified version of the virus was then run in our IDS, and was falsely classified by it as benign. As expected, the malicious functionality of the code remained intact.

6.1 Comparison to Other Classification Algorithms

We've implemented and compared the effectiveness of different classification algorithms, using the same features, training set and test set. In-order to take into account true and false positives and negatives, we tried to maximize the Matthews correlation coefficient (MCC), which is used in machine learning as a measure of the quality of binary classifications [1].

The results appear in Table 1.

Table 1. Detection rate of the IDS by classifier type

Classifier type	Malware detection rate (TPR)	Benign software detection rate (TNR)	MCC
Decision tree	84.3	88.9	0.76
Random forest	86.1	89.5	0.77
K-Nearest neighbors	89.4	86.0	0.77
Naïve Bayes (Gaussian)	87.0	54.5	0.50
Naïve Bayes (Bernoulli)	97.9	59.9	0.64
Ada-Boost	87.4	84.8	0.74
Support vector machine (Linear)	87.5	86.4	0.76
Support vector Machine (RBF)	96.3	74.9	0.74
Linear discriminant analysis	82.6	82.6	0.68

The Random Forest classifier and k-Nearest Neighbors classifier were the best overall, taking into account both malware and benign software detection rate (by maximizing the MCC).

6.2 Countering the Camouflage: Section-Based Transformations

The basic form of decision tree node condition is: $system\_call[i]=?system\_call\_type[k]$. However, using this kind of input makes the IDS classification fragile: It's enough that we add a single system call in the middle of the sequence or switch the positions of two system calls, to change the entire decision path.

Therefore, we want to transform the input data (the system calls array) in a way that would make a modification of the inspected code harder to impact the decision tree path of the modified code, thus counter the camouflage algorithm. In-order to define those transformations, we first divide the system calls sequence to small sections of consecutive system calls. Each system calls Section would have a fixed length, m. Thus, $section[i] = (sys\_call[(i-1)*m+1], .., sys\_call[i*m])$.

In an *order-preserving without duplicates removal section-based transformation*, we define the discrete values of the decision nodes in the tree to be: $section[i]$ $=?$ $(sys\_call[(i-1)*m+1], sys\_call[(i-1)*m+2], .., sys\_call[i*m])$.

However, this transformation is more specific than the basic model - so it would be easier to fool - and thus we didn't use it. This changes when adding *duplicates removal*: If there is more than a single system call of the same type in a section - only the first instance (which represent all other instances) appears in the section. This transformation prevents the possibility to split a system call into separate system calls (e.g. two *NtWriteFile()* calls, each writing 100 bytes, instead of a single call writing 200 bytes). Therefore, this was the first transformation we used.

The second transformation we examined is *non-order-preserving without duplicates removal*. This transformation is identical to the *order-preserving without duplicates removal transformation*, except for the fact that the system calls in each section are ordered in a predetermined order (lexicographically), regardless of their order of appearance in the trace. Using this transformation makes the probability of affecting the decision tree path by switching the places of two arbitrary system calls much smaller. Only the switching of two system calls from different sections might affect the decision path.

The last transformation we considered is *non-order-preserving with duplicates removal*. It is identical to the former, except for the fact that if there is more than a single system call of the same type in a section - only one instance (which represent all other instances) would appear in the section. This transformation handles both system calls switching and splitting. Notice that this transformation makes a section similar to a set of system calls: Each value can appear at most once, without position significance.

In-order to test the detection rate of our modified IDS, we used the same test set used for the basic model. A section size of $m=10$ was chosen. The detection rate, computed by the definitions specified in Sect. 3, appear in Table 2.

As can be seen from this table, section-based transformations are effective, by the definition in Sect. 3.

In-order to test our camouflage algorithm effectiveness vs. the modified IDS, we have used the camouflage algorithm shown in Algorithm 1 to modify the system calls trace. Then we have applied the input transformation on the modified system calls trace - and then we fed it to the input-transformed IDS variant. Without transformation we got a false-negative rate of 100 %. With section-based transformation, non order-preserving, without duplicates removal - we got 18.8 %. With section-based transformation, non order-preserving, with

Table 2. Detection rate of the IDS by input transformation type

Input type	Malware detection rate	Benign software detection rate
No transformation (original DB)	84.3	88.9
Non order-preserving, without duplicates removal	87.4	90.7
Non order-preserving, with duplicates removal	86.5	88.1
Order-preserving, with duplicates removal	87.6	91.3
No transformation (updated DB)	86.5	88.7

duplicates removal we got 17.2 %. With section-based transformation, order-preserving, with duplicates removal - we got 17.4 %.

We see that each input transformation reduces the effectiveness of the camouflage dramatically, since the camouflage we applied was designed against individual system calls and not against input transformations.

Countering the Input Transformations with Custom-Fit Camouflage Algorithm. One might argue that camouflaging a system calls trace in our basic IDS (without the transformations suggested in Sect. 6.2) is an easy task. One needs to add only a single system call at the beginning to change all following system calls positions, thus affecting the decision path in the tree. Can we apply our camouflage algorithm on our section-based IDS with the same effectiveness?

In-order to fit our camouflage algorithm to section-based transformations, we have used Algorithm 1, except that in each iteration we added an entire system calls section, instead of a single system call. This is done in step 4: Assuming the condition is:

$section[i] =?$ $(sys\_call[(i-1)*m+1], sys\_call[(i-1)*m+2],.., sys\_call[i*m])$, if the edit_op is Sub_L, Add_R, or Del_L then:

Add $section[i] = (sys\_call[(i-1)*m+1], sys\_call[(i-1)*m+2],.., sys\_call[i*m])$ (add the same section).

Else: Add $section[i]=(sys\_call'[(i-1)*m+1],$ $sys\_call[(i-1)*m+2],..,$ $sys\_call[i*m])$ s.t. $sys\_call'[(i-1)*m+1]$ $!=$ $sys\_call[(i-1)*m+1]$ (add a section with a different first system call).

The section is added with the same transformation type as the IDS: either *order preserving* or not, and either with or without *duplicates removal*.

We have applied this algorithm on all section-based transformations described in Sect. 6.2. Like Algorithm 1, there is no guarantee that the algorithm would converge. However, all 436 modified section traces were classified as benign by our IDS, with all input transformations, i.e., camouflage algorithm effectiveness of 100 %. This is due-to the same rationale mentioned in Sect. 5. This was also the case when modifying the random forest camouflage algorithm mentioned in Sect. 5.1 to counter input transformations by replacing Algorithm 1 used by it with this variant.

6.3 Partial Knowledge of the IDS

So far, we assumed that the attacker has full knowledge of both the classifier type, the training set used to create it and its features, in-order to generate the exact same classifier and then use it to camouflage the malicious code. We can alleviate this assumption: If the attacker can gain partial knowledge about the training set, he can construct the simulated classifier using *only* the training set he knows about and use it in Algorithm 1. Such partial knowledge is easy to gather, e.g., using the VirusTotal[7] samples closest to the IDS release date, which are very probable to be used by the IDS. We have trained the attacker classifier using a part of the training set which is used by the IDS classifier, as mentioned in Sect. 6. We then camouflaged the entire test set using Algorithm 1, based on the attacker partial knowledge based classifier.

We discovered that a knowledge of 86.4 % of the IDS training set is enough to create a camouflage that is 56.6 % effective. A knowledge of 77.7 % of the training set provides camouflage effectiveness of 31.3 % and 69.1 % of it provides effectiveness of 25.4 %. We also tested a full knowledge of the training set, with different features being selected (in case of chi-square equality). In this case, the camouflage is 64 % effective. Finally, we tested a full knowledge of the attacker on the training set and features, followed by an update of the IDS training set size by 1.7 %, without the attacker knowledge. In this case, the generated camouflage was 75.5 % effective. This means that training set updates can decrease the camouflage algorithm effectiveness, which was supported by our results, which are not shown due to space limitation.

From all the experiments, it is clear that the camouflage algorithm is useful to an attacker even with partial knowledge of the classifier.

7   Conclusions

In this article, we have shown that malware code which has been identified by a specific machine learning classifiers (decision tree or random forest) can be camouflaged in-order to be falsely classified as benign. We have done so by modifying the actual code being executed, without harming its malicious functionality. We then applied a defense mechanism to the camouflage algorithm, called input transformations, making it more robust, and showed that it can also be evaded.

This suggests that it is not enough to use a machine learning classifier with a large DB of benign and malicious samples to detect malware - one must also be aware of the possibility that such classifier would be fooled by a camouflage algorithm - and try to counter it with techniques such as continuous updating

---

[7] https://www.virustotal.com/.

of the classifier's training set or application of the input transformation that we discussed. However, as we have shown, even such transformations are susceptible to camouflage algorithms designed against them.

Our future work in this area would examine the effectiveness of our camouflage algorithm on other machine-learning classifiers (e.g. SVM, boosted trees, etc.) and find other algorithms to cope with such classifiers and with other types of features (e.g., anomaly based detection, [12]), currently not supported.

References

1. Baldi, P., Brunak, S., Chauvin, Y., Andersen, C.A., Nielsen, H.: Assessing the accuracy of prediction algorithms for classification: an overview. Bioinformatics **16**(5), 412–424 (2000)
2. Biggio, B., Rieck, K., Ariu, D., Wressnegger, C., Corona, I., Giacinto, G., Rol., F.: Poisoning behavioral malware clustering. In: Proceedings of the 7th ACM Workshop on Artificial Intelligence and Security (2014)
3. Firdausi, I., Lim, C., Erwin, A.: Analysis of machine learning techniques used in behavior based malware detection. In: Proceedings of 2nd International Conference on Advances in Computing, Control and Telecommunication Technologies, pp. 201–203 (2010)
4. Forrest, S., Hofmeyr, S., Somayaji, A., Longsta, T.: A sense of self for Unix processes. In: IEEE Symposium on Security and Privacy, pp. 120–128. IEEE Press, USA (1996)
5. Forrest, S., Hofmeyr, S., Somayaji, A.: The evolution of system-call monitoring. In: Proceedings of the Annual Computer Security Applications Conference, pp. 418–430 (2008)
6. Gambs, S., Gmati, A., Hurfin, M.: Reconstruction attack through classifier analysis. In: Proceedings of the 26th Annual IFIP WG 11.3 Working Conference on Data and Applications Security and Privacy, pp. 274–281 (2012)
7. Hamlen, K.W., Mohan, V., Masud, M.M., Khan, L., Thuraisingham, B.: Exploiting an antivirus interface. Comput. Stand. Interfaces **31**(6), 1182–1189 (2009)
8. Kolter, J.Z., Maloof, M.A.: Learning to detect malicious executables in the wild. In: Proceedings of the 10th International Conference on Knowledge Discovery and Data Mining, pp. 470–478 (2004)
9. Navarro, G.: A guided tour to approximate string matching. ACM Comput. Surv. **33**(1), 31–88 (2001)
10. Ming, J., Xin, Z., Lan, P., Wu, D., Liu, P., Mao, B.: Replacement attacks: automatically impeding behavior-based malware specifications. In: Malkin, T., et al. (eds.) ACNS 2015. LNCS, vol. 9092, pp. 497–517. Springer, Heidelberg (2015). doi:10. 1007/978-3-319-28166-7_24
11. Moser, A., Kruegel, C., Kirda, E.: Limits of static analysis for malware detection. In: 23rd Annual Computer Security Applications Conference, pp. 421–430 (2007)
12. Moskovitch, R., Gus, I., Pluderman, S., Stopel, D., Fermat, Y., Shahar, Y., Elovici, Y.: Host based intrusion detection using machine learning. In: Proceedings of Intelligence and Security Informatics, pp. 107–114 (2007)
13. Raffetseder, T., Kruegel, C., Kirda, E.: Detecting system emulators. In: Garay, J.A., Lenstra, A.K., Mambo, M., Peralta, R. (eds.) ISC 2007. LNCS, vol. 4779, pp. 1–18. Springer, Heidelberg (2007)

14. Rozenberg, B., Gudes, E., Elovici, Y., Fledel, Y.: Method for detecting unknown malicious executables. In: Kirda, E., Jha, S., Balzarotti, D. (eds.) RAID 2009. LNCS, vol. 5758, pp. 378–379. Springer, Heidelberg (2009)
15. Somayaji, A., Forrest, S.: Automated response using system-call delays. In: Proceedings of the 9th USENIX Security Symposium, pp. 185–198 (2000)
16. Sufatrio, Yap, R.H.C.: Improving host-based IDS with argument abstraction to prevent mimicry attacks. In: Valdes, A., Zamboni, D. (eds.) RAID 2005. LNCS, vol. 3858, pp. 146–164. Springer, Heidelberg (2006)
17. Tandon, G., Chan, P.: On the learning of system call attributes for host-based anomaly detection. Int. J. Artif. Intell. Tools 15(6), 875–892 (2006)
18. Wagner, D., Soto, P.: Mimicry attacks on host-based intrusion detection systems. In: Proceedings of the 9th ACM Conference on Computer and Communications Security, pp. 255–264 (2002)

Network Security and Forensic

HeapRevolver: Delaying and Randomizing Timing of Release of Freed Memory Area to Prevent Use-After-Free Attacks

Toshihiro Yamauchi$^{(\boxtimes)}$ and Yuta Ikegami

Graduate School of Natural Science and Technology,
Okayama University, 3-1-1 Tsushima-naka, Kita-ku, Okayama 700-8530, Japan
yamauchi@cs.okayama-u.ac.jp

Abstract. Recently, there has been an increase in use-after-free (UAF) vulnerabilities, which are exploited using a dangling pointer that refers to a freed memory. Various methods to prevent UAF attacks have been proposed. However, only a few methods can effectively prevent UAF attacks during runtime with low overhead. In this paper, we propose HeapRevolver, which is a novel UAF attack-prevention method that delays and randomizes the timing of release of freed memory area by using a memory-reuse-prohibited library, which prohibits a freed memory area from being reused for a certain period. In this paper, we describe the design and implementation of HeapRevolver in Linux and Windows, and report its evaluation results. The results show that HeapRevolver can prevent attacks that exploit existing UAF vulnerabilities. In addition, the overhead is small.

Keywords: Use-after-free (UAF) vulnerabilities · UAF attack-prevention · Memory-reuse-prohibited library · System security

1 Introduction

Recently, there has been an increase in use-after-free (UAF) vulnerabilities, which can be exploited by referring a dangling pointer to a freed memory. A UAF attack abuses the dangling pointer that refers to a freed memory area and executes an arbitrary code by reusing the freed memory area. Figure 1 shows the number of UAF vulnerabilities investigated in [1]. The figure shows that the number of UAF vulnerabilities has rapidly increased since 2010 [1]. Further, the number of exploited UAF vulnerabilities has increased in Microsoft products [2]. In particular, large-scale programs such as browsers often include many dangling pointers, and the UAF vulnerabilities are frequently exploited by drive-by download attacks. For example, many UAF attacks exploit the vulnerabilities of plug-ins (e.g. Flash Player) in browsers. As a modern browser has a JavaScript engine, an attacker can exploit the UAF vulnerabilities using JavaScript, which creates and frees memory area.

© Springer International Publishing AG 2016
J. Chen et al. (Eds.): NSS 2016, LNCS 9955, pp. 219–234, 2016.
DOI: 10.1007/978-3-319-46298-1_15

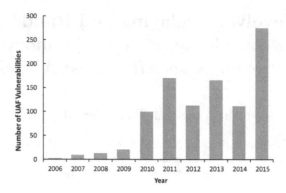

Fig. 1. Number of UAF vulnerabilities

To show the characteristics of a UAF attack, we investigated CVE-2012-4792, CVE-2012-4969, CVE-2013-3893, and CVE-2014-1776 as UAF vulnerabilities used for attacks in real world. Investigation results show that in a UAF attack, memory is reused immediately after a target freed-object is reused to reduce the possibility of a target memory area being reused by another process after it is released. Various methods to prevent UAF attacks have been proposed [3–13]. However, only a few methods can effectively prevent UAF attacks during runtime with low overhead. Furthermore, the memory usage of existing methods is inefficient, and these methods utilize considerable memory area for preventing UAF-attacks.

Thus, many related works have used techniques such as the DelayFree deploy technique that delays the time of freeing a memory object. In [15–17], methods were proposed to prevent UAF attacks against Internet Explorer (IE) by calling functions that have recently taken measures against UAF attacks. However, DelayFree [16] and Memory Protector [17] do not release the freed memory areas for a fixed period, thus complicating UAF attacks. This period remains until the total size of the freed memory area is more than the threshold (beyond 100 KB). However, when the freed total memory size increases beyond the threshold, all memory areas that were prevented to be released are released and can be reused. In addition, each program must be altered to apply these methods, resulting in the increase in man-day requirement to modify a program and develop a patch. An attack against DelayFree is reported in [18], indicating that an attack against DelayFree will succeed. In addition, an attack against IE secured using Isolated Heap and Memory Protector was reported in [19]. Therefore, new countermeasures are required to prevent UAF attacks.

In this paper, we propose HeapRevolver, which is a novel UAF-attack prevention method that delays and randomizes the release timing of a freed memory area by using a memory-reuse-prohibited library. By delaying release of freed memory area, HeapRevolver prohibits the reuse of the memory area for a certain period. Thus, the abovementioned UAF attacks are prevented. The threshold for the conditions of reuse of the freed memory area can be randomized by

HeapRevolver. This function makes it more difficult to reuse memory area for UAF attacks by randomizing the timing of the release of the memory area. In addition, we added a reuse condition in which the freed memory area is merged with an adjacent freed memory area before release. By adding this condition, a UAF attack will fail if an offset of the dangling pointer to the memory area is not appropriately calculated. Furthermore, HeapRevolver can be implemented in a library and be applied without altering the targeted program for protection. Thus, applying HeapRevolver to targeted programs is not difficult. As HeapRevolver can reuse the freed memory area under the reuse conditions, the memory can be efficiently used. Finally, we describe the design and implementation of HeapRevolver in Linux and Windows and report the evaluation results. The results show that the performance overhead of HeapRevolver is relatively smaller than that of DieHarder [14], which is one of the representative methods to prevent UAF attacks by library replacement.

2 Problem and HeapRevolver Design

2.1 Problem of Existing Methods

The problems of the related studies [15–17] are as follows:

(Problem 1) The reuse timing can be guessed by attackers: The related methods do not release the freed memory area for a fixed period and complicates UAF attacks. Owing to the period being fixed, attackers can guess the reuse timing. Thus, the reuse time estimation must be made difficult.

(Problem 2) Need to alter the program code: Some methods alter the program of IE and call the recently added functions, thus preventing a UAF attack. Therefore, altering a program is necessary.

(Problem 3) Target application and OS's are limited: The methods protect IE in Windows against UAF attacks. Therefore, a more easy deployment method for various OS's and application programs is required for UAF attack mitigation.

In this paper, we propose a novel UAF attack-prevention method to resolve these three problems.

2.2 Design of HeapRevolver

In this paper, we focus on the objective that UAF attacks can be prevented by preventing reuse of the freed memory area. However, when the reuse of freed memory area is prevented, memory usage becomes extremely inefficient. In addition, the overhead of creating new memory area increases because *brk* and *sbrk* system calls are issued to expand the heap area. To solve this problem, we prohibit the reuse of a memory area for a certain period after it is freed. When a certain period has passed, the memory area can be reused. We assume that if this period is fixed, the reuse timing can be predicted by the attackers. Therefore, we randomize the prohibited period of reuse in HeapRevolver.

To prevent UAF attacks by reusing the memory objects, HeapRevolver prevents a UAF attack by altering an existing library. The altered library prohibits reuse of the freed memory for a certain period. The conditions for reuse are as follows.

(Condition 1). The total size of the freed memory area is beyond the designated size.

(Condition 2). The freed memory area is merged with an adjacent freed memory area.

When condition 1 is satisfied, the memory area that satisfies condition 2 is released. The released memory size is at most half of the designated total size in the freed memory. Condition 1 refers to technique used in DelayFree [16] and Memory Protector [17]. The designated total size (threshold) in the freed memory in these techniques is constant. The threshold is 100 KB. When an attacker creates a memory area of 100 KB, the freed memory is released; thus, an attacker can attempt to reuse a memory area by creating a memory area.

In HeapRevolver, we develop two countermeasures for this problem. First, the total size threshold of the freed memory area is set to a larger value than that in DelayFree. This measure increases the threshold entropy against UAF attacks because threshold estimation becomes more difficult. Second, the threshold is randomized in some ranges. In addition, the threshold is randomly updated when condition 1 is satisfied. Furthermore, HeapRevolver releases at most only half of the freed memory area, implying that the randomly selected memory is delayed. This results in a certain memory area that cannot be reused for a long period. Furthermore, by adding condition 2, a UAF attack fails if an offset of a dangling pointer to the memory area is not appropriately calculated.

3   Implementation of HeapRevolver

3.1   Implementation of HeapRevolver in Linux

In this section, we describe the implementation of HeapRevolver for glibc (x86_64) in Linux by altering only the *free()* function of the malloc algorithm that releases the memory area. Figure 2 shows the memory structure of malloc in HeapRevolver.

The *free()* function process of HeapRevolver is explicated as follows. *Lock_bins* and *wait_bins* are added to the *malloc_state* structure for HeapRevolver.

(1) The freed memory area (chunk) is stored in the head of the list (*lock_bins*).
(2) When the total size of the freed chunk stored in *lock_bins* and *wait_bins* is beyond the threshold limit, the freed chunks are released from the *lock_bins* list until half of the designated total size is released. The freed chunks must be merged with a *chunk* located in an adjacent memory cell before the chunks are released. When a freed chunk is removed from the *lock_bins*, HeapRevolver searches for a freed chunk that can be merged with the adjacent chunk from the *wait_bins* and *unsorted_chunks*. If HeapRevolver finds a chunk for merging, the freed chunk is merged with it and is entered into the *unsorted_chunks* for release.

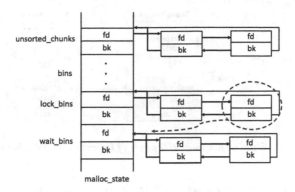

Fig. 2. Memory structure of malloc in HeapRevolver

(3) If no chunk can be merged, the chunks in *lock_bins* are moved to *wait_bins* after attaching an attribute, indicating means that the chunk must be merged before reuse.

We believe that the threshold for the total size of the freed chunks is 1 MB, which is sufficient to complicate UAF attacks. In glibc of Linux/x86_64, a memory area that is larger or equal to 128 KB is created by the *mmap()* function. Thus, if the chunk size is smaller than 128 KB, the chunk is entered in the *lock_bins*. Therefore, more than seven chunks are entered in *lock_bins* when threshold ≥ 1 MB. Furthermore, HeapRevolver randomizes the threshold of the total size when the total size of freed memory is larger than the threshold value.

The proposed method is applied to a library, which is introduced by replacing an existing library in a specific directory or changing a linked dynamic library before it is loaded. For example, a linked dynamic library can be changed by modifying the path names of LD_PRELOAD and LD_LIBRARY_PATH.

3.2   Implementation of HeapRevolver in Windows

The Windows' APIs *kernel32.dll* and *ntdll.dll* provide similar memory management processing as the glibc library in Linux. In addition, the *HeapFree()* function in *kernel32.dll* is often used to release a heap area. Thus, we implemented a function of HeapRevolver in the *HeapFree()* function. In our implementation, the *HeapFree()* function is hooked by our original function.

The hook function of HeapRevolver is implemented using a dynamic link library (DLL) injection and Windows API hook. DLL injection is a DLL mapping method to other processes and executes DLL processing in the processes. Windows API hook is a method that hooks a Windows API call and executes a certain processing before the hooked Windows API call. We deployed an import address table (IAT) hook for the Windows API hook. IAT hook is a method that modifies the address of APIs in IAT to call a target function.

Figure 3 shows the flow of hooking the *HeapFree()* function to the target process. When the *Hook_HeapFree()* function of *Hook.dll* is called by IAT

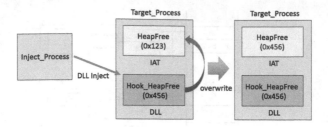

Fig. 3. Flow of hooking *HeapFree()* function on Windows

hook, the *Hook_HeapFree()* function of *Hook.dll* obtains the arguments of the *HeapFree()* function and stores them in a ring buffer. Next, the *Hook_HeapFree* function checks whether the sum of the freed memory are beyond the threshold. If the sum exceeds the threshold, the *Hook_HeapFree()* function obtains the arguments of the *HeapFree()* function and calls the *HeapFree()* function to release the freed memory area. The *Hook_HeapFree()* function calls the *HeapFree()* function until half of the threshold is released. If the sum of the freed memory does not exceed the threshold, the proposed function returns without any operation. Thus, the *Hook_HeapFree()* function delays the release of the freed memory area until the sum of the freed memory area exceeds the threshold.

The implementation of HeapRevolver in Windows is almost the same as in Linux. However, the prototype implementation of Windows does not include the determination of whether a memory area is already merged with an adjacent memory area. This needs to be further studied. In addition, the prototype implementation in Windows uses the number of freed memory areas as a threshold instead of the sum of the freed memory area sizes because the process of managing the size is complex. Even when the amount of freed memory area is used as a threshold, the entropy can increase and can complicate UAF attacks using a large number of thresholds and randomizing them.

4   Evaluation

4.1   Security Analysis

Possibility of Success of UAF Attacks in HeapRevolver. We analyzed the possibility of attacks against HeapRevolver. For an attack to succeed, an attacker must reuse the freed memory area and overwrite the memory. Subsequently, malicious codes must be executed by referring to a dangling pointer. In HeapRevolver, the freed memory area cannot be reused until it satisfies the reuse condition because the area is entered into a wait_bin queue. Thus, most of the aforementioned UAF attacks can be prevented using HeapRevolver. Only when a memory area is freed, the sum of the freed memory area exceeds the threshold and the target memory area is merged to an adjacent memory area. The freed memory area can then be immediately reused after it is released. However, in this case, reusing the freed memory area is difficult because the attacker must predict the size of the merged memory area (described in the next paragraph). In addition, the attacker must understand the number and total size of the freed memory areas. Because the threshold of reuse is randomly set when the freed memory area is released and large-scale programs such as browsers process many memory allocations and releases, predicting when the sum of the freed memory area exceeds the threshold is very difficult.

The additional condition for attacks is the immediate reuse of the freed memory area after it is released. In many attacks, the requested size of memory allocation is the same as that of the target freed memory area. In HeapRevolver, the reusable memory area must be merged to an adjacent memory area. Thus, the possibility of reuse is considerably reduced when the same size is designated for the memory allocation. For example, in Linux, unused memory area with a size is the same as the requested size is reused prior to the reuse of the memory area with another size.

If a dangling pointer is referred to before all the previous conditions are satisfied, the attacks will fail because of segmentation or other faults. After the faults, the application is terminated, and the next attack becomes impossible. Because such failure in attacks reveals the attempts of attacks, we believe that attackers will avoid performing low-possibility attacks.

Attack Possibility Against HeapRevolver. To defeat HeapRevolver, attackers consider repeating memory allocation and releasing memory. In addition, to increase the probability of successful attacks, heap spraying is used. Heap spraying is effective when the memory layout is predictable or memory fragmentation in the heap area is suppressed. In HeapRevolver, freeing the memory area is randomly delayed, and memory fragmentation such as external fragmentation in the heap area frequently occurs. In this situation, large area of heap spraying is often allocated in the last part of the heap area, and we believe that the success of heap spraying is low. For the attacks against HeapRevolver to succeed, both UAF attacks and heap spraying must succeed; thus, the possibility of the success of two attacks is low, and the risk of revealing attack attempt is high because of failures.

As a typical attack, to overwrite a freed memory area referred by dangling pointer, the attacker attempts to allocate a large memory area after the target memory area is freed. Next, the attacker overwrites the entire target memory area. Overwriting a large memory area is expected to improve the possibility of a successful attack. This type of attack can succeed after the target memory area is freed and reused. As aforementioned, reuse of the target memory area is difficult. In addition, the timing of freeing the target memory area is non-deterministic; thus, creating attack codes with a high success probability against HeapRevolver is difficult.

4.2   Evaluation Environment

We used a computer with Intel Core i7-3770 (3.40 GHz) and 4-GB main memory for the evaluation. The OS's and versions used in the evaluations are Linux

3.13.0-45-generic/x86_64 (Ubuntu 14.04 LTS) and Windows 7 (64 bit). The
HeapRevolver was implemented in glibc-2.19 in Linux.

```
yuta@debian:~$ ./uaf 100 10
result = 110
Addnum = 0x602010
buf = 0x602010
$
```

(A) Before application of HeapRevolver

```
yuta@debian:~$ LD_PRELOAD="/usr/local/test2
/lib/libc.so.6" ./uaf 100 10
result = 110
Addnum = 0x602010
buf = 0x602030
Segmentation fault
```

(B) After application of HeapRevolver

Fig. 4. Experimental results of UAF attack prevention in Linux

To show the feasibility and overhead of the HeapRevolver, we evaluated its
performance on Linux and Windows. The following experiments were performed.
The UAF-attack prevention experiments in Linux and Windows show that UAF
attacks can be prevented by HeapRevolver. In addition, we evaluated the performance overhead and memory usage of HeapRevolver. Finally, we compared
HeapRevolver with DieHarder, which is one of the UAF prevention methods that
use library replacement. In the overhead evaluations, we used fixed thresholds
on HeapRevolver because we clarified the relationship between the threshold size
and performance and memory overhead of HeapRevolver.

4.3   Prevention Experiments of UAF Attack in Linux

We describe the experimental results of attempting UAF attacks using a program. In the program, an object of an *Addnum* class is created and deleted.
Subsequently, when a memory area with the same size as that of the *Addnum*
object is created, the memory area of the deleted *Addnum* object is reused.
The address where a pointer of the shell code is stored is overwritten on the
vtable address of the *Addnum* object. The shell code is executed by a call to
the overwritten vtable. The program was executed when address space layout
randomization and data execution prevention were disabled.

Figure 4 shows the execution results before and after the application of
HeapRevolver in Linux. Figure 4-(A) shows that the *Addnum* object and *buf*
were allocated in the same memory area. Next, the UAF attack was performed
by referring to a dangling pointer. Thus, the shell codes were executed. In contrast, Fig. 4-(B) shows that an *Addnum* object and *buf* were allocated in different
memory areas. Here, the UAF attack failed due to segmentation fault because
the memory area accessed by referring to the dangling pointer did not have
access rights. Therefore, HeapRevolver can prevent the UAF attack.

Table 1. Overheads in malloc-test.

Memory size	lib	Thread num		
		1	3	5
100 B	glibc	0.335	1.02	1.71
	HeapRevolver (100 KB)	0.398 (18.8 %)	1.200 (17.6 %)	2.015 (18.1 %)
	HeapRevolver (1 MB)	0.399 (19.1 %)	1.205 (18.1 %)	2.020 (18.4 %)
512 B	glibc	0.371	1.132	1.885
	HeapRevolver (100 KB)	0.425 (14.5 %)	1.310 (15.7 %)	2.195 (16.4 %)
	HeapRevolver (1 MB)	0.437 (17.8 %)	1.324 (17.1 %)	2.210 (17.2 %)
1024 B	glibc	0.374	1.137	1.903
	HeapRevolver (100 KB)	0.526 (40.6 %)	1.495 (31.5 %)	2.481 (30.4 %)
	HeapRevolver (1 MB)	0.543 (45.2 %)	1.503 (36.6 %)	2.509 (31.8 %)

4.4 Evaluation of Performance Overhead in Linux

To compare the performances of HeapRevolver and the original glibc, they were evaluated using several program types. The thresholds of HeapRevolver in evaluation were 100 KB and 1 MB.

First, the malloc-test benchmark was used to evaluate the processing time. The malloc-test benchmark contains some tests for the malloc and freeing processes. The tests were performed by multi-threading. The processing time was measured when the process was repeated 10,000,000 times. The requested memory sizes were 100, 512, and 1,024 bytes. The number of threads was changed from one to five.

Table 1 lists the evaluation results, which shows that the overhead of HeapRevolver was less than 20 % in the malloc-test when the memory sizes were 100 and 512 bytes. The overhead of HeapRevolver increased by approximately 30 %–45 % when the requested memory size was 1024 bytes. We believe that this increase caused the repeated issue for the *sbrk* system call to change the size of the data segment in this evaluation. The evaluation results show that the large threshold of the HeapRevolver involved large overhead for every requested memory size.

Next, the performance overhead of the HeapRevolver was measured using UnixBench, SysBench and Himeno benchmarks. Table 2 lists the evaluation results, which show that the overhead of HeapRevolver was less than 0.25 % in every benchmark evaluation. The performance overhead of the 1-MB HeapRevolver is greater than that of the 100-KB HeapRevolver. We suppose that performance overhead increases according to the size of the threshold and that the performance overhead is small and acceptable.

Next, the overhead in applying the proposed method to glibc was measured using browser benchmarks; we used Firefox and Chrome as browsers for the evaluation. The processing time of the browser benchmarks was measured using Google's Octane 2.0, Apple's SunSpider 1.0.2, Mozilla's Kraken 1.1, Microsoft's LiteBrite, FutureMark's Peacekeeper, and Mozilla's Dromaeo. Figures 5 and 6

Table 2. Evaluation results on UnixBench, SysBench, and Himeno benchmark.

lib	UnixBench	SysBench (s)	Himeno benchmark
glibc	4,139.18	25.98	2,690.24
HeapRevolver (100 KB)	4,131.38 (0.19 %)	26.21 (0.23 %)	2,689.64 (0.02 %)
HeapRevolver (1 MB)	4,130.57 (0.21 %)	26.22 (0.24 %)	2,688.05 (0.08 %)

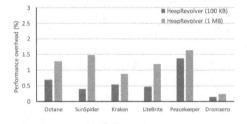

Fig. 5.   Performance   overhead   of browser benchmarks on Firefox

Fig. 6.   Performance   overhead   of browser benchmarks on Chrome

show the comparison results of HeapRevolver with glibc in Firefox and Chrome respectively, considering their performance overhead.

Figure 5 shows that the overhead was less than 1.8 % in both 100 KB and 1 MB in Firefox. The overhead in the 1 MB HeapRevolver, in which the duration of reuse was longer, was larger than that in the 100 KB HeapRevolver because the change in the amount of data segment size (heap area), such as *sbrk* system call, increased when allocating a new memory area. Furthermore, Fig. 6 shows that the overhead in Chrome was less than 2.6 % in both the 100 KB and 1 MB HeapRevolvers. The overhead of the 1 MB HeapRevolver in Chrome was larger than that of 100 KB in Firefox.

Finally, the response time of a web server was measured. The thttpd 2.25 b was used as a web server, and ApacheBench was used as a benchmark in measuring the response time of the web server in this evaluation. The size of the requested file varied from 100 bytes, 1 KB, 10 KB, and 100 KB.

Table 3 lists the evaluation results of the response time of thttpd. It shows that the overhead of HeapRevolver in every result was small. However, the overhead of HeapRevolver increased when the requested file size was 0.1 KB. This process included network and CPU processes. Thus, we assume that the overhead of the memory allocation and release were hidden by these processes.

4.5   Evaluation of Memory Consumption in Linux

We performed three experiments to evaluate the memory consumption of HeapRevolver in Linux. The thresholds of HeapRevolver were 100 KB and 1 MB.

We measured the memory usage of the malloc algorithm with HeapRevolver and compared it with that of original glibc. We used a malloc-test program. In this experiment, five threads were run, and the allocation and freeing processes

Table 3. Response time (overheads) of thttpd web server (ms)

Method	Request file size (KB)			
	0.1	1	10	100
glibc	74.0	75.3	131.1	1,057.8
HeapRevolver (100 KB)	77.1 (4.2%)	80.0 (6.3%)	130.6 (-0.4%)	1,053.4 (-0.4%)
HeapRevolver (1 MB)	77.6 (4.9%)	76.4 (1.5%)	131.4 (0.2%)	1,057.9 (0.0%)

Table 4. Memory usage of the malloc-test.

Method	Memory usage (KB)
glibc	588
HeapRevolver (100 KB)	588
HeapRevolver (1 MB)	1452

Table 5. Memory usage after Firefox finished browsing the 10 websites

Method	Memory usage (MB)
glibc	282
HeapRevolver (100 KB)	279
HeapRevolver (1 MB)	294

were performed when the memory size was 512 bytes. Each thread repeated this process 10 million times. We measured the memory usage when the processing of the five threads was finished.

Table 4 lists that the memory usages of glibc and 100-KB and 1 MB HeapRevolver were almost the same. The size of the freed memory area was less than the threshold. When the threshold was 1 MB, the size of the exceeded memory usage was within the threshold limit. Therefore, these results show that the maximum overhead of the memory usage for each process is less than the threshold.

We used Firefox 31.0 and Selenium IDE to evaluate the memory consumption when browsing 10 websites continuously. We then measured the memory consumption after Firefox finished browsing the 10 websites.

Table 5 lists the evaluation results of the website browsing. The memory usage of glibc and HeapRevolver were almost the same. The memory usage was between 280 and 320 MB because the memory usage overhead of HeapRevolver was small and the variation in memory usage was relatively large.

To compare HeapRevolver with glibc, the change in the amount of virtual memory consumption when a browser benchmark was run was measured. In this evaluation, Octane, SunSpider, and Kraken were used.

Figures 7 and 8 show the memory consumption of Octane in Firefox and Chrome. The evaluation results of Octane in Firefox and Chrome show that the memory consumption of HeapRevolver was almost the same as that of glibc. Furthermore, the memory consumptions of SunSpider and Kraken of the browser benchmarks in both browsers were almost the same as those of glibc. Therefore, the overhead in the memory consumption in HeapRevolver was also small. Table 6 lists the maximum memory consumption under each condition. The evaluation results show the overhead of maximum memory consumption is small.

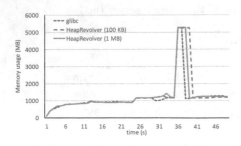

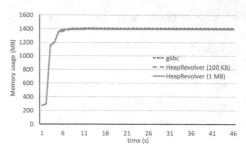

Fig. 7. Memory usage of Octane on Firefox

Fig. 8. Memory usage of Octane on Chrome

Table 6. Maximum memory consumption on browser benchmarks (KB)

Browser	lib	Octane	SunSpider	Kraken
Firefox	glibc	5,375,276	917,996	1,158,092
	HeapRevolver (100 KB)	5,382,988 (0.14 %)	922,416 (0.48 %)	1,124,996 (−2.86 %)
	HeapRevolver (1 MB)	5,407,820 (0.61 %)	949,344 (3.41 %)	1,151,620 (−0.56 %)
Chrome	glibc	1,441,932	1,431,016	1,421,312
	HeapRevolver (100 KB)	1,427,148 (−1.03 %)	1,414,824 (−1.13 %)	1,406,628 (−1.03 %)
	HeapRevolver (1 MB)	1,428,172 (−0.95 %)	1,415,848 (−1.06 %)	1,406,628 (−1.03 %)

4.6   Prevention Experiments Against UAF Attack in Windows

We experimented on whether UAF attacks using real attack codes distributed in Metasploit could be prevented. The attack codes used in the environments exploited CVE-2011-1260 and CVE-2012-4969 of IE 7 on Windows XP and CVE-2014-0322 of IE10 on Windows 7. We determined that approximately 3,000 freed memory areas existed and were reserved for reuse in Linux when a threshold of 1 MB was set. Thus, we used 3,000 as the threshold for the Windows experiments.

We applied HeapRevolver to IE on Windows as described earlier. Then, the attack codes were executed in each environment. Thus, HeapRevolver successfully prevented all the UAF attacks that reused memory objects.

4.7   Evaluation of Performance Overhead in Windows

We measured the overhead of HeapRevolver both before and after the introduction of HeapRevolver on Windows 7. We ran three types of browser benchmark, namely, Octane, SunSpider, and Kraken, on IE 10. The threshold of HeapRevolver was 3,000. The measured overhead of HeapRevolver in the three browser benchmarks was less than 2.5 %. These browser benchmarks are CPU-intensive and require large memory. Thus, we suppose that the influence on the performance of the browser benchmarks can explicitly be observed. Nevertheless, the results show that the overhead of HeapRevolver in Windows is small, and the overhead is acceptable.

4.8   Comparison with Existing Method

We compared HeapRevolver with DieHarder [14], which can be classified to be the same as HeapRevolver. The threshold of HeapRevolver in this evaluation was 1 MB.

Figures 9 and 10 show the performance overhead of HeapRevolver compared with that of glibc when Octane, SunSpider, and Kraken were executed in Firefox and Chrome. The performance overhead of HeapRevolver was less than that of DieHarder except in Kraken. The performance overhead of HeapRevolver was less than 3.0 % but the overhead of DieHarder in SunSpider was relatively large (approximately 4 %). We will analyze the resultant factor of DieHarder in future; however, we believe some inefficient processing in the reuse of objects in DieHarder occurred.

Table 7. Evaluation results of malloc-test.

Memory size	lib	Thread num				
		1	2	3	4	5
512 B	HeapRevolver (1 MB)	0.437 (17.8 %)	0.880 (17.6 %)	1.324 (17.1 %)	1.765 (16.2 %)	2.210 (17.2 %)
	DieHarder	1.247 (236 %)	2.586 (245 %)	4.094 (262 %)	5.421 (259 %)	6.982 (270 %)

Table 7 lists the evaluation results of the malloc-test. The performance overhead of DieHarder was more than 200 % that of glibc because DieHarder allocated memory area at random from some ranges in the memory area. In addition, we evaluated the performance overhead results of original glibc using UnixBench, SysBench, and Himeno benchmarks (Table 8). The results show that the performance overhead of HeapRevolver was smaller than that of DieHarder in all benchmarks.

Finally, we evaluated the change in the amount of memory consumption under three browser benchmarks in Firefox. Figure 11 shows that the memory consumption of DieHarder in Octane was more than twice that of HeapRevolver. Figure 12 shows that the memory consumption of DieHarder in SunSpider was approximately three times more than that of HeapRevolver. However,

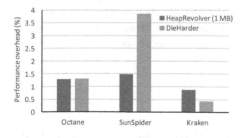

Fig. 9. Comparison of HeapRevolver and DieHarder for browser benchmarks in Firefox

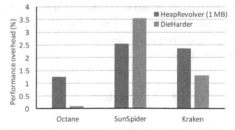

Fig. 10. Comparison of HeapRevolver and DieHarder for browser benchmarks in Chrome

Table 8. Evaluation results of UnixBench, SysBench, and Himeno benchmarks.

lib	UnixBench (KB/s)	SysBench (s)	Himeno benchmark
HeapRevolver (1 MB)	4,130.57 (0.21 %)	26.22 (0.24 %)	2,688.05 (0.08 %)
DieHarder	4,124.77 (0.35 %)	26.25 (1.04 %)	2,674.44 (0.60 %)

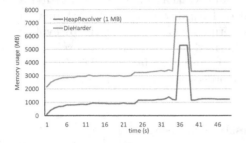

Fig. 11. Overheads of Firefox browser memory usage (Octane)

Fig. 12. Overheads of Firefox browser memory usage (SunSpider)

the overhead of DieHarder was very heavy to use in real world. Comparatively, the results show that the memory usage of HeapRevolver was efficient because HeapRevolver delayed the reuse of freed memory within the threshold size.

Next, we discuss the results in the Chrome browser. We evaluated the total memory consumption of the processes created by Chrome because Chrome creates more than one process. Therefore, we measured the total memory consumption of virtual memory in all Chrome processes, and compared HeapRevolver with DieHarder. The total memory consumption of HeapRevolver in Octane was 45,904,020 KB and that of DieHarder was 87,906,816 KB. These results show that the memory consumption of DieHarder in Octane was approximately twice that of HeapRevolver. In addition, the memory usage trend in Chrome is similar to that in Firefox.

All comparison results show that the overhead of HeapRevolver is smaller than that of DieHarder in most cases and the amount of memory consumption of HeapRevolver is less than that of DieHarder. In addition, to apply DieHarder in Windows, source codes are necessary, and the allocator must be linked and compiled during the development process. In comparison, HeapRevolver does not need a source code and can be applied to programs where source codes cannot be obtained.

5   Related Work

Dangling pointer-detection approaches [3–7] include dynamic binary translation, shadow memory, and taint analysis. These approaches detect dangling pointers before program execution. However, if the dangling pointers are abused, which cannot be detected before a practical use, UAF attacks cannot be prevented in runtime. In [8–10], UAF attacks were prevented by replacing a malloc library with a new library in which the allocation unit is a page. However, because the allocation unit of the created memory area consists of pages, the memory usage is inefficient. In [11–13], a UAF attack was prevented using a method that prevents alteration of vtable. However, these methods cannot handle a UAF attack that does not alter vtable.

6   Conclusions

In this paper, HeapRevolver was proposed, and its design and implementation in Linux and Windows were described. As the memory-reuse-prohibited library prevents the freed memory area from being reused during a certain period, the HeapRevolver can prevent UAF attacks without altering the targeted program for protection. As the timing of reuse of the freed memory area is randomized in HeapRevolver by randomizing the maximum total size of the freed memory areas (the threshold of HeapRevolver), UAF attacks become more difficult.

The evaluation results in Linux show that the HeapRevolver overhead is sufficiently small. However, the process of repeating memory allocation and releasing memory slightly influences the performance. Further, the evaluation results show that the increase in the memory consumption is slight compared with that in the original glibc, and the overhead is acceptable. The experimental results in Windows using UAF exploit codes show that UAF attacks can be prevented using HeapRevolver. In addition, the performance evaluation results by using browser benchmarks show that the HeapRevolver overhead is less than 2.5%. Finally, we compared HeapRevolver with DieHarder through evaluations. The results of the browser benchmarks show that the HeapRevolver overhead is smaller than that of DieHarder in most cases and the amount of memory consumption of HeapRevolver is approximately half that of DieHarder.

Moreover, HeapRevolver can be easily deployed in existing systems and programs and can make UAF attacks more difficult. In addition, the HeapRevolver overhead is sufficiently small to be deployed in real systems. We believe that HeapRevolver can prevent UAF attacks by exploiting zero-day vulnerability.

Acknowledgement. This research was partially supported by Grant-in-Aid for Scientific Research 16H02829.

References

1. Common Vulnerabilities and Exposures. https://cve.mitre.org/index.html
2. Microsoft Security Intelligence Report, vol. 16. http://www.microsoft.com/en-us/download/details.aspx?id=42646
3. Serebryany, K., Bruening, D., Potapenko, A., Vyukov, D.: Addresssanitizer: a fast address sanity checker. In: 2012 USENIX Conference on Annual Technical Conference (USENIX ATC 2012), pp. 309–318 (2012)

4. Caballero, J., et al.: Undangle: early detection of dangling pointers in use-after-free and double-free vulnerabilities. In: 2012 International Symposium on Software Testing and Analysis (ISSTA 2012), pp. 133–143 (2012)

5. Nethercote, N., Seward, J.: Valgrind: a framework for heavyweight dynamic binary instrumentation. In: 28th ACM SIGPLAN Conference on Programming Language Design and Implementation (PLDI 2007), pp. 89–100 (2007)

6. Bruening, D., Zhao, Q.: Practical memory checking with Dr. memory. In: 9th Annual IEEE/ACM International Symposium on Code Generation and Optimization, pp. 213–223 (2011)

7. Lee, B., et al.: Preventing use-after-free with dangling pointers nullification. In: 2015 Network and Distributed System Security Symposium (NDSS) (2015)

8. GFlags and PageHeap. https://msdn.microsoft.com/en-us/library/windows/hardware/ff549561%28v=vs.85%29.aspx

9. Electric Fence. http://elinux.org/Electric_Fence

10. D.U.M.A. - Detect Unintended Memory Access. http://duma.sourceforge.net/

11. Younan, Y.: FreeSentry: protecting against use-after-free vulnerabilities due to dangling pointers. In: 2015 Network and Distributed System Security Symposium (NDSS) (2015)

12. Zhang, C., et al.: VTint: protecting virtual function tables' integrity. In: 22nd Annual Network and Distributed System Security Symposium (NDSS) (2015)

13. Gawlik, R., Holz, T.: Towards automated integrity protection of C++ virtual function tables in binary programs. In: 30th Annual Computer Security Applications Conference (ACSAC 2014), pp. 396–405 (2014)

14. Novark, G., Berger, E.D.: DieHarder: securing the heap. In: 17th ACM Conference on Computer and Communications Security (CCS 2010), pp. 573–584 (2010)

15. Tang, J.: Isolated heap for internet explorer helps mitigate uaf exploits. http://blog.trendmicro.com/trendlabs-security-intelligence/isolated-heap-for-internet-explorer-helps-mitigate-uaf-exploits/

16. Tang, J.: Mitigating uaf exploits with delay free for internet explorer. http://blog.trendmicro.com/trendlabs-security-intelligence/mitigating-uaf-exploits-with-delay-free-for-internet-explorer/

17. Security Intelligence, Understanding IE's New Exploit Mitigations: The Memory Protector and the Isolated Heap. https://securityintelligence.com/understanding-ies-new-exploit-mitigations-the-memory-protector-and-the-isolated-heap/

18. Security Week: Microsoft's Use-After-Free Mitigations Can Be Bypassed: Researcher. http://www.securityweek.com/microsofts-use-after-free-mitigations-can-be-bypassed-researcher

19. Hariri, A.-A., et al.: Abusing Silent Mitigations - Understanding Weaknesses Within Internet Explorers Isolated Heap and MemoryProtection. https://www.blackhat.com/us-15/briefings.html

Timestamp Analysis for Quality Validation of Network Forensic Data

Nikolai Hampton[1][(✉)] and Zubair A. Baig[2]

[1] Edith Cowan University, Joondalup, Australia
nikolaih@our.ecu.edu.au
[2] School of Science & Security Research Institute,
Edith Cowan University, Joondalup, Australia
z.baig@ecu.edu.au

Abstract. Digital forensics is a fast-evolving field of study in contemporary times. One of the challenges of forensic analysis is the quality of evidence captured from computing devices and networks involved in a crime. The credibility of forensic evidence is dependent on the accuracy of established timelines of captured events. Despite the rising orders of magnitude in data volume captured by forensic analysts, the reliability and independence of the timing data source may be questionable due to the underlying network dynamics and the skew in the large number of intermediary system clocks that dictate packet time stamps. Through this paper, we propose a mechanism to verify the accuracy of forensic timing data through collaborative verification of forensic evidence obtained from multiple third party servers. The proposed scheme does analysis of HTTP response headers extracted from network packet capture (PCAP) files and validity testing of third party data through the application of statistical methods. We also develop a proof of concept universal time agreement protocol to independently verify timestamps generated by local logging servers and to provide a mechanism that may be adopted in digital forensics procedures.

1 Introduction

Timing accuracy is one of the most overlooked aspects of digital forensic evidence. While standards such as the Network Time Protocol (NTP) exist for clock synchronisation, they frequently suffer from many issues including incorrect configuration, clock drift and configuration issues with virtual server environments [8]. Casey and Rose (2010) identify the need to establish reliable timelines as part of the digital forensics process and cite several cases in which timing discrepancies in digital evidence have caused difficulties for investigators, prosecutors and defence attorneys alike [5]. So crucial is the accuracy of timing data, many criminal and civil cases have invested significant time verifying the validity of forensic timestamps [5,8,14]. Even significant tools in use by law enforcement have been shown to suffer from timing and integrity issues. For example, an independent report in to the FBI's Carnivore system found significant deficiencies with integrity, including the lack of time synchronisation on logging servers [15].

© Springer International Publishing AG 2016
J. Chen et al. (Eds.): NSS 2016, LNCS 9955, pp. 235–248, 2016.
DOI: 10.1007/978-3-319-46298-1_16

Accurate event timing allows forensic investigators to establish relationships between events and actors to ascertain weight of evidence i.e., to facilitate solid foundations of evidence for presentation in a court of law. The ultimate goal of a forensic investigator is to preserve, provide and assess evidence to determine what actions, in particular mal-actions, were taken [17] and whether they were deliberate. By building an accurate and trusted timeline, an investigator may draw a clear "picture" that demonstrates a sequence of events, a suspect's thought process, actions and intent [5]. In order to prove the intent of the perpetrators of the cybercrime, an investigation often needs to demonstrate the link between cause and effect, which requires accurate timestamps of data or evidence. However, timestamp data is frequently called in to question, with different devices and pieces of evidence reporting significantly different and conflicting timestamps. Where the variation is small, this may not pose a problem, however timestamps may vary by hours, days, or even more, due to factors like timezone and configuration errors. At best, these discrepancies add cost and complexity to an investigation, at worst they may affect the course of a civil or criminal trial [5, 14].

Network forensic evidence may appear in several formats, from log files to captured packets from the computing devices involved in the crime. Most log data contains timing data in a certain format to enable comparison between events, however the reliability and independence of the timing data source may be questionable. The Apache log format, the Syslog format and PCAP packet capture formats all specify dedicated fields to represent time-stamp data of network traffic captures [2, 7, 18]; however, in each case, the timing data is provided by in-built local processes and is reliant upon the system clock of the logging device at the destination network. While services such as the Network Time Protocol (NTP) [3] can provide high accuracy time stamps, it is necessary for system administrators to configure, enable and verify the correct functioning of NTP clients, to maintain evidence quality. Data analysis is the fundamental function of forensic investigators. With questionable accuracy in identified data timestamps, the reliability of forensic evidence may be challenged.

One of the steps in forensic analysis is validation of evidence, process and tools [5, 13], including server and time stamp validation for any captured data. Simple validation may be possible where direct access to a logging system is available, and the configuration and status of the server at the time of capture is known. Sometimes this information may be pieced together from system log-files, which may prove that a logging server was recently synchronised using a mechanism like NTP, however such type of evidence is independent of the actual log data being examined. Time-stamp data presented in log-files is also be dependent on local server configuration; for example, the NTP protocol does not include any mechanism for synchronising time zones or daylight saving information, thus an NTP synchronised server may still provide incorrect time stamp data if time zone information or daylight savings parameters are incorrectly set [3].

Standards and processes are a cornerstone of digital forensics; processes for identifying the validity of timing data have been recognised as critical since the early days of computer forensic investigations [9]. The work by Stevens (2004) examined a way to synchronise timing data across multiple devices by building a clock model which takes in to account local RTC errors and timezones [16]. However, the method requires direct access to the devices and known clock states "close" to the time of capture. While most work on defining best practices for standardising timing analysis has involved the validation of device real-time-clocks (RTCs) to verify file-creation times, there is a clear need for forensic investigators to apply these same synchronisation disciplines to all forensic evidence, including network capture data. The same issues that plague time synchronisation on end-user devices also affect servers, routers and other logging equipment. The method proposed by Stevens used relative time offsets across devices and timezones and allowed investigators to normalise the time between multiple devices by comparing their RTCs to calculate their differences.

Our method extends the concept of relative time offsets by reducing packet capture timestamp data to a single dimension elapsed-time offset, and then applies a statistical analysis technique to compare the offsets to timing data returned by independent 3rd party servers. This allows us to verify timing data integrity without relying on any individual device's accuracy, rather our method allows an investigator to state that an event occurred at a specific time according to multiple independent "virtual witnesses" (servers). Our method provides a formalised framework for forensics investigators to verify timing integrity regardless of whether any verifiable timing sources are available.

2   Timing Data Sources and Errors

In an Internet-connected network environment, network packet capture data arrives from a range of sources. Several of these sources may include time-stamps that could be used to verify logging server data accuracy and variations from established baselines; web requests frequently provide response headers with a time-stamp generated by a responding server [6]; email headers frequently include time-stamps from Mail Transfer Agents MTA's and client machines; and web application content may include a range of time-sources from cookies to embedded HTML code and JavaScript variables. Some of the issues associated with time stamp validation are: ascertaining the timestamps of response data received from web servers and the lack of a standard encoding technique between the clients and servers. Our statistical method for obtaining timing agreement from multiple 3rd parties, identifies only coherent timing-data sources, thus eliminating multiple sources of error.

While packet capturing tools such as Wireshark [18] include timestamp data, this data is also collected from the local clock on the logging device and may suffer from the aforementioned errors. Reliable remote network time sources such as the Network Time Protocol (NTP) exist, however their use as a forensic tool may be limited depending on whether NTP events are included in a packet capture and also on the integrity of the configured NTP server. As such, the forensic verification of the data is left to the examiner; a process which usually

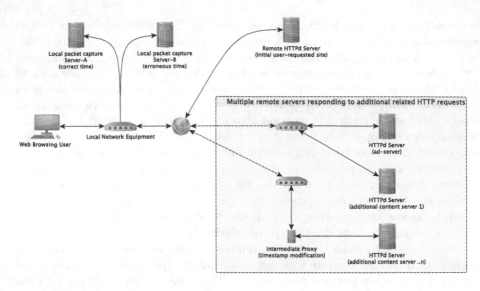

Fig. 1. Example network configuration for logging packet capture data

requires manual examination. In addition, normalisation of time stamps requires interpretation and analysis to remove time zone offsets and errors.

In Fig. 1, a typical network configuration is presented that comprises end-users accessing the web, and intermediary packet capture servers for packet logging. When additional HTTP requests are transmitted by an end-user's network router to pertinent web servers, multiple servers may respond to the request. Therefore, the process of data logging and correlation for responses to a common query also entails high precision in analysis and accurate correlation between the received HTTP response packets. The ability for a forensic investigator to perform standardised time analysis and verification on captured data could improve the forensic integrity of an investigation and assist investigators by allowing them to focus on the identification and extraction of other relevant evidence.

3   Problem Definition

Everyday web-browsing activities of clients generate a large number of web requests and corresponding responses. In a 2014 survey on web-page metrics, Butkiewicz, Madhyastha, and Sekar [4] found that for a single web browsing session, the median number of requests solicited from a web server is equal to 40, with a large volume of web pages referencing content from multiple web servers. This implies that a single end-user action will frequently result in a large amount of returned data and meta-data to the requesting end users. Almost every HTTP server response contains an HTTP Date field, and many responses also include Expiry time fields, Last Modified time fields, and Cookies. Content may also include timing data embedded in links, JavaScript or meta-data.

A typical example of HTTP date headers and embedded arrival times as captured in the local capture/logging servers, is illustrated in Table 1. HTTP date headers reflect the time when the HTTP response was generated by the remote server [6]. As independent 3rd party servers generate the HTTP date headers, they may act as witnesses to assist a forensic investigator in validating event timing; either by verifying any embedded real-time clock (RTC) data in a PCAP file and subsequently correcting RTC errors if the local logging servers are incorrectly configured, or by providing an RTC estimate if no RTC data is present.

As can be seen from the examples in Table 1, the arrival times for user responses corresponding to a user query vary from one log entry to another, and thus the accuracy of collected data is questionable. The examples show both accurate ("tick") and erroneous ("cross") timestamp data. Specifically, the table illustrates how a logging server with a correctly set clock (Server-A) can be relied upon to provide forensically accurate timing data, while a server with an approximate clock error of +3 h (Server-B) will tag all packet data as incorrect. While a forensic investigation using Server-A would yield accurate evidence; a forensic investigation relying on PCAP timing data provided by Server-B could result in questionable reliability of evidence, or even incorrect conclusions. In both cases, the integrity of the captured data can be tested and validated against HTTP date header data; Server-A's integrity can be assured through agreement with accurate 3rd party response data. Server-B's error can be detected, identified, analysed and corrected using the same data.

The challenge for forensic investigators using 3rd party servers as witnesses is in determining which witness responses are accurate, and which are erroneous. In the same way that Table 1 PCAP logging servers (Server-A and Server-B) may be set correctly or incorrectly, so to remote servers may have correct or incorrect internal clocks. These servers produce HTTP Date headers that is either accurate or erroneous.

Attaching a packet capture server on to the same network as the end-user machine allows data to be intercepted, collected and analysed. Packet capture data contains the raw low-level network interactions for transferring data from a web server to an end-user. This traffic can be easily parsed to extract requests matching certain parameters. For data generators that keep perfect time, the time-stamps extracted from packet data would agree with a known start time. Perfect time beacons are defined as those beacons that are in agreement with each other. These two beacons in the context of forensically sound evidence are: the observed time stamps from network traffic packets and the real time (given by the summation of the actual logging start time and the elapsed i.e., offset time). As can be seen from Fig. 4, perfect time beacons must agree with each other. Perfect time is when the observed time is in agreement with the real time. An observed time stamp above the perfect-time-line implies the time stamp lies in the future, and an observed time below the perfect-time-line would imply that the time stamp lies in the past.

Table 1. Categorisation of time stamps as accurate or erroneous based on user interaction and server state

User Action	Related / Automatic Actions	Description	RTC	Captured HTTP Date response	PCAP Log Entry (Server A)	PCAP Log Entry (Server B)
Examples of logged HTTP Date responses and PCAP embedded Arrival Time data in response to a single user action in comparison to an accurate Real Time Clock (RTC)						
User requests WWW site		User visits an initial website	08:00:00.00 0 1/1/2000		Arrival Time: 08:00:00.000 ✓	Arrival Time: 11:15:20.012 ✗
	User HTTP response	HTTP data are returned to the user. With references to related resources	08:00:01.08 6 1/1/2000	HTTP.Date: 1/1/2000 08:00:01 ✓	Arrival Time: 08:00:01.086 ✓	Arrival Time: 11:15:21.098 ✗
	Browser automated HTTP requests	The web browser parses the returned HTTP data, identifies and retrieves related resources.	08:00:01.15 6 1/1/2000		Arrival Time: 08:00:01.156 ✓	Arrival Time: 11:15:21.168 ✗
	Ad-server response with correct timestamp	Additional resource retrieved from advertising server with correct HTTP date field	*08:00:01*.21 0 1/1/2000	HTTP.Date: 1/1/2000 *08:00:02* ✓	Arrival Time: *08:00:01.210* ✓	Arrival Time: *11:15:21.222* ✗
	Additional content server response with erroneous timestamp	Additional resource retrieved from additional content/resource server.	*08:00:01*.25 0 1/1/2000	HTTP.Date: 1/1/2000 *06:55:22* ✗	Arrival Time: *08:00:01.250* ✓	Arrival Time: *11:15:21.262* ✗
	Additional content server response with timestamp removed in transit	Additional resource retrieved via proxy which manipulates or removes timestamp	08:00:02.10 0 1/1/2000	HTTP.Date: *(not set)* ✗	Arrival Time: 08:00:02.100 ✓	Arrival Time: 11:15:22.112 ✗
				✓ Indicates agreement between the captured evidence and RTC ✗ Indicates a timing error or discrepancy		

4   Proposed Time-Stamp Analysis Scheme

The Network Time Protocol (NTP) allows computer devices to remain in synchronisation not simply within local networks but also across corporate as well as geographical borders. In theory, devices that have their clocks synchronised through the NTP protocol should be accurate to within a few seconds. Unfortunately, due to misconfigurations or errors this isn't always the case. Thus, network timestamps will vary from highly accurate to significantly inaccurate or in error.

As the timing signal observed from remote server packets is destined to progress at a constant and linear rate, it is easy to convert our timing data down to a single-dimension which represents the offset from the perceived start-of-capture time i.e., the PCAP time of origin (T0). Because the accurate timing beacons are more likely to agree on a similar value, the distribution of perceived T0 will peak at the real T0 (Fig. 4). Variance in the peak distribution indicates a disagreement between the Real-Time-Clock and a mass of 3rd party timing beacons.

Normalising of the timing signal to remove outliers can be achieved through any number of noise reduction methods. We examine the use of k-means clustering as well as statistical analysis to determine the most reliable method for identifying 'good' remote servers with a high degree of probability, where 'good' remote servers refers to those servers that report high accuracy timing data.

Timestamp data may be inserted in to metadata or traffic payload for identification of the data's age. The data may represent the real-item, or it may represent another "arbitrary" time. Real timing data would identify the time of creation of the data point; this indicates an attempt to transmit a time that can

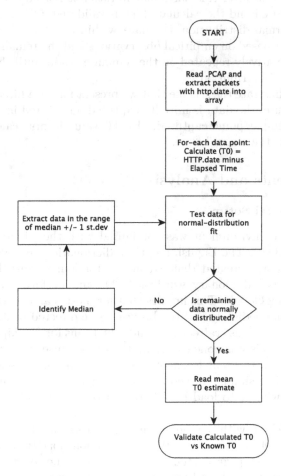

Fig. 2. Flowchart representing the data correlation procedure adopted for time stamp analysis

be used to determine factors such as the data's age. Arbitrary time may represent events that have either occurred in the past or will occur in the future: it may be set through a predefined formula, such as the current time plus one-hour.

In addition, arbitrary time may reflect a particular point in time for example, the closing date for student course enrolment; or it may reflect an event in the past. Consideration must also be given to erroneous timestamps that may arise through multiple reasons including inaccurate system clocks or even calculation errors.

For the proposed scheme, for any given instance of the packet capture, the current time is determined by adding the time of origin (T0) to the elapsed time since the beginning of capture, where the value T0 is unknown. Subsequently, 3rd party timing data is subtracted from the elapsed time to determine the final value. Subsequently, the test data is subject to normal distribution fit. If the data that remains after this particular iteration is normally distributed, the mean T0 is estimated and the calculated T0 is validated. Otherwise, if the data does not fit a normal distribution, the data within (± 1) standard deviation of the median is kept based on empirical observations and the remainder discarded. The process is iteratively repeated on the remaining data until they approach a sufficiently normal distribution.

In Fig. 2, we illustrate the scheme that we present for data filtering. As can be seen from the figure, the data is initially captured and stored in PCAP format. For each data sample/point captured, the T0 value is first calculated as the HTTP.date minus the elapsed time.

5   Experiments and Analysis

5.1   Experimental Setup

A virtual machine environment was configured with the Firefox web browser (Mozilla Firefox 39.0). The English language dictionaries were also installed. A Linux shell script was created that extracts a random English language word from the Linux user dictionary wordlist [1,11] and performs an "I'm feeling lucky" search using Google. This implies that for most searches, the top-ranking page is returned immediately and the browser is re-directed to it.

The Google search was crafted to exclude the terms for "Wikipedia", "Wiki", and "Dictionary"; this was done to eliminate excessive user traffic to these sites, which were observed to occur frequently due to the nature of searching for uncommon words. The simulated web-browsing activity was set up to retrieve a random site, allowing it to load for 20 to 40 s then quit and retrieve the next website.

A virtual machine with a random Internet browsing client was configured to access a new website every 20–40 s, this random load/wait cycle provided enough time for most page content to load entirely, i.e. enough time for the HTML page source to load, and the client side javascript to trigger and HTTP requests-response pairs for 3rd party and rich media content to be captured. A separate logging server was configured on the host machine.

The logging server captured network traffic from the simulated Internet client. The data were extracted and analysed using the R programming language [12]. The host machine was synchronised with a Stratum 1 NTP server operated by the Australian National Measurement Institute [10]; this ensured high clock accuracy. tcpdump was used to extract packet capture data for ten-minute blocks. The packet capture was configured to filter all traffic not originating or destined for the virtual machine that was simulating the browsing activity. Each tcpdump packet capture of browsing activity was also stamped with NTP clock statistics for the logging server. Packet captures were only included in the sample data where the logging server accuracy was better than or equal to 10ms from the Stratum 1 NTP servers.

It was hypothesized that accurate timing data obtained from 3rd party servers would be distributed around a 'high' central peak distribution. The packet capture timing data were extracted from twenty automated 10-minute browsing sessions. The HTTP timestamp, and the RTC timestamp data were extracted from the packet captures. The HTTP timestamp was compared to the RTC timestamp. A time-difference value was calculated for each timestamp received by subtracting the RTC recorded timestamp on the observed packet.

$$T_d = T_h + 0.5 - T_r - T_l \tag{1}$$

where: T_d is the time-difference (error) equivalent to the HTTP timestamp (T_h) plus 0.5 s; minus the RTC timestamp (T_r); minus the reported latency (T_l). The value of 0.5 is added because the HTTP headers have an error tolerance of 1 s and was observed to not ignore the floor of the value of the embedded HTTP time field.

Data for each automated packet capture were tested for goodness of fit against a standard normal distribution. The absolute error $|T_d|$ was progressively reduced by extracting subsets of data at $|T_d|$ (Un-filtered, 120, 60, 30, 15, 5, 2). The subset data were compared to normal distributions using a Kolmogorov–Smirnov goodness-of-fit test. The mean error and 95 % confidence interval values were recorded for each subset of data.

Verification of the process was done by testing datasets in the absence of RTC timestamp (Tr) data, utilising the median timestamp Th as an initial estimate of signal centrality, testing for normality, discarding outliers, and then repeating as per Fig. 2.

5.2   Results Analysis

By examining the distribution of timing beacons with reduced absolute error, we were able to eliminate outliers and examine the distribution of 'known & acceptable' timing data. Each iteration tested the distribution of the HTTP timestamp on either side of the accurate RTC timestamps by a reduced margin of absolute error. The resulting time errors for 4 types of experiments, namely, unfiltered data, +/− 120 s, +/− 10 s and +/− 2 s are presented in Fig. 3. As the absolute error on $|T_d|$ was reduced, the distribution approached normal; this can be seen as in the improvement of Q-Q and P-P probability plots of observed data vs normally distributed data in Fig. 3.

Typically data with a $|T_d|$ maximum less than 10 s was found to fit a normal distribution when tested using a (Kolmogorov-Smirnov goodness of fit test $p > 0.1$). While other data from similarly size slices did not. This indicates that when the maximum error was reduced, the data approached a normal distribution. The intuition for this can be summarised as follows: most servers are likely to have their clocks in general agreement with global master clocking sources and where remote servers have no such clock agreement, the reported times were found to digress from the norm unpredictably. Or in terms of reliable witnesses to an event: reliable witnesses will agree when an event occurred, those that disagree will disagree unpredictably. Timing data were found to be either accurately distributed around the RTC or highly inaccurate with errors ranging from minutes to years.

As can be seen from Table 2 and Fig. 3, the data shows a strong and tight correlation to the accurate RTC signal present in the packet capture data; most importantly, the data show a high correlation in the $T0$ region. This indicates that it is possible to use 3rd party timing beacons to ensure the quality and accuracy of the logging RTC; or, where the RTC is absent or known to be inaccurate, 3rd party timing beacons can be used to calculate an estimated RTC with a high degree of accuracy.

Packet capture data frequently includes a packet capture elapsed time $T_{elapsed}$ value for each recorded packet. $T_{elapsed}$ represents the elapsed time since the beginning of the capture window. As there is a known duration between 3rd party timing beacon events, it is possible to collapse all timing data to a single time-difference T_d 'error' dimension; i.e. each T_h timestamps deviation from the linear progression of the RTC timestamp T_r. It is also clear that the 'start of capture' time can be determined by subtracting any known accurate RTC value from $T_{elapsed}$.

$$T0 = T_r - T_{elapsed} \tag{2}$$

In the absence of an RTC, timing beacon events can be used to calculate a T0 estimate $(T0_{est})$ using the arithmetic mean after repeating the method of progressively removing outliers until $T0_{est}$ is normally distributed and the confidence interval is within an acceptable range for the data being investigated.

$$T0_{est} = \frac{1}{n} \sum_{i=1}^{n} T_{h(i)} - T_{elapsed(i)} \tag{3}$$

The results show that an efficient algorithm for identifying accurate 3rd party timing beacons within PCAP data can be achieved by reducing timestamps to a single dimension array containing $T0$ estimates from multiple sources; and repeatedly eliminating outliers until the remaining data approaches a normal distribution fit. This was confirmed through testing to evaluate $T0$ without knowledge of RTC values using the process outlined in Fig. 4.

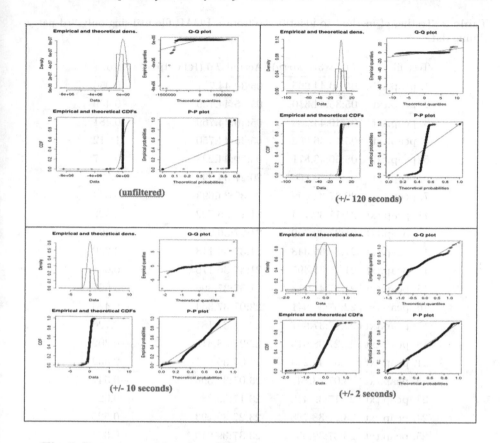

Fig. 3. Data approaching normal distribution as outlying data are discarded

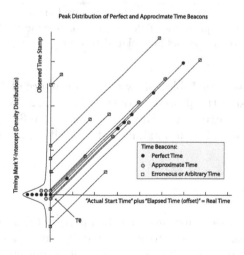

Fig. 4. Reduction of 3rd party timing beacons extracted from HTTP time to 1-Dimensional array and the resulting probability density histogram

Table 2. Testing of method to identify T0 from a PCAP file utilising only 3rd party timing data

Test file	$T0_{est}(3rdparty)$	Actual $T0$ (RTC time)	Error (s)
1. pcap.txt	05:30:44.665	05:30:44.721	−0.056
2. pcap.txt	05:35:44.310	05:35:44.739	−0.429
3. pcap.txt	05:40:44.288	05:40:44.769	−0.481
4. pcap.txt	05:45:46.062	05:45:44.750	1.312
5. pcap.txt	05:50:43.871	05:50:44.228	−0.357
6. pcap.txt	20:27:33.868	20:27:34.594	−0.726
7. pcap.txt	20:37:34.099	20:37:34.693	−0.594
11. pcap.txt	21:17:39.244	21:17:36.722	2.522
12. pcap.txt	21:27:39.752	21:27:36.258	3.494
13. pcap.txt	21:37:39.348	21:37:36.118	3.230
14. pcap.txt	21:47:35.495	21:47:36.176	−0.681
15. pcap.txt	21:57:41.273	21:57:37.306	3.967
16. pcap.txt	22:07:36.941	22:07:37.364	−0.423
17. pcap.txt	22:17:37.907	22:17:37.181	0.726
18. pcap.txt	22:27:38.013	22:27:38.315	−0.302
21. pcap.txt	22:57:42.243	22:57:39.681	2.562
22. pcap.txt	23:07:38.849	23:07:39.396	−0.547
23. pcap.txt	23:17:39.412	23:17:39.384	0.028
24. pcap.txt	23:27:38.768	23:27:39.293	−0.525
25. pcap.txt	23:37:39.558	23:37:39.919	−0.361
26. pcap.txt	23:47:39.483	23:47:40.103	−0.620
		Mean squared error:	2.705

Note: missing capture files failed import or parsing in the Python script due to data errors not related to time

Results as illustrated in Table 2 show the performance of $T0$ estimation with absent RTC data using the procedure outlined in Fig. 2. We successfully identified T0 with a high degree of accuracy using only the 3rd party HTTP time data. $T0$ and $T0_{est}$ varied by a maximum of 4 s, with a mean squared error of 2.7 s.

6   Conclusions

Through this paper we demonstrated that 3rd party servers provide an accurate timing signal that may be used to independently verify local forensic timing data; and, where local timing data is not present or inaccurate, the agreement between several 3rd party servers can be used to accurately estimate the timing of events required for forensic examination of evidence.

HTTP response headers frequently contain a date field supplied by 3rd party servers. The quality of the data from individual servers varies from accurate within a few seconds, to wildly inaccurate. The 3rd party time data were found to cluster around the real-time value; servers within a margin of error ± 10 s was found to be normally distributed around the accurate real time clock. This indicated that a statistical sampling of server responses could prove to be useful for excluding data obtained from inaccurate servers through the HTTP date responses.

We tested the statistical analysis method for examining and classifying 3rd party HTTP time stamp data as accurate or erroneous, and provided validation that 3rd party timing data may be a viable resource for forensic investigators. The opportunity exists to extend the analysis to other timing sources embedded in network packets. It may be possible to detect a wide range of timing data using simple regular expressions, and subsequently apply the filtration processes described in the paper to include only data that accurately reflects the time. Other methods of clustering, noise-reduction, and outlier reduction may also be examined as part of future work.

References

1. Aitkinson, K.: Spell Checking Oriented Word Lists (SCOWL) (2016). http://wordlist.aspell.net/scowl-readme/
2. Apache Software Foundation: Apache HTTP Server Version 2.2 Configuration (2015). https://httpd.apache.org/docs/2.2/mod/mod_log_config.html#logformat
3. Burbank, J., Mills, D., Kasch, W.: Network Time Protocol Version 4: Protocol and Algorithms Specification, June 2010. https://tools.ietf.org/html/rfc5905
4. Butkiewicz, M., Madhyastha, H., Sekar, V.: Characterizing Web Page Complexity and Its Impact, June 2014
5. Casey, E., Rose, C.W.: Chapter 2 - Forensic Analysis (2010). http://www.sciencedirect.com/science/article/pii/B9780123742674000021
6. Fielding, R., Reschke, J.: Hypertext Transfer Protocol (HTTP/1.1): Semantics and Content, June 2014. https://tools.ietf.org/html/rfc7231#section-7.1.1.2
7. Gerhards, R.: RFC 5424 - The Syslog Protocol, March 2009. https://tools.ietf.org/html/rfc5424#section-6.2.3
8. Marangos, N., Rizomiliotis, P., Mitrou, L.: Time synchronization: pivotal element in cloud forensics, April 2016. http://onlinelibrary.wiley.com/doi/10.1002/sec.1056/abstract
9. Meyers, M., Rogers, M.: Computer forensics: the need for standardization and certification (2004). http://www.123seminarsonly.com/Seminar-Reports/044/59032742-Computer-Forensics.pdf
10. National Measurement Institute: Time and Frequency Dissemination Service (2016). http://www.measurement.gov.au/
11. Open Source Software: wbritish. https://packages.debian.org/sid/text/wbritish
12. R Core Team: R: A Language and Environment for Statistical Computing (2015). https://www.R-project.org/
13. Scientific Working Group on Digital Evidence: SWGDE recommended guidelines for validation testing, September 2014. https://www.swgde.org/

14. Bratus, S., Lembree, A., Shubina, A.: Software on the Witness Stand: What Should it Take for us to Trust it? http://www.cs.dartmouth.edu/~sergey/trusting-e-evidence.pdf
15. Smith, S.P., Perrit, H.J., Krent, H., Mencik, S., Crider, J.A., Shyong, M., Reyonalds, L.L.: Independent Review of the Carnivore System, November 2000. https://www.justice.gov/archive/jmd/carnivore_draft_1.pdf
16. Stevens, M.W.: Unification of relative time frames for digital forensics, September 2004. http://www.sciencedirect.com/science/article/pii/S174228760400057X
17. US-CERT: Computer Forensics (2008). https://www.uscert.gov/sites/default/files/publications/forensics.pdf
18. Wireshark.org: FileFormatReference/libpcap - The Wireshark Wiki (2008). https://wiki.wireshark.org/FileFormatReference/libpcap

Searchable Encryption

An Efficient Secure Channel Free Searchable Encryption Scheme with Multiple Keywords

Tingting Wang[1], Man Ho Au[2], and Wei Wu[1]([✉])

[1] Fujian Provincial Key Laboratory of Network Security and Cryptology,
School of Mathematics and Computer Science, Fujian Normal University,
Fuzhou 350007, China
tingtingwang90@126.com, weiwu81@gmail.com
[2] Department of Computing, The Hong Kong Polytechnic University,
Kowloon, Hong Kong
csallen@comp.polyu.edu.hk

Abstract. Pubilc Key Encrytion with Keyword Search (PEKS) scheme allows users to search encrypted messages by using a particular keyword without leaking any information. Practically, users might need to relate multiple keywords to one message. To effectively encrypt multiple keywords, Baek et al. first presented a PEKS scheme with multiple keywords (MPEKS). In this paper, we come up with a new efficient secure channel free PEKS scheme with multiple keywords named SCF-MPEKS. We give formal definitions and a concrete construction of SCF-MPEKS. The proposed SCF-MPEKS scheme is secure in the presented models of indistinguishability for SCF-MPEKS. Our scheme removes the secure channel assumption between the server and the receiver, which has much better performance in terms of both computational and communication overhead than Baek et al.'s MPEKS scheme for building a secure channel is very costly.

Keywords: Pubilc key encrytion · Keyword search · Multiple keywords · Secure channel free

1 Introduction

With the amazing speed of development of cloud computing, more and more enterprises and individuals choose to store data in the cloud to achieve lower costs and more efficient management. However, the confidentiality and privacy of data cannot be guaranteed when the user uploads some of his own sensitive data, to an untrusted cloud server, since the untrusted cloud server can directly view, delete, or even leak the sensitive data uploaded by the user. To protect the security of data, a user usually needs to encrypt the data before uploading the data into the server. A practical example is the personal health records (PHR) system [12–15]. The personal health records (PHR) system is an emerging patient-centric platform of health information exchange, which is usually outsourced to be stored at a third party, such as cloud service providers. Although it is very convenient

© Springer International Publishing AG 2016
J. Chen et al. (Eds.): NSS 2016, LNCS 9955, pp. 251–265, 2016.
DOI: 10.1007/978-3-319-46298-1_17

to facilitate the management and sharing of patients' personal health information (PHI) in the cloud computing environment, there has been big concerns on security and privacy matters as the sensitive personal health information could be exposed to these untrusted third party servers. To ensure the patients control over access to their own privacy, it is a promising solution to encrypt the PHRs before outsourcing. However, when patients' PHR files are encrypted, it produces another problem of a PHR system, that is how users can perform search over the encrypted data to find some patients' information. For instance, a medical researcher may want to find out fellow patients with the same disease and symptoms in order to do further investigation. A naive solution for him is to download the whole data base, then he should try to decrypt all encrypted records to find his target data. This is undoubtedly time-consuming and inefficient for it needs a large amount of calculation overhead to decrypt and too much of his device's space to store the data. To achieve the goal of retrieving on encrypted data directly, searchable encryption [5,8,10,16] has been proposed as a promising method. The basic idea is to build an encrypted keyword indexes appended to the encrypted documents. At this time, users can retrieve the encrypted data with certain keywords. For example, when a medical researcher wants to find out fellow patients with the same disease and symptoms, he can submit a query request like "$age = 20$", "$sex = male$" and "$ilness = birdflu$" to the server. The server can help find out the corresponding patients' encrypted documents and returns them to him without learning anything else about the query including the keywords. In recent years, except the application in PHRs system, searchable encryption study has improved rapidly. More and more schemes [2,5,9,10,17,18] are designed to satisfy users' increasing requirements of query types and focus on improving the search efficiency. And all of them can be divided into two different kinds of searchable encryption techniques, one is the "Searchable Symmetric Encryption" scheme and the other one is the "Searchable Asymmetric Encryption" scheme. Both of them have respective importance in functions and properties. In a symmetric searchable encryption system [8,16,17], a user can retrieve his own encrypted data with a certain keyword from the server. Unfortunately, they cannot be used to retrieve the encrypted data from the third party, which means that they can not be applied in many practical applications. Considering the scenario of an email routing system. Suppose Alice has a number of devices: mobile phones, laptops, pagers, etc. Now she is on a holiday from work and wishes to read only urgent emails that require her attention but not all of them. At this time, Alice's mail gateway is supposed to route her emails containing the keyword "urgent" to her pager equipped with her. That is to say, the mail gateway should be given the ability by Alice to define which email matches to the keyword "urgent" and help Alice to pick out corresponding emails. To preserve the security and privacy of emails from even inside attackers such as an untrusted mail server, her public key will be used to encrypt emails sent to her. So how to pick out the encrypted emails directly without showing any other information about her emails to the untrusted server is a significant research project. To address this issue, Boneh et al. [5] first proposed public key encryptions with keyword search scheme (PEKS). In their scheme, the user Bob wishes to send an email M with keywords $w_1, \cdots, w_n$ to user Alice. Bob first encrypts the email M using Alice's public key. He then appends ciphertexts of keywords PEKS(pk_A, w_1), $\cdots$, PEKS(pk_A, w_n) to the encrypted email. After that, Bob sends the ciphertexts with the following form to Alice's mail server:

$$E(pk_A, M) \parallel PEKS(pk_A, w_1) \parallel \cdots \parallel PEKS(pk_A, w_n)$$

where pk_A is Alice's public key. Alice could send the server a trapdoor T_w of the "business", if Alice wants to select some emails containing the keyword "business". The server can help find out the emails that contain the keyword "business" using the information of the T_w. More generally, whenever Alice wants to conduct search on her encrypted emails receiving from anyone knowing Alice's public key, she can achieve this by sending the server a certain trapdoor T_w to test which email contains the keyword w. Upon receiving the PEKS(pk_A, w') ciphertest and the corresponding T_w, the server can check whether $w = w'$. An idea PEKS system should ensure that during the whole search procedure, the server can only learn the result about whether $w = w'$ and obtain nothing more about w itself and the email body.

Just as discussed in the above, Boneh et al.'s [5] PEKS scheme can be applied in the email routing system. In this mechanism, user Alice achieves her goal of searching for the encrypted emails that include the keyword w by giving the server the trapdoor associated with w, while the PEKS value reveals nothing else about the message to the server and other parties. In addition to this application, Waters et al. [18] pointed out that the PEKS scheme can be used to construct an encrypted and searchable audit log system.

However, Boneh et al.'s [5] PEKS scheme needs a secure channel between the server and the receiver, for it is not safe if trapdoor is transferred through the public network. But as stated in [2], building a secure channel using established techniques such as Secure Socket Layer (SSL) is costly and may not be suitable for all situations. In [2], Baek et al. first presented the notion of "secure channel free PEKS scheme" (SCF-PEKS) which deletes the secure channel by making the server keep its own public/private key pairs. In the SCF-PEKS scheme, Bob may encrypt the email using Alice's public key and the server's public key. Only the server's corresponding private key can execute the test algorithm.

Furthermore, in the real-life application, users often need to attach several keywords to one message. For example, if Alice wants to search an email from "Bob" on "Monday", both "Bob" and "Monday" should be used as keywords. Surely, we can relate appropriate amount of keywords to one message to satisfy our searching requirements. For this reason, it usually requires a number of keywords in an email to support the user's searching, furthermore, all the keywords need to be encrypted and it is very important to create a simple and efficient PEKS ciphertexts for multiple keywords to minimize the computation and storage overhead. In [5], Boneh et al. suggested one can simply create the PEKS ciphertexts with the form of "$E(pk_A, M) \parallel PEKS(pk_A, w_1) \parallel \cdots \parallel PEKS(pk_A, w_n)$". However, no formal definition for PEKS scheme with multiple keywords was proposed in [5]. To solve this issue, Baek et al. [2] provided the notion of "PEKS scheme with multiple keywords" (MPEKS). They achieved the goal of encrypting multiple keywords efficiently by using the *randomness re-use* technique [3, 11]. They defined the security notion for MPEKS and proved its security in the random oracle model.

We come up with a new efficient secure channel free searchable encryption scheme with multiple keywords (SCF-MPEKS) by integrating the notions of "SCF-PEKS" and "MPEKS" in this paper. Compared with Baek et al.'s [2] MPEKS scheme, our scheme does not need any secure channel and gives a better performance than Baek et al.'s MPEKS scheme.

The rest of the paper is organized as follows. In Sect. 2, we go through the bilinear map and hardness assumptions required by the paper. In Sect. 3, we propose formal definitions of SCF-MPEKS and its security model. In Sect. 4, we describe our SCF-MPEKS scheme, discuss its efficiency, and prove its security in the random oracle model. Finally, we conclude this paper in Sect. 5.

2   Preliminaries

2.1   Bilinear Map

Let G_1 and G_2 be two cyclic groups of large prime order p. Let g be a generator of G_1. We say that a map $\hat{e} : G_1 \times G_1 \longrightarrow G_2$ is an admissible bilinear map if it satisfies the following three properties:

1. Bilinear: $\hat{e}(R_1^\alpha, R_2^\beta) = \hat{e}(R_1, R_2)^{\alpha\beta}$ for all $R_1, R_2 \in G_1$, and $\alpha, \beta \in Z_p$.
2. Non-degenerate: If g is the generator of G_1, then $\hat{e}(g, g)$ is the generator of G_2.
3. Computable: There is an efficient polynomial time algorithm to compute $\hat{e}(R_1, R_2)$ for any $R_1, R_2 \in G_1$.

We can obtain the above bilinear map such as modified Weil or Tate pairing [6] from certain elliptic curves.

2.2   Complexity Problems

Now, let we go through two complexity problems: q-Bilinear Diffie-Hellman (BDH) [6] problem and Bilinear Diffie-Hellman Inversion (BDHI) [4, 19] problem.

Bilinear Diffie-Hellman Problem (BDH): Given $g, g^\alpha, g^\beta, g^\gamma \in G_1$ as input, where $\alpha, \beta, \gamma \xleftarrow{R} Z_p$, output $\hat{e}(g, g)^{\alpha\beta\gamma} \in G_2$. We define the advantage of an algorithm $\mathcal{A}$ to solve the BDH problem in G_1 as ϵ if

$$Pr[\mathcal{A}(g, g^\alpha, g^\beta, g^\gamma) = \hat{e}(g, g)^{\alpha\beta\gamma}] \geq \epsilon.$$

Definition 1. *We say that BDH is intractable if no polynomial time algorithm has a non-negligible advantage ϵ in solving BDH.*

1-Bilinear Diffie-Hellman Inversion Problem (1-BDHI): Given (g, g^x) $\in G_1^2$, where $x \xleftarrow{R} Z_p$, output $\hat{e}(g,g)^{1/x} \in G_2$. We define the advantage of an algorithm $\mathcal{A}$ to solve the 1-BDHI problem in G_1 as ϵ if

$$Pr[\mathcal{A}(g, g^x) = \hat{e}(g,g)^{1/x}] \geq \epsilon.$$

Definition 2. *We say that 1-BDHI is intractable if no polynomial time algorithm has a non-negligible advantage ϵ in solving 1-BDHI.*

3   A Secure Channel Free PEKS Scheme with Multiple Keywords (SCF-MPEKS)

3.1   Generic Model for SCF-MPEKS

Similar to the scheme in [5], three entities called *"sender"*, *"receiver"* and *"server"* are involved in our construction. The sender uses the server's public key and the receiver's public key to generate MPEKS ciphertexts and sends MPEKS ciphertexts to the server. The server receives MPEKS ciphertexts and performs search upon receiving the trapdoors from the receiver. The receiver creates trapdoors and sends them to the server via a public network. Now we define a formal SCF-PEKS scheme with multiple keywords (SCF-MPEKS) consisting of the following five polynomial-time algorithms:

1. $\mathsf{KeyGen}_{receiver}(\lambda)$: Takes a security parameter λ as input and returns the receiver's public and private key pair (pk_r, sk_r).
2. $\mathsf{KeyGen}_{server}(\lambda)$: Takes a security parameter λ as input and returns the server's public and private key pair (pk_s, sk_s).
3. $\mathsf{SCF\text{-}MPEKS}(pk_r, pk_s, W)$: Takes the receiver's public key pk_r, the server's public key pk_s and a keyword-vector $W = (w_1, w_2, \cdots, w_n)$ as input, and returns a searchable MPEKS ciphertext S of W, we write $S = \mathsf{SCF\text{-}MPEKS}(pk_r, pk_s, W)$.
4. $\mathsf{Trapdoor}(sk_r, w)$: Takes the receiver's secret key sk_r and a keyword w as input, and returns a trapdoor T_w.
5. $\mathsf{Test}((pk_r, sk_s, S, T_w)$: Takes the receiver's public key pk_r, the server's private key sk_s, the searchable encryption $S = \mathsf{SCF\text{-}MPEKS}(pk_r, pk_s, W)$ and the trapdoor T_w as input, and returns "1" if W includes w, and "0" otherwise.

3.2   Consistency Definition for Our SCF-MPEKS Scheme

Here, we will define the consistency of our SCF-MPEKS scheme as discussed in [1]:

Definition 3. *Let $\mathcal{B}$ be an adversary and λ a security parameter. We consider the experiment $\mathbf{Exp}_{\mathcal{B}}^{\text{SCF-MK-consist}}(\lambda)$ addressed in [1]: If there exists a keyword $w' \neq w$, where $w \in W$, and Test function outputs 1. We define the advantage of $\mathcal{B}$ as $\mathbf{Adv}_{\mathcal{B}}^{\text{SCF-MK-consist}}(\lambda)$ as follows:*

$$\mathbf{Adv}_{\mathcal{B}}^{\text{SCF-MK-consist}}(\lambda) = Pr[\mathbf{Exp}_{\mathcal{B}}^{\text{SCF-MK-consist}}(\lambda) = 1].$$

The proposed SCF-MPEKS scheme is to be computationally consistent if the advantage $\mathbf{Adv}_{\mathcal{B}}^{\text{SCF-MK-consist}}(\lambda)$ is negligible for all polynomial-time adversaries.

3.3   Adversarial Models for SCF-MPEKS

As discussed in [2], we say that a SCF-MPEKS scheme is SCF-MPEKS cipher-texts secure if it satisfies the following two conditions:

- A malicious server cannot distinguish which MPEKS ciphertexts matches which keyword if it has not obtained the corresponding trapdoor for the keyword.
- A malicious outside attacker(including the receiver) cannot make any decision about the MPEKS ciphertexts even if he can generates all trapdoors for any keyword of his choice.

Now, we formally define the security models for our SCF-MPEKS scheme. Let two polynomial time algorithms A_1 and A_2 be chosen keyword adversaries against a SCF-PEKS with multiple keywords (SCF-MPEKS) scheme. We will define the indistinguishability of secure channel free PEKS with multiple keywords against chosen keyword attacks (IND-SCF-MK-CKA) via the following two games between the adversary A_1(or A_2) and the challenger C:

Game$_1$: Assume that A_1 is a malicious server.

1. The KeyGen(λ) algorithm is run by the challenger C to generate public and private key pair (pk_r, sk_r) and (pk_s, sk_s) for the receiver and server, respectively, where λ is a security parameter. It gives the server's key pair (pk_s, sk_s) to the attacker A_1 as well as the receiver's public key pk_r
2. Adaptively, the adversary A_1 can ask C for the trapdoor T_w for any keyword $w \in \{0,1\}^*$ of his choice.
3. A_1 sends two new keyword-vector pairs (W_0, W_1) on which it wishes to be challenged to C, where $W_0 = (w_{01}, \cdots, w_{0n})$ and $W_1 = (w_{11}, \cdots, w_{1n})$. A_1 has not queried both components of W_0 and W_1. Upon receiving this, C chooses a random $\beta \in \{0,1\}$ and creates a target MPEKS ciphertext $S_\beta =$ SCF-MPEKS (pk_r, pk_s, W_β) and returns it to A_1.
4. A_1 can continue to ask C for the trapdoor of any keyword except the challenged keyword-vectors W_0 and W_1.
5. Eventually, A_1 outputs its guess $\beta' \in \{0,1\}$ and wins the game if $\beta = \beta'$.

The success of a chosen keyword adversary A_1 winning the above game is defined as

$$\text{Succ}_{\text{SCF-MPEKS},A_1}^{\text{IND-SCF-MK-CKA}}(\lambda) = |Pr[\beta' = \beta] - 1/2|.$$

Game$_2$: Assume that A_2 is a malicious outside attacker.

1. The KeyGen(λ) algorithm is run by the challenger C to generate public and private key pair (pk_r, sk_r) and (pk_s, sk_s) for the receiver and server's, respectively, where λ is a security parameter. It gives the receiver's key pair (pk_r, sk_r) to the attacker A_2 as well as the server's public key pk_s.
2. A_2 can adaptively ask C for the trapdoor T_w for any keyword $w \in \{0,1\}^*$ of his choice.

3. $\mathcal{A}_2$ sends two new keyword-vector pairs (W_0, W_1) on which it wishes to be challenged to $\mathcal{C}$, where $W_0 = (w_{01}, \cdots, w_{0n})$ and $W_1 = (w_{11}, \cdots, w_{1n})$. The challenger $\mathcal{C}$ chooses a random $\beta \in \{0,1\}$ and creates a target MPEKS ciphertexts $S_\beta = \mathsf{SCF\text{-}MPEKS}(pk_r, pk_s, W_\beta)$ and returns it to $\mathcal{A}_2$.
4. Eventually, $\mathcal{A}_2$ outputs its guess $\beta' \in \{0,1\}$ and wins the game if $\beta = \beta'$

The success of a chosen keyword adversary $\mathcal{A}_2$ winning the above game is defined as

$$\mathbf{Succ}_{\mathsf{SCF\text{-}MPEKS},\mathcal{A}_2}^{\mathrm{IND\text{-}SCF\text{-}MK\text{-}CKA}}(\lambda) = |Pr[\beta' = \beta] - 1/2|.$$

Definition 4. *The* SCF-MPEKS *scheme is said to be* IND-SCF-MK-CKA *secure under chosen keyword attacks if* $\mathbf{Succ}_{\mathsf{SCF\text{-}MPEKS},\mathcal{A}_1}^{\mathrm{IND\text{-}SCF\text{-}MK\text{-}CKA}}$ *and* $\mathbf{Succ}_{\mathsf{SCF\text{-}MPEKS},\mathcal{A}_2}^{\mathrm{IND\text{-}SCF\text{-}MK\text{-}CKA}}$ *are negligible in* λ.

4   Proposed SCF-MPEKS Scheme

4.1   Construction of SCF-MPEKS

Let G_1 and G_2 be two cyclic groups of large prime order p, a map $\hat{e}: G_1 \times G_1 \to G_2$ a bilinear map. Let g be the generator of G_1. We make use of two one-way and collision-resistant hash functions $H_1: \{0,1\}^* \longrightarrow G_1$ and $H_2: G_2 \longrightarrow \{0,1\}^{log\ p}$. The scheme is described as following:

1. $\mathsf{KeyGen}_{receiver}(\lambda)$: Take the security λ as input. Choose a random value $x \in Z_p^*$, a generator g of G_1 and computes $X = g^x$. It outputs the receiver's public key $pk_r = X$ and secret key $sk_r = x$.
2. $\mathsf{KeyGen}_{server}(\lambda)$: Take the security λ as input. Choose a random value $y \in Z_p^*$, a generator g of G_1 and computes $Y = g^y$. It outputs the server's public key $pk_s = Y$ and secret key $sk_s = y$.
3. $\mathsf{SCF\text{-}MPEKS}(pk_r, pk_s\ W)$ where $W = (w_1, \ldots, w_n)$: Choose two randomly values $r \in Z_p^*$ and compute $S = (U, V_1, \ldots, V_n)$ such that $U = X^r$, $V_1 = H_2(\hat{e}(H_1(w_1), Y)^r), \ldots, V_n = H_2(\hat{e}(H_1(w_n), Y)^r)$. It outputs S as a MPEKS ciphertext.
4. $\mathsf{Trapdoor}(sk_r, w')$: Compute $T_{w'} = H_1(w')^{1/x}$ and output $T_{w'}$ as a trapdoor for a keyword w'.
5. $\mathsf{Test}((U, V_i), sk_s, T_{w'})$ for $i \in \{1, \ldots, n\}$: If $H_2(\hat{e}(T_{w'}^y, U)) = V_i$ holds, output "1", and "0" otherwise.

4.2   Consistency Proof and Performance Analysis

Consistency Proof. Here, we will show that our SCF-MPEKS scheme satisfies the computational consistency. For some $i \in \{1, \ldots, n\}$, w.l.o.g, we take $i = 1$, supposed $w' = w_1$, computational consistency of the scheme is easily proved as follows:

$$H_2(\hat{e}(T^y_{w'}, U)) = H_2(\hat{e}(H_1(w')^{\frac{y}{x}}, X^r))$$
$$= H_2(\hat{e}(H_1(w')^{\frac{y}{x}}, g^{xr}))$$
$$= H_2(\hat{e}(H_1(w'), g^y)^r)$$
$$= H_2(\hat{e}(H_1(w'), Y)^r)$$
$$= H_2(\hat{e}(H_1(w_1), Y)^r)$$
$$= V_1.$$

From the above equation, we can see that if $w' \neq w_1$, then the equation holds with a negligible probability for the hash function H_1 is collision-resistant.

Performance Analysis. We compare the performance of our SCF-MPEKS scheme with Baek et al.'s MPEKS scheme [2] by showing the time cost of its sub algorithms. The simulation is conducted using type A pairings in the pairing-based library (version 0.5.12)[1]. The conditions of the platform we use are shown in Table 1. The time cost is shown in Table 2. As shown in the Table 2, the running time of our scheme is almost the same as Baek et al.'s MPEKS scheme [2], with a slightly worse performance in the test procedure. However, we remove the secure channel requirement so that the trapdoor can be transferred directly via the public network. This in turns reduces the computation and communication overhead for building a secure channel which is very costly. Therefore, our scheme achieves a better performance and is more practical in real life.

4.3 Security Proof

Theorem 1. *The* SCF-PEKS *scheme with multiple keywords* (SCF-MPEKS) *above is* IND-SCF-MK-CKA *secure against chosen keyword attacks in* $Game_1$ *under the random oracle model assuming 1-BDHI problem is intractable.*

Proof. Suppose $\mathcal{A}_1$ is a malicious server which has advantage ϵ in breaking the SCF-MPEKS. Assume $\mathcal{A}_1$ makes at most q_1 hash function queries to H_1, q_2 hash function queries to H_2 and q_T trapdoor queries (Here, assume that q_T is sufficiently large). An algorithm $\mathcal{B}$ is going to be constructed to solve the 1-BDHI problem with probability at least $\epsilon' = (\frac{q_T}{q_T+1})^{2n-2} \frac{\epsilon}{eq_2(q_T+1)}$, where e is the base

Table 1. Simulation platform

OS	Ubuntu 10.10
CPU	Pentium(R) T4400
Memory	2.00 GB RAM
Hard disk	250 GB/5400 rpm
Programming language	C

---

[1] http://crypto.stanford.edu/pbc/.

Table 2. Performances comparison between MPEKS and SCF-MPEKS

MPEKS [2]	KeyGen$_{receiver}$	MPEKS($n = 10$)	Trapdoor	Test
Average time	0.016 s	0.338 s	0.026 s	0.014 s
SCF-MPEKS	KeyGen$_{receiver}$/KeyGen$_{server}$	SCF-MPEKS($n = 10$)	Trapdoor	Test
Average time	0.016 s	0.336 s	0.029 s	0.026 s

of the natural logarithm and n is the number of keywords. The running time of the algorithm $\mathcal{B}$ is approximately the same as $\mathcal{A}_1's$.

On input parameters of pairing $(g, G_1, G_2, \hat{e})$ and a random instance (g, g^x), algorithm $\mathcal{B}$'s goal is to output $R = \hat{e}(g, g)^{1/x}$. Algorithm $\mathcal{B}$ works by interacting with $\mathcal{A}_1$ as follows:

KeyGen. Select a random value $y \in Z_p^*$ and computes $Y = g^y$. It starts by giving $\mathcal{A}_1$ the receiver's public key $X = g^x$ and $\mathcal{A}_1$'s key pair (y, Y).

H_1 Queries. $\mathcal{A}_1$ can query the random oracle H_1 at any time. To respond, $\mathcal{B}$ maintains a list of tuples $< w_j, l_j, e_j, \nu_j >$ denoted as H_1-list. The list is empty initially. When $\mathcal{A}_1$ sends the query $w_i \in \{0, 1\}^*$ to the random oracle H_1, $\mathcal{B}$ responds as follows:

1. If w_i already in the II_1 list in a tuple $< w_i, l_i, e_i, \nu_i >$, then $H_1 = l_i$ will be responded by $\mathcal{B}$.
2. Otherwise, a random coin $\nu_i \in \{0, 1\}$ will be generated by $\mathcal{B}$ so that $Pr[c_i = 0] = 1/(q_T + 1)$. Then a random value $e_i \in Z_p^*$ will be picked by $\mathcal{B}$.

   If $\nu_i = 0$, $\mathcal{B}$ computes $l_i = g^{e_i} \in G_1$.

   If $\nu_i = 1$, $\mathcal{B}$ computes $l_i = (g^x)^{e_i} \in G_1$.
3. $\mathcal{B}$ adds the tuple$< w_i, l_i, e_i, \nu_i >$to the H_1 list and responds with $H_1 = l_i$.

H_2 Queries. To respond to H_2 queries, $\mathcal{B}$ maintains a list of tuples $< \kappa_j, U_j >$ denoted as the H_2-list. The list is empty initially. When $\mathcal{A}_1$ queries the random oracle H_2 at a point $\kappa_j \in G_2$, $\mathcal{B}$ responds as follows:

1. If the query κ_j already appears in the H_2-list in a tuple $< \kappa_j, U_j >$, then $\mathcal{B}$ responds with $H_2(\kappa_j) = U_j$.
2. Otherwise, $\mathcal{B}$ picks up a $U_j \in \{0, 1\}^{\log p}$ randomly, and adds the tuple $< \kappa_j, U_j >$ to the H_2 list. $\mathcal{B}$ responds with $H_2(\kappa_j) = U_j$.

Trapdoor Queries. When $\mathcal{A}_1$ sends a query for the trapdoor corresponding to the word w_i.

1. $\mathcal{B}$ executes the above algorithm for responding to H_1 queries to create a tuple $< w_i, l_i, e_i, \nu_i >$. If $\nu_i = 0$, then $\mathcal{B}$ reports failure and terminates.
2. Otherwise, we know $\nu_i = 1$ and hence $l_i = (g^x)^{e_i}$. Compute $T_{w_i} = g^{e_i}$. Observe that $T_{w_i} = H_1(w_i)^{1/x}$ and therefore T_{w_i} is the correct trapdoor for the keyword w_i. $\mathcal{B}$ sends T_{w_i} to $\mathcal{A}_1$.

Challenge. Eventually, $\mathcal{A}_1$ generates a pair of keyword-vector (W_0, W_1), where $W_0 = (w_{01}, \cdots, w_{0n})$ and $W_1 = (w_{11}, \cdots, w_{1n})$ which is going to be challenged on. Upon receiving the target keyword-vector, $\mathcal{B}$ responds as follows:

1. $\mathcal{B}$ chooses $a \in \{1, \cdots, n\}$ randomly.
2. $\mathcal{B}$ runs the above algorithm for responding to H_1-queries to get two tuples $< w_{0a}, l_{0a}, e_{0a}, \nu_{0a} >$ and $< w_{1a}, l_{1a}, e_{1a}, \nu_{1a} >$ corresponding to (w_{0a}, w_{1a}). If both $\nu_{0a} = \nu_{1a} = 1$ then $\mathcal{B}$ reports failure and terminates. Otherwise, we can see one of ν_{0a} and ν_{1a} equals to 0, $\mathcal{B}$ responds as follows:
   - Run the above algorithm for responding to H_1-queries $2n - 2$ times to get two vectors of tuples $< w_{01}, l_{01}, e_{01}, \nu_{01} >, \cdots, < w_{0a-1}, l_{0a-1}, e_{0a-1}, \nu_{0a-1} >, < w_{0a+1}, l_{0a+1}, e_{0a+1}, \nu_{0a+1} >, \cdots, < w_{0n}, l_{0n}, e_{0n}, \nu_{0n} >$ and $< w_{11}, l_{11}, e_{11}, \nu_{11} >, \cdots, < w_{1a-1}, l_{1a-1}, e_{1a-1}, \nu_{1a-1} >, < w_{1a+1}, l_{1a+1}, e_{1a+1}, \nu_{1a+1} >, \cdots, < w_{1n}, l_{1n}, e_{1n}, \nu_{1n} >$. If one of ν_{0k} and ν_{1k} are equal to 0 for all $k = 1, \cdots, a-1, a+1, \cdots, n$, $\mathcal{B}$ reports failure and terminates. Otherwise, $\mathcal{B}$ responds as follows:
     * Chooses $\beta \in \{0, 1\}$ uniformly at random such that $\nu_{\beta a} = 1$.
     * $\mathcal{B}$ chooses $k' \in Z_p^*$ at random. Let $r = \frac{k'}{yx} \in Z_p^*$ for the unknown value x.

     Define $V_a = H_2(\hat{e}(g, g)^{\frac{e_{\beta a} k'}{x}})$. Create a target SCF-MPEKS ciphertext S as follows:

     $$S = (U, V_1, \cdots, V_n) = (g^{\frac{k'}{y}}, H_2(\hat{e}(g, g)^{e_{\beta 1} k'}), \cdots, H_2(\hat{e}(g, g)^{e_{\beta a-1} k'}),$$
     $$H_2(\hat{e}(g, g)^{\frac{e_{\beta a} k'}{x}}), H_2(\hat{e}(g, g)^{e_{\beta a+1} k'}), \cdots, H_2(\hat{e}(g, g)^{e_{\beta n} k'}).$$

     Note that by the definition of Y, then we can get

     $$V_a = H_2(\hat{e}(g, g)^{\frac{e_{\beta a} k'}{x}}) = H_2(\hat{e}(g^{e_{\beta a}}, g^y)^{\frac{k'}{yx}}) = H_2(\hat{e}(H_1(w_{\beta a}), Y)^{\frac{k'}{yx}}).$$

     Note also that

     $$V_k = H_2(\hat{e}(g, g)^{e_{\beta k} k'}) = H_2(\hat{e}(g^{e_{\beta k}}, g^y)^{\frac{k'}{yx}}) = H_2(\hat{e}(H_1(w_{\beta k}), Y)^{\frac{k'}{yx}}).$$

     for $k = 1, \cdots, a-1, a+1, \cdots, n$

More Trapdoor Queries. $\mathcal{A}_1$ can continue to issue trapdoor queries for keywords w_j with the only restriction $w_j \notin W_0, W_1$. $\mathcal{B}$ answers these queries as before.

Output. Eventually, $\mathcal{A}_1$ outputs its guess $\beta' \in \{0, 1\}$ showing whether the challenge S is the result of W_0 or W_1. At this point, $\mathcal{B}$ picks a random pair $< \kappa_j, U_j >$ from the H_2-list and computes $\rho = \kappa_j^{\frac{1}{e_j k'}}$. Then $\mathcal{B}$ outputs $\kappa_j^{\frac{1}{e_j k'}}$ as its guess for $\hat{e}(g, g)^{1/x}$. (Note that if $\kappa_j = \hat{e}(g, g)^{\frac{e_{\beta a} k'}{x}}$, then $\kappa_j^{\frac{1}{e_j k'}} = R = \hat{e}(g, g)^{1/x}$)

Analysis. This completes the description of $\mathcal{B}$. Next we will show that $\mathcal{B}$ outputs the correct $\hat{e}(g,g)^{1/x}$ with probability at least ϵ'. Firstly, we analyze the probability that $\mathcal{B}$ does not abort during the simulation. Denote ε_1 and ε_2 as events that $\mathcal{B}$ does not abort during the simulation of the trapdoor queries and the simulation of the challenge phase. The probability that ε_1 happens is $(1 - \frac{1}{q_T+1})^{q_T} \geq 1/e$. At the same time, the probability that ε_2 happens is $(1 - \frac{1}{q_T+1})^{2n-2}[1 - (1 - \frac{1}{q_T+1})^2] \geq (\frac{q_T}{q_T+1})^{2n-2}\frac{1}{q_T+1}$. Observe that since $\mathcal{A}_1$ can never issue a trapdoor query for the challenged keyword-vectors, the two events ε_1 and ε_2 are independent. Therefore, the probability that $\mathcal{B}$ does not abort during the above simulation is $Pr[\varepsilon_1 \bigcap \varepsilon_2]$, that is at least $(\frac{q_T}{q_T+1})^{2n-2}\frac{1}{e(q_T+1)}$.

Now, supposing $\mathcal{B}$ does not abort, then $\mathcal{B}$ simulates a real attack game when $\mathcal{A}_1$ issues a query for either $H_2(\hat{e}(H_1(w_{0a}),Y)^{\frac{k'}{yx}})$ or $H_2(\hat{e}(H_1(w_{1a}),Y)^{\frac{k'}{yx}})$. Let ε_3 be the event that in the real attack $\mathcal{A}_1$ sends a query for either $H_2(\hat{e}(H_1(w_{0a}),Y)^{\frac{k'}{yx}})$ or $H_2(\hat{e}(H_1(w_{1a}),Y)^{\frac{k'}{yx}})$, then we will analyze the probability of the event ε_3 happening. Our analysis is based on the hybrid argument [2]. As discussed in [2], let $Hybrid_k$ where $k \in \{1,\cdots,n\}$ is an event that $\mathcal{A}_1$ successfully guesses the keyword of the left part of a "hybrid" MPEKS ciphertext formed with k, coordinates from w_β followed by $(n-k)$ coordinates from $w_{1-\beta}$. We can get $Pr[\varepsilon_3] = 2\sum_{k=1}^{n}(Pr[Hybrid_k] - Pr[Hybrid_{k-1}]) = 2(Pr[Hybrid_n] - Pr[Hybrid_0]) = 2\epsilon$. Then $\mathcal{A}_1$ issues a query for $H_2(\hat{e}(H_1(w_{\beta a}),Y)^{\frac{k'}{yx}})$ with probability ϵ. Therefore, the value $\hat{e}(g,g)^{\frac{e_{\beta a}k'}{x}}$ will appear on the left hand side of some pair in the H_2-list. $\mathcal{B}$ will choose the correct pair with probability at least $1/q_2$. Thus, $\mathcal{B}$ will generate the right answer with probability at least ϵ/q_2. As $\mathcal{B}$ does not abort during the simulation with probability at least $(\frac{q_T}{q_T+1})^{2n-2}\frac{1}{e(q_T+1)}$, we know that $\mathcal{B}$'s success probability overall is at least $(\frac{q_T}{q_T+1})^{2n-2}\frac{\epsilon}{eq_2(q_T+1)}$.

Theorem 2. *The* SCF-PEKS *scheme with multiple keywords* (SCF-MPEKS) *above is* IND-SCF-MK-CKA *secure against chosen keyword attacks in* Game$_2$ *under the random oracle model assuming BDH problem is intractable.*

Proof. Assume $\mathcal{A}_2$ is a receiver which enjoys advantage ϵ in breaking the SCF-MPEKS. Assume $\mathcal{A}_2$ makes at most q_1 hash function queries to H_1, q_2 hash function queries to H_2 and q_T trapdoor queries. An algorithm $\mathcal{B}$ will be generated to solve the BDH problem with probability at least $\epsilon' = \epsilon/eq_2$, where e is the base of the natural logarithm. The running time of the algorithm $\mathcal{B}$ is approximately the same as $\mathcal{A}_2's$.

On input parameters of pairing $(g,G_1,G_2,\hat{e})$ and a random instance (g,g^a, g^b, g^c), algorithm $\mathcal{B}$'s goal is to output $T = \hat{e}(g,g)^{abc}$. Algorithm $\mathcal{B}$ works by interacting with $\mathcal{A}_2$ as follows:

KeyGen. Select a value $\alpha \in Z_p^*$ randomly, compute $X = g^\alpha$. It starts by giving $\mathcal{A}_2$ the server's public key $Y = g^a$ and $\mathcal{A}_2$'s key pair (α, X).

H_1 Queries. $\mathcal{A}_2$ can query the random oracle H_1 at any time. To respond, $\mathcal{B}$ maintains a list of tuples $< w_j, l_j, e_j >$ denoted as the H_1-list. The list is empty initially. When $\mathcal{A}_2$ queries the random oracle H_1 at a point $w_i \in \{0,1\}^*$, $\mathcal{B}$ answers as follows:

1. If the query w_i already in the H_1 list in a tuple $< w_i, l_i, e_i >$, then $\mathcal{B}$ responds with $H_1 = l_i$.
2. Otherwise, $\mathcal{B}$ chooses a random value $e_i \in Z_p^*$ and computes $l_i = g^{be_i}$.
3. The tuple $< w_i, l_i, e_i >$ is added to the H_1 list and $\mathcal{B}$ responds with $H_1 = l_i$.

H_2 Queries. To respond to H_2 queries, $\mathcal{B}$ maintains a list of tuples $< \kappa_j, U_j >$ denoted as H_2-list. The list is empty initially. When $\mathcal{A}_2$ queries the random oracle H_2 at a point $\kappa_j \in G_2$, $\mathcal{B}$ responds:

1. If the query κ_j already appears in the H_2-list in a tuple $< \kappa_j, U_j >$, then $\mathcal{B}$ responds with $H_2(\kappa_j) = U_j$.
2. Otherwise, $\mathcal{B}$ selects a $U_j \in \{0,1\}^{logp}$ randomly, and adds the tuple $< \kappa_j, U_j >$ to the H_2 list. $\mathcal{B}$ sends $H_2(\kappa_j) = U_j$ back.

Trapdoor Queries. As $\mathcal{A}_2$ sends a query for the trapdoor corresponding to the word w_i, $\mathcal{B}$ executes the above algorithm for answering to H_1 queries to get a tuple $< w_i, l_i, e_i >$. Then $\mathcal{B}$ computes $T_{w_i} = (g^{be_i})^{1/\alpha}$ and gives T_{w_i} to $\mathcal{A}_2$.

Challenge. Eventually, $\mathcal{A}_2$ generates a pair of keyword-vector (W_0, W_1), where $W_0 = (w_{01}, \cdots, w_{0n})$ and $W_1 = (w_{11}, \cdots, w_{1n})$ which will be challenged on. Upon receiving the target keyword-vector, $\mathcal{B}$ picks $\beta \in \{0,1\}$ uniformly at random and generates a target SCF-MPEKS ciphertext as follows:

$$S = (U, V_1, \cdots, V_n) = (g^{\alpha c}, H_2(\hat{e}(g^{be_i}, g^a)^c), \cdots, H_2(\hat{e}(g^{be_n}, g^a)^c))$$

By the definition of Y, then

$$V_i = H_2(\hat{e}(g^{be_i}, g^a)^c) = H_2(\hat{e}(H_1(w_i), Y)^c).$$

for $k = 1, \cdots, n$.

Output. Eventually, $\mathcal{A}_2$ outputs its guess $\beta' \in \{0,1\}$ showing whether the challenge S is the result of W_0 or W_1. Then $\mathcal{B}$ picks a pair $< \kappa_j, U_j >$ randomly from the H_2-list and computes $\eta = \kappa_j^{\frac{1}{e_j}}$. Then $\mathcal{B}$ outputs $\kappa_j^{\frac{1}{e_j}}$ as its guess for $\hat{e}(g, g)^{abc}$.

Analysis. This completes the description of $\mathcal{B}$. We will show that $\mathcal{B}$ outputs the right $\hat{e}(g, g)^{abc}$ with probability at least ϵ'. Firstly we analyze the probability that $\mathcal{B}$ does not abort during the simulation. Let ε_1 and ε_2 be events that $\mathcal{B}$ does not abort during the challenge phase and $\mathcal{A}_2$ issues a query for neither one of $H_2(\hat{e}(g^{ae_i}, g^b)^c)$, for $i = 1, \cdots, n$. As there is no restriction on the challenge phase, $\mathcal{B}$ does not abort during the challenge phase. Thus, $Pr[\varepsilon_1] = 1$. Finally, it needs to show that during the simulation $\mathcal{A}_2$ issues a query for one of $H_2(\hat{e}(g^{ae_i}, g^b)^c)$, for $i = 1, \cdots, n$, with a probability of at least 2ϵ. When ε_2 occurs, the bit $\beta \in \{0, 1\}$ indicates whether S is a SCF-MPEKS ciphertext of W_0 or W_1 is independent of $\mathcal{A}_2's$ view. Thus, $\mathcal{A}_2$ outputs β' will satisfy $\beta' = \beta$ with probability at most $\frac{1}{2}$. By definition of $\mathcal{A}_2$, it is clear that in the real attack $|Pr[\beta' = \beta] - 1/2| \geq \epsilon$. We explain that the above two facts imply that $Pr[\neg\varepsilon_2] \geq 2\epsilon$:

$$
\begin{aligned}
Pr[\beta' = \beta] &= Pr[\beta' = \beta|\varepsilon_2]Pr[\varepsilon_2] + Pr[\beta' = \beta|\neg\varepsilon_2]Pr[\neg\varepsilon_2] \\
&\leq Pr[\beta' = \beta|\varepsilon_2]Pr[\varepsilon_2]Pr[\varepsilon_2] + Pr[\neg\varepsilon_2] \\
&= \frac{1}{2}Pr[\varepsilon_2] + Pr[\neg\varepsilon_2] \\
&= \frac{1}{2} + \frac{1}{2}Pr[\neg\varepsilon_2].
\end{aligned}
$$

$$
Pr[\beta' = \beta] \geq Pr[\beta = \beta|\varepsilon_2]Pr[\varepsilon_2] = \tfrac{1}{2}Pr[\varepsilon_2] = \tfrac{1}{2} - \tfrac{1}{2}Pr[\neg\varepsilon_2].
$$

Then $\epsilon \leq |Pr[\beta' = \beta] - \frac{1}{2}| \leq \frac{1}{2}Pr[\neg\varepsilon_2]$. Hence, $Pr[\neg\varepsilon_2] \geq 2\epsilon$ as required. Consequently, $\mathcal{B}$ will select the correct pair with a probability of at least $1/q_2$ (here, we can assume that q_2 is sufficient large) and thereby the correct answer with a probability of at least $2\epsilon/q_2 \geq \epsilon/q_2$. $\mathcal{B}$ does not abort with a probability 1, hence, $\mathcal{B}$'s overall probability of success is at least ϵ/eq_2.

5 Conclusion

In this paper, we integrate the notions of "SCF-PEKS" and "MPEKS" schemes to obtain a new efficient secure channel free searchable encryption scheme with multiple keywords (SCF-MPEKS). We define the security property-indistinguishability of SCF-MPEKS and present a concrete scheme. The scheme is proved to be secure in the random oracle model assuming that the BDH and 1-BDHI problems are intractable. Efficiency analysis shows that our scheme is more efficient than Baek et al.'s MPEKS scheme.

Acknowledgement. This work is supported by National Natural Science Foundation of China (61472083, 61402110), Program for New Century Excellent Talents in Fujian University (JA14067), Distinguished Young Scholars Fund of Fujian (2016J06013) and Fujian Normal University Innovative Research Team (IRTL1207).

References

1. Abdalla, M., Bellare, M., Catalano, D., Kiltz, E., Kohno, T., Lange, T., Malone-Lee, J., Neven, G., Paillier, P., Shi, H.: Searchable encryption revisited: consistency properties, relation to anonymous IBE, and extensions. J. Cryptology **21**(3), 350–391 (2008)
2. Baek, J., Safavi-Naini, R., Susilo, W.: Public key encryption with keyword search revisited. In: Gervasi, O., Murgante, B., Laganà, A., Taniar, D., Mun, Y., Gavrilova, M.L. (eds.) ICCSA 2008. LNCS, vol. 5072, pp. 1249–1259. Springer, Heidelberg (2008). doi:10.1007/978-3-540-69839-5_96

3. Bellare, M., Boldyreva, A., Staddon, J.: Randomness re-use in multi-recipient encryption schemeas. In: Desmedt, Y.G. (ed.) PKC 2003. LNCS, vol. 2567, pp. 85–99. Springer, Heidelberg (2003). doi:10.1007/3-540-36288-6_7

4. Boneh, D., Boyen, X.: Efficient selective-ID secure identity-based encryption without random oracles. In: Cachin, C., Camenisch, J. (eds.) [7], pp. 223–238

5. Boneh, D., Di Crescenzo, G., Ostrovsky, R., Persiano, G.: Public key encryption with keyword search. In: Cachin, C., Camenisch, J. (eds.) [7], pp. 506–522

6. Boneh, D., Franklin, M.: Identity-based encryption from the weil pairing. In: Kilian, J. (ed.) CRYPTO 2001. LNCS, vol. 2139, pp. 213–229. Springer, Heidelberg (2001). doi:10.1007/3-540-44647-8_13

7. Cachin, C., Camenisch, J.L. (eds.): EUROCRYPT 2004. LNCS, vol. 3027. Springer, Heidelberg (2004)

8. Curtmola, R., Garay, J.A., Kamara, S., Ostrovsky, R.: Searchable symmetric encryption: improved definitions and efficient constructions. J. Comput. Secur. 19(5), 895–934 (2011)

9. Chunxiang, G., Zhu, Y.: New efficient searchable encryption schemes from bilinear pairings. I. J. Netw. Secur. 10(1), 25–31 (2010)

10. Hwang, Y.H., Lee, P.J.: Public key encryption with conjunctive keyword search and its extension to a multi-user system. In: Takagi, T., Okamoto, T., Okamoto, E., Okamoto, T. (eds.) Pairing 2007. LNCS, vol. 4575, pp. 2–22. Springer, Heidelberg (2007). doi:10.1007/978-3-540-73489-5_2

11. Kurosawa, K.: Multi-recipient public-key encryption with shortened ciphertext. In: Naccache, D., Paillier, P. (eds.) PKC 2002. LNCS, vol. 2274, pp. 48–63. Springer, Heidelberg (2002). doi:10.1007/3-540-45664-3_4

12. Li, M., Yu, S., Cao, N., Lou, W.: Authorized private keyword search over encrypted data in cloud computing. In: 2011 International Conference on Distributed Computing Systems, ICDCS 2011, Minneapolis, Minnesota, USA, 20–24 June 2011, pp. 383–392. IEEE Computer Society (2011)

13. Li, M., Shucheng, Y., Zheng, Y., Ren, K., Lou, W.: Scalable and secure sharing of personal health records in cloud computing using attribute-based encryption. IEEE Trans. Parallel Distrib. Syst. 24(1), 131–143 (2013)

14. Liu, J., Huang, X., Liu, J.K.: Secure sharing of personal health records in cloud computing: ciphertext-policy attribute-based signcryption. Future Gener. Comp. Syst. 52, 67–76 (2015)

15. Löhr, H., Sadeghi, A.-R., Winandy, M.: Securing the e-health cloud. In: Veinot, T.C., Çatalyürek, Ü.V., Luo, G., Andrade, H., Smalheiser, N.R. (eds.) Proceedings of the ACM International Health Informatics Symposium, IHI 2010, Arlington, VA, USA, 11–12 November 2010, pp. 220–229. ACM (2010)

16. Song, D.X., Wagner, D., Perrig, A.: Practical techniques for searches on encrypted data. In: 2000 IEEE Symposium on Security and Privacy, Berkeley, California, USA, 14–17 May 2000, pp. 44–55. IEEE Computer Society (2000)

17. Liesdonk, P., Sedghi, S., Doumen, J., Hartel, P., Jonker, W.: Computationally efficient searchable symmetric encryption. In: Jonker, W., Petković, M. (eds.) SDM 2010. LNCS, vol. 6358, pp. 87–100. Springer, Heidelberg (2010). doi:10.1007/978-3-642-15546-8_7

18. Waters, B.R., Balfanz, D., Durfee, G., Smetters, D.K.: Building an encrypted and searchable audit log. In: Proceedings of the Network and Distributed System Security Symposium, NDSS 2004, San Diego, California, USA. The Internet Society (2004)

19. Zhang, F., Safavi-Naini, R., Susilo, W.: An efficient signature scheme from bilinear pairings and its applications. In: Bao, F., Deng, R., Zhou, J. (eds.) PKC 2004. LNCS, vol. 2947, pp. 277–290. Springer, Heidelberg (2004). doi:10.1007/978-3-540-24632-9_20

Searchable Symmetric Encryption Supporting Queries with Multiple-Character Wildcards

Fangming Zhao[1,2](✉) and Takashi Nishide[2]

[1] TOSHIBA Corporation, 72-34, Horikawa-cho, Saiwai-ku, Kawasaki 212-8585, Japan
fangming.zhao@toshiba.co.jp
[2] University of Tsukuba, 1-1-1 Tennoudai, Tsukuba, Ibaraki 305-8573, Japan
nishide@risk.tsukuba.ac.jp

Abstract. We consider the problem of searchable encryption scheme which allows a user to search over encrypted data without decrypting it. Existing schemes in the symmetric setting only deal with equality search or a limited similarity keyword search. In this paper, we study Bloom filter-based searchable symmetric encryption schemes which make search on encrypted keywords more expressive and flexible, i.e., support fuzzy search or wildcard search by using multiple wildcard characters. Our schemes are more efficient than previous solutions on both computation cost and communication cost. Security of our main construction is analyzed based on a formal, strong security model for searchable symmetric encryption.

Keywords: Searchable encryption · Bloom filter · Wildcard

1 Introduction

1.1 Background

Cloud services are spreading rapidly and widely due to advance in computer and telecommunication technology. Both individual and enterprise users outsource not only data but also processing to cloud servers for reasons of management cost and convenience. Because most cloud services are provided by third-party service providers, encryption/decryption at the server's side becomes inappropriate because the server is not fully trusted. Therefore the data should be encrypted before outsourced to the cloud storage servers. However, even if the encryption will ease user's concerns about data leakage, it also introduces some new problems: because the encrypted data (or, ciphertext) is not meaningful to the cloud servers, many useful data operations performed by cloud servers, such as the search functionality, become infeasible.

Searchable encryption is a technique that allows a client to outsource documents to an honest but curious server in the encrypted form, such that the stored documents can be retrieved selectively while revealing as little information as possible to the server. Compared with the traditional *equality search*,

© Springer International Publishing AG 2016
J. Chen et al. (Eds.): NSS 2016, LNCS 9955, pp. 266–282, 2016.
DOI: 10.1007/978-3-319-46298-1_18

which means the keywords which match the query completely hit, to support various typical users' searching behaviors and typing habits, advanced search functionalities also include a *wildcard search*, in which the keywords that match any character other than wildcard characters obtain hits, and here wildcard characters (e.g. "?" or "*") represent any characters; a *fuzzy search*, in which the keywords within a certain edit distance from the query obtain hits. As a common scene, a user may search and retrieve the data of their respective interests using any keywords they might come up with. For example, after a cloud server administrator gets error information "*Error (code = 131415): an automatic reboot by Segmentation fault*" from one server, he may want to know whether any other similar errors happened among other servers from numerous log files, which include similar keywords like "*Error (code = 13????): *reboot**". In such a situation, search keywords with wildcards (e.g. "*" and "?") will also be useful because his search input might not exactly match those preset keywords due to the lack of exact knowledge about the entire keyword, typing habits, possible typos, and representation inconsistencies (e.g. "*BO BOX*" and "*B.O. BOX*").

In this paper, we study the searchable symmetric encryption (SSE) utilizing both two kind of wildcards, i.e., "*" and "?", to conveniently satisfy users' various searching behaviors and requirements in an outsourced cloud environment.

- "*" matches zero or more non-space characters, and it can be used as a multiple-character wildcard.
- "?" matches exactly one non-space character, and it can be used as a single-character wildcard.

For example, "he*" will match any word starting with he, such as "he", "her", "help", "hello", "helicopter", and so on. On the other hand, "he?" will only match three-letter words starting with "he", such as "hem", "hen", and so on. Wildcard searches over encrypted data enable the cloud server to return results (e.g. an encrypted document) that match combinations of characters and wildcards. Such an advanced SSE scheme using multiple-character wildcard search will be helpful in the following usecases:

Wildcard search in a more expressive manner ———————————

- "*2013*.*, 2013*tokyo*.*, module*.c*"
  (Search a file name)
- "PC-MA??TCNZ*6, V83-P?83TS*-NW??"
  (Search model numbers of some products)
- "Ta* Ni*, Fa*M* ?hao"
  (Search an author name from initial characters)
- "Error (code=????): * reboot * ."
  "[Urgent]: troubleshooting * decryption *"
  "Bug Report: * func_a * error return *"
  (Search an important information from a log file)
- "192.168.???.13"
  "200?:*:*:1a2b:1a2b"
  (Search an IP address)
- "1-*-*, *[Tennodai], Tsukuba, Ibaraki 305-8577 Japan"
  (Search an address)

1.2   Related Works

In the literature, searchable encryption is a subject started in 2000 from the work of Song et al. [SWP00], in which they introduced for the first time a symmetric searchable scheme. They have introduced three basic searchable encryption security properties: the hidden queries, the controlled searching and the query isolation. However, their scheme does not appear to be efficient and practical because the complexity is linear in the number of keywords multiplying the number of outsourced documents. Later, practical schemes using Bloom filters, which consider both efficiency and adversary model for searching in encrypted data were proposed [Goh03, BBH+11, SNS12, ME14]. Goh [Goh03] first introduced an approach based on Bloom filters. Goh introduced the concept of semantic security against *adaptive chosen keywords attack (IND-CKA)* and a second slightly stronger security model *IND2-CKA*. Later, Bösch et al. [BBH+11] proposed a conjunctive wildcard search scheme over encrypted data and presented a new security property taking into account an adaptive adversary, called *adaptive semantic security for SSE*. Being superior to Goh [Goh03] which mainly supports only the exact keyword search, [BBH+11] supports flexible conjunctive wildcard searches, where a conjunction is the union of any number of keywords. Suga et al. [SNS12] proposed a flexible fuzzy search scheme which supports a keyword query containing single-wildcard characters based on the subset query technique [MIP02]. Recently, Mohan et al. [ME14] also proposed a fuzzy keyword search scheme for similarity search using a single-wildcard character, but no security model was considered.

Cash et al. [CJJ+13] and Faber et al. [FJ+15] presented another kind of SSE solution without utilizing the Bloom filter. Their schemes support Boolean queries on multiple keywords. In particular, [FJ+15] extends the basic Boolean query on exact keywords of [CJJ+13] to support wildcard queries, phrase queries, range queries and substring queries. Compared with their complicated computing process, our Bloom filter-based schemes that use only hash-based operations will allow simpler implementations.

1.3 Our Contributions

In this paper, we study advanced wildcard searches over encrypted data and propose an SSE scheme supporting queries with multiple-character wildcards. Compared with existing works [Goh03, BBH+11, SNS12, ME14], our scheme supports a more flexible, expressive query where the server can search for partially matched encrypted keywords by taking advantage of both the single-character wildcard "?" and the multiple-character wildcard "*". Our second construction is analyzed and proved secure based on a formal model, *adaptive semantic security for SSE*, and especially, the second construction prevents an information leakage threat, called a correlation attack. This approach is much more cost-effective in terms of both the network traffic and the storage cost than [BBH+11]. Besides, we also give efficient and secure document update mechanisms of both variants for practical use in real world applications.

2 Preliminaries

2.1 Definitions and Notations

Bloom Filter [B70]. A Bloom filter (BF) is a space-efficient probabilistic data structure to represent a set of elements. Usually a Bloom filter is realized by a bit array and we assume the length of the array is m. Also the filter has several independent hash functions and here we assume that there are k hash functions $\{h_i : \{0,1\}^* \to [1, m]\}_{1 \leq i \leq k}$.

An empty Bloom filter is a bit array a of m bits that are set to all 0's. To store an element e in the Bloom filter a, we compute $h_i(e)$ for $1 \leq i \leq k$ and set $a[h_i(e)]$ to 1 for $1 \leq i \leq k$. We can perform set membership queries on a Bloom filter. For example, to see whether a Bloom filter a has an element e, we check whether all of $a[h_i(e)]$'s are 1's for $1 \leq i \leq k$ and if so, the Bloom filter includes e. Similarly we can also perform subset queries. We note that false positives can happen, but the probability of false positives can be made sufficiently small by choosing appropriate parameters.

Pseudo-Random Generators. A polynomial time deterministic algorithm $G : \{0,1\}^n \to \{0,1\}^{\ell(n)}$ is said to be a pseudo-random generator, if for all *PPT* D, there exists a negligible function $negl(\cdot)$ such that $| \Pr_{s \in_R \{0,1\}^n} [D(G(s)) = 1]$

$- \Pr_{r \in_R \{0,1\}^{\ell(n)}} [D(r) = 1] | < negl(n)$

A distribution is pseudo-random if a string chosen according to it cannot be efficiently distinguished from a random string. The probabilities above are also over the random bits used by D and the random choices of the seed and the string r.

Random Oracle Model [BR93]. All oracle queries, regardless of the identity of the party making them, are answered by a single function, that is uniformly selected among all possible functions. The set of possible functions is determined by a length function, $\ell_{out}(\cdot)$, and by the security parameter of the system. Specifically, given security parameter k we consider functions mapping $\{0,1\}^* \rightarrow \{0,1\}^{\ell_{out}(k)}$ to be a random oracle. Security of an ideal system is defined as usual. That is, an ideal system is considered secure if any adversary with the given abilities (including oracle access) has only a negligible probability of success (or only a negligible advantage). We also stress that a random oracle is a function: if it is queried twice on the same input then the output is the same.

2.2 SSE Syntax

We consider a user U who stores a set of encrypted documents on an *honest-but-curious* cloud server S which can be trusted to adhere to the protocols, but which tries to learn as much information as possible, e.g., what kind of information U always accesses. U later may want to retrieve some of the encrypted documents containing a specific keyword (or, a search expression), from S. To do so, U first stores both encrypted documents and their secure indexes that are generated from each keyword that he may search for later, in S. The secure indexes allow U to search encrypted documents containing a specific keyword. Then, to search for a specific keyword from S, U creates a trapdoor for that keyword and sends this trapdoor to the server which then returns the result indicating which documents match the query. U then decides which of the documents she wants to retrieve and sends the document IDs to S. S returns the requested documents. Our searchable symmetric encryption schemes consist of the following four algorithms:

- *Keygen(1^s)*: Given a security parameter s, *Keygen* outputs the master private key K. This algorithm is run by the client.
- *BuildIndex(K, D)*: Given the master key K and a document collection D, the algorithm outputs an index I. This algorithm is run by the client.
- *Trapdoor(K, w)*: Given the key K and a keyword w, *Trapdoor* outputs the trapdoor Td_w for w. This algorithm is run by the client.
- *SearchIndex(Td_w, I)*: Given a trapdoor Td_w for word w and the index I, the algorithm outputs a bit string which indicates the matched documents. This algorithm is run by the server.

2.3 Security Model

Security for searchable encryption is intuitively characterized as the requirement that no information beyond the outcome of a search is leaked. In this paper, we use the security definitions for searchable symmetric encryption (SSE) from [CGK+11]. Being different from their original security definitions, in this paper we extend the definition of a basic "Keyword" to a "Keyword/Token Characteristic Set", which includes more than one element for supporting a more expressive search with one or more wildcard characters. Next, in the following description of security definitions, we still use the "keyword" to represent the meanings of both a "Keyword" and an element of the "Keyword/Token Characteristic Set" for simplicity and easy understanding. There are mainly three auxiliary notions: the history, which defines the user's input to the scheme; the server's view, or everything he sees during the protocols; and the trace, which defines the information we allow to leak to the server.

An interaction between the client and the server will be determined by a document collection and a set of keywords that the client wishes to search for (and that we wish to hide from the adversary). An instantiation of such an interaction is called a history.

Definition 1 (History). *Let W be a dictionary consisting of all possible keywords. A history H_q, is an interaction between a client and a server over q queries, consisting of a collection of documents D and the keywords w_i used for q consecutive search queries. The partial history H_q^t of a given history $H_q = (D, w_1, ..., w_q)$, is the sequence $H_q^t = (D, w_1, ..., w_t)$, where $t \leq q$.*

The server's view consists of all the information the server can gather during a protocol run. Basically, the view consists of the encrypted files $E(d_{FID_i})$, and their identifier FID_i, indexes I, and the trapdoors Td_{w_i}. It will also contain some additional common information, such as the number of BFs attached to each specific document, $(Nbf_1, ..., Nbf_n)$, and if any, the ID sets of existing BFs of each file, $(Set_{FID_1}, ..., Set_{FID_n})$, and the position information of all trapdoors, $(P_{w_1}, ..., P_{w_q})$ where $P_{w_j} = \{pos_1, ..., pos_{v_{w_j}}\}$, $j \in [1, q]$. Here, $\{pos_1, ..., pos_{v_{w_j}}\}$ is named as an *abstract position set*, where v_{w_j} is a variable which depends on each w_j and is decided by the number of positions to be checked by the server (e.g., to be checked to see whether the values equal "1"). The server's view also includes the real values of bit positions of the indexes that are checked by the server (because in some case those indexes are masked before sent to the server, then the real value of each position may be masked). This kind of information for each w_j, called R_{w_j}, will be learned by the server after executing a keyword search. Specifically, if a position p is checked for one of the BFs and the $BF[p]$ did not match while searching the trapdoor of w_j, such information will be recorded in a bit array as $BA[p] = 0$ otherwise 1 for each BF with a unique identifier, BID_{w_j}, such that $BA_{BID_{w_j}} = \{BA[1], ..., BA[v_{w_j}]\}$, and $R_{w_j} = \{BA_{BID_{w_1}}, ..., BA_{BID_{w_q}}\}$.

Definition 2 (View). *Let D be a collection of n documents and let $H_q = (D, w_1, ..., w_q)$ be a history over q queries. An adversary's view under secret key K of the SSE scheme is defined as $V_K(H_q) = (FID_1, ..., FID_n, E(d_{FID_1}), ..., E(d_{FID_n}), I, Td_{w_1}, ..., Td_{w_q}, Nbf_1, ..., Nbf_n, P_{w_1}, ..., P_{w_q}, R_{w_1}, ..., R_{w_q}, Set_{FID_1}, ..., Set_{FID_n})$ The partial view $V_K^t(H_q)$ of a history H_q under secret key K is the sequence $V_K^t(H_q) = (FID_1, ..., FID_n, E(d_{FID_1}), ..., E(d_{FID_n}), I, Td_{w_1}, ..., Td_{w_t}, Nbf_1, ..., Nbf_n, P_{w_1}, ..., P_{w_t}, R_{w_1}, ..., R_{w_q}, Set_{FID_1}, ..., Set_{FID_n})$*

Definition 3 (Access Pattern). *Let D be a collection of n documents and H_q = $(D, w_1, ..., w_q)$ be a history over q queries. The access pattern induced by a q-query history $H = (D, w)$, is the tuple $\alpha(H) = (D(w_1), ..., D(w_q))$.*

Finally, the trace consists of all the information that we are willing to leak or the server is allowed to learn. The information includes the file IDs and their related query words in the history and information that describes which trapdoors in the view correspond to the same underlying words in the history. The index and encrypted files are also stored on the server, so the size of files $|d_{FID_i}|$, the length of the a bloom filter $|BF|$ and the number of BFs attached with each document, $(Nbf_1, ..., Nbf_n)$, will be leaked. In some case, it may also leak the ID sets of existing BFs of each file, $Set_{FID_1}, ..., Set_{FID_n}$, We add also the sequence $(D(w_1), ..., D(w_n))$ which denotes the access pattern of a client, and the search pattern Π_q of a client as any information that can be derived from knowing whether two arbitrary searches were performed for the same word or not to the trace. More formally, Π_q can be thought of as a symmetric binary matrix where $\Pi_q[i, x] = 1$ if $w_i = w_x$, and 0 otherwise, for $1 \leq i, x \leq q$. Since the server will search for a keyword by checking the stored BFs (i.e., bit arrays) with the received trapdoor, the following two kind of information, (1) the abstract position set of each trapdoor, $P_{w_j} = \{pos_1, ..., pos_{v_{w_j}}\}$ for trapdoor Td_{w_j}, and, (2) $(R_{w_1}, ..., R_{w_q})^1$, the real values of each meaningful bit position $BF[p]$ that are checked by the server (because in some case that indexes are masked before sent to the server).

Definition 4 (Trace). *Let D be a collection of n documents and H_q = $(D, w_1, ..., w_q)$ be a history over q queries. The trace of H_q is the sequence $Tr(H_q)$ = $(FID_1, ..., FID_n, |d_{FID_1}|, ..., |d_{FID_n}|, |BF|, Set_{FID_1}, ..., Set_{FID_n}, Nbf_1, ..., Nbf_n, D(w_1), ..., D(w_q), \Pi_q, P_{w_1}, ..., P_{w_q}, R_{w_1}, ..., R_{w_q})$*

We use a simulation-based approach from Curtmola et al. [CGK+11] to introduce the security definition for semantic security. Here we assume the client initially stores a number of documents and afterwards does an arbitrary number of search queries. Intuitively, it says that given all the information the server is allowed to learn (*Trace*), he learns nothing from the information he receives (*View*) about the user's input (*History*) that he could not have generated on his own.

Definition 5 (Adaptive Semantic Security for SSE). *An SSE scheme is adaptively semantically secure if for all $q \in \mathbb{N}$ and for all (non-uniform) probabilistic polynomial-time adversaries $\mathcal{A}$, there exists a (non-uniform) probabilistic polynomial-time algorithm (the simulator) S such that for all traces Tr_q of length q, and for all polynomially samplable distributions $\mathcal{H}_q = \{H_q : Tr(H_q) = Tr_q\}$ (i.e., the set of histories with trace Tr_q), all functions $f : \{0,1\}^m \to \{0,1\}^{\ell(m)}$ (where $m = |H_q|$ and $\ell(m) = poly(m)$), all $0 \leq t \leq q$ and all polynomials p and*

---

[1] The access pattern, i.e., a sequence $(D(w_1), ..., D(w_n))$, may be deduced from $(R_{w_1}, ..., R_{w_q})$.

sufficiently large k:

$$| \, Pr[\mathcal{A}(V_K^t(H_q)) = f(H_q^t) \,] - Pr[\mathcal{S}(Tr(H_q^t)) = f(H_q^t)] \, | < \frac{1}{p(k)}$$

where $H_q \xleftarrow{R} \mathcal{H}_q$, $K \leftarrow Keygen(s)$, *and the probabilities are taken over* $\mathcal{H}_q$ *and the internal coins of Keygen,* $\mathcal{A}, \mathcal{S}$ *and the underlying BuildIndex algorithm.*

3 Our Constructions

We extend the approach of Suga et al. [SNS12] supporting single-character wild-cards such that we can also use multiple-character wildcards. We assume that there is an upper bound u of the keyword length in our schemes. In [SNS12], one Bloom filter (i.e., array) is created from one keyword. For example, if the keyword is "abc\0"[2], a *keyword characteristic set* {'1:a', '2:b', '3:c', '4:\0'} is extracted from the keyword and stored in the Bloom filter. To perform a search with a search expression "?bc" which means that the second character should be 'b' and the third character should be 'c', a search token (which is also a Bloom filter) is created with a *token characteristic set* {'2:b', '3:c'}. As a result, the search operation is reduced to a subset query on the Bloom filters, and in this case, the search token "?bc" can match the keyword "abc" because {'2:b', '3:c'} $\subseteq$ {'1:a', '2:b', '3:c', '4:\0'}. In [SNS12], only single-character wildcards (i.e., '?') are supported. We extend how to create keyword/token characteristic sets to support multiple-character wildcards in the search expressions.

3.1 Keyword/Token Characteristic Sets

We begin by explaining how to create a keyword/token characteristic set from a keyword with a simple example. First, let's consider a simple keyword $w =$ "abcc\0" and its keyword characteristic set $S_K(w)$. In our construction, the set $S_K(w)$ consists of two sets $S_K^{(o)}(w), S_K^{(p)}(w)$, i.e., $S_K(w) = S_K^{(o)}(w) \cup S_K^{(p)}(w)$. The set $S_K^{(o)}(w)$ is set to {'1:a', '2:b', '3:c', '4:c', '5:\0'} similarly to [SNS12]. Further the set $S_K^{(p)}(w)$ consists of two sets $S_K^{(p_1)}(w), S_K^{(p_2)}(w)$ that are created by considering all the pairs of two characters[3] (including \0) in w.

More specifically, $S_K^{(p_1)}(w)$ is computed as

$$S_K^{(p_1)}(w) = \{ \text{'1:1:a,b', '2:1:a,c', '3:1:a,c', '4:1:a,\0', '1:1:b,c', '2:1:b,c', '3:1:b,\0',}$$
$$\text{'1:1:c,c', '2:1:c,\0', '1:1:c,\0'} \}.$$

For example, the element '3:1:a,c' in $S_K^{(p_1)}(w)$ comes from the subsequence of 'a' and 'c' (i.e., "ab<u>c</u>c") and the first 3 means the distance between 'a' and 'c' and the second 1 means that this is the first appearance of the sequence of 'a' and 'c' with distance 3.

---

[2] \0 is a null character and we include it in the keyword explicitly.

[3] in other words, all the subsequences of length 2.

Similarly $S_K^{(p_2)}(w)$ is computed as

$$S_K^{(p_2)}(w) = \{\text{'-:1:a,b', '-:1:a,c', '-:2:a,c', '-:1:a,\textbackslash 0', '-:1:b,c', '-:2:b,c', '-:1:b,\textbackslash 0',}$$
$$\text{'-:1:c,c', '-:1:c,\textbackslash 0', '-:2:c,\textbackslash 0'}\}.$$

The element '-:2:a,c' in $S_K^{(p_2)}(w)$ comes from the subsequence of 'a' and 'c' (i.e., "a<u>bc</u>c") and this time we do not specify the distance between 'a' and 'c', so we use -, and the second 2 means that this is the second appearance of the subsequence of 'a' and 'c' with distance being unspecified. $S_K(w)$ is defined as $S_K^{(o)}(w) \cup S_K^{(p_1)}(w) \cup S_K^{(p_2)}(w)$. Then, the user can query any part she want form the set $S_K(w)$.

Next we explain how to create a token characteristic set from a search expression with another example, a case that the search expression contains some wildcard characters. Let's consider an extended search expression $e' = $ "*aa*b$^{(5)}$*x??z*c$^{(13)}$*\textbackslash 0" and its token characteristic set $S_T(e')$. First we mention the difference between the search expression in [SNS12] and our extended one. Similarly the set $S_T(e')$ consists of two sets $S_T^{(o)}(e'), S_T^{(p)}(e')$, i.e., $S_T(e') = S_T^{(o)}(e') \cup S_T^{(p)}(e')$. The set $S_T^{(o)}(e')$ is set similarly to [SNS12]. Further the set $S_T^{(p)}(e')$ consists of two sets $S_T^{(p_1)}(e'), S_T^{(p_2)}(e')$ that are created by considering all the pairs of two characters (including *null*) in e'. The token characteristic set generation process are described here.

Input: an extended search expression, e.g., $e' = $ "*aa*b$^{(5)}$*x??z*c$^{(13)}$*\textbackslash 0"

Output: a token characteristic set including $S_K^{(o)}(e'), S_K^{(p_1)}(e'), S_K^{(p_2)}(e')$

1. $S_T^{(o)}(e') = \{\text{'5:b', '13:c'}\}$. If there is any character with a specific appearance order in the search expression, extract each character with its appearance order, then add to $S_T^{(o)}(e')$.

2. $S_T^{(p_1)}(e') = \{\text{'2:1:x,z', '1:1:a,a', '1:1:a,b', '2:1:a,b', '1:1:z,c'}\}$.
   If there is any single-wildcard character(s) "?" sandwiched between two characters or any consecutive characters, extract all the possible character pairs then add to $S_T^{(p_1)}(e')$. Next, if the search expression contains one or several single-wildcard character(s) '*', extract all subsequence of two-character pairs together with their specific distance while respecting the appearance order.

3. $S_T^{p_2}(e') = \{\text{'-:1:a,a', '-:1:a,b', '-:1:a,x', '-:1:a,z', '-:1:a,c', '-:1:a,\textbackslash 0',}$
   $\text{'-:2:a,b', '-:2:a,x', '-:2:a,z', '-:2:a,c', '-:2:a,\textbackslash 0', '-:1:b,x',}$
   $\text{'-:1:b,z', '-:1:b,c', '-:1:b,\textbackslash 0', '-:1:x,z', '-:1:x,c', '-:1:x,\textbackslash 0',}$
   $\text{'-:1:z,c', '-:1:z,\textbackslash 0', '-:1:c,\textbackslash 0'}\}$.
   Remove all "?" and "*" from the search expression to form a new string, e.g. aabxzc\textbackslash 0. Then extract all possible two-character pairs, and set its appearance order if there exists a duplicated pair.

3.2   First Construction with Higher Efficiency but Weaker Security

We first introduce the first construction which supports efficiently the updateable search on encrypted documents. Since the same keyword (or, element of the token characteristic set) will be translated to the same BF for all documents, the degree of BF similarity (which also means document similarity) is not protected in this scheme although the higher efficiency is realized compared with our second construction.

- **Keygen(1^s)**: Given a security parameter s, generate a secret master key $K = \{k_1, k_2, ..., k_r\}$, consisting of r independent secret keys.
- **BuildIndex(K, D)**: The input is the master secret key K and a document collection D consisting of a set of n documents. FID_i denotes the file identifier of a specific document d_{FID_i}, where $i \in [1, n]$. For each document, generate a list of all its keywords and their attached keyword characteristic sets $S_K(w) = \{e_1, e_2, ..., e_\ell\}$ as described in Sect. 3.1. This construction prepares one Bloom filter per keyword characteristic set. The index thus can be represented as an $m \times b$ binary matrix where m means the number of keywords in a document and b is the size of a single Bloom filter in bits. To generate the Bloom filters for each $S_K(w)$ of the documents D and then to output the index, the user executes the following processes:
  1. For each element e_j ($j \in [1, \ell]$) in $S_K(w)$:
     (a) Generate its trapdoor: $Td_{e_j} = \{pos_1, pos_2, ..., pos_r\}$, where $pos_x = RO(k_x, e_j)$ for $x \in [1, r]$. RO means a hash function modeled as a random oracle [BR93].
     (b) Set the Bloom Filter BF: Set the bits at the positions of Td_{e_j} in its BF to 1.
  2. Create the index I_{FID_i} from all BFs: $I_{FID_i} = (BF_1, ..., BF_m)^T$.
- **Trapdoor(K, w)**: Given the key $K = \{k_1, k_2, ..., k_r\}$, for a search expression w, first generate its token characteristic set $S_T(w)$ as described in Sect. 3.1. For each element e_j of $S_T(w)$, calculate its trapdoor $Td_{e_j} = \{pos_1, pos_2, ..., pos_r\}$, where $pos_x = RO(k_x, e_j)$ for $x \in [1, r]$, $j \in [1, \ell]$. Then, output the trapdoor for the search expression: $Td = \{Td_{e_1}, Td_{e_2} ..., Td_{e_\ell}\}$.
- **SearchIndex(Td, I)**: Given a trapdoor $Td = \{Td_{e_1}, Td_{e_2}, ..., Td_{e_j}\}$ and all the indexes I_{FID_i} for all $i \in n$, $j \in [1, \ell]$ documents are checked as follows. Check if any BF from I_{FID_i} contains 1's in all locations denoted by any Td. If some BF matches, the server returns the related FID_i to the client.

3.3   Second Construction with Higher Security

In the 1st construction, each element of the keyword characteristic set is represented by the same r positions in all Bloom filters. Anyone (e.g. the server) who can access the index will know the similarity of documents from their indexes because two similar Bloom filters mean the similar keyword/element is included in both documents. Such an information leakage is called *correlation attack* [BBH+11]. To prevent such an correlation attack and to gain a higher level resilience against information leakage, we also extend our first construction to a "masked" index scheme with higher security. Compared with the existing work [BBH+11], our construction is much more cost-effective both on the network traffic and on the storage cost of the client.

- **Keygen**(1^s): Given a security parameter s, generate a secret master key $K = \langle K_H, K_G \rangle$, with $K_H = \{k_x\}_{x \in [1,r]}$ being r independent keys and $K_G \in \{0,1\}^*$.
- **BuildIndex**(K, D): The input are the secret key K_H, K_G and a document collection D consisting of a set of n documents. FID_i denotes the file identifier of a specific document d_{FID_i}, where $i \in [1,n]$. For each document, generate a list of all its keywords and their attached keyword characteristic sets, $S_K(w)$. This construction also prepares one Bloom filter per keyword, which means each BF is prepared for a unique set, $S_K(w)$, in one documents. Then the index can be represented as an $m \times b$ binary matrix where m is the number of keywords and b is the size of a single Bloom filter in bits. To generate the Bloom filter for each $S_K(w)$ and finally output the index of a document, executes the following algorithms:
  1. Generate a unique identifier, BID, as the ID of the BF (for each set $S_K(w)$). To distinguish each BID and ensure its uniqueness on each keyword/document, it uses both the file ID, FID_i, and the keyword w, to generates the BID:
     $BID_w = RO(K_G, FID_i \parallel w)$
     For each document, the number of its attached BIDs is the number of its keywords. Then, for each element e_j where $j \in [1, \ell]$ in the set $S_K(w)$:
     (a) Generate the trapdoor, Td_{e_j}: Given the key $K_H = \{k_1, k_2, ..., k_r\}$, for each element e_j, it calculates the trapdoor $Td_{e_j} = \{pos_1, pos_2, ..., pos_r\}$, where $pos_x = RO(k_x, e_j)$ for $x \in [1, r]$.
     (b) Set the Bloom filter, BF: Set the bits at the positions of Td_{e_j} in BF to 1.
  2. Create a mask for the BF. For each position (or, bit), $BF[p]$ where $p \in [1, b]$, compute its *mask-bit*, $MB[p]$:
     $MB[p] = \overline{RO}(BID, RO(K_G, p))$
     Here, the output of $\overline{RO}$ is the first bit of the output of $RO()$.
  3. Mask each bit in $BF[p]$ with $MB[p]$ using the bitwise XOR operation:
     $BF[p] = BF[p] \oplus MB[p]$
     then output each (masked) BF_i for $i \in [1, m]$, an $m \times b$ binary matrix, together with its BID. Finally, the index of a document, $I = (BF_1, ..., BF_m)^T$ with the BIDs of each BF_i, will be sent to and saved on the server.
- **Trapdoor**(K, w): Given the secret keys K_H and K_G, for a search expression w, first generate its token characteristic set $S_T(w)$ as described in Sect. 3.1. For each element e_j of $S_T(w)$, where $j \in [1, \ell]$,
  1. It first calculates the first part of the trapdoor $Td_{1st} = \{pos_1, pos_2, ..., pos_r\}$, where $pos_x = RO(k_x, e_j)$ for $x \in [1, r]$.
  2. Using another secret key K_G, it calculates $Td_{2nd} = \{RO(K_G, pos_1), RO(K_G, pos_2), ..., RO(K_G, pos_r)\}$ as the second part of the trapdoor.

Then, output the trapdoor $Td = \{Td_{e_1}, Td_{e_2}, ..., Td_{e_\ell}\}$, where $Td_{e_j} = \langle Td_{1st}, Td_{2nd} \rangle$ to query the server.

- **SearchIndex**(Td, I): Given the trapdoor $Td = \{Td_{e_1}, Td_{e_2}, ..., Td_{e_\ell}\}$, where $Td_{e_j} = \langle Td_{1st}, Td_{2nd} \rangle$, the server checks all its stored indexes, I, for the matching document(s). The server executes the following processes:

  1. According to each position of $\{pos_1, pos_2, ..., pos_v\}$ from the received Td_{1st} (v is decided by the number of elements in Td), it extracts corresponding columns as a Sub-Index, $S\text{-}I$, from all stored indexes.
  2. Based on the received $Td_{2nd} = \{RO(K_G, pos_1), RO(K_G, pos_2), ..., RO(K_G, pos_v)\}$ and all stored $BIDs$, it generates the *mask-bits* using pos_x and BID_i, where $i \in [1, m]$ and $x \in [1, v]$.
     $MB_i'[x] = \overline{RO(BID_i, RO(K_G, pos_x))}$
  3. Unmask $S\text{-}I$ with $MB_i'[x]$ where $x \in [1, v]$. For each bit of $S\text{-}I$, it calculates:
     $S\text{-}I'[i][x] = S\text{-}I[i][x] \oplus MB'_i[x]$
     and then output the bitwise AND result $S\text{-}I'$ that is an $m \times v$ unmasked subindex.
  4. Check if any row $S\text{-}I'[i]$ in the subindex $S\text{-}I'$ contains 1's in all v locations. If so, output the related file ID(s) d_{FID_i} as the matching document(s).

3.4   A Discussion on the Document Updates

Both of our constructions support efficient and secure updates on the document collection, D, in the sense that the valid user is allowed to *add* and *delete* any document to/from D.

In our first construction, since the same keyword (or, element of the token characteristic set) is translated to an identical BF for all documents, the server can integrate all identical BFs (which are generated from different documents) to a unique BF for managing documents more efficiently. Thus, the server appends all the files IDs (FID_i) which contain the same keyword/element, to the unique BF. We give a toy example which shows a binary search tree based BF in Fig. 1. In this example, the tree has five indexes, 110, 101, 011, 010, 001 (i.e., the length of a Bloom filter is three here). If we want to add a document, d_5, which has two BFs, 101 and 010, then we just link the file ID to the corresponding nodes of the tree. If we want to delete a document, d_5, then we just need to delete its file ID which is linked to the corresponding nodes of the tree.

We can add the following two algorithms to our first construction:

- **Add**(K, D). This algorithm is equal to *BuildIndex()*. The new index I (including BFs) and its FID_i is sent to the server. Then, based on BFs included in the I, the server links the FID_i to the corresponding nodes of the binary search tree.
- **Delete**(FID_i). Given a file ID FID_i, delete it from the binary search tree.

During such an update operation, the algorithm reveals only the processed file ID and the number of its related BFs.

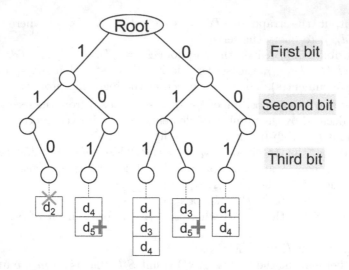

Fig. 1. Binary search tree based document updates

In our second construction, because the similarity between documents (BFs) is considered as an information leakage, each BF is masked before it is stored on the server. Then, the same keyword/element will be transformed to different BFs for each documents. Sharing the identical BF among different documents (as in our first construction) will not work, so the server must maintain a unique index (or, a set of BFs), for each document. Thus, the operations (update/add/delete) for a document will be quite simple where the server just needs to add or delete the new FID_i and its unique index I without leaking extra information. Owing to the proposed BID where $BID_w = RO(K_G, FID_i \parallel w)$, the server can identify duplicated BFs (and avoid storing the same BF twice) of a document.

- **Add(K, D).** This algorithm is equal to $BuildIndex()$. The new index I (including BFs appended with their corresponding $BIDs$) and its FID is sent to the server. If the FID already exists, the server checks the BID to avoid a duplicated BF.
- **Delete(FID_i).** Given a file ID FID_i, the server deletes it together with its I (including all its BFs) from its storage.

4   Security Proof

In this section, we give the security proof of our second construction. At this point, we do not take the external update algorithms (in Sect. 3.4) into account.

Theorem 1 *In the random oracle model, our second construction with secure extension described in Sect. 3.3 is secure in the sense of Adaptive Semantic Security for SSE scheme in Definition 5.*

Proof Let $q \in \mathbb{N}$, and let $\mathcal{A}$ be a probabilistic polynomial-time adversary. We will describe a probabilistic polynomial-time simulator $\mathcal{S}$ as in Definition 5 such that for all polynomially-bounded functions f and all distributions $\mathcal{H}_q$, $\mathcal{S}$ can simulate the partial view of an adversary $\mathcal{A}(V_K^t(\mathcal{H}_q))$ given only the trace of a partial history $Tr(H_q^t)$ for all $0 \leq t \leq q$ with probability negligibly close to 1. For all $0 \leq t \leq q$, we show that $\mathcal{S}(Tr(H_q^t))$ can generate a simulated view $V'^t_K(\mathcal{H}_q)$ is indistinguishable from $V_K^t(\mathcal{H}_q)$. Let $Tr(H_q) = (FID_1, ..., FID_n,$ $|d_{FID_1}|,...,|d_{FID_n}|, |BF|, Set_{FID_1}, ..., Set_{FID_n}, Nbf_1, ..., Nbf_n, D(w_1),..., D(w_q),$ $\Pi_q, P_{w_1}, ..., P_{w_q}, R_{w_1}, ..., R_{w_q})$ be the trace of an execution after q search queries and let H_q be a history consisting of q search queries such that $Tr(H_q) = Tr_q$. Then the simulator $\mathcal{S}$ works as follows: $\mathcal{S}$ chooses n random values $Rnd_1, ...,$ Rnd_n such that $|Rnd_i| = |d_{FID_i}|$ for all $i \in [1,n]$. $\mathcal{S}$ also includes the $FID_1,$ ..., $FID_n, Nbf_1, ..., Nbf_n, P_{w_1}, ..., P_{w_q}, R_{w_1}, ..., R_{w_q}, Set_{FID_1}, ..., Set_{FID_n}$ known from the trace, in the partial view.

Then the simulator $\mathcal{S}$ generates a simulated index $I' = (B_1,...,B_n)^T$ with random $B_i \in \{0,1\}^b$, for $i \in [1,n]$. I' will be included in all partial views $V'^t_K(\mathcal{H}_q)$ used to simulate $\mathcal{A}$. Next, $\mathcal{S}$ simulates the trapdoor for query w_t, $1 \leq t \leq q$ in sequence. If $\Pi_q[j, t] = 1$ for some $1 \leq j < t$ set $Td'_{w_t} = Td'_{w_j}$, and otherwise, $\mathcal{S}$ generates the simulated trapdoor for the query t, $Td'_{w_t} = \{Td'_{e_1}, Td'_{e_2}, ..., Td'_{e_\ell}\}$, where $Td'_{e_c} = \langle Td'_{1st}, Td'_{2nd}\rangle$. For each Td'_{e_c}, $\mathcal{S}$ first randomly picks each $pos_v \in [1, b]$ from the abstract position set of the trace, and generates Td'_{1st}, such that $Td'_{1st} = \{pos_1, ..., pos_{v_{w_t}}\}$. Then, $\mathcal{S}$ picks a random value Rnd'_{e_c} as an "element" for $c \in [1, \ell]$ and calculates $Td'_{2nd} = \{RO(K_G, RO(k_1, Rnd'_{e_c})), RO(K_G, RO(k_2, Rnd'_{e_c})), ..., RO(K_G, RO(k_r, Rnd'_{e_c}))\}$

Note, during the simulation, $\mathcal{S}$ controls random oracle $RO()$. Whenever the adversary $\mathcal{A}$ queries x to the $RO()$, to evaluate $RO(x)$, $\mathcal{S}$ first checks if it has already recorded a pair (x, r), in which case $RO(x)$ evaluates to the value r. Otherwise, $\mathcal{S}$ picks a random value r, records (x, r) and evaluates $RO(x)$ to r. Finally, $\mathcal{S}$ constructs a simulated view $V'^t_K(\mathcal{H}_q) = (FID_1, ...,$ $FID_n, E(d_{Rnd_1}), ..., E(d_{Rnd_n}), I', Td'_{w_1}, ..., Td'_{w_t}, Nbf_1, ..., Nbf_n, P_{w_1}, ...,$ $P_{w_t}, R_{w_1}, ..., R_{w_t}, Set_{FID_1}, ..., Set_{FID_n})$ and eventually outputs $\mathcal{A}(V'^t_K)$. We now prove that $V'^t_K(\mathcal{H}_q)$ is indistinguishable from $V_K^t(\mathcal{H}_q) = (FID_1, ..., FID_n,$ $E(d_{FID_1}), ..., E(d_{FID_n}), I, Td_{w_1}, ..., Td_{w_t}, Nbf_1, ..., Nbf_n, P_{w_1}, ..., P_{w_t}, R_{w_1},$ $..., R_{w_t}, Set_{FID_1}, ..., Set_{FID_n})$

We now claim that $V'^t_K(\mathcal{H}_q)$ is indistinguishable from $V_K^t(\mathcal{H}_q)$ and thus that the output of $\mathcal{A}$ on $V_K^t(\mathcal{H}_q)$ is indistinguishable from the output of $\mathcal{S}$ on input $Tr(H_q)$. Therefore we first state that: for all FID_i and all Nbf_i, Set_{FID_i} where $i \in [1,n]$, $P_{w_1}, ..., P_{w_t}, R_{w_1}, ..., R_{w_t}$, in $V'^t_K(\mathcal{H}_q)$ and $V_K^t(\mathcal{H}_q)$ are identical, thus indistinguishable. $E(\cdot)$ is semantically secure encryption algorithm (IND-CPA) [GM84], thus $E(d_{FID_i})$ is indistinguishable from $E(Rnd_i)$ of the same length. It is also clear that I' is indistinguishable form I, otherwise one could distinguish between a random string $I' = (B_1, ..., B_n)^T$ of size b and $[BF[p] \oplus MB[p]]_{p \in [1,b]}$, which means the bitwise XOR of a BF-bit (the former) and the mask-bit (the latter) that are both generated from the $RO()$. Then, what is left is to show that the simulated trapdoor Td'_{w_j} is indistinguishable from Td_{w_j}, where $1 \le j < t$. For each element e_c of the trapdoor, $Td'_{e_c} = \langle Td'_{1st}, Td'_{2nd} \rangle$, because Td'_{1st} is picked from the trace as an abstract position set, it is identical, and thus is indistinguishable. For the Td'_{2nd} which is calculated from the $RO()$, it is easy to see that the it is also indistinguishable, otherwise one could distinguish $RO(K_G, RO(k_t, e_c))$ from $RO(K_G, RO(k_t, Rnd_{e_c}))$. Consequently, each Td'_{e_c} is indistinguishable thus a trapdoor Td'_{w_j} is also indistinguishable from Td_{w_j}. Since $V'^t_K(H_q)$ is indistinguishable from $V^t_K(H_q)$ for all $0 \le t \le q$, the output of $\mathcal{A}$ will also be indistinguishable. This completes the proof.   □

5   Related Work and Discussion

To the best of our knowledge, previous schemes, except that of [BBH+11], did not consider the Bloom filter based wildcard search in the adaptive semantic security model, which is a stronger security model for searchable symmetric encryption. Hereafter, we mainly discuss the Bloom filter based schemes.

First, the work of [Goh03] only realized the Bloom filter based equality search (or, full-text search) and was proved secure under a weaker IND-CKA model. [SNS12] extends the search expression to support general fuzzy search using a single-character wildcard, i.e., "?", and their security model is based on the IND-CKA model. In [BBH+11], being similar to ours scheme, their first scheme use the Bloom filter "as-is" for efficiency. Because each keyword is represented by the same positions among all Bloom filters, this scheme leaks the information of document similarity to cloud servers. Their second scheme, called a 2-round masked scheme, is proposed to prevent such an information leakage problem: the user first masks all of the indexes locally before sending them to the cloud server. Then, the masked indexes are saved on the cloud server to ensure no such similarity information is leaked. After receiving a query from the user, i.e., a trapdoor, the server has to search and generate the masked answer which contains both real and fake file IDs. Finally, the searcher unmasks the answer and obtains the real file IDs, and then access the document by the real file IDs. Obviously, this 2-round masked scheme increases both the communication traffic and storage cost for transferring and managing those fake answers.

To solve this kind of similarity information leakage problem, we proposed the secure 1-round scheme using a novel *BID*. This construction does not increase the communication cost and storage (management) cost for the user and the *BIDs* do not need to be maintained on the user side. Moreover, our constructions also considered the application of secure and efficient document updates (i.e., addition and deletion of documents).

6   Conclusion

We proposed SSE schemes supporting encrypted keyword queries in a more expressive and flexible manner. Both of our two variants use Bloom filter for efficiency. The first scheme is more efficient in terms of computation and storage cost on the cloud server side, while the second scheme is more secure in the sense that we prevent the *correlation attack* by masking the indexes before sending to cloud servers. Our second scheme is proven secure against adaptive adversaries.

Acknowledgments. This work was supported in part by JSPS KAKENHI Grant Number 26330151, JSPS A3 Foresight Program, and JSPS and DST under the Japan - India Science Cooperative Program.

References

[BR93] Bellare, M., Rogaway, P.: Random oracles are practical: a paradigm for designing efficient protocols. In: ACM CCS 1993. ACM Press, New York (1993)

[EO97] Kushilevitz, E., Ostrovsky, R.: Replication is not needed: single database, computationally-private information retrieval. In: FOCS. IEEE (1997)

[FJ+15] Faber, S., Jarecki, S., Krawczyk, H., Nguyen, Q., Rosu, M., Steiner, M.: Rich queries on encrypted data: beyond exact matches. In: Pernul, G., Ryan, P.Y.A., Weippl, E. (eds.) ESORICS 2015. LNCS, vol. 9327, pp. 123–145. Springer, Heidelberg (2015). doi:10.1007/978-3-319-24177-7_7

[SWP00] Song, D.X., Wagner, D., Perrig, A.: Practical techniques for searches on encrypted data. In: Proceedings 2000 IEEE Symposium on Security and Privacy S&P 2000. IEEE (2000)

[B70] Bloom, B.H.: Space/time trade-offs in hash coding with allowable errors. Commun. ACM **13**(7), 422–426 (1970)

[BBH+11] Bösch, C., Brinkman, R., Hartel, P., Jonker, W.: Conjunctive wildcard search over encrypted data. In: Jonker, W., Petković, M. (eds.) SDM 2011. LNCS, vol. 6933, pp. 114–127. Springer, Heidelberg (2011)

[CJJ+13] Cash, D., Jarecki, S., Jutla, C., Krawczyk, H., Roşu, M.-C., Steiner, M.: Highly-scalable searchable symmetric encryption with support for boolean queries. In: Canetti, R., Garay, J.A. (eds.) CRYPTO 2013, Part I. LNCS, vol. 8042, pp. 353–373. Springer, Heidelberg (2013)

[CK10] Chase, M., Kamara, S.: Structured encryption and controlled disclosure. In: Abe, M. (ed.) ASIACRYPT 2010. LNCS, vol. 6477, pp. 577–594. Springer, Heidelberg (2010)

[CGK+11] Curtmola, R., Garay, J.A., Kamara, S., Ostrovsky, R.: Searchable symmetric encryption: improved definitions and efficient constructions. J. Comput. Secur. **19**(5), 895–934 (2011)

[Goh03] Goh, E.-J.: Secure indexes. In: Cryptology ePrint Archive 2003/216 (2003)

[GO96] Goldreich, O., Ostrovsky, R.: Software protection and simulation on oblivious RAMs. J. ACM **43**(3), 431–473 (1996)

[KP13] Kamara, S., Papamanthou, C.: Parallel and dynamic searchable symmetric encryption. In: Sadeghi, A.-R. (ed.) FC 2013. LNCS, vol. 7859, pp. 258–274. Springer, Heidelberg (2013)

[KPR12] Kamara, S., Papamanthou, C., Roeder, T.: Dynamic searchable symmetric encryption. In: ACM Conference on Computer and Communications Security (CCS), pp. 965–976 (2012)

[KL14] Katz, J., Lindell, Y.: Introduction to Modern Cryptography, 2nd edn. CRC Press, Boca Raton (2014). ISBN 9781466570269

[KO12] Kurosawa, K., Ohtaki, Y.: UC-secure searchable symmetric encryption. In: Keromytis, A.D. (ed.) FC 2012. LNCS, vol. 7397, pp. 285–298. Springer, Heidelberg (2012)

[ME14] Mohan, L., Sudheep, E.M.: An efficient file storage implementation in cloud based on suffix trees for encrypted data access. Int. J. Adv. Res. Comput. Sci. Softw. Eng. 4(3), 1256–1261 (2014)

[MIP02] Charikar, M., Indyk, P., Panigrahy, R.: New algorithms for subset query, partial match, orthogonal range searching, and related problems. In: Widmayer, P., Triguero, F., Morales, R., Hennessy, M., Eidenbenz, S., Conejo, R. (eds.) ICALP 2002. LNCS, vol. 2380, pp. 451–462. Springer, Heidelberg (2002)

[GM84] Goldwasser, S., Micali, S.: Probabilistic encryption. J. Comput. Syst. Sci. 28(2), 270–299 (1984)

[SNS12] Suga, T., Nishide, T., Sakurai, K.: Secure keyword search using bloom filter with specified character positions. In: Takagi, T., Wang, G., Qin, Z., Jiang, S., Yu, Y. (eds.) ProvSec 2012. LNCS, vol. 7496, pp. 235–252. Springer, Heidelberg (2012)

A System of Shareable Keyword Search on Encrypted Data

Wei-Ting Lu[1], Wei Wu[2], Shih-Ya Lin[1], Min-Chi Tseng[1],
and Hung-Min Sun[1(✉)]

[1] Department of Computer Science, National Tsing Hua University, Hsinchu, Taiwan
hmsun@cs.nthu.edu.tw
[2] Fujian Provincial Key Laboratory of Network Security and Cryptology,
School of Mathematics and Computer Science,
Fujian Normal University, Fujian, China

Abstract. Nowadays the cloud security becomes a significant issue: while the single user keyword search on encrypted data has been proposed, encrypting files before uploading scarifies the advantage of the convenience of sharing data with others on the cloud.

We design a searchable encryption for the multi-user case. We combine the advantage of efficiency of the symmetric encryption with authentication of the asymmetric encryption to provide a secure and efficient system of shareable keyword search on encrypted data.

Keywords: Shareable keyword search · Multi-user keyword search · Encrpyted data

1 Introduction

People are worried about the confidentiality and the security of their data. Most of the intuitive solutions are to encrypt the data before outsourcing to the cloud. But it brings the difficulty of finding data when the file names and contents are ciphertext.

Many symmetric encryption (SE) schemes [1–3,6,7,10,11,13] etc. have been proposed, including both the searchable symmetric encryption schemes (SSE) and the public key encryption with keyword search schemes (PEKS). Called the single-user searchable encryption (SUSE). There are many paper proposed schemes for the multiple-user searchable encryption (MUSE) as well. Files owners broadcast the key of the SUSE to authorize users to achieve a MUSE. The advantage of the scheme is that there is no need to apply trusted server and the key management is simple. Unluckily, the key exposure becomes the inherited problem.

To solve this problem, ID-based encryption schemes have been presented [4,5, 12]. However the ID-based encryption is hard to implement in some programming languages. Another scheme [14] combines the hybrid cloud with the broadcast encryption (BE) and applies the two-phase operation to achieve MUSE. The workload is too heavy for the trusted center.

J. Chen et al. (Eds.): NSS 2016, LNCS 9955, pp. 283–299, 2016.
DOI: 10.1007/978-3-319-46298-1_19

We propose an efficient multi-user keyword-based search on encrypted data, in which, original documents and a set of keywords are encrypted with owners' different data keys, stored on the public server and the public server performs the second encryption to the data with different server keys stored on the private server.

2   Related Works

2.1   Single-User Searchable Encryption

The method used in SUSE could be either the symmetric encryption or the public key encryption. While solving the big outsourcing data problem, symmetric encryption schemes are better solution because of its efficiency. They can be described as following.
(Setup, Encrypt, Trpdr, Search, Decrypt):

$Setup(1^k)$: It is executed by the user to set up the scheme. It takes a security parameter as input, and outputs the necessary keys.

$Encrypt(K_D, K_W, Data)$: It is executed by the user to encrypt the data and its keywords. It takes the data and its necessary keys for data K_D and the key for keywords K_W as input, and outputs ciphertexts of data and its keywords. The key could be either symmetric or asymmetric depending on the scheme.

$Trpdr(K_W, W)$: It is executed by the user. It takes the key for keyword K_W and the keyword set W as input, and outputs the trapdoor set of keyword T_r.

$Search(T_r)$: It is executed by the server to do the keyword search. It takes the trapdoor set T_r as input, and outputs a set of data or the failure symbol. Note that users could only search his own data.

$Decrypt(K_D, C)$: It is executed by the user to decrypt the ciphertexts of data C, and gets the original data D.

2.2   Multi-user Searchable Encryption

The MUSE scheme is based on the SUSE, and it should meet more requirements such as:

(1) It could dynamically add and remove users.
(2) For different users, the visibility of the same file is distinct. Users could only see the files which he is allowed to access.

Due to the above two requirements, we need to add some functions. Collection of a general MUSE scheme are *(Setup, AddUser, Encrypt, Trpdr, Search, Decrypt, RevokeUser, Update)*.

$Setup(1^k)$: It is executed by the data owner to set up the scheme. It takes a security parameter as input, and outputs the necessary keys.

$AddUser(u)$: It is executed by the data owner to add a new authorized user u by using owner's secret key. If necessary the owner may update or store other information for access control in trusted third party.

Encrypt($K_D, K_W, Data, Group$): It is executed by the data owner to encrypt data and its keyword. It takes the data, the keys K_D for data and K_W for keywords, and a set of the authorized user G that can access the data, and outputs ciphtexts of data and its keyword.

Trpdr(K_W, W): It is executed by the user. It takes key for keyword K_W and keyword set W as input, and outputs the trapdoor set of keywords T_r.

Search(u, T_r): It is executed by the server to perform the keyword search. It takes user u and trapdoor set T_r as input, and outputs a set of data or the failure symbol.

Decrypt(u, K_D, C): It is executed by the user u to decrypt the ciphertexts of data C by using owner's key for data, and gets the original data D.

RevokeUser(u): It is executed by the data owner to revoke authorized user u.

Update(): It usually executed by the data owner to update data and its keywords.

2.3 Long-Term Key & Session Key

The key is intended to be used at multiple points in time. In our system, every user generates a long-term key during the setup phase. The key is stored in the client PC.

A session key is not intentionally stored, and is not re-creatable. Session keys arc used only for communications protocols. We extend the concept of the session key to create the short-term key. The short-term key in our system is not re-creatable and only can be used once. Every shared data has its own short-term keys.

2.4 Searching on Encrypted Data [9]

A query generated at the client-side, is transformed into a representation so that it can be evaluated directly on encrypted data at the cloud storage server.

3 Design

3.1 Design Goal

We propose an efficient multi-user keyword-based search on encrypted data. In our scheme, we store the user data and its corresponding set of keywords on the public server, encrypted with owner different data keys and the corresponding user server key. Meanwhile, we store users' secret information on the private server. Furthermore, our scheme can transform a query to a special form that server could directly search on the database and return the results that obtain certain keywords. The proposed scheme is designed with the following primary objectives:

- Security: Our scheme uses the symmetric encryption and the asymmetric encryption to ensure the efficiency and confidentiality of data. The files are encrypted using the AES-CBC algorithm and the keyword is generated by using the AES-CFB algorithm. Every shared data uses different short-term keys. Meanwhile, we use the two-phase operation on the data to guarantee the security when users have been revoked. In order to protect owners' data keys and the corresponding server key, we utilize the public key encryption to encrypt them.
- Shareable: Data owner could share his data to authorize users and dynamically add or revoke users.
- Efficiency: We apply the symmetric encryption on data to ensure the efficiency of our system and make use of the asymmetric one to protect owner's data key.
- Search Options: The search options of our system also includes the conjunctive keyword search (AND/OR), common prefix keyword search and Chinese keyword search.

3.2 Basic Model

As shown in Fig. 1, we propose a new multi-user searchable symmetric encryption scheme. There are four separate roles in our scheme {data owner, public server, private server, authorized users}.

- The public server stores data and keywords that are encrypted and uploaded by data owners. It would ask the private server for the server key of the data owner. And it encrypts them again and stores the ciphertexts in the server. It copes with trapdoor when receiving from authorized users and performs the keyword search.
- The private server is used to build a trusted center to provide access control and key management, and therefore it must be fully trusted. Private server stores keys of every user and every file.
- The data owner encrypts data and defines a group of authorized users who can access the data before outsourcing to the public server.
- Authorized users are allowed to access the data. They could do different kinds of keyword search to the data, and ask the private server for the keys of data to generate the trapdoor and decrypt the data.

In order to make the proposed model more practical, three key ideas are proposed:

1. Different kinds of keys: After the step of setup, the user would possess different kinds of keys including secret data keys, secret keyword keys, a server key, a master key and a symmetric master key.
2. Encrypt twice: Before uploading to the public server, the owner encrypts his data and keywords by using his short-term data key and short-term keyword key. When public server receives the ciphertext, it would ask the private server for the corresponding server key to encrypt the data again.

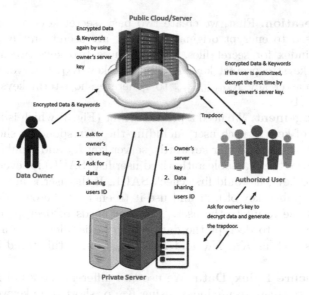

Fig. 1. Basic model of shareable keyword search on encrypted data

3. Public key encryption: Our scheme makes use of the public key encryption to protect keys. When the public server asks the private server for the owner's server key, the private server would first encrypt it with server's public key. And the public server would decrypt the received key by using its own private key before using it. Similarly, when an authorized user asks the private server for owner's short-term data key or short-term keyword key, the private server would encrypt it with the user's public key to protect the security of keys.

The advantages of our scheme include:

1. When owner adds a new authorized user or revokes a user, there is no influence to other authorized users.
2. Every file has different short-term key to enhance the security of owners' data.
3. By using the asymmetric encryption to protect keys, authorized users could not be forged.
4. The access control of different files is achieved.

3.3 Design of Proposed Scheme

We divided our system into the following main areas.

- Key Generation
- Key Management
- Create Secure Index/Data
- Authentication Mechanism

Key Generation. First, we create two basis secret keys for an individual user. K_D is used to encrypt original files that are secret and K_W is used to create secure index for secret files. Besides these two keys, we also create a pair of public keys to protect keys K_P, private key K_M, a server key K_S and a symmetric master key $K_{Msymmetric}$ to generate short-term keys (for details please see Sect. 4).

Key Management. We need a private server (Fig. 3) which is fully trusted. It stores a set of keys of each user, including the corresponding short-term key for data, the short-term key for keywords, server key K_S and a public key K_P of user. Also it stores the shareable authorized user list (SAUL) for every file. When an user asks for keys, it would first check SAUL. If the user is authenticated, it would find the public key of user and use it to encrypt the owner's short-term key, then send the result to the user. The user needs to decrypt the key with his own master key to decrypt the data which he is allowed to access. Other long-term keys such as K_D, K_W and $K_{Msymmetric}$ are still stored in the client side.

Create Secure Index/Data. We use two different modes of AES. One is the CFB mode to create secure index, using K_W or short-term keyword key. The other one is CBC mode to encrypt the original file, using K_D or short-term data key.

Authentication Mechanism. We use the Password-Based Key Derivation Function 2 (PBKDF2). We also utilize the public key encryption to implement the key protection system. Before the private server sending any key to anyone (either the server or the user), it would use their public keys to encrypt the key to prevent intruders from hijacking users' short-term keys or the server key K_S.

3.4   Definition of Shareable Keyword Search

According to the Multi-user Searchable Encryption of Sect. 2, the basic collection of a general MUSE scheme are *(Setup, AddUser, Encrypt, Trpdr, Search, Decrypt, RevokeUser)*. Below are the definition of our system. It consists of 10 algorithms.

1. *Setup(1^k)* It is run by every user to generate the secure parameter $K = (K_D, K_W, K_M, K_P, K_S, K_{Msymmetric})$, where K_D and K_W are symmetric keys which are used to encrypt secret data and its keywords and are stored in the client side. K_M and K_P are the master key and the public key, respectively. K_P is public and stored on private server while K_M is private and stored in the client side to identify users. K_S is the corresponding server key used to encrypt the data and keywords after data owner encrypt them at first time.

2. *AddUser(K_M, id_{ui})* It is run by the data owner to add a new authorized user u_i. The data owner encrypts authorized user id by using K_M and sends the result to the private server. After receiving the ciphertext, the private server decrypts the user id by using K_P. If the user u_i exists, then it adds u_i to the shareable authorized user list (SAUL).

3. *Semi-Encrypt(short-term K_D, short-term K_W, Data)* It is run by the data
   owner to encrypt the data and create the secure index. When the owner
   uploads a shared data, the system would generate two short-term keys (short-
   term K_D, short-term K_W) based on $K_{\text{Msymmetric}}$ (please refer to Sect. 4 for
   more details). The owner would use them (short-term K_D, short-term K_W)
   to encrypt the data and generate index. The outputs of this function is the
   semi-ciphertext semi-C and semi-index semi-I which will be sent to the public
   server.
4. *Encrypt(semi-C,semi-I, K_S)* It is run by the public server. After receiving
   semi-C and semi-I from the data owner u_i, the public server would act as
   below:

   (a) Ask the private server for the server key of u_i, it runs *AskServerkey(u_i)*.
   The output of this function is the ciphertext of the server key serverkey-C by
   using the public key of server K_{Pserver}.
   (b) After receiving serverkey-C, the public server would decrypt it with its
   own master key K_{Mserver} and get the K_S of u_i.
   (c) Run Encrypt(semi-C,semi-I,K_S) and get final ciphertext of data C and
   index I.

5. *Semi-Trpdr(short-term K_W, W)* It is run by the user u_i to generate the trapdoor of keyword W semi-T_r. Short-term K_W is a key set including the short-
   term K_W of data. Before executing the function, user would act as below:

   (a) Ask the private server for the keyword key of other users, the private
   server first checks SAUL and gets the keyword key short-term K_W of data.
   (b) The private server encrypts the short-term K_W by using K_P of the user
   u_i then sends keywordkey-C to the user u_i.
   (c) User u_i decrypts the keywordkey-C and gets short-term K_W set. User uses
   those short-term K_W to create semi-T_r and other users set G including u_i,
   and sends them to the public server.

6. *Trpdr(K_S, semi-T_r, G)* It is run by the public server. Before executing this,
   the public server executes *AskServerkey(G)* to get K_S of G. And use them
   to generate the final trapdoors.
7. *Search(I, T_r)* It is run by the public server to search trapdoor T_r and return
   the results which contain keyword W to the user.
8. *Semi-Decrpyt(K_S, C)* It is run by the public cloud. Before executing this,
   the public cloud needs to execute *AskServerkey(u_i)* and gets semi-plaintext
   semi-P.
9. *Decrypt(K_D, semi-P)* It is run by the user. Before executing the function,
   user would first do the actions below:
   (a) Ask the private server for data key of the data owner, the private server
   first checks SAUL and gets the data key short-term K_D of data.
   (b) Private server encrypts the short-term K_D by using K_P of user u_i then
   sends datakey-C to user u_i.
   (c) User u_i decrypts the datakey-C and gets short-term K_D. User uses short-
   term K_D to decrypt semi-P and gets the original data.

10. *RevokeUser*(K_M, id_{ui}) It is run by the data owner to revoke the autho-
    rized user u_i. After receiving it, the private server removes the user u_i from
    shareable authorized user list (Table 1).

Table 1. Notations used in this thesis

Notation	Description
K_D	The symmetric key used to encrypt/decrypt secret data (data without sharing) and is stored in the client side
short-term K_D	The symmetric key used to encrypt/decrypt shared data, it is generated before data upload and stored on the private server
K_W	The symmetric key used to generate the secure index of the secret data (data without sharing) and it is stored in client side
short-term K_W	The symmetric key used to generate secure index of shared data, is generated before data upload and is stored on the private server
K_P	The public key for every user and it is stored on the private server
K_M	The private key(master key) for every user and is stored secretly in the client side
$K_{Msymmetric}$	The symmetric private key(symmetric master key) to create short-term K_D and short-term K_W
K_S	The symmetric server key used to encrypt/decrypt data and generate final trapdoor
$K_{Pserver}$	The public key for public server and is stored in private server
$K_{Mserver}$	The private key (master key) for public server and is stored secretly on public server
SAUL	Shareable Authorized User List
u_i	User i
G	A group of data owners who allow users to access their files
semi-C	Semi-Ciphertext of data. It is generated by the data owner by using short-term K_D and sends to public server
semi-I	Semi-Index. It is generated by data owner by using short-term K_W and sends to public server
semi-T_r	Semi-Trapdoor. It is generated by users by using short-term K_W and sends to public server
semi-P	Semi-Plaintext of data. It is generated by the public cloud by using K_S to decrypt Ciphertext C
C	Ciphertext of data. The public server encrypts semi-C by using K_S and stores it
I	Secure Index. Public server receives semi-I and generate it by using K_S
T_r	Final Trapdoor. After the public server receives semi-T_r, it uses K_S to generate T_r

4   Key Generation

4.1   Generating Password for Authentication

We concatenate users' password with his email address, username and domain name. After concatenation, we need to do PBKDF2 function to generate user passwords for authentication. We illustrate it as: (Table 2)

concat $= (pw\|email\|username\|domainname)$

pw' $=$ PBKDF2(concat,S,c,dkLength)

Table 2. Notations used for password generation

pw	The original password that users type in
S	Salt which is stored on the private server
c	Iteration count
dkLength	Intended length in octets of the derived
pw'	The password stored on private server and used in our system to authenticate the identity of users

4.2   Generating Short-Term K_D and Short-Term K_W for Different Shared Files

As described before, we apply different short-term data keys and short-term keyword keys to different shared data to enhance security. Our long-term key is $K_{Msymmetric}$ stored in the client side and no one else would have the knowledge of it. We use it to generate our short-term key for different files. Notations we would use is described below (Table 3).

To obtain higher entropy for generated keys, we create semi-key by performing bit-wise exclusive or operator with two different random numbers (R_1, R_2).

Table 3. Notations used in generating short-term K_D and short-term K_W

pw'	The user password stored on private server
short-term K_D	The short term symmetric key used to encrypt/decrypt shared data
short-term K_W	The short term symmetric key used to generate secure index of shared data
R_1	Random number is generated when data upload and used for creating short-term K_D
R_2	Random number is generated when data upload and used for creating short-term K_W

These random numbers are generated when data uploaded and every file uses different random numbers. To protect semi-keys, we apply AES encryption. We use owners' master symmetric key $K_{\text{Msymmetric}}$ to generate final short-term keys by encrypting semi-keys. This method makes dictionary and brute-force attacks too slow.

$semi\text{-}key_D = pw' \oplus R_1$	semi-key for data
$semi\text{-}key_W = pw' \oplus R_2$	semi-key for index
short-term $K_D = \text{AES}(semi\text{-}key_D, K_{\text{Msymmetric}})$	Short term symmetric key used to encrypt/decrypt a file
short-term $K_W = \text{AES}(semi\text{-}key_W, K_{\text{Msymmetric}})$	Short term symmetric key used to create index

5   Implementation

5.1   Programming Language and Server Database

The proposed system is implemented in the C#.Net programming language. Users can only install some .Net Framework by clicking some buttons and could easily execute the system. We employ Virtual Studio 2012 to design an user interface that is simple for users. For cryptography operations, we use *System.Security.Cryptography* namespace (Fig. 2).

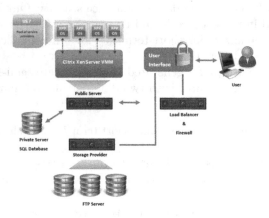

Fig. 2. Architecture overview of our system

In the public server part, we use FTP server as data storage. Xenserver as the service provider. Internet Information Server (IIS) 7 as a Web Server software application running on Windows Server 2008. We also build a Zen load balancer between users and the public server to achieve optimal resource utilization, maximize throughput and minimize response time.

In the private server part, we use Microsoft SQL server 2010 to store keywords of different files, SAUL (Shareable Authorized User List), different keys of different shared data, and distinct keys (K_P, K_S, $K_{Pserver}$) of every user.

5.2   System Operations

Signup. After registered, they could upload and perform various keyword search on their data.

Login Process. We concatenate user's password with his username, email and domain name, perform PBKDF2 function, transfer to the server and compare with pw' on the private server.

Upload the File. We divide this operation into two parts, one is uploading a secret file without sharing, the other one is uploading shared files and let authorized users have access to them. Meanwhile all files would be compressed before being encrypted. In order to improve the efficiency of the keyword search, we apply the same data key K_D and keyword key K_W to these files. Hence, we introduce how we generate data key K_D and keyword key K_W for secret files.

As described in Sect. 4, to obtain higher entropy, we calculate semi-keys by doing bit-wise exclusive or operator with two different random numbers (R'_1, R'_2) generated when users signing up. These two random numbers are stored in the client PC and they are different from R_1 and R_2 in Sect. 4. The comparison between (R_1, R_2) and (R'_1, R'_2) is shown in Table 4.

We also apply a slow hash function to avoid dictionary attacks. It computes the hash value by re-hashing it many times. We derive the real keys for secret files in the following steps:

If only the owner can access the file, the procedure of uploading is shown in Fig. 3. For every unsharable file, we use the same K_D to encrypt data and the same K_W to generate index. These keys could only be accessed by the data owner and are stored in the client side. For the secret data, we only encrypt once to improve the efficiency of uploading and retrieval.

If the data owner wants to share his file with others, he needs to fill the usernames of authorized users in the Shared_Id field when uploading the data.

Table 4. Comparison between (R_1, R_2) and (R'_1, R'_2)

(R_1, R_2)	(R'_1, R'_2)
Is used to generate short-term key for shared data	Is used to generate K_D and K_W for secret data
Is generated when uploading a shared file	Is generated when users signing up
Stored on the private server	Stored secretly in the client side
Every shared file has different R1, R2	R'1, R'2 is always the same number for an user

$semi\text{-}K_D = pw' \oplus R_1'$	semi-key for data
$semi\text{-}K_W = pw' \oplus R_2'$	semi-key for index
$K_D = \mathrm{SHF}(semi\text{-}K_D)$	Used to encrypt/decrypt a secret file
$K_W = \mathrm{SHF}(semi\text{-}K_W)$	Used to create index for a secret file

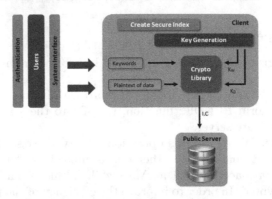

Fig. 3. Flow chart of uploading a secret file

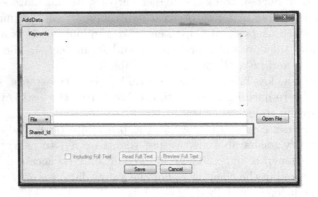

The system would generate two random number R_1 and R_2, and use pw', R_1, R_2 and $K_{\mathrm{Msymmetric}}$ of data owner to create the short-term K_D for data and short-term K_W for keyword. We also generate another index when uploading. That is encrypted by the owners' secret K_W. And this index set is stored on our server. After encrypting the data and keywords, the ciphertext semi-C and semi-I (encrypted by short-term K_W) would be uploaded to public server and encrypted by using data owner's K_S where the ciphertext is stored on the public server (before encryption, the public server would ask the private server for data owner's K_S.). SAUL, short-term K_D and short-term K_W of the data would stored on the private server. The flow chart of uploading procedure is shown in Fig. 4.

Retrieval. Secure index generation for secret files.

After the user types the keywords that he wants to search, our system would first search keywords on secret files and run procedure below:

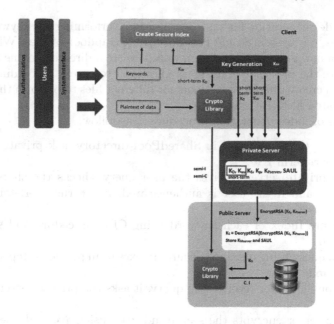

Fig. 4. Flow chart of uploading a shared file

1. Create Secure Index of each keyword by using CFB procedure and K_W.
2. Generate a query using obtained Secure Indexes from previous step.
3. Submit the query to the public server.
4. Decrypt the result query by using K_W from the public server to obtain the final result.

   Download the desired secret files from the result of query:

1. Create a connection to the public server and download the encrypted file.
2. Decrypt them by using K_D and decompress the file.

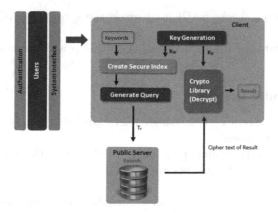

Fig. 5. Retrieval for secret files

Secure index generation for shared files: After performing the keyword search on secret files, our system would generate index trapdoor of files. When a user signs up for a new account, the system would create a directory named "Shared-Pool" to store the files that other users allow you to access. According to these files, we could create different trapdoors for different files to perform the keyword search on shared files (Figs. 5 and 6).

The steps of index generation procedure is as follow:

- According to the files stored in SharedPool directory, ask private server for different short-term K_W.
- When the private server receives the user query, checks the shared_Id filed from SAUL, and if the user is authenticated, it returns short-term K_W of data to the user.
- Create Secure Index of each keyword using CFB procedure and short-term K_W of data.
- Generate a query using obtained Secure Indexes from previous step and submit it to the public server.
- After the public server receives the query, it asks the private server for K_S of data owner.
- The public server encrypts the secure index by using K_S and does keyword search.
- The public server decrypts result query by using K_S and sends to the user.
- After the user receives the query from the public server, system would decrypt it by using short-term K_W to obtain the final result.

Download the desired shared files from the result of query:

- Create the connection to the public server, public server would first check SAUL for authentication.
- If the user is authenticated, public server would ask private server for K_S of data owner and decrypt the file.
- User downloads the encrypt file, and asks the private server for short-term K_D of data.
- The private server checks SAUL and sends the short-term K_D of the file to user.
- The user decrypts the file by using short-term K_D and decompresses it.

5.3   Experimental Results

We compared our system with the single user searchable encryption [8] with the same documents and users.

Here we increase the number of users. In this test, the database contains greater than 50,000,000 documents and each document contains more than 100 keywords.

Table 5 is the result of single user searchable encryption system. An user stores 50, 100, 200 documents on his own storage and generates queries of different numbers of keywords and common prefix search.

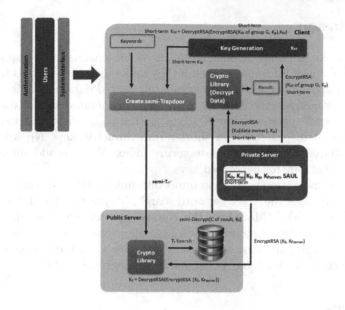

Fig. 6. Retrieval for shared files

Table 5. Search duration of single user searchable encryption system

Number of queried keywords	50 documents	100 documents	200 documents
1 keyword	1.5 s	2.98 s	6.62 s
5 keywords	4.2 s	5.71 s	9.31 s
10 keywords	7.55 s	9.32 s	12.92 s
Common prefix search	1.15 s	1.18 s	1.29 s

Table 6. Search duration of our system (Shareable Keyword Search on Encrpyted Data System)

Number of queried keywords	50 documents	100 documents	200 documents
1 keyword	1.768 s	6.02 s	10.821 s
5 keywords	2.97 s	6.98 s	12.4 s
10 keywords	5.74 s	10.07 s	17.76 s
Common prefix search	1.685 s	1.768 s	1.943 s

Table 6 below is the result of our system (MUSE system). And the search duration of common prefix search would not increase while adding more documents.

6   Conclusion

We described an authentication mechanism which ensures it is impossible for hijacker to steal user information even if they apply users' credentials from other systems. Our special key generation system for shared data uses different short-term keys to guarantee the security. Each key is generated by the data owner, who owns a secret symmetric key $K_{\text{Msymmtric}}$. $K_{\text{Msymmtric}}$ and Random number R_1, R_2 are used to generate two short-term symmetric keys K_D and K_W for encrypting shared data and generate secure index. We also add some steps to obtain higher entropy for generated keys.

In the implementation part, most important functional requirements is search functionality. Besides the exact keyword search, conjunctive (And, Or) keyword search is also included. Moreover, the common prefix search is also available which enhances system functionality and makes system more practical. The experimental results are shown in Sect. 5. If we construct them on real server instead of virtual machine, our performance will become better.

References

1. Chen, R., Mu, Y., Yang, G., Guo, F., Wang, X.: A new general framework for secure public key encryption with keyword search. In: Foo, E., Stebila, D. (eds.) ACISP 2015. LNCS, vol. 9144, pp. 59–76. Springer, Heidelberg (2015). doi:10.1007/978-3-319-19962-7_4

2. Boneh, D., Crescenzo, G., Ostrovsky, R., Persiano, G.: Public key encryption with keyword search. In: Cachin, C., Camenisch, J.L. (eds.) EUROCRYPT 2004. LNCS, vol. 3027, pp. 506–522. Springer, Heidelberg (2004). doi:10.1007/978-3-540-24676-3_30

3. Gu, C., Zheng, Y., Kang, F., Xin, D.: Keyword search over encrypted data in cloud computing from lattices in the standard model. In: Qiang, W., Zheng, X., Hsu, C.-H. (eds.) CloudCom-Asia 2015. LNCS, vol. 9106, pp. 335–343. Springer, Heidelberg (2015). doi:10.1007/978-3-319-28430-9_25

4. Li, J., Jia, C., Li, J., Liu, Z.: A novel framework for outsourcing and sharing searchable encrypted data on hybrid cloud. In: 2012 4th International Conference Intelligent Networking and Collaborative Systems (INCoS) (2012)

5. Li, J., Li, J., Liu, Z., Jia, C.: Enabling efficient and secure data sharing in cloud computing. Concurrency Comput. Pract. Exp. **26**, 1052–1066 (2013)

6. Li, J., Wang, Q., Wang, C., Cao, N., Ren, K., Lou, W.: Fuzzy keyword search over encrypted data in cloud computing. In: INFOCOM 2010. IEEE Press (2010)

7. Golle, P., Staddon, J., Waters, B.: Secure conjunctive keyword search over encrypted data. In: Jakobsson, M., Yung, M., Zhou, J. (eds.) ACNS 2004. LNCS, vol. 3089, pp. 31–45. Springer, Heidelberg (2004)

8. Amir, R.: Efficient Common Prefix Search on Encrypted Data as an Additional Service on the Top of the Storage Providers (2013)

9. Rezapour, A., Chen, S.-T., Sun, H.-M.: Efficient common prefix search on encrypted data as an additional service on the top of the storage providers. In: 2015 IEEE International Conference on Smart City/SocialCom/SustainCom (SmartCity), pp. 975–981 (2015)

10. Zittrower, S., Zou, C.C.: Encrypted phrase searching in the cloud. In: Global Communications Conference (GLOBECOM). IEEE (2012)
11. Song, X., Wagner, D., Perrig, A.: Practical techniques for searches on encrypted data. In: IEEE Symposium on Security and Privacy (2000)
12. Zhang, Y., Jia, Z., Wang, S.: A multi-user searchable symmetric encryption scheme for cloud storage system. In: 2013 5th International Conference Intelligent Networking and Collaborative Systems (INCoS) (2013)
13. Zhao, Y., Chen, X.F., Ma, H., et al.: A new trapdoor-indistinguishable public key encryption with keyword search. J. Wireless Mobile Netw. (2012)
14. Liu, Z., Wang, Z., Cheng, X., Jia, C., Yuan, K.: Multi-user searchable encryption with coarser-grained access control in hybrid cloud. In: 2013 4th International Conference on Emerging Intelligent Data and Web Technologies (2013)

Security Policy and Access Control

An Attribute-Based Protection Model for JSON Documents

Prosunjit Biswas[✉], Ravi Sandhu, and Ram Krishnan

Institute for Cyber Security, University of Texas at San Antonio,
San Antonio, USA
prosun.csedu@gmail.com, {ravi.sandhu,ram.krishnan}@utsa.edu

Abstract. There has been considerable research in specifying authorization policies for XML documents. Most of these approaches consider only *hierarchical structure* of underlying data. They define authorization policies by directly identifying XML nodes in the policies. These approaches work well for hierarchical structure but are not suitable for other required characteristics we identify in this paper as *semantical association* and *scatteredness*.

This paper presents an attribute based protection model for JSON documents. We assign *security-label* attribute values to JSON elements and specify authorization policies using these values. By using security-label attribute, we leverage semantical association and scatteredness properties. Our protection mechanism defines two types of policies called authorization and labeling policies. We present an operational model to specify authorization policies and different models for defining labeling policies. Finally, we demonstrate a proof-of-concept for the proposed models in the Swift service of OpenStack IaaS cloud.

1 Introduction

JavaScript Object Notation (JSON) is a human and machine readable representation for text data. It is widely used because of its simple and concise structure. For example, Twitter uses JSON as the only supported format for exchange of data starting from API v1.1 [5] and YouTube recommends uses of JSON for speed from its latest API [6]. JSON is being adapted increasingly in large and scalable document databases such as MongoDB [4], Apache Casandra [2] and CouchDB [3]. Besides these, JSON is also widely used in lightweight data storages for example in configuration files, online catalogs or applications with embedded-storage.

In spite of high adoption from industries, JSON has received little attention from academic researchers. To the best of our knowledge, there is no formal work published on the protection of JSON documents.

On the other hand, considerable work has been done for protection of XML documents. Although syntactically JSON and XML formats are different, semantically both of them form a rooted tree hierarchical structure. In fact, JSON data can equivalently be represented in XML form and vice versa. This brings

© Springer International Publishing AG 2016
J. Chen et al. (Eds.): NSS 2016, LNCS 9955, pp. 303–317, 2016.
DOI: 10.1007/978-3-319-46298-1_20

an obvious question - whether we can utilize authorization models used for XML documents for protection of JSON data.

Before we answer the preceding question, we look into some of the salient characteristics of data represented in JSON (or XML) format, given below.

- **Hierarchical relationship.** Data often exhibits hierarchical relationship. For example, a residential address consists of pieces like house number, street name, district/town and state name organized into an strictly hierarchical structure.
- **Semantical association.** Different pieces of data are often related semantically and may need same level of protection. For example, phone number, email address, Skype name may all represent contact information and require same level of protection.
- **Scatteredness.** Related information can be scattered around a document. For example, different pieces of contact information might be located in different places in a document. Some pieces of data can even be repeated in more than one place in the same document or across documents.

Interestingly, most of XML authorization models [8–10, 17] consider *structural hierarchy* only. These models have an implicit assumption that information has been organized in the intended hierarchical form. These models attach authorization policies directly on nodes in the XML tree and propagate them using the hierarchical structure. For example, Damiani et al. [15] specify authorization policy as a tuple ⟨*subject, object, action, sign, type*⟩ where subject is specified as user, user group, IP address or semantic name; object is specified with XPath expression; example of actions are read or write; signs are positive and negative; and example of types are local, global and DTD which determines the level of propagation. In this model, if similar data items requiring same level of protection are placed in structurally unrelated nodes, it is required to attach same authorization policy to all these nodes. This results in duplication of authorization policies which is caused by lack of recognition of semantic association and scatteredness properties.

Duplication incurs significant overhead in maintenance of authorization policies. For instance, if requirements for storing or publishing contact information (e.g. email, phone, fax) change, it is required to update policies for all different pieces of data that represent contact information. Organizations often collect different types of data including personal identifiable information of employees and customers. So, they are compliant to different internal and external parties including government and standard bodies. This increases the likelihood that authorization requirements change frequently over time.

While most XML authorization models directly identify nodes in their authorization policies, our proposed model adds a level of abstraction by using *security-label* attribute values. The proposed model specifies two types of policies called *authorization policies* and *labeling policies*. Authorization policies are specified using *security-label* attribute values. These values are assigned to JSON data using labeling policies. A conceptual overview of existing XML authorization models and our proposed model is shown schematically in Fig. 1(a) and (b) respectively. By using security-label attribute values to connect nodes and policies, we can assign semantically related or scattered data same attribute values. This eliminates the need to specify duplicated policies.

(a)   (b)

Fig. 1. (a) Existing XML models (b) the proposed model

The proposed model additionally offers flexibility in specification and maintenance of authorization and labeling policies. These two types of policies can now be managed separately and independently. For instance, given *security-label* attribute values, higher level, organization-wide policy makers can specify authorization policies using these values without knowing details of JSON structure. On the other hand, local administrators knowledgeable about details of specific JSON documents can specify labeling policies.

We believe, the presented model can easily be generalized for data represented in trees and be instantiated for other representations, for example, YAML [1]. For simplicity, we only focus on JSON here.

The contributions of this paper are as follows. We have identified underlying characteristics of data represented in XML/JSON form. While, existing XML authorization models address only *structural hierarchy*, we additionally focus on *semantical association* and *scatterredness* properties. We have designed an attribute-based protection mechanism for JSON documents including an operational and two different labeling models. We have demonstrated a proof-of-concept for the proposed models in the Swift service of OpenStack IaaS cloud platform.

The rest of the paper is organized as follows. In Sect. 2, we discuss underlying concepts of JSON documents and existing works relating to the protection of these documents. Section 3 presents the operational model. The labeling models are described in Sect. 4. Section 5 discusses the proof-of-concept implementation of our proposed models. Finally, we conclude the paper in Sect. 6.

2   Background and Related Work

In this section, we briefly review JSON and discuss related work.

2.1   JSON (JavaScript Object Notation)

JSON or JavaScript Object Notation is a format for representing textual data in a structured way. In JSON, data is represented in one of two forms—as an

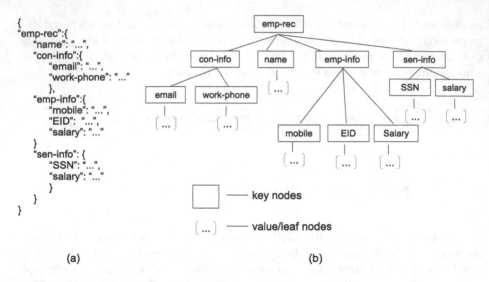

```
{
"emp-rec":{
    "name": "...",
    "con-info":{
        "email": "...",
        "work-phone": "..."
    },
    "emp-info":{
        "mobile": "...",
        "EID": "...",
        "salary": "..."
    }
    "sen-info": {
        "SSN": "...",
        "salary": "..."
    }
  }
}
```

          (a)   (b)

Fig. 2. Example of (a) JSON data (b) corresponding JSON tree

object or an *array* of values. A JSON object is defined as a collection of *key, value* pairs where a *key* is simply a string representing a name and a *value* is one of the following primitive types—string, number, boolean, null or another object or an array. The definition of a JSON object is recursive in that an object may contain other objects. An array is defined as a set of an ordered collection of values. JSON data manifests following characteristics.

– JSON data forms a rooted tree hierarchical structure.
– In the tree, leaf nodes represent values and a non-leaf nodes represent keys.
– A node in the tree, can be uniquely identified by a unique path.

Figure 2(a) shows the content of a JSON document where strings representing values have been replaced by "..." for ease of presentation. Figure 2(b) shows the corresponding tree representation. Any node in the tree can be uniquely represented by JSONPath [18] which is a standard representation of paths for JSON documents.

2.2   Related Work

There is limited academic research published on security of JSON data. To the best of our knowledge, we are the first to propose a protection model for it.

On the other hand, XML security has long been investigated by many researchers. A fundamental line of work in this area is about specifying authorization policies for the protection of XML documents [8–10,17]. All of these models attach authorization policies directly on nodes in the XML tree. Most of these models use XPath [14] to specify a node in the tree. For example, Damiani et al. [15] specify authorization policies as a tuple of ⟨*subject, object, action, sign, type*⟩

where an *object* is identified by an URI (Uniform Resource Identifier) along with a XPath expression.

Another direction of work is about effective enforcement of authorization mechanisms for secure and efficient query evaluation. For example, in [16] the authors derive *security views* comprising exactly the set of accessible nodes for different user groups. Based on the security view, they provide a unique DTD view for each user group. Similar works in this direction include [19,20] which use query preprocessing approaches. These models uses preprocessed finite automatas for authorization policies, document and Schema/DTD, and determine if a query is safe before running it. Unsafe queries can be rewritten.

The idea of associating labels with protected objects has been proposed before. For example, in *purpose based access control (PBAC)* [13], the authors associate *intended purposes* with data items and *access purpose* with users. If *access purpose* of a user is included in the *intended purposes* of the requested objects, the request is granted. Our approach is similar. While PBAC manages intended purposes using RBAC [22], we use attributes with attribute-based access control (ABAC). Most significantly, PBAC does not specify how to annotate objects with *access purposes*, which we emphasize in this paper via labeling policies. Adam et al. [7], have applied *concepts* and *slots* on digital objects which work at a finer grained content level. They have also specified an access control model based on expressions using concepts and slots. This model also does not specify how to assign concepts and slots to objects.

The concept of attaching organized labels to users and objects and controlling access based on these labels is the underlying idea of Lattice Based Access Control (LBAC [21]), sometime also referred as Mandatory Access Control (MAC). The operational model, *AtOM*, presented in Sect. 3 resembles LBAC but it is fundamentally different from LBAC. *AtOM* is based on enumerated authorization policy ABAC model named EAP-ABAC [11,12]. EAP-ABAC is a general purpose ABAC model which supports larger set of attributes contrary to single label in LBAC and based on enumerated authorization policies. Correlation between EAP-ABAC and LBAC is presented in [12].

3   The Operational Model

This section presents the Attribute-based Operational Model (*AtOM*) for protection of JSON documents. *AtOM* adapts enumerated authorization policies from [11,12].

Figure 3 presents components of *AtOM*. In the figure, the set of users is represented by U. Each user is assigned to one or more values of an attribute named *user-label* or *uLabel* in short. These values are selected from the set of all possible user-label values UL which are partially ordered. The partial order is represented by ULH. An example showing user-label values and hierarchy is presented in Fig. 4(a). On the other hand, the set of JSON elements are specified as JE. JSON elements may subsume other JSON elements, and form a tree structured hierarchy. The hierarchy is represented by JEH. Each JSON element is assigned values of an attribute named *security-label* or *sLabel* in short.

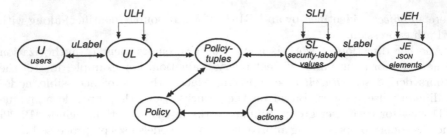

Fig. 3. The Attribute-based Operational Model ($AtOM$)

Table 1. Definition of $AtOM$

<u>*I. Sets and relations*</u>
- U, JE and A (set of users, JSON elements and actions resp.)
- JEH (hierarchy of JSON elements, represented by $\succeq_j$)
- UL and ULH (finite set of uLabel values and their partial order denoted as $\succeq_{ul}$ resp)
- SL and SLH (finite set of security-label values and their partial denoted as $\succeq_{sl}$ resp)
- $uLabel$ and $sLabel$ (attribute functions on users and JSON objects resp.) Formally,
$$uLabel : U \rightarrow 2^{UL};\ sLabel : JO \rightarrow 2^{SL}$$
<u>*II. Policy components*</u>
- $Policy\text{-}tuples = UL \times SL$
- $Policy_a \subseteq Policy\text{-}tuples$ for $a \in A$
- $Policy = \{Policy_a | a \in A\}$
<u>*III. Authorization function*</u>
- $can\_access(u : U, a : A, o : JE) = (\exists (ul, sl) \in Policy_a)[ul \in uLabel(u) \wedge sl \in sLabel(o)]$
- $is\_authorized(u : U, a : A, je_i : JE) = (can\_access(u, a, je_j))[je_i \succeq_{sl} je_j]$

These values are selected from the set of security-label values SL which are also partially ordered. The partial order is represented by SLH. An example showing security-label values and hierarchy is presented in Fig. 4(b). A JSON tree annotated with security-label values is given in Fig. 4(c). These components and relationship among them are formally specified in Segment I of Table 1.

In Fig. 3, the set of authorization policies is represented by $Policy$. There exists one authorization policy per action which is shown by the one-to-one relation between $Policy$ and A. In Table 1, $Policy_{read}$ presents the authorization policy for action read. An authorization policy may contain one or more micro-policies and one micro-policy can be associated with more than one authorization policies. This is represented by the many-to-many relation between $Policy$ and $Policy\text{-}tuples$. $Policy_{read}$, as mentioned above, contains four policy-tuples including *(manager, sensitive)*. The tuple *(manager, sensitive)* while contained in policy $Policy_{read}$ specifies that users who are manager can read objects that have been assigned values sensitive. Formally, we represent a policy-tuple a pair of atomic values (ul, sl) where $ul \in UL$ and $sl \in SL$. The formal definition of policies and policy-tuples is given in Segment II of Table 1. We use the terms policy-tuples and micro-policies equivalently to represent sub-policies.

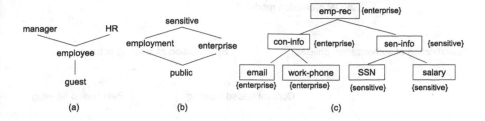

Fig. 4. (a) User-label values, (b) security-label values and (c) annotated JSON tree

Table 2. Example of an authorization policy and authorization requests

I. Enumerated authorization policies
$Policy_{read} \equiv \{$ *(manager,sensitive), (HR,employment),*
(employee, enterprise), (guest, public) $\}$
II. Authorization requests
$is\_authorized(Alice, read, emp\text{-}rec) = true$, assuming $uLabel(Alice) = \{manager\}$
$is\_authorized(Bob, read, emp\text{-}rec) = false$, assuming $uLabel(Bob) = \{employee\}$
$is\_authorized(Bob, read, con\text{-}info) = true$, assuming $uLabel(Bob) = \{employee\}$
$is\_authorized(Charlie, read, sen\text{-}info) = false$, assuming $uLabel(Charlie) = \{HR\}$

The authorization function $is\_authorized()$ is specified in Section III of Table 1. We define the helper function $can\_access(u, a, o)$ which specifies that the user u can access the object o for action a if there exists a policy-tuple in $Policy_a$ for that allows it. A user is authorized to perform an action on the requested JSON element if he can access the requested element and all its sub-elements. For example, let us assume, Alice as a manager wants to read *emp-rec* which has been assigned value *enterprise* as shown in Fig. 4(c). The tuple *(manager, sensitive)* in $Policy_{read}$ specifies that Alice can read object labeled with sensitive or junior values. Thus, the request $is\_authorized(Alice, read, emp\_rec)$ is evaluated true. On the other hand, assuming Bob as an employee, the request $is\_authorized(Bob, read, emp\text{-}rec)$ is evaluated false as an employee cannot read *sen-info* which is sub-element of *emp-rec*. Additional examples of authorization request is given in Segment II of Table 2.

4   Labeling Policies

In this section, we discuss specification of labeling policies for the operational model given in Sect. 3. We broadly categorize the policies used in the operational model into specification of authorization policies and assignment of security-label values or labeling policies. Policy scope of the operational model is schematically shown in Fig. 5. Here, we focus on the later type of policies.

We specify two different approaches to assign security-label values to elements in a JSON document, viz. content-based and path-based. These approaches are

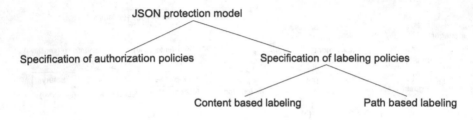

Fig. 5. Policy scope

fundamentally different in how a JSON element is specified. While a path is described starting from the root node of the tree, content is specified starting from the leaf nodes of the tree. These two contrasting approaches offer flexibility in assignments and propagation of security-label values.

4.1   Control on Labeling Policies

For specification of labeling policies, we define two types of restriction that control assignments and propagations of *security-label* values. In the first type, we restrict how security-label values are selected and assigned on tree nodes. We call this *assignment-control*. In the second type, we specify how assigned values are propagated along nodes in the tree. We call this *propagation-control*.

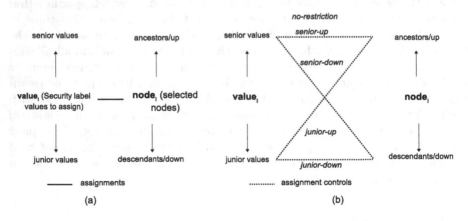

Fig. 6. (a) Assignment of security label values (b) assignment controls

The motivation of *assignment-control* is to restrict arbitrary assignments of security-label values. This enables administrators to restrict future assignments after some assignments have been carried out. These controls are specified during the assignments. If any attempting assignment does not comply with *assignment-control*s of existing assignments, it will be discarded. We define five possible options for *assignment-control* as *no-restriction, senior-up, senior-down, junior-up* and *junior-down*. The type *no-restriction* does not specify any restriction. If we assign a value $value_i$ in $node_i$, with *senior-up* restriction, all up/ancestors of $node_i$ must be assigned values senior to $value_i$ possibly including $value_i$. In type *senior-down* restriction, all down/descendants of $node_i$ must be assigned values senior to $value_i$ possibly including $value_i$. Similarly, the types *junior-up* and *junior-down*, specify that ancestors and descendants of $node_i$ must be assigned values junior to $value_i$, possibly including $value_i$. Figure 6 schematically illustrates *assignment-control*. In Fig. 7, the node *con-info* is assigned a value *enterprise* with option *junior-down* which regulates that its descendant nodes namely {email, work-phone} must be assigned values *enterprise* or its juniors, in this case from the set {enterprise, public} (using security-label values given in Fig. 4(b)). In the same figure, the node *sen-info* is assigned value *sensitive* with option *senior-down* which mandates that its descendant nodes namely {SSN, salary} must be assigned values from *sensitive* or its seniors in this case from the set {sensitive}.

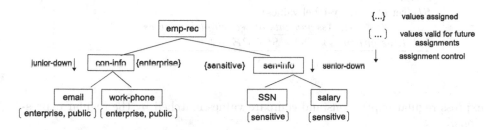

Fig. 7. Assignments with assignment controls

Once we assign security-label values on an element in a JSON tree, the value can be propagated to other elements in the tree. We define following types for *propagation-control* as *no-prop, one-level up, one-level down, cascading up* and *cascading down*. Assigned values are not propagated in type *no-prop*. From a node, assigned values are propagated to parent and all its siblings in the type *one-level up*. Assigned values are propagated to all ancestor nodes in type *cascading up*. Similarly, from a selected item, assigned values are propagated to direct children in type *one-level down* and to all descendants in type *cascading down*.

4.2 Content-Based Labeling

This section shows how to assign security-label values by matching content and propagating the labels.

We adapt the concept of *query object* available in MongoDB [4] which matches content in a JSON document. Query objects discover content starting from the *value nodes* of the JSON tree. It accepts regular expression to find *value nodes* or *key nodes* conveniently. MongoDB has built-in functions to

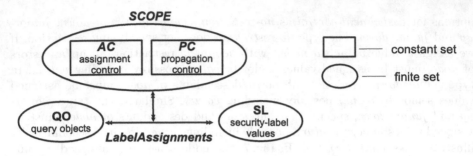

Fig. 8. Content-based labeling model

Table 3. Definition of content-based labeling

I. Basic sets and relations
- *QO* (set of query objects).
- *AC* (assignment control) *AC*= {*no-restriction, senior-up, junior-up*}.
- *PC* (propagation control) *PC* = {*no-prop, one-level-up, cascade-up*}.
- *SCOPE* ⊆ *AC* × *PC*
- *SL* (set of security-label values).
II. Assignments of security-label values
- *LabelAssignments* ⊆ *QO* × *SCOPE* × 2^{SL}

express regular expressions and compare values matched by the regular expressions.

A model to assign security-label values based on query objects is given in Fig. 8. In the figure, QO represents the set of all query objects and SL is the set of security-label values. The set AC represents *assignment-control* and PC represents *propagation-control* discussed earlier. AC and PC together define labeling scopes. A labeling scope determines how values are assigned and propagated in the tree. As content is matched from the value/leaf nodes of the tree, we consider assignment and propagation control only for the ancestors of the matching nodes.

The formal definition of the model is given in Table 3. Segment I of the table specify basic sets and relations. In Segment II, the relation *LabelAssignments* defines rules for assigning security-label values. An assignment rule is a triple of a query object to match content, a scope and a set of values to be assigned. Section I of Table 4 gives some examples of query objects and their interpretation in plain English. Segment II of Table 4, presents examples of assignment policies based on query objects.

4.3 Path-Based Labeling

In this section, we show how we assign security-label values by matching paths in the JSON tree and propagate them along the tree.

Table 4. Examples of query objects and content-based labeling policies

I. Query objects
- ob1 = { "email": { \$regex: "/.*@example.com/" } } (matches email addresses from domain example.com)
- ob2 = { \$elemMatch: { \$regex: "RE_EMAIL" } } (matches any key having value corresponding to the given regular expression)
- ob3 = {\$elemMatch:{ \$regex: "RE_SSN"}, \$elemMatch: {"RE_CREDIT_CARD"}} (matches all objects containing both social security and credit card number)
II. LabelAssignments
- LabelAssignments= { (ob1, (no-prop, unrestricted), {enterprise}), (ob2, (no-prop, unrestricted), {enterprise}), (ob3, (no-prop, restricted), { sensitive} }

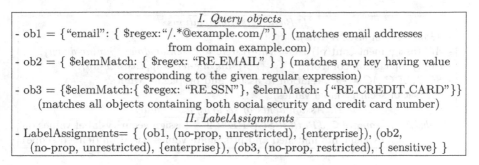

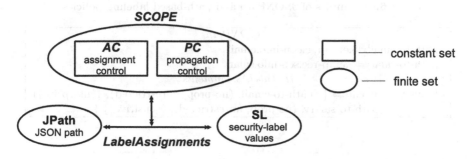

Fig. 9. Path-based labeling model

We adapt *JSONPath* [18] to specify path-based labeling policies. This model is very similar to the content-based labeling model except we use JSONPath instead of query objects. While, query objects are matched starting from the leaf nodes, JSONPath specifies elements starting from the root node (or any node in case of relative path) and traverses towards leaf of the tree. As a result, this model apply assignment control and propagation control towards descendants of matching nodes. The components of the model and its formal definition are given in Fig. 9 and Table 5 respectively. Examples of JSON paths and path based labeling policies are presented in Segment I and II of Table 6.

5 Implementation in OpenStack Swift

We have implemented our proposed operational model and path-based labeling scheme in OpenStack IaaS cloud platform using OpenStack Keystone as the authorization service provider and OpenStack Swift as the storage service provider. Our choice of OpenStack is motivated by its support for independent and inter-operable services and a well defined RESTful API set.

We have modified OpenStack Keystone and Swift services to accommodate required changes. A reference architecture of our testbed is given in Fig. 10. Details of the implementation is shown in Fig. 11. Required changes are presented as highlighted rectangles in Fig. 11.

Table 5. Definition of path-based labeling

I. Basic sets and relations
- *JPath* (set of JSONPaths).
- *AC* (assignment control) $AC=\{no\text{-}restriction,\ senior\text{-}down,\ junior\text{-}down\}$.
- *PC* (propagation control) $PC=\{no\text{-}prop,\ one\text{-}level\text{-}up,\ cascade\text{-}up\}$.
- $SCOPE \subseteq AC \times PC$, relation to assign and propagate values.
- *SL* (set of security-label values).
II. Assignments of security-label values
- $LabelAssignments \subseteq JPath \times SCOPE \times 2^{SL}$ (assign security-label values on JSON elements matched and propagate values based on defined scope)

Table 6. Examples of JSONPath and path-based labeling policies

I. JSONPaths
- path-to-email=$.emp-rec.con-info.email
- path-to-salary=$.emp-rec.sen-info.salary
II. LabelAssignments
- LabelAssignments= { (path-to-email, (no-prop, unrestricted), {enterprise}), (path-to-salary, (no-prop, unrestricted), {sensitive}) }

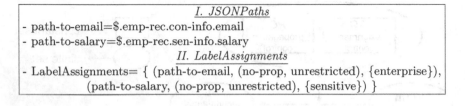

Fig. 10. Reference architecture of the implementation testbed

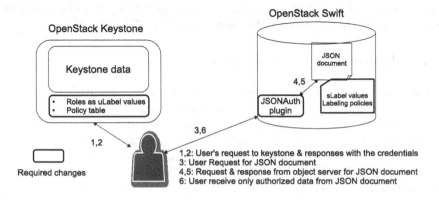

Fig. 11. Implementation in OpenStack IaaS cloud platform

5.1 Changes in OpenStack Keystone

OpenStack Keystone uses roles and role-based policies to provide authorization decisions. In our implementation, we uses roles to hold user-label attribute values. A set of valid security-label values are also stored as part of the Keystone service.

Among two different types of policies - authorization and labeling policies, the former is managed in the Keystone service. We assume, a higher level administrators (possibly at the level of organization) adds, removes or updates these authorization policies. We add a policy table in Keystone database to store these enumerated authorization policies.

5.2 Changes in OpenStack Swift

In Swift side, we store *security-label* values assigned to JSON objects and path-based labeling policies applied to them. Security-label values and labeling policies are stored as metadata of the stored objects, JSON documents in this case. For simplicity, we assume object owner (Swift account holder in this case) can update security-label values or labeling policies for stored JSON document.

During evaluation, we intercept every requests to Swift (from the Swift-proxy server) and reroute a request to be passed through *JSONAuth plugin* if it is a request for a JSON document. In this case, the request additionally carries a requested path and authorization policies applicable to the user. JSONAuth plug-in retrieves the requested JSON document, apply path-based labeling policies to annotate the document and uses authorization policies to determine if the user is authorized for the requested content of the file.

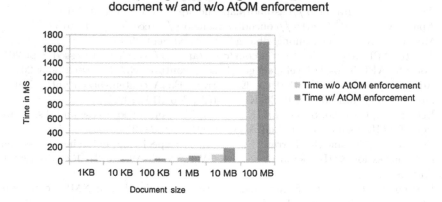

Fig. 12. Performance evaluation

5.3   Evaluation

An evaluation of our implementation is shown in Fig. 12. The evaluation has been made against concurrent download requests to the Swift proxy server. The X-axis shows size of the JSON document requested for download while the Y-axis shows the average download time for 10 concurrent request. Our evaluation shows a performance hit of nearly 60 % over no authorization protection.

6   Conclusion

This paper presents an attribute based protection model for JSON documents. In the proposed model, JSON elements are annotated with *security-label* attribute values with *labeling policies*. We specify *authorization policies* using these attribute values. The advantage of the separation of labeling and authorization policies is that they can be specified and administered independently possibly by different level of administrators. In this regard, we have presented an operational model to specify authorization policies that evaluates access request. Further, we have specified two different models for assigning security-label attribute values on JSON elements based on content and paths. We have presented a proof-of-concept of the proposed models in OpenStack IaaS cloud platform.

Acknowledgement. This research is partially supported by NSF Grants CNS-1111925 and CNS-1423481.

References

1. The official YAML website. www.yaml.org. Accessed July 2016
2. Apache Cassandra. http://cassandra.apache.org/. Accessed Sept 2015
3. Apache CouchDB^TM. http://couchdb.apache.org/. Accessed Sept 2015
4. MongoDB. http://www.mongodb.org/. Accessed Sept 2015
5. Twitter API. https://dev.twitter.com/docs/api/1.1/overview. Accessed Sept 2015
6. Youtube API. https://developers.google.com/youtube/v3/. Accessed Sept 2015
7. Adam, N.R., Atluri, V., Bertino, E., Ferrari, E.: A content-based authorization model for digital libraries. IEEE KDE **14**(2), 296–315 (2002)
8. Bertino, E., Castano, S., Ferrari, E., Mesiti, M.: Controlled access and dissemination of XML documents. In: 2nd ACM WIDM, pp. 22–27 (1999)
9. Bertino, E., Castano, S., Ferrari, E., Mesiti, M.: Specifying, enforcing access control policies for XML document sources. World Wide Web **3**(3), 139–151 (2000). Springer
10. Bertino, E., Ferrari, E.: Secure and selective dissemination of XML documents. ACM TISSEC **5**(3), 290–331 (2002)
11. Biswas, P., Sandhu, R., Krishnan, R.: A comparison of logical-formula and enumerated authorization policy ABAC models. In: Ranise, S., Swarup, V. (eds.) DBSec 2016. LNCS, vol. 9766, pp. 122–129. Springer, Heidelberg (2016). doi:10.1007/978-3-319-41483-6_9

12. Biswas, P., Sandhu, R., Krishnan, R.: Label-based access control: an ABAC model with enumerated authorization policy. In: Proceedings of the 2016 ACM International Workshop on Attribute Based Access Control, pp. 1–12 (2016)
13. Byun, J.-W., Bertino, E., Li, N.: Purpose based access control of complex data for privacy protection. In: 10th ACM SACMAT (2005)
14. Clark, J., DeRose, S.: XML path language (XPath) version 1.0 (1999)
15. Damiani, E., De Capitani di Vimercati, S., Paraboschi, S., Samarati, P.: A fine-grained access control system for XML documents. ACM TISSEC 5(2), 169–202 (2002)
16. Fan, W., Chan, C.-Y., Garofalakis, M.: Secure XML querying with security views. In: ACM SIGMOD/PODS, pp. 587–598 (2004)
17. Fundulaki, I., Marx, M.: Specifying access control policies for XML documents with XPath. In: 9th ACM SACMAT, pp. 61–69 (2004)
18. Goessner, S.: JSONPath Syntax. http://goessner.net/articles/JsonPath/. Accessed Sep 2015
19. Luo, B., Lee, D., Lee, W.-C., Liu, P., Qfilter: fine-grained run-time XML access control via NFA-based query rewriting. In: ACM CIKM (2004)
20. Murata, M., Tozawa, A., Kudo, M., Hada, S.: XML access control using static analysis. ACM TISSEC 9(3), 292–324 (2006)
21. Sandhu, R.S.: Lattice-based access control models. IEEE Comput. 26(11), 9–19 (1993)
22. Ravi, S.S., Coyne, E.J., Feinstein, H.L., Youman, C.E.: Rolebased access control models. IEEE Comput. 29(2), 38–47 (1996)

The GURA$_G$ Administrative Model
for User and Group Attribute Assignment

Maanak Gupta$^{(\boxtimes)}$ and Ravi Sandhu

Institute for Cyber Security, Department of Computer Science,
University of Texas at San Antonio,
One UTSA Circle, San Antonio, TX 78249, USA
gmaanakg@yahoo.com, ravi.sandhu@utsa.edu

Abstract. Several attribute-based access control (ABAC) models have been recently proposed to provide finer-grained authorization and to address the shortcomings of existing models. In particular, Servos et al. [33] presented a hierarchical group and attribute based access control (HGABAC) model which introduces a novel approach of attribute inheritance through user and object groups. For authorization purposes the effect of attribute inheritance from groups can be equivalently realized by direct attribute assignment to users and objects. Hence the practical benefit of HGABAC-like models is with respect to administration. In this paper we propose the first administration model for HGABAC called GURA$_G$. GURA$_G$ consists of three sub-models: UAA for user attribute assignment, UGAA for user-group attribute assignment and UGA for user to user-group assignment.

Keywords: Attribute based access control · Attribute inheritance · Group hierarchy · Group attribute administration · User-group assignment

1 Introduction

Interest in attribute-based access control (ABAC) has been developing over the past two decades, in part due to limitations of the widely deployed role-based access control (RBAC) model [32]. A number of ABAC models have been published over the years [10–12,15,27,34,36,37], although none of these is quite regarded as the definitive characterization of ABAC.

Since ABAC access mechanism revolves around the attributes of entities, Servos et al. [33] proposed the hierarchial group and attribute-based (HGABAC) model, which leverages user and object groups for allocating attribute values to users and objects. In this model, a user can be assigned to a user-group and instead of assigning attributes individually to each user in the group, a collection of attribute values is assigned to the group and inherited by all users in that group. A similar mechanism applies on the object side with object groups.

The essential benefit of HGABAC is convenient administration of attribute values for users and objects. Our contribution in this paper is to present the

© Springer International Publishing AG 2016
J. Chen et al. (Eds.): NSS 2016, LNCS 9955, pp. 318–332, 2016.
DOI: 10.1007/978-3-319-46298-1_21

first administrative model for HGABAC, called GURA$_G$. GURA$_G$ builds upon the GURA model [14] for user attribute assignment (UAA) but further adds components for user-group attribute assignment (UGAA) and user to user-group assignment (UGA). For this purpose we introduce an alternate formalization of the HGABAC model which is compatible with the GURA and GURA$_G$ models.

Remaining paper has been organized as follows. An overview of HGABAC followed with re-formalized model is discussed and specified in Sect. 2. In Sect. 3, we propose a formal role and attribute based administration model for user and user groups (GURA$_G$). Section 4 discusses some limitations of the proposed model. Section 5 reviews previous work related to ABAC and administration models, followed by conclusion in Sect. 6.

2   HGABAC Model

This section gives an informal characterization of groups in HGABAC [33], followed by a formal specification. Our formalization is in the style of ABAC$_\alpha$ [15], different from but equivalent to the formalization of Servos et al. [33]. Our alternate formalization of HGABAC enables us to build upon the GURA administrative model [14] for ABAC$_\alpha$ in Sect. 3.

2.1   Groups in HGABAC

Similar to many ABAC models, HGABAC recognizes the entities of users, subjects and objects. A user is a human being which interacts directly with the computer, while subjects are active entities (like processes) created by the user to perform actions on objects. Objects are system resources like files, applications etc. Operations correspond to access modes (e.g. read, write) provided by the system and can be exercised by a subject on an object. The properties of entities in the system are reflected using attributes. Users and subjects hold the same set of attributes whereas objects have a separate set of attributes reflecting their characteristics. We assume all attributes are set valued. Also each attribute has a finite set of possible atomic values from which a subset can be assigned to appropriate entities.

In addition to the above familiar ABAC entities, HGABAC further introduces the notion of a group as a named collection of users or objects. Each group has attribute values assigned to it. A member of the group inherits these values from the group. Users will inherit attributes from user groups and objects from object groups. A partially ordered group hierarchy also exists in the system where senior groups inherit attribute values from junior groups.

An example user-group hierarchy is illustrated in Fig. 1. Senior groups are shown higher up and the arrows indicate the direction of attribute inheritance. Since Graduate group (G) is senior to both CSD and UN, G will hold the attribute values directly assigned to it as well as values inherited from CSD and UN. The values of univId and college attributes for group G are respectively inherited from UN and CSD, values of userType and studType are directly

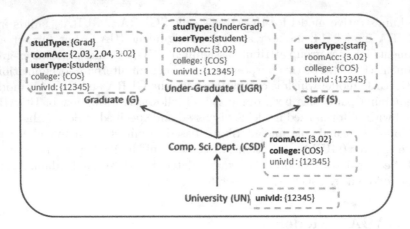

Fig. 1. Example User Groups (values in black are direct and in gray are inherited)

assigned to G while the values of roomAcc are a mix of directly assigned values, 2.03 and 2.04, and inherited value 3.02 from CSD. Each user is assigned to a subset of user groups. Similarly there is an object-group hierarchy wherein attribute values of objects are analogously inherited.

The core advantage of introducing groups is simplified administration of user and object attributes where an entity obtains a set of attributes values by group membership in lieu of assigning one value at a time. In context of Fig. 1 assigning an attribute value to CSD potentially saves hundreds or thousands of assignments to individual student and staff. Likewise changing the CSD level room from 3.02 to, say, 3.08, requires only one update as opposed to thousands.

2.2   HGABAC Model: An Alternate Formalization

We now develop a formalization of the HGABAC model different from that of Servos et al. [33]. This alternate formalization will be useful in the next section where we develop the GURA$_G$ for administration of HGABAC. Our formalization uses the conceptual model of HGABAC shown in Fig. 2. The complete HGABAC formalization is given in Table 1, which we will discuss in the remainder of this subsection. An example configuration of HGABAC is given in the next subsection.

Basic sets and functions of HGABAC are shown at the top of Table 1. U, S, O and OP represent the finite set of existing users, subjects, objects and operations respectively. UG and OG represent sets of user and object groups in the system. UA is the set of user attributes for users, user groups and subjects. OA is similarly the set of object attributes for objects and object groups. All these sets are disjoint.

Attribute values can be directly assigned to users, objects, user groups and object groups (we will consider subjects in a moment). These are collectively called entities. Each attribute of an entity is set valued. The value of an attribute

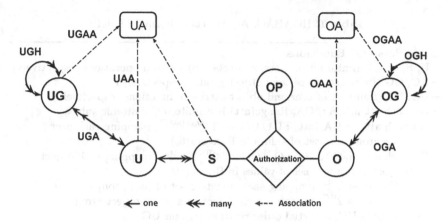

Fig. 2. A Conceptual Model of HGABAC

att for an entity is some subset of Range(att) which is a finite set of atomic values, as indicated by the functions att_u and att_o in Table 1. These functions specify the attribute values that are directly assigned to entities. The function directUg specifies the user groups to which the user is assigned, and similarly the function directOg specifies the object groups to which an object is assigned.

User group hierarchy (UGH) is a partial order on UG, written as $\succeq_{ug}$, where $ug_1 \succeq_{ug} ug_2$ denotes ug_1 is senior to ug_2 or ug_2 is junior to ug_1. This many to many hierarchy results in attribute inheritance where the effective values of user attribute function att_u for a user-group ug (defined by effectiveUG$_{att_u}(ug)$) is the union of directly assigned values for att_u and the effective attribute values of all groups junior to ug. The assignment of a user to a user-group will inherit values from this group to that user. The function effective$_{att_u}$ maps a user to the set of values which is the union of the values of att_u directly assigned to the user and the effective values of attribute att_u from all user groups directly assigned to the user. Similar sets and functions are specified for objects and object groups.

A subject is created by a user, denoted by the SubUser function. The effective attribute values of a subject are under control of its creating user. These values are required to be a subset of the corresponding effective attribute values for the creator. In general these values can change with time but cannot exceed the creator's effective values. The exact manner in which a subject's effective attributes are modified by its creator is not specified in the model, and can be realized differently in various implementations.

Each operation op $\in$ OP in the system has an associated boolean authorization function Authorization$_{op}$(s,o) which specifies the conditions under which subject s $\in$ S can execute operation op on object o $\in$ O. The condition is specified as a propositional logic formula using the policy language given in Table 1. This formula can only use the effective attribute values of the subject and object in

Table 1. HGABAC: An Alternate Formal Model

Basic Sets and Functions

- U, S, O, OP (finite set of users, subjects, objects and operations respectively)
- UG, OG (finite set of user and object groups respectively)
- UA, OA (finite set of user and object attribute functions respectively)
- For each att in $UA \cup OA$, Range(att) is a finite set of atomic values
- For each att_u in UA, $att_u : U \cup UG \rightarrow 2^{Range(att_u)}$, mapping each user and user group to a set of values in $Range(att_u)$
- For each att_o in OA, $att_o : O \cup OG \rightarrow 2^{Range(att_o)}$, mapping each object and object group to a set of values in $Range(att_o)$
- $directUg : U \rightarrow 2^{UG}$, mapping each user to a set of user groups
- $directOg : O \rightarrow 2^{OG}$, mapping each object to a set of object groups
- $UGH \subseteq UG \times UG$, a partial order relation $\succeq_{ug}$ on UG
- $OGH \subseteq OG \times OG$, a partial order relation $\succeq_{og}$ on OG

Effective Attributes (Derived Functions)

- For each att_u in UA,
  - $effectiveUG_{att_u} : UG \rightarrow 2^{Range(att_u)}$, defined as
    $$effectiveUG_{att_u}(ug_i) = att_u(ug_i) \cup (\bigcup_{\forall g \in \{ug_j | ug_i \succeq_{ug} ug_j\}} effectiveUG_{att_u}(g))$$
  - $effective_{att_u} : U \rightarrow 2^{Range(att_u)}$, defined as
    $$effective_{att_u}(u) = att_u(u) \cup (\bigcup_{\forall g \in directUg(u)} effectiveUG_{att_u}(g))$$
- For each att_o in OA,
  - $effectiveOG_{att_o} : OG \rightarrow 2^{Range(att_o)}$, defined as
    $$effectiveOG_{att_o}(og_i) = att_o(og_i) \cup (\bigcup_{\forall g \in \{og_j | og_i \succeq_{og} og_j\}} effectiveOG_{att_o}(g))$$
  - $effective_{att_o} : O \rightarrow 2^{Range(att_o)}$, defined as
    $$effective_{att_o}(o) = att_o(o) \cup (\bigcup_{\forall g \in directOg(o)} effectiveOG_{att_u}(g))$$

Effective Attributes of Subjects (Assigned by Creator)

- SubUser : $S \rightarrow U$, mapping each subject to its creator user
- For each att_u in UA, $effective_{att_u} : S \rightarrow 2^{Range(att_u)}$, mapping of subject s to a set of values for its effective attribute att_u. It is required that : $effective_{att_u}(s) \subseteq effective_{att_u}(SubUser(s))$

Authorization Function

For each $op \in OP$, $Authorization_{op}$ (s:S, o:O) is a propositional logic formula, returning true or false and is defined using the following policy language:

- $\alpha ::= \alpha \wedge \alpha \mid \alpha \vee \alpha \mid (\alpha) \mid \neg\alpha \mid \exists x \in set.\alpha \mid \forall x \in set.\alpha \mid set \triangle set \mid$ atomic $\in$ set | atomic $\notin$ set
- $\triangle ::= \subset \mid \subseteq \mid \nsubseteq \mid \cap \mid \cup$
- set ::= $effective_{att_{u_i}}(s) \mid effective_{att_{o_i}}(o)$ for $att_{u_i} \in UA$, $att_{o_i} \in OA$
- atomic ::= value

Access Decision Function

A subject $s_i \in S$ is allowed to perform an operation $op \in OP$ on a given object $o_j \in O$ if the effective attributes of the subject and object satisfy the policies stated in $Authorization_{op}(s : S, o : O)$. Formally, $Authorization_{op}(s_i, o_j) = True$

Table 2. Example HGABAC Configuration

Basic Sets and functions

- UA = {studId, userType, skills, studType, univId, roomAcc, college, jobTitle, studStatus}
- OA = {readerType}
- OP = {read}
- UG = {UN, CSD, G, UGR, S}, OG = { }
- UGH is given in Fig. 1, OGH = { }
- Range of each att$_u$ in UA, denoted by Range(att$_u$):

    studId = {er35, abc12, fhu53},   userType = {faculty, staff, student},

    skills = {c, c++, java},   studType = {Grad, UnderGrad},

    univId = {12345},   roomAcc = {1.2, 2.03, 2.04, 3.02},

    college = {COS, COE, BUS},   jobTitle = {TA, Grader, Admin},

    studStatus = {graduated, part-time, full-time}
- Range of each att$_o$ in OA, Range(readerType) = {faculty, staff, student}

Authorization Function:

Authorization$_{read}$(s : S, o : O) $\equiv$ effective$_{userType}$(s) $\in$ effective$_{readerType}$(o) $\wedge$ java $\in$ effective$_{skills}$(s)

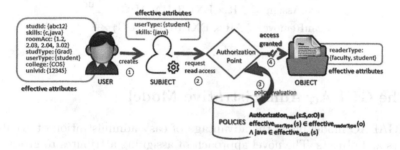

Fig. 3. Example Access Request Flow

question. The authorization functions are specified by the security policy archi-
tects when the system is created. Thereafter, a subject $s_i \in S$ is allowed to
execute operation op on object o $o_j \in O$ if and only if Authorization$_{op}$(s_i, o_j)
evaluates to True.

2.3 Example HGABAC Configuration

An example HGABAC configuration is given in Table 2, utilizing the user group
hierarchy of Fig. 1. For simplicity, we do not include any object groups. The
authorization policy for the read operation is specified. The access request flow
in Fig. 3 assumes the user has the set of effective attributes shown. The subject
has the given subset of its creator's effective attributes. The subject is thereby
allowed to read the object as the authorization policy for read is satisfied by the
effective attributes of the subject and object.

Table 3. GURA$_G$ Administrative Model

Administrative Roles and Expressions

– AR: a finite set of administrative roles

– EXPR(UA): a finite set of prerequisite expressions composed of user attribute functions as defined in Sects. 3.1 and 3.2

– EXPR(UA ∪ UG): a finite set of prerequisite expressions composed of user attribute functions and user groups as defined in Sect. 3.3

Administrative Relations

– User Attribute Assignment **(UAA)** & User-Group Attribute Assignment **(UGAA)**:

For each att$_u$ in UA,

$$\text{canAdd}_{att_u} \subseteq AR \times EXPR(UA) \times 2^{Range(att_u)}$$
$$\text{canDelete}_{att_u} \subseteq AR \times EXPR(UA) \times 2^{Range(att_u)}$$

– User to User-Group Assignment **(UGA)**:

$$\text{canAssign} \subseteq AR \times EXPR(UA \cup UG) \times 2^{UG}$$
$$\text{canRemove} \subseteq AR \times EXPR(UA \cup UG) \times 2^{UG}$$

---

3   The GURA$_G$ Administrative Model

The HGABAC model offers the advantage of easy administration of attributes for users and objects. The novel approach of assigning attributes to groups and users to groups is analogous to the permission-role and user-role assignment in RBAC [32]. By assigning a user to a user-group, the user inherits all the effective attribute values of that group in a single step, as compared to one by one attribute value assignment. Further, if an inherited attribute value has to be changed for multiple users, instead of changing per user, the value in a group can be changed, making administration very convenient.

The essence of HGABAC model is in simple administration as the effect of attribute inheritance can also be realized by direct attribute assignment for authorization purposes. Changing the attribute values of a group can impact large numbers of users and objects, thus reducing the administrative effort, and leading to better comprehension of attribute values. For example, in Fig. 1 the fact that groups G, UGR and S inherit the roomAcc value 3.02 from CSD is visible because of the group structure.

This section presents the GURA$_G$ administrative model for managing the user side of HGABAC. GURA$_G$ is inspired by the GURA model [14] which in turn evolved from URA97 [30]. All these models require a set of administrative roles AR that will be assigned to security administrators. Administrative role hierarchy also exists, wherein senior administrative roles inherit permissions from junior ones. GURA$_G$ regulates the powers of an administrative role with respect to user attribute assignment (UAA), user-group attribute assignment (UGAA) and user to user-group assignment (UGA) (see Fig. 2). The *Add* and

Table 4. Example rules in UAA

---

canAdd$_{jobTitle}$ rule:

(DeptAdmin, Grad $\in$ effective$_{studType}$(u), {TA, Grader})

canDelete$_{roomAcc}$ rule:

(BuildAdmin, graduated $\in$ effective$_{studStatus}$(u), {1.2, 2.03, 2.04, 3.02})

Delete operations enable addition or deletion of attribute values from user and user groups. Assignment or removal of a user from a user-group is accomplished by *Assign* and *Remove* operations. Table 3 depicts the various sets and administrative relations required to administer the user side of HGABAC. The prerequisite conditions are specified with slight modifications to the policy language described in Table 1. We now define the three sub-models of GURA$_G$.

3.1   The UAA Sub-model of GURA$_G$

The UAA sub-model deals with addition or deletion of values to a set-valued attribute of a user. It is composed of two relations as shown in Table 3. The meaning of $(ar, Expr(ua), Z) \in$ canAdd$_{att_u}$ is that a member of an administrator role ar (or senior to ar) is authorized to add any value in the allowed range Z of attribute att$_u$ of a user whose attributes satisfy the condition specified in Expr(ua). EXPR(UA) is the set of all prerequisite conditions represented as propositional logic expressions. The expressions return true or false and are specified using earlier defined policy language (Table 1) with following changes.

$$set ::= att_{u_i}(u) \mid effective_{att_{u_i}}(u) \mid constantSet \qquad for\ att_{u_i} \in UA$$
$$atomic ::= constantAtomic$$

The meaning of $(ar, Expr(ua), Z) \in$ canDelete$_{att_u}$ is that the member of administrator role ar (or senior) is authorized to delete any value in allowed range Z of attribute att$_u$ of a user whose attributes satisfy the condition specified in Expr(ua). The delete operation will only impact directly assigned attribute value of the user (i.e. $val \in att_u(u)$). If the value to be deleted is inherited from a group, the operation will not have any effect. Further, if a value is both inherited and directly assigned to user, deletion will only delete the direct value, thereby, the user will still hold the value inherited from the group. It is worth mentioning that any change in prerequisite conditions after the attribute value assignment has been made, will not have any retrospective effect and the entity involved will still retain the value. This is consistent with the GURA and URA97 models.

Table 4 illustrates example UAA relation. First rule allows administrator role DeptAdmin (or senior to DeptAdmin) to add any value in {TA, Grader} to user attribute jobTitle if the user's studType attribute includes Grad. Second rule allows administrator role BuildAdmin (or senior to BuildAdmin) to remove any of the specified room values from the roomAcc attribute of a user whose status includes graduated.

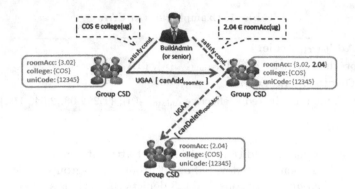

Fig. 4. Example User-Group Attribute Assignment (UGAA)

Table 5. Example rules in UGAA

canAdd$_{roomAcc}$ rule:	(BuildAdmin, COS ∈ college(ug), {2.04})
canAdd$_{skills}$ rule:	(DeptAdmin, Grad ∈ studType(ug), {c++})
canDelete$_{roomAcc}$ rule:	(BuildAdmin, 2.04 ∈ roomAcc(ug), {3.02})

3.2 The UGAA Sub-model of GURA$_G$

This sub-model controls addition and deletion of attributes to user-groups as shown in Table 3. The relations for UAA and UGAA have slightly different policy languages for EXPR(UA), which in UGAA is defined as follows.

$$\text{set} ::= att_{u_i}(ug) \mid \text{effectiveUG}_{att_{u_i}}(ug) \mid \text{constantSet} \qquad \text{for } att_{u_i} \in UA$$
$$\text{atomic} ::= \text{constantAtomic}$$

The meaning of canAdd and canDelete are similar to those in UAA sub-model. In particular, the delete operation in UGAA only impacts directly assigned attribute values of a user-group (i.e. $val \in att_u(ug)$) and will not delete inherited values from junior groups.

Figure 4 shows addition and deletion of attribute values to user-group CSD in context of Table 5. Addition of value 2.04 to roomAcc attribute of CSD group by administrator role BuildAdmin (or senior to BuildAdmin) is allowed by first rule in Table 5. Figure also shows deletion of 3.02 value from roomAcc attribute authorized by third rule.

3.3 The UGA Sub-model of GURA$_G$

The UGA sub-model is composed of two authorization relations in the lower part of Table 3. These control the assignment of user to user-groups, as well as removal of a user from a user-group. The meaning of $(ar, expr, \{g_1, g_2, g_3\}) \in$ canAssign is that member of administrator role ar (or senior) can assign any user-group

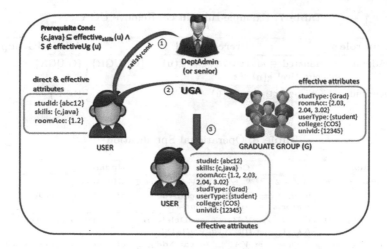

Fig. 5. Example User to User-Group Assignment (UGA)

Table 6. Example rules in canAssign UGA

Admin role	Prereq. cond	AllowedGroups
DeptAdmin	$\{c, java\} \subseteq effective_{skills}(u) \wedge S \notin effectiveUg(u)$	$\{G, CSD\}$
StaffAdmin	$\{G, UGR\} \cap effectiveUg(u) = \emptyset \wedge Admin \in effective_{jobTitle}(u)$	$\{S\}$
DeptAdmin	$U \in directUg(u) \wedge 3.02 \in roomAcc(u) \wedge S \notin effectiveUg(u)$	$\{UGR, CSD\}$

in $\{g_1, g_2, g_3\}$ to a user which satisfy the conditions in expr. EXPR(UA $\cup$ UG) now includes the current membership or non-membership of user in user-groups along with user attributes. The policy language has the following changes.

$$set ::= att_{u_i}(u) \mid effective_{att_{u_i}}(u) \mid directUg(u) \mid effectiveUg(u) \mid constantSet$$
$$atomic ::= constantAtomic$$
$$where\ effectiveUg(u) = directUg(u) \cup \left(\bigcup_{\forall ug_i \in directUg(u)} \{ug_j | ug_i \succeq_{ug} ug_j\} \right)$$

The canRemove relation in Table 3 controls the removal of a user from user-group memberships. The remove operation is said to be weak in that it will only impact explicit memberships of user. A user is an explicit member of group ug if $ug \in directUg(u)$ whereas a user is an implicit member of ug if for some $ug_i \in directUg(u)$, $ug \in \{ug_j | ug_i \succeq_{ug} ug_j\}$ exists. It should be mentioned that removal of a user from any explicit membership ug will automatically result in removal from all implicit membership due to ug.

Figure 5 shows assignment of user to user-group G allowed by first rule in Table 6. This assignment results in updates on effective attributes of user as user now inherits all attributes from group G along with direct attributes assigned through UAA. In case of weak removal (using Fig. 1), suppose a user is an explicit member of groups CSD and G and administrator role DeptAdmin

Table 7. Example rules in canRemove UGA

Admin role	Prereq. cond	AllowedGroups
UniAdmin	graduated $\in$ effective$_{\text{studStatus}}$(u) $\wedge$ {G, UGR} $\cap$ effectiveUg(u) $\neq \emptyset$	{G,UGR}
DeptAdmin	COS $\notin$ effective$_{\text{college}}$(u)	{CSD}

Table 8. Operational Specification

Operations	Conditions	Updates
In following operations: $VAL' \in 2^{\text{Range}(att_u)}$, $val \in VAL'$, $expr \in \text{EXPR(UA)}$		
Add(ar, u, att_u, val)	if $\exists \langle ar, expr, VAL' \rangle \in \textbf{canAdd}_{att_u}$ $\wedge$ $expr(u) = \text{True} \wedge val \notin att_u(u)$	$att'_u(u) = att_u(u) \cup \{val\}$
Delete(ar, u, att_u, val)	if $\exists \langle ar, expr, VAL' \rangle \in \textbf{canDelete}_{att_u}$ $\wedge$ $expr(u) = \text{True} \wedge val \in att_u(u)$	$att'_u(u) = att_u(u) \setminus \{val\}$
Add(ar, ug, att_u, val)	if $\exists \langle ar, expr, VAL' \rangle \in \textbf{canAdd}_{att_u}$ $\wedge$ $expr(ug) = \text{True} \wedge val \notin att_u(ug)$	$att'_u(ug) = att_u(ug) \cup \{val\}$
Delete(ar, ug, att_u, val)	if $\exists \langle ar, expr, VAL' \rangle \in \textbf{canDelete}_{att_u}$ $\wedge$ $expr(ug) = \text{True} \wedge val \in att_u(ug)$	$att'_u(ug) = att_u(ug) \setminus \{val\}$
In following operations: $UG' \in 2^{\text{UG}}$, $ug \in UG'$, $expr \in \text{EXPR(UA} \cup \text{UG)}$		
Assign(ar, u, ug)	if $\exists \langle ar, expr, UG' \rangle \in \textbf{canAssign}$ $\wedge$ $expr(u) = \text{True} \wedge ug \notin \text{directUg}(u)$	$\text{directUg}'(u) = \text{directUg}(u) \cup \{ug\}$
Remove(ar, u, ug)	if $\exists \langle ar, expr, UG' \rangle \in \textbf{canRemove}$ $\wedge$ $expr(u) = \text{True} \wedge ug \in \text{directUg}(u)$	$\text{directUg}'(u) = \text{directUg}(u) \setminus \{ug\}$

removes user from CSD (authorized by second rule in Table 7), the user will still have attributes of CSD through its membership in G.

3.4 Operational Specification of GURA$_G$

Table 8 outlines administrative operations required for user-group membership and attribute assignment. In all operations: $ar \in \text{AR}, u \in \text{U}, att_u \in \text{UA}, ug \in \text{UG}$. A request (first column) succeeds only if a tuple exists in administrative relation and the entity satisfies the conditions (second column), in which case the update (third column) is performed.

3.5 GURA$_G$ Model Extensions

This section proposes some enhancements to GURA$_G$.

Strong Removal: We can define a strong removal operation as per the following example using Fig. 1. If a user is explicit member of CSD and G and administrator role DeptAdmin removes this user from CSD (allowed by second rule in Table 7), the user will also be removed from group G along with CSD if allowed by authorization rules. If the user cannot be deleted from G, the operation will have no effect.

Inherited Value Deletion in User: Let Alice have administrator role r_1 and Alice tries to delete inherited value val from attribute att_u of user u_1. Let there be a $canDelete_{att_u}$ rule $(r, cond, allowedVal)$ and if $r_1 \geqslant r, val \in allowedVal$ and u_1 satisfies $cond$, find all user groups ug in directUg(u_1) from where the attribute value val is inherited. There are two possibilities: (i) If there exists a $canRemove$ rule $(r, cond, allowedGroup)$ and if $r_1 \geqslant r, ug \in allowedGroup$ and u_1 satisfies the $cond$, remove u_1 from all such ug groups. (ii) If such a rule doesn't exist or u_1 cannot be removed from some ug groups, the operation will have no effect.

Inherited Value Deletion in User Group: Let Alice have role r_1, and Alice tries to delete inherited value val from attribute att_u of user group ug_1. Let there exists a $canDelete_{att_u}$ rule $(r, cond, allowedVal)$ and if $r_1 \geqslant r, val \in allowedVal$ and ug_1 satisfies $cond$, find all user groups ug junior to ug_1 which has val directly assigned. Delete val from all such ug as if Alice did this delete. If any delete fails this operation is aborted.

4   Discussion and Limitations

The principal advantage of HGABAC model is convenient and simplified administration of attributes. GURA$_G$ proposes first administration model for HGABAC. Reachability analysis in GURA [16] discusses whether a user can be assigned specific values with a given set of administrator roles. Since GURA$_G$ proposes the authorization relations in line with GURA, we conjecture that similar reachability analysis is feasible for GURA$_G$.

At the same time, GURA$_G$ inherits some weaknesses of URA97 and GURA as discussed in [23]. Authorization rules in UAA and UGAA may require a user or user-group to have attribute values to satisfy prerequisite conditions to get other attribute values. To attain prerequisite attribute values, entity might need to satisfy another condition which itself would require some other attributes and so on. A single GURA$_G$ attribute assignment may require multiple attribute assignments to get final attribute values, possibly involving several administrators. These multi-step assignments may also result in some attribute values to be assigned to an entity solely for administrative purposes, but not otherwise needed.

Likewise, UGA rules may require a user having existing attribute values or membership in groups, which might also require multiple user groups or attribute pre-assignments and security administrators. If some rule has prerequisite junior groups requirement to assign a senior group membership, it will unnecessarily necessitate a user to be explicit member of junior groups, though same attribute inheritance can be achieved through senior group membership only. Thus, junior group assignments would be redundant and may lead to multiple step revocations when the user is deleted from system. An approach similar to [23] could be proposed to resolve these shortcomings where users and user-groups are assigned to organizational structure based user or group pools. Organizational pool is a group of users or user-groups with similar goals. Entities are assigned to pools and then attribute values depending on the requirements. Pools are used in prerequisite conditions instead of attributes overcoming multiple pre-assignments for user and user-groups. A similar approach can also be followed in user to user-group assignment.

The object side of HGABAC has not been discussed but it seems to be a pragmatic approach to extend URA97 for object administration as well. Though user and object have different properties, for attribute assignments we believe it will not make any difference. For user and object group hierarchies, RRA97 [30] could be a base model to be worked upon.

5   Related Work

Several papers [4,7,8,22] have been published to associate attributes to encrypted data, policies and keys. A fine grained ABAC for data outsourcing system is discussed in [12]. Work in [28] proposes key distribution center and encryption using cloud owner attributes. RBAC has been extended to use attributes for role assignment [5,24]. [20] discussed approaches to relate roles and attributes while RB-RBAC [3] dynamically assign roles to users using attribute based rules. Role activation based on time constraints is explored in [17]. Mutable attributes in access decisions is discussed in [25]. Xin et al. [15] also presented an ABAC model with DAC, MAC and RBAC configurations. Lang et al. [21] proposed a model by extending XACML [1] and SAML [2] to support multi-policy ABAC. Using location attribute to secure social networks is discussed in [9]. [13] enforces separation of duty in ABAC systems. Automatic security risk adjustment based on attributes is presented in [18]. Yuan et al. [37] presented an authorization architecture and policy formulation for ABAC in web services. Wang et al. [36] provided framework using logic based programming to model ABAC. Preference based authorization [19] is proposed by extending XACML. Context based policy redeployment is discussed in [26]. [35] proposes an extension to assertion based policy language for federated systems. Administrative models include URA97 [31], PRA97 [29], ARBAC97 [30], GURA [14] and work by Crampton et al. [6].

6   Conclusion and Future Work

The paper presents first generalized URA97, called GURA$_G$, for HGABAC administration. Propositional logic conditions together with administrative roles are used to make administrative authorization decisions. GURA$_G$ has three sub-models: user attribute assignment (UAA), user-group attribute assignment (UGAA) and user to user-group assignment (UGA). The authorization relations in UAA and UGAA control addition and deletion of direct attributes from user and user-group. UGA governs assignment and removal of a user from user-groups based on the current membership (or non-membership) and attributes of user. Some extensions to GURA$_G$ have also been discussed. As GURA$_G$ proposes manual assignment of attribute values and user-groups to users, a potential foray can be to develop automated GURA$_G$ like model. An administrative model for group hierarchies and objects can also be a future prospect.

Acknowledgement. This research is partially supported by NSF Grants CNS-1111925 and CNS-1423481.

References

1. https://www.oasis-open.org/committees/tc_home.php?wg_abbrev=xacml
2. https://www.oasis-open.org/committees/tc_home.php?wg_abbrev=security
3. Al-Kahtani, M.A., Sandhu, R.: A model for attribute-based user-role assignment. In: Proceedings of IEEE ACSAC, pp. 353–362 (2002)
4. Bethencourt, J., Sahai, A., Waters, B.: Ciphertext-policy attribute-based encryption. In: Proceedings of IEEE Security and Privacy, pp. 321–334 (2007)
5. Chadwick, D.W., Otenko, A., Ball, E.: Role-based access control with X.509 attribute certificates. IEEE Internet Comput. **7**(2), 62–69 (2003)
6. Crampton, J., Loizou, G.: Administrative scope: a foundation for role-based administrative models. ACM TISSEC **6**(2), 201–231 (2003)
7. Emura, K., Miyaji, A., Nomura, A., Omote, K., Soshi, M.: A ciphertext-policy attribute-based encryption scheme with constant ciphertext length. In: Bao, F., Li, H., Wang, G. (eds.) ISPEC 2009. LNCS, vol. 5451, pp. 13–23. Springer, Heidelberg (2009)
8. Goyal, V., Pandey, O., Sahai, A., Waters, B.: Attribute-based encryption for fine-grained access control of encrypted data. In: Proceedings of ACM CCS, pp. 89–98 (2006)
9. Hsu, A.C., Ray, I.: Specification and enforcement of location-aware attribute-based access control for online social networks. In: Proceedings of ACM ABAC 2016, pp. 25–34 (2016)
10. Hu, V.C., Ferraiolo, D., Kuhn, R., Friedman, A.R., Lang, A.J., Cogdell, M.M., Schnitzer, A., Sandlin, K., Miller, R., Scarfone, K.: Guide to attribute based access control (ABAC) definition and considerations. NIST Special Publication 800–162 (2014)
11. Hu, V.C., Kuhn, D.R., Ferraiolo, D.F.: Attribute-based access control. IEEE Comput. **2**, 85–88 (2015)
12. Hur, J., Noh, D.K.: Attribute-based access control with efficient revocation in data outsourcing systems. IEEE TPDS **22**(7), 1214–1221 (2011)
13. Jha, S., Sural, S., Atluri, V., Vaidya, J.: Enforcing separation of duty in attribute based access control systems. In: Jajodia, S., et al. (eds.) ICISS 2015. LNCS, vol. 9478, pp. 61–78. Springer, Heidelberg (2015). doi:10.1007/978-3-319-26961-0_5
14. Jin, X., Krishnan, R., Sandhu, R.: A role-based administration model for attributes. In: Proceedings of ACM SRAS, pp. 7–12 (2012)
15. Jin, X., Krishnan, R., Sandhu, R.: A unified attribute-based access control model covering DAC, MAC and RBAC. In: Cuppens-Boulahia, N., Cuppens, F., Garcia-Alfaro, J. (eds.) DBSec 2012. LNCS, vol. 7371, pp. 41–55. Springer, Heidelberg (2012)
16. Jin, X., Krishnan, R., Sandhu, R.: Reachability analysis for role-based administration of attributes. In: Proceedings of ACM DIM, pp. 73–84. ACM (2013)
17. Joshi, J.B., Bertino, E., Latif, U., Ghafoor, A.: A generalized temporal role-based access control model. IEEE TKDE **17**(1), 4–23 (2005)
18. Kandala, S., Sandhu, R., Bhamidipati, V.: An attribute based framework for risk-adaptive access control models. In: Proceedings of IEEE ARES, pp. 236–241, August 2011

19. Kounga, G., Mont, M.C., Bramhall, P.: Extending XACML access control architecture for allowing preference-based authorisation. In: Katsikas, S., Lopez, J., Soriano, M. (eds.) TrustBus 2010. LNCS, vol. 6264, pp. 153–164. Springer, Heidelberg (2010)

20. Kuhn, D.R., Coyne, E.J., Weil, T.R.: Adding attributes to role-based access control. IEEE Comput. **43**(6), 79–81 (2010)

21. Lang, B., Foster, I., Siebenlist, F., Ananthakrishnan, R., Freeman, T.: A flexible attribute based access control method for grid computing. J. Grid Comput. **7**(2), 169–180 (2009)

22. Liang, K., Fang, L., Susilo, W., Wong, D.: A ciphertext-policy attribute-based proxy re-encryption with chosen-ciphertext security. In: Proceedings of IEEE INCoS, pp. 552–559 (2013)

23. Oh, S., Sandhu, R., Zhang, X.: An effective role administration model using organization structure. ACM TISSEC **9**(2), 113–137 (2006)

24. Oppliger, R., Pernul, G., Strauss, C.: Using attribute certificates to implement role-based authorization and access controls. In: Sicherheit in Informationssystemen, pp. 169–184 (2000)

25. Park, J., Sandhu, R.: The UCON ABC usage control model. ACM TISSEC **7**(1), 128–174 (2004)

26. Preda, S., Cuppens, F., Cuppens-Boulahia, N., Garcia-Alfaro, J., Toutain, L.: Dynamic deployment of context-aware access control policies for constrained security devices. J. Syst. Softw. **84**(7), 1144–1159 (2011)

27. Priebe, T., Dobmeier, W., Kamprath, N.: Supporting attribute-based access control with ontologies. In: Proceedings of IEEE ARES, p. 8 (2006)

28. Ruj, S., Nayak, A., Stojmenovic, I.: DACC: Distributed Access Control in Clouds. In: Proceedings of IEEE TrustCom, pp. 91–98 (2011)

29. Sandhu, R., Bhamidipati, V.: An Oracle implementation of the PRA97 model for permission-role assignment. In: Proceedings of ACM RBAC Workshop, pp. 13–21 (1998)

30. Sandhu, R., Bhamidipati, V., Munawer, Q.: The ARBAC97 model for role-based administration of roles. ACM TISSEC **2**(1), 105–135 (1999)

31. Sandhu, R.S., Bhamidipati, V.: The URA97 model for role-based user-role assignment. In: DBSec, pp. 262–275. Chapman & Hall, Ltd. (1998)

32. Sandhu, R.S., Coyne, E.J., Feinstein, H.L., Youman, C.E.: Role-based access control models. IEEE Comput. **2**, 38–47 (1996)

33. Servos, D., Osborn, S.L.: HGABAC: towards a formal model of hierarchical attribute-based access control. In: Cuppens, F., Garcia-Alfaro, J., Zincir Heywood, N., Fong, P.W.L. (eds.) FPS 2014. LNCS, vol. 8930, pp. 187–204. Springer, Heidelberg (2015)

34. Shen, H., Hong, F.: An attribute-based access control model for web services. In: Proceedings of IEEE PDCAT, pp. 74–79 (2006)

35. Squicciarini, A.C., Hintoglu, A.A., Bertino, E., Saygin, Y.: A privacy preserving assertion based policy language for federation systems. In: Proceedings of ACM SACMAT, pp. 51–60 (2007)

36. Wang, L., Wijesekera, D., Jajodia, S.: A logic-based framework for attribute based access control. In: Proceedings of ACM FMSE, pp. 45–55 (2004)

37. Yuan, E., Tong, J.: Attributed based access control (ABAC) for web services. In: Proceedings of IEEE ICWS (2005)

On the Relationship Between Finite Domain ABAM and PreUCON$_A$

Asma Alshehri$^{(\boxtimes)}$ and Ravi Sandhu$^{(\boxtimes)}$

Department of Computer Science, Institute for Cyber Security,
University of Texas at San Antonio,
One UTSA Circle, San Antonio 78249, USA
nmt366@my.utsa.edu, ravi.sandhu@utsa.edu

Abstract. Several access control models that use attributes have been proposed, although none so far is regarded as a definitive characterization of attribute-based access control (ABAC). Among these a recently proposed model is the attribute-based access matrix (ABAM) model [14] that extends the HRU model [4] by introducing attributes. In this paper we consider the finite case of ABAM, where the number of attributes is finite and the permissible values (i.e., domain) for each attribute is finite. Henceforth, we understand ABAM to mean finite ABAM. A separately developed model with finite attribute domains is PreUCON$_A$ [10], which is a sub-model of the usage control UCON model [9]. This paper explores the relationship between the expressive power of these two finite attribute domain models. Since the safety problem for HRU is undecidable it follows safety is also undecidable for ABAM, while it is known to be decidable for PreUCON$_A$ [10]. Hence ABAM cannot be reduced to PreUCON$_A$. We define a special case of ABAM called RL-ABAM2 and show that RL-ABAM2 and PreUCON$_A$ are equivalent in expressive power, but each has its own advantages. Finally, we propose a possible way to combine the advantages of these two models.

1 Introduction

Attribute-Based Access Control (ABAC) is a form of access control that has recently caught the interest of both academic and industry researchers. High-level definitions and descriptions of ABAC are generally accepted, but heretofore there has been no particular unified model or standardization of ABAC. The National Institute of Standards and Technology (NIST) recently described a high level access control model that uses attributes [5,6]. Jin et al. [7] have proposed a unified ABAC model that can be configured to the traditional access control models (i.e., DAC, MAC and RBAC). Researchers have also studied combining attributes with RBAC. Kuhn et al. [8] presented models that combine ABAC and RBAC in various ways, while Yong et al. [13] proposed extending the roles of the RBAC with attributes. Al-Kahtani et al. [1] introduced the notion of using attributes in user-role assignment of RBAC model. Chadwick et al. [3] describe the use of X.509 certificates to enforce RBAC. Bennett et al. [2] showed that

© Springer International Publishing AG 2016
J. Chen et al. (Eds.): NSS 2016, LNCS 9955, pp. 333–346, 2016.
DOI: 10.1007/978-3-319-46298-1_22

online social network policies can be cast in an ABAC framework. Thus there has been a tradition of research on combining or relating attributes to various access control models, old and new.

A novel approach to combining attributes with the access matrix was developed by Zhang et al. [14], who defined the attribute-based access matrix (ABAM) model by adding attributes to the classic HRU model [4]. In the HRU model each cell $[s_i, o_j]$ of the access matrix contains a set of rights that subject s_i can exercise over object o_j. In general, a subject is also an object while every object is not necessarily a subject. Subjects and objects are collectively called entities. ABAM additionally associates a set of attributes $ATT(o)$ with each entity o. A notable aspect of ABAM is that its commands not only test for and modify rights in access matrix cells like in HRU, but can further test for and modify attribute values. In the finite ABAM the set of attributes is finite and each attribute can take values from only a finite fixed set. Henceforth we understand ABAM to mean finite ABAM. The ABAM model is reviewed in Sect. 2.1.

The features of attribute testing and modification, also called attribute mutability, were adapted in ABAM [14] from the earlier UCON model [9]. UCON incorporates various additional features such as ongoing authorization and updates, as well as obligations and conditions. Here we focus on a sub-model of UCON called PreUCON$_A$ [9,10] where attribute testing and modification are carried out prior to allowing access. Similar to finite ABAM, in finite PreUCON$_A$ the set of attributes is finite and each attribute of an entity can only take on a finite set of permissible values. Henceforth, we understand PreUCON$_A$ to mean finite PreUCON$_A$. PreUCON$_A$ is reviewed in Sect. 2.2.

In this paper we investigate the theoretical relationship between ABAM and PreUCON$_A$. Our first observation is that ABAM is an extension of HRU and thereby inherits the undecidable safety results of HRU. On the other hand PreUCON$_A$ is known to have decidable safety analysis [10]. It follows that ABAM cannot be reduced to PreUCON$_A$. On the other hand, we show how PreUCON$_A$ can be reduced to ABAM (Sect. 3). This construction inspires us to define a restricted version of ABAM named RL-ABAM2, which stands for right-less ABAM with two parameters as will be explained (Sect. 4). We then prove that PreUCON$_A$ and RL-ABAM2 theoretically have equivalent expressive power (Sect. 5). Section 6 concludes the paper.

2   Background

In the following we respectively review the ABAM and PreUCON$_A$ models.

2.1   The ABAM Model

ABAM is defined in terms of access control matrix and commands in the tradition of HRU [4], TAM [11] and other access matrix based formal models. The basic components of the ABAM model are subjects and their attributes, objects and their attributes, access rights, access matrix, primitive operations and commands. These are explained below.

Subjects and Objects. Entities in ABAM are objects O and subjects S. Subjects are active entities that can invoke access requests or execute permissions on objects. Subjects can be the target of access requests so $S \subseteq O$. Objects that are not subjects are called pure objects. When an object is created, a unique identity (ID) recognized by the system is given to that object and cannot be changed after the creation. This ID is never reused.

Attributes and Attribute Tuples. In ABAM, the set of attributes G_{ATT} is attached to each entity. Each attribute is a variable with a specific data type. An attribute of an entity can be assigned an atomic value v_i, which comes from domain V_i for that attribute, or a set value $\{v_1, .., v_i, .., v_k\} \subseteq V_i$. Also, a *null* value will be assigned if the entity does not have that attribute. For entity o, the set of attributes of o come from $G_{ATT} = \{a_1, .., a_i, .., a_n\}$, and the value v_i of each attribute a_i is from the domain $V(a_i) = \{v_1, .., v_i, .., v_m\}$. The ordered set of attributes and domains $G_v = [a_1 : V(a_1), ... , a_i : V(a_i) , ... , a_n : V(a_n)]$ is a combination of G_{ATT} and $V(a_i)$. The attribute value tuple for entity o is $ATT(o) = (a_1 = v_1, ... , a_i = v_i, ... , a_n = v_n)$, where $v_i \in V_i$ or $v_i \subseteq V_i$ for $1 \le i \le n$. The result of updating a_i from v_i to v_i' changes $ATT(o)$ to $ATT'(o)$ $= (a_1 = v_1, ... , a_i = v_i', ... , a_n = v_n)$. An entity attribute is denoted as *ent.att* where *ent* refers to entity name and *att* is the attribute name.

	$s_1: ATT(s_1)$	$s_2: ATT(s_2)$	$o_1: ATT(o_1)$	$o_2: ATT(o_2)$
$s_1: ATT(s_1)$		{parent}	{read, write}	
$s_2: ATT(s_2)$			{read}	

Fig. 1. ABAM access matrix [14]

Rights and Access Matrix. An access matrix is a matrix with columns representing all objects (subjects and pure objects), and rows representing the set of all subjects. Each object in the columns and rows is associated with its attribute tuple. Access rights in the $[s_i, o_j]$ cell of the matrix specify the access that subject s_i has to object o_j. All entities in rows (subjects) can access other entities in the column (subjects and pure objects) by executing given access rights (e.g., read, write, execute). The set of all access rights is denoted by R and each cell $[s, o]$ is a subset of R. Figure 1 shows an example of an access matrix [14].

Attribute Predicates. A predicate P is a Boolean expression constructed using attributes and constants with appropriate relation symbols. There are two kinds of predicates. A unary predicate has one attribute variable and a constant, e.g. *Alice.credit* ≤ 100. A binary predicate has two different attribute variables, e.g. *s1.roles* $\subset$ *s2.roles*. Binary predicates can be built over attributes from the same entity or two different entities.

Primitive Operations. A primitive operation is the basic action that a subject can execute over an object which cause changes in the status of the access matrix. The primitive operations are defined as follows.

1. Enter r into [s,o]: Enters generic right r into cell [s, o] in the access matrix.
2. Delete r from [s,o]: Deletes generic right r from cell [s, o] in the access matrix.
3. Create subject s:ATT(s): Creates a new subject s with attribute tuple $ATT(s)$.
4. Destroy subject s: Removes subject s and its attribute tuple from the system.
5. Create object o:ATT(o): Creates a new object o with attribute tuple $ATT(o)$.
6. Destroy subject s: Removes object o and its attribute tuple from the system.
7. Update attribute ent.att $= v'$: Updates the attribute tuple $ATT(o)$ to $ATT'(o) = (a_1 = v_1, \ldots, a_i = v'_i, \ldots, a_n = v_n)$ where $v_i \in V_i$ and $v_i \neq v'_i$.

The first six are essentially similar to their counterparts in HRU, whereas the seventh is new to ABAM.

Commands. A command in ABAM involves three parts: parameters (entities with possibly new attribute values), conditions, and a sequence of primitive operations. ABAM commands allow primitive operation to be executed if the condition on existing rights is satisfied, as well as the specified predicates on attributes of the entities evaluate to true. The set of all commands is $G_\alpha = \{\alpha_1, \alpha_2, .., \alpha_h\}$. Each individual command is defined as follows.

Command $\alpha_i(X_1 : ATT(X_1), X_2 : ATT(X_2), .., X_k : ATT(X_k))$
if $r_1 \in [X_{s1}, X_{o1}] \wedge r_2 \in [X_{s2}, X_{o2}] \wedge ...r_m \in [X_{sm}, X_{om}] \wedge p_1 \wedge p_2 \wedge ...p_n$
then $op_1; op_2; ...; op_l$ **end**

The name of the command is α_i. $X_1, X_2, \ldots, X_k$ are subject or object parameters; $r_1, r_2, \ldots, r_m$ are generic rights; $s_1, s_2, \ldots, s_m$ and $o_1, o_2, \ldots, o_m$ are integers between 1 and k; $ATT(X_1), ATT(X_2), \ldots, ATT(X_k)$ specify new values of attributes for the respective entities (if any is updated by the command); $p_1, p_2, \ldots, p_n$ are predicates built over old or new attribute tuples of $X_1, X_2, \ldots, X_k$. The "if" part of the command is called the condition of α. Update operations can update an attribute from an old value $v_i \in V_i$ to a different new value $v'_i \in V_i$ or from an old value set $\{v_1, v_2, .., v_r\} \subseteq V_i$ to a new different subset of V_i. The operations $op_1; op_2; ...; op_l$ in the body of the command are executed sequentially and the entire command executes atomically. Each op_i consists of one of the seven primitive operations enumerated above.

Command Example. The following ABAM command enables the first subject to update attribute a_2 of the second subject to v'_i, provided the specified condition is true.

Command $Update(s_1 : ATT(s_1), s_2 : ATT(s_2))$
if $r_1 \in [X_{s1}, X_{s2}] \wedge s_1.a_1 = v_i \wedge s_1.a_2 \leq s_2.a_2$
then $update\ attribute\ s_2.a_2 = v'_i$ **end**

An ABAM command allows only conjunctive form of condition. In case of a disjunctive form of condition, we need to have one command for each component condition. For negated predicates, ABAM command accomodates it by simply defining a normal predicate for a negated one. Therefore, without loss of generality, we can consider the condition of ABAM command to be an arbitrary propositional logic formula.

2.2   The PreUCON$_A$ Model

We now describe the PreUCON$_A$ model.

Subject, Objects, Attributes, and Rights. The PreUCON$_A$ model has objects as resources and subjects as user processes. Similar to the ABAM model, subjects are a subset of objects. Each object has a finite set of attributes and a unique name. Object attributes can be accessed by using dot notation to associate object name with attribute name, as in $name_{object}.name_{attribute}$, e.g., o.security = 'high'. This model supports the dynamic creation and deletion of objects. The permission defined over an object is called a usage right.

Usage Control Scheme. There are three components of a usage control scheme U_Θ.

- an object schema OS_Δ,
- a set of usage rights UR $= \{r_1, r_2, ..., r_m\}$, and
- a set of usage control commands $\{UC_1, UC_2, ..., UC_n\}$.

The object schema OS_Δ is the combination of the attributes of objects and domains from which attribute values come. $OS_\Delta = (a_1 : \Omega_1, a_2 : \Omega_2, ..., a_n : \Omega_n)$, where each a_i is the name of an attribute, and Ω_i is the domain of a_i that has a finite set of values which can be assigned to the attribute a_i. Each object will have an ordered attribute value tuple $AVT = < v_1, v_2, ..., v_n >$, where n is the number of attributes in the object schema and each $v_i \in \Omega_i$. Attributes can be assigned to an atomic value or a set value. Also, attributes can be set to a default value from the domain at creation time.

Usage rights defines the rights r_i that can be granted by a usage control command. UR is finite. Giving a right to a subject to be executed on an object depends on the attribute value of subjects and objects as specified by usage control commands discussed below.

The usage control commands comprise a finite set of commands. Each command has a name that is linked with the authorized right r when executing this command. There are two formal parameters for each command, s and o. Subject s is the actor that seeks to access the target object o with right r. Also, commands can be either non-creating commands in which the object o exists before the execution of the command, or creating commands in which the object o is created during the execution of the command. The structure of creating and non-creating commands is shown in Table 1.

Table 1. PreUCON$_A$ commands

Non-Creating Commands	Creating Commands
Command-Name$_r$ (s, o)	**Command-Name$_r$ (s)**
PreCondition: $f_b(s,o) \rightarrow \{yes, no\}$;	**PreCondition:** $f_b(s) \rightarrow \{yes, no\}$;
PreUpdate:	**PreUpdate:** create o;
$\quad s.a_{i_1} := f_1, a_{i1}(s,o)$;	$\quad s.a_{i_1} := f_1, a_{i1}(s)$;
$\quad \ldots$	$\quad \ldots$
$\quad s.a_{i_p} := f_1, a_{ip}(s,o)$;	$\quad s.a_{i_p} := f_1, a_{ip}(s)$;
$\quad o.a_{j_1} := f_2, a_{j1}(s,o)$;	$\quad o.a_1 := f_2, a_1(s)$;
$\quad \ldots$	$\quad \ldots$
$\quad o.a_{j_q} := f_2, a_{jq}(s,o)$;	$\quad o.a_n := f_2, a_n(s)$;

In the PreCondition section, the Boolean function $f_b(s, o)$ takes the attribute values of s and o as input and returns true or false. In case of false, the command terminates without executing any updating or granting rights r, while in case of true, the update attribute operations in the PreUpdate section will be executed, and the operation permitted by right r is allowed. Zero or more of the attributes of the input s and o are updated individually to new values that are calculated from their old values, which existed before the command execution.

The structure of a creating command is mostly similar. The input parameter is only s, and the function $f_b(s)$ is a Boolean function that takes the attributes of s as an input and returns a *true* or *false* value. In case of *false*, the command terminates without executing any creating, updating, or granting rights r, while in the case of true, the command of creating an object should be executed before doing any updating of the object attributes. Zero or more of the attributes of the input s and new object o are updated individually to new values that are calculated from old values of s, which existed before the command execution.

3   Expressing PreUCON$_A$ IN ABAM

In this section we consider how to express PreUCON$_A$ in ABAM. The reductions we consider in this paper are state-matching reductions [12], which is the accepted formal criteria for theoretical equivalence of access control models.

There are two challenges in reducing PreUCON$_A$ to ABAM. First, the formulas in the PreCondition part of Table 1 are arbitrary computable Boolean functions, whereas ABAM only permits propositional logic formulas. Second, the update functions in the body of a PreUCON$_A$ command are arbitrary computable functions. In ABAM only specific new values are allowed in the update operation. However, due to the finite domain assumption these functions from PreUCON$_A$ can be computed for all possible attribute values of s and o, and the results can be "compiled" into multiple ABAM commands. We show how to do this for the body of the PreUCON$_A$ command. An analogous construction applies to the PreCondition part, but is not shown here for lack of space and straightforward similarity.

The attributes assignment formulas can be handled by having an ABAM command for each possible combination of attribute values. Consider an update operation $s.a_i := f(s, o)$. There are only a finite number of possible results for the value of $s.a_i$, depending on the value domain of a_i and whether a_i is atomic or set valued. For each possible value of a_i we can determine which input combinations of the attribute values of s and o will produce that result, if only by exhaustive enumeration of f for these combinations. The example below illustrates this idea more concretely.

The PreUCON$_A$ components are subjects (S), objects (O), usage rights (UR) and an object schema OS_Δ. To express PreUCON$_A$ in ABAM, we can define the following analogous ABAM components where the subscript ABAM is used to distinguish the ABAM component from the corresponding PreUCON$_A$ component.

- $O_{ABAM} = O$ and $S_{ABAM} = S$
- $R_{ABAM} = UR = \{ur_1, ur_2, ..., ur_k\}$
- M_{ABAM} with a row for every S_{ABAM} with its attribute tuple, and a column for every O_{ABAM} with its attribute tuple.
- $[s_i, o_j] = \phi$, where $s_i \in S_{ABAM}$, and $o_i \in O_{ABAM}$
- $G_{ATT} = \{a_1, .., a_i, .., a_n\}$
- $G_V = OS_\Delta = [a_1 : \Omega_1, a_2 : \Omega_2, ..., a_n : \Omega_n]$.

We illustrate the construction of ABAM commands by the following example. Let the object schema $OS_\Delta = [a_1 : \{1, 2\}, a_2 : \{2, 3\}, a_3 : \{1, 2, 3\}]$ and usage rights $UR = \{update\}$. The initial values for s and o attributes are $[1,2,3]$ and $[2,3,1]$ respectively for $[a_1, a_2, a_3]$. Command$_{update}$ is as follows:

Command$_{update}$ (s, o)
PreCondition: $s.a_1 \leq 2 \vee o.a_2 \leq 3$
PreUpdate: $o.a_3 := max(s.a_3, o.a_3)$;

Since $s.a_3 = 3$ and $o.a_3 = 1$, the new value of $o.a_3$ is 3 which is the maximum of two values. The corresponding ABAM components of the PreUCON$_A$ schema will be as follows.

- $O_{ABAM} = O$ and $S_{ABAM} = S$
- $R_{ABAM} = UR = \{update\}$
- M_{ABAM} with a row for every S_{ABAM} with its attribute tuple, and a column for every O_{ABAM} with its attribute tuple.
- $[s_i, o_j] = \phi$, where $s_i \in S_{ABAM}$, and $o_i \in O_{ABAM}$
- $G_{ATT} = \{a_1, a_2, a_3\}$
- $G_V = OS_\Delta = [a_1 : \{1, 2\}, a_2 : \{2, 3\}, a_3 : \{1, 2, 3\}]$.

The possible ABAM commands for PreUCON$_A$ command$_{update}$ are given in Table 2. Since attribute a_3 has only three possible values we need three ABAM commands. This construction easily extends to multiple attributes. It is evident will need a large number of commands for each PreUCON$_A$ command that uses such formulas.

Table 2. Possible ABAM commands

Updating to value 1	Updating to value 2	Updating to value 3
Command $update(s{:}ATT(s), o{:}ATT(o))$	**Command** $update(s{:}ATT(s), o{:}ATT(o))$	**Command** $update(s{:}ATT(s), o{:}ATT(o))$
if $s.a_1 \leq 2 \lor o.a_2 \leq 3 \land (s.a_3 = 1 \lor o.a_3 = 1)$	**if** $s.a_1 \leq 2 \lor o.a_2 \leq 3 \land ((s.a_3 = 1 \land o.a_3 = 2) \lor (s.a_3 = 2 \land o.a_3 = 1))$	**if** $s.a_1 \leq 2 \lor o.a_2 \leq 3 \land ((s.a_3 = 1 \land o.a_3 = 3) \lor (s.a_3 = 2 \land o.a_3 = 3) \lor (s.a_3 = 3 \land o.a_3 = 1) \lor (s.a_3 = 3 \land o.a_3 = 2) \lor (s.a_3 = 3 \land o.a_3 = 3))$
update attribute $o.a_3 = 1$	update attribute $o.a_3 = 2$	update attribute $o.a_3 = 3$
enter $update$ into $[s, o]$;	enter $update$ into $[s, o]$;	enter $update$ into $[s, o]$;
delete $update$ from $[s, o]$;	delete $update$ from $[s, o]$;	delete $update$ from $[s, o]$;
end	**end**	**end**

4   Right-Less ABAM with Two Parameters (RL-ABAM2)

PreUCON$_A$ has the ability to grant a non-persistent right for each command. In other words, by the end of any command execution, the given right is taken back from the actor. In contrast, an ABAM command has the power of granting one or more rights to the actor, maintaining the given rights in the corresponding cell of the actor, and permitting two or more parameters (more targets) for each command. These ABAM features will cause difficulties for expressing ABAM in PreUCON$_A$. Moreover, unrestricted use of rights in ABAM will result in undecidable safety as in HRU [4], whereas PreUCON$_A$ has decidable safety [10]. Therefore, in general it is not possible to reduce ABAM to PreUCON$_A$. These considerations lead us to focus on a restricted form of ABAM inspired by the construction in the previous section.

4.1   RL-ABAM2 Definition

RL-ABAM2 is the reduced model of ABAM, where RL indicates "right less" and the two denotes the number of parameters required in a command. Object, subject, attributes, attribute tuples, rights, access matrix, predicates, and primitive operations are all the same as in ABAM. However, an RL-ABAM2 command has more limited characteristics than an ABAM command in terms of number of parameters, the if statement section, and the existence of rights. In RL-ABAM2, a command is defined as follows:

Command $\alpha_i(X_1 : ATT(X_1), X_2 : ATT(X_2))$
if $p_1 \land p_2 \land ...p_n$
then
$op_1; op_2; ...; op_l$;
enter r_1 into $[X_1, X2]$;
delete r_1 from $[X_1, X2]$;
...

enter r_k into $[X_1, X2]$;
delete r_k from $[X_1, X2]$;
end

In the above RL-ABAM2 command, the number of parameters is only two. Moreover, the rights check part is eliminated in the "if" statement section, so the predicates P are the only part that appears. The body of the command will have all kinds of operations, but every right entered into any cell needs to be deleted prior to the end of the command. In general, the RL-ABAM2 model is a special case of ABAM model.

4.2   Expressing PreUCON$_A$ in RL-ABAM2

In Sect. 3, we discussed how to express the PreUCON$_A$ in the ABAM. In fact, the result of expressing PreUCON$_A$ commands to ABAM commands is RL-ABAM2 commands which have two parameters, no check for rights, and a delete right operation for each entered right. Thus, we can state that Sect. 3 is already expressing PreUCON$_A$ in RL-ABAM2.

5   Expressing RL-ABAM2 in PreUCON$_A$

In this section we show how to reduce RL-ABAM2 to PreUCON$_A$.

5.1   General Construction

Given an RL-ABAM2 schema with the following components: objects $O_{RL-ABAM2}$, subjects $S_{RL-ABAM2}$, access rights $R_{RL-ABAM2} = \{r_1, .., r_k\}$, attributes tuple $ATT(o_i) = < a_1 = v_1, .., a_n = v_n >$, where $o_i \in O_{RL-ABAM2}$, and a list of all attributes which are linked with their domains $G - V_{\{RL-ABAM2\}} = [a_1{:}V(a_1), \, ... \, , a_i{:}V(a_i), \, ... \, , a_n{:}V(a_n)]$, each RL-ABAM2 commands will have the following structure:

Command α_i $(s_i : ATT(s_i), o_j : ATT(o_j))$
if $p_1 \wedge p_2 \wedge ...p_n$
then
create object $X2 : ATT(X2)$;
update attribute $s_i.a_k = v_i'$;
update attribute $o_i.a_s = v_j'$;
enter r_i into $[s_i, o_j]$;
delete r_i from $[s_i.o_j]$;
end

This structure for RL-ABAM2 commands can be assumed without loss of generality. The create operation (if present) comes first, followed by update operations, and at the end, all enter and delete operations. For each parameter, zero or more attributes of $o_j \in O_{RL-ABAM2}$ or $s_i \in S_{RL-ABAM2}$ can be updated from v_i to v_i', as well as one or more rights $r_i \in (R_{RL-ABAM2})$ can be entered into cell $[s_i, o_j]$ and deleted.

The corresponding PreUCON$_A$ components of the RL-ABAM2 schema are as follows:

- Entity in PreUCON$_A$ are objects $O_{Pre\_UCON_A}$
- $O_{Pre\_UCON_A} = O_{RL-ABAM2}$
- $S_{Pre\_UCON_A} = S_{RL-ABAM2}$
- $UR_{Pre\_UCON_A} = R_{RL-ABAM2}$
- $OS_\Delta = G - V_{\{RL-ABAM2\}}$

As discussed above, RL-ABAM2 has the power of entering and deleting many rights in one command, while a PreUCON$_A$ command grants a single right. In the case of executing many operations over rights in the body of RL-ABAM2, applying a singleton PreUCON$_A$ command can only cover one of the RL-ABAM2 rights. Consequently, multiple PreUCON$_A$ commands are required to cover RL-ABAM2 rights. To preserve atomicity of the RL-ABAM2 command specific attributes are added as well as a special object for synchronization. Some parts of the corresponding PreUCON$_A$ components of the RL-ABAM2 schema are extended as follows:

- Entity in PreUCON$_A$ are objects $O_{Pre\_UCON_A}$
- $O_{Pre\_UCON_A} = O_{RL-ABAM2} \cup O_{lock}$
- $S_{Pre\_UCON_A} = S_{RL-ABAM2}$
- $UR_{Pre\_UCON_A} = Command - R_{RL-ABAM2}$
- $Auxiliary - OS_\Delta = [lock{:}V(lock),\ type{:}V(type),\ R\_to\_select{:}V(R\_to\_select),\ position{:}V(position)]$
- $OS_\Delta = G - V_{\{RL-ABAM2\}} \cup Auxiliary - OS_\Delta$

The domain for each of these additional attributes is as follows: $V(lock)$ = {0, 1}, $V(type)$ = {ordinary, lock}, $V(R\_to\_select)$ = $UR_{Pre\_UCON_A}$, and $V(position)$ = {1,2}. The initial values for the proposed attributes are set as follows: For all $o \in O_{RL-ABAM2}$: o.type = ordinary, o.lock = 0, o.position = ϕ, and o.R_to_select = ϕ. For O_lock: O_lock.type = lock, O_lock.lock = 1, O_lock.position = ϕ, O_lock.R_to_select = ϕ.

To apply a RL-ABAM2 command in PreUCON$_A$ commands, a sequence of steps is introduced as follows:

1- Give a lock to the first parameter of the RL-ABAM2 command
2- Decide the second parameter of the Rl-ABAM2 command
3- Implement a sequence of PreUCON$_A$ commands
4- Release the lock from the first parameter (actor) of the RL-ABAM2 command.

To implement the first step, a command called get_lock will be executed with the first parameter of RL-ABAM2 s_i and the special object O_lock:

Command get_lock $(s_i : ATT(s_i), O\_lock : ATT(O\_lock))$
if $s_i.type = ordinary \land O\_lock.type = lock \land s_i.lock = 0 \land O\_lock.lock = 1$
then
update attribute $s_i.lock = 1$;
update attribute $O\_lock.lock = 0$;
update attribute $s_i.position = 1$;
update attribute $s_i.R\_to\_select = UR_{Pre\_UCON_A}$
end

Then, the actor needs to decide the second parameter, and the below command will take care of the second step:

Command $pick\_target(s_i : ATT(s_i), o_j : ATT(o_j))$
if $s_i.type = ordinary \land s_i.lock = 1 \land o_j.lock = ordinary \land s_i.position = 1 \land$
$o_j.position = \phi$
then
update attribute $o_j.position = 2$;
end

The third step contains an ordered series of PreUCON$_A$ commands which depend on the number of the operation over rights in the body of an RL-ABAM2 command ($UR_{Pre\_UCON_A} = \{r_1, r_2, ..., r_k\}$). The structure of the ordered series of commands is as follows:

> **Command**$-r_1(s_i, o_j)$
> **PreCondition:** $f_b(s_i, o_j) \land$
> $s_i.R\_to\_select = UR_{Pre\_UCON_A} \land s_i.lock = 1$
> $\land s_i.position = 1 \land o_j.position = 2$;
> **PreUpdate:**
> $create\ o$;
> $s_i.a_k = v_i'$;
> $o_j.a_s = v_j'$;
> $s_i.R\_to\_select = UR_{Pre\_UCON_A} - \{r_1\}$

> **Command**$-r_2(s_i, o_j)$
> **PreCondition:** $s_i.R\_to\_select = UR_{Pre\_UCON_A} - \{r_1\} \land s_i.lock = 1$
> $\land s_i.position = 1 \land o_j.position = 2$;
> **PreUpdate:**
> $s_i.R\_to\_select = UR_{Pre\_UCON_A} - \{r_1, r_2\}$

....

....

Command$-r_k(s_i, o_j)$
    PreCondition: $s_i.R\_to\_select = \{r_k\} \wedge s_i.lock = 1 \wedge s_i.position = 1$
                          $\wedge\ o_j.position = 2;$

    PreUpdate:

            $o_j.position = \phi$
            $s_i.R\_to\_select = \phi$

Finally, the user can release the lock and give it back to the special object O_lock by using the following command:

Command $release\_lock$ $(s_i : ATT(s_i), O\_lock : ATT(O\_lock))$
if $s_i.type = ordinary \wedge O\_lock.type = lock \wedge s_i.lock = 1 \wedge O\_lock.lock = 0 \wedge$
$s_i.R\_to\_select = \phi$
then
update attribute $s_i.lock = 0$;
update attribute $O\_lock.lock = 1$;
update attribute $s_i.position = \phi$; **end**

5.2 An Example

The following example shows components of RL-ABAM2 schema. The command add-survey allows contributors to add a new health survey to their list. The contributors are required to be diabetics and never participated before. Moreover, the add-survey command permits contributors to post answers to questions and to close the survey after finishing. By the end of the survey, post and close rights will be taken away. The RL-ABAM2 schema is as follows: $(R_{RL-ABAM2}) = \{post, close\}$, $G - V_{\{RL-ABAM2\}} = [disease:\{diabetic, epileptic\}, X:\{0, 1\}]$. Furthermore, RL-ABAM2 command will have the following structure:

Command $add - survey$ $(s : ATT(s), o : ATT(o))$
if $s.disease = diabetic \wedge s.X = 0$
then
create object $o : ATT(o)$;
update attribute $o.disease = diabetes$;
update attribute $X = 1$;
enter $post$ into $[s, o]$;
delete $post$ from $[s, o]$;
enter $close$ into $[s, o]$;
delete $close$ from $[s, o]$; **end**

The corresponding PreUCON$_A$ components of the RL-ABAM2 schema will be as follows:

- $O_{Pre\_UCON_A} = O_{RL-ABAM2} \cup O_{lock}$
- $S_{Pre\_UCON_A} = S_{RL-ABAM2}$

- $UR_{Pre\_UCON_A} = \{post, close\}$
- $Auxiliary - OS_\Delta = [lock:\{0,1\}, \quad type:\{ordinary, lock\},$
  $R\_to\_select:\{post, close\}, position:\{1,2\}]$
- $OS_\Delta = [\text{disease}:\{\text{diabetic, dpileptic}\}, X:\{0,1\}] \cup Auxiliary - OS_\Delta$

$V(lock) = \{0, 1\}$, $V(type) = \{ordinary, lock\}$, $V(R\_to\_select) = UR_{Pre\_UCON_A}$, and $V(position) = \{1,2\}$.

The initial values for the Auxiliary attributes are set as above, and to apply a RL-ABAM2 command in PreUCON$_A$ commands, the four sequence steps will be implemented as follows:

1- Give a lock to the first parameter of the RL-ABAM2 command by using the *get_lock* command.
2- Decide the second parameter of the Rl-ABAM2 command by using the *pick_target* command.
3- Implement a sequence of PreUCON$_A$ commands as follows:

Command$_{post}(s, o)$
  PreCondition: $s.disease = disease \wedge s.X = 0 \wedge$
  $s.R\_to\_select = \{post, close\} \wedge s.lock = 1 \wedge$
  $s.position = 1 \wedge o.position = 2;$

  PreUpdate:
  $create\ o;$
  $o.disease = diabetes;$
  $s.X = 1;$
  $s.R\_to\_select = \{close\};$

Command$_{close}(s, o)$
  PreCondition: $s.R\_to\_select = \{close\} \wedge s.lock = 1 \wedge$
  $s.position = 1 \wedge o.position = 2;$

  PreUpdate:
  $o.position = \phi$
  $s.R\_to\_select = \phi$

4- Release the lock from the first parameter (actor) of the RL-ABAM2 command by using *release_lock* command.

6 Conclusion

In this paper we have formally demonstrated the equivalence of PreUCON$_A$ and RL-ABAM2, which are two finite domain ABAC models. We have argued that ABAM being a superset of HRU cannot be reduced to PreUCON$_A$, because of the latter's decidable safety result. Hence, equivalence of PreUCON$_A$ can only be established to some proper sub-model of ABAM such as RL-ABAM2. Our constructions suggest the power of using formulas in PreUCON$_A$, absence of which in ABAM leads to having to an explosion of ABAM commands in the PreUCON$_A$ to ABAM reduction. Conversely, the ability to activate multiple rights in a single

RL-ABAM2 command leads to multiple PreUCON$_A$ commands in the ABAM to PreUCON$_A$ reduction. These features could be combined in a more usable model. Finally, the study of ABAM indicates that a safe application of access rights could be based on the following principles. Firstly, do not use rights in the if part of commands. Secondly, some rights could be left behind by commands so their next use is more efficient. Our comparative study of PreUCON$_A$ and ABAM suggests there is a meaningful place for access matrix rights, even as access control research and practice is tending towards attributes.

Acknowledgement. This research is partially supported by NSF Grant CNS-1111925 and CNS-1423481.

References

1. Al-Kahtani, M.A., Sandhu, R.: Rule-based RBAC with negative authorization. In: 20th IEEE ACSAC, pp. 405–415 (2004)
2. Bennett, P., Ray, I., France, R.: Modeling of online social network policies using an attribute-based access control framework. In: Jajodia, S., Mazumdar, C. (eds.) ICISS 2015. LNCS, vol. 9478, pp. 79–97. Springer, Heidelberg (2015). doi:10.1007/978-3-319-26961-0_6
3. Chadwick, D.W., Otenko, A., Ball, E.: Role-based access control with X. 509 attribute certificates. IEEE Internet Comput. **7**(2), 62–69 (2003)
4. Harrison, M.A., Ruzzo, W.L., Ullman, J.D.: Protection in operating systems. Commun. ACM **19**(8), 461–471 (1976)
5. Hu, V.C., Ferraiolo, D., Kuhn, R., Friedman, A.R., Lang, A.J., Cogdell, M.M., Schnitzer, A., Sandlin, K., Miller, R., Scarfone, K.: Guide to attribute based access control (ABAC) definition and considerations. NIST Spec. Publ. **800**, 162 (2014)
6. Hu, V.C., Kuhn, D.R., Ferraiolo, D.F.: Attribute-based access control. IEEE Comput. **48**(2), 85–88 (2015)
7. Jin, X., Krishnan, R., Sandhu, R.: A unified attribute-based access control model covering DAC, MAC and RBAC. In: Cuppens-Boulahia, N., Cuppens, F., Garcia-Alfaro, J. (eds.) DBSec 2012. LNCS, vol. 7371, pp. 41–55. Springer, Heidelberg (2012)
8. Kuhn, D.R., Coyne, E.J., Weil, T.R.: Adding attributes to role-based access control. IEEE Comput. **43**(6), 79–81 (2010)
9. Park, J., Sandhu, R.: The UCON ABC usage control model. ACM Trans. Inf. Syst. Secur. (TISSEC) **7**(8), 128–174 (2004)
10. Rajkumar, P.V., Sandhu, R.: Safety decidability for pre-authorization usage control with finite attribute domains. IEEE Trans. Dependable Secure Comput. no. 1, p. 1, PrePrints PrePrints. doi:10.1109/TDSC.2015.2427834
11. Sandhu, R.S.: The typed access matrix model. In: Research in Security and Privacy, pp. 122–136 (1992)
12. Tripunitara, M.V., Li, N.: A theory for comparing the expressive power of access control models. J. Comput. Secur. **15**(2), 231–272 (2007)
13. Yong, J., Bertino, E., Roberts, M.T.D.: Extended RBAC with role attributes. In: PACIS 2006 Proceedings, p. 8 (2006)
14. Zhang, X., Li, Y., Nalla, D.: An attribute-based access matrix model. In: The 2005 ACM Symposium on Applied Computing, pp. 359–363 (2005)

Security Protocols

MD-$\mathcal{VC}_{Matrix}$: An Efficient Scheme for Publicly Verifiable Computation of Outsourced Matrix Multiplication

Gang Sheng[1]($\boxtimes$), Chunming Tang[1], Wei Gao[2], and Ying Yin[3]

[1] College of Mathematics and Information Science,
Guangzhou University, Guangzhou 510006, China
`shenggang@neusoft.edu.cn`
[2] School of Mathematics and Statistics Science,
Ludong University, Yantai 264025, China
[3] College of Computer Science and Engineering,
Northeastern University, Shenyang 110004, China

Abstract. Cloud service provider that is equipped with tremendous resources enables the terminals with constrained resources to perform outsourced query or computation on large scale data. Security challenges are always the research hotspots in the outsourced computation community. In this paper, we investigate the problem of publicly verifiable outsourced matrix multiplication. However, in the state-of-the-art scheme, a large number of computationally expensive operations are adopted to achieve the goal of public verification. Thus, the state-of-the-art scheme works inefficiently actually due to the fact that most of the time is spent on the verification-related computing. To lower the verification-related time cost, we propose an efficient scheme for public verification of outsourced matrix multiplication. The two-dimensional matrix is transformed into a one-dimensional vector, which retains the computing ability and is used as the substitute for subsequent verification-related work. The security analysis demonstrates the security of the proposed outsourcing scheme, and the performance analysis shows the running efficiency of the scheme.

Keywords: Cloud computing · Outsourced computation · Public verification · Matrix multiplication

1 Introduction

Cloud computing offers a new choice for the entity including the company, the organization and the individual. With cloud computing, there is no need for the entity to deploy high performance hardware, and thus the trivial but indispensable routine maintenance work of hardware and system will decrease greatly. The burdensome task of computation or data storage can be outsourced to the cloud service provider that is equipped with tremendous resources. Benefiting

© Springer International Publishing AG 2016
J. Chen et al. (Eds.): NSS 2016, LNCS 9955, pp. 349–362, 2016.
DOI: 10.1007/978-3-319-46298-1_23

from the cloud service, the entity can control the computation or manage the data with resource-constrained terminal such as a personal computer, or even a mobile phone. Almost all of the work previously done locally can be outsourced to the cloud, such as data storage, database management, scientific computation, data mining, etc. The cloud service enables the entity to work with high efficiency and low cost.

The research on outsourced computation started in the scientific computation community in the 1990s, and with the advent of cloud computing, computation outsourcing nowadays becomes a hot research topic. The focus of the outsourced computation research concentrates mainly on the security challenges, among which two have attracted intense attention. The first security challenge is the data privacy. As the request data and the obtained result often contain sensitive information, the service provider in the outsourced computation research community is generally assumed to be unreliable. Security measures, such as data disguise, problem transformation, and homomorphic encryption, etc., should be done on the data and the result to protect them from being detected by the cloud service provider. The second security challenge is the result verification. As the cloud service provider may be lazy or error may occur in the algorithm, wrong result may be returned to the service requester. The service requester should have some mechanism to check whether or not the result is correct.

Matrix, as a fundamental mathematical primitive, has been extensively utilized in the scientific and engineering fields. In the outsourced computation research community, the existing research on secure matrix computation now covers matrix multiplication, matrix inversion, matrix determinant, systems of linear equations, etc. For the problem of publicly verifiable outsourcing of matrix multiplication, many efforts have been done [1–3]. Fiore et al. proposed a scheme $\mathcal{VC}_{Matrix}$ for publicly verifiable matrix multiplication in the amortized model [1], where new pseudo-random functions with closed-form efficiency were developed to handle matrix multiplication. Jia et al. developed an efficient scheme ESO-LMM [3], where the security requirements in terms of unforgeability of proof and privacy protection of outsourced data are achieved. Li et al. proposed an efficient scheme [2], where only an element is computed for the verification key in the ProbGen stage and the efficiency is improved correspondingly.

However, in light of our observation most of the time is wasted by the verification-related computation in the state-of-the-art scheme. A large number of computationally expensive operations are adopted in each step of the outsourced computation. In the KeyGen step, each element $w_{i,j}$ of the verification matrix W is computed accordingly by the element $m_{i,j}$ of the matrix M, whose time complexity is $O(n^2)$. In the subsequent Compute step, the verification-related computing works with the same time complexity $O(n^2)$. Thus, the publicly verifiable scheme works inefficiency due to the adoption of a large number of computationally expensive operations for verification-related computing.

In this paper, we propose an efficient scheme MD-$\mathcal{VC}_{Matrix}$ for publicly verifiable matrix multiplication. To lower the time cost of the verification-related computation, matrix digest(MD) is constructed. By MD, the two-dimensional matrix is transformed into a one-dimensional vector, which retains the computing ability and is used as the substitute for subsequent verification-related work. The time complexity of verification-related work in the two algorithms **KeyGen** and **Compute** reduces dramatically from $O(n^2)$ to $O(n)$.

Our main contributions of this paper are:

- We construct matrix digest for the original matrix as the substitute for the verification-related work in each algorithm of the outsourced computation.
- We propose an efficient scheme MD-$\mathcal{VC}_{Matrix}$ for publicly verifiable computation of outsourced matrix multiplication.
- We show the security of the proposed scheme.
- We give theoretic analysis and experiment results, which demonstrate the efficiency of the proposed scheme.

The rest of the paper is organized as follows. The models and definitions are given in Sect. 2. We propose a secure scheme for the outsourced matrix multiplication and analyze the correctness in Sect. 3. In Sect. 4, we analyze the security of the proposed scheme. The performance analysis is given in Sect. 5 including theoretic analysis and experiment results. Section 6 overviews the related works. Finally, we conclude the paper in Sect. 7.

2 Models and Definitions

2.1 System Model and Security Model

We study the problem of publicly verifiable computation of outsourced matrix multiplication in this paper. The system model is illustrated in Fig. 1.

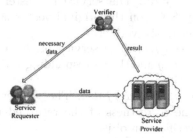

Fig. 1. System model.

There are three parties involved in the system model, i.e., the service provider, the service requester, and the verifier. The service provider is a specific cloud service provider deployed with abundant computing resources. The service requester with constrained resources owns a large-scale matrix M and a vector x, and outsources the operation of $M \cdot x$ to the service provider. The verifier is a third party verifier, which performs public verification with necessary verification data on the result from the service provider. The overall working process of outsourced computation is given as follows:

- The service requester performs computation on M, x to obtain necessary data for later verification, and sends part of the obtained data to the verifier.
- At the same time, the service provider sends M, x and related data to the service provider.
- Upon receiving the request from the service requester, the service provider performs matrix multiplication to get the result and the related operation to get the verification object, and sends the obtained result and the verification object to the verifier.
- With the data from the service requester and the service provider, the verifier checks whether or not the returned result is correct. If the result is correct, the result is returned to the service requester.

In the given system model, the service requester is assumed honest, and the service provider and the verifier is assumed semi-honest. The security issue of public verification is taken into consideration, and privacy preservation is not considered in this paper.

2.2   Definitions

Definition 1. *A secure scheme $\mathcal{VC}$ for publicly verifiable computation of outsourced matrix multiplication is a four-tuple (**KeyGen, ProbGen, Compute, Verify**) [1,4].*

- **KeyGen**$(1^\lambda, M) \to (SK_M, EK_M, PK_M)$: The service requester invokes the algorithm KeyGen with the security parameter λ on the original matrix M to get the secret key SK_M, public key PK_M, and EK_M for later verification. PK_M is sent to the verifier.
- **ProbGen**$(SK_M, x) \to VK_x$: The service requester invokes the algorithm ProbGen with the key SK_M on the original vector x to get the verification key VK_x, which is sent to the verifier.
- **Compute**$(EK_M, x) \to (y, v)$: The service provider invokes the algorithm Compute to get the result y and the corresponding verification object v, which are both sent to the verifier.
- **Verify**$(PK_M, VK_x, y, v) \to true/false$: The verifier invokes the algorithm Verify to determine the correctness of the returned result y with the keys PK_M, VK_x and the verification object v.

Definition 2. *Matrix Digest is a vector generated by a matrix together with chosen parameters.*

By the characteristics of matrix, a matrix can be viewed as a set of column vectors. Then, for a matrix $A \in \mathbb{Z}^{n \times d}$, we have $A = (a_1, \ldots, a_d)$, where for $i = 1$ to d, $a_i \in \mathbb{Z}^n$ is a column vector.

Then, for a matrix $A \in \mathbb{Z}^{n \times d}$ and a vector $p = (p_1, \ldots, p_n) \in \mathbb{Z}^n$, the matrix digest m of A can be obtained by

$$m = p \cdot A \in \mathbb{Z}^d. \tag{1}$$

By (1), the matrix digest has the following properties:

- **deterministic.** Given a matrix, the matrix digest is determined only that the parameters, i.e. the vector p, are determined.
- **computable.** The obtained matrix digest is essentially a vector, which has all the properties of vector and can be applied to the operation of vectors.
- **irreversible.** The computation of matrix digest is a one-way mapping. Given a matrix digest, the matrix and the parameters cannot be detected. Even if the matrix digest and the parameters are given simultaneously, the matrix cannot be detected, too.

2.3 Security Preliminaries

Let q be a big prime, and G_1, G_2, G_T be multiplicative cyclic groups of the same order q, and g_1, g_2 be a generator of group G_1, G_2, respectively.

Definition 3. *Unsymmetrical Bilinear Paring.*
Suppose G_1, G_2, G_T are equipped with a pairing $e : G_1 \times G_2 = G_T$, which should satisfy the conditions described as follows:

- **bilinear.** $\forall a, b \in \mathbb{Z}_q$, *equation $e(g_1^a, g_2^b) = e(g_1, g_2)^{ab}$ holds.*
- **non-degenerate.** *For any $g \in G_1$, if $\forall h \in G_2$, equation $e(g, h) = 1$ holds, $g = 1$.*
- **computable.** *The operations in groups G_1, G_2, G_T, and operations of bilinear map e are solvable in PPT.*

Definition 4. *co-Computational Diffie-Hellman problem (co-CDH).*
The advantage of solving the co-CDH by an adversary $\mathcal{A}$ is defined as

$$\mathcal{ADV}_{\mathcal{A}}^{cdh}(\lambda) = \Pr[(q, g_1, g_2, g_1^a, g_2^b) = g_1^{ab}],$$

where $a, b \in \mathbb{Z}_q$.
Then we say the co-CDH assumption ϵ-holds in G_1, G_2, if for every PPT algorithm $\mathcal{A}$ we have $\mathcal{ADV}_{\mathcal{A}}^{cdh} \leq \epsilon$.

Definition 5. *External Diffie-Hellman problem (XDH).*
The advantage of $\mathcal{ADV}_{\mathcal{A}}^{cdh}(\lambda)$ of deciding the XDH problem by an adversary is defined as

$$\mathcal{ADV}_{\mathcal{A}}^{cdh}(\lambda) = |\Pr[\mathcal{A}(q, g_1, g_2, g_1^a, g_2^b, g_1^{ab})] - \Pr[\mathcal{A}(q, g_1, g_2, g_1^a, g_2^b, g_1^c)]| \leq \epsilon,$$

where $a, b, c \in \mathbb{Z}_q$.
We say the XDH assumption ϵ-holds over G_1, G_2, G_T, if for every PPT algorithm $\mathcal{A}$ we have $\mathcal{ADV}_{\mathcal{A}}^{xdh} \leq \epsilon$.

For any verifiable computation scheme $\mathcal{VC}$, we follow Fiore et al. to define the following experiment [1].

Definition 6. *Experiment $Exp_{\mathcal{A}}^{PubVer}[\mathcal{VC}, f, \lambda]$.*

$(SK_f, EK_f, Pk_f) \leftarrow KeyGen(1^\lambda, f)$

For $i = 1$ *to* q

$\quad x_i \leftarrow \mathcal{A}(EK_f, \hat{x}_1, VK_{x,1}, \dots, \hat{x}_{i-1}, PK_{x,i-1}, VK_{x,i-1})$

$\quad (\hat{x}_i, PK_{x,i}, VK_{x,i}) \leftarrow ProbGen(f_\lambda, PK_f, E, \hat{M}, SK_f, x_i)$

$x^* \leftarrow \mathcal{A}(EK_f, \hat{x}_1, PK_{x,1}, VK_{x,1}, \dots, \hat{x}_q, PK_{x,q}, VK_{x,q})$

$(\hat{x}^*, PK_{\hat{x}^*}, VK_{\hat{x}^*}) \leftarrow ProbGen(f_\lambda, PK_f, E, \hat{E}, SK_f, \hat{x}^*)$

$REs' \leftarrow \mathcal{A}(EK_f, \hat{x}_1, PK_{x,1}, VK_{x,1}, \dots, \hat{x}_q, PK_{x,q}, VK_{x,q}, \hat{x}^*, PK_{\hat{x}^*}, SK_{\hat{x}^*})$

$\hat{y}' = Verify(PK_{\hat{x}^*}, VK_{\hat{x}^*}, Res')$

$y' \leftarrow Decryption(\hat{y}', H(\hat{E}'))$

IF $\hat{y}' \neq \bot$ *and* $y' \neq f(x^*)$ *output 1, otherwise output 0.*

In our scheme x, y are matrixes, x is in the domain of function f (where $f = M \cdot x$) is a function which will be delegated).

For any $\lambda \in \mathcal{N}$, we define the advantage of an adversary $\mathcal{A}$ making at most $q = poly(\lambda)$ queries in the above experiment against $\mathcal{VC}$ as:

$$Adv_{\mathcal{A}}^{PubVer}[\mathcal{VC}, f, q, \lambda] = \Pr[Exp_{\mathcal{A}}^{PubVer}[\mathcal{VC}, f, \lambda] = 1].$$

A verifiable computation scheme $\mathcal{VC}$ is secure for $\mathcal{F}$ if for any $f \in \mathcal{F}$ and any PPT adversary $\mathcal{A}$ it holds that $Adv_{\mathcal{A}}^{PubVer}[\mathcal{VC}, f, q, \lambda]$ is negligible.

3   MD-$\mathcal{VC}_{Matrix}$: Proposed Scheme

We mainly focus on the security issue of public verification of outsourced matrix multiplication in this paper. For the purpose of privacy preservation, an alternative would be that the original matrices can be hidden by multiplying sparse matrices, which is utilized and analyzed in [5,6], etc. In this section, we propose a scheme $MD - \mathcal{VC}_{Matrix}$ for public verification of outsourced matrix multiplication, which works efficiently by using the matrix digest for the verification-related computation.

3.1   Scheme

The main trick is to construct matrix digest for the original matrix, which converts the two-dimensional matrix into a one-dimensional vector. The one-dimensional vector is used as the substitute for the verification-related computation. The computationally expensive computation of exponentiation is then decreased dramatically.

Let p be a large prime, and $n \geq 1, d \geq 1$ be integers. For a matrix $M \in \mathbb{Z}_p^{n \times d}$ and a vector $\boldsymbol{x} \in \mathbb{Z}_p^d$, the operation of $\boldsymbol{y} = M \cdot \boldsymbol{x}$ is to be obtained, which is outsourced to the service provider. The verifier should have the ability to publicly check the correctness of the result $\boldsymbol{y}$.

The details of our proposed scheme MD-$\mathcal{VC}_{Matrix}$ are given as follows.

KeyGen$(1^\lambda, M)$. Let $M \in \mathbb{Z}_p^{n \times d}$ be a matrix. The service requester generates a description of bilinear groups $(p, g_1, g_2, \mathbb{G}_1, \mathbb{G}_2, \mathbb{G}_T, e) \leftarrow \mathcal{G}(1^\lambda)$ with the security parameter λ, a random vector $\boldsymbol{p} \in \mathbb{Z}_p^n$, an integer $\alpha \in \mathbb{Z}_p$, and a secret key $K = (k_0, k_1, \dots, k_d)$, where for $i = 0$ to d, $k_i \in \mathbb{Z}_p$.

The service requester computes $PK_p, \boldsymbol{m}, \boldsymbol{w}$ as follows:

- $PK_p = (PK_1, \ldots, PK_n)$, where $PK_i = e(g_1^{\alpha p_i}, g_2)$.
- $\boldsymbol{m} = \boldsymbol{p} \cdot M$.
- $\boldsymbol{w} = (w_1, \ldots, w_d)$, where $w_i = g_1^{\alpha m_i} \cdot F_K(i)$.

Here, $F_K(i)$ is an algebraic pseudorandom function, which is adopted in [2] and is computed as follows:
$$F_K(i) = g_1^{k_0 k_i},$$
where $i = 1, \ldots, d$.

Output $SK_M = K$, $EK_M = (M, \boldsymbol{w})$, and $PK_M = PK_p$.

ProbGen$(SK_M, \boldsymbol{x})$. Let $\boldsymbol{x} = (x_1, \ldots, x_d) \in \mathbb{Z}_p^d$ be the input. The service requester computes $\rho_x = \prod_{i=1}^d F_K(i)^{x_i}$, and defines the verification key $VK_x = e(\rho_x, g_2)$. Output $(\boldsymbol{x}, VK_x)$.

Compute$(EK_M, \boldsymbol{x})$. The service provider computes the result $\boldsymbol{y} = M \cdot \boldsymbol{x}$, and the verification object $v = \prod_{i=1}^d w_i^{x_i}$ as the proof. Output $(\boldsymbol{y}, v)$.

Verify$(PK_M, VK_x, \boldsymbol{y}, v)$. The verifier checks if

$$e(v, g_2) = \prod_{i=1}^n (PK_i)^{y_i} \cdot VK_x. \tag{2}$$

If the equation holds then output $\boldsymbol{y}$, otherwise output $\bot$.

3.2 Correctness Analysis

Theorem 1. *The proposed algorithm Verify is correct.*

Proof. By the two algorithms KeyGen and Compute, we have $\boldsymbol{m} = \boldsymbol{p} \cdot M$ and $\boldsymbol{y} = M \cdot \boldsymbol{x}$, respectively.

Then, $\boldsymbol{m} \cdot \boldsymbol{x} = \boldsymbol{p} \cdot \boldsymbol{y}$. Thus, we have

$$\sum_{i=1}^d m_i x_i = \sum_{i=1}^n p_i y_i. \tag{3}$$

Then, in the Stage **Verify**, when the verifier checks if $e(v, g_2) = \prod_{i=1}^d (PK_i)^{y_i} \cdot VK_x$, we have

$$e(v, g_2) = e(\prod_{i=1}^d w_i^{x_i}, g_2)$$

$$= e(\prod_{i=1}^d g_1^{a m_i x_i}, g_2) \cdot e(\prod_{i=1}^d F_K(i)^{x_i}, g_2)$$

$$= e(g_1^{\sum_{i=1}^d a m_i x_i}, g_2) \cdot VK_x$$

$$= \prod_{i=1}^n e(g_1^{a p_i y_i}), g_2) \cdot VK_x$$

$$= \prod_{i=1}^n (PK_i)^{y_i} \cdot VK_x$$

Thus, the algorithm Verify is correct.

4   Security Analysis

In this section, we follow the framework of [1,2] to give the security analysis of our proposed scheme MD-$\mathcal{VC}_{Matrix}$ for publicly verifiable computation of outsourced matrix multiplication.

Theorem 2. *If $\mathcal{G}$ is such that co-CDH assumption ϵ_{cdh}-holds, and F is ϵ_{prf}-secure, then any PPT adversary $\mathcal{A}$ making at most $q = poly(\lambda)$ queries has advantage*

$$ADV_{\mathcal{A}}^{PubVer}[MD - \mathcal{VC}_{Matrix}, f, q, \lambda] \leq \epsilon_{cdh} + \epsilon_{prf}.$$

Then we define the following games, where $G_i(\mathcal{A})$ is the output of Game i run by the adversary $\mathcal{A}$.

Game 0. this game is the same as $Exp_{\mathcal{A}}^{PubVer}[MD - \mathcal{VC}_{Matrix}, f, q, \lambda]$.

Game 1. this game is similar to Game 0, except that $PK_M = (e(g_1^{ap_1}, g_2), \ldots, e(g_1^{ap_n}, g_2))$ in the evaluation of the **KeyGen** algorithm.

Game 2. this game is similar to Game 1, except that the verification matrix $\boldsymbol{w} = (w_1, \ldots, w_d)$, where $w_i = g_1^{am_i} \cdot R_i$.

The proof of this theorem is based on Games defined above, and is obtained by proving the following claims.

Claim 1. $\Pr[G_0(\mathcal{A}) = 1] = \Pr[G_1(\mathcal{A}) = 1]$

Proof. The only difference between the two games is the computation of public key in the **ProbGen** algorithm. However, due to the security bilinear map, the probability of the adversary winning in Game 1, i.e., $\Pr[G_1(\mathcal{A}) = 1]$, remains the same.

Claim 2. $|\Pr[G_1(\mathcal{A}) = 1] - \Pr[G_2(\mathcal{A}) = 1]| \leq \epsilon_{prf}$

Proof. The difference between Game 2 and Game 1 is that we replace each pseudorandom function FK with a random value of group R_i. Obviously, for any adversary $\mathcal{A}$, the difference between the possibility of winning two Games accounts on the possibility of winning the pseudorandom function. Thus, the possibility of winning Game must be lower than winning a pseudorandom function.

Claim 3. $\Pr[G_2(\mathcal{A}) = 1] \leq \epsilon_{cdh}$

Proof. Assume by contradiction that there exists a PPT adversary $\mathcal{A}$ such that the probability of $\mathcal{A}$ winning in Game 2 is a non-negligible function ϵ. Then, we show that we can build an efficient algorithm $\mathcal{B}$ which uses $\mathcal{A}$ to solve the co-CDH problem with probability $\epsilon_{cdh} \geq \epsilon$.

$\mathcal{B}$ takes as input a group description $(q, g_1, g_2, G_1, G_2, G_T, e)$ and 2 random elements g_1^a, g_2^b and proceeds as following steps.

First, $\mathcal{B}$ randomly chooses $\boldsymbol{p} = (p_1, \ldots, p_n) \in \mathbb{Z}_p^n$, $\mathcal{B}$ randomly chooses $\boldsymbol{w} = (w_i)_d \leftarrow G_1$ for $i = 1, \ldots, d$, sets $EK_M = (M, \boldsymbol{w})$. Let $PK_M = (e(g_1^a, g_2^b)^{p_1}, \ldots, e(g_1^a, g_2^b)^{p_n})$. Then, $e(F_K(i), g_2) = e(w_i, g_2)/e(g_1^a, g_2^b)^{m_i}$. Obviously, the public keys, evaluation keys and $e(F_K(i), g_2)$ are distributed as same as in Game 2.

Next, $\mathcal{B}$ runs $\mathcal{A}(PK_M, EK_M, e(F_K(i), g_2))$ and answers its queries as follows. Let $\boldsymbol{x}$ be the queried value. $\mathcal{B}$ computes

$$VK_x = e(\prod_{i=1}^{d} F_K(i)^{x_i}, g_2) = \prod_{i=1}^{d} e(F_K(i), g_2)^{x_i} = \prod_{i=1}^{d} (e(w_i, g_2)/e(g_1^a, g_2^b)^{m_i})^{x_i}$$

and returns it to $\mathcal{A}$. By the bilinear property of $e(\cdot, \cdot)$, this computation of VK_x is equivalent to the one in Game 2.

Finally, let $\hat{\sigma}_y = (\hat{y}, \hat{v})$ be the output of $\mathcal{A}$ at the the end of the game, such that for some $\boldsymbol{x}^*$ chosen by $\mathcal{A}$ it holds $Verify(PK_M, VK_{x^*}, \hat{\sigma}_y) = \hat{y}$, $\hat{y} \neq \perp$ and $y \neq M \cdot \boldsymbol{x}^*$. By verification, this means that

$$e(\hat{v}, g_2) = \prod_{i=1}^{n} PK_i^{\hat{y}_i} \cdot VK_{x^*} = \prod_{i=1}^{n} e(g_1^a, g_2^b)^{p_i \hat{y}_i} \cdot VK_{x^*} \tag{4}$$

Let $y = M \cdot \boldsymbol{x}^*$ be the correct output of the computation. The, by correctness it also holds:

$$e(v, g_2) = \prod_{i=1}^{n} e(g_1^a, g_2^b)^{p_i y_i} \cdot VK_{x^*} \tag{5}$$

So, dividing the two verification Eqs. (4),(5), we obtain that

$$e(\hat{v}/v, g_2) = \prod_{i=1}^{n} e(g_1^{ab}, g_2)^{\sum_{i=1}^{d} p_i(\hat{y}_i - y_i)} \tag{6}$$

Because $\hat{y}_i \neq y_i$ for $i = 1$ to n, $\sum_{i=1}^{d} p_i(\hat{y}_i - y_i)$ in (6) is generally not 0. Thus,

$$g_1^{ab} = (\hat{v}/v)^{(\sum_{i=1}^{d} p_i(\hat{y}_i - y_i))^{-1}} \bmod q$$

Therefore, if $\mathcal{A}$ wins in Game 2 with probability ϵ_{cdh}, then $\mathcal{B}$ solves co-CDH with the same probability.

5   Performance Analysis

In this section, we evaluate the performances of our proposed scheme in terms of computation overhead by theoretic analysis and experimental result.

5.1   Theoretic Analysis

Due to the difference of magnitude between the operations in $\mathbb{Z}$ and $\mathbb{G}$, it is difficult to differentiate $\mathcal{VC}_{Matrix}$ and MD-$\mathcal{VC}_{Matrix}$ by the traditional notation O for the analysis of time complexity. In this section, we give two notations O_I, O_E to make as clear as possible comparisons. O_I denotes the time complexity of operations in $\mathbb{Z}$ including integer addition, multiplication, etc. O_E denotes the time complexity of operations in $\mathbb{G}_1, \mathbb{G}_2, \mathbb{G}_T$ including multiplication, exponentiation, bilinear map, etc.

Let n denote the line number of matrix M and d denote the column number of matrix M. The analysis result is given in Table 1.

Table 1. Comparison of computation overhead

Algorithm	$\mathcal{VC}_{Matrix}$	MD-$\mathcal{VC}_{Matrix}$
KeyGen	$O_E(nd)$	$O_I(nd)+O_E(d)$
ProbGen	$O_E(n+d)$	$O_E(d)$
Compute	$O_I(nd)+O_E(nd)$	$O_I(nd)+O_E(d)$
Verify	$O_E(n)$	$O_E(n)$

It is obvious that MD-$\mathcal{VC}_{Matrix}$ is superior to $\mathcal{VC}_{Matrix}$ in the algorithms **ProbGen** and **Compute**. The computation overhead of MD-$\mathcal{VC}_{Matrix}$ for the verification-related computation is $O_E(d)$ in the two algorithms. The computation overhead of $\mathcal{VC}_{Matrix}$ for the verification-related computation is $O_E(n+d)$ and $O_E(nd)$ respectively in the two algorithms. The computation overhead for verification-related computation of $\mathcal{VC}_{Matrix}$ and MD-$\mathcal{VC}_{Matrix}$ in the algorithm **KeyGen** is $O_E(d)$ and $O_E(nd)$ respectively, but $O_I(nd)$ is added for computing the matrix digest in MD-$\mathcal{VC}_{Matrix}$. Thus, it is ambiguous to differentiate $\mathcal{VC}_{Matrix}$ and MD-$\mathcal{VC}_{Matrix}$ using O_I and O_E. The computation overhead of the two schemes is same in the algorithm **Verify**, i.e. $O_E(n)$.

5.2   Experiment Results

We now discuss the running efficiency in practice of our proposed scheme for publicly verifiable outsourced matrix multiplication with experiments. We implement the proposed algorithms including **ProbGen**, **KeyGen** and **Compute**. The computation overhead of the two schemes in the algorithm **Verify** is same according to the theoretic analysis, which will not be discussed by experiment. The algorithms are implemented with Java program language and JPBC library is used [7]. The experiments are conducted on a laptop with an Intel Core i5 CPU running at 2.50 GHz with 4 GB RAM. Each experiment is executed 100 times, and the average time cost is obtained. The comparison results are shown in Fig. 2. For clarity, d is set to be equal to n in Fig. 2. The horizontal axis represents the scale of the data, and the vertical axis represents the running time of the algorithm.

It is ambiguous by theoretic analysis to compare the algorithm **KeyGen** owning to the different magnitude of operations in $\mathbb{Z}$ and $\mathbb{G}$. The computation overhead of computing matrix digest is $O(nd)$ in MD-$\mathcal{VC}_{Matrix}$, but the computation is performed in $\mathbb{Z}$, which works with high efficiency. The computation in $\mathbb{G}$ is computationally expensive including exponentiation, bilinear map, etc. The experiment result of the algorithm **KeyGen** is shown in Fig. 2(a), which demonstrates the efficiency of MD-$\mathcal{VC}_{Matrix}$ is superior to that of $\mathcal{VC}_{Matrix}$.

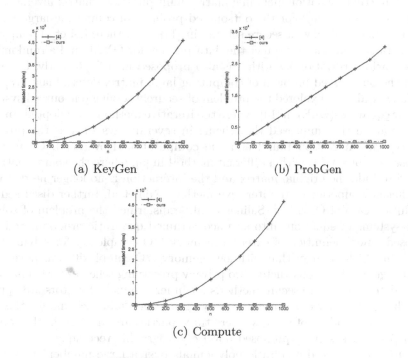

(a) KeyGen   (b) ProbGen

(c) Compute

Fig. 2. Comparison of two schemes

The experiment results of the algorithm **ProbGen** and **Compute** are shown in Fig. 2(b) and (c) respectively. The running efficiency of MD-$\mathcal{VC}_{Matrix}$ is superior to that of $\mathcal{VC}_{Matrix}$, which demonstrates the consistency with the the theoretic analysis.

6   Related Works

Atallah et al. first investigated the problem of outsourced scientific computations and gave an outsourcing computation framework [8]. Benjamin et al. gave private and cheating-free protocols for outsourcing expensive algebraic computations to two remote servers [9]. Combined with the Shamir's secret share scheme, Mohassel presented multiple non-interactive authorization protocols for private and verifiable linear algebra calculation [10]. Atallah et al. proposed the improved outsourcing protocols for secure outsourced matrix multiplication(OMM) [8]. With the techniques of bilinear map and random number, Fiore et al. presented a publicly verifiable protocol for OMM [1].

Sparse matrix plays an important role in the research community of OMM, with which the time cost of matrix multiplication decreases from $O(n^3)$ to $O(n^2)$. Matrix multiplication using sparse matrix is used as the fundamental technique. Hu et al. designed secure and efficient outsourcing protocols for outsourced matrix calculation including matrix multiplication, matrix inversion and matrix determinant [5]. For the outsourced problem of computing large matrix inversion, Lei et al. gave a secure scheme in [11]. And then, Lei et al. employed matrix transformation to protect the data privacy for OMM, and a randomized Monte Carlo verification algorithm is also proposed in [12]. Recently, Lei et al. solved the outsourced problem of computing large matrix determinant [13].

Wang et al. first explored the problem of securely solving outsourced systems of linear equations(OLE) in [14], where the iterative method was adopted. In [15], Chen et al. further improved the scheme in several ways such as the protocol security, the interaction round and the computational overhead. Chen et al. proposed to solve OLE with a different method in [6], where the sparse matrix is applied to hide the original matrix and the interaction is no longer needed with the efficiency superior to the iterative method. Nie et al. further discussed the no-solution case of OLE [16]. Salinas et al. transformed the problem of solving linear systems of equations into an unconstrained quadratic program, and first proposed a new definition of external memory I/O complexity for solving OLE in [17], in which an algorithm with low memory I/O complexity was developed.

Murugesan et al. constructed two privacy preserving schemes for similar document detection, where secure methods for inner product of vectors are applied [18]. Sheng et al. gave a privacy preserving and verifiable scheme for the outsourced inner product of vectors where three parties are involved in the computation [19]. Backes et al. proposed novel cryptographic techniques to solve the problem of outsourced quadratic polynomials over a large number of variables [20]. Wang et al. first proposed and solved the problem of outsourced linear programming in [21], where data privacy preservation and result verification are both accomplished. Xiang et al. studied the problem of privacy preserving face recognition in [22], where the large computation task is chosen to outsource to the cloud server. In [23], Liu et al. focused on the secure computation problem of privacy preserving trajectory similarity. Jung et al. provided a solution for privacy-preserving sum and product calculation respectively without secure channel [24].

7   Conclusion

In this paper, we study the problem of outsourced large-scale matrix multiplication in the model where three parties are involved. We propose a secure and efficient scheme, which aims at the security goal of both data privacy preservation and result correctness verification simultaneously. Concretely according to the algebraic properties of matrix and matrix multiplication, we generate the matrix digests for the original matrices involved in the matrix multiplication calculation, with which the service requester can determine whether or not the returned result matrix is correct, and the result verification can be done without the original matrices. The data privacy is also preserved by multiplying sparse matrices. The users and the server both work with high efficiency because only basic numerical operation is used including addition and multiplication, and no computationally expensive calculations used. In the future work, we plan to extend the proposed secure scheme for outsourced matrix multiplication to be publicly verifiable.

Acknowledgments. This work is supported in part by the National Natural Science Foundation of China under Grant No. 11271226,61272182, the National Research Foundation for the Doctoral Program of Higher Education of China under Grant No. 20134410110003, High Level Talents Project of Guangdong, Guangdong Provincial Natural Science Foundation under Grant No. S2012010009950, the Project of Department of Education of Guangdong Province under Grant No. 2013KJ-CX0146, the Natural Science Foundation of Bureau of Education of Guangzhou under Grant No. 2012A004, the basic research major projects of Department of Education of Guangdong Province under Grant No. 2004KZDXM044, and the Guangzhou Zhujiang Science and Technology Future Fellow Fund under Grant No. 2012J2200094.

References

1. Fiore, D., Gennaro, R.: Publicly verifiable delegation of large polynomials and matrix computations, with applications. In: 19th ACM Conference on Computer and Communications Security, pp. 501–512. ACM, New York (2012)
2. Li, H., Zhang, S., Luan, T.H., Ren, H., Dai, Y., Zhou, L.: Enabling efficient publicly verifiable outsourcing computation for matrix multiplication. In: International Telecommunication Networks and Applications Conference (ITNAC), pp. 44–50. IEEE Press, New York (2015)
3. Jia, K., Li, H., Liu, D., Yu, S.: Enabling efficient and secure outsourcing of large matrix multiplications. In: IEEE Global Communications Conference (GLOBECOM), pp. 1–6. IEEE Press, New York (2015)
4. Gennaro, R., Gentry, C., Parno, B.: Non-interactive verifiable computing: outsourcing computation to untrusted workers. In: Rabin, T. (ed.) CRYPTO 2010. LNCS, vol. 6223, pp. 465–482. Springer, Heidelberg (2010). doi:10.1007/978-3-642-14623-7_25
5. Hu, X., Pei, D., Tang, C., Wong, D.: Verifiable and secure outsourcing of matrix calculation and its application. Scientia inica (Informationis) **43**(7), 842–852 (2013)
6. Chen, X., Huang, X., Li, J., Ma, J., Lou, W., Wong, D.: New algorithms for secure outsourcing of large-scale systems of linear equations. IEEE Trans. Inf. Forensics Secur. **10**(1), 69–78 (2015)
7. Caro, D., Iovino, V.: jPBC: java pairing based cryptography. In: IEEE Symposium on Computers and Communications, pp. 850–855. IEEE Press, New York (2011)

8. Atallah, M., Frikken, K.: Securely outsourcing linear algebra computations. In: 5th ACM Symposium on Information, Computer and Communications Security, pp. 48–59. ACM Press, New York (2010)
9. Benjamin, D., Atallah, M.J.: Private and cheating-free outsourcing of algebraic computations. In: Sixth Annual Conference on Privacy, Security and Trust (PST 2008), pp. 240–245. IEEE Press, New York (2008)
10. Mohassel, P.: Efficient and secure delegation of linear algebra. Technical report, Cryptology ePrint Archive, Report 2011/605 (2011)
11. Lei, X., Liao, X., Huang, T., Li, H., Hu, C.: Outsourcing large matrix inversion computation to a public cloud. IEEE Trans. Cloud Comput. 1(1), 1 (2013). http://ieeexplore.ieee.org/xpls/abs_all.jsp?arnumber=6613485&tag=1
12. Lei, X., Liao, X., Huang, T., Heriniaina, F.: Achieving security, robust cheating resistance, and high-efficiency for outsourcing large matrix multiplication computation to a malicious cloud. Inf. Sci. 280, 205–217 (2014)
13. Lei, X., Liao, X., Huang, T., Li, H.: Cloud computing service: the case of large matrix determinant computation. IEEE Trans. Serv. Comput. 8(5), 688–700 (2015)
14. Wang, C., Ren, K., Wang, J., Wang, Q.: Harnessing the cloud for securely outsourcing large-scale systems of linear equations. IEEE Trans. Parallel Distrib. Syst. 24(6), 1172–1181 (2013)
15. Chen, F., Xiang, T., Yang, Y.: Privacy-preserving and verifiable protocols for scientific computation outsourcing to the cloud. J. Parallel Distrib. Comput. 74(3), 2141–2151 (2014)
16. Nie, H., Ma, H., Wang, J., Chen, X.: Verifiable algorithm for secure outsourcing of systems of linear equations in the case of no solution. In: Ninth International Conference on Broadband and Wireless Computing, Communication and Applications, pp. 572–577. IEEE Press, New York (2014)
17. Salinas, S., Luo, C., Chen, X., Li, P.: Efficient secure outsourcing of large-scale linear systems of equations. In: IEEE INFOCOM 2015, pp. 1035–1043. IEEE Press, New York (2015)
18. Murugesan, M., Jiang, W., Clifton, C., Si, L., Vaidya, J.: Efficient privacy-preserving similar document detection. VLDB J. 19(4), 457–475 (2010)
19. Sheng, G., Wen, T., Guo, Q., Yin, Y.: Secure scalar product computation of vectors in cloud computing. J. Northeast. Univ. 34(6), 786–791 (2013)
20. Backes, M., Fiore, D., Reischuk, R.M.: Verifiable delegation of computation on outsourced data. In: 2013 ACM SIGSAC Conference on Computer & Communications Security, pp. 863–874. ACM, New York (2013)
21. Wang, C., Ren, K., Wang, J.: Secure practical outsourcing of linear programming in cloud computing. In: IEEE INFOCOM 2011, pp. 820–828. IEEE Press, New York (2011)
22. Xiang, C., Tang, C., Cai, Y., Xu, Q.: Privacy-preserving face recognition with outsourced computation. Soft Comput. 20(9), 3735–3744 (2016)
23. Liu, A., Zhengy, K., Liz, L., Liu, G., Zhao, L., Zhou, X.: Efficient secure similarity computation on encrypted trajectory data. In: IEEE 31st International Conference on Data Engineering, pp. 66–77. IEEE Press, New York (2015)
24. Jung, T., Mao, X., Li, X.Y., Tang, S.J., Gong, W., Zhang, L.: Privacy-preserving data aggregation without secure channel: multivariate polynomial evaluation. In: IEEE INFOCOM 2013, pp. 2634–2642. IEEE Press, New York (2013)

Expressive Rating Scheme by Signatures with Predications on Ratees

Hiroaki Anada[1]($\boxtimes$), Sushmita Ruj[2], and Kouichi Sakurai[3,4]

[1] Department of Information Security, University of Nagasaki,
W408, 1-1-1, Manabino, Nagayo-cho,
Nishisonogi-gun, Nagasaki 851-2195, Japan
anada@sun.ac.jp

[2] R.C. Bose Center for Cryptology and Security, Indian Statistical Institute,
Kolkata, No 921, S.N. Bose Bhavan, 203 B.T. Road, Kolkata 700108, India
sush@isical.ac.in

[3] Department of Informatics, Kyushu University,
W2-712, 744 Motooka, Nishi-ku, Fukuoka 819-0395, Japan
sakurai@inf.kyushu-u.ac.jp

[4] Institute of Systems, Information Technologies and Nanotechnologies,
7F, Fukuoka SRP Center Bldg. 2-1-22, Momochihama, Sawara-ku,
Fukuoka 814-0001, Japan

Abstract. Reputation boards are popular tools because of their useful information of products for consumers. In this paper, we propose a rating scheme for the reputation boards. The feature of our rating scheme is that it enables users to rate not only products but also their providers expressively by using digital signatures with predications on ratees. First, we define a syntax of such an expressive rating scheme. Then, we provide a generic conversion of a cryptographic primitive called an attribute-based signature scheme (ABS) into an expressive rating scheme. Using a boolean formula on attributes of ratees, signatures with predications on ratees are generated, which we call expressive ratings. Public linkability of ABS is effectively used to prohibit double ratings. Also, employing an ABS scheme of the Fiat-Shamir type, we construct a concrete efficient expressive rating scheme.

Keywords: Reputation · Rating · Attribute · Predication · Digital signature

1 Introduction

Reputation is fundamental phenomenon in our world, even on the Internet. A typical example can be seen as a reputation board in a website for transactions such as "amazon.com", where products by providers are rated by consumers. Later, the system manager merges those individual ratings into a reputation on a product by using a reputation function which is typically a statistical procedure.

Such reputation boards have been explored widely from the paradigm to realistic problems (for example, [3,9,11]). Especially, from the cryptographic point

© Springer International Publishing AG 2016
J. Chen et al. (Eds.): NSS 2016, LNCS 9955, pp. 363–379, 2016.
DOI: 10.1007/978-3-319-46298-1_24

of view, reputation boards have been studied with interest [3,14,18] because of the required functionality such as being unforgeable, anonymous, prohibiting double rating, and being traceable. In cryptographic constructions, the central building block is a group signature scheme [4–6,8].

A rating scheme for a reputation board consists of one authority called the system manager (like "amazon.com"), and providers and consumers. A provider's product is purchased by a consumer through a transaction and used. The system manager is assumed to be honest, and controls registrations of both providers of products and consumers. In this paper, we also assume that providers are honest because users of a product by a provider rate it and it is critical for activity of the provider. On the other hand, we care the registration of consumers, and simply call a consumer a user.

Here the above cryptographic requirements arise [7,13,19]; first, a rating by impersonation should be prevented. Hence unforgeability of ratings is a requirement. Second, when a user rates a product, he should be anonymous to providers and other users. That is, for honest ratings, a rating scheme must have anonymity of raters. Third, double ratings on a single product should be detected. Publicly linkability of ratings by a single user is useful for the detection. Fourth, when a user acts illegitimately, he should be traced by the system manager; that is, traceability is needed for realistic operation.

In the usage of a reputation board, a rater looks at a product he bought from various points of view such as price, cost, functionality, quality, reliability, warranty, etc. Currently the above properties are treated separately despite the dependence among those properties. For example, price and cost should not be separated when a user purchases a product repeatedly. In the case a rating can be expressed as "price or cost is three stars ($\star\star\star$)". Moreover, it is often the case for users (consumers) to need reputation not on individual products but on a provider of them. For example, it will be useful if it exists statements of the following type: "The provider's products are either two stars on price and three stars on reliability or three stars on price and four stars on reliability, while they have five stars on warranty". These examples show that there is a need for users (raters) to evaluate products or providers (ratees) by ratings of predication-type over attributes of ratees, which we call *expressive* ratings.

1.1 Our Contribution

In this paper, keeping this functionality in mind, we will provide an expressive rating scheme in which a rating accompanies a predication over attributes of ratees.

The first contribution is to define a syntax of an expressive rating scheme over attributes of ratees. In previous works of Liu et al. [15] and Guo et al. [13], rating schemes based on attributes of raters have been proposed. In contrast to those works [13,15], our emphasis is on ratees' attributes, and it enables an expressive rating not only on, for example, products, but also on providers of products. Note that treating attributes of *raters* functions as checking expressive *rights* of voters, whereas treating attributes of *ratees* functions as describing *predication* of voting. For example, our rating scheme is capable to rate a provider in the above way; in other words, "the price balances with quality, while the warranty is always good".

The second contribution is to provide a generic conversion of an attribute-based signature (ABS) scheme into an expressive rating scheme. This conversion is not trivial because in the construction of the conversion, public linkability of ratings generated by a single user must be attained (carefully) from an ABS scheme with attribute privacy. In the construction, a tag is chosen at random, and the name of a product or a provider is concatenated with the tag to form a message. The message is signed by ABS, and a rating is output as a concatenation of the signature with the tag. Hence, none of the name, the tag and the signature can be forged.

The third contribution is to provide an efficient expressive rating scheme in an ad hoc manner. Using an ABS scheme of the Fiat-Shamir type, we construct an expressive rating scheme concretely. In the construction, public linkability of the ABS scheme is used as opposed the above generic conversion from ABS schemes with attribute privacy; that is, no publicly linkable. The resulting scheme has a feature of pairing-free. The (different but comparable) constructions in the previous works [13,15] employ the ABS scheme of Maji et al. [17] which needs more computational amount due to pairing-computations

The fourth contribution is to display a use-case of our rating scheme to a reputation board. There is a system manager and he makes both *quantitative* attributes (stars: $\star \cdots \star$) and *qualitative* attributes (*price, reliability,* ...: $at_1, at_2, \ldots$) available to users, publicly. Then the system manager issues a rating ticket to each user for a user to rate a product or a provider. Technically, the rating ticket is a private key for the above quantitative attributes. The public linkability (of two ratings issued by a single user) of our rating scheme enables the reputation board to restrain double rating.

1.2 Related Work

Nakanishi and Funabiki [19] gave a simple efficient anonymous reputation system. In their reputation system, users are seller and buyers, and seller anonymity is achieved by employing a group signature scheme. Blömer et al. [7] gave an anonymous and publicly linkable reputation system by employing a group signature scheme. Guo et al. [13] gave a definition and construction of a privacy-preserving attribute-based reputation system. Their system differs from our work at the point that, in their scheme, attribute are of raters, not of ratees. Liu et al. [15] proposed a survey system. The spirit is similar to ours, but their proposal is a survey system based on attributes of raters.

The contributions and comparison are summarized in the Table 1. All schemes of the above four approaches as well as ours have basic properties of unforgeability, anonymity of rater and traceability. The requirement of prohibiting double ratings is attained by public linkability in [7] and our approach, while other schemes attain the property by other functionalities. The feature of our scheme is characterized by fine-grained ratings on ratees (in other words, expressive ratings).

Table 1. Comparison of functionalities.

	Unforgeability	Anonymity (Rater)	Anonymity (Seller)	Public link	Traceability	Fine grained (Rater)	Fine grained (Ratee)
Nakanishi et al. [19]	✓	✓	✓	-	✓	-	-
Blömer et al. [7]	✓	✓	-	✓	✓	-	-
Guo et al. [13]	✓	✓	✓	-	✓	-	-
Liu et al. [15]	✓	✓	-	-	✓	✓	-
Our approach	✓	✓	-	✓	✓	-	✓

1.3 Organization of the Paper

In Sect. 2, we summarize needed notations and notions. In Sect. 3, we define the syntax of our expressive rating scheme with predication over attributes of ratees. In Sect. 4, we provide a generic conversion of ABS into an expressive rating scheme. In Sect. 5, we construct an expressive rating scheme in an ad hoc manner. In Sect. 6, we explain a use-case of our expressive rating scheme in a reputation board. In Sect. 7, we conclude our work and mention a future direction.

2 Preliminaries

The security parameter is denoted by λ. A uniformly random sampling of an element a from a set $\mathcal{S}$ is denoted as $a \in_R \mathcal{S}$.

2.1 Rating Scheme, Reputation System

Based on previous work [4–6,8], we summarize the requirements for a rating scheme for a reputation board from the cryptographic point of view.

Unforgeability means that no one without a legitimate secret key can produce a rating on behalf of an honest user.

Anonymity means that signatures of honest users are indistinguishable.

Public linkability requires that any entity can determine whether two ratings for a single product are generated by a single rater or not, where no secret key is required. Note that public linkability, together with an "open" algorithm operated by a system manager, implies that every rater can stay anonymous so long as he rates a product only once.

Traceability means that it is impossible for any set of colluding users to create ratings that can not be traced back to a user of the system.

2.2 Attribute-Based Signature[1,2,16]

Scheme. An attribute-based signature scheme, ABS, consists of four PPT algorithms: ABS =(**ABS.Setup, ABS.KG, ABS.Sign, ABS.Vrfy**).

ABS.Setup$(1^\lambda, \mathcal{U}) \to$ (MPK, MSK). It takes as input the security parameter 1^λ and an attribute universe $\mathcal{U} = \{at_1, \ldots, at_u\}$. Each at_i is an attribute. It outputs a public key MPK and a master secret key MSK.

ABS.KG(MPK, MSK, id, S) $\to$ SK$_{id,S}$. It takes as input the public key MPK, the master secret key MSK, and an identity string id and an attribute set $S \subset \mathcal{U}$. It outputs a private key SK$_{id,S}$ that corresponds to the pair(id, S).

ABS.Sign(MPK, SK$_{id,S}$, (m, f)) $\to \sigma$. It takes as input a public key MPK, a private key SK$_{id,S}$, a pair (m, f) of a message $\in \{0, 1\}^*$ and an access formula. It outputs a signature σ.

ABS.Vrfy(MPK, $(m, f), \sigma) \to 1/0$. It takes as input a public key MPK, a pair (m, f) of a message and an access formula, and a signature σ. It outputs a decision 1 or 0. When it is 1, we say that $((m, f), \sigma)$ is *valid*. When 0, we say that $((m, f), \sigma)$ is *invalid*.

We demand correctness of ABS; for any λ, any $\mathcal{U}$, any $S \subset \mathcal{U}$ and any (m, f) such that $f(S) = 1$,

$$\Pr[(\text{MPK}, \text{MSK}) \leftarrow \textbf{ABS.Setup}(1^\lambda, \mathcal{U}), \text{SK}_{id,S} \leftarrow \textbf{ABS.KG}(\text{MPK}, \text{MSK}, S),$$
$$\sigma \leftarrow \textbf{ABS.Sign}(\text{MPK}, \text{SK}_{id,S}, (m, f)), b \leftarrow \textbf{ABS.Vrfy}(\text{MPK}, (m, f), \sigma) : b = 1] = 1.$$

Chosen-Message Attack on ABS. Intuitively, an adversary $\mathcal{F}$'s objective is to make an *existential forgery*. $\mathcal{F}$ tries to make a forgery $((m^*, f^*), \sigma^*)$ that consists of a message, a target access policy and a signature. The following experiment $\textbf{Exprmt}_{\text{ABS}, \mathcal{F}}^{\text{euf-cma}}(\lambda, \mathcal{U})$ of a forger $\mathcal{F}$ defines the *chosen-message attack on ABS to make an existential forgery*.

$\quad$ $\textbf{Exprmt}_{\text{ABS}, \mathcal{F}}^{\text{euf-cma}}(\lambda, \mathcal{U})$:

$\quad\quad$ (MPK, MSK) $\leftarrow$ **ABS.Setup**$(1^\lambda, \mathcal{U})$

$\quad\quad$ $((m^*, f^*), \sigma^*) \leftarrow \mathcal{F}^{\mathcal{ABSKG}(\text{MPK}, \text{MSK}, \cdot, \cdot), \mathcal{ABSSIGN}(\text{MPK}, \text{SK}_{\cdot,\cdot}, (\cdot, \cdot))}(\text{MPK})$

$\quad\quad$ If **ABS.Vrfy**(MPK, $(m^*, f^*), \sigma^*) = 1$, then Return WIN

$\quad\quad$ else Return LOSE

In the experiment, $\mathcal{F}$ issues key-extraction queries to its key-generation oracle $\mathcal{ABSKG}$ and signing queries to its signing oracle $\mathcal{ABSSIGN}$. Giving an identity string id$_i$ and an attribute set S_i, $\mathcal{F}$ queries $\mathcal{ABSKG}$(MPK, MSK, $\cdot, \cdot$) for the secret key SK$_{id_i, S_i}$. In addition, giving (id$_j$, S_j) and a pair (m, f) of a message and an access formula, $\mathcal{F}$ queries $\mathcal{ABSSIGN}$(MPK, SK$_{\cdot,\cdot}$, $(\cdot, \cdot)$) for a signature σ that satisfies **ABS.Vrfy**(MPK, $(m, f), \sigma) = 1$ when $f(S_j) = 1$.

The access formula f^* declared by $\mathcal{F}$ is called a *target access formula*. Here we consider the *adaptive* target in the sense that $\mathcal{F}$ is allowed to choose f^* after seeing MPK and issuing some key-extraction queries and signing queries. Two restrictions are imposed to $\mathcal{F}$ on f^*. In key-extraction queries, S_i that satisfies $f^*(S_i) = 1$ was never queried. In signing queries, (m^*, f^*) was never queried and

S_j that satisfies $f^*(S_j) = 1$ was never queried.. The numbers of both queries are bounded by a polynomial in λ.

The *advantage* of $\mathcal{F}$ over ABS in the game of chosen-message attack to make existential forgery is defined as: $\mathbf{Adv}_{\mathrm{ABS},\mathcal{F}}^{\mathrm{euf\text{-}cma}}(\lambda) \stackrel{\mathrm{def}}{=} \Pr[\mathrm{WIN} \leftarrow \mathbf{Exprmt}_{\mathrm{ABS},\mathcal{F}}^{\mathrm{euf\text{-}cma}}(\lambda, \mathcal{U})]$.

Definition 1 (Unforgeability ([16,20])). *ABS is called* existentially unforgeable against chosen-message attacks *if, for any PPT $\mathcal{F}$ and for any $\mathcal{U}$,* $\mathbf{Adv}_{ABS,\mathcal{F}}^{euf\text{-}cma}(\lambda)$ *is negligible in λ.*

Attribute Privacy of ABS. Roughly speaking, ABS is called to have attribute privacy if any unconditional cheating verifier cannot distinguish two distributions of signatures each of which is generated by different attribute set.

Definition 2 (Attribute Privacy (Perfect Privacy[16,20])). *ABS is called to have* attribute privacy *if, for all $(MPK, MSK) \leftarrow \mathbf{ABS.Setup}(1^\lambda, \mathcal{U})$, for all message m, for all attribute sets S_1 and S_2, for all signing keys $SK_{S_1} \leftarrow$*
$\mathbf{ABS.KG}(MPK, MSK, S_1)$ and $SK_{S_2} \leftarrow \mathbf{ABS.KG}(MPK, MSK, S_2)$ and for all access formula f such that $f(S_1) = 1$ and $f(S_2) = 1$ or $f(S_1) \neq 1$ and $f(S_2) \neq 1$, two distributions $\mathbf{ABS.Sign}(MPK, SK_{S_1}, (m, f))$ and $\mathbf{ABS.Sign}(MPK, SK_{S_2}, (m, f))$ are identical.

3 Syntax of Expressive Rating Scheme with Predication over Attributes of Ratees

In this section, we define the syntax of our expressive rating scheme based on attributes. We need unforgeability, anonymity, public linkability and traceability on our expressive rating scheme for later application to secure reputation boards. For this sake we give definitions of those properties.

3.1 Terminologies of Entities

First, we define entities of our expressive rating scheme over attributes of ratees.

A *system manager* is an authority of our expressive rating scheme, and is assumed to be honest. It issues a pair of system manager's public key and secret key, (MPK, MSK).

An *item* is a name of either a product or a provider of a product.

An *attribute universe* $\mathcal{U}$ is the set of all possible attributes of items.

A subset of $\mathcal{U}$ is denoted by S.

A *rater* is a user of a product, who is identified by an identity string id.

An *id-List* is the list of rater's identities $(\mathrm{id}_i)_i$. id-List is updated when a rater, given a private key $\mathrm{SK}_{\mathrm{id},S}$, is registered by the system manager.

A *ratee* is an item which is rated.

3.2   Expressive Rating Scheme Based on Attributes of Ratees

A expressive rating scheme RS with predication over attributes of ratees consists of seven PPT algorithms: (**RS.Setup, RS.Reg, RS.Rate, RS.Vrfy, RS.Eval, RS.Open, RS.PubLink**).

$\quad$ **RS.Setup**$(1^\lambda, \mathcal{U}) \to (\text{MPK}, \text{MSK}, \text{id-List})$.

$\quad$ This PPT algorithm is run by the system manager in the set up phase. On input the security parameter 1^λ and the attribute universe $\mathcal{U}$, it outputs a master public key MPK, a master secret MSK and an empty id-List.

$\quad$ **RS.Reg**$(\mathcal{U}, \text{MPK}, \text{MSK}, \text{id}, S, \text{id-List}) \to (\mathcal{U}, \text{MPK}, \text{SK}_{\text{id},S}, \text{id-List})$.

$\quad$ This PPT algorithm is run by the system manager in each registration of a user. On input $\mathcal{U}$, MPK, MSK, id that is a user's ID, $S \subset \mathcal{U}$ and id-List, it outputs the updated attribute universe $\mathcal{U}$, the updated master public key MPK, a private key $\text{SK}_{\text{id},S}$ and the updated id-List.

$\quad$ **RS.Rate**$(\text{MPK}, \text{SK}_{\text{id},S}, (item, f)) \to rate$.

$\quad$ This PPT algorithm is run by a user in each rating. On input MPK, $\text{SK}_{\text{id},S}$ and $(item, f)$ that is a pair of an item $item$ (typically it is a product's name or a provider's name) and a boolean predicate f on $\mathcal{U}$ (which describes a rating content), it outputs a rating string $rate$.

$\quad$ **RS.Vrfy**$(\text{MPK}, (item, f), rate) \to 1/0$.

$\quad$ This deterministic polynomial-time algorithm is run by a provider in each verification of a rating to the provider's $item$. On input MPK, $(item, f)$ and $rate$, it outputs 1 or 0.

$\quad$ **RS.PubLink**$(\text{MPK}, item, (f_0, rate_0), (f_1, rate_1)) \to 1/0/\bot$.

$\quad$ This deterministic polynomial-time algorithm can be run by any user to decide whether two ratings, $rate_0$ on $(item, f_0)$ and $rate_1$ on $(item, f_1)$, are generated by a single user or not. On input MPK, $((item, f_0), rate_0), ((item, f_1), rate_1)$, it outputs 1 or 0.

$\quad$ **RS.Open**$(\text{MPK}, \text{MSK}, \text{id-List}, (item, f), rate) \to \text{id}/\bot$.

$\quad$ This deterministic polynomial-time algorithm is run by the system manager to open a rating string $rate$. On input MPK, MSK, id-List, $(item, f)$ and $rate$, it outputs id or $\bot$ (that means no ID is output).

RS.Eval$((item, f), (rate_i)_i) \to r\text{-}count.$

This deterministic polynomial-time algorithm is run by the system manager in the phase of evaluating a rating value on an *item*. Let each $rate_i$ be a rating string on $(item, f)$ for all i. On input $(item, f)$ and $(rate_i)_i$, it outputs an integer *r-count*.

Correctness should hold: $\Pr[(MPK, MSK) \leftarrow$ **RS.Setup**$(1^\lambda, \mathcal{U}), (\mathcal{U}, MPK,$ $SK_{id,S}, id\text{-}List) \leftarrow$ **RS.Reg**$(\mathcal{U}, MPK, MSK, id, S, id\text{-}List), rate \leftarrow$ **RS.Rate** $(MPK, SK_{id,S}, (item, f)) : 1 \leftarrow$ **RS.Vrfy**$(MPK, (item, f), rate)] = 1.$

3.3 Definition of Properties

Given the above syntax, the properties of unforgeability, anonymity, public linkability and traceability are defined as follows.

Unforgeability. Informally speaking, unforgeability of an expressive rating scheme RS assures that a rating *rate* cannot be generated without a secret key $SK_{id,S}$ for some id and S. We assume that the communication between users and the system manager is via secure channel. Let us think about the following experiment.

Exprmt$_{RS,\mathcal{A}}^{\text{euf-cia}}(\lambda, \mathcal{U})$:

$(MPK, MSK) \leftarrow$ **RS.Setup**$(1^\lambda, \mathcal{U})$

$((item^*, f^*), rate^*) \leftarrow \mathcal{A}^{\mathcal{RSREG}(\mathcal{U}, MPK, MSK, \cdot, \cdot, \cdot), \mathcal{RSRATE}(MPK, SK_{\cdot, \cdot}, (\cdot, \cdot))}(MPK)$

If **RS.Vrfy**$(MPK, (item^*, f^*), rate^*) = 1$, then Return WIN

else Return LOSE

In the experiment, $\mathcal{A}$ issues registration queries and rating-queries. Giving an identity string id_i, an attribute set S_i and id-List, $\mathcal{A}$ queries its registration oracle $\mathcal{RSREG}(\mathcal{U}, MPK, MSK, \cdot, \cdot, \cdot)$ for the secret key SK_{id_i, S_i}. Note that $\mathcal{A}$ receives not only SK_{id_i, S_i} but also the updated $\mathcal{U}, MPK$ and id-List. In addition, Giving an identity string id_i, an attribute set S_i and a pair $(item, f)$ of a name of an item and a boolean predicate, $\mathcal{A}$ queries its rating oracle $\mathcal{RSRATE}(MPK, SK_{\cdot, \cdot}, (\cdot, \cdot))$ for a rating *rate* that satisfies **RS.Vrfy**$(MPK, (item, f), rate) = 1$ when $f(S_i) = 1$.

The boolean predicate f^* declared by $\mathcal{A}$ is called a *target boolean predicate*. Here we consider the *adaptive* target in the sense that $\mathcal{A}$ is allowed to choose f^* after seeing MPK and issuing some key-extraction queries and signing queries. Two restrictions are imposed to $\mathcal{A}$ on f^*. In registration queries, S_i that satisfies $f^*(S_i) = 1$ was never queried. In rating queries, $(item^*, f^*)$ was never queried and S_j that satisfies $f^*(S_j) = 1$ was never queried. The numbers of both queries are bounded by a polynomial in λ.

The *advantage* of $\mathcal{A}$ over RS in the game of chosen-item attack to make existential forgery of a rating is defined as:

$$\mathbf{Adv}_{RS,\mathcal{A}}^{\text{euf-cia}}(\lambda) \stackrel{\text{def}}{=} \Pr[\text{WIN} \leftarrow \mathbf{Exprmt}_{RS,\mathcal{A}}^{\text{euf-cia}}(\lambda, \mathcal{U})].$$

Definition 3 (Unforgeability). *An expressive rating scheme* RS *is called* existentially unforgeable against chosen-item attacks *if, for any PPT* $\mathcal{A}$ *and for any* $\mathcal{U}$, $\mathbf{Adv}_{RS,\mathcal{A}}^{euf\text{-}cia}(\lambda)$ *is negligible in* λ.

Note that the above unforgeability is usually called existential unforgeability [1,2,20].

Anonymity. Informally speaking, anonymity of an expressive rating scheme RS assures that an identity string id of a rater is hidden from a rating *rate*. Let us think about the following experiment.

$\mathbf{Exprmt}_{RS,\mathcal{A}}^{anonym}(\lambda,\mathcal{U})$:

$(MPK, MSK, \text{id-List}) \leftarrow \mathbf{RS.Setup}(1^\lambda, \mathcal{U})$

$(\text{id}_0, S_0), (\text{id}_1, S_1) \leftarrow \mathcal{A}(MPK)$

$(\mathcal{U}, MPK, SK_{\text{id}_0, S_0}, \text{id-List}) \leftarrow \mathbf{RS.Reg}(\mathcal{U}, MPK, MSK, \text{id}_0, S_0, \text{id-List})$

$(\mathcal{U}, MPK, SK_{\text{id}_1, S_1}, \text{id-List}) \leftarrow \mathbf{RS.Reg}(\mathcal{U}, MPK, MSK, \text{id}_1, S_1, \text{id-List})$

$(item^*, f^*) \leftarrow \mathcal{A}$, If $f^*(S_0) \neq f^*(S_1)$, then abort

$b \in_R \{0,1\}$, $\hat{rate} \leftarrow \mathbf{RS.Rate}(MPK, SK_{\text{id}_b, S_b}, (item^*, f^*))$

$b^* \leftarrow \mathcal{A}(\hat{rate})$

If $b = b^*$, then Return WIN, else Return LOSE

The *advantage* of $\mathcal{A}$ over RS in the anonymity game is defined as:

$$\mathbf{Adv}_{RS,\mathcal{A}}^{anonym}(\lambda) \stackrel{\text{def}}{=} |\Pr[\text{WIN} \leftarrow \mathbf{Exprmt}_{RS,\mathcal{A}}^{anonym}(\lambda,\mathcal{U})] - 1/2|.$$

Definition 4 (Anonymity). *An expressive rating scheme* RS *is called to have* anonymity *if, for any PPT* $\mathcal{A}$ *and for any* $\mathcal{U}$, $\mathbf{Adv}_{RS,\mathcal{A}}^{anonym}(\lambda)$ *is negligible in* λ.

Public Linkability. Informally speaking, public linkability of an expressive rating scheme RS assures that it is possible for any entity to decide whether two ratings $rate_1$ and $rate_2$ on a single *item* are generated by a single rater or not. Let us think about the following experiment.

$\mathbf{Exprmt}_{RS,\mathcal{A}}^{pub\text{-}link}(\lambda,\mathcal{U})$:

$(MPK, MSK, \text{id-List}) \leftarrow \mathbf{RS.Setup}(1^\lambda, \mathcal{U})$

$(\text{id}_0, S_0), (\text{id}_1, S_1) \leftarrow \mathcal{A}(MPK)$

$(\mathcal{U}, MPK, SK_{\text{id}_0, S_0}, \text{id-List}) \leftarrow \mathbf{RS.Reg}(\mathcal{U}, MPK, MSK, \text{id}_0, S_0, \text{id-List})$

$(\mathcal{U}, MPK, SK_{\text{id}_1, S_1}, \text{id-List}) \leftarrow \mathbf{RS.Reg}(\mathcal{U}, MPK, MSK, \text{id}_1, S_1, \text{id-List})$

$b \in_R \{0,1\}$, $\qquad ((item^*, f_x^*), rate_x^*) \leftarrow \mathcal{A}(MPK, SK_{\text{id}_b, S_b})$

Initialize state of $\mathcal{A}$, $((item^*, f_1^*), rate_1^*) \leftarrow \mathcal{A}(MPK, SK_{\text{id}_1, S_1}, item^*)$

$\hat{b} \leftarrow \mathbf{RS.PubLink}(MPK, item^*, (f_x^*, rate_x^*), (f_1^*, rate_1^*))$

If $b \neq \hat{b}$, then Return WIN else Return LOSE

The *advantage* of $\mathcal{A}$ over RS in the public-linkability game is defined as:

$$\mathbf{Adv}_{\mathrm{RS},\mathcal{A}}^{\mathrm{pub\text{-}link}}(\lambda) \overset{\mathrm{def}}{=} \Pr[\mathrm{WIN} \leftarrow \mathbf{Exprmt}_{\mathrm{RS},\mathcal{A}}^{\mathrm{pub\text{-}link}}(\lambda,\mathcal{U})].$$

Definition 5 (Public Linkability). *An expressive rating scheme RS is called to have* public linkability *if, for any PPT $\mathcal{A}$ and for any $\mathcal{U}$, $\mathbf{Adv}_{\mathrm{RS},\mathcal{A}}^{pub\text{-}link}(\lambda)$ is negligible in λ.*

Traceability. Informally speaking, traceability of an expressive rating scheme RS assures that an identity string id can be determined from a rating *rate* by the system manager. Let us think about the following experiment.

> $\mathbf{Exprmt}_{\mathrm{RS},\mathcal{A}}^{\mathrm{trace}}(\lambda,\mathcal{U}) :$
>
>   (MPK, MSK, id-List) $\leftarrow$ **RS.Setup**$(1^\lambda, \mathcal{U})$
>
> $((item^*, f^*), rate^*) \leftarrow \mathcal{A}^{\mathcal{RSREG}(\mathcal{U},\mathrm{MPK},\mathrm{MSK},\cdot,\cdot,\cdot)}(\mathrm{MPK})$
>
> $d \leftarrow$ **RS.Open**(MPK, MSK, id-List, $(item^*, f^*), rate^*)$
>
>   If **RS.Vrfy**(MPK, $(item^*, f^*), rate^*) = 1 \ \wedge \ [d =\perp]$,
>
>   then Return WIN, else Return LOSE

The *advantage* of $\mathcal{A}$ over RS in the public-linkability game is defined as:

$$\mathbf{Adv}_{\mathrm{RS},\mathcal{A}}^{\mathrm{trace}}(\lambda) \overset{\mathrm{def}}{=} \Pr[\mathrm{WIN} \leftarrow \mathbf{Exprmt}_{\mathrm{RS},\mathcal{A}}^{\mathrm{trace}}(\lambda,\mathcal{U})].$$

Definition 6 (Traceability). *An expressive rating scheme RS is called to have* traceability *if, for any PPT $\mathcal{A}$ and for any $\mathcal{U}$, $\mathbf{Adv}_{\mathrm{RS},\mathcal{A}}^{trace}(\lambda)$ is negligible in λ.*

4 Our Generic Conversion of ABS into Expressive Rating Scheme

In this section, we provide a generic construction of an expressive rating scheme based on attributes of ratees by converting an attribute-based signature scheme (ABS). Basically, an attribute-based signature is used as a rating string. We adapt ABS so that the resulting expressive rating scheme possesses public linkability and traceability defined in Sect. 3. We assume that the employed ABS is able to add a new attribute after its setup phase with keeping all the components of the input attribute universe $\mathcal{U}$ and the input master public key MPK without changing the master secret key. Most of known ABS schemes (for example, [16,17,20]) has this property, and we denote this algorithm as **ABS.MPKUp**$(1^\lambda, \mathcal{U}, \mathrm{MPK}, \mathrm{MSK}) \to (\mathcal{U}, \mathrm{MPK})$.

4.1 Our Generic Conversion

RS.Setup$(1^\lambda, \mathcal{U}) \to$ (MPK, MSK). This algorithm runs **ABS.Setup**$(1^\lambda, \mathcal{U})$ to obtain (MPK, MSK), and initialize id-List $:= \phi$. It returns (MPK, MSK, id-List).

RS.Reg$(\mathcal{U}, \mathrm{MPK}, \mathrm{MSK}, \mathtt{id}, S, \mathtt{id}\text{-List}) \to (\mathcal{U}, \mathrm{MPK}, \mathrm{SK}_{\mathtt{id},S}, \mathtt{id}\text{-List})$. This algorithm first chooses a string which we call a *tag* uniformly at random: $\tau \in_R \{0,1\}^\lambda$. Treating the tag τ as a new attribute, it updates the attribute universe as well as the attribute set $S\colon \mathcal{U} := \mathcal{U} \cup \{\tau\}, \overline{S} := S \cup \{\tau\}$. Then it runs the algorithm of adding a new attribute: $(\mathcal{U}, \mathrm{MPK}) \leftarrow \mathbf{ABS.MPKUp}(1^\lambda, \mathcal{U}, \mathrm{MPK}, \mathrm{MSK})$. Then it runs $\mathbf{ABS.KG}(\mathrm{MPK}, \mathrm{MSK}, \mathtt{id}, \overline{S})$ to obtain $\mathrm{SK}_{\mathtt{id},\overline{S}}$. Finally it updates $\mathtt{id}\text{-List} := \mathtt{id}\text{-List} \cup \{\mathtt{id} \parallel \tau\}$. It returns the updated attribute universe $\mathcal{U}$, the updated master public key MPK, a private key $\mathrm{SK}_{\mathtt{id},\overline{S}}$ that is re-named as $\mathrm{SK}_{\mathtt{id},S}$ and the updated $\mathtt{id}\text{-List}$. Note that $\mathrm{SK}_{\mathtt{id},S}$ includes the tag string τ.

RS.Rate$(\mathrm{MPK}, \mathrm{SK}_{\mathtt{id},S}, (item, f)) \to rate$. This algorithm first extracts the tag string τ (that is an attribute) from the secret key $\mathrm{SK}_{\mathtt{id},S}$. and puts $m := item$ and $\overline{f} := f \wedge \tau$. Then it runs $\mathbf{ABS.Sign}(\mathrm{MPK}, \mathrm{SK}_{\mathtt{id},\overline{S}}, (m, \overline{f}))$ to obtain an ABS signature σ. Then it outputs a rating string $rate$ as $rate := \sigma \parallel \tau$.

RS.Vrfy$(\mathrm{MPK}, (item, f), rate) \to 1/0$. This algorithm first parses $rate$ as $\sigma \parallel \tau$, and puts $m := item$ and $\overline{f} := f \wedge \tau$. Then it runs $\mathbf{ABS.Vrfy}(\mathrm{MPK}, (m, \overline{f}), \sigma)$ to obtain a decision $1/0$. It returns the decision: 1 or 0.

RS.PubLink$(\mathrm{MPK}, item, (f_0, rate_0), (f_1, rate_1)) \to 1/0/\bot$. This algorithm parses $rate_0$ and $rule_1$ as $\sigma_0 \parallel \tau_0$ and $\sigma_1 \parallel \tau_1$, respectively. Then it puts $m := item$ and $\overline{f_0} := f_0 \wedge \tau_0$ and $\overline{f_1} := f_1 \wedge \tau_1$. It runs, for each $(\overline{f}, \sigma) = (\overline{f_0}, \sigma_0), (\overline{f_1}, \sigma_1)$, $\mathbf{ABS.Vrfy}(\mathrm{MPK}, (m, \overline{f}), \sigma)$ to obtain decisions $1/0$. If at least one decision is not 1, then it returns $\bot$. Otherwise, it checks whether $\tau_0 = \tau_1$ holds or not. If it holds, then it returns 1, and otherwise, 0.

RS.Open$(\mathrm{MPK}, \mathrm{MSK}, \mathtt{id}\text{-List}, (item, f), rate) \to \mathtt{id}/\bot$. This algorithm parses $rate$ as $\sigma \parallel \tau$. It puts $m := item$ and $\overline{f} := f \wedge \tau$. Then it runs $\mathbf{ABS.Vrfy}(\mathrm{MPK}, (m, \overline{f}), \sigma)$. If 0, then it returns $\bot$. Otherwise, it searches τ in $\mathtt{id}\text{-List}$ to find the corresponding $\mathtt{id}$; if it finds $\mathtt{id}$, then it returns $\mathtt{id}$, and otherwise, $\bot$.

RS.Eval$((item, f), (rate_i)_i) \to r\text{-}count$. This algorithm parses $rate_i$ as $\sigma_i \parallel \tau_i$ for each i. It puts $m := item$, $\overline{f}_i := f \wedge \tau_i$, and $r\text{-}count := 0$. For each i, it runs $\mathbf{ABS.Vrfy}(\mathrm{MPK}, (m, \overline{f}_i), \sigma_i)$; if 1, then $r\text{-}count := r\text{-}count + 1$, otherwise it retains the count $r\text{-}count$. After all the verification, it outputs $r\text{-}count$.

For the above generic construction, correctness holds from the correctness of the employed ABS scheme.

4.2   Security

Security is discussed for our expressive rating scheme so that all properties which an expressive rating scheme should have are attained.

Theorem 1 (Unforgeability). *If the employed ABS is existentially unforgeable against chosen-message attacks, then our expressive rating scheme RS is existentially unforgeable against chosen-item attacks.*

Proof. For any given PPT adversary $\mathcal{A}$ on our RS, there exists a PPT adversary $\mathcal{F}$ on the employed ABS; this is due to the following observation. The simulation of the registration oracle of $\mathcal{A}$ goes perfectly by choosing a random string $\tau \in_R \{0,1\}^\lambda$, putting $\overline{S} := S \cup \{\tau\}$, and asking the key-extraction oracle of $\mathcal{F}$ for $\mathrm{SK}_{\mathrm{id},\overline{S}}$. The simulation of the rating oracle of $\mathcal{A}$ goes perfectly by asking the signing oracle of $\mathcal{F}$. Getting a forgery $((item^*, f^*), rate^*)$ from $\mathcal{A}$, $\mathcal{F}$ parses $rate^*$ as $\sigma^* \parallel \tau^*$. Setting $m^* := item^*$ and $\overline{f}^* := f^* \wedge \tau^*$, $\mathcal{F}$ returns an existential forgery $((m^*, \overline{f}^*), \sigma^*)$; hence we have an equality $\mathbf{Adv}_{\mathrm{RS},\mathcal{A}}^{\mathrm{euf\text{-}cia}}(\lambda) = \mathbf{Adv}_{\mathrm{ABS},\mathcal{F}}^{\mathrm{euf\text{-}cma}}(\lambda)$.   □

Theorem 2 (Anonymity). *If the employed ABS has attribute privacy, then our expressive rating scheme RS has anonymity.*

Proof. If ABS has attribute privacy, a rating $((item^*, f^*), \hat{rate})$ where $\hat{rate} = \hat{\sigma} \parallel \hat{\tau}$ in the experiment $\mathbf{Exprmt}_{\mathrm{RS},\mathcal{A}}^{\mathrm{anonym}}(\lambda, \mathcal{U})$ leaks no information on the rater's identity string id_b because σ leaks no information and τ is chosen uniformly at random. That is, $\mathbf{Adv}_{\mathrm{RS},\mathcal{A}}^{\mathrm{anonym}}(\lambda) = 0$.   □

Theorem 3 (Public Linkability). *If the employed ABS is existentially unforgeable against chosen-message attacks, then our expressive rating scheme RS has public linkability.*

Proof. For any given PPT adversary $\mathcal{A}$ on our RS in the public linkability game $\mathbf{Exprmt}_{\mathrm{RS},\mathcal{A}}^{\mathrm{pub\text{-}link}}(\lambda, \mathcal{U})$, we construct a PPT adversary $\mathcal{F}$ on the employed ABS in the euf-cma game $\mathbf{Exprmt}_{\mathrm{ABS},\mathcal{F}}^{\mathrm{euf\text{-}cma}}(\lambda, \mathcal{U})$, as follows. Receiving (id_0, S_0) and (id_1, S_1) from $\mathcal{A}$, $\mathcal{F}$ chooses random string $\tau_0, \tau_1 \in_R \{0,1\}^\lambda$, putting $\overline{S_0} := S_0 \cup \{\tau_0\}$ and $\overline{S_1} := S_1 \cup \{\tau_1\}$, and asks its key-extraction oracle for $\mathrm{SK}_{\mathrm{id}_0,\overline{S_0}}$ and $\mathrm{SK}_{\mathrm{id}_1,\overline{S_1}}$ to give each of them to $\mathcal{A}$ according to the game. Suppose $\mathcal{A}$ wins with $b = 0$ and $\hat{b} = 1$. There are a valid two ratings $((item^*, f_0^*), rate_0^*)$ and $((item^*, f_1^*), rate_1^*)$ with a common tag τ^* satisfying either $\tau^* \neq \tau_0$ or $\tau^* \neq \tau_1$. In the former case, $\mathcal{F}$ parses $rate_0^*$ as $\sigma_0^* \parallel \tau^*$, puts $m^* := item^*$, $\overline{f}^* := f_0^* \wedge \tau^*$ and returns $((m^*, \overline{f}^*), \sigma_0^*)$. This is a valid signature with $\overline{f}^*(\overline{S_0}) = 0$; that is, an existential forgery. Thus we have an inequality $\mathbf{Adv}_{\mathrm{RS},\mathcal{A}}^{\mathrm{pub\text{-}link}}(\lambda) \leq \mathbf{Adv}_{\mathrm{ABS},\mathcal{F}}^{\mathrm{euf\text{-}cma}}(\lambda)$. The discussions for the rest of cases are essentially the same.   □

Note that, though ratings generated by our generic RS is not unlinkable, it has anonymity of raters. This is because the tag τ which is attached to id is chosen uniformly at random.

Theorem 4 (Traceability). *If the employed ABS is existentially unforgeable against chosen-message attacks, then our expressive rating scheme RS has traceability.*

Proof. For any given PPT adversary $\mathcal{A}$ on our RS in the traceability game $\mathbf{Exprmt}_{\mathrm{RS},\mathcal{A}}^{\mathrm{trace}}(\lambda, \mathcal{U})$, we construct a PPT adversary $\mathcal{F}$ on the employed ABS in the euf-cma game $\mathbf{Exprmt}_{\mathrm{ABS},\mathcal{F}}^{\mathrm{euf\text{-}cma}}(\lambda, \mathcal{U})$, as follows. A similar discussion to that of the proof of unforgeability allows $\mathcal{F}$ to reply to the query $(\mathrm{id}, S, \mathrm{id\text{-}List})$ of $\mathcal{A}$. Suppose $\mathcal{A}$ wins. $\mathcal{F}$ parses $rate^*$ as $\sigma^* \parallel \tau^*$. Setting $m^* := item^*$ and $\overline{f}^* := f^* \wedge \tau^*$,

$\mathcal{F}$ returns $((m^*, \overline{f^*}), \sigma^*)$. By the definition of the traceability game, σ^* is a valid signature on $(m^*, \overline{f^*})$, and τ^* is not in id-List. this is an existential forgery of ABS. $\qquad\qquad\qquad\qquad\qquad\qquad\qquad\qquad\qquad\qquad\qquad\qquad\qquad\qquad\qquad$ □

5 Our Ad Hoc Concrete Construction of an Expressive Rating Scheme

In this section, employing an ABS scheme of the Fiat-Shamir type [1,2], we construct an efficient expressive rating scheme concretely. Roughly speaking, attribute privacy of ABS is hard to attain, but fortunately we do not necessarily need the strong property; that is, even if we employ an ABS scheme without attribute privacy and with public linkability, there is possibility to obtain an expressive rating scheme with even more efficiency in signature length and computational amount. In addition, there is no need for the algorithm **ABS.MPKUp** which is needed in Sect. 4.

5.1 Scheme

We will borrow the notation in [1,2] and describe the points of modification to obtain an expressive rating scheme, RS — (**RS.Setup, RS.Reg, RS.Rate, RS.Vrfy, RS.Eval, RS.Open, RS.PubLink**). Below, $\Sigma = (\Sigma^1, \Sigma^2, \Sigma^3, \Sigma^{\text{vrfy}})$ is a given Σ-protocol [10] and $\Sigma_f = (\Sigma_f^1, \Sigma_f^2, \Sigma_f^3, \Sigma_f^{\text{vrfy}})$ is the boolean proof system obtained from Σ and a boolean predicate f [1,2], which is a generalization of the so-called OR-proof [10] to any monotone formula f.

RS.Setup$(1^\lambda, \mathcal{U}) \to (\text{MPK}, \text{MSK}, \text{id-List})$: This algorithm chooses, on input 1^λ and $\mathcal{U}$, a pair $(x_{\text{mst}}, w_{\text{mst}})$ at random from $R = \{(x, w)\}$ by running $\text{Inst}_R(1^\lambda)$ which are a statement and a witness of a Σ-protocol [10]. It also chooses a hash key μ at random from a hash-key space $\textit{Hashkeysp}(\lambda)$. It outputs a public key $\text{MPK} = (x_{\text{mst}}, \mathcal{U}, \mu)$ and a master secret key $\text{MSK} = (w_{\text{mst}})$ as well as an empty id-List.

> **RS.Setup**$(1^\lambda, \mathcal{U})$:
>
> $(x_{\text{mst}}, w_{\text{mst}}) \leftarrow \text{Inst}_R(1^\lambda), \mu \leftarrow \textit{Hashkeysp}(\lambda)$
>
> $\text{MPK} := (x_{\text{mst}}, \mu), \text{MSK} := (w_{\text{mst}}), \text{id-List} := \phi$
>
> $\text{Return}(\text{MPK}, \text{MSK}, \text{id-List})$

RS.Reg$(\mathcal{U}, \text{MPK}, \text{MSK}, \text{id}, S, \text{id-List}) \to (\mathcal{U}, \text{MPK}, \text{SK}_{\text{id},S}, \text{id-List})$: This PPT algorithm chooses, on input $\mathcal{U}, \text{MPK}, \text{MSK}, S$, a pseudo-random function key k from $\textit{PRFkeysp}(\lambda)$ and a string τ from $\{0,1\}^\lambda$ uniformly at random. Then it applies the credential bundle technique [16,17] to strings $m_{\text{at}} := (\tau \parallel \text{at}), \text{at} \in S$.

Here we employ the Fiat-Shamir signing algorithm $FS(\Sigma)^{\text{sign}}$.

> **RS.Reg**$(\mathcal{U}, MPK, MSK, \text{id}, S, \text{id-List})$:
>
> $k \leftarrow PRFkeysp(\lambda), \tau \in_R \{0,1\}^\lambda$
>
> For $\text{at} \in S$:
>
> $\quad m_{\text{at}} := (\tau \parallel \text{at}), a_{\text{at}} \leftarrow \Sigma^2(x_{\text{mst}}, w_{\text{mst}})$
>
> $\quad c_{\text{at}} \leftarrow Hash_\mu(a_{\text{at}} \parallel m_{\text{at}}), w_{\text{at}} \leftarrow \Sigma^3(x_{\text{mst}}, w_{\text{mst}}, a_{\text{at}}, c_{\text{at}})$
>
> $SK_{\text{id},S} := (k, \tau, (a_{\text{at}}, w_{\text{at}})_{\text{at} \in S}), \text{id-List} := \text{id-List} \cup \{\text{id} \parallel \tau\}$
>
> Return $(\mathcal{U}, MPK, SK_{\text{id},S}, \text{id-List})$.

RS.Rate$(MPK, SK_{\text{id},S}, (item, f)) \rightarrow rate$: This PPT algorithm is obtained by adding **Supp** and **StmtGen** to Σ^3.

> **Supp**$(MPK, SK_{\text{id},S}, f) \rightarrow (a_{\text{at}_j}, w_{\text{at}_j})_{1 \leq j \leq \text{arity}(f)}$
>
> $w := (w_{\text{at}_j})_{1 \leq j \leq \text{arity}(f)}$
>
> **StmtGen**$(MPK, \tau, (a_{\text{at}_j})_{1 \leq j \leq \text{arity}(f)})$
>
> $\quad \rightarrow (x_{\text{at}_j})_{1 \leq j \leq \text{arity}(f)} =: x$

The above procedures are needed to input a pair of statement and witness, $(x = (x_{\text{at}_j})_{1 \leq j \leq \text{arity}(f)}, w = (w_{\text{at}_j})_{1 \leq j \leq \text{arity}(f)})$, to Σ^1_f. Note here that $(x_{\text{at}_j}, w_{\text{at}_j}) \in R$ for any $i_j \in S$. On the other hand, $(x_{\text{at}_j}, w_{\text{at}_j}) \notin R$ for any $i_j \notin S$, without a negligible probability, $\text{neg}(\lambda)$.

Therefore, the message on the first move has to include not only commitments $(\text{CMT}_l)_l$ but also a string τ and elements $(a_{\text{at}_j})_{1 \leq j \leq \text{arity}(f)}$ for the verifier $\mathcal{V}$ to be able to produce the same statement x.

Hence a rating string is $rate := (\tau, (a_{\text{at}_j})_{1 \leq j \leq \text{arity}(f)}, (\text{CMT}_l)_l, (\text{CHA}_n)_n, (\text{RES}_l)_l)$.

RS.Vrfy$(MPK, (item, f), rate) \rightarrow 1/0$: This deterministic algorithm utilizes **StmtGen** and Σ^{vrfy}_f to check validity of the pair of message and boolean predicate, (m, f), and the rating string $rate$, under the public key MPK.

RS.PubLink$(MPK, item, (f_0, rate_0), (f_1, rate_1)) \rightarrow 1/0$: This deterministic algorithm decides whether two tags τ_0 and τ_1 which are in $rate_0$ and $rate_1$, respectively, are the same or not. If so, then it returns 1 and otherwise, 0.

RS.Open$(MPK, MSK, (item, f), rate) \rightarrow \{\text{id}, \perp\}$: This deterministic algorithm searches, in id-List, the tag τ that is in $rate$, and returns the corresponding id. If it finds no such id, it returns $\perp$.

RS.Eval$((item, f), (rate_i)_i) \rightarrow r\text{-}count$: This deterministic algorithm counts the number $r\text{-}count$ of $rate_i$ each of which has a different tag τ_i. It returns $r\text{-}count$.

6 Use-Case to a Reputation Board

In this section, to show the features of our expressive rating scheme, we give here examples of use-case to a reputation board (like "amazon.com").

As quantitative attributes, let $quant_i$ be $\star \cdots \star$ (i-stars). As qualitative attributes, let at_1, at_2, at_3 and at_4 be price, cost, reliability and warranty, respectively.

Example 1 [Rating a Product]. An enhanced rating such as attaching stars ($\star$) for an "OR-statement" is possible by our expressive rating scheme. Suppose that the following boolean predicate is chosen by a user.

$$f_1 = [at_1 \vee at_2] \wedge quant_3.$$

The boolean predicate f_1 means "price or cost is three stars ($\star\star\star$)".

Example 2 [Rating a Provider of Products]. Our expressive rating scheme is expressive when it is applied to a higher level predication; especially in the case of rating providers of products. Suppose that the following boolean predicate is chosen by a user.

$$f_2 = [\ [\ [at_1 \wedge quant_2] \wedge [at_3 \wedge quant_3]\ ]$$
$$\vee\ [\ [at_1 \wedge quant_3] \wedge [at_3 \wedge quant_4]\ ]\ ]$$
$$\wedge\ [at_4 \wedge quant_5].$$

The boolean predicate f_2 means "The provider's products have either two stars on price and three stars on reliability or three stars on price and four stars on reliability, while they have five stars on warranty". In other words, the boolean predicate f_2 is saying that the price balances with quality, while the warranty is always very good.

7 Conclusions

In this paper, we defined an expressive rating scheme that enables a rater to generate a expressive rating as predication over attributes of ratees. We used as an individual rating an attribute-based signature (ABS) on a boolean predicate. We made the reputation function take as an input those signatures. Then, using an ABS scheme of the Fiat-Shamir style, we constructed an expressive rating scheme concretely.

In our generic construction, public linkability is for prohibiting double ratings on a single ratee by a single rater. From a point of view of privacy, it is a useful option if an expressive rating scheme has a property that two ratings on two ratees by a single rater looks independent (that is, cannot be publicly linkable). This property is called *user-controlled linkability* in the ABS scheme of Ghadafi et al. [12]. To construct an efficient expressive rating scheme with user-controlled linkability is a challenging problem.

Acknowledgements. Concerning the first author, this work is partially supported by a Kakenhi Grant-in-Aid for Scientific Research (C) JP15K00029 from Japan Society for the Promotion of Science.

Concerning the third author, this work is partially supported by a Kakenhi Grant-in-Aid for Scientific Research (C) JP15H02711 from Japan Society for the Promotion of Science.

References

1. Anada, H., Arita, S., Sakurai, K.: Attribute-based signatures without pairings via the fiat-shamir paradigm. In: Proceedings of the 2nd ACM Wookshop on ASIA Public-Key Cryptography, ASIAPKC 2014, 3 June, 2014, Kyoto, Japan, pp. 49–58 (2014)
2. Anada, H., Arita, S., Sakurai, K.: Proof of knowledge on monotone predicates and its application to attribute-based identifications and signatures. Cryptology ePrint Archive, Report 2016/483 (2016). http://eprint.iacr.org/2016/483
3. Androulaki, E., Choi, S.G., Bellovin, S.M., Malkin, T.: Reputation systems for anonymous networks. In: Borisov, N., Goldberg, I. (eds.) PETS 2008. LNCS, vol. 5134, pp. 202–218. Springer, Heidelberg (2008)
4. Ateniese, G., Camenisch, J.L., Joye, M., Tsudik, G.: A practical and provably secure coalition-resistant group signature scheme. In: Bellare, M. (ed.) CRYPTO 2000. LNCS, vol. 1880, pp. 255–270. Springer, Heidelberg (2000)
5. Bellare, M., Micciancio, D., Warinschi, B.: Foundations of group signatures: formal definitions, simplified requirements, and a construction based on general assumptions. In: Biham, E. (ed.) EUROCRYPT 2003. LNCS, vol. 2656, pp. 614–629. Springer, Heidelberg (2003). doi:10.1007/3-540-39200-9_38
6. Bellare, M., Shi, H., Zhang, C.: Foundations of group signatures: the case of dynamic groups. In: Menezes, A. (ed.) CT-RSA 2005. LNCS, vol. 3376, pp. 136–153. Springer, Heidelberg (2005)
7. Blömer, J., Juhnke, J., Kolb, C.: Anonymous and publicly linkable reputation systems. In: 19th International Conference on Financial Cryptography and Data Security, FC 2015, San Juan, Puerto Rico, 26–30 January, 2015, Revised Selected Papers, pp. 478–488 (2015)
8. Boneh, D., Boyen, X., Shacham, H.: Short group signatures. In: Franklin, M. (ed.) CRYPTO 2004. LNCS, vol. 3152, pp. 41–55. Springer, Heidelberg (2004)
9. Clauß, S., Schiffner, S., Kerschbaum, F.: k-anonymous reputation. In: 8th ACM Symposium on Information, Computer and Communications Security, ASIA CCS 2013, 08–10 May 2013, Hangzhou, China, pp. 359–368 (2013)
10. Damgård, I.: On σ-protocols. In: Course Notes (2011). http://www.cs.au.dk/ivan/Sigma.pdf
11. Dellarocas, C.: Immunizing online reputation reporting systems against unfair ratings and discriminatory behavior. In: EC, pp. 150–157 (2000)
12. El Kaafarani, A., Chen, L., Ghadafi, E., Davenport, J.: Attribute-based signatures with user-controlled linkability. In: Gritzalis, D., Kiayias, A., Askoxylakis, I. (eds.) CANS 2014. LNCS, vol. 8813, pp. 256–269. Springer, Heidelberg (2014)
13. Guo, L., Zhang, C., Fang, Y., Lin, P.: A privacy-preserving attribute-based reputation system in online social networks. J. Comput. Sci. Technol. **30**(3), 578–597 (2015)

14. Kerschbaum, F.: A verifiable, centralized, coercion-free reputation system. In Proceedings of the 2009 ACM Workshop on Privacy in the Electronic Society, WPES 2009, Chicago, Illinois, USA, 9 November 2009, pp. 61–70 (2009)
15. Liu, J.K., Au, M.H., Huang, X., Susilo, W., Zhou, J., Yu, Y.: New insight to preserve online survey accuracy and privacy in big data era. In: Kutyłowski, M., Vaidya, J. (eds.) ICAIS 2014, Part II. LNCS, vol. 8713, pp. 182–199. Springer, Heidelberg (2014)
16. Maji, H.K., Prabhakaran, M., Rosulek, M.: Attribute-based signatures. IACR Cryptology ePrint Archive, p. 595 (2010)
17. Maji, H.K., Prabhakaran, M., Rosulek, M.: Attribute-based signatures. In: Kiayias, A. (ed.) CT-RSA 2011. LNCS, vol. 6558, pp. 376–392. Springer, Heidelberg (2011)
18. Michalas, A., Komninos, N.: The lord of the sense: a privacy preserving reputation system for participatory sensing applications. In: IEEE Symposium on Computers and Communications, ISCC 2014, Funchal, Madeira, Portugal, 23–26 June 2014, pp. 1–6 (2014)
19. Nakanishi, T., Funabiki, N.: An anonymous reputation system with reputation secrecy for manager. IEICE Trans. 97(A(12)), 2325–2335 (2014)
20. Okamoto, T., Takashima, K.: Efficient attribute-based signatures for non-monotone predicates in the standard model. In: Catalano, D., Fazio, N., Gennaro, R., Nicolosi, A. (eds.) PKC 2011. LNCS, vol. 6571, pp. 35–52. Springer, Heidelberg (2011)

Symmetric Key Cryptography

A New Adaptable Construction of Modulo Addition with Scalable Security for Stream Ciphers

Min Hsuan Cheng, Reza Sedaghat$^{(\boxtimes)}$, and Prathap Siddavaatam

OPR-AL Labs, Department of Electrical and Computer Engineering,
Ryerson University, Toronto, ON M5B 2K3, Canada
{minhsuan.cheng,rsedagha,prathap.siddavaatam}@ryerson.ca
http://www.ee.ryerson.ca/opr

Abstract. In recent years, attacks involving polynomial cryptanalysis have become an important tool in evaluating encryption algorithms involving stream ciphers. Stream cipher designs are difficult to implement since they are prone to weaknesses based on usage, with properties being similar to one-time pad key-stream are subjected to very strict requirements. Contemporary stream cipher designs are highly vulnerable to Algebraic cryptanalysis based on linear algebra, in which the inputs and outputs are formulated as multivariate polynomial equations. Solving a nonlinear system of multivariate equations will reduce complexity, which in turn yields the targeted secret information. Recently, Addition Modulo 2^n has been suggested over logic XOR as a mixing operator to guard against such attacks. However, it has been observed that the complexity of Modulo Addition can be drastically decreased with the appropriate formulation of polynomial equations and probabilistic conditions. A new model for enhanced Addition Modulo is proposed. The framework for the new design is characterized by user-defined expandable security for stronger encryption and does not impose changes in the existing layout for stream ciphers such as SNOW 2.0, BIVIUM, CryptMT, Grain Family, etc. The structure of the proposed design is highly scalable, boosts the Algebraic degree and thwarts the probabilistic conditions by maintaining the original hardware complexity without changing the integrity of the Addition Modulo 2^n.

Keywords: Algebraic attack · Modulo addition · Algebraic degree · Scalability · SNOW 2.0 · Trivium · S-Box · LFSR · NFSR · SAT solver · Stream cipher

1 Introduction

Algebraic cryptanalysis focuses on formulating multivariate polynomial equations between the inputs and outputs with low Algebraic degree. Stream ciphers were first subjected to Algebraic Attacks in [8], where the keystream is used to solve a system of multivariate polynomial equations related to the initial states

© Springer International Publishing AG 2016
J. Chen et al. (Eds.): NSS 2016, LNCS 9955, pp. 383–397, 2016.
DOI: 10.1007/978-3-319-46298-1_25

of the cipher. The significance of the attack is that the formulae exist with probability 1 or close to 1, unlike traditional probabilistic attacks, such as differential cryptanalysis [1] and linear cryptanalysis [5]. As a result, solving such equations successfully will always yield the desired value of the targeted variable. The procedure to set up the attack typically starts with the attacker finding a set of equations that can describe the relationship between the input and the output. Each equation in the set contains an Algebraic degree. Higher degree results in higher difficulty to solve the equations. At the same time, it is very common that the number of multivariate equations is less than the number of variables. Therefore, an attacker would try to uncover ways that will lower the Algebraic degree of the existing equations or new independent equations that will help describe the relationship between input and output. Moreover, it is often possible that the degree can be lowered or that new equations can be formed based on some probabilistic condition. Finally, solving the set of equations can be done through techniques such as Gaussian reduction or methods described in [6,9].

1.1 Preview of Related Work

Addition Modulo 2^n has been widely used as an elementary cryptographic module in stream ciphers, such as CAST [1] and MARS [4], and block ciphers, such as SOBER-t32 [12] and SNOW 2.0 [10]. Typically, it is used for mixing, which combines two data sources to provide security. While the logic XOR operation is also often used for mixing, Modulo Addition offers better security against Algebraic Attack [7] because it is partly non-linear in GF(2). A linear operation in GF(2), such as XOR, can be described by an equation of Algebraic degree 1. Modulo Addition is linear only at its least significant bit (LSB); therefore, it is harder for an attacker to solve using Algebraic Attack.

1.2 Scope of Our Contribution

The Algebraic degree of formulae describing Modulo Addition can be reduced to quadratic [7]. At the same time, conditional properties of the Modulo Addition have been found to lower the Algebraic degree and create new independent equations. These techniques help tremendously to reduce the complexity of solving Modulo Addition. As a result, this paper aims to devise a new structure that will increase the Algebraic degree when compared to traditional Modulo Addition and simultaneously increase the difficulty of using the conditional properties. The size of our structure is user-defined and highly adaptable to security requirements, providing users a scalable security model against Algebraic Attack.

1.3 Organization

Section 2 outlines basic notations and definitions used in the paper. Section 3 illustrates the details of the proposed design. Section 4 outlines design analysis and differentiates the new model from traditional Modulo Addition. Section 5 demonstrates the application with analysis of the new design in a common stream cipher like SNOW 2.0. Section 6 concludes the paper by discussing future opportunities.

2 Notation and Definitions

2.1 Algebraic Immunity

The study on Algebraic Attack identified an important property for Boolean functions, called Algebraic Immunity [13] used as a metric in crypto-systems. Using good Algebraic Immunity, resistance against Algebraic Attacks can be achieved i.e., using linearization. Defined as the minimum Algebraic degree in the system of equations, Algebraic Immunity was deemed to be insufficient and consequently a Describing Degree was devised. The Describing Degree $\mathfrak{D}$ is defined as the minimum Algebraic degree that an S-Box can be defined by system of equations using corresponding degree [7].

2.2 Complexity for Generic Stream Cipher

The complexity for a stream cipher employing Algebraic Attacks is estimated as the summation of binomial coefficients $_N C_{\mathfrak{D}}$ given by,

$$\mathfrak{T} = \sum_{k=0}^{\mathfrak{D}} {_N C_{\mathfrak{D}}} \tag{1}$$

where N is the number of variables or states in the stream cipher and $\mathfrak{T}$ is the number of monomials of degree $\leq \mathfrak{D}$. The calculation for estimated complexity is derived by multiplying $\mathfrak{T}$ with the number of operations and the cycle time required for each operation. As these parameters are either algorithm or platform dependent or both, $\mathfrak{T}$ by itself can be used to provide estimation.

2.3 Overview of Modulo Addition

A set of equations describing the relationship between the input and outputs must be derived while viewing Modulo Addition from the perspective of Algebraic Attack. This is outlined in [11] for the n-bit Modulo Addition of $Z = X \boxplus Y$, and shown in (2).

$$\begin{aligned} Z_i &= X_i + Y_i, \quad \text{for } i = 0 \\ Z_i &= X_i + Y_i + C_{i-1}, \quad \text{with C = carry bit}, 1 \leq i \leq n - 1 \end{aligned} \tag{2}$$

The addition operation is denoted by $+$ sign in $GF(2)$, which is the logic XOR operation. The carry variable obtained above can be described by (3).

$$C_i = \begin{cases} X_iY_i \text{, for } i = 0 \\ X_iY_i + (X_i + Y_i)(C_{i-1}) \text{, for } 1 \leq i < 2 \\ X_iY_i + (X_i + Y_i)(X_{i-1}Y_{i-1}) + \\ \displaystyle\sum_{k=0}^{i-2} X_kY_k \prod_{l=k+1}^{i} (X_l + Y_l) \text{, with } 2 \leq i < n - 2 \end{cases} \tag{3}$$

By merging (2) and (3), we can observe that the Modulo Addition is not completely nonlinear since the least significant bit(LSB) of the resulting output always stays linear. Also the carry terms dominate all other terms of the resulting Algebraic degree. Consequently, the degree increases linearly with the carry terms as in (3). This is due to the fact that the more significantly positioned carry terms not only depend on their corresponding input variables, which have a degree 1, but also on the previous carry terms. As C_0 is generated by X_0 and Y_0, the degree of Z_1 becomes 2. Similarly, C_1 is generated by X_1 and Y_1, and the degree of Z_2 becomes 3. In general, for an n-bit output, we can define the Algebraic degree for each output bit i as:

$$deg(i) = i + 1 \text{, where } 0 < i \leq n \tag{4}$$

Thus, the complexity of solving the equations is directly proportional to the Algebraic degree. In [7], a set of equations was devised that describes Modulo Addition but limits the Algebraic degree to 2. This property is described using (5). Moreover the methods in [7] produced $6n - 3$ independent equations instead of the original n equations. This effectively reduces the complexity of Algebraic Attack on Modulo Addition even before the deployment of conditional properties.

$$Z_i = \begin{cases} X_i + Y_i & \text{for } i = 0 \\ X_i + Y_i + X_iY_i & \text{for } i = 1 \\ X_i + Y_i + X_{i-1}Y_{i-1} + \\ (X_{i-1} + Y_{i-1})(X_{i-1} + Y_{i-1} + Z_{i-1}) & 1 < i \leq n - 1 \end{cases} \tag{5}$$

2.4   The Characteristics of Modulo Addition

Output Characteristic. This can abet in linearizing the equations when the output bits of the addition are all 1's, or when the output is $2^n - 1$. In fact when the carry-in is 0, all the output bits are 1's only when the input bits are of opposite polarity. Alternatively, for each pair of input bits, the two bits are either $\{1, 0\}$ or $\{0, 1\}$. This process is referred to as propagate [14] and the probability of this occurring is 2^{-n}. In this case, the Algebraic degree of the equations is lowered to 1.

Input Characteristic. Two input characteristics are utilized as a means to linearize the equations. First, no carry is generated when one of the input is simply 0. Second, there can be no carries generated when one of the inputs is the two's complement of the other input. The output bits of this input pairing are always 0 in Modulo Addition. The distribution of the carry bits is as follows: There will be no carries generated from the input pairs until the first $\{1,1\}$ pair. Subsequent input pairs will always generate a carry. This provides a controlled distribution to the carry bits. Consequently, if one of the inputs is a power of 2 and the other input is a two's complement, then there is no generation of a carry. Although these conditions can reduce the Algebraic degree, the probability attached to these conditions is 2^{-n}.

Carry Absence in Modulo Addition. A carry-less Modulo Addition will have a completely linearized equation, i.e., the Algebraic degree of (2) is unity when all carries are 0. The probability of occurrence for this condition can be evaluated using (6) and can be approximated to $2^{-(n-1)}$.

The Conditional Properties of Modulo Addition. This concept includes all the characteristics for Modulo Addition outlined in the preceding sections and was first introduced in [11]. The concept was later adapted to Modulo Addition [3] and improved with expansion capability [7]. The aim of adapting conditional equations in Modulo Addition is to lower the Algebraic degree of the equations or to create more independent equations with lower degree. The occurrence of these conditions is based solely on the manipulation of input bits and carry bits. As discussed in preceding sections, the cost of these conditions is the probability. When considering the input bits, the probability is assumed to be uniform, or $1/2$; when considering carry bits, the probability can be generalized using (6). The probability of a carry being 1 approaches $1/2$ as the number of bits increases.

$$\left.\begin{array}{l} Pr(C_i = 1) = \dfrac{2^i - 1}{2^{i+1}} \\[2mm] Pr(C_i = 0) = 1 - Pr(C_i = 1) \end{array}\right\} 1 \leq i \leq n \tag{6}$$

3   Our Design

In our proposed design, a new type of cryptographic model is devised that provides user-defined scalable security against Algebraic Attack. The Algorithm 1 clearly contrasts our new design with the traditional Modulo Addition.

The Expandable Input function $\mathcal{F}^{in}()$ performs expansion of each input bit into a 2^m–bit string based on an $n * m$-bit control string KI. The parameter m is user-defined based on user security requirements. The input control string KI can typically be generated within a cipher. In essence the expansion function is very flexible. The user can substitute either existing or custom expanding functions instead of the proposed function defined here and the expanding function can be an Algebraic function or an S-Box. Our proposed expansion function is an arithmetic relationship that can be easily scaled. Also, every output bit is 0–1 balanced. We can define the Expandable Input function as follows: for any $X = \{x_{n-1}, \ldots x_1, x_0\}$ in $\mathbb{Z}$ be an n-bit input and let $KI_X = \{KI_{x_{n-1}}, KI_{x_{n-2}} \ldots KI_{x_1}, KI_{x_0} \mid KI_{x_i} \in \{0,1\}^m, 0 \leq i \leq n-1\}$. In addition, we have $KI_{x_i} \triangleq KI_{x_{i,m-1}}, \ldots, KI_{x_{i,1}}, KI_{x_{i,0}} \; \forall \; KI_{x_{i,j}} \in \{0,1\}$ with $0 \leq i \leq n-1, 0 \leq j \leq m-1$. Furthermore, let X' be the expanded input where $X' = \{x'_{n-1}, \ldots x'_1, x'_0\}$ and $x'_i \in \{\{0,1\}^w \mid w = 2^m\}$ and KI_{x_i} are treated as decimal numbers in (7) as follows.

$$\left. \begin{aligned} x'_i &= \mathcal{F}^{in}(x_i, \; KI_{x_i}) \\ \mathcal{F}^{in}(x_i, \; KI_{x_i}) &= 2^w - 1 - 2^{KI_{x_i}}, \text{for } x_i = 0 \\ \mathcal{F}^{in}(x_i, \; KI_{x_i}) &= 2^{KI_{x_i}}, \text{for } x_i = 1 \end{aligned} \right\} \tag{7}$$

It is recommended to define an user-defined parameter $m \geq 2$ for (7) in order to avoid repeating values. Figure 1 illustrates an example for $m = 2$.

Algorithm 1. New Design Model for Modulo Addition

Data: n-bit inputs $X \longleftarrow \{x_i \mid 0 < i \leq n\}$ and
$Y \longleftarrow \{y_i \mid 0 < i \leq n\} \; \forall \; X, Y \in \mathbb{Z}$, 3 sets of control strings
$\forall \; KI_{x_i}, KI_{y_i}, KO_i \in \{0,1\}^m$, for some user-defined $m \in \mathbb{Z}^*$.
Result: n-bit output $Z \longleftarrow \{z_i \mid 0 < i \leq n\}$

1 **begin**
2   perform input expansion for X
3   **forall the** $x_i \in X$ **do**
4       $\mid$ $x'_i \longleftarrow \mathcal{F}^{in}(x_i, \; KI_{x_i})$
5   **end**
6   perform input expansion for Y
7   **forall the** $y_i \in Y$ **do**
8       $\mid$ $y' \longleftarrow \mathcal{F}^{in}(y_i, \; KI_{y_i})$
9   **end**
10   use expanded inputs and do modulo addition
11    $Z' \longleftarrow X' \boxplus Y'$
12   perform output compaction for Z'
13   **forall the** $z'_i \in Z'$ **do**
14       $\mid$ $z_i \longleftarrow \mathcal{F}^{out}(z'_i, \; KO_i)$
15   **end**
16 **end**

Modulo Addition component of our new design takes the inputs $X' = \{x'_{n-1}, \ldots, x'_1, x'_0\} \triangleq \{x'_{(n-1)(w-1)}, \ldots, x'_{(n-1)1}, x'_{(n-1)0}, \ldots, x'_{1(w-1)}, \ldots, x'_{11}, x'_{10}, x'_{0(w-1)1}, \ldots, x'_{01}, x'_{00}\}$ and $Y' = \{y'_{n-1}, \ldots, y'_1, y'_0\} \triangleq \{y'_{(n-1)(w-1)}, \ldots, y'_{(n-1)1}, y'_{(n-1)0}, \ldots, y'_{1(w-1)}, \ldots, y'_{11}, y'_{10}, y'_{0(w-1)1}, \ldots, y'_{01}, y'_{00}\}$ which were

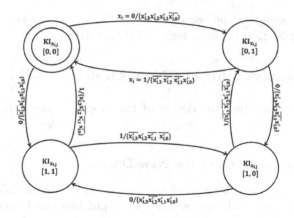

Fig. 1. Input expansion output states $x'_{i,j}$ depending on control input $KI_{x_{i,j}}$ for $m = 2$

the resultant outputs of the previous component after its expansion process was completed. It is now apparent that the number of additions to be performed by this particular component has increased from 2^n to $2^{(n)(w)}$ with $w = 2^m$ for some user-defined $m \in \mathbb{Z}^*$. The output for the Modulo Addition component is given by $Z' = \{z'_{n-1}, \ldots, z'_1, z'_0\} \triangleq \{z'_{(n-1)(w-1)}, \ldots, z'_{(n-1)1}, z'_{(n-1)0}, \ldots, z'_{1(w-1)}, \ldots, z'_{11}, z'_{10}, z'_{0(w-1)1}, \ldots, z'_{01}, z'_{00}\}$. In general, we can derive (8) using (5) or (2) and (3) as follows.

$$z'_{ij} = \begin{cases} x'_{ij} + y'_{ij} & \text{for } i = 0,\ j = 0; \\ x'_{ij} + y'_{ij} + x'_{ij-1}y'_{ij-1} + \\ (x'_{ij-1} + y'_{ij-1})(x'_{ij-1} + y'_{ij-1} + z'_{ij-1}) \\ \qquad \text{for } \begin{subarray}{l} 0<i\leq n-1 \\ 0<j\leq w-1 \end{subarray} \end{cases} \tag{8}$$

Output Compaction forms the last component of our new design. It is a contraction function $\mathcal{F}^{out}$ that compresses $\{z'_i \mapsto z_i \mid \{0,1\}^{nw} \mapsto \{0,1\}^n, n, w \in \mathbb{Z}^*\}$ based on a $n * m$-bit control string KO. This function is very flexible depending on the type of contraction method chosen to implement the task of compressing the summation output. In our design, we propose a $2^m : 1$ multiplexer (MUX) function (Note: The choice of function can be dependent on the user's security requirement). Let $KO = \{KO_{n-1}, \ldots, KO_i, \ldots, KO_1, KO_0 \mid KO_i \in \{0,1\}^m, 0 < i \leq n - 1\}$. Thereby we have, $Z = \{z_{n-1}, \ldots, z_1, z_0\} = \{\mathcal{F}^{out}(z'_{n-1}, KO_{n-1}), \ldots, \mathcal{F}^{out}(z'_1, KO_1), \mathcal{F}^{out}(z'_0, KO_0)\}$. Therefore the expression for $\mathcal{F}^{out}$ can be generalized as in (9).

$$\left. \begin{aligned} z_i &= \mathcal{F}^{out}(z'_i,\ KO_i) \\ \mathcal{F}^{out}(z'_i,\ KO_i) &= \sum_{\ell=0}^{w-1} z'_{i\ell} \prod_{b=0}^{m-1} (-1)^{\frac{\ell}{2^b}+1} KO_{\ell b} \end{aligned} \right\} \tag{9}$$

In (9), (-1) refers to the complement of $KO_{\ell b}$; summation refers to logic XOR and multiplication refers to logic AND operations.

4   Design Analysis for the New Model

In this section, we analyze the design of the proposed model using Algebraic cryptanalysis.

4.1   The Characteristics of the New Design

Output characteristic can be defined for the new design by initially considering the traditional Modulo Addition where the output bits can be used directly to derive potential carries and input pairings. In the new design however, the Output Compaction function is lossy; thus, the attacker can only obtain n bits out of 2^{nw} bits even if the output control string KO is known. Therefore, these n bits cannot provide enough information to derive the potential carries and input pairings. It is still possible to have all 1's in the sum of the Modulo Addition component in the new design. This requires specific combinations of the two m-bit input control strings KI_{x_i} and KI_{y_i}. In particular, the two input control strings should to be the same while the corresponding inputs should be a propagate pair. As discussed before, the probability of output being all 1's in a traditional Modulo Addition is 2^{-n}. Thus the probability of this condition occurring in the new design is decreased to $(2^{-n})(2^{-mn})$.

Input characteristic can be evaluated by employing a similar procedure while considering input characteristics of the traditional Modulo Addition component. To begin with the expanded inputs will never be all 0's when using the input expansion function given in (7). Therefore, this characteristic becomes invalid. Nevertheless, it is possible for the expanded inputs to be the Two's Complement of one another. By observing (7) carefully, it is evident that there are only 3 such cases given any m and $m \geq 2$. Thus, the probability is derived to be $(3/2^{2m+2})$, which is significantly less than 2^{-n}.

4.2   Carry Absence in Modulo Addition

We observe that the probability of carry has decreased from $2^{-(n-1)}$ to $2^{-(wn-1)}$ for the same n-bit input pair as evident in (10). This results in an increase of difficulty for an attacker to create a scenario without any carry, as discussed in Sect. 2.4.

4.3   The Carry Probability

We can estimate the probability of carry for traditional Modulo Addition using (6). As discussed in preceding sections, each bit of the expanded input is $0 - 1$ balanced. We can view the Input Expansion component as an amalgamation of

Boolean functions wherein each output bit corresponds to a $\{0,1\}^{m+1} \mapsto \{0,1\}$ function. However in this case, each Boolean function is $0-1$ balanced since the output of the function has an equal chance of producing either a 0 or 1. Using this assumption, the probability of carry for the new design can be deduced as given below. The ensuing result produces an equation which is very similar to (6). Suppose the carry bits generated due to the summation of two expanded inputs is given by $C' = \{c'_{n-1}, \ldots, c'_1, c'_0\} \triangleq \{c'_{(n-1)(w)}, \ldots, c'_{(n-1)0}, \ldots, c'_w, \ldots, c'_{11}, c'_{10}, c'_{0w}, \ldots, c'_{01}, c'_{00} \mid w = 2^m, m \in \mathbb{Z}^*\}$, the probability as expressed as

$$\left. \begin{aligned} Pr(c'_{ij} = 1) &= \frac{2^{i*w+j} - 1}{2^{i*w+j+1}} \\ Pr(c'_{ij} = 0) &= 1 - Pr(C_i = 1) \end{aligned} \right\} \text{ for } \begin{aligned} 1 &\le i \le n - 1 \\ 1 &\le j \le w, w = 2^m \end{aligned}$$

$$(10)$$

4.4   The Complexity Analysis for the New Model

The Algebraic degree must be obtained in order to evaluate the complexity of solving the new design under an Algebraic Attack. This is possible by expressing the new design in its Algebraic normal form (ANF), which describes a Boolean function using logic XOR gates [9]. The Algebraic degree of each component is first studied before considering the degree of whole design.

Algebraic Degree of Expanded Input is the monomial with the largest degree in the Algebraic normal form. With regard to the Expanded Input function, each expanded variable can be expressed in the ANF by considering itself a Boolean function. Intuitively, the value of the expanded variable is a manipulation of the original input value based on the value of the user-defined parameter m.

Effective Algebraic Degree of Addition Modulo can be evaluated for the new model using (5) or (2) and (3). We notice that (5) limits the Algebraic degree to quadratic in the original Modulo Addition by utilizing the output variables when output is observable. However, in the new design, the output variables of the Modulo Addition component may not be observable. But it is possible to define them as additional variables so that the Algebraic degree of the expression can be reduced. Assuming that additional variables are used, the Algebraic degree of the Modulo Addition component is at most 2m. This is due to the fact that each input variable now has a degree of m and the largest degree is quadratic using (5). At this point, it can be observed that the Algebraic degree has already increased by the user-defined parameter m. It is possible to express the Modulo Addition using (2) and (3), and its Algebraic degree is outlined by (4). As mentioned before, each input variable now has a degree of m. The LSB of the addition then has a degree of m and the rest of output bits have a degree of $(i * w + j + 1)m$ with $0 \le i \le n - 1, 0 \le j \le 2^m - 1, w = 2^m$. The derivation approach is similar to what is outlined in the preceding section. We also notice that the degree of the carry terms increases linearly according to their bit positions. However, the degree increases in multiples of m because the expanded input variables have a degree of m. As a result, the degree of z'_{01} is generated by the multiplication of two degree m variables x'_{00} and y'_{00}. Similarly, the degree of z'_{02} can be generated by the multiplication of x'_{01}, x'_{00}, and y'_{00}, or the combination of y'_{01}, x'_{00} and y'_{00} whose degrees are $2m$ and $3m$ respectively. Therefore, each output variable of the Modulo Addition, z'_{ij}, has a degree of $(i * w + j + 1)m$. By comparison the effective increase of Algebraic degree is m with regard to the traditional Modulo Addition. A comparison summary of Algebraic degree is given in Table 1.

Table 1. A comparison of algebraic degrees for summation

	In traditional modulo addition	In our new design
Algebraic degree using (5)	$1 \to 2$	$m \to 2m$
Algebraic degree using (2) and (3)	$1 \to i + 1$	$m \to (i * w + j + 1)m$

Algebraic Degree of Output Compaction is determined. As specified in preceding sections, this function is a 2m:1 logic Multiplexer (MUX) function defined by (9). As this equation is itself in the Algebraic normal form (ANF), the degree can be determined by observing (9). Consequently, the degree is $m + 1$ since the output of the MUX function depends on the values of all the select lines and the input. The 1 comes from the assumption that the degree of input to the MUX is 1. When the degree changes, it must be substituted accordingly.

4.5   Overall Algebraic Degree of New Design

The overall algebraic degree can be estimated by an union of degrees of all the components in our new model. Table 1 provides a summary of the Algebraic degree of the new design and a comparison to the traditional Modulo Addition. Here the Algebraic degree of the traditional Modulo Addition is calculated using (5). As described in Table 2, the Algebraic Immunity has increased by $2m$, or at least 4 for $m = 2$. The Describing Degree $\mathfrak{D}$ has increased from 2 to at least 10 for $m = 2$ and $n = 1$. Also, an attacker can seek to lower the degree of the new design by looking for additional independent equations with lower degree or by creating extra variables. The benefit of these methods is to be determined by the attacker. A corner case study is provided in Sect. 4.6 as a starting point.

4.6   A Corner Case Analysis for the New Design

A corner case for the new design can be derived by carefully observing for a conditional property; a probabilistic condition can help reduce the Algebraic degree. As described in Sect. 4.4, it is clear that the Algebraic degree of the Input Expansion function depends on the multiplication of the input control string variables. Therefore, if the variables are all known, the degree falls to 1.

Table 2. A comparison of algebraic properties for traditional and new design modulo addition

		Traditional Modulo Addition	New Design Modulo Addition
Algebraic Degree of	Input	1	m
	Addition	2	$m \rightarrow (i * w + j + 1)m$
	Output	–	$m + 1$
	Total	$1 \rightarrow 2$	$2m \rightarrow m + (i * w + j + 1)m$
	Algebraic Immunity	1	$2m$
	Describing Degree($\mathfrak{D}$)	2	$m+$ $((n-1) * 2^m + (2^m - 1) + 1)m$

Specifically, if the input control string has all 0's, the expanded inputs are either the same as the inputs or the complement of the inputs. Under this condition, the degree of addition becomes at least 1, which is the same as the traditional Modulo Addition. In each block of expanded inputs, the expression of the summation of expanded input variables can be reduced because many of the variables are the same. In fact, the degree of the LSB in each block of expanded inputs is $i + 1$, for $0 \leq i \leq n - 1$. The rest of the summation bits from adding each block of the expanded inputs have a degree of $i + 2$. Furthermore, the attacker would notice that if the Output Compaction function is able to select the LSB in each block of the summation, i.e., z'_{i0}, the Algebraic degree is the lowest. To reproduce this condition, the output control string needs to be all 0's. As a result, the degree of the new design becomes $i + 1$ for z'_i with $0 \leq i \leq n - 1$. Incidentally, this is the same as the traditional Modulo Addition as shown in Table 1. The cost of this condition has a probability of 2^{-3mn} as all control bits need to be 0's. The traditional Modulo Addition and our new design can be viewed as S-Boxes and their complexity against Algebraic Attack can be approximated as S-Boxes. For the traditional Modulo Addition, the required parameters have been studied in [7]. A comparison for the same has been listed in Table 3. While referring to the corner case, the $\mathfrak{T}$ is still larger because of the increased number of variables and Algebraic degree. Simultaneously, the complexity has also increased by attaching the conditional cost.

5   Case Study: New SNOW 2.0

In this section, we demonstrate the application of our new design using a stream cipher, which utilizes combiner with memory [10]. SNOW 2.0 uses a length 16 LFSR over $GF(2^{32})$. In other words, the LFSR has 16 elements, or states, but each state contains a 32-bit word. Let $S_0, S_1, \ldots, S_{15}$ denote the states of the LFSR. The feedback function is defined as the XOR combination of S_0 multiplied by α, S_2 and S_{11} divided by α. To produce the output key stream, a Finite State Machine (FSM) is used in conjunction with the LFSR. The FSM contains two 32-bit registers R1 and R2. The value of R2 is determined by feeding the value

Table 3. A complexity comparison for the corner case analysis

	Input Variables	Output Variables	Extra Variables Equations (R)	Algebraic Degree (deg)	Condition Cost	Number of Monomials (Σ)	Complexity (Γ)
Traditional Modulo Addition	$2n$	n	0 $6n-3$	2	0	$\sum_{i=0}^{2}\binom{3*n}{i}$	$(\Sigma/2n)^{\lceil\Sigma/R\rceil}$
New Design Modulo Addition	$3mn+2n$	n	0 n	$n+1$	2^{3mn}	$\sum_{i=0}^{n+1}\binom{3n(1+m)}{i}$	$(\Sigma/3mn+2n)^{\lceil\Sigma/R\rceil}$

of R1 through a set of AES S-Boxes and the AES Mix Column function. The value of R1 is determined by performing Addition Modulo 2^{32} between R2 and S_5. Finally, the output combiner function is defined as first performing Addition Modulo 2^{32} between R1 and S_{15}, then XOR-ing the result with R2, and finally XORing the result of the former with S_0.

Applications Using the New Design. The new design is used to replace the two Modulo Additions and the user-defined parameter m is chosen to be 3. There are 288 extra bits required to supply the input and output control strings of each addition, because for each input bit of the 32-bit addition, a 3-bit control string is needed. Therefore, 576 bits in total are required for two additions. The extra bits can be generated in my ways. In this case, S_{14} is used to generate 288 bits and the same set of bits is used for the two insertions of the new design. The logic behind this generation is as follows:

1. For each bit of the first input X, a total of 3 input control bits are needed. They will be the 3 LSBs of the 3-bit circular-left-shifted S_{14}. For example: $KI_{x_0} = (S_{14,2}, S_{14,1}, S_{14,0})$ and $KI_{x_1} = (S_{14,31}, S_{14,30}, S_{14,29})$.
2. For each bit of the second input Y, the 3 input control bits will propagate from the 3 LSBs of the 3-bit circular-right-shifted and inverted S_{14}. Let S'_{14} denote the bit-wise inverted S_{14}. Then, $KI_{y_0} = (S'_{14,2}, S'_{14,1}, S'_{14,0})$ and $KI_{y_1} = (S'_{14,5}, S'_{14,4}, S'_{14,3})$.
3. For the output control string, each 3 output control bits arrives from the 3 LSBs of the 3-bit circular-right-shifted S_{14}. For example: $KO_0 = (S_{14,2}, S_{14,1}, S_{14,0})$ and $KO_1 = (S_{14,5}, S_{14,4}, S_{14,3})$.

This setup can at least guarantee that the input control bits for the first input pair will not be all 0's simultaneously. The new SNOW 2.0 setup is shown in Fig. 2.

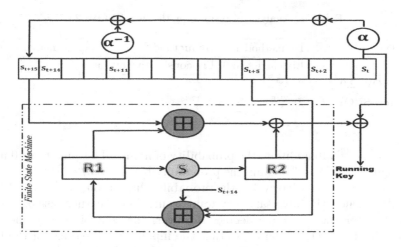

Fig. 2. Schematic for the new SNOW 2.0 design

5.1 Analysis of New SNOW 2.0

The Algebraic Attack on SNOW 2.0 has been studied extensively in [3,7]. Two methods have been proposed to linearize the Addition Modulo 2^{32} in the stream cipher. The first method is relatively straightforward, as the Modulo Addition can be completely linearized when there are no carries. The probability of this occurring can be estimated using (6). The condition is satisfied as long as each input pair does not generate a carry. The probability of this happening is $(3/4)^{31}$ because the probability of an input pair generating no carries is $(3/4)$. The author in [3] seeks to use this condition for both additions and for 17 consecutive cycles. The probability of this is $(3/4)^{31*2*17} \approx 2^{-438}$, which is close to exhaustive search 2^{-576}. In SNOW 2.0, the exhaustive search includes the search for 512 bits in the LFSR states and two 32-bit registers. In the new SNOW 2.0, the cost of having no carries has greatly increased. As $m = 3$ in this application, the length of the Modulo Addition component in the new design becomes $32 * 2^3 = 256$. To fix the carries for one Modulo Addition, the probability is estimated to be $2^{-(31*8*17)}$ $= 2^{-4216}$ by using (6). This is much larger than exhaustive search. The second method sees the attacker trying to manipulate the output characteristics of the Modulo Addition to linearize the equations, as described in [7]. In particular, 9 consecutive values of the register R1 are fixed. The desired output values from the summation are $R1_1 = 0$, $R1_2 = 2^{32} - 1$, $R1_3 = 0$, $R1_4 = 0$, $R1_5 = 0$, $R1_6 = 0$, $R1_7 = 0$, $R1_8 = 0$, and $R1_9 = 0$. The value of R1 comes from summing R2 and S_5 but the value of R2 comes from feeding R1 through the ASE S-Boxes and Mix Column operation. Therefore, only S_5 needs to be fixed. Due to the nature of LFSR, 9 states need to be fixed, namely: S_5, S_6, S_7, S_8, S_9, S_{10}, S_{11}, S_{12}, and S_{13}. The associated probability is $2^{-32*9} = 2^{-288}$. With the new design applied; however, the output characteristic may not be applicable. As discussed in Sect. 4, the probability of fixing all outputs to be 1 in the new design is $2^{-n(m+1)}$. In this scenario, the probability has become

Table 4. Analysis of results for the new SNOW 2.0

Type	By method 1	By method 2	Corner case
	Fix carries to 0	Fix consecutive outputs	
SNOW 2.0	2^{-248}	2^{-288}	–
New SNOW 2.0	2^{-4216}	2^{-1768}	NA

$2^{-32(3+1)} = 2^{-128}$. In addition, the probability of fixing all outputs to be 0 in the new design is $(3/2^{2m+2})^n$. Again, the probability becomes $(3/2^{2*3+2})^{32} \approx 2^{-205}$. For a total of 9 consecutive cycles, the probability has become $2^{-205*8} * 2^{-128} = 2^{-1768}$. In essence, the adversary may want to utilize the corner case of the new design to lower the Algebraic degree. However, the control string generation logic, outlined in Sect. 5, guarantees that the input control strings for the LSBs of the two inputs will not be 0 simultaneously. Therefore, the set of equations cannot be completely linearized, as illustrated in Table 4.

6   Conclusion and Future Work

In this paper, a new type of Modulo Addition is proposed to defend against Algebraic Attack. It contains three components: Input Expansion, Addition Modulo, and Output Compaction. In addition, the new design utilizes an expanding and compacting structure that can be user-defined to fit into various cryptographic systems. Our model develops more adaptable functions to substitute the existing Input Expansion and Output Compaction modules in order to provide different requirement based security enhancements. Future plans involve further investigation and development of additional Algebraic cryptanalysis to create extra independent equations with lower degrees [2].

References

1. Adams, C.M.: Constructing symmetric ciphers using the cast design procedure. Des. Codes Crypt. **12**(3), 283–316 (1997)
2. Armknecht, F.: On the existence of low-degree equations for algebraic attacks. IACR Cryptology ePrint Archive 2004, 185 (2004)
3. Billet, O., Gilbert, H.: Resistance of SNOW 2.0 against algebraic attacks. In: Menezes, A. (ed.) CT-RSA 2005. LNCS, vol. 3376, pp. 19–28. Springer, Heidelberg (2005)
4. Burwick, C., Coppersmith, D., D'Avignon, E., Gennaro, R., Halevi, S., Jutla, C., Matyas Jr., S.M., O'Connor, L., Peyravian, M., Luke, J., Peyravian, O.M., Stafford, D., Zunic, N.: Mars - a candidate cipher for aes. In: NIST AES Proposal (1999)
5. Carlet, C., Feng, K.: An infinite class of balanced functions with optimal algebraic immunity, good immunity to fast algebraic attacks and good nonlinearity. In: Pieprzyk, J. (ed.) ASIACRYPT 2008. LNCS, vol. 5350, pp. 425–440. Springer, Heidelberg (2008). doi:10.1007/978-3-540-89255-7_26

6. Courtois, N., Klimov, A., Patarin, J., Shamir, A.: Efficient algorithms for solving overdefined systems of multivariate polynomial equations. In: Preneel, B. (ed.) EUROCRYPT 2000. LNCS, vol. 1807, pp. 392–407. Springer, Heidelberg (2000). doi:10.1007/3-540-45539-6_27

7. Courtois, N.T., Debraize, B.: Algebraic description and simultaneous linear approximations of addition in SNOW 2.0. In: Chen, L., Ryan, M.D., Wang, G. (eds.) ICICS 2008. LNCS, vol. 5308, pp. 328–344. Springer, Heidelberg (2008)

8. Courtois, N.T., Meier, W.: Algebraic attacks on stream ciphers with linear feedback. In: Biham, E. (ed.) EUROCRYPT 2003. LNCS, vol. 2656, pp. 345–359. Springer, Heidelberg (2003). doi:10.1007/3-540-39200-9_21

9. Courtois, N.T., Patarin, J.: About the XL algorithm over $GF(2)$. In: Joye, M. (ed.) CT-RSA 2003. LNCS, vol. 2612, pp. 141–157. Springer, Heidelberg (2003)

10. Ekdahl, P., Johansson, T.: A new version of the stream cipher SNOW. In: Nyberg, K., Heys, H. (eds.) SAC 2002. LNCS, vol. 2595, pp. 47–61. Springer, Heidelberg (2003). doi:10.1007/3-540-36492-7_5

11. Fischer, S., Meier, W.: Algebraic immunity of S-Boxes and augmented functions. In: Biryukov, A. (ed.) FSE 2007. LNCS, vol. 4593, pp. 366–381. Springer, Heidelberg (2007)

12. Hawkes, P., Rose, G.: Primitive specification and support documentation for SOBER-t32 submission to NESSIE. In: Proceedings of the First Open NESSIE Workshop (2000)

13. Meier, W., Pasalic, E., Carlet, C.: Algebraic attacks and decomposition of boolean functions. In: Cachin, C., Camenisch, J.L. (eds.) EUROCRYPT 2004. LNCS, vol. 3027, pp. 474–491. Springer, Heidelberg (2004). doi:10.1007/978-3-540-24676-3_28

14. Weste, N.H., Harris, D.: Datapath subsystems. In: CMOS VLSI Design: A Circuits and Systems Perspective, pp. 637–711. Addison Wesley, Heidelberg (2004)

Extension of Meet-in-the-Middle Technique for Truncated Differential and Its Application to RoadRunneR

Qianqian Yang[1,2,3], Lei Hu[1,2(✉)], Siwei Sun[1,2], and Ling Song[1,2]

[1] State Key Laboratory of Information Security, Institute of Information Engineering, Chinese Academy of Sciences, Beijing 100093, China
hu@is.ac.cn
[2] Data Assurance and Communication Security Research Center, Chinese Academy of Sciences, Beijing 100093, China
[3] University of Chinese Academy of Sciences, Beijing 100049, China

Abstract. In the FSE 2015 conference, Li *et al.* introduced a new method to construct differential characteristics of block ciphers by exploiting the meet-in-the-middle like technique. Inspired by the method, in this paper we obtain general results on truncated differential characteristics of block ciphers with Feistel structure. Applying the result to RoadRunneR, which is a fast bit-slice lightweight block cipher proposed in the LightSec 2015 conference for low cost 8-bit processors, we find 5-round truncated differential characteristics with probability 2^{-56}. Using the truncated differential characteristics, we present a attack on 7-round RoadRunneR-128 without whitening keys, with data complexity of 2^{55} chosen plaintexts, time complexity of 2^{121} encryptions, and memory complexity of 2^{68}. This is the currently best known attack on RoadRunneR block cipher.

Keywords: Truncated differential · Meet-in-the-middle technique · Lightweight block cipher · RoadRunneR

1 Introduction

With the applications of small embedded devices such as RFIDs and sensor networks, lightweight block ciphers (with smaller block and key sizes) designed for such environment are increasingly popular. Many lightweight block ciphers have been proposed in recent years, including PRESENT [9], LED [14], LBlock [29], PRINCE [10], and two lightweight block ciphers SIMON and SPECK [3] designed by the U.S. National Security Agency. In this context, evaluating the security of such lightweight ciphers is currently receiving considerable attention.

Differential cryptanalysis [5], which was proposed by Biham and Shamir in 1990 to analyze the block cipher DES, is one of the most principal and effective attacks on block ciphers. Based on the differential cryptanalysis, there are many variants of differential analysis, such as related-key differential attack [4],

© Springer International Publishing AG 2016
J. Chen et al. (Eds.): NSS 2016, LNCS 9955, pp. 398–411, 2016.
DOI: 10.1007/978-3-319-46298-1_26

high-order differential attack [16], multiple differential attack [8], impossible differential attack [6], boomerang attack [28], truncated differential attack [16] and so forth.

Truncated differential cryptanalysis, developed by Knudsen in 1994, is a generalization of differential cryptanalysis. Different from the differential characteristic, the truncated differential considers differences that are only partially determined. Namely, the truncated differential includes a set of differential trails that have the same active S-boxes. Truncated differential cryptanalysis has been applied to many ciphers, such as SAFER [17], IDEA [18], Skipjack [19], E2 [22], Twofish, Camellia [20,25], CRYPTON [15], and even a stream cipher Salsa20 [11]. In FSE'15, by exploiting the meet-in-the-middle like technique, Li *et al.* [21] proposed a new method to construct truncated differential characteristics of block ciphers.

RoadRunneR [2] is a new lightweight block cipher which was recently proposed by Adnan Baysal and Sähap Şahin in LightSec'15. RoadRunneR is a small and fast bit-slice block cipher designed for low cost 8-bit processors. While most of lightweight block ciphers with high software implementation efficiency lack thorough security proofs, the security of RoadRunneR is provable against differential and linear attacks. RoadRunneR is a Feistel-type block cipher with 64-bit block size and 80-bit or 128-bit key size. Its two versions for 80-bit and 128-bit key, i.e., RoadRunneR-80 and RoadRunneR-128, have respectively 10 and 12 rounds of Feistel iterations.

Our Contribution. First, inspired by a meet-in-the-middle technique recently proposed by Li *et al.* [21] for finding truncated differentials of block ciphers, we obtain general results on truncated differential characteristics of block ciphers with Feistel structure. Second, applying the result we find to RoadRunneR, we get its 5-round truncated differential characteristics. By extending the truncated differential characteristic to two rounds forwards, we successfully launch a truncated differential attack on 7-round RoadRunneR-128 without whitening keys, with data complexity of 2^{55} chosen plaintexts, time complexity of 2^{121} encryptions and memory complexity of 2^{68}.

Organization of this paper. Sect. 2 presents a brief description of the block cipher RoadRunneR. In Sect. 3, extending the method of meet-in-the-middle technique for truncated differential, we propose a general result on truncated differential characteristic of Feistel structure ciphers. In Sect. 4, applying the result to RoadRunneR, we launch a truncated differential attack on 7-round RoadRunneR-128. The paper is concluded in Sect. 5.

2   Brief Description of RoadRunneR

2.1   Description of RoadRunneR Block Cipher

In this section, we briefly review the design of the block cipher RoadRunneR, and refer the reader to [2] for more details.

Recently, there are many lightweight ciphers designed for better performance in hardware implementation. RoadRunneR is a small and fast bit-slice block cipher suitable for low cost 8-bit processors. The designers of RoadRunneR pointed out that this cipher has a very low code size and is efficient for 8-bit software implementation. Moreover, RoadRunneR is proved to be resistant to differential and linear attacks.

RoadRunneR is based on the iterative Feistel structure, with 64-bit block size and 80-bit or 128-bit key size. The version of 80-bit key size needs 10 rounds of iterations and the other needs 12 rounds.

The F-Function. The F-function is a 4-round SPN structure, and the detail can be seen in Fig. 1, which is redrawn from [2]. The first three rounds have the same function called SLK, which is the consecutive application of S-box layer, diffusion layer and key addition, and the last round only has S-box layer. After the second SLK function, a round constant is XORed to the least significant byte of the state. For round $i = 0, 1, \cdots, NR - 1$, the round constant is $C_i = NR - i$, where NR is the number of total rounds. The 4-round SPN-like structure ensures a high number of active S-boxes for an active F-function.

The S-box Layer. Lately, bit-slice techniques increase in popularity. Block ciphers such as NOEKEON [12], SEA [24], PRIDE [1] and RECTANGLE [30] all use bit-slice S-boxes but with different S-box layer design strategies. Bit-slice S-box structure has advantages in both hardware and software implementations [13]. In RoadRunneR, the designers adopted an efficient bit-slice S-box, as illustrated in Table 1.

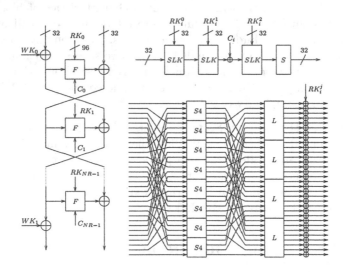

Fig. 1. Feistel structure (on left), F function (on top right), and SLK function (on bottom right)

Table 1. S-box of RoadRunneR

x	0×0	0×1	0×2	0×3	0×4	0×5	0×6	0×7	0×8	0×9	0×a	0×b	0×c	0×d	0×e	0×f
S(x)	0×0	0×8	0×6	0×d	0×5	0×f	0×7	0×c	0×4	0×e	0×2	0×3	0×9	0×1	0×b	0×a

The Diffusion Layer. In the block cipher RoadRunneR, the linear layer L is of the form as

$$L(x) = (x \lll i) \oplus (x \lll j) \oplus (x \lll k),$$

where $x \lll i$ represents the i−bit left rotation of the word x. This form of L guarantees that the linear layers are invertible and all have branch number 4. Due to good diffusion and performance of L, the designers chose $L(x) = x \oplus (x \lll 1) \oplus (x \lll 2)$ as the diffusion layer matrix.

The Key Schedules. RoadRunneR has two versions: RoadRunneR-80 and RoadRunneR-128, which take 80-bit and 128-bit key respectively. For these two versions, the key scheduling part generates 96-bit round keys with the same method. The initial whitening key starts from the beginning of the master key. Then for the round keys, when a new 32-bit of key material is required, the key schedule generates a 32-bit from the master key in a circular way. At last, the final whitening key is generated by the same way. The details of round keys used in RoadRunneR-80 and RoadRunneR-128 are given in Table 2.

2.2 Security Analysis on RoadRunneR Against Standard Differential Attack

In [2], RoadRunneR is proved immune to standard differential attack. The designers have given the minimum number of active S-boxes in standard differential characteristics. Carrying out the mixed integer programming based method [23,26,27], we have computed the same results of the minimum number of active

Table 2. Key schedules of RoadRunneR

80-bit key schedule		128-bit key schedule	
Master key: $A\|B\|C\|D\|E$		Master key $= A\|B\|C\|D$	
Initial whitening $= A\|B$		Initial whitening: A	
Rounds	Key words	Rounds	Key words
0,5	$(C\|D) - (E\|A) - (B\|C)$	0,4,8	$B - C - D$
1,6	$(D\|E) - (A\|B) - (C\|D)$	1,5,9	$A - B - C$
2,7	$(E\|A) - (B\|C) - (D\|E)$	2,6,10	$D - A - B$
3,8	$(A\|B) - (C\|D) - (E\|A)$	3,7,11	$C - D - A$
4,9	$(B\|C) - (D\|E) - (A\|B)$		
Final whitening: $C\|D$		Final whitening: B	

Table 3. Minimum number of active S-boxes

No. of rounds	4	5	6
Min.# Act. S-boxes	26	36	48

S-boxes as in [2]. As shown in Table 3, the highest probability of 5-round differential characteristic is at most 2^{-72} which is smaller than 2^{-64}, it follows that there is no useful differential in 5 or more rounds of RoadRunneR.

3   Extension of Meet-in-the-Middle Technique for Truncated Differential

In [21], Li *et al.* proposed the meet-in-the-middle technique to find the truncated differential of block ciphers. Inspired by the method, we obtain general results on truncated differential characteristics of block ciphers with Feistel structure. We first give the definition of truncated differential and the proposition proposed by Li *et al.*

Definition 1 *[7]. For a block cipher E with a parameter key K, the truncated differential characteristic $(\Gamma_{in} \xrightarrow{E} \Gamma_{out})$ is a set of differential trails, where Γ_{in} is a set of input differences, and Γ_{out} is a set of output differences. The expected probability of such truncated differential $(\Gamma_{in} \xrightarrow{E} \Gamma_{out})$ is defined by*

$$Pr(\Gamma_{in} \xrightarrow{E} \Gamma_{out}) = \frac{1}{|\Gamma_{in}|} \sum_{a \in \Gamma_{in}} Pr((E_K(X) \oplus E_K(X \oplus a)) \in \Gamma_{out})$$

$$= \frac{1}{|\Gamma_{in}|} \sum_{a \in \Gamma_{in}} Pr(a \to \Gamma_{out}).$$

Proposition 1 *[21]. For a block cipher $E = E_1 \circ E_0$, there are two truncated differential characteristics with high probability, i.e., $Pr(\Gamma_0 \xrightarrow{E_0} \Gamma_1) = p$, and $Pr(\Gamma_2 \xrightarrow{E_1^{-1}} \Gamma_1) = 1$, where Γ_0 is the input difference set of E, and Γ_1 and Γ_2 are the output difference sets of E_0 and E, respectively. Then the probability of the truncated differential $\Gamma_0 \xrightarrow{E} \Gamma_2$ is $p \times \frac{|\Gamma_2|}{|\Gamma_1|}$, where $|\Gamma_2| \le |\Gamma_1|$, displayed in Fig. 2.*

For a block cipher E with Feistel structure, we assume that the block size is n bits, thus the branch size is $n/2$ bits. The input value of round i is denoted by (L_{i-1}, R_{i-1}), and the round function is denoted by f.

Theorem 1. *For a block cipher E with Feistel structure, if there exists a 1-round truncated differential $(\Gamma_\alpha, 0) \xrightarrow{1-round} (\Gamma_\alpha, \Gamma_\beta)$ with probability 1 $(|\Gamma_\alpha| = 2^a, |\Gamma_\beta| = 2^b, a < n/2, b < n/2)$, there is a 5-round truncated differential characteristic with high probability, i.e., $Pr((0, \Gamma_\alpha) \xrightarrow{5-round} (0, \Gamma_\alpha)) = 2^{-n+a+n/2-b}$.*

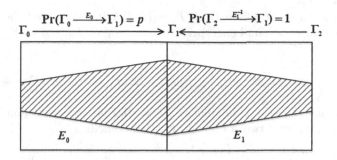

$$\Pr(\Gamma_0 \xrightarrow{E_0} \Gamma_1) = p \qquad \Pr(\Gamma_2 \xrightarrow{E_1^{-1}} \Gamma_1) = 1$$

Fig. 2. Meet-in-the-middle technique for truncated differentials

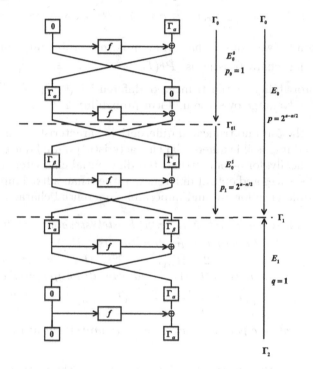

Fig. 3. The 5-Round truncated differential characteristic

The probability of the truncated differential characteristic $(\mathbf{0}, \Gamma_\alpha) \xrightarrow{5-round}$ $(\mathbf{0}, \Gamma_\alpha)$ *obtains* $2^{n/2-b}$ *advantage over the uniform probability* 2^{-n+a}.

Proof. We first denote the 5-round cipher as E with the first three rounds defined as E_0 (the first two rounds defined as E_0^0 and the third round defined as E_0^1) and the last two rounds defined as E_1, as indicated in Fig. 3.

Since the set of input differences is $\Gamma_0 = (\mathbf{0}, \Gamma_\alpha)$, it follows that the set of output differences after 3-round encryption satisfies $\Gamma_1 = (\Gamma_\alpha, \Gamma_\beta)$ with probability $2^{-(n/2-a)}$, i.e.,

$$Pr(\Gamma_0 \xrightarrow{E_0} \Gamma_1) = Pr(\Gamma_0 \xrightarrow{E_0^0} \Gamma_{01}) \times Pr(\Gamma_{01} \xrightarrow{E_0^1} \Gamma_1) = 1 \times 2^{-n/2+a} = 2^{-n/2+a}.$$

Similarly, for the set of differences $\Gamma_2 = (\mathbf{0}, \Gamma_\alpha)$, the corresponding set of output differences after two rounds decryption coincides to $\Gamma_1 = (\Gamma_\alpha, \Gamma_\beta)$ with probability 1, i.e., $Pr(\Gamma_2 \xrightarrow{E_0} \Gamma_1) = 1$.

By the Proposition 1, the probability of 5-round truncated differential characteristic is

$$Pr((\mathbf{0}, \Gamma_\alpha) \xrightarrow{5-round} (\mathbf{0}, \Gamma_\alpha)) = Pr(\Gamma_0 \xrightarrow{E} \Gamma_2) = 2^{-(n/2-a)} \times 2^a/2^{a+b} = 2^{-n+a+n/2-b}.$$

By Definition 1, we know that the uniform probability of the truncated differential characteristic is $Pr(\Gamma_0 \xrightarrow{E} \Gamma_2) = \frac{|\Gamma_2|}{2^n-1} = \frac{2^a}{2^n-1} \approx 2^{-n+a}$. The probability of the truncated differential $(\mathbf{0}, \Gamma_\alpha) \xrightarrow{5-round} (\mathbf{0}, \Gamma_\alpha)$ obtains $2^{n/2-b}$ advantage over the uniform probability 2^{-n+a}. □

Noted that the 5-round truncated differential characteristic is much different from the 5-round impossible differential characteristic pointed out by the designers in [2]. Specifically, for 5-round truncated differential characteristic, there is a set of input differences and output differences rather than a fixed input difference and a output difference for 5-round impossible differential characteristic.

Theorem 2. *For a block cipher E with Feistel structure, if there exists a $R-round$ truncated differential characteristic $(\Gamma_{\alpha_0}, \Gamma_{\alpha_1}) \xrightarrow{R-round} (\Gamma_{\beta_0}, \Gamma_{\beta_1})$ with probability 1 $(|\Gamma_{\alpha_0}| = 2^{a_0}, |\Gamma_{\alpha_1}| = 2^{a_1}, |\Gamma_{\beta_0}| = 2^{b_0}, |\Gamma_{\beta_1}| = 2^{b_1}, a_0, a_1, b_0, b_1 < n/2)$, there is a $(2R+1)-round$ truncated differential characteristic with probability $Pr((\Gamma_{\alpha_0}, \Gamma_{\alpha_1}) \xrightarrow{(2R+1)-round} (\Gamma_{\alpha_0}, \Gamma_{\alpha_1})) = 2^{-n+(a_0+a_1)+n/2-b_1}$, which is relatively high compared with the corresponding probability $2^{-n+(a_0+a_1)}$ for a random iterative cipher and achieves an improvement of factor $2^{n/2-b_1}$.*

Proof. The proof of this theorem can be completed by the method analogous to Theorem 1. Define the $(2R+1)$-round cipher as E with the first $R+1$ rounds defined as E_0 and the last R rounds defined as E_1, as shown in Fig. 4.

The probability of truncated differential characteristics is $2^{b_0-n/2}$, i.e.,

$Pr(\Gamma_0 \xrightarrow{E_0} \Gamma_1) = Pr(\Gamma_0 \xrightarrow{E_0^0} \Gamma_{01}) \times Pr(\Gamma_{01} \xrightarrow{E_0^1} \Gamma_1) = 1 \times 2^{-n/2+b_0} = 2^{b_0-n/2}$. Due to truncated characteristics with the probability 1, i.e., $Pr(\Gamma_2 \xrightarrow{E_0} \Gamma_1) = 1$, the probability of $2R + 1$ round truncated differential is $Pr((\Gamma_{\alpha_0}, \Gamma_{\alpha_1}) \xrightarrow{(2R+1)-round} (\Gamma_{\alpha_0}, \Gamma_{\alpha_1})) = Pr(\Gamma_0 \xrightarrow{E} \Gamma_2) = 2^{b_0-n/2} \times 2^{a_0+a_1}/2^{b_0+b_1} = 2^{-n+(a_0+a_1)+(n/2-b_1)}$. Clearly, the probability of the truncated differential obtains $2^{n/2-b_1}$ advantage over the uniform probability $2^{-n+(a_0+a_1)}$. □

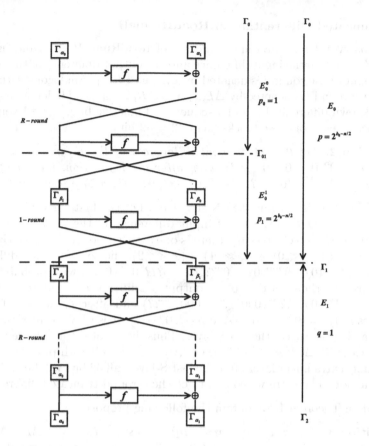

Fig. 4. $(2R + 1)$-round truncated differential characteristic

Obviously, Theorem 1 is a special case for Theorem 2. Combining the property that a cipher has an R-round truncated differential with probability 1 and the meet-in-the-middle technique for truncated differential, we obtain $(2R+1)$-round truncated differential characteristic. Without loss of generality, the result can be used to estimate the security of block ciphers with Feistel structure. Applying to RoadRunneR, we present a truncated differential attack.

4   Application to RoadRunneR

In this section, we describe our truncated differential attack on the 7-round RoadRunneR-128 without whitening key. Applying the result of Sect. 3 to Road-RunneR, we gain 5-round high probability truncated differentials. Further we provide the truncated differential attack on RoadRunneR-128 in detail.

4.1   Truncated Differentials of RoadRunneR

Notations. We define the round function of RoadRunneR as F and use ΔF^I and ΔF^O to denote the input difference and the output difference of the function F. The input of the round i is denoted by L_{i-1} and R_{i-1}. Analogously, the input difference of round i is denoted by ΔL_{i-1} and ΔR_{i-1}. 0, ? and **0** denote a inactive bit, a unknown difference bit and a sequence of inactive bits, respectively. With two branches, each of these blocks has $n/2 = 32$ bits.

Proposition 2. *Let the set of input differences of the F-function is* $\Delta F^I = (0 \cdots 0?, 0 \cdots 0?, 0 \cdots 0?, 0 \cdots 0?)$, *then after the F-function, the set of output differences is* $\Delta F^O = (0? \cdots ?, 0? \cdots ?, 0? \cdots ?, 0? \cdots ?)$ *with probability 1.*

Proof. F-function is a 4-round SPN structure. Let the first three SLK function as f_1, f_2 and f_3. Due to the set of input differences of the F-function $\Delta F^I = (0 \cdots 0?, 0 \cdots 0?, 0 \cdots 0?, 0 \cdots 0?)$, there is one active S-box in f_1. Since the linear layer is $L(x) = (x \lll 0) \oplus (x \lll 1) \oplus (x \lll 2)$, the set of output differences after f_1 is $f_1^O = (0 \cdots 0???, 0 \cdots 0???, 0 \cdots 0???, 0 \cdots 0???)$ with probability 1.

Similarly,   the   set   of   output   differences   after f_2 is $f_2^O = (000?????, 000?????, 000?????, 000?????)$ and after f_3 the set of output differences is $f_3^O = (0? \cdots ?, 0? \cdots ?, 0? \cdots ?, 0? \cdots ?)$. It is easy to show that there is only 7 active S-boxes at the last S-layer. Thus the set of output differences after the F-function is $\Delta F^O = (0? \cdots ?, 0? \cdots ?, 0? \cdots ?, 0? \cdots ?)$ with probability 1.

If adding extra linear layer after the last S-layer, all 32 bits will be active after the F-function. Therefore we couldn't get the 5-round truncated differential. □

Based on Theorem 1, we obtain the following proposition.

Proposition 3. *Let a set of input differences be* $\Gamma_{in} = (\Delta L_0, \Delta R_0) = ((\mathbf{0}, \mathbf{0}, \mathbf{0}, \mathbf{0}), (0 \cdots 0?, 0 \cdots 0?, 0 \cdots 0?, 0 \cdots 0?))$, *then after a 5-round encryption of RoadRunneR, the probability of a set of output differences satisfying* $\Gamma_{out} = (\Delta R_5, \Delta L_5) = \Gamma_{in} = ((\mathbf{0}, \mathbf{0}, \mathbf{0}, \mathbf{0}), (0 \cdots 0?, 0 \cdots 0?, 0 \cdots 0?, 0 \cdots 0?))$ *is about* 2^{-56}.

Proof. Similar to Theorem 1, we denote the 5-round cipher as E with the first three rounds defined as E_0 (the first two rounds defined as E_0^0 and the third round defined as E_0^1) and the last two rounds defined as E_1. Since

$$\Gamma_0 = \Gamma_{in} = (\Delta L_0, \Delta R_0) = (\mathbf{0}, \Gamma_\alpha)$$
$$= ((\mathbf{0}, \mathbf{0}, \mathbf{0}, \mathbf{0}), (0 \cdots 0?, 0 \cdots 0?, 0 \cdots 0?, 0 \cdots 0?)),$$
$$\Gamma_1 = (\Delta L_3, \Delta R_3) = (\Gamma_\alpha, \Gamma_\beta)$$
$$= ((0 \cdots 0?, 0 \cdots 0?, 0 \cdots 0?, 0 \cdots 0?), (0? \cdots ?, 0? \cdots ?, 0? \cdots ?, 0? \cdots ?)),$$
$$\Gamma_2 = \Gamma_{out} = (\Delta R_5, \Delta L_5) = (\mathbf{0}, \Gamma_\alpha)$$
$$= ((\mathbf{0}, \mathbf{0}, \mathbf{0}, \mathbf{0}), (0 \cdots 0?, 0 \cdots 0?, 0 \cdots 0?, 0 \cdots 0?)),$$

we acquire that $a = 4, b = 28$. By Theorem 1, the probability of the 5-round truncated differential is

$$Pr(\Gamma_{in} \xrightarrow{5-round} \Gamma_{out}) = Pr(\Gamma_0 \xrightarrow{E} \Gamma_2) = 2^{-64+4+32-28} = 2^{-56}.$$

From Definition 1, we know that the uniform probability of the truncated differential characteristic is $Pr(\Gamma_0 \xrightarrow{E} \Gamma_2) = \frac{|\Gamma_2|}{2^{64}-1} = \frac{2^4}{2^{64}-1} \approx 2^{-60}$.

For both RoadRunneR-80 and RoadRunneR-128, there is 5-round truncated differential characteristic with probability 2^{-56}. $\qquad\qquad\qquad\qquad\qquad$ □

4.2   Truncated Differential Attack on 7-Round RoadRunneR-128

With the 5-round truncated differential characteristic on 1–5 round, we are able to extend this truncated differential characteristic by adding two rounds to the output and attack 7-round RoadRunneR-128. Our proposed attack consists of two phases:

Data Collection Phase. By expanding two rounds after the 5-round truncated differential characteristic, we deduce that the set of plaintexts differences is

$$\Delta P = (\Delta L_0, \Delta R_0) = ((\mathbf{0}, \mathbf{0}, \mathbf{0}, \mathbf{0}), (0 \cdots 0?, 0 \cdots 0?, 0 \cdots 0?, 0 \cdots 0?))$$

and the set of ciphertexts differences should satisfy

$$\begin{aligned}\Delta C =&(\Delta R_7, \Delta L_7)\\ =&((0? \cdots ?, 0? \cdots ?, 0? \cdots ?, 0? \cdots ?), (? \cdots ?, ? \cdots ?, ? \cdots ?, ? \cdots ?)),\end{aligned}$$

referring to Fig. 5 for the detail. The gray color nibbles stand for active S-boxes and the white nibbles symbolize passive S-boxes.

Construct $N_s = 2^{51}$ structures, in each of which, plaintexts fix in bits 24, 16, 8, 0 and traverse in other 60 bits. For one structure, there are 2^4 plaintexts and corresponding ciphertexts which consist of 2^7 pairs. The expected number of right pairs is $2^{51} \times 2^7 \times 2^{-56} = 4$. After 7-round encryption, the ciphertexts differences satisfy $\Delta C = ((0? \cdots ?, 0? \cdots ?, 0? \cdots ?, 0? \cdots ?), (? \cdots ?, ? \cdots ?, ? \cdots ?, ? \cdots ?))$, which makes $2^{N_s} \times 2^7 \times 2^{-4} = 2^{N_s+3}$ pairs left.

Key Recovery Phase.

–**Step 1.** Guess 68 bits: D, A and $B[24, 16, 8, 0]$, then do the following steps for every remaining pair of plaintexts. We use the method of table look-up to recovery the following 56 bits of key: $B[31 : 25, 23 : 17, 15 : 9, 7 : 1]$ and $C[30 : 24, 22 : 16, 14 : 8, 6 : 0]$.

(a) In the 7-th round, because of knowing D, A and ciphertexts' values C_L, we could calculate each pair's the input difference and output difference of the last S-box layer. Then looking up the concrete distribution table by its input difference and output difference of 7 S-boxes, we get 28 bits values $B[31 : 25, 23 : 17, 15 : 9, 7 : 1]$ of 7 nibbles. In general, each pair of plaintexts will be excluded with probability $1/2$. For each of remaining pairs, we get 2 candidates for $B[31 : 25, 23 : 17, 15 : 9, 7 : 1]$.

(b) In the 6-th round, for each pairs of remaining plaintexts we obtain the values of A, B and the input values of F-function. Therefore, we could calculate each pair's input difference and output difference of the last S-box layer. Similar to (a), we get 28 bits values $C[30 : 24, 22 : 16, 14 : 8, 6 :$

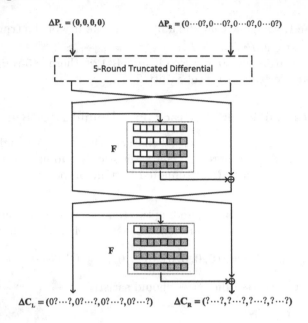

Fig. 5. The truncated differential attack on 7-round RoadRunneR-128

0] of 7 nibbles by looking up the concrete distribution table. On average, each pair of remaining plaintexts will be excluded with probability $1/2$. For each of remaining pairs, we get 2 candidates for $C[30:24, 22:16, 14:8, 6:0]$.

(c) In this way, about 4 pairs expected left for the right key and about 2^{-2} pairs expected to left for the wrong keys. Choose the key whose count is the largest as the candidate of right key.

–**Step 2.** Ultimately, there are 2^{68} survived candidates after Step 1. For each survived candidate, we compute the seed key by doing an exhaustive search for other 4 bits.

Complexity Analysis.

– *Data Complexity.* In our work, we choose $N_s = 51$, the expected count of the right key is $2^{-56} \times 2^{51} \times 2^7 = 4$. The data complexity is $2^{51} \times 2^4 = 2^{55}$.
– *Time Complexity.* We analyze the time complexity in each step. In the data collection phase, the time complexity is 2^{55} 7-round encryptions. In step 1, we need $2^{N_s+3} = 2^{54}$ pairs chosen plaintexts, which cost $2^{68} \times (2^{54} \times 2 \times 1/7 + 2^{54} \times 2 \times 1/7) \approx 2^{121}$ encryptions. In step 2 for the exhaustive searching, the time complexity is $2^{68} \times 2^4 \times 1 = 2^{72}$ encryptions. Therefore, the total time complexity is 2^{121} encryptions.
– *Memory Complexity.* For storing the counters of 56 bits key, the memory complexity is 2^{56}. For storing the 2^{68} survived candidates in Step 1, the memory complexity is 2^{68}. Hence, the memory complexity is 2^{68}.

Overall, we have proposed a successful attack on 7-round RoadRunneR-128 with the data, time and memory complexities are $2^{55}, 2^{121}$ and 2^{68}, respectively.

5 Conclusion

In this paper, by exploiting the meet-in-the-middle technique for truncated differential introduced in FSE 2015, we present a general result on truncated differential characteristics of block ciphers with Feistel structure. Based on our observation, we obtain 5-round truncated differential characteristic of Road-RunneR, and accordingly propose a truncated differential attack on 7-round RoadRunneR-128 without whitening key, with data complexity of 2^{55} chosen plaintexts, time complexity of 2^{121} encryptions and memory complexity of 2^{68}.

Acknowledgements. The authors would like to thank anonymous reviewers for their helpful comments and suggestions. The work of this paper was supported by the National Key Basic Research Program of China (2013CB834203), the National Natural Science Foundation of China (Grants 61472417, 61402469 and 61472415), the Strategic Priority Research Program of Chinese Academy of Sciences under Grant XDA06010702, and the State Key Laboratory of Information Security, Chinese Academy of Sciences.

References

1. Albrecht, M.R., Driessen, B., Kavun, E.B., Leander, G., Paar, C., Yalçın, T.: Block ciphers – focus on the linear layer (feat. PRIDE). In: Garay, J.A., Gennaro, R. (eds.) CRYPTO 2014. LNCS, pp. 57–76. Springer, Heidelberg (2014). doi:10.1007/978-3-662-44371-2_4
2. Baysal, A., Sahin, S.: Roadrunner: a small and fast bitslice block cipher for low cost 8-bit processors. Technical report, IACR Cryptology ePrint Archive, 2015: 906 (2015)
3. Beaulieu, R., Shors, D., Smith, J., Treatman-Clark, S., Weeks, B., Wingers, L.: The SIMON and SPECK families of lightweight block ciphers. Cryptology ePrint Archive (2013). https://eprint.iacr.org/2013/404
4. Biham, E.: New types of cryptanalytic attacks using related keys. In: Helleseth, T. (ed.) EUROCRYPT 1993. LNCS, vol. 765, pp. 398–409. Springer, Heidelberg (1994). doi:10.1007/3-540-48285-7_34
5. Biham, E., Shamir, A.: Differential cryptanalysis of DES-like cryptosystems. J. Cryptology 4(1), 3–72 (1991)
6. Biryukov, A.: Impossible Differential Attack. In: Encyclopedia of Cryptography and Security. pp. 597–597. Springer, Heidelberg (2011)
7. Blondeau, C.: Improbable differential from impossible differential: on the validity of the model. In: Paul, G., Vaudenay, S. (eds.) INDOCRYPT 2013. LNCS, pp. 149–160. Springer, Heidelberg (2013). doi:10.1007/978-3-319-03515-4_10
8. Blondeau, C., Gérard, B.: Multiple differential cryptanalysis: theory and practice. In: Joux, A. (ed.) FSE 2011. LNCS, vol. 6733, pp. 35–54. Springer, Heidelberg (2011). doi:10.1007/978-3-642-21702-9_3
9. Bogdanov, A.A., Knudsen, L.R., Leander, G., Paar, C., Poschmann, A., Robshaw, M., Seurin, Y., Vikkelsoe, C.: PRESENT: an ultra-lightweight block cipher. In: Paillier, P., Verbauwhede, I. (eds.) CHES 2007. LNCS, vol. 4727, pp. 450–466. Springer, Heidelberg (2007). doi:10.1007/978-3-540-74735-2_31

10. Borghoff, J., et al.: PRINCE – a low-latency block cipher for pervasive computing applications. In: Wang, X., Sako, K. (eds.) ASIACRYPT 2012. LNCS, pp. 208–225. Springer, Heidelberg (2012). doi:10.1007/978-3-642-34961-4_14

11. Crowley, P.: Truncated differential cryptanalysis of five rounds of salsa20. In: The State of the Art of Stream Ciphers SASC 2006, 198–202 (2006)

12. Daemen, J., Peeters, M., Van Assche, G., Rijmen, V.: Nessie proposal: noekeon. In: First Open NESSIE Workshop, pp. 213–230 (2000)

13. Grosso, V., Leurent, G., Standaert, F.-X., Varıcı, K.: LS-designs: bitslice encryption for efficient masked software implementations. In: Cid, C., Rechberger, C. (eds.) FSE 2014. LNCS, pp. 18–37. Springer, Heidelberg (2015). doi:10.1007/978-3-662-46706-0_2

14. Guo, J., Peyrin, T., Poschmann, A., Robshaw, M.: The LED block cipher. In: Preneel, B., Takagi, T. (eds.) CHES 2011. LNCS, vol. 6917, pp. 326–341. Springer, Heidelberg (2011). doi:10.1007/978-3-642-23951-9_22

15. Kim, J., Hong, S., Lee, S., Song, J., Yang, H.: Truncated differential attacks on 8-round CRYPTON. In: Lim, J.-I., Lee, D.-H. (eds.) ICISC 2003. LNCS, pp. 446–456. Springer, Heidelberg (2004). doi:10.1007/978-3-540-24691-6_33

16. Knudsen, L.R.: Truncated and higher order differentials. In: Preneel, B. (ed.) FSE 1994. LNCS, pp. 196–211. Springer, Heidelberg (1995). doi:10.1007/3-540-60590-8_16

17. Knudsen, L.R., Berson, T.A.: Truncated differentials of SAFER. In: Gollmann, D. (ed.) FSE 1996. LNCS, pp. 15–26. Springer, Heidelberg (1996). doi:10.1007/3-540-60865-6_38

18. Knudsen, L.R., Rijmen, V.: Truncated differentials of idea. Department of Electrical Engineering, ESAT-COSIC Technical report 97 1 (1997)

19. Knudsen, L.R., Robshaw, M.J.B., Wagner, D.: Truncated differentials and skipjack. In: Wiener, M. (ed.) CRYPTO 1999. LNCS, pp. 165–180. Springer, Heidelberg (1999). doi:10.1007/3-540-48405-1_11

20. Lee, S., Hong, S., Lee, S., Lim, J., Yoon, S.: Truncated differential cryptanalysis of camellia. In: Kim, K. (ed.) ICISC 2001. LNCS, pp. 32–38. Springer, Heidelberg (2002). doi:10.1007/3-540-45861-1_3

21. Li, L., Jia, K., Wang, X., Dong, X.: Meet-in-the-middle technique for truncated differential and its applications to CLEFIA and camellia. In: Leander, G. (ed.) FSE 2015. LNCS, vol. 9054, pp. 48–70. Springer, Heidelberg (2015). doi:10.1007/978-3-662-48116-5_3

22. Moriai, S., Sugita, M., Aoki, K., Kanda, M.: Security of E2 against truncated differential cryptanalysis. In: Heys, H., Adams, C. (eds.) SAC 1999. LNCS, pp. 106–117. Springer, Heidelberg (2000). doi:10.1007/3-540-46513-8_8

23. Mouha, N., Wang, Q., Gu, D., Preneel, B.: Differential and linear cryptanalysis using mixed-integer linear programming. In: Wu, C.-K., Yung, M., Lin, D. (eds.) Inscrypt 2011. LNCS, pp. 57–76. Springer, Heidelberg (2012). doi:10.1007/978-3-642-34704-7_5

24. Standaert, F.-X., Piret, G., Gershenfeld, N., Quisquater, J.-J.: SEA: a scalable encryption algorithm for small embedded applications. In: Domingo-Ferrer, J., Posegga, J., Schreckling, D. (eds.) CARDIS 2006. LNCS, vol. 3928, pp. 222–236. Springer, Heidelberg (2006). doi:10.1007/11733447_16

25. Sugita, M., Kobara, K., Imai, H.: Security of reduced version of the block cipher camellia against truncated and impossible differential cryptanalysis. In: Boyd, C. (ed.) ASIACRYPT 2001. LNCS, pp. 193–207. Springer, Heidelberg (2001). doi:10.1007/3-540-45682-1_12

26. Sun, S., Hu, L., Wang, M., Wang, P., Qiao, K., Ma, X., Shi, D., Song, L.: Automatic enumeration of (related-key) differential and linear characteristics with predefined properties and its applications. In: IACR Cryptology ePrint Archive 2014, 747 (2014)
27. Sun, S., Hu, L., Wang, P., Qiao, K., Ma, X., Song, L.: Automatic security evaluation and (Related-key) differential characteristic search: application to SIMON, PRESENT, LBlock, DES(L) and other bit-oriented block ciphers. In: Sarkar, P., Iwata, T. (eds.) ASIACRYPT 2014. LNCS, pp. 158–178. Springer, Heidelberg (2014). doi:10.1007/978-3-662-45611-8_9
28. Wagner, D.: The boomerang attack. In: Knudsen, L. (ed.) FSE 1999. LNCS, pp. 156–170. Springer, Heidelberg (1999). doi:10.1007/3-540-48519-8_12
29. Wu, W., Zhang, L.: LBlock: a lightweight block cipher. In: Lopez, J., Tsudik, G. (eds.) ACNS 2011. LNCS, vol. 6715, pp. 327–344. Springer, Heidelberg (2011). doi:10.1007/978-3-642-21554-4_19
30. Zhang, W., Bao, Z., Lin, D., Rijmen, V., Yang, B., Verbauwhede, I.: Rectangle: a bit-slice lightweight block cipher suitable for multiple platforms. Sci. China Inform. Sci. **58**(12), 1–15 (2015)

System Security

DF-ORAM: A Practical Dummy Free Oblivious RAM to Protect Outsourced Data Access Pattern

Qiumao Ma, Wensheng Zhang$^{(\boxtimes)}$, and Jinsheng Zhang

Department of Computer Science, Iowa State University, Ames, USA
{qmma,wzhang,alexzjs}@iastate.edu

Abstract. Oblivious RAM (ORAM) is a security-provable model that can be used to protect a client's access pattern to remote storage. Existing ORAM constructions were designed mainly for communication efficiency, but the server-side storage efficiency was generally neglected. This paper proposes DF-ORAM, which has the following features when N blocks each of B bits are outsourced: (i) server-side storage overhead is $3N$ bits (i.e., no dummy blocks); (ii) no server-side computational cost; (iii) server-client communication cost is $O(\log N \cdot B)$ bit per query; and (iv) client-side storage cost is $O(\lambda \cdot B)$ bits where λ is a security parameter. Asymptotical and implementation-based evaluation demonstrate DF-ORAM to be the most communication-efficient and storage-efficient one among the existing ORAMs that do not require server-side computation.

1 Introduction

Cloud storage services have become popular, but clients of these services may outsource their data with reservation. As a base line of security and privacy defense, the clients may encrypt their sensitive data before outsourcing. Data encryption alone is however insufficient, because a client' privacy and data secrecy can still be exposed, if her access pattern to the data is revealed [7].

The oblivious RAM (ORAM) model [2], which works by continuously shuffling data as the data are accessed, is a well-known security-provable approach for data access pattern protection. Recently, numerous ORAM constructions [1,3–6,8–20] have been proposed to reduce the cost of employing this technology. Most research on ORAM has focused on the communication efficiency improvement, but the storage efficiency has not received much attention. To host N data blocks, the state-of-the-art ORAM constructions generally need the storage server to also store $O(N)$ or $O(N \log N)$ dummy data blocks. Hence, a new design is needed to reduce both the storage and communication overhead.

This paper proposes *DF-ORAM*, a ORAM construction that simultaneously accomplishes the following features: (i) The server storage does not store any dummy block; instead, it introduces only a small overhead of $3N$ bits, given that N real data blocks are outsourced. (ii) The server is not required to conduct

© Springer International Publishing AG 2016
J. Chen et al. (Eds.): NSS 2016, LNCS 9955, pp. 415–432, 2016.
DOI: 10.1007/978-3-319-46298-1_27

computation. (iii) The client-server communication cost is $O(\log N \cdot B)$ bits per query, given that a block size is B bit. (iv) The client storage cost is $O(\lambda \cdot B)$ bits, where λ is security parameter.

DF-ORAM organizes the server-side storage as a binary tree. Initially, all outsourced data blocks are randomly stored to the nodes of this storage tree. When a block is queried by the client, the path that contains the query target is accessed. For each non-leaf node on the selected path, two blocks are accessed: one has been accessed before and the other has not; for each leaf node on the path, one block that has not been accessed is accessed. Such an access pattern is followed in every query process to make the process oblivious. After every a certain fixed number of queries, an eviction process is launched, which evicts the data stored at the client back to the server-side storage tree. For obliviousness, every eviction process selects a path from the tree following the reverse-lexicographic order, and the eviction operations regarding each node on the selected path follow the same pattern: all blocks on the node are retrieved to the client, updated and re-encrypted, and then uploaded back to the node.

In addition, DF-ORAM evicts data blocks from a node to its child nodes only when the node has at least $3s$ blocks, where $s \geq 4.2\lambda$ and λ is a security parameter; then, among these blocks, at most s blocks are selected to evict to the left child, and meanwhile the same number of blocks are selected to evict to the right child. This is based on the following observation: among any $3s$ or more blocks in a node, with a probability of $1 - O(2^{-\lambda})$, at least s blocks can be evicted to the left child and at least s blocks can be evicted to the right child, given that each of the $3s$ blocks can choose to be evict-able to the left or right child uniformly at random. Therefore, data blocks can always be found for eviction and there is no need to introduce dummy blocks.

Extensive analysis has verified the security of the DF-ORAM construction. Asymptotical and implementation-based comparisons have also been conducted for DF-ORAM, Path ORAM, and SE-ORAM, the state-of-the-art ORAM constructions without server-side computation. Compared to Path ORAM, DF-ORAM reduces the communication cost by a factor of 2, the query delay by a factor of 4 to 5, and data access delay per query by a factor of 2, besides reducing the server-side storage overhead from $9N \cdot B$ bits to $3N$ bits. Compared to SE-ORAM, DF-ORAM reduces the communication cost by a factor of $\log N$, though increasing the server-side storage overhead by $3N$ bits.

In the following, Sect. 2 reviews related works. Section 3 presents security definition. Section 4 presents DF-ORAM, followed by security analysis in Sect. 5. Section 6 compares DF-ORAM to state-of-the-art ORAM schemes, asymptotically and via implementation-based evaluation. Section 7 concludes the paper.

2   Related Work

ORAM constructions fall roughly into two classes: hash-based and index-based ORAMs.

Hash-based ORAMs [2–6,8,11,18–20] organize the server storage as a hierarchy of layers. Each layer contains either a series of buckets [2,18–20], or a pair of Cuckoo Hash tables with stash [3–6,8,11]. In a bucket ORAM proposed in [2], the server needs to additionally store $(2 \log N - 1)N$ dummy blocks in order to host its client's N real data blocks; its communication cost is $O(\log^3 N)$ blocks per query, with a constant client-side storage. In a bucket ORAM proposed in [18–20], the server additionally stores at least N dummy blocks and cN bits $(0 < c < 1)$ of Bloom Filters for each layer; its communication cost is $O(\log^2 N \log \log N)$ blocks per query, with a client-side storage of $O(\log^2 N)$ blocks. In a Cuckoo Hash ORAM [3–6,8,11], the server stores at least $7N$ dummy data blocks; its communication cost is $O(\log^2 N)$ blocks per query with a constant client-side storage, or $O(\log N)$ blocks per query with a client-side storage of $O(N^c)$ blocks $(0 < c < 1)$.

Index-based ORAMs [1,9,10,12–16] use index table for data lookup. They require the client to either store the index table locally, or outsource it to the server recursively in a way similar to storing their data, at the expense of increased communication cost. Representative index-based ORAMs include Path ORAM [13], C-ORAM [10] and SE-ORAM [9]. Path ORAM [13] stores data blocks in a binary tree. In order to store N real data blocks, the height of tree needs to be $\log N$, each tree node stores Z (a system parameter with default value 5) data blocks, and therefore, $2Z \cdot N$ data blocks (including $(2Z - 1) \cdot N$ dummy blocks) are stored on the tree. To query a data block, the client retrieves all the data blocks along a path containing the query target, finds the target, re-encrypts the blocks, and uploads as many as possible of the blocks back to server. The blocks that cannot be stored back are kept in a local stash. Overall, Path ORAM incurs a communication cost of $O(\log N \cdot B)$ bits and a server-side storage overhead of $O(N \cdot B)$ bits; it does not require server computational cost. C-ORAM [10] also stores data blocks in a binary tree. To accommodate N real data blocks, the height of tree is set as L, $L \in O(\log N)$. Each node can store up to z data blocks (z is a system parameter and $N \le z \cdot 2^{L-1}$). Therefore, at least $4N$ data blocks (note: the $4N$ blocks include $3N$ noisy or empty blocks; the size of each block has to be expanded due to being encrypted with some homomorphic encryption algorithm) are stored on the tree. To query a data block, the client first obliviously merges all blocks along a path containing the query target to leaf node, then issues a PIR-read to retrieve the query target. After accesses the query target, client re-encrypts it and writes it back to root node using PIR-write and then conducts an eviction process. In eviction process, client guides server to obliviously merge all blocks along the evicting path from root to leaf node. A post eviction process is used to remove one noise block from leaf node to avoid leaf node from overflow. Overall, C-ORAM incurs a communication cost of $O(B)$ bits and server-side storage overhead is $O(N \cdot B)$ bits; but it requires expensive server computational cost.

3   System Model and Security Definition

We consider a system as follows. A client exports N equal-size data blocks to a remote storage server. The client accesses the exported data every now and then, and wishes to hide the pattern of the accesses from the server.

Each data request from the client, which should be kept private, is one of the following two types: (i) read a data block D of unique ID i from the storage, denoted as a 3-tuple $(read, i, D)$; or (ii) write or modify a data block D of unique ID i to the storage, denoted as a 3-tuple $(write, i, D)$. To accomplish a private data request, the client needs to access some locations at the remote storage. Each access to a location at the remote storage, which is observable by the server, can be one of the following types: (i) retrieve (i.e., read) a data block D from a location l at the remote storage, denoted as a 3-tuple $(read, l, D)$; or (ii) upload (i.e., write) a data block D to a location l at the remote storage, denoted as a 3-tuple $(write, l, D)$.

We assume the client is trusted, while the remote server is *honest but curious*; that is, the server stores data and serves the client's requests according to the protocol that we deploy, but it may attempt to figure out the client's access pattern. The network connection between the client and the server is assumed secure; in practice, this can be achieved using well-known techniques such as SSL. Similar to the security definition of existing ORAMs [2,13,16], we define the security of our proposed ORAM as follows.

Definition 1. *Let $x = \langle (op_1, i_1, D_1), (op_2, i_2, D_2), \cdots \rangle$ denote a private sequence of the client's intended data requests, where each op is either a read or write operation. Let $A(x) = \langle (op_1', l_1, D_1'), (op_2', l_2, D_2'), \cdots \rangle$ denote the sequence of the client's accesses to the locations at the remote storage (observable by the server), in order to accomplish the client's private data requests. Let λ be a security parameter. An ORAM system is said to be secure if (i) for any two equal-length private sequences x and y of intended data requests, their corresponding observable location access sequences $A(x)$ and $A(y)$ are computationally indistinguishable; and (ii) the probability that the ORAM system fails to operate is $O(2^{-\lambda})$.*

4   The DF-ORAM Construction

4.1   Server-Side Storage

The server-side storage is organized as a binary tree, on which each node has a unique ID. The root node n_0 has ID 0. For any other node n_x whose parent node is n_p, if n_x is the left child of n_p, $x = 2p + 1$; if n_x is the right child of n_p, $x = 2p + 2$.

Each node n_i contains the following components: a container of data blocks, an access bitmap (denoted as AB_i) indicating which blocks have been accessed, an *encrypted* tag bitmap (denoted as TAG_i) indicating each block's eviction orientation (1 if the block must be evicted to the right child of this node, or 0 if the block can be evicted to the left or right child with equal possibility), a tag counter (denoted as TC_i) indicating the number of blocks tagged with 1, and an eviction bit (denoted as EB_i) indicating the next evicting node (0 if left child or 1 if right child).

The storage tree is initially a *full* binary tree. Each node stores $2s$ data blocks, where $s \geq 4.2\,\lambda$. The AB_i, TAG_i, TC_i and EB_i for each node n_i are initialized to all-zero. Let $h + 1$ denote the height of tree. Then, the total number of data blocks stored in the tree is $N = 2(2^{h+1} - 1)s$. Note that, the storage does not store any dummy data block.

Each data block d_i is encrypted probabilistically to D_i, using a symmetric cipher (e.g., AES), before exported to the server. Specifically, $D_i = E(r_i | d_i)$, where r_i is a random nonce. Then, the blocks are randomly distributed to the nodes on the tree.

As the data blocks are queried and evicted, the tree may become unbalanced. Specifically, if a node does not contain any data block, the node is deleted; if a leaf node contains more than $3s$ blocks, the node will be expanded into a 2-level binary subtree rooted at itself.

4.2   Client-Side Storage

The client maintains an *index table* at its local storage. Each of the N outsourced data blocks has an entry in this table. The entry for the block of ID i is a $\langle node(i), offset(i), tag(i) \rangle$ tuple, which indicates that the data block is stored at node $node(i)$ with offset $offset(i)$ and the block is tagged with $tag(i)$. The client also allocates a permanent *stash* space to store up to s data blocks that have been queried most recently, and a temporary *cache* space to facilitate data query and shuffling.

4.3   Data Query

When the client wants to query data block D_t, it checks whether D_t is in its local stash. If so, the block is accessed and retained in its original position; otherwise, the client looks up its local index table to obtain $node(t)$, $offset(t)$ and $tag(t)$. Then, the client acts as follows.

The client randomly selects a layer-$(h + 2)$ node, denoted as $n_{t'}$, which is a descendant of $node(t)$. Note that, we select the descendant node from layer $h+2$ is because the height of the tree is bounded by $h+3$ with an overwhelming probability of $1-2^{-\lambda}$ according to our analysis in Sect. 5.3. Moreover, if $tag(t) = 1$, $n_{t'}$ must be a descendant of the right child of $node(t)$; otherwise, $n_{t'}$ can be any layer-$(h + 2)$ descendant of $node(t)$. Then, the client sends a message $bitmapReq(t')$ to the server.

On receiving $bitmapReq(t')$, the server constructs an ordered sequence that contains all the existing nodes on the path from the root to $n_{t'}$, and returns the access and tag bitmaps of these nodes.

Let us denote the sequence as $n_0', n_1', \cdots, n_l'$, where n_0' is the root and n_l' is the furthest away from the root. Depending on the current topology of the server-side storage tree, there are four cases regarding the shape of the subtree rooted at node n_l' (as shown in Fig. 2): shape (i) - n_l' itself is a leaf node; shape (ii) - n_l' has only right child node; shape (iii) - n_l' has only left child and its tag

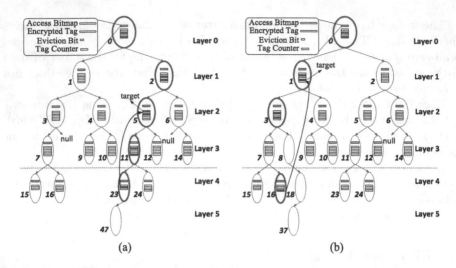

Fig. 1. Query examples. The initial tree height $h + 1 = 4$. In (a), query target D_t is at node n_5. The client randomly selects node n_{47} as the layer-5 (i.e., layer-$(h + 2)$) descendant of n_5; that is, it selects the path from the root to n_{47} to access. As n_{47} does not exist in the current storage tree, the client actually accesses two data blocks (including D_t) from each of the nodes n_0, n_2, n_5, n_{11} and n_{23}. n_{23} is a leaf node; hence, the block read from n_{23} is moved to the position where D_t resided, after the query. In (b), query target D_t is at node n_1, and the client randomly n_{37} as the layer-5 descendant of n_1. As nodes n_8, n_{18} and n_{37} on the path from n_0 to n_{37} do not exist, the client actually accesses two blocks (including D_t) from each of the nodes n_0, n_1 and n_3 on the selected path. Because n_3 is a non-leaf node and all of its blocks are tagged with 0, the server allows the client to access a block from node n_{16}, which is one of the furthest descendants of n_3. Also, the block accessed from n_{16} is moved to the place where D_t resided after the query.

count (TC) is greater than 0 (i.e., at least one block in n'_l is tagged with 1); shape (iv) - n'_l has only left child and its TC is 0. If n'_l is a non-leaf node, and meanwhile it has a right child or TC is 0 (i.e., shape (ii) or (iv) in Fig. 2), the server further finds a leaf node (denoted as n'_{l+1}) which is the furthest descendant node of n'_l, and returns the access bitmap of n'_{l+1}.

According to the access bitmaps received from the server, the client selects two blocks $D'_{i,0}$ and $D'_{i,1}$ from each n'_i where $i = 0, \cdots, l$, as follows.

- *Case I: D_t is in n'_i.* Depending on if D_t has already been accessed, the following are two subcases. (i) *Case I-A: D_t has been accessed in n'_i.* In this case, $D'_{i,0}$ is set to D_t, and a data block $D'_{i,1}$ is randomly selected from the blocks that have not been accessed in n'_i. (ii) *Case I-B: D_t has not been accessed in n'_i.* In this case, a data block $D'_{i,0}$ is randomly selected from the set of blocks that have been accessed in n'_i, and $D'_{i,1}$ is set to D_t.

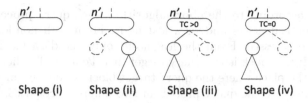

Fig. 2. Shapes of the subtree rooted at n'_l

- *Case II: D_t is not in n'_i.* In this case, a block $D'_{i,0}$ is randomly selected from the blocks that have been accessed in n'_i; another block $D'_{i,1}$ is randomly selected from the blocks that have not been accessed in n'_i.

If n'_l is not a leaf node, the client needs to take further actions as follows.

- *Case I: n'_l has right child or TC of n'_l is 0 (i.e., shape (ii) or (iv) in* Fig. 2*).* In this case, the access bitmap of n'_{l+1} should have been returned to the client. In response, the client randomly selects one block, denoted as $D'_{l+1,0}$, from the blocks that have been accessed in n'_{l+1}.
- *Case II: n'_l has left child and TC of n'_l is not 0 (i.e., shape (iii) in* Fig. 2*).* In this case, n'_l is the last node to access during this query process. After the client has selected the blocks to access, as elaborated above, if the selected block $D'_{l,1}$ is tagged with 0, it should update the tag bitmap of n'_l by changing one of the 1 bits to 0; this way, one less block is tagged with 1. In response, server decreases TC by one.

The client sends the positions of the above selected blocks to the server, and the server returns the blocks requested by the client in an ordered sequence as

$$D'_{0,0}, D'_{0,1}, \cdots, D'_{l,0}, D'_{l,1}$$

if n'_l is last node to access, or

$$D'_{0,0}, D'_{0,1}, \cdots, D'_{l,0}, D'_{l,1}, D'_{l+1,0}$$

if n'_{l+1} is the last node to access.

On receiving the ordered sequence of data blocks from the server, the client accesses block D_t and stores it in its local stash. Meanwhile, the client re-encrypts the rest blocks, and then permutes and uploads them back to the server such that: if D_t is the last one of the returned blocks, all but the last one of the returned blocks are uploaded; otherwise, the last of the returned block replaces the position where D_t resided. Consequently, the position at the server-side storage tree that is previously occupied by the last one of the returned blocks becomes empty.

Finally, the client updates the access bitmaps to reflect which blocks have been recently accessed, re-encrypts the tag bitmaps of the nodes, and upload them back to the server. The client also updates its local index tables to reflect the permutation of data blocks.

Note that, according to the above algorithm, each query process accesses a sequence of non-leaf nodes and/or a leaf node. From each non-leaf node, two data blocks are accessed. From the leaf node, only one data block is accessed and removed. If the block is the query target, it is kept by the client; otherwise, it is moved to the place where the query target block resides. Figure 1 shows two examples to illustrate the query process in two different scenarios.

4.4 Data Eviction

After every s queries, the client launches a data eviction process, in which the client evicts the s data blocks in its stash to a path on the tree. The eviction operations can be evenly spread over the time period of s queries; however, to simplify the presentation, we elaborate the eviction as an isolated process as follows.

At the beginning, the client re-encrypts the s data blocks in its stash, and selects the root node as the first evicting node.

Let e denote the ID of the current evicting node. The procedure of evicting data blocks from stash of the client to node n_e, denoted as $evict(n_e)$, is as follows. The client downloads for n_e the eviction bit EB_e, the tag bitmap TAG_e and all the data blocks in the node. Then, it decrypts TAG_e and re-encrypts the data blocks. Based on whether n_e is a leaf node, as well as the values of EB_e and TAG_e, there are the following cases.

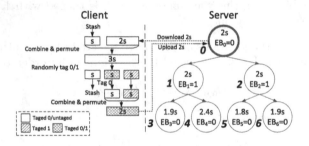

Fig. 3. Eviction case I.

Case I: n_e is a non-leaf node and $EB_e = 0$. In this case, n_e has $2s$ data blocks. As illustrated in Fig. 3, the client merges the s blocks in its stash with the $2s$ blocks downloaded from n_e, randomly permutes them, and tags each of these $3s$ blocks with 0 or 1 randomly. According to our analysis in Sect. 5.1, with a probability of $1 - O(2^{-\lambda})$, at least s among the all $3s$ blocks are tagged with 0 and at least s data blocks are tagged with 1.

From the $3s$ blocks, the client selects s blocks tagged with 0, and retains them in its stash. For the rest $2s$ blocks, the client selects s blocks tagged with 1, re-tags the rest s blocks with 0, encrypts and stores the tags in TAG_e, and uploads the $2s$ blocks together with TAG_e back to n_e. In response, the server updates its EB_e to 1, initializes AB_e to all-zero and sets TC_e to s.

Further, the client updates its index table to record which blocks are now stored at node n_e as well as the offsets and tags of these blocks, and then acts as follows: (i) if n_e has a left child, the client selects the left child as the new evicting node, denotes it as n_e, and repeats the procedure $evict(n_e)$ to evict the data blocks in its stash to n_e; (ii) otherwise (i.e., n_e has no left child), the client requests the server to construct a left child for n_e, uploads the s blocks in its stash to this left child, uploads an all-zero tag bitmap for these blocks, and finishes this round of eviction. In response, the server initializes AB_e and EB_e to all-zero.

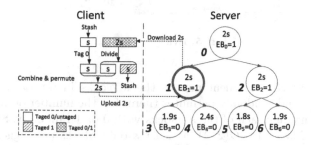

Fig. 4. Eviction case II.

Case II - n_e is a non-leaf node and $EB_e = 1$. In this case, node n_e has s blocks tagged with 0, but TC ranges from 0 to s. Figure 4 illustrates one example for this case.

The client merges the s blocks in its stash with the s blocks tagged with 0, permutes them randomly, and uploads them back to n_e. Also, it initializes TAG_e to all zero, re-encrypts it, and then uploads it back to n_e as well. In response, the server initializes AB_e, EB_e and TC_e to all zero. Meanwhile, the client keeps the blocks tagged with 1 in its stash.

Next, regarding whether n_e has right child, there are the following sub-cases. (i) *Sub-case II-A: n_e has a right child.* In this sub-case, n_e has s blocks tagged with 1. Hence, the client selects the right child as the new evicting node, denotes it as n_e, and repeats procedure $evict(n_e)$ to evict the s data blocks in its stash to n_e. (ii) *Sub-case II-B: n_e has no right child.* If n_e has no block tagged with 1, the client finishes the current round of eviction. Otherwise, the client requests the server to construct a right child for n_e, uploads the blocks in its stash to this right child, and finishes this round of eviction.

Case III - n_e is a leaf node and it has no more than $2s$ data blocks. In this case, the client merges the s blocks in its stash with the blocks from n_e, permutes these blocks randomly, and uploads them back to n_e. The client also uploads an encrypted all-zero tag bitmap for the node. In response, the server updates the access bitmap and tag bitmap of n_e to all zero. Finally, the client updates its local index table accordingly, and finishes this round of eviction.

Case IV - n_e is a leaf node and it has more than $2s$ blocks. Note that n_e cannot have $3s$ or more blocks according to our query and eviction algorithms. As

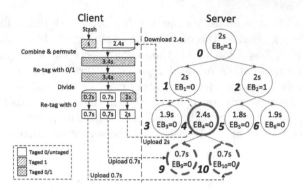

Fig. 5. Eviction case IV.

illustrated by Fig. 5, the client merges the s blocks in its stash with all the blocks from n_e, and randomly permutes them. Let the number of merged blocks be s'. The client tags each of the s' blocks with 0 or 1 randomly. Since $s' > 3s$, with a probability of $1 - O(2^{-\lambda})$, at least s data blocks are tagged with bit 0 and at least s data blocks are tagged with bit 1. Then, from these blocks, the client requests the server to create a left child for n_e, and selects $\lceil \frac{s'-2s}{2} \rceil$ (which is less than s) blocks tagged with 0 to be stored at this left child node. Also, the client requests the server to create a right child for n_e, and selects $\lfloor \frac{s'-2s}{2} \rfloor$ blocks tagged with 1 to be stored at this right child node. The rest $2s$ blocks are uploaded back to node n_e. The client also uploads encrypted all-zero tag bitmaps to the above three nodes. In response, the server initializes the access bitmaps, tag bitmaps, eviction bits and TC of these three nodes to all-zero. Finally, the client updates its index table to reflect the current distribution of the blocks on these three nodes, and then finishes this round of eviction.

5   Analysis

In this section, we study the security strength of DF-ORAM in terms of failure probability and obliviousness. We also analyze the upper bound of the height of the server-side storage tree, which is important for the design and cost evaluation of DF-ORAM.

5.1   Failure Probability Analysis

The probabilities for DF-ORAM to fail in a query process and an eviction process are stated in Lemmas 1 and 3, respectively.

Lemma 1. *DF-ORAM fails in a query process with a probability no larger than* $2^{-\lambda}$.

Proof. During a query process, two data blocks are accessed from each non-leaf node on a selected path that contains the query target. Among them, one block has been accessed since the most recent eviction process involving this node, while the other block has not. The query process fails at a non-leaf node if the client cannot find a block that has not been accessed in the node.

For each non-leaf node n_l on layer l, it is selected as an evicting node after every $s \cdot 2^l$ queries; and for each query, it has a probability of $\frac{1}{2^l}$ to be on the query path. Let X be a random variable counting the number of query processes which (i) access n_l and (ii) occur between two consecutive eviction processes that access n_l. Hence,

$$\mathbf{E}[X] = s \cdot 2^l \cdot \frac{1}{2^l} = s.$$

According to the Chernoff bound and the fact that $s \geq 4.2\lambda \geq 3\lambda$ in DF-ORAM, the probability for $X \geq 2s$ is

$$\mathbf{Pr}[X \geq 2s] \leq e^{-s/3} < 2^{-s/3} \leq 2^{-\lambda}.$$

Given the fact each non-leaf node n_l in DF-ORAM has $2s$ data blocks, the probability for a query process to fail in accessing n_l is upper-bound by $2^{-\lambda}$.

For each leaf node accessed by a query process, one data block is accessed and removed. If the block is the query target, it is retrieved and kept by the client; otherwise, it is moved to replace the query target. Hence, the process will not fail at a leaf node.

Therefore, we have proved that DF-ORAM fails in a query process with a probability upper-bounded by $2^{-\lambda}$. $\square$

To facilitate the probability for DF-ORAM to fail in an eviction process, we first introduce and prove the following lemma.

Lemma 2. *Consider* $3s$ *data block, where* $s \geq 4.2\,\lambda$. *Each of the blocks is randomly tagged with* 0 *or* 1. *Let* k_0 *and* k_1 *represent the number of blocks that are tagged with* 0 *and* 1, *respectively. Then,*

$$Pr[k_0 < s] = Pr[k_1 < s] < 2^{-\lambda}.$$

Proof. Due to the symmetry between 0 and 1, it is obvious that $Pr[k_0 < s] = Pr[k_1 < s]$. Hence, we only consider $Pr[k_0 < s]$ in the following.

$$Pr[k_0 < s] = \sum_{k=0}^{s-1} \binom{3s}{k}(\frac{1}{2})^{3s} < s\binom{3s}{s}(\frac{1}{2})^{3s} = s \cdot \frac{(3s)!}{s!(2s)!}(\frac{1}{2})^{3s} \tag{1}$$

$$\leq s \cdot \frac{e(3s)^{3s+\frac{1}{2}}e^{-3s}}{\sqrt{2\pi}e^{-s}s^{s+\frac{1}{2}}\sqrt{2\pi}e^{-2s}(2s)^{2s+\frac{1}{2}}}(\frac{1}{2})^{3s} \tag{2}$$

$$= \frac{es}{2\pi} \cdot \frac{3^{3s+\frac{1}{2}}s^{3s+\frac{1}{2}}}{s^{s+\frac{1}{2}}2^{2s+\frac{1}{2}}s^{2s+\frac{1}{2}}}(\frac{1}{2})^{3s} = \frac{e}{2\pi} \cdot \sqrt{\frac{3}{2s}} \cdot (\frac{27}{32})^s \leq (\frac{1}{2})^{\frac{s}{4.2}} \leq 2^{-\lambda} \tag{3}$$

Here, Inequality (2) is due to Stirling's approximation, and Inequality (3) is due to $\frac{e}{2\pi} \cdot \sqrt{\frac{3}{2s}} < 1$ and $(\frac{27}{32})^s < (\frac{1}{2})^{\frac{s}{4.2}}$.

Lemma 3. *The probability for DF-ORAM to fail in an eviction process is* $O(2^{-\lambda})$.

Proof. As elaborated in Sect. 4, the process of evicting data blocks to an evicting node n_e has one of four cases. Among them, Case III will never fail, but Case I, II or IV can fail if the client cannot find s blocks tagged with 0 or s blocks tagged with 1 after each of $3s$ blocks has been tagged randomly with 0 or 1. According to Lemma 2, each of these cases occurs with a probability no greater than $2^{-\lambda}$. So, DF-ORAM fails in an eviction process with a probability no greater than $O(2^{-\lambda})$.

According to the above lemmas, we have the following theorem.

Theorem 1. *The probability for DF-ORAM to fail is* $O(2^{-\lambda})$.

5.2   Obliviousness Analysis

Lemma 4. *When a data block is queried, it has the same probability to be on any of the paths that connecting the root and a layer-$(h + 2)$ node.*

Proof. (sketch) The proof includes three parts. Part I: At the first time when a data block is queried, it is obvious that it has the same probability to be on any of the $(h+2)$-hop paths due to the initially random distribution of blocks to the server-side storage tree.

Part II: After a block has been queried, we can prove by induction that the block can be evicted back to the server-side storage tree on any of the $(h+2)$-hop paths with the same probability. (i) Base case: As elaborated in the DF-ORAM eviction algorithm, when a data block is evicted from the client's stash to the server-side storage tree, it has the same probability to be evicted to the left or right child of the tree root, or it is evicted to the root node tagged with 0, and thus it can be queried from any $(h + 2)$-hop path with the same probability. (ii) Inductive step: Once a block is in a node of the tree, with the DF-ORAM eviction algorithm, it can be evicted to the left or right child with the same probability or stay in the node tagged with 0, and therefore can be queried from any path from the node towards a layer-$(h + 2)$ node with the same probability.

Part III: In a query process, a data block on a lower layer may be moved to an upper layer to replace the query target block. This case is equivalent to backtrack to an earlier step in the process of evicting this data block. Hence, the backtracking does not change the probability that a data block can be queried from any $(h + 2)$-hop path with the same probability.

Theorem 2. *The query and eviction processes in DF-ORAM are oblivious.*

Proof. (sketch) According to Lemma 4, a block has the same probability to be distributed on any of the paths from the root to a layer-$(h + 2)$ node. Hence, the distribution of querying path is uniformly random. Also, during each query process, location access follows the same pattern: each non-leaf node on the querying path has two data blocks accessed, among which one has been accessed and the other has not; each leaf node has one block accessed and removed. Therefore, the query process is oblivious.

An eviction process is launched after every s queries. The paths selected for eviction follows the reverse lexicographic order. During each eviction process, the location access on the selected path also follows the same pattern: all blocks in each evicting node are downloaded to the client; then client re-encrypts, permutes and then stores blocks back to the server. The permutation is kept unknown from the server, and each data block is re-encrypted before uploaded. Hence, the eviction process is also oblivious.

5.3 Upper Bound of the Height of Storage Tree

Lemma 5. *In DF-ORAM, the height of the storage tree is upper-bounded by $h + 3$ with a probability of at least $1 - 2^{-\lambda}$, given that $s \geq 4.2(\lambda + 1)$.*

Proof. In DF-ORAM, the total number of outsourced data blocks is $N = 2(2^{h+1} - 1)s$, and the total number of layer-$(h+2)$ nodes is $P = 2^{h+2}$. Both the initial distribution and the eviction process distribute the N data blocks to the P paths each connecting the root and a layer-$(h+2)$ node, uniformly at random.

Next, we estimate the maximum number of data blocks that are distributed to each path that connects the root and a layer-$(h+2)$ node. This can be achieved by utilizing the standard balls and bins model, where $N = 2(2^{h+1} - 1)s$ balls thrown into $P = 2^{h+2}$ bins. The average number of balls distributed to each bin is $N/P < s$. According to the Chernoff bound, if each bin has a capacity of $2s$, the probability for a bin to overflow is bounded by $e^{-s/3}$, which is less than $2^{-\lambda}$, due to $s \geq 4.2\lambda$. As a capacity of a leaf node in DF-ORAM is $3s$, a layer-$(h + 2)$ node overflows only with a probability lower than $2^{-\lambda}$. Hence, the theorem has been proved.

6 Performance Comparison

We first compare DF-ORAM with several state-of-the-art ORAM constructions, including Path ORAM [13], C-ORAM [10] and SE-ORAM [9], in terms of asymptotical storage, communication, and computational costs. Then, based on system implementations of DF-ORAM and Path ORAM, we compare their performance in practical settings.

6.1 Asymptotical Comparison

From Table 1, we can see that both Path ORAM and C-ORAM incurs a server-side storage overhead of $O(N \cdot B)$ bits. Particularly, Path ORAM needs the server to store $9N \cdot B$ bits when the client exports $N \cdot B$ bits of data; C-ORAM needs to store $3N \cdot B$ extra dummy and empty blocks; also, each data and dummy block should be encrypted with a certain homomorphic encryption, which incurs

Table 1. Asymptotical Comparison of Communication and Storage Cost. N data blocks each of B bits are outsourced. λ is the security parameter for DF-ORAM. For all the listed ORAM constructions, the index table is supposed to be stored at the client and thus its storage cost is not considered in the comparison. The server storage overhead is defined as the extra cost in addition to the outsourced data blocks (i.e., the $N \cdot B$ bits).

ORAM	Client storage cost	Server storage overhead	Communication cost
Path ORAM [13]	$O(\log N \cdot B) \cdot \omega(1)$	$O(N \cdot B)$	$O(\log N \cdot B)$
C-ORAM [10]	$O(B)$	$O(N \cdot B)$	$O(B)$
SE-ORAM [9]	$O(\log^2 N \cdot B)$	0	$O(\log^2 N \cdot B)$
DF-ORAM	$O(\lambda \cdot B)$	$< 3N$	$O(\log N \cdot B)$ 0

further storage overhead. The recently proposed SE-ORAM incurs no server-side storage overhead. Though DF-ORAM does incur storage overhead at the server, the overhead is less than $3N$ bits. In practical settings where $B \geq 16\,\mathrm{KB}$ is typical, this overhead is less than a small fraction (i.e., less than $\frac{1}{2^{18}}$) of the amount of data exported by the client.

As shown in Table 1, the client-side storage cost of DF-ORAM is $O(\lambda \cdot B)$ bits, because both the permanent stash and temporary cache are of size $O(s \cdot B)$ bits and $s \geq 4.2\,\lambda$. Path ORAM requires the client to maintain a cache of $O(\log N \cdot B) \cdot \omega(1)$ bits in order to store blocks that cannot be written back to server. C-ORAM only needs a client-side storage of $O(B)$ bits and SE-ORAM requires a client-side storage of $O(\log^2 N \cdot B)$ bits. Though DF-ORAM requires a larger client-side storage than the compared schemes, the cost is not high in practice. Particularly, even when $\lambda = 80$ and $B = 256\,K$ bytes, the cost is only $336\,M$ bytes, which is affordable by a mobile phone.

From Table 1 we can see that, DF-ORAM has the same level of asymptotical communication cost as Path ORAM. As we will show in Sect. 6.2, the actual communication cost of DF-ORAM is around $1/2$ of that of Path ORAM. Compared to SE-ORAM, DF-ORAM reduces the communication overhead by an order of $\log N$. Although DF-ORAM has higher communication cost than C-ORAM, C-ORAM incurs expensive computational cost which can overshadow the reduction in communication cost and result in even longer data access delay [10].

From Table 2 we can see that, C-ORAM requires the server and the client to conduct expensive homomorphic encryption, decryption, addition and multiplications. None of DF-ORAM, Path ORAM and SE-ORAM requires the server to conduct computation, and DF-ORAM incurs the same level of client-side computational cost as Path ORAM, i.e., encryption and decryption of data blocks with symmetric cryptographical primitives. Also, as we will show in Sect. 6.2, DF-ORAM reduces the client computational cost by a factor of 2, compared to Path ORAM. Compared with SE-ORAM, DF-ORAM reduces the client computational cost by an order of $\log N$.

Table 2. Asymptotical comparison of computational cost. N data blocks each of B bits are stored. For C-ORAM, since it uses additive homomorphic encryption as primitives, we use the following two parameters to measure the performance of homomorphic encryption: b denotes the plaintext size in bits and C_{AH} denotes the computational cost for one homomorphic operation, including encryption/decryption, addition and multiplication. C_{Reg} denotes the computational cost of one symmetric encryption/decryption operation.

ORAM	Client computational cost	Server computational cost
Path ORAM [13]	$O(B \log N \cdot C_{Reg})$	0
C-ORAM [10]	$O(C_{AH} \cdot B/b)$	$O(\log^2 N \cdot C_{AH} \cdot B/b)$
SE-ORAM [9]	$O(B \log^2 N \cdot C_{Reg})$	0
DF-ORAM	$O(B \log N \cdot C_{Reg})$	0

Also note that, Path ORAM, SE-ORAM and DF-ORAM support small block size, i.e. they only require $B \in \Omega(\log^2 N)$ bits, while C-ORAM requires block size $B \in \Omega(\log^4 N)$ bits.

6.2 Implementation-Base Comparison

We implement DF-ORAM and compare it with Path ORAM [13] which is the state-of-the-art ORAM scheme without server computational cost. Note that, we do not compare DF-ORAM with C-ORAM [10], as C-ORAM requires expensive computations at both the server and client sides, which can overshadow the benefit introduced from the reduced communication cost. Particularly, as reported in [10], it costs 7 min to retrieve a data block of size $100k$ bits, and most of the time is spent on computation. Also, as DF-ORAM has much lower communication cost than SE-ORAM, we do not compare them in this section either.

Parameter and System Settings. We choose $2^{16} \leq N \leq 2^{24}$ and $16\,\text{KB} \leq B \leq 256\,\text{KB}$ in the implementation-based evaluation. For DF-ORAM, we set $\lambda = 20$ and $s = 100$. For Path ORAM, we set the node size $Z = 5$. Such a setting makes both schemes to have a failure probability of around 2^{-20}. We use two virtual machines as the client and the server, respectively. Each of them has a CPU of AMD Opteron 63xx 2.4 GHz and 8 GB memory. The network bandwidth between them is 20 Mbps.

Storage Cost. The server storage cost in Path ORAM is $10N \cdot B$ bits; in DF-ORAM, the data blocks take $N \cdot B$ bits and the meta-data takes less than 6 MB. In both schemes, the index tables are stored locally and have same size of $O(N \cdot \log N)$. But each entry in DF-ORAM is bigger than that of Path ORAM. In our experimental setting, $node(i)$ takes 32 bits, $offset(i)$ takes 16 bits and $TAG(i)$ takes 8 bits. So the index table in Path ORAM is less than 64 MB., while the one in DF-ORAM is less than 112 MB.

Path ORAM has a permanent stash of $O(\log N \cdot B)$ bits to store blocks that cannot be sent back to server, and a temporary cache of $5 \log N \cdot B$ bits to store blocks retrieved from server. These two parts consumes less than 42 MB. In DF-ORAM, a stash can hold s data blocks and a cache can hold $3s$ data blocks. In our setting, $s = 100$, so these two parts consume less than 100 MB.

To sum up, the client-side storage cost in DF-ORAM is less than 212 MB and in Path ORAM is less than 106 MB.

Communication Cost. Table 3 shows the communication cost of Path ORAM and DF-ORAM, in terms of the number of blocks transferred between the client and the server per query. As we can see, DF-ORAM incurs a communication cost between 75 to 127 while Path ORAM incurs 160 to 240. DF-ORAM reduces the communication cost by a factor of 2, compared with Path ORAM.

Table 3. Communication Cost.Unit: number of blocks. Path ORAM has $10 \log N$ communication cost and DF-ORAM incurs around $1/2$ as of Path ORAM.

ORAM	$N = 2^{16}$	$N = 2^{18}$	$N = 2^{20}$	$N = 2^{22}$	$N = 2^{24}$
DF-ORAM	75	90	102	115	127
Path ORAM [13]	160	180	200	220	240

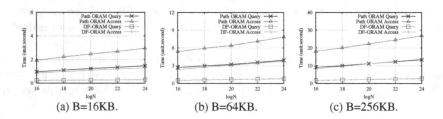

(a) B=16KB.   (b) B=64KB.   (c) B=256KB.

Fig. 6. Response time for DF-ORAM and Path ORAM [13]. Compared with Path ORAM, DF-ORAM reduces query delay by a factor of 4 to 5 and access delay with a factor of 2.

Response Time. We define the query delay as the time from when the query request is issued until when the client receives and decrypts the target data block. We also define the access delay as the time from the moment when the client issues the query request to the moment when both the query and the associated eviction task completes. Note that, both the query delay and the access delay include the computational time and the block transfer time. From Fig. 6(a), (b) and (c), we can see that DF-ORAM reduces the query delay by a factor of 4 to 5, and the access delay by a factor of 2, compared with Path ORAM. We can also see that, the access delay of DF-ORAM is between 800 milliseconds to 14 s, which is much shorter than that incurred by C-ORAM [10].

7 Conclusion

This paper proposes DF-ORAM, a practical dummy-free ORAM construction which incurs $O(\log N \cdot B)$ communication cost and small storage overhead at the server. Asymptotical analysis and implementation-based evaluations demonstrate that DF-ORAM is the most communication-efficient and storage-efficient one among the existing ORAM constructions that do not require server-side computation. Specifically, compared with Path ORAM in practical settings, DF-ORAM reduces communication cost by a factor of 2, reduces query delay by a factor of 4 to 5 and has access delay by a factor of 2, while introducing less than 6 MB. storage overhead to the server.

Acknowledgement. This work was partly supported by NSF under grant CNS-1422402.

References

1. Gentry, C., Goldman, K.A., Halevi, S., Julta, C., Raykova, M., Wichs, D.: Optimizing ORAM and using it efficiently for secure computation. In: De Cristofaro, E., Wright, M. (eds.) PETS 2013. LNCS, vol. 7981, pp. 1–18. Springer, Heidelberg (2013). doi:10.1007/978-3-642-39077-7_1
2. Goldreich, O., Ostrovsky, R.: Software protection and simulation on oblivious RAMs. J. ACM **43**(3), 431–473 (1996)
3. Goodrich, M.T., Mitzenmacher, M.: Mapreduce parallel cuckoo hashing and oblivious RAM simulations. In: Proceedings of the CoRR (2010)
4. Goodrich, M.T., Mitzenmacher, M.: Privacy-preserving access of outsourced data via oblivious RAM simulation. In: Aceto, L., Henzinger, M., Sgall, J. (eds.) ICALP 2011. LNCS, pp. 576–587. Springer, Heidelberg (2011). doi:10.1007/978-3-642-22012-8_46
5. Goodrich, M.T., Mitzenmacher, M., Ohrimenko, O., Tamassia, R.: Oblivious RAM simulation with efficient worst-case access overhead. In: Proceedings of the CCSW (2011)
6. Goodrich, M.T., Mitzenmacher, M., Ohrimenko, O., Tamassia, R.: Privacy-preserving group data access via stateless oblivious RAM simulation. In: Proceedings of the SODA (2012)
7. Islam, M., Kuzu, M., Kantarcioglu, M.: Access pattern disclosure on searchable encryption: ramification, attack and mitigation. In: Proceedings of the NDSS (2012)
8. Kushilevitz, E., Lu, S., Ostrovsky, R.: On the (in)security of hash-based oblivious RAM and a new balancing scheme. In: Proceedings of the SODA (2012)
9. Ma, Q., Zhang, J., Zhang, W., Qiao, D.: SE-ORAM: a storage-efficient oblivious RAM for privacy-preserving access to cloud storage. In: Proceedings of the 3rd IEEE International Conference on Cyber Security and Cloud Computing, Bejing, China (2016)
10. Moataz, T., Mayberry, T., Blass, E.O.: Constant communication ORAM with small blocksize. In: Proceedings of the CCS (2015)
11. Pinkas, B., Reinman, T.: Oblivious RAM revisited. In: Rabin, T. (ed.) CRYPTO 2010. LNCS, vol. 6223, pp. 502–519. Springer, Heidelberg (2010). doi:10.1007/978-3-642-14623-7_27

12. Shi, E., Chan, T.-H.H., Stefanov, E., Li, M.: Oblivious RAM with $O((\log N)^3)$ worst-case cost. In: Lee, D.H., Wang, X. (eds.) ASIACRYPT 2011. LNCS, pp. 197–214. Springer, Heidelberg (2011). doi:10.1007/978-3-642-25385-0_11

13. Stefanov, E., Dijk, M.V., Shi, E., Fletcher, C., Ren, L., Yu, X., Devadas, S.: Path ORAM: an extremely simple oblivious RAM protocol. In: Proceedings of the CCS (2013)

14. Stefanov, E., Shi, E.: Multi-cloud oblivious storage. In: Proceedings of the CCS (2013)

15. Stefanov, E., Shi, E.: ObliviStore: high performance oblivious cloud storage. In: Proceedings of the S&P (2013)

16. Stefanov, E., Shi, E., Song, D.: Towards practical oblivious RAM. In: Proceedings of the NDSS (2011)

17. Wang, X.S., Huang, Y., Chan, T.H.H., Shelat, A., Shi, E.: SCORAM: oblivious RAM for secure computation. In: Proceedings of the CCS (2014)

18. Williams, P., Sion, R.: Single round access privacy on outsourced storage. In: Proceedings of the CCS (2012)

19. Williams, P., Sion, R., Carbunar, B.: Building castles out of mud: practical access pattern privacy and correctness on untrusted storage. In: Proceedings of the CCS (2008)

20. Williams, P., Sion, R., Tomescu, A.: PrivateFS: a parallel oblivious file system. In: Proceedings of the CCS (2012)

PMFA: Toward Passive Message Fingerprint Attacks on Challenge-Based Collaborative Intrusion Detection Networks

Wenjuan Li[1], Weizhi Meng[2,3]([✉]), Lam-For Kwok[1], and Horace Ho Shing Ip[1]

[1] Department of Computer Science, City University of Hong Kong,
Kowloon Tong, Hong Kong
wenjuan.li@my.cityu.edu.hk
[2] Infocomm Security Department, Institute for Infocomm Research,
Singapore, Singapore
yuxin.meng@my.cityu.edu.hk
[3] Department of Applied Mathematics and Computer Science,
Technical University of Denmark, Kongens Lyngby, Denmark

Abstract. To enhance the performance of single intrusion detection systems (IDSs), collaborative intrusion detection networks (CIDNs) have been developed, which enable a set of IDS nodes to communicate with each other. In such a distributed network, insider attacks like collusion attacks are the main threat. In the literature, challenge-based trust mechanisms have been established to identify malicious nodes by evaluating the satisfaction between challenges and responses. However, we find that such mechanisms rely on two major assumptions, which may result in a weak threat model and make CIDNs still vulnerable to advanced insider attacks in practical deployment. In this paper, we design a novel type of collusion attack, called *passive message fingerprint attack (PMFA)*, which can collect messages and identify normal requests in a passive way. In the evaluation, we explore the attack performance under both simulated and real network environments. Experimental results indicate that under our attack, malicious nodes can send malicious responses to normal requests while maintaining their trust values.

Keywords: Intrusion Detection System · Collaborative network · Insider threats · Collusion attacks · Challenge-based trust mechanism

1 Introduction

Intrusion detection systems (IDSs), either *network-based (NIDS)* or *host-based (HIDS)*, have been deployed in computer networks at large, aiming to identify various intrusions [17]. In particular, HIDSs protect an end system or network

---

W. Meng was previously known as Yuxin Meng.

© Springer International Publishing AG 2016
J. Chen et al. (Eds.): NSS 2016, LNCS 9955, pp. 433–449, 2016.
DOI: 10.1007/978-3-319-46298-1_28

application through auditing system and event logs. By contrast, NIDSs can monitor network traffic for attacks, by sitting outside the firewall on the demilitarized zone (DMZ), or anywhere inside the private network [8].

With the increasing complexity of intrusions, former studies have revealed that a single or isolated IDS may be easily bypassed by novel attacks and cannot detect some certain attacks such as denial-of-service (DoS) attacks, which may cause potential damage if failed to detect timely (i.e., causing paralysis of the entire network) [21]. In order to enhance the detection capability of single IDSs, collaborative intrusion detection networks (CIDNs) have been developed that enable various IDS nodes to communicate required information with each other [4,21]. Although CIDNs can help improve the overall detection performance, such networks are vulnerable to insider attacks [3], e.g., *collusion attacks* where malicious nodes may collaborate to provide false alarm ranking information to reduce the effectiveness of alarm aggregation. As a result, identification of insider attacks is a major challenge for current CIDNs.

In order to protect CIDNs against insider threats, trust mechanisms should be built in such networks. In the literature, challenge-based trust mechanisms (shortly *challenge mechanisms*) are proposed, where *challenges* are sent to evaluate the trustworthiness of other nodes. Under this mechanism [4–7], a challenge can contain a set of alarms requesting for severity. As the testing node knows the severity of the alert located in the requests, it can use the received feedback to derive a trust value (e.g., satisfaction level) for the tested node. It is proved that such mechanism can prevent insider attacks like collusion attacks.

Contributions. However, we identify that such challenge mechanism depends heavily on two assumptions [4,5]: (a) challenges are sent out in a way that makes them difficult to be distinguished from normal messages; and (b) malicious nodes always send feedback opposite to its truthful judgment. In practical implementations, it is aware that malicious nodes may act more dynamic and complex; thus, these assumptions may be not realistic and leave CIDNs still vulnerable to advanced insider attacks. In this work, we develop a novel type of collusion attack, called *passive message fingerprint attack (PMFA)*, which can compromise the challenge mechanism in real scenarios, through passively collecting messages and distinguishing normal requests. Our contributions of this work can be summarized as below:

- We begin by reviewing existing challenge-based CIDNs and then analyze the adopted threat model including assumptions. It is shown that challenge-based CIDNs may still be vulnerable to advanced insider attacks.
- Based on our analysis, we develop a novel type of collusion attack, called *passive message fingerprint attack (PMFA)*, where a set of malicious nodes can collaborate to collect messages and distinguish normal requests from messages. In this case, these nodes can send false information to only normal requests but give truthful feedback to challenges. This may enable malicious nodes to maintain their trust values.
- In the evaluation, we explore the attack performance under both simulated and real CIDN environments. Experimental results demonstrate that our attack

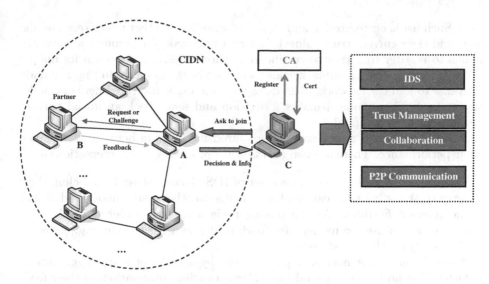

Fig. 1. The high-level architecture of a typical challenge-based CIDN including its major components.

is feasible and effective to compromise the challenge mechanism in real world applications. Afterwards, we discuss some potential countermeasures to defend against our attack.

It is worth noting that challenge mechanisms are an important means to protect CIDNs against common insider attacks. The major purpose of this work is to analyze its robustness on some advanced attacks. Our work aims to stimulate more research in enhancing challenge-based CIDNs in practical scenarios.

The remainder of this paper is organized as follows. We introduce the background of challenge-based CIDNs in Sect. 2. In Sect. 3, we analyze the adopted threat model by challenge mechanisms and describe *passive message fingerprint attack (PMFA)* in detail. Section 4 presents our evaluation and analyzes the results. Section 5 reviews related work. Finally, we conclude the work with future directions in Sect. 6.

2   Background of Challenge-Based CIDNs

In the literature, challenge-based trust mechanisms are one of the effective solutions to defend collaborative networks against insider attacks. Figure 1 depicts the high-level architecture of a typical challenge-based CIDN.

Network Interactions. In the architecture, each IDS node can choose its partners or collaborators based on to its own policies and experience. These IDS nodes can be associated if they have a collaborative relationship. Each node can maintain a list of their collaborated nodes, called *partner list* (or *acquaintance list*). Such list is customizable and stores information of other nodes (e.g., public keys and their current trust values). Before a node asks for joining the network, it has to register to a trusted certificate authority (*CA*) and obtain its unique proof of identity (e.g., a public key and a private key). As shown in Fig. 1, if node *C* wants to join the network, it needs to send an application to a network node, say node *A*. Then, node *A* makes a decision and sends back an initial *partner list*, if node *C* is accepted.

CIDNs allow IDS nodes exchange required messages in-between to enhance their performance. There are two major types of messages for interactions.

- *Challenges.* A challenge contains a set of IDS alarms asking for labeling their severity. A testing node can send a challenge to other tested nodes and obtain the relevant feedback. As the testing node knows the severity of the sent alarms, it can use the received feedback to derive a trust value (e.g., satisfaction level) for the tested node.
- *Normal requests.* A normal request is sent by a node for alarm aggregation. Other IDS nodes should send back alarm ranking information as their feedback. Alarm aggregation is an important feature for CIDNs, which can help improve the detection performance, and it usually considers the feedback from trusted nodes.

Network Components. Intuitively, an IDS component is essential for a CIDN node. Besides, A node in a typical challenge-based CIDN often contains several components including *trust management component, collaboration component* and *P2P communication*.

- *Trust management component.* This component is responsible for evaluating the trustworthiness of other nodes. Under the challenge mechanism, the trustworthiness of other nodes is mainly computed by evaluating the received feedback. Each node can send out either normal requests or challenges for alert ranking (consultation). To protect challenges, it is worth noting that challenges should be sent out in a random manner and in a way that makes them difficult to be distinguished from a normal alarm ranking request.
- *Collaboration component.* This component is mainly responsible for assisting a node to evaluate the trustworthiness of others by sending out *normal requests* or *challenges*, and receiving the relevant *feedback*. If a tested IDS node receives a request or challenge, this component will help send back its feedback. As shown in Fig. 1, if node *A* sends a *request/challenge* to node *B*, then node *B* will send back relevant feedback.
- *P2P communication.* This component is responsible for connecting with other IDS nodes and providing network organization, management and communication among IDS nodes.

Effectiveness. Challenge-based trust mechanisms can enhance a CIDN framework in detecting common insider attacks including Sybil attack, newcomer attack, betrayal attack and collusion attack [4–7].

- *Sybil attack.* This attack occurs when a malicious node creates a lot of fake identities [2]. This malicious node can utilize fake identities to gain larger influence on the alert aggregation. Referred to Fig. 1, an IDS node should register to a *CA* and obtain a unique proof identity, hence this kind of attack can be mitigated.
- *Newcomer (re-entry) attack.* This attack occurs when a malicious node registers as a new user aiming to erase its bad history. Challenge-based CIDNs begin by giving low initial trust values to all newcomers, so that they cannot make an impact on alarm aggregation.
- *Betrayal attack.* This attack occurs when a trusted node becomes a malicious one suddenly. To defend this attack, the above model employs a strategy: a high trust should be taken a long-time interaction and consistent good behavior to build, while only a few bad actions to ruin it. In particular, it employs a forgetting factor to give more credits to recent behaviors.
- *Collusion attack.* This attack happens when a group of malicious peers cooperate together by providing false alarm rankings in order to compromise the network. Challenge-based trust mechanisms can uncover malicious peers through sending challenges. The trust values of malicious nodes can decrease rapidly if their untruthful feedback is detected.

Overall, challenge-based CIDNs can not only provide collaboration among IDS nodes, but also detect common insider threats. However, in real deployment [11,12], we find that challenge-based trust mechanisms rely on two main assumptions, which may be vulnerable to some advanced insider attacks.

3   Our Developed Attack

In this section, we analyze the threat model made by challenge-based trust mechanisms, discuss adopted assumptions and describe our developed attack.

3.1   Threat Model Analysis

As stated above, challenge-based trust mechanisms are effective to defend against most common attacks. However, in real implementations [11,12], we notice that the defense of collusion attacks depends primarily on two assumptions (or conditions) as below.

- Challenges are sent out in a random way and in a way that makes them difficult to be distinguished from normal messages.
- Malicious nodes always send feedback opposite to its truthful judgment.

Basically, these two assumptions aim to protect *challenges*, as they are the key to identify malicious nodes under various insider attacks. The first assumption has two conditions: *random manner* and *hard to distinguish*. These two conditions ensure that an IDS node cannot distinguish a challenge from normal requests, so that malicious nodes have a trivial possibility of identifying and bypassing challenges, and have to give response to each message.

The second assumption describes that malicious nodes always send feedback opposite to its truthful judgment, resulting in a rapid decrease of trust values of malicious nodes. Based on [6,7], this is called *maximal harm model* where an adversary always chooses to report false feedback with the intention to bring the most negative impact to the request sender. For example, when a malicious node receives a ranking request, it will send feedback 'no risk' for an alarm whose real risk level should be 'medium', because this feedback can maximally deviate the aggregated result at the sender side.

Discussions. These assumptions are reasonable in some cases, in which attackers are naive and choose a *maximal harm model* (we call these attacks as *naive attacks*). However, in real scenarios, advanced attackers may perform more dynamic and complex behaviors to compromise a CIDN (i.e., attackers may employ different strategies to reduce the detection risk). Even for a malicious node, it can send out truthful feedback, pretending to be a benign one in order to maintain its trust value. In this work, 'advanced attack' refers to the situation where attackers can perform complicated operations, as compared to naive attacks (under *maximal harm model*).

Thus, these assumptions may result in a weak threat model in real-world applications and leave CIDNs still vulnerable to advanced attacks. For example, we accept that challenges can be send out in a random way and in a way that makes them difficult to be distinguished from messages. However, it is still possible for attackers to distinguish normal requests from messages.

3.2 Passive Message Fingerprint Attacks

As analyzed above, challenge-based CIDNs are effective to detecting common insider attacks, but may be still vulnerable to advanced attacks. In this part, we develop a kind of advanced collusion attack, called *passive message fingerprint attack (PMFA)*, where malicious nodes are able to maintain their trust, through passively exchanging received messages and distinguishing normal requests.

Basic idea. Under the challenge-based trust mechanism, it is a difficult task for an IDS node to distinguish challenges from messages. However, it is possible to distinguish normal requests from messages. It is worth noting that normal requests are sent out for alarm ranking of one or several alarms (i.e., used for alarm aggregation). Therefore, a set of (trusted) IDS nodes can receive this request and give feedback. We notice that such request will contain the same alarm set, so that a request is distinguishable through comparing the received messages among several nodes. If several nodes receive the message containing the same alarm set, this message should be a normal request rather than a challenge. Taking advantage of this, malicious nodes can choose to send untruthful feedback to only requests, but give truthful response to other messages.

In Fig. 2, we illustrate how this attack works. Suppose node A is a testing node that sends out messages including challenges to its partner nodes, where

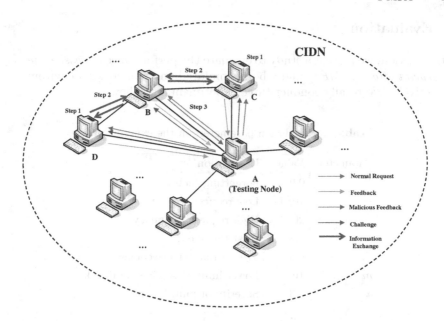

Fig. 2. A case of passive message fingerprint attack (PMFA) on challenge-based CIDNs.

a challenge is used to evaluate their trustworthiness. After receiving a message, all tested nodes will give feedback. If nodes B, C and D are malicious, then the steps in *PMFA* can be described as below:

- **Step 1.** Under the attack, each malicious node can collect and store all received messages from the testing node. We accept that a challenge is sent in a random manner and cannot be distinguished from normal messages, so that all malicious nodes are not able to identify a challenge.
- **Step 2.** Malicious nodes start exchanging information of received messages with each other. In real scenarios, normal requests will be sent out to all trusted nodes for alarm ranking, so it is possible to compare the messages and check whether it is a normal request. For instance, nodes B, C and D exchange their received messages and update others' database. Then, nodes B compares the messages received by nodes C and D. If a match is identified, then the relevant message should be a normal request.
- **Step 3.** After identifying a normal request, node B can send back malicious feedback to this message (i.e., affect the alarm aggregation of node A). But for other messages, node B still sends back its truthful answers.

To summarize, our attack enables malicious nodes to collaboratively distinguish normal requests from messages, and give untruthful feedback to only requests but truthfully response to other messages. This can greatly reduce the possibility of detection by challenges. As a result, malicious nodes can make a negative impact on alarm aggregation while maintaining their trust values.

4   Evaluation

In this section, we present a study to evaluate the performance of *passive message fingerprint attack (PMFA)* under both simulated and real network environment, respectively. We totally conduct three experiments as follows.

Table 1. Simulation parameters in the experiment.

Parameters	Value	Description
λ	0.9	Forgetting factor
ε_l	10/day	Low request frequency
ε_h	20/day	High request frequency
r	0.8	trust threshold
T_s	0.5	Trust value for newcomers
m	10	Lower limit of received feedback
d	0.3	Severity of punishment

– *Experiment-1.* In this experiment, we aim to explore the performance of naive collusion attacks under the assumptions discussed in Sect. 3.1.
– *Experiment-2.* In the second experiment, we aim to study the feasibility of *passive message fingerprint attack (PMFA)* in attacking a simulated challenge-based CIDN.
– *Experiment-3.* In this experiment, we cooperate with an information center and evaluate the real attack performance in a real wired CIDN.

In the remaining parts, we introduce CIDN settings (i.e., how to compute trust values and satisfaction levels) and discuss experimental results.

4.1   CIDN Settings

There are 20 nodes in the simulated CIDN environment, which are randomly distributed in a 5×5 grid region. We use Snort [19] as IDS plugin that can be implemented in a node. Each IDS node can connect to other nodes and establish an initial *partner list* based on the distance. The initial trust values of all nodes in the *partner list* are set to $T_s = 0.5$ based on [5,6].

To evaluate the trustworthiness of partner nodes, each IDS node can send out challenges randomly to its partners with an average rate of ε. There are two levels of request frequency: ε_l and ε_h. For a highly trusted or highly untrusted node, the request frequency is low, since it should be very confident about the decision of their feedback. On the other hand, the request frequency should be high for other nodes whose trust values are close to threshold. To facilitate comparisons, all the settings can be referred to [5,6,12]. It is worth emphasizing that we set low request frequency to 10 per day, which is more strict than [5,6]. The detailed parameters are summarized in Table 1.

Node Expertise. Three expertise levels are employed for an IDS node as low (0.1), medium (0.5) and high (0.95). The expertise of an IDS can be using a beta function described as below:

$$f(p'|\alpha,\beta) = \frac{1}{B(\alpha,\beta)}p'^{\alpha-1}(1-p')^{\beta-1}$$
$$B(\alpha,\beta) = \int_0^1 t^{\alpha-1}(1-t)^{\beta-1}dt$$

(1)

where $p'(\in [0,1])$ is the probability of intrusion examined by the IDS. $f(p'|\alpha,\beta)$ means the probability that a node with expertise level l responses with a value of p' to an intrusion examination of difficulty level $d(\in [0,1])$. A higher value of l means a higher probability of correctly identifying an intrusion while a higher value of d means that an intrusion is more difficult to detect. In particular, α and β can be defined as [5]:

$$\alpha = 1 + \frac{l(1-d)}{d(1-l)}r$$
$$\beta = 1 + \frac{l(1-d)}{d(1-l)}(1-r)$$

(2)

where $r \in \{0,1\}$ is the expected result of detection. For a fixed difficulty level, the node with higher level of expertise can achieve higher probability of correctly detecting an intrusion. For example, a node with expertise level of 1 can accurately identify an intrusion with guarantee if the difficulty level is 0.

Node Trust Evaluation. To evaluate the trustworthiness of a target node, a testing node can send a *challenge* to the tested node through a random generation process. The testing node then can compute a score to reflect its satisfaction level. Based on [4], we can evaluate the trustworthiness of a node i according to node j as follows:

$$T_i^j = \left(w_s \frac{\sum_{k=0}^n F_k^{j,i}\lambda^{tk}}{\sum_{k=0}^n \lambda^{tk}} - T_s\right)(1-x)^d + T_s$$

(3)

where $F_k^{j,i} \in [0,1]$ is the score of the received feedback k and n is the total number of feedback. λ is a *forgetting factor* that assigns less weight to older feedback response. w_s is a *significant weight* depending on the total number of received feedback, if there is only a few feedback under a certain minimum m, then $w_s = \frac{\sum_{k=0}^n \lambda^{tk}}{m}$, otherwise $w_s = 1$. x is the percentage of "don't know" answers during a period (e.g., from $t0$ to tn). d is a positive incentive parameter to control the severity of punishment to "don't know" replies. More details about equation derivation can be referred to [4,5].

Satisfaction Evaluation. Suppose there are two factors: an expected feedback ($e \in [0,1]$) and an actual received feedback ($r \in [0,1]$). Then, a function

F ($\in [0,1]$) can be used to reflect the satisfaction by measuring the difference between the received answer and the expected answer as below [5,6]:

$$F = 1 - (\frac{e-r}{max(c_1 e, 1-e)})^{c_2} \quad e > r \tag{4}$$

$$F = 1 - (\frac{c_1(r-e)}{max(c_1 e, 1-e)})^{c_2} \quad e \leq r \tag{5}$$

where c_1 controls the degree of penalty for wrong estimates and c_2 controls satisfaction sensitivity. A large c_2 means more sensitive. In this work, we set $c_1 = 1.5$ and $c_2 = 1$ based on the simulation in [5].

4.2 Experiment-1

In this simulation, we conduct an experiment to show the robustness of challenge-based CIDNs against naive collusion attacks, where a set of dishonest nodes collaborate to always send false alarm ranking. We accept the assumptions that challenges are sent out in a random way and malicious nodes always send feedback opposite to its truthful judgment (maximal harm model). The results are depicted in Figs. 3 and 4.

In Fig. 3, we show the convergence of trust values regarding different expert nodes. It is worth emphasizing that there are three expertise levels: low ($I = 0.1$), medium ($I = 0.5$) and high ($I = 0.95$). Our results are in line with the results in [4,5], in which nodes with higher expertise can achieve bigger trust values. In addition, it is noticed that the trust values of all nodes become stable after around 20 days in the simulated network.

As a study of naive collusion attacks, we randomly select three expert nodes ($I = 0.95$) starting to send out untruthful feedback in a constant way from Day 45. For simplicity, we name these nodes as *malicious node 1*, *malicious node 2* and *malicious node 3*. Figure 4 describes the trust values of these malicious nodes

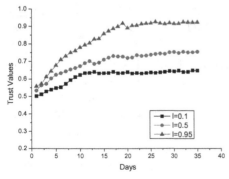

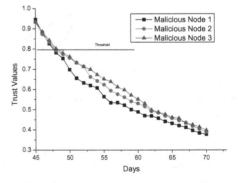

Fig. 3. Convergence of trust values of IDS nodes regarding three expertise levels.

Fig. 4. Trust values of malicious nodes under naive collusion attacks.

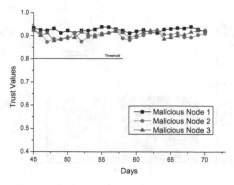
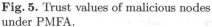
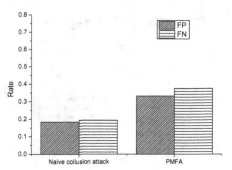

Fig. 5. Trust values of malicious nodes under PMFA.

Fig. 6. Average false rates in alarm aggregation under different attack models.

during the attack period. It is noted that trust values of malicious nodes can drop quickly below the threshold of 0.8 (within 2–3 days). Because malicious nodes always send untruthful feedback to messages including challenges, challenge-based CIDNs are able to detect naive collusion attacks in a short period. The results demonstrate that the challenge-based trust mechanisms work well in identifying malicious nodes under the naive collusion attack and disables them to make any impact on alarm aggregation.

4.3   Experiment-2

In this experiment, we aim to investigate the feasibility of *passive message fingerprint attack (PMFA)* on attacking challenge-based CIDNs. Similar to the above experiment, we also use the same expert nodes of *malicious node 1*, *malicious node 2* and *malicious node 3* to launch our attack. The trust values of malicious nodes and average false rates are depicted in Figs. 5 and 6, respectively. The main observations can be described as below.

- Figure 5 illustrates that the trust values of three malicious nodes are maintained above the threshold and cannot be detected by the challenges. This validates that normal requests can be distinguished from messages under our attack. As a result, these nodes can still make an impact on alarm aggregation.
- Figure 6 describes the average false rates in alarm aggregation under two different attack models. False rates include both *false positions (FP)* and *false negatives (FN)*. The false rates are about 18.3 %−20 % under naive collusion attack, whereas reach 30 %−38 % under our attack.

Overall, these results demonstrate the feasibility of our attack, where malicious nodes can send malicious feedback to only normal requests, but still give truthful response to other messages. This enables them to act abnormally (i.e., increasing false rates in alarm aggregation), but maintain their trust values (i.e., without detection by challenges).

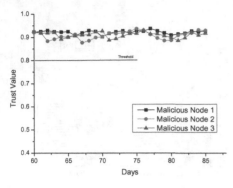
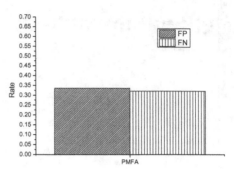

Fig. 7. Trust values of malicious nodes under PMFA and a real CIDN.

Fig. 8. Average false rates in alarm aggregation under PMFA and a real CIDN.

4.4 Experiment-3

In this experiment, we mainly evaluate our attack in a real CIDN environment to explore its practical performance. We cooperate with an information center and utilize a wired CIDN that consists of 15 nodes, in which the incoming network traffic is about 1105 packets/s on average. The basic network settings can be referred to Table 1. Before the experiment, we first run the whole network and wait trust values to become stable. Then, we randomly select three expert nodes as malicious ones to perform *passive message fingerprint attack (PMFA)*. The results are described in Figs. 7 and 8, respectively. The major observations can be summarized as follows.

- Figure 7 depicts that no malicious node can be identified under our attack (i.e., none of their trust values are below the threshold of 0.8). Thus, they can keep making a negative impact on alarm aggregation.
- As malicious nodes can keep sending malicious feedback to cause a large disagreement in alarm agreation, false rates would be increased. Figure 8 presents that average false rates in a real CIDN can reach 30 %−33 %.

These results demonstrate the effectiveness of our attack in a real CIDN and uncover that challenge-based trust mechanisms should be further improved to deal with more advanced insider threats in real deployment.

4.5 Mitigation Strategies

As stated above, we have demonstrated the feasibility and effectiveness of *passive message fingerprint attack (PMFA)* in compromising the robustness of challenge-based CIDNs. To defend against such advanced attacks, several potential countermeasures can be considered to improve the challenge mechanisms.

- *Challenge improvement.* In practice, each node can receive a challenge, but the contained alarms may be different. This because challenges are sent in random, so that alarms will be extracted randomly from an alarm database. To defend against our attack, challenges can be designed to contain the same alarms, making malicious nodes unable to identify normal requests.
- *Sending strategy improvement.* To further increase the difficulty of identifying normal requests, CIDNs can send normal requests and challenges in a cross way. In this case, nodes may not receive the messages with the same content, causing that malicious nodes have to give truthful feedback.

It is worth noting that the above strategies can mitigate but may not completely prevent advanced attacks. Hence, there is a need to combine several strategies and employ a more robust CIDN framework. To sum up, our study validates that advanced insider attacks may compromise challenge-based CIDNs in real scenarios. To defend against these threats, more advanced threat models should be considered in designing practical trust mechanisms for CIDNs.

5 Related Work

It is intuitive that a single IDS has no information about the whole environment that it was deployed, so that it is very likely to be bypassed by some complex intrusions [21]. To mitigate this issue, collaborative intrusion detection networks (CIDNs) have been proposed and implemented, which enable an IDS node to achieve more accurate detection by collecting and communicating information from/with other IDS nodes. Several related distributed systems can be classified as below.

- *Centralized/Hierarchical systems:* Emerald [16] and DIDS [18];
- *Publish/subscribe systems:* COSSACK [15] and DOMINO [22];
- *P2P Querying-based systems:* Netbait [1] and PIER [9].

More specifically, the system of EMERALD (Event Monitoring Enabling Responses to Anomalous Live Disturbances) [16] was a distributed tool suite, which tracks malicious activity across various abstract layers in a large network. It combines models from distributed high-volume event-correlation with traditional intrusion detection. Similarly, distributed Intrusion Detection System (DIDS) [18] aimed to combine distributed monitoring and data reduction with centralized data analysis module to monitor a heterogeneous computer network. COSSACK system [15] was developed for mitigating DDoS attack in an automate way. Such system requires no manual intervention and supports independent attack signature. Moreover, DOMINO (Distributed Overlay for Monitoring InterNet Outbreaks) [22] was an architecture for a distributed intrusion detection system, which enhances collaboration among heterogeneous nodes within a network. The overlay design enables this system to be heterogeneous, scalable, and robust to attacks and failures. Also, it can detect spoofed IP sources, reduce false positives, and enable attack classification in a timely manner. For querying-based systems, PIER [9] was an Internet-scale query engine, which supports massively distributed, database-style dataflows for snapshot and continuous queries. It is intended to serve as a building block for a diverse set of Internet-scale information centric applications (i.e., tapping into the standardized data).

However, it is well-recognized by the literature that such collaborative networks are vulnerable to insider attacks. For example, Li *et al.* [10] identified that most distributed intrusion detection systems (DIDS) relied on centralized fusion, or distributed fusion with unscalable communication mechanisms, and then proposed a DIDS based on the emerging decentralized location and routing infrastructure. However, their approach assumes that all peers are trusted which is vulnerable to insider attacks (i.e., betrayal attacks where some nodes suddenly become malicious).

To protect CIDNs against insider threats, building proper trust models is one of the promising solutions. Following this idea, Duma *et al.* [3] proposed a P2P-based overlay for intrusion detection (Overlay IDS) that mitigated the insider threat by using a trust-aware engine for correlating alerts and an adaptive scheme for managing trust. The trust-aware correlation engine is capable of filtering out warnings sent by untrusted or low quality peers, while the adaptive trust management scheme uses past experiences of peers to predict their trustworthiness. Tuan [20] then utilized game theory to model and analyze the processes of reporting and exclusion in a P2P network. They identified that if a reputation system was not incentive compatible, the more numbers of peers in the system, the less likely that anyone will report about a malicious peer.

Later, challenge-based trust mechanism have been proposed. For example, Fung *et al.* proposed challenge-based CIDNs, in which the trustworthiness of a node depends on the received answers to the challenges. Initially, they proposed a HIDS collaboration framework [4] that enables each HIDS to evaluate the trustworthiness of others based on its own experience by means of a forgetting factor. The forgetting factor can give more emphasis on the recent experience of the peer. Then, they improved their trust management model by using a Dirichlet-based model to measure the level of trustworthiness among IDS nodes according to their mutual experience [5]. This model had strong scalability properties and was robust against common insider threats and the experimental results demonstrated that the new model could improve robustness and efficiency. As feedback aggregation is a key component in a challenge mechanism, Fung *et al.* [6] further applied a Bayesian approach to feedback aggregation to minimize the combined costs of missed detection and false alarm.

Following the framework, Li *et al.* [11] identified that different IDS nodes may have different levels of sensitivity in detecting different types of intrusions, so they proposed a notion of *intrusion sensitivity* that measures the detection sensitivity of an IDS in detecting different kinds of intrusions. For example, if a signature-based IDS node has more numbers of signatures (or rules) in detecting DoS attacks, then it should be considered as more powerful in detecting such attacks than other nodes (which have relatively fewer related signatures). This notion is very helpful when making decisions based on the collected information from different nodes, as it can help detect intrusions and correlate IDS alerts through emphasizing the impact of an *expert IDS*.

Later, They proposed an *intrusion sensitivity-based trust management model* [12] for CIDNs and automated the allocation of *intrusion sensitivity* using machine learning techniques in practice (e.g., knowledge-based KNN classifier [14]). As a study, they described how to apply *intrusion sensitivity* for aggregating alarms and investigated its effect on defending against pollution attacks in which a group of malicious peers cooperate together by providing false alert rankings [13]. The experimental results indicated that the use of *intrusion sensitivity* can decrease the trust values of malicious nodes more quickly. They also pointed out several challenges in this field. For instance, it is a big challenge to objectively and correctly assign the values of *intrusion sensitivity* based on expert knowledge, as experts may have different views regarding the settings of IDS nodes. To address this issue, one of the potential solutions is to study the criterion for evaluating the *intrusion sensitivity*.

6 Conclusion

Challenge-based trust mechanisms are well-developed to protect CIDNs against insider threats like collusion attacks. However, in real-world applications, we identify that such mechanisms rely on two major assumptions and may be still vulnerable to advanced insider attacks. In this paper, we develop an advanced collusion attack, called *passive message fingerprint attack (PMFA)*, where malicious nodes can maintain their trust values, through passively exchanging received messages and distinguishing normal requests. Under this attack, malicious nodes are able to give untruthful feedback to only requests but truthfully response to other messages. The evaluation, under both simulated and real network environments, validates the feasibility and effectiveness of our attack. Our work attempts to stimulate more research in designing robust CIDN frameworks in real-world scenarios. There are many future directions, which could include exploring other advanced insider attacks on challenge-based CIDNs and enhancing existing framework to against complex attacks.

Acknowledgments. We would like to thank all anonymous reviewers for their helpful comments in improving the paper.

References

1. Chun, B., Lee, J., Weatherspoon, H., Chun, B.N.: Netbait: a distributed worm detection service. Technical report IRB-TR-03-033, Intel Research Berkeley (2003)
2. Douceur, J.R.: The sybil attack. In: Druschel, P., Kaashoek, F., Rowstron, A. (eds.) IPTPS 2002. LNCS, vol. 2429, pp. 251–260. Springer, Heidelberg (2002). doi:10.1007/3-540-45748-8_24
3. Duma, C., Karresand, M., Shahmehri, N., Caronni, G.: A trust-aware, P2P-based overlay for intrusion detection. In: DEXA Workshop, pp. 692–697 (2006)

4. Fung, C.J., Baysal, O., Zhang, J., Aib, I., Boutaba, R.: Trust management for host-based collaborative intrusion detection. In: De Turck, F., Kellerer, W., Kormentzas, G. (eds.) DSOM 2008. LNCS, vol. 5273, pp. 109–122. Springer, Heidelberg (2008)

5. Fung, C.J., Zhang, J., Aib, I., Boutaba, R.: Robust and scalable trust management for collaborative intrusion detection. In: Proceedings of the 11th IFIP/IEEE International Conference on Symposium on Integrated Network Management (IM), pp. 33–40 (2009)

6. Fung, C.J., Zhu, Q., Boutaba, R., Basar, T.: Bayesian decision aggregation in collaborative intrusion detection networks. In: NOMS, pp. 349–356 (2010)

7. Fung, C.J., Boutaba, R.: Design and management of collaborative intrusion detection networks. In: Proceedings of the 2013 IFIP/IEEE International Symposium on Integrated Network Management (IM), pp. 955–961 (2013)

8. Gong, F.: Next Generation Intrusion Detection Systems (IDS). McAfee Network Security Technologies Group (2003)

9. Huebsch, R., Chun, B.N., Hellerstein, J.M., Loo, B.T., Maniatis, P., Roscoe, T., Shenker, S., Stoica, I., Yumerefendi, A.R.: The architecture of PIER: an internet-scale query processor. In: Proceedings of the 2005 Conference on Innovative Data Systems Research (CIDR), pp. 28–43 (2005)

10. Li, Z., Chen, Y., Beach, A.: Towards scalable and Robust distributed intrusion alert fusion with good load balancing. In: Proceedings of the 2006 SIGCOMM Workshop on Large-Scale Attack Defense (LSAD), pp. 115–122 (2006)

11. Li, W., Meng, Y., Kwok, L.-F.: Enhancing trust evaluation using intrusion sensitivity in collaborative intrusion detection networks: feasibility and challenges. In: Proceedings of the 9th International Conference on Computational Intelligence and Security (CIS), pp. 518–522. IEEE (2013)

12. Li, W., Meng, W., Kwok, L.-F.: Design of intrusion sensitivity-based trust management model for collaborative intrusion detection networks. In: Zhou, J., Gal-Oz, N., Zhang, J., Gudes, E. (eds.) Trust Management VIII. IFIP AICT, vol. 430, pp. 61–76. Springer, Heidelberg (2014)

13. Li, W., Meng, W.: Enhancing collaborative intrusion detection networks using intrusion sensitivity in detecting pollution attacks. Inf. Comput. Secur. 24(3), 265–276 (2016). Emerald

14. Meng, W., Li, W., Kwok, L.-F.: Design of intelligent KNN-based alarm filter using knowledge-based alert verification in intrusion detection. Secur. Commun. Netw. 8(18), 3883–3895 (2015). Wiley

15. Papadopoulos, C., Lindell, R., Mehringer, J., Hussain, A., Govindan, R.: COSSACK: Coordinated Suppression of Simultaneous Attacks. In: Proceedings of the 2003 DARPA Information Survivability Conference and Exposition (DISCEX), pp. 94–96 (2003)

16. Porras, P.A., Neumann, P.G.: Emerald: event monitoring enabling responses to anomalous live disturbances. In: Proceedings of the 20th National Information Systems Security Conference, pp. 353–365 (1997)

17. Scarfone, K., Mell, P.: Guide to Intrusion Detection and Prevention Systems (IDPS). NIST Special Publication 800–94 (2007)

18. Snapp, S.R., et al.: DIDS (Distributed Intrusion Detection System) - motivation, architecture, and an early prototype. In: Proceedings of the 14th National Computer Security Conference, pp. 167–176 (1991)

19. Snort: An an open source network intrusion prevention and detection system (IDS/IPS). http://www.snort.org/

20. Tuan, T.A.: A game-theoretic analysis of trust management in P2P systems. In: Proceedings of ICCE, pp. 130–134 (2006)

21. Wu, Y.-S., Foo, B., Mei, Y., Bagchi, S.: Collaborative Intrusion Detection System (CIDS): a framework for accurate and efficient IDS. In: Proceedings of the 2003 Annual Computer Security Applications Conference (ACSAC), pp. 234–244 (2003)
22. Yegneswaran, V., Barford, P., Jha, S.: Global intrusion detection in the DOMINO overlay system. In: Proceedings of the 2004 Network and Distributed System Security Symposium (NDSS), pp. 1–17 (2004)

Iris Cancellable Template Generation Based on Indexing-First-One Hashing

Yen-Lung Lai[✉], Zhe Jin, Bok-Min Goi, Tong-Yuen Chai, and Wun-She Yap

Lee Kong Chian Faculty of Engineering and Science,
Universiti Tunku Abdul Rahman, Sungai Long, Malaysia
yenlung92@hotmail.com, {jinzhe,goibm,chaity,yapws}@utar.edu.my

Abstract. Iris recognition system has demonstrated its strong capability in performing personal verification and identification with promising recognition accuracy. However, the conventional iris recognition system stores the unprotected iris templates in a database, which is potentially being compromised. Even though biometric template protection provides a feasible solution to secure biometric template, a trade-off between security and recognition accuracy is incurred. That is, the higher security level always trades with poor recognition accuracy and vice versa. In this paper, a new iris template protection scheme is proposed, namely "Indexing-First-One" (IFO) hashing. IFO hashing transforms the binary feature into index value with Jacaard distance preservation. The resultant template offers a good indication of inheriting similarity from the IrisCode and strong concealment of IrisCode against inversion attack as well as other major security and privacy attacks. Experiments on CASIA-v3 data set substantiate that the proposed scheme can achieve as low as 0.54 % equal error rate and well preservation of recognition performance before and after IFO hashing.

Keywords: Biometric · IrisCode · Cancellable · Template protection · Security

1 Introduction

Traditional authentication mechanisms rely on user's password, PIN numbers or physical keys to allow the legitimate individual get access into the system. However, this method has suffered from certain inherent limitations such as "too-many-passwords". Moreover, password, ID cards or access card are easy to be forgotten, stolen and lost. That leads to the compromise of security, especially when all of this information is known and shared by others. On the other hand, biometric traits have been used to identify individuals based on the physiological and behavioral characteristics of human being. The most popular traits used in biometric-based authentication systems are irises, face, and fingerprint [10]. Since the biometric traits/identifiers are inherently bound to individual, this means that people no longer need to worry about the password or ID card being stolen or forgotten. Furthermore, biometrics cannot be share and lost.

© Springer International Publishing AG 2016
J. Chen et al. (Eds.): NSS 2016, LNCS 9955, pp. 450–463, 2016.
DOI: 10.1007/978-3-319-46298-1_29

Among all the biometric identifiers, human iris is considered as a highly reliable biological trait for personal identification and verification [5,6]. It is generally conceded that iris recognition is the most promising approach as compare to others biometric recognition system [4,16].

Conventional iris recognition system stores the generated iris templates in database, which is potentially being attacked or compromised. Once this database is compromised, the attacker can use the stolen template to perform impersonation. Due to the fact that human iris is permanently associated with each individual, this implies a permanent loss of identity for each user. Moreover, information of human iris is very limited as every individual only possesses two irises for iris template generation. Thus, the compromised template cannot be revoked easily and further hinders the usage of the human iris in recognition purpose. The security and privacy issues become a major concern for a user and a solution is needed.

Biometric template protection is introduced to solve the existing security and privacy problems for a biometric recognition system. The notions of cancellable biometric [10,19] that achieves the following properties was introduced:

1. Diversity: Different templates are used for different purposes. There is no cross-matching between the generated templates for different applications.
2. Revocability: The generated template must be able to be revoked when a database is compromised.
3. Non-invertibility: Generated template need to be non-invertible to make sure it is computationally hard for the attacker to reconstruct the original template.
4. Performance: The newly generated template must preserve or at least come with insignificant degradation on the recognition performance.

2   Literature Review

For cancellable biometric, it can be classified into biometric salting and non-invertible transformation [10]. Generally, in biometric salting, independent auxiliary data such as user specific password or token are combined with original biometric data to generate a distorted version of the new biometric template in order to protect the original biometric data. On the other hand, non-invertible transformation refers to one-way transformation function is used to transform the original biometric data into its non-invertible version.

In biometric salting, a well-known instant, S-IrisCode encoding is proposed by Chong et al. [4] to generate cancellable iris template. It is essentially an extension of biometric salting approach (i.e. Biohashing [19]). The amplitude of the complex iris Gabor-feature was projected into a lower and more discriminative feature space through iterated inner products with a set of user-specific random vectors. Similar in salting approach, the original iris information is distorted due to the inner product multiplication with a random vectors. The projected vectors are then quantized into binary bits. A noise mask is introduced to eliminate the weak inner product and improve the recognition performance. Cancellability is achieved through replacing the user-specific random vectors to allow new template to be generated in case of compromised database event happen. Another cancellable iris template based on biometric salting approach was proposed by Pillai et al. [16]. Pillai et al. partitioned the iris into several sectors and projected these sectors to a lower dimensional space by using a external token (i.e. random Gaussian matrix). The projected vectors are further quantized into binary bits to generate cancellable iris template whereby new random Gaussian matrix can be used to reissue a new iris template and replace the old template.

For non-invertible transformation, one way transformation function is applied to generate cancellable Iris template. In [21], cancellable iris template is generated through non-invertible transformation by combining the rows of the iris feature or IrisCode. Before this, the iris feature or IrisCode is row shifted. Non-invertibility was achieved due to the distortion of the original iris information after different rows of iris feature or IrisCode were combined through certain operation (e.g. addition/multiplication or XOR). User-specific keys are used to select two number of rows as the input of aforementioned operation. This method can preserve the original recognition performance. However, the recognition performance will be deteriorated when same key is used. This implies that the vulnerability in stolen token case occurred in Biohashing would be suffered in this method as well.

Block remapping method is used to perform non-invertible transform in [7]. The normalized iris texture is first partitioned into several image blocks. Then, the image blocks are permuted by using random permutation key. A many-to-one image blocks remapping technique is then used to generate cancellable iris template. Same image blocks can be remap to a target texture (same size with original iris texture) during block remapping process. The redundant iris texture not involve during remapping process induced some information loss. Thus non-invertibility can be archived. Different permutation keys can be used for new template generation to replace the compromised template.

A tokenless non-invertible transformation named Bio-encoding was proposed by Ouda et al. [14,15]. Ouda et al. first extracted the consistent bits from the original IrisCode generated from several iris image samples for each user. After that, the consistent bits are split into multiple binary codewords and encoded by a random generated binary sequence to produce a new random set, namely BioCode which can be securely stored in database. However, the IrisCode can be regenerated from the BioCode when the Boolean function used to generate the random sequence is known by an adversary [12].

A new alignment-free non-invertible transformation is used to generate cancelable iris template from IrisCode using bloom filter [17]. A bloom filter b is a bit array of length n initialized with zero. In this method, the IrisCode is split into i equal size blocks. Each block constitute to a single bloom filter b_i. Then, a number of hash functions h_i are used to add an elements of '1' into a bloom filter. The hash function can be described as $h_i = T \oplus x_j$, where T denotes a secret key to enable cancellability while x_j denotes the column codewords in each block with size w where $\forall j \in [1, w]$. Same columns code words will output same hashing result induced a many-to-one mapping, thus, non-invertibility can be achieved. The recognition performance is able to be preserved after the transformation is employed. However, Hermans et al. [8] proposed a false positive matching attack against bloom filter approach with a undesired low time complexity of 2^{25}.

Vast majority of existing iris template protection scheme is able to maintain the recognition performance but still noted with certain vulnerabilities:

1. Token storage problem: Biometric salting technique [4,16] showed significant degradation in recognition performance when same seed is used [11]. This implies the user-specific token used in salting technique is required to be securely stored in order to achieve better recognition performance.
2. Trade-off problem: [7,17], failed to achieve non-invertibility as the adversary can launch false positive matching attack. This is the drawback of maintaining the recognition performance by preserving more original iris features. Notice that information loss is required to achieve stronger non-invertibility [13].

In this paper, a new iris template protection scheme inspired from the concept of Min-hashing is proposed. The proposed scheme generates protected iris template while breaking the tradeoff between accuracy and security. Essentially, the scheme utilizes the implicit ordering of IrisCode (location of binary bits) instead of absolute binary value of IrisCode, which permits more original binary information can be loss from the IrisCode while maintaining its discriminative representation to achieve stronger non-invertibility without significant deteriorates the recognition performance. Besides, no user-specific token is required, hence, eliminated the key storage issue.

3   Preliminary

MinHash is a method for speedy estimating how similar two sets are. MinHash was initially used in the search engine to detect duplicate web pages and remove them from search results as well as in the large-scale clustering problems [1,2]. Min-hashing, records the index of first '1' occurrence for a number of permutation, i of binary vectors, for $i = 1, 2, \ldots, m$ where m denoted the number of permutations applied. Different index vectors, which may encoded in binary form, can be formed by using the different permutation seeds on a binary vector. Let $\mathbf{A}$ and $\mathbf{B}$ be two index vectors generated from the binary vector and h be a hash function that maps the members of $\mathbf{A}$ and $\mathbf{B}$ to distinct indexes, and for any set S define min $h_i(S)$ to be the minimal member of S with respect to h. Now, if we apply min h to both $\mathbf{A}$ and $\mathbf{B}$, we will get the same value exactly when the element of the union $\mathbf{A} \cup \mathbf{B}$ with minimum hash value lies in the intersection $\mathbf{A} \cap \mathbf{B}$. The probability of this being true, which also known as hash collision rate, is the ratio above, and hence $Pr[\min h_i(\mathbf{A}) = \min h_i(\mathbf{B})] = JS(\mathbf{A}, \mathbf{B}) \pm \epsilon$ with an estimation error ϵ, and $JS(\mathbf{A}, \mathbf{B})$ is the Jaccard similarity defined as $JS(\mathbf{A}, \mathbf{B}) = \frac{|\mathbf{A} \cap \mathbf{B}|}{|\mathbf{A} \cup \mathbf{B}|}$, $0 \leqslant JS \leqslant 1$, where $JS = 1$ indicates a perfect match. The error ϵ can be minimized by increase the number of m with a pay back of higher hashed code storage is required [9] (Fig. 1).

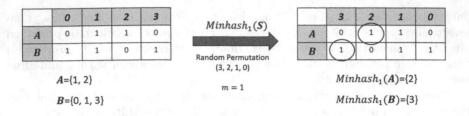

Binary representation

$$\Pr[Minhash_i(A){=}Minhash_i(B)] = JS(A, B)$$

Fig. 1. Min-hashing process ([1]).

4 The Proposed Scheme

Inspired from the concept of Min-hashing, the IFO hashing has utilizes m independent hash functions $h_1, h_2, \ldots, h_m$, each hash function is derived from different permutation set which contain P number of random generated permutation vectors. The iris template is generated by concatenating all the hashed output values of an IrisCode ($\mathbf{X}$) which can be described by an IFO hashing function denoted as $H(\mathbf{X}) = \{h_i(\mathbf{X})|i = 1, 2, \ldots, m\}$. The detailed procedure of IFO hashing function is described as follow:

1. Random Permutation: Generate a permutation set contains P number of random generated permutation vectors. Column-wise permute the input IrisCode $\mathbf{X} \in \{0, 1\}^{n_1 \times n_2}$ using the permutation vectors to generate permuted IrisCode $\mathbf{X}' = \{\mathbf{X}_l'|l = 1, 2, \ldots, P\}$
2. Hadamard product code generation: Generate the Pth- ordered conjunctions Hadamard product code $\mathbf{X}^P$ by multiplying all the permuted IrisCode which can be described as $\mathbf{X}^P = \prod_{l=1}^{P}(\mathbf{X}_l')$.
3. For each row in the product code $\mathbf{X}^P$, select the first K elements, while $1 \leq K \leq n_2$.
4. Among the selected first K elements, record down the index value denoted as C_X corresponding to the first binary bit '1'.
5. Modulo thresholding: A simple threshold function is imposed to alleviate the leakage of the original IrisCode by choosing a security threshold value τ, where $0 \leq \tau < K$. For every $C_X > K - \tau$, output $\mathbf{C}_X' = C_X \bmod (K - \tau)$.
6. Continue step 1 to 5 using different permutations set $\theta_{(i,l)}$, while $i \in [1, m]$, $l \in [1, P]$ to form an $n_1 \times m$ iris template $\mathbf{C}_X' = \{\mathbf{C}_{Xi}' \in \mathbf{Z}^{n_1} \mid i = 1, 2, \ldots, m\}$, while $\mathbf{C}_X' \in [0, K - \tau - 1]$.

Each single permutation constitute to a independent hash function $h_i(\mathbf{X})$, thus, $h_i(\mathbf{X}) = \mathbf{C}_{Xi}'$ (Fig. 2). The final IFO hashed code formed by concatenating $\mathbf{C}_{Xi}'$ for $i = 1, 2 \ldots, m$ as discussed in step 6.

IFO as an extension version of Min-hashing not only increased the complexity in generating the hash code through hardamard multiplication and modulo thresholding, it inherited the useful properties which the similarity between two input feature vector $\mathbf{X}$ and $\mathbf{Y}$ can be estimated based on the probability of their hashed code to be identical. This similarity measure can be described as $Pr[h_i(\mathbf{X}) = h_i(\mathbf{Y})]$ and is essentially equivalent to the Jacaard similarity measurement as discussed in Min-hashing [1,9]. IFO hashing enjoys this benefit in protecting the IrisCode with Jacaard distance preservation for the original IrisCode recognition.

Before matching, a pre-align process is needed to tackle the rotational inconsistencies caused by the head tilt of a person. Before apply the proposed scheme, The IrisCode is column-wise shifted left for $1, 2, \ldots, 16$ bits, and then followed by right shifted with $1, 2, \ldots, 16$ bits. Each of the shifted IrisCode is then applied the proposed scheme yielding $16 * 2 = 32$ shifted query instances. Matching is perform between each of the query instances with the enrolled IFO hashed code.

Let denotes the IFO hashed code for enrolled IrisCode ($\mathbf{X}$) as $\mathbf{C}_X'$ and the IFO hashed code for the query IrisCode ($\mathbf{Y}$) as $\mathbf{C}_Y'$. The similarity $S \in [0, 1]$ between $\mathbf{C}_X'$ and $\mathbf{C}_Y'$ can be calculated based on the probability for their hashed output value to be the same. This refers to the case when $C_{X(j,i)} = C_{Y(j,i)}$, for $i \in [1, m]$ and $j \in [1, n_1]$. In practice, the failure case in locating the first binary '1' need to be filter out in order to increase the matching efficiency. This can be done by only included the non-zero elements in the matching process which can be described as:

$$S(\mathbf{C}_X', \mathbf{C}_Y') = \frac{|\mathbf{B}_X \cap \mathbf{B}_Y \cap \mathbf{Q}_{XY}|}{|\mathbf{B}_X \cap \mathbf{B}_Y|}, \quad |\mathbf{B}_X \cap \mathbf{B}_Y| \neq 0 \qquad (1)$$

In Eq. (1), $\mathbf{B}_X$, $\mathbf{B}_Y \in \{0,1\}^{n_1 \times m}$ denotes the binary vector which is '1' when $C_{X(j,i)}', C_{Y(j,i)}' \neq 0$, and '0' when $C_{X(j,i)}', C_{Y(j,i)}' = 0$. Hence, $|\mathbf{B}_X \cap \mathbf{B}_Y|$ actually act as a filter mask for both $\mathbf{C}_X'$ and $\mathbf{C}_Y'$. This ensure only non-zero elements in both $\mathbf{C}_X'$ and $\mathbf{C}_Y'$ are included during matching process. By doing so, the failure case in locating the first binary '1' during IFO hashing can be excluded for matching. Meanwhile, $\mathbf{Q}_{XY} \in \{0,1\}^{n_1 \times m}$ denotes the binary vector which recorded the collision event. This collision event refers to the scenario when $Pr[h_i(\mathbf{X}) = h_i(\mathbf{Y})]$. The collision event is measured in element-wise manner during matching. For instant, $\mathbf{Q}_{XY}$ is initiated with all zeros. By comparing $\mathbf{C}_X'$ and $\mathbf{C}_Y'$, each $Q_{X(j,i)Y(j,i)}$ will be added an element '1' into it when $C_{X(j,i)}' = C_{Y(j,i)}'$. Together with the filter mask, the validity of the recorded collision between $\mathbf{C}_X'$ and $\mathbf{C}_Y'$ also can be confirmed. In this context, any failure case in locating the binary '1' during IFO hashing, neither contribute to a collision nor non-collision event. Hence, the matching efficiency can be increased. By measuring the collision between $\mathbf{C}_X'$ and $\mathbf{C}_Y'$, the Jacaard similarity between the enrolled IrisCode $\mathbf{X}$ and the query IrisCode $\mathbf{Y}$ able to obtained. Higher

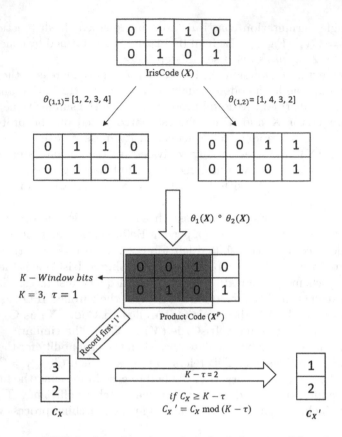

Fig. 2. Example of IFO hashing based on single hash function (h) with setting $K = 3, \tau = 1$

collision imply higher similarity between $\mathbf{C}_X{}'$ and $\mathbf{C}_Y{}'$. Where $S(\mathbf{C}_X{}', \mathbf{C}_Y{}') = 1$ indicates perfect match.

5   Experiment Studies

To measure the recognition performance of the proposed iris template protection scheme, CASIA database v3-interval [3] is used. This dataset contains 2639 iris images from 396 different classes (eyes). In our experiments, only left eye images are considered. To standardize the matching, from all the left eye images, we only selected the classes which included at least 7 iris samples, resulted a total classes of 124 classes are selected, and $124 * 7 = 868$ iris images are used. For intra-class comparisons, each iris template is matched against the templates generated from other iris samples of the same classes, leading to a total of 2604 genuine comparisons. For inter-class comparisons, every template is matched with all other templates generated from different iris samples of different classes, yielding a total 373674 impostor comparisons. Equal error rate (EER) has been used to evaluate the recognition performance where the false acceptance rate (FAR) and false rejection rate (FRR) are equal.

5.1 IrisCode Generation

The IrisCode generation technique is adopted from Rathgeb et al. [17]. The iris region is first detected by applying the weighted adaptive Hough transform. After that, a 2-stages segmentation process is used to segment the iris and pupil boundaries [20]. Followed by a normalization process is used to unwrap the iris region into a fixed dimension array namely rubber sheet model [6]. The normalized iris texture is enhanced as a rectangular texture, lower fourteen rows are eliminated to form the new iris texture with size of 50×512. The purpose of eliminating the lower fourteen rows is to reduce the effect of pupil dilation/contraction which induce noises during matching. The pixels of every five rows are averaged to result a new one-dimensional signal. By convolving this signal with 1-D log-Gabor filter, a complex iris Gabor features with the size of 10×512. Finally each complex value of the iris Gabor features is phase-quantized into 2 binary bits to generate the IrisCode with the length of $2 \times 10 \times 512 = 10240$ bits.

5.2 Recognition Performance Evaluation

The recognition performance for the original IrisCode [17] is first evaluated by calculating their hamming distance during matching with shifted bits of ± 16. Next, The same experiment has been carried out by applying the proposed iris template protection scheme on the original IrisCode with the setting of $m = 10, 20, 30, 40, 50, 100$, and 200, $P = 3$ and $\tau = 0$. The result shown in Table 1 implies that the increase of m yields the decrease of EER (increased recognition performance) for different selected K-window size.

Table 1. EER for different number of hash functions m, Hadamard multiplication with order $P = 3$ and security threshold $\tau = 0$

K	Equal error rate (%)						
	$m = 10$	$m = 20$	$m = 30$	$m = 40$	$m = 50$	$m = 100$	$m = 200$
50	3.37	1.46	1.17	0.99	0.94	0.58	0.54
100	3.41	1.41	0.98	0.88	0.86	0.76	0.54
200	3.05	1.29	0.97	0.86	0.82	0.60	0.54
Original IrisCode [17]	0.38						

Notice that the template generated from the proposed scheme is with the EER that is very close to the original IrisCode. This shows that the recognition performance can almost preserved after the proposed scheme is applied.

5.3   Non-invertible Analysis

In this section, we analyze the security of proposed scheme in term of non-invertibility. For non-invertibility analysis, the proposed transformation has transformed the binary IrisCode into real index values. It is difficult for an adversary to guess the original IrisCode information directly from any stolen iris template. Thus, the adversary first needs to reconstruct the K-window bits in order to obtain the binary information of the input IrisCode($\mathbf{X}$).

The modulo thresholding technique is included to prevent the case happen when $C_{X(j,i)} = K$ for $i \in [1, m]$ and $j \in [1, n_1]$. When $C_{X(j,i)} = K$, this implies the first binary bit '1' appeared in the last index of the K-window, an adversary can easily conclude that the entire row of the product code is $[0, 0, 0, \ldots, 1_K]$. Consequently, the adversary can reconstruct the K-window bits information by only a single trial.

In this case, the security threshold (τ) indicates the minimum number of trials to reconstruct the K-window bits. This can be explained by Letting $\tau = K - C_{X(j,i)}$, then $C_{X(j,i)} = K - \tau$. For $0 \leq \tau < K$, the max $(C_{X(j,i)})$ of the IFO hashed codes can be changed by computing $C_{X(j,i)}' = C_{X(j,i)} \bmod (K - \tau)$ when $C_{X(j,i)} > K - \tau$. By doing so, $C_{X(j,i)}'$ is always smaller than K where $C_{X(j,i)}' \in [0, K - \tau - 1]$. Thus, $C_{X(j,i)}'$ will never equal to K and subsequently increased the minimum number of trials for an adversary to reconstruct the K-window bits which can be described as 2^τ (Fig. 3).

To evaluate the effect of the security threshold on recognition performance in term of EER, another experiment has carried out for different value of τ and K, while $m = 50$, $P = 3$. Figure 4 shows the EER versus security threshold τ for different values of K. Based on the result shown in Fig. 4, the recognition performance has maintained by increasing τ up to certain threshold (approximately 90 % of K). As discussed, the non-invertibility properties able to strengthen up by increasing the value of τ. This imply the proposed scheme has constrained the trade-off problem between recognition and non-invertibility in a very small

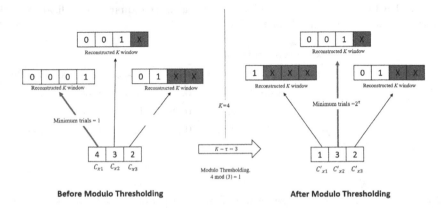

Fig. 3. K-window bits information reconstruction before and after thresholding

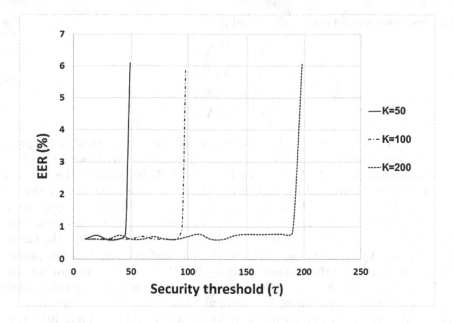

Fig. 4. Graph equal error rate (EER) vs security threshold (τ)

range of τ (when $\tau > 0.9K$). When out of this range, the non-invertibility able to increased without deteriorating the recognition performance.

Attack via Record Multiplicity (ARM): ARM refers to the attack which utilized multiple compromised templates and keys to reconstruct the original template information [18]. We have make used of an simple example to study the non-invertibility of proposed scheme from the effect of ARM. For non-invertibility analysis, we always assume all the parameters (i, P, K, τ) and permutation token being known by adversary.

Let the input Iriscode denotes as $\mathbf{X} \in \{0, 1\}^{1 \times N}$, the product code formed by carry out P permutation of the IrisCode and followed Hadamard multiplication denoted as $\mathbf{X}^P$. Each of the elements in the product code X_q^P, for $q \in [1, N]$ can be described as multiplication of P elements randomly choose from X_1, X_2, X_3, ..., X_N which refer to the 1st, 2nd, 3rd, ..., Nth elements of the original IrisCode ($\mathbf{X}$) respectively. Let $P = 2$, $\tau = 1$, and $K = N = 4$. When $P = 2$, means two permutation is used to generate the product code. In this case, we simply described the two permutation to be $[1, 2, 4, 3]$ and $[2, 4, 3, 1]$. For one single hashing ($i = 1$), the equations described each elements in the product code X_q^P can be formed when the permutation token is known by an adversary.

This equations formed can be described as:

$$X_1^2 = X_1 X_2,$$
$$X_2^2 = X_2 X_4,$$
$$X_3^2 = X_4 X_3,$$
$$X_4^2 = X_3 X_1.$$

(2)

As mentioned, $K = N = 4$, the K-window bits essentially equal to the product code can be described as $\mathbf{X}_K^P = \{X_q^2 | q = 1, 2 \ldots, K\}$. By follows Eq. (2), it is obvious when $X_1^2 = 1$, $X_1 X_2$ must be also '1'. This indicates the first and second elements of original IrisCode are both '1'. By repeating this for the following X_q^2 for $q = 1, 2, \ldots, K$, certain amount of binary '1' able to regenerate in the original IrisCode ($\mathbf{X}$). For this instant, by simply initiate a sparse code same size with $\mathbf{X}$, the entire original IrisCode ($\mathbf{X}$) able to regenerate with the knowledge of when $X_q^P = 1$. On the other words, the IrisCode regeneration process now merely depend on the number of binary bits '1' left inside the product code (or K-window, when $K \neq N$) after Hadamard multiplication. By using single compromised IFO hashed code, it is computational infeasible to regenerate the IrisCode due to the loss of information induced by the Hadamard multiplication, hence, resulted a lot of '0' in the product code. For ARM, multiple IFO hashed code are assumed to be compromised which makes the regeneration of entire IrisCode become probable.

However, due to the incorporated modulo thresholding in IFO hashing, this increased the difficulty of ARM to regenerate the original IrisCode. For instant, based on Eq. (2), let $X_1^2 = 0$, $X_2^2 = 0$, $X_3^2 = 0$, and $X_4^2 = 1$. During IFO hashing, the position of the first binary '1' will be encoded which refers to $C_X = 4$. Previously, we have defined $\tau = 1$, and $K = N = 4$. Now, the modulo thresholding process will output $C_X' = C_X \bmod (K - \tau)$. After modulo operation, C_X will set to $C_X' = 1$ which denotes the final IFO hashed value. When the adversary has constructed the equation $X_1^2 = X_1 X_2$ as shown in Eq. (2), this will lead to a wrong reconstruction due to the shifted output C_X from 3 to 1. As the actual initial value of $X_1^2 = 0$ will be wrongly defined by the adversary as $X_1^2 = 1$. This resulted an invalid equation formed and consequently the regenerated IrisCode will comes out with error. Although new equations can be constructed from different compromised IFO hashed codes, the adversary is still hard to determine the actual value of C_X from the final IFO hashed value C_X'. This shows how the proposed ARM withstand to ARM.

5.4   Cancellability Analysis

To evaluate the cancellability, 100 hashed codes for each IrisCode have been generated with 100 random permutation sets. The first hashed code is matched and compared with other 99 new hashed codes. The whole process is repeated and produce in a $99 * 7 * 124 = 85932$ pseudo-imposter scores. The genuine, imposter, and pseudo-imposter distribution are given in Fig. 5 and computed

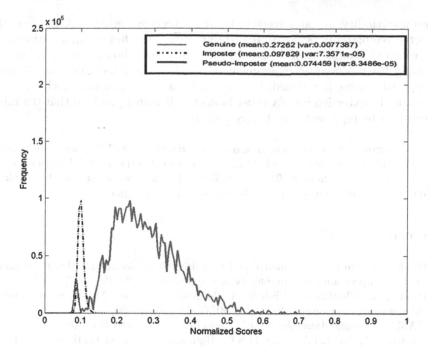

Fig. 5. The genuine, imposter and pseudo-imposter distribution plot

with experiment setting of $P = 3, K = 50, m = 50$ and $\tau = 0$. Note that the numbers of computed scores are different for the imposter and pseudo-imposter matching, this is because in pseudo- imposter matching, we only focus on the matching scores between the first hashed code and the newly generated hashed code for each iris image (same user) for cancellability evaluation.

From Fig. 5, a large degree of overlapping occurs between the imposter and pseudo-imposter distributions. This implies the newly generated templates using the given 100 random permutation sets act as different iris template even though it is generated from the same IrisCode (same users). In terms of verification performance, we obtain EER = 0.12 % in which intersection of genuine and pseudo-imposter distribution is taken. This verifies that IFO Hashing satisfies the cancellability property requirement.

6   Conclusion

We have proposed a robust hashing technique to protect the iris template stored in a database. The robust hashing technique has been applied on the original IrisCode. A comprehensive experimental evaluation shows that a very close equal error rate has been obtained as compared with the recognition performance of original IrisCode without template protection. Besides, the protected template is represented in real features domain. This offers another layer of security in term of non-invertibility. For an adversary trying to regenerate the IrisCode from the protected template, he/she required to reconstruct the binary information from the protected template which experiment result has shown that it is computationally hard. Moreover, experiment result also supported that cancellability of proposed scheme is satisfied. Last but not least, the proposed technique can potentially be extended for any other biometric features provided that the input features can be represented as binary vectors.

Acknowledgments. This works is under supports by MOSTI Science Fund number 01-02-11-SF0201. Wun-She Yap would like to acknowledge the financial support by the MOSTI Science Fund number 01-02-11-SF0189. The authors would like to thank C. Rathgeb for his helpful advice and data sets used in this paper.

References

1. Broder, A.: On the resemblance and containment of documents. In: Proceedings of the Compression and Complexity of Sequences, pp. 21–29 (1997)
2. Broder, A., Charikar, M., Frieze, A., Mitzenmacher, M.: Min-wise independent permutations. J. Comput. Syst. Sci. **60**(3), 630–659 (2000)
3. CASIA iris image database. http://www.cbsr.ia.ac.cn/Databases.htm
4. Chong, S.C., Jin, A.T.B., Ling, D.N.C.: High security iris verification system based on random secret integration. Comput. Vis. Image Underst. **102**(2), 169–177 (2006)
5. Daugman, J.: How iris recognition works. IEEE Trans. Circ. Syst. Video Technol. **14**(1), 21–30 (2004)
6. Daugman, J.: Probing the uniqueness and randomness of iris codes: results from 200 billion iris pair comparisons. Proc. IEEE **94**(11), 1927–1935 (2006)
7. Hämmerle-Uhl, J., Pschernig, E., Uhl, A.: Cancelable iris biometrics using block re-mapping and image warping. In: Samarati, P., Yung, M., Martinelli, F., Ardagna, C.A. (eds.) ISC 2009. LNCS, vol. 5735, pp. 135–142. Springer, Heidelberg (2009)
8. Hermans, J., Mennink, B., Peeters, R.: When a bloom filter is a doom filter: security assessment of a novel iris biometric template protection system. In: Proceedings of the Biometrics Special Interest Group. Lecture Notes in Informatics (LNI), vol. 230, pp. 75–86 (2014)
9. Indyk, P.: A small approximately min-wise independent family of hash functions. In: Proceedings of 10th Annual ACM-SIAM Symposium on Discrete Algorithms (SODA 1999), pp. 454–456 (1999)
10. Jain, A.K., Nandakumar, K., Nagar, A.: Biometric template security. EURASIP J. Adv. Signal Process. **2008**(113), 1–17 (2008). Special issue on Biometrics
11. Kong, A., Cheung, K.H., Zhang, D., Kamel, M., You, J.: An analysis of biohashing and its variants. Pattern Recogn. **39**(7), 1359–1368 (2006)
12. Lacharme, P.: Analysis of the iriscodes bioencoding scheme. Int. J. Comput. Sci. Softw. Eng. (IJCSSE 2012) **6**(5), 315–321 (2012)
13. Nagar, A., Nandakumar, K., Jain, A.K.: Biometric template transformation: a security analysis. In: Proceedings of the SPIE7541, Media Forensics and Security II, 75410O (2010)
14. Ouda, O., Tsumura, N., Nakaguchi, T.: Tokenless cancelable biometrics scheme for protecting iris codes. In: Proceedings of 20th International Conference on Pattern Recognition (ICPR 2010), pp. 882–885 (2010)

15. Ouda, D., Tsumura, N., Nakaguchi, T.: On the security of bioencoding based cancelable biometrics. IEICE Trans. Inf. Syst. **E94**–**D**(9), 1768–1777 (2011)
16. Pillai, J.K., Patel, V.M., Chellappa, R., Ratha, N.K.: Sectored random projections for cancelable iris biometrics. In: Proceeding IEEE International Conference on Acoustics Speech and Signal Processing, pp. 1838–1841 (2010)
17. Rathgeb, C., Breitinger, F., Busch, C.: Alignment-free cancelable iris biometric templates based on adaptive bloom filters. In: IEEE International Conference on Biometrics (ICB 2013), pp. 1–8 (2013)
18. Scheirer, W.J., Boult, T.E.: Cracking fuzzy vaults and biometric encryption. In: Proceedings of the Biometrics Symposium, pp. 1–6 (2007)
19. Teoh, A.B.J., Goh, A., Ngo, D.C.L.: Random multispace quantization as an analytic mechanism for biohashing of biometric and random identity inputs. IEEE Trans. Pattern Anal. Mach. Intell. **28**(12), 1892–1901 (2006)
20. Uhl, A., Wild, P.: Weighted adaptive hough and ellipsopolar transforms for real-time iris segmentation. In: Proceedings of the 5th IAPR International Conference on Biometrics (ICB 2012), pp. 283–290 (2012)
21. Zuo, J., Ratha, N.K., Connel, J.H.: Cancelable iris biometric. In: Proceedings of 19th International Conference on Pattern Recognition (ICPR 2008), pp. 1–4 (2008)

Web Security

Detecting Malicious URLs Using Lexical Analysis

Mohammad Saiful Islam Mamun$^{(\boxtimes)}$, Mohammad Ahmad Rathore,
Arash Habibi Lashkari, Natalia Stakhanova, and Ali A. Ghorbani

University of New Brunswick, Fredericton, NB, Canada
{msi.mamun,mahmad.rathore,a.habibi.l,natalia,ghorbani}@unb.ca

Abstract. The Web has long become a major platform for online criminal activities. URLs are used as the main vehicle in this domain. To counter this issues security community focused its efforts on developing techniques for mostly blacklisting of malicious URLs. While successful in protecting users from known malicious domains, this approach only solves part of the problem. The new malicious URLs that sprang up all over the web in masses commonly get a head start in this race. Besides that Alexa ranked trusted websites may convey compromised fraudulent URLs called *defacement* URL. In this work, we explore a lightweight approach to detection and categorization of the malicious URLs according to their attack type. We show that lexical analysis is effective and efficient for proactive detection of these URLs. We provide the set of sufficient features necessary for accurate categorization and evaluate the accuracy of the approach on a set of over 110,000 URLs. We also study the effect of the obfuscation techniques on malicious URLs to figure out the type of obfuscation technique targeted at specific type of malicious URL.

Keywords: Malicious URLs · Lexical features · URL obfuscation · Machine learning

1   Introduction

With ubiquitous use of Internet technology, the concern with security comes to the forefront. The web has been used as a hub for a variety of malicious activities from malware hosting and propagation to phishing websites' tricking users to provide their personal user information. Malicious URLs are intended for malicious purposes. Visitors of such URLs are under the threat of being victim to certain attacks [9]. According to the latest Google Safe browsing report, Google search blacklisted over 50,000 malware sites and over 90,000 phishing sites monthly [1].

Blacklisting is a typical approach to deal with malicious websites which is simple and provide better accuracy. This technique is effective only when lists are timely updated and websites are visited extensively for finding malicious webpages. Unfortunately, it falls short for providing timely protection of online

© Springer International Publishing AG 2016
J. Chen et al. (Eds.): NSS 2016, LNCS 9955, pp. 467–482, 2016.
DOI: 10.1007/978-3-319-46298-1_30

users. Since blacklists (IP addresses and URLs information) are extracted from expensive and sometimes complex filtering technologies, companies would not sell their updated list to market for free. Moreover, due to the cloaking applied on webpages and attackers recurrently change the URL and IP of the malicious webpages, new webpages are less likely to get checked against the blacklists. Besides that trusted websites may host fraudulent or hidden URL known as a *defacement* URL that contains both malicious and legitimate web pages. These URLs cannot be reached by crawling the legitimate web site within up to the third level of depth. Detection of these malicious URLs are effective when they perform in real time, detect new URLs with high accuracy, and specially recognize specific attack type (e.g., phishing URL).

Heuristic-based technique in [18] can identify newly created malicious websites in real-time by using signatures of known attack payloads. However, this approach would fail to detect novel attacks that result in zero-day exploits and signature detection is often evaded by attackers using change in patterns and obfuscation techniques.

Machine learning techniques are used to classify malicious websites through features taken from URLs, web content and network activity. The detection methods and tools which adopt the approach of patrolling web content may consume more computation time and resource. Therefore, URL based detection techniques for malicious URL detection are largely limited to classification of URLs in general or any specific attack i.e. spam [3,6,20]. Meanwhile research shows that the characteristics of malicious URLs differ with the type of technique used for exploitation (e.g., spam, adware, phishing, drive-by-downloads etc.) [19].

In this study, we adapted machine learning techniques to the detection and categorization of the malicious URLs. We look at four types of malicious use of URLs such as spam URLs, phishing URLs, website URLs distributing malware, and defacement URLs where pages belong to the trusted but compromised sites and identify a set of significant lexical features that can be used in recognizing the types of URL attack.

Obfuscation techniques used by the attacker to evade static detection in malicious URLs. Since obfuscation based features have been widely used for phishing attacks [3,23], we also study the effect of the obfuscation techniques on different type of malicious URLs to determine which attack type is mostly affected with what kind of obfuscation technique.

We select 79 features related to lexical analysis and 4 features related to obfuscation techniques for primary analysis. After applying the feature selection algorithm on the dataset, we end up with five sets of mostly *relevant* features for multi label and multi-class classification for any type of malicious URL detection.

We evaluated this approach on around 110,000 URLs taken from different sources, and achieved a prediction accuracy (with low false positive rate) of nearly 99 % in detecting URLs of the attack type and approx. 93–99 % in identifying attacks with multi-class classifier. It appears that selective lexical features can find the better accuracy for identifying the different types of URL attacks. Although obfuscation techniques are widely used in the literature as a part of

Malicious URL detection (e.g. [23]). However, from our experiment, we found no significant impact on statistical analysis.

2 Related Work

Using lexical features with a proposed classification engine gives high accuracy in classifying the URLs. Domains used for phishing purpose have shown to have different lengths and diverse location. McGrath et al. in [14] analyze the differences between benign and phishing URLs using features such as URL and domain length.

Based on the behavior of domains in phishing websites, Ma et al. in [6], manage to identifying suspicious URLs by using lexical and blacklisted host based features. They believe that there are certain red flag *keywords* tend to appear in malicious URLs such as appearing *ebayisapi* for spoofing *ebay* web pages. However, in the following works, Ma et al. in [15] use supervised learning across both lexical and host-based features. In this case, authors argue that their approach is complementary to both blacklisting and system based evaluation such as site content and behavior analysis where one cannot predict seeing only the status of previously unseen URLs. Moreover, this requires visiting potentially dangerous sites. They figure out that using appropriate classifiers, it is possible to identify most predictive features for automatically classifying malicious or benign URLs.

In [5], authors use lexical, host and page-content based features for identifying malicious URLs collected from spam messages in twitter and emails. Choi et al. in [8], present a machine learning method to detect malicious URLs and identify attack types such as spamming, phishing, and malware. Their studies include multiple types of malicious URLs using features from six different areas namely lexicon, link popularity, web page content, DNS, DNS fluxing and network traffic. However, their result shows that using lexical features yield *lower* accuracy for spam and malware URL dataset.

Authors in [21] use descriptive features of URL to complement lexical features. They combine the lexical information and static characteristics of URL string to classify malicious URLs. Without host and content based analysis, in this experiment, they were able to deal with two million URLs in five minutes and their proposed method misses around 9 % of malicious instances.

The effectiveness of machine learning based phishing detection with known protected websites has been studied by Chu et al. in [10]. Based on only lexical and domain features authors propose several highly effective features with detection rate over 91 %. In [22], authors study hidden fraudulent URLs which are embedded to the trusted URLs and also defacement URLs which are legitimate pages belonging to trusted but compromised web sites. They provide a dataset that can be useful for evaluating the performance of a classifier for aforementioned malicious URLs.

Obfuscation techniques are commonly used by spammers and scammers in order to obscure (hide and confuse) any malicious URL. It's often appeared in unsolicited emails, ad-related URLs and web-site owner intending to evade recognition of a linked address. Obfuscated URL parts can help the malicious URL parts to evade the detection system. In this work, our target was to see the obfuscation techniques used by Malicious, Phishing and Spam URLs separately. Gerara et al. in [23] mentioned several URL obfuscation techniques used in malicious URLs. Le et al. in [3] identified four of them that are commonly used in domain are obfuscating with IP address, another domain, large host names or, unknown and misspelled. Ma et al. [6] mentioned three prominent obfuscation types for avoiding detection. They are benign tokens in the URL, free hosting services used, sites with international TLD.

However, the malicious owner can also use these obfuscation techniques to evade detection and tempt users to hit. Therefore, Su et al. in [2] proposes to dissect URLs to several portions and use logistic regression for detection. Apart from the work of Choi et al. in [8] where authors evaluates the performance of a classifier for discriminating three types of malicious URLs (Spam, Phishing, Malware), most of the related works focus on either *malicious* URLs *in general* or any specific type of URLs (e.g. Phishing). Regarding feature selections, most of the works depend on various kind of features: lexical, content, obfuscation, DNS etc. In this work, we consider four different types of malicious URLs (Defacement, Spam, Phishing, Malware) for experiments. By applying only static lexical features for classifying URLs (to achieve high performance), our malicious URL detector produces a promising as well as competitive performance to some existing works.

3   Background

3.1   Lexical Analysis

Lexical features are the textual properties of URL such as length of hostname, URL length, tokens found in the URL etc. Due to lightweight computation[1], safety[2] and high classification accuracy lexical features become one of the most popular sources of features in machine learning [3].

Features collected from URLs are not dependent on any application like email, social networking websites, games etc. Since many malicious URLs have short life span, lexical features remain available even when malicious webpage are unavailable [10].

In this research, we study five main components of the URLs to be inspected for analysis: URI, domain, path, argument and file name. Following are the brief description of all the features considered for analysis.

---

[1] Using web content as features requires downloading and analysis of page contents. Moreover inspecting millions of URL and its contents per unit of time may create a bottleneck.

[2] Access to malicious webpage may cause risk since such webpages may contain malicious content such as Javascript functions.

- *Entropy Domain and Extension:* Malicious websites often insert additional characters in the URL to make it look like a legitimate. e.g, CITI can be written as CIT1, by replacing last alphabet I with digit 1. English text has fairly low entropy i.e., it is predictable. By inserting characters the entropy changes than usual. For identifying the randomly generated malicious URLs, alphabet entropy is used.

- *CharacterContinuityRate:* Character Continuity Rate is used to find the sum of the longest token length of each character type in the domain, such as abc567ti $= (3 + 3 + 1)/9 = 0.77$. Malicious websites use URLs which have variable number of character types. Character continuity rate determine the sequence of letter, digit and symbol characters. The sum of longest token length of a character type is divided by the length of the URL [21].

- *Features related with Length Ratio:* The length ratio of the parts of URL is computed to find the abnormal parts [21]. The combination of URL part consist of argument, path, domain and URL such as *argPathRatio* (Ratio of argument and path), *argUrlRatio* (Ratio of argument and URL), *argDomain-Ratio* (Argument divided by domain), *domainUrlRatio* (Domain divided by URL), *pathUrlRatio* (Path divided by URL), *PathDomainRatio* (Path divided by Domain).

- *Features related to count of Letter, Token and Symbol:* The frequency of characters in the URL are calculated in the form of letters, tokens and symbol [5,10,18]. These characters are categorized and counted from these components of URLs:
  - *Symbol Count Domain:* A dictionary of delimiters such as ://.:/?=,;()]+ are calculated from domain. Phishing URLs e.g. have more dots compared to benign ones [15,17].
  - *Domain token count:* Tokens are taken from the URL String. The Malicious URLs use multiple domain tokens. Number of tokens in the domains are calculated.
  - *Query Digit Count:* Number of digits in the query part of the URL.
  - *tld:* Some phishing URL use multiple top level domain within a domain name.

- *Number Rate of Domain, DirectoryName, FileName, URL, AfterPath:* Number rate calculate the proportion of digits in the URL parts of directory name, domain, filename, URL itself and part after the path. [21].

- *Features related to Length:* Length of URL gets longer due to addition of variables or redirected URL. [11,18]. such as, Length of URL (url Len), domain (domain Len) and file name (file Name Len), Arguments' Longest-WordLength[3], Longest Path Token Length [8], Average length of path token [10] (avgpathtokenlen).

- *ldl getArg:* In phishing URLs masquerading is done by adding digits in the letters. For detection of these deceiving URLs, sequence of letter digit letter in URL and path is calculated [21].

---

[3] URLs which originating from pages that are written in server side scripting languages, often have arguments [3]. The longest variable value length from arguments of URL is calculated.

– *spcharUrl:* URLs use special characters which are suspicious such as // and they have higher risk of redirection [11].

Table 1. Feature selection for lexical analysis

Dataset	Features
Spam (CfsSub + Best First)	Domain token count, tld, ldl getArg, Number of Dots in URL, delimiter path, Symbol Count Domain
Phishing (CfsSub + Best First)	Domain token count, tld, url Len, domain length, file Name Len, dpath url Ratio, Number of Dots in URL, Query Digit Count, Longest Path Token Length, delimiter Domain, delimiter path, Symbol Count Domain, Entropy Domain
Malware (CfsSub + Best First)	Domain token count, tld, url Len, arg Doman Ratio, Number of Dots in URL, Number Rate Domain, Symbol Count Domain, Entropy Domain, Entropy Extension
Defacement (CfsSub + Best First)	Domain token count, avgpathtokenlen, tld, ArgUrlRatio, NumberofDotsinURL, Arguments LongestWordLength, spcharUrl, delimeter Domain, delimeter path, NumberRate DirectoryName, SymbolCount Domain, Entropy Domain
All (Infogain + Ranker)	Entropy Domain, argPathRatio, ArgUrlRatio, ArgDomanRatio, pathurlRatio, CharacterContinuityRate, NumberRate FileName, domainUrlRatio, NumberRate URL, PathDomainRatio, NumberRate AfterPath, avgpathtokenlen

3.2   Obfuscation

Obfuscation is used as a common method for masking malicious URLs. An attacker intending to evade static analysis on lexical URL features use obfuscation techniques so that malicious URLs become statistically similar to the benign ones [11]. The obfuscation techniques on URLs is analyzed for the intent of malicious activity in this research. We analyzed mainly two type of URL obfuscation techniques used by attackers:

– Type I: Obfuscating the hostname:
  • Obfuscating the domain with IP (IP_obfus): In this type of attack host name is obfuscated by the IP address instead of domain name. Use of IP address as a domain name of the URL alludes the owner is tempting to access private information of the user [16,18].

- Obfuscating domain with legitimate name (Prefix_obfus): In this type of attack the domain is a prefix with a legitimate domain such as brand name. The purpose of brand name prefix is to find the URL which use legitimate, benign domain in their prefix. Therefore, the user might be tempted to click on the URL through the brand prefix. Legitimate domain name such as domain name from Alexa is used in variation to make the malicious URL look like a legitimate one [12]. For example, in the following legiti-mate URL http://widget.b2b.com/relationship/, *b2b* is a benign first level domain name known as a *brand name*. However, in case a custom domain name that has name or brand in it, http://detail.b2b.hc360.com/detail/ or http://detail.b2b1.com/detail/, although *hc360* or *ab2b* is not a benign domain, a brand name *b2b* is used as a *second level* domain or a *prefix* to distract users.
- Type II: Obfuscating the directory:
  - Obfuscation with encoding (Encoding_obfus): In this attack type string of characters are obfuscated by the use of alternate encoding schemes i.e., Unicode, Base64, Hexadeimal, Decimal characters [7]. Unicode encoding allow the characters to be referenced and saved in multiple bytes. UTF-8 is a common encoding format. It preserves the full ASCII character code range. The standard character can be encoded in longer escape-code sequence.
  - Obfuscating using redirected URLs (RedirectURL_obfus): The content coming between protocol name and the '@' character is ignored which allow the addition of obfuscated URLs. URLs for redirection are embedded in the links. These links deviate the user to link which has no link to the actual page [18]. These redirected URL are attached in malicious links by attackers [13].
  - Obfuscating using hexadecimal form (Hex_obfus): Characters of a path is represented by their corresponding numbers in the hexadecimal form where numbers are preceded by a "%" symbol to recognize a hexadecimal repre-sentation of the character. For instance, "%63ur%65" is the hexamdedimal form of "cure". It is mainly used to use spaces and special characters in the URL. However, the same techniques can be used to inject malicious items.
  - Authentication type obfuscation (AuthString_Obfus): This type of obfus-cation is used for automatic authentication when login name or password is required for accessing a web page. But if the site requires no authentication, the additional authentication text will have no effect e.g. http://www.xyz.com/index.htm.

4   Experiment

4.1   Dataset

Around 114,400 URLs were collected initially containing benign and malicious URLs in *four* categories: Spam, Malware, Phishing and Defacement. Four single-class datasets by mixing benign and malicious URLs and one multi-class dataset

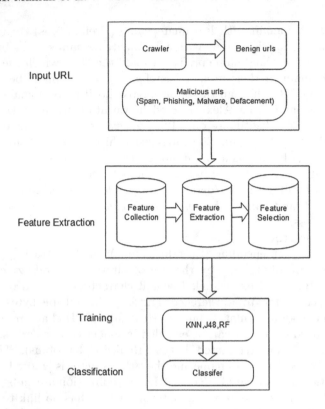

Fig. 1. URL classification architecture

by combining all four malicious URLs and benign URLs were generated for experiment (See Fig. 1).

- Benign URLs: Over 35,300 benign URLs were collected from Alexa top websites. The domains have been passed through Heritrix webcrawler to extract the URLs. Around half a million unique URLs are crawled initially and then parsed to remove duplicate and domain only URLs. Later the extracted URLs have been checked through virustotal to filter the benign URLs.
- Spam URLs: Around 12,000 spam URLs were collected from publicly available web spam dataset in [24].
- Phishing URLs: Around 10,000 phishing URLs were taken from OpenPhish website [26] which is a repository of active phishing sites.
- Malware URLs: More than 11,500 URLs related to malware websites were obtained from DNS-BH [25] which is a project that maintain list of malware sites.
- Defacement URLs: In [27], authors select 2500 URLs provided by Zone-H [28] and extend the lists by adding URLs of pages reached by crawling the compromised sites up to the third level. After necessary filtration (e.g. URLs whose path is empty or equal to index.html, URLs whose domain is an IP address),

they labelled 114,366 URLs as *Defacement*. However, for our experiment we randomly choose 45,457 URLs.

4.2 Features Selection, Test and Validation

The motive of evaluation and search strategy is to find the features which are significant and contribute most in the analysis. In this paper, we used CFSSubsetEval and Infogain as feature selection algorithms.

CfsSubsetEval evaluates the worth of a subset of features by considering the individual predictive ability of each feature along with the degree of redundancy. Infogain searches the space of feature subsets by greedy hill-climbing strategy augmented with a backtracking facility. Later a ranker ranks features by their individual evaluations.

Initially 79 features were selected from components such as URL, domain, path, file-name and argument. After applying feature selection algorithm on each dataset, different sets of features have been chosen (See Table 1) for further experiment.

Classification of data is done through two groups of algorithms. K-Nearest Neighbours algorithm (KNN) [30], a pattern recognition method used for classification by assigning weight to the neighbours according to the their contributions. Euclidean function was used as a distance function for KNN. Tree based classifiers namely C4.5 [29] and RandomForest [31] used to present results as a tree. To evaluate the quality of the classifiers, we used two common metrics: Precision (Positive Predictive value) and Recall (Sensitivity).

$$\text{Precision}(\texttt{Pr}) = \frac{TP}{TP+FP} \qquad \text{Recall}(\texttt{Rc}) = \frac{TP}{TP+FN}$$

During training we tuned up several parameters of Random Forest to achieve better and efficient model with less error. For example, the number of trees to be generated is set to 80 for Spam, 100 for Malware and Phishing, 150 for Defacement, 120 for multi-class datasets.

We divided our experiment in testing and validation, therefore, split the datasets accordingly (80 % for test - 20 % for validation) using pre-processing function (resample with noReplacement) in Weka.

5 Analysis and Results

As mentioned earlier two set of features have been selected as part of the analysis: (i) Analyzing lexical features to recognize benign and malicious URLs based on selected set of features in Table 1, (ii) Analyzing Obfuscation techniques against different attack types.

Table 2. Classification results (single-class)

Dataset	Algorithm	Result	
		Pr	Re
Spam	C4.5	0.98	0.98
	KNN	0.98	0.98
	RF	**0.99**	**0.99**
Phishing	C4.5	0.97	0.97
	KNN	0.97	0.97
	RF	**0.99**	**0.99**
Malware	C4.5	0.98	0.98
	KNN	0.98	0.98
	RF	**0.99**	**0.99**
Defacement	C4.5	0.99	0.99
	KNN	0.99	0.99
	RF	**0.99**	**0.99**

(a) Lexical Features

Dataset	Algorithm	Result	
		Pr	Re
Spam	C4.5	0.752	0.388
	KNN	0.753	0.388
Phishing	C4.5	0.382	0.844
	KNN	0.383	0.844
Malware	C4.5	0.857	0.398
	KNN	0.857	0.398
Defacement	C4.5	0.795	0.741
	KNN	0.795	0.741

(b) Obfuscation Features

Table 3. Classification results based on lexical features (multi-class)

Dataset	Labels	C4.5		KNN		RF	
		Pr	Rc	Pr	Rc	Pr	Rc
Multi class	Spam	0.96	0.971	0.96	0.97	0.962	0.986
	Phishing	0.92	0.856	0.92	0.85	0.926	0.928
	Malware	0.96	0.97	0.96	0.97	0.979	0.983
	Defacement	0.93	0.97	0.93	0.97	0.969	0.973
	Average	0.94	0.94	0.94	0.94	**0.97**	**0.97**

5.1   Lexical Analysis

Table 2a shows the results of lexical analysis on single-class datasets, the accuracy of the all datasets with selected set of features are higher than 97 %. For example in Spam and Malware datasets the accuracy were more than 98 % with 6 and 9 features or in the Defacement dataset, accuracy was 99 % with 13 features. The same analysis has been done in the multi-class dataset which was the combination of all four different types of malicious URLs with Benign ones. As Table 3 shows, the average of accuracy in all ML algorithms are more than 95 %.

We observe that tree based classifiers, with Random Forest yields highest accuracy among the classifiers tested. While efficient in identifying certain type of URL individually (≈99 %), Random Forest has also outperformed as a multiclass classifier (≈97 %). Among other classifiers examined, KNN and C4.5 classifiers have approximately the same performance (≈94 %) for multiclass classifer with the worst accuracy for phishing (around 80 %). Since Random Forest appears

Table 4. Soft pediction based on SD (C0 = Benign, C1 = Dataset class)

Dataset	Filters									
	Yellow $(0 < \text{SD} \leq .1)$		Green $(.1 < \text{SD} \leq .2)$		Orchid $(.2 < \text{SD} \leq .3)$		Blue $(.3 < \text{SD} \leq .4)$		Red $(\text{SD} > .4)$	
	C0	C1	C0	C1	C0	C1	C0	C1	C0	C1
Defacement	847	640	341	247	119	95	50	27	17	21
Phishing	2077	725	810	534	308	295	192	285	72	125
Malware	1793	1496	997	804	349	288	142	111	75	43
Spam	3974	94	124	177	54	218	39	158	2	2

to be effiencient in both *binary* and *multiclass* classification, we select Random Forest classifier for further investigation.

Confidence interval of a prediction known as *prediction interval*, a well-defined concept in statistical inference, estimates the prediction interval based on member decision tree scores. At the time of prediction Random Forest produces a *hard decision* based on the maximum votes of the individual trees for a class to get elected [4]. However, a *soft prediction* can also be determined from the individual trees' voting which provides a confidence score for the prediction. This confidence score can be used for *hard decision* once it exceeds a threshold value. For this experiment, we train a regression-type Random Forest model for the datasets. For all binary classifiers (Spam, Phishing, Malware, Defacement), Benign is labelled as 0 and any respected class (e.g. Spam) is labelled as 1.

The scatter plot of experiment ("Actual class" versus "Predicted class") are given in the Fig. 2 below. Figure 2 depicts the data points overlaid with error bars. The error bars corresponding to a *soft prediction* is represented by a Standard Deviation (SD) of uncertainty for a certain class. Due to the large number of data points and to achieve a holistic view of data, we filter the result in four steps:

- Yellow-filter contains data points whose SD is greater than 0 but less than or equal to .1
- green-filter contains data points whose SD is greater than .1 but less than or equal to .2
- Orchid-filter subset contains data points whose SD is greater than .2 but less than or equal to .3
- Blue-filter contains data points whose SD is greater than .3 but less than or equal to .4
- Red-filter contains data points whose SD is greater than .4

Results of four binary classifiers are given in Table 4. Lifted SD indicates considerable fluctuating among member decision tree scores. Higher lifting can be realized with prospective statistical outliers.

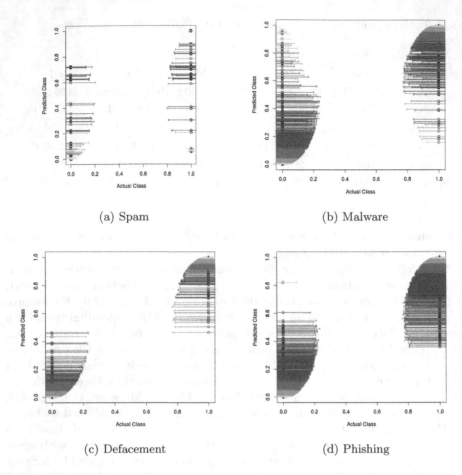

(a) Spam

(b) Malware

(c) Defacement

(d) Phishing

Fig. 2. Predection interval based on decision tree score (Color figure online)

Most of the URLs are grouped into the closest range of its respective class
(0 or 1). For instance, in case of Defacement dataset a total of 13,308 URLs
out of 15,712 observed in extremity of the range (aligned with average) while
2404 URLs with any SD and in the worst case Phishing dataset shows a total
of 5423 URLs out of 15,368 observed with any SD. In addition there is no URL
data point with (SD > .5) and the majority of URLs are overlaid with yellow
and Green error bars. It is interesting to note that the highest SD (Red filter)
corresponding to overestimating/underestimating errors, has very few of either
kind of URL, in the range of 2 (Spam) and 75 (Malware) for Benign URL and 2
(Spam) to 125 (Phishing) for any other URLs. This ensures that soft prediction
is not uniformly distributed. Some range of *soft prediction* values where the SD
is very small for example Yellow, Green, and Orchid filters must be used for an
infallible prediction. Considering these facts, we can answer how much risky a
URL is? If the soft prediction is closer to 1 with a small threshold value of SD

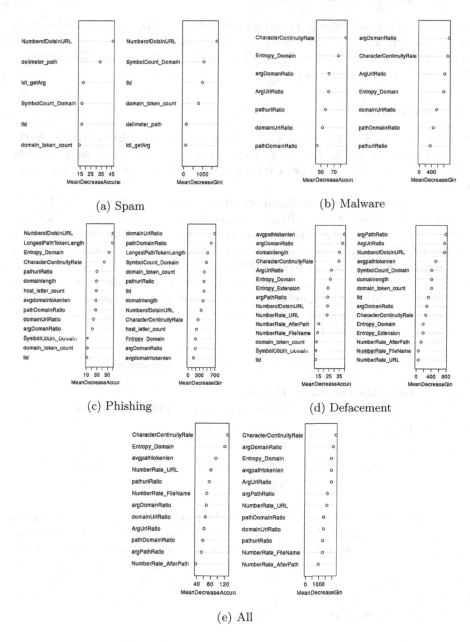

(a) Spam

(b) Malware

(c) Phishing

(d) Defacement

(e) All

Fig. 3. Random forest variable importance

score (e.g. up to Orchid filter), the URL is risky. In the opposite way, the closer the URL is to 0 with a small SD score, the more secure it is.

Random forest computes various measure of variable importance that can be very informative to understand how much each variable contributing to the accuracy of the model. Figure 3 exhibits two different Variable importance graph for all four binary-class and a multi-class: MeanDecreaseAccuracy that is the mean decrease in accuracy and MeanDecreaseGini that is the Gini index or *Mean decrease in Node Impurity*.

5.2   Obfuscation

As mentioned in Sect. 3.2, we study six obfuscation types (Brand name, Auth-String, IP, RedirectURL, Encoding, Hex) for analysis. However, no significant output has been noticed for obfuscation type AuthString and Hex for any of our datasets.

Obfuscation detection rate found on all four dataset is shown in the Table 5. As the result shows, Spam URLs contains the most number of Prefix_obfus (brand name) obfuscation (38 %), that refers using of legitimate domains in the spam URLs to trick the user for visiting the webpage. The phishing URLs have some amount of brand name (13 %) and redirect obfuscation (5 %). The malware URLs have a large number of encoding obfuscation (40 %), which shows that malware URLs use a number of encoding techniques to evade from static detection. A few percentage of URLs shows combination of multiple encoding techniques applied in a URL.

Table 5. Obfuscation detection rate in the malicious URL

Obfuscation technique	Dataset			
	Defacement	Spam	Phishing	Malware
Brand name	0.71 %	**38 %**	**13.33 %**	1.58 %
Redirect	0.64 %	5.20 %	4.61 %	0.08 %
Encoding	**5.57 %**	4.48 %	2.04 %	**39.01 %**
IP	0.73 %	-	**1.54%**	0.29 %

Using AttributeSelection with InfoGainAttributeEval as attribute evaluator and Ranker as search method, we found three features Encoding, Brand name, RedirectURL to be useful. We try to use machine learning classifiers on the obfuscation features with no promising result (See Table 5). For instance, C4.5 can distinguish phishing URL with 84 % TP rate (the best result in our experiment). However, the Precision (40 %) and ROC area (.65) value for the same classifier is too low to accept the result.

5.3   Comparison

Our research result is very close to that of the work done by Choi et al. in [8]. Although a major part of our experiment datasets (benign, phishing, malware, a portion of spam) are identical, we have extended our dataset with Defacement dataset. Regarding lexical classification outcomes of Choi et al. (Spam 73 % Phishing 91.6 % and Malware 70.3 %), authors did not mention precisely whether their result stems from applying multi-class or single-class classifier. Note that using multi-class classification with additional dataset must degrade the overall performance and accuracy. However, our Random Forest classifier outperforms their lexical feature results in either case of individual and aggregated (multi-class) classifiers yielding around 99 % and 97 % accuracy respectively even with an addition of Defacement URL dataset.

6   Conclusion

This paper explored an approach for classifying different attack types of URL automatically as benign, defacement, spam, phishing and malware through supervised learning relying on lexical features. This technique is an addon for the blacklist techniques, in which new malicious URLs cannot be identified and efficient for analyzing large number of URLs. Selected feature sets applied on supervised classification on a ground truth dataset yields a classification accuracy of 97 % with a low false positive rate. Our prediction interval filtering experiment can also be helpful to improve classifier accuracy. In addition, it can be extended to calculate risk rating of a malicious URL after parameter adjustment and learning with huge training data. Despite random forest classification accuracy is able to identify approx. 97 % of the malicious or benign URL, by using proper SD filter we could reach up to around 99 % accuracy. As future work we are planning to develop a real time tool for computing SD filter dynamically and detection of malicious URLs.

References

1. Google Safe Browsing Transparency Report (2015). www.google.com/transparencyreport/safebrowsing/
2. Su, K.-W., et al.: Suspicious URL filtering based on logistic regression with multi-view analysis. In: 8th Asia Joint Conference on Information Security (Asia JCIS). IEEE (2013)
3. Le, A., Markopoulou, A., Faloutsos, M.: PhishDef: URL names say it all. In: Proceedings IEEE, INFOCOM. IEEE (2011)
4. Breiman, L.: Random forests. Mach. Learn. **45**(1), 5–32 (2001)
5. Thomas, K., et al.: Design and evaluation of a real-time URL spam filtering service. In: Proceeding of the IEEE Symposium on Security and Privacy (SP) (2011)
6. Ma, J., et al.: Identifying suspicious URLs: an application of large-scale online learning. In: Proceedings of the 26th Annual International Conference on Machine Learning. ACM (2009)
7. Nunan, A.E., et al.: Automatic classification of cross-site scripting in web pages using document-based and URL-based features. In: IEEE Symposium on Computers and Communications (ISCC) (2012)
8. Choi, H., Zhu, B.B., Lee, H.: Detecting malicious web links and identifying their attack types. In: Proceedings WebApps (2011)
9. Huang, D., Kai, X., Pei, J.: Malicious URL detection by dynamically mining patterns without pre-defined elements. World Wide Web **17**(6), 1375–1394 (2014)

10. Chu, W., et al.: Protect sensitive sites from phishing attacks using features extractable from inaccessible phishing URLs. In: IEEE International Conference on Communications (ICC) (2013)
11. Xu, L., et al.: Cross-layer detection of malicious websites. In: Proceedings of the Third ACM Conference on Data and Application Security and Privacy. ACM (2013)
12. Garera, S., et al.: A framework for detection and measurement of phishing attacks. In: Proceedings of the ACM Workshop on Recurring Malcode (2007)
13. Radu, Vasile: Application. In: Radu, Vasile (ed.) Stochastic Modeling of Thermal Fatigue Crack Growth. ACM, vol. 1, pp. 63–70. Springer, Heidelberg (2015)
14. Kevin, M.D., Gupta, M.: Behind phishing: an examination of phisher modi operandi. In: Proceedings of the 1st Usenix Workshop on Large-Scale Ex-ploits and Emergent Threats (2008)
15. Ma, J., et al.: Beyond blacklists: learning to detect malicious web sites from suspicious URLs. In: Proceedings of the 15th ACM SIGKDD International Conference on Knowledge Discovery and Data Mining. ACM (2009)
16. Davide, C., et al.: Prophiler: a fast filter for the large-scale detection of malicious web pages. In: Proceedings of the 20th International Conference on World Wide Web. ACM (2011)
17. Xiang, G., et al.: CANTINA+: a feature-rich machine learning framework for detecting phishing web sites. ACM Trans. Inf. Syst. Secur. (TISSEC) **14**(2), 21 (2011)
18. Abdelhamid, N., Aladdin, A., Thabtah, F.: Phishing detection based associative classification data mining. Expert Syst. Appl. **41**(3), 5948–5959 (2014)
19. Eshete, B., Villafiorita, A., Binspect, K.W.: Holistic Analysis and Detection of Malicious Web Pages. Security and Privacy in Communication Networks. Springer, Heidelberg (2012)
20. Cao, C., Caverlee, J.: Behavioral detection of spam URL sharing: posting patterns versus click patterns. In: IEEE International Conference on Advances in Social Networks Analysis and Mining (ASONAM) (2014)
21. Lin, M.-S., et al.: Malicious URL filtering- a big data application. IEEE International Conference on Big Data (2013)
22. Enrico, S., Bartoli, A., Medvet, E.: Detection of hidden fraudulent urls within trusted sites using lexical features. In: Proceeding 18th International Conference on Availability, Reliability and Security (ARES). IEEE (2013)
23. Garera, S., Provos, N., Chew, M., Rubin, A.: A framework for detection and measurement of phishing attacks. In: Proceedings of the ACM workshop on Recurring malcode, pp. 1–8. ACM (2007)
24. WEBSPAM-UK2007 dataset. http://chato.cl/webspam/datasets/uk2007/
25. Malware domain dataset. http://www.malwaredomains.com/
26. OpenPhish dataset. https://openphish.com/
27. Davanzo, M., Bartoli, A.: Anomaly detection techniques for a web defacement monitoring service. Expert Syst. Appl. (ESWA) **38**(10), 12521–12530 (2011)
28. Zone-h, unrestricted information. http://www.zone-h.org/
29. Quinlan, J.R.: C4.5: Programs for Machine Learning. Morgan Kaufmann Publishers Inc., San Francisco (1993)
30. Keller, J.M., Gray, M.R., Givens, J.A.: A fuzzy k-nearest neighbor algorithm. IEEE Trans. Syst. Man Cybern. **4**, 580–585 (1985)
31. Liaw, A., Wiener, M.: Classification and regression by randomForest. R news **2**(3), 18–22 (2002)

Gatekeeping Behavior Analysis for Information Credibility Assessment on Weibo

Bailin Xie[1], Yu Wang[2(✉)], Chao Chen[2], and Yang Xiang[2]

[1] Cisco School of Informatics, Guangdong University of Foreign Studies, Guangzhou, China
xiebailin96@126.com
[2] School of Information Technology, Deakin University, Geelong, Australia
{y.wang,chao.chen,yang}@deakin.edu.au

Abstract. Microblogging sites, such as Sina Weibo and Twitter, have gained significantly in popularity and become an important source for real-time information dissemination. Inevitably, these services are also used to spread false rumors and misinformation, usually with the unintentional collaboration from innocent users. Previous studies show that microblog information credibility can be assessed automatically based on the features extracted from message contents and users. In this paper, we address this problem from a new perspective by exploring the human input in the propagation process of popular microblog posts. Specifically, we consider that the users are the gatekeepers of their own media portal on microblogging sites, as they decide which information is filtered for dissemination to their followers. We find that truthful posts and false rumors exhibit distinguishable patterns in terms of which gatekeepers forward them and what the gatekeepers comment on them. Based on this finding, we propose to assess the information credibility of popular microblog posts with Hidden Markov Models (HMMs) of gatekeeping behavior. The proposed approach is evaluated using a real life data set that consists of over ten thousand popular posts collected from Sina Weibo.

Keywords: Online social networks · Microblogging · Weibo · Information credibility · HMM

1 Introduction

Microblogging sites like Sina Weibo [1] and Twitter [2, 3] have gained significantly in popularity in recent years. With the large active user base and the natural, effortless and instantaneous way to share information in the form of microblog, these sites become an important source for real-time information sharing and news dissemination. Inevitably, false rumors and misinformation also find their way to attract public interest and spread widely through these sites. A series of incidents show that such malicious messages can pose significant threats of damages far beyond the social media platforms. For example, a hoax Tweet posted by the compromised Twitter account of Associated Press claimed that two explosions in the White House injured the US President [4]. The message not only caused a nationwide panic but also rocked the financial market with a $200 billion lost. Moreover, a Twitter spam campaign that

© Springer International Publishing AG 2016
J. Chen et al. (Eds.): NSS 2016, LNCS 9955, pp. 483–496, 2016.
DOI: 10.1007/978-3-319-46298-1_31

spread DDoS attack malware in the guise of leaked nude photos of Hollywood celebrities caused a nationwide Internet meltdown in New Zealand [5].

In order to mitigate the threats of misinformation and false rumors, a number of prior studies have addressed the problem of information credibility assessment on microblogging sites. In general, the state of the art approaches can be divided into two categories, i.e., assessment with external information sources and assessment using only the signals on the social media platform itself. The approaches in the first category resort to either the verified content from external news sources or the help of active human experts. In contrast, the approaches in the second category extract a range of features from message content, user, topic, and propagation attributes, and then build classifiers using machine learning (ML) algorithms. In this work, we revisit the problem from a new perspective, in which we take advantage of the human input that is already available on the platform. The idea is to infer the information credibility by mining the opinions of interested and relevant users who participate in the propagation of popular microblog posts.

In this paper, we introduce the concept of gatekeepers on microblogging platforms. The rationale is that the users are not only information consumers but also information gatekeepers. They decide which message is filtered for dissemination to their followers and they can append their personal comments. Moreover, these interactions will affect the further propagation of the message. Being a gatekeeper here does not mean that the user has the authority or resources to confirm whether the information is truthful or not. Instead, the gatekeepers just make their own judgement based on their knowledge and background, and their motivation can be either personal interest or other purposes. In addition, they may have different beliefs about the message they are gatekeeping, such that they may show positive, neutral or negative attitude towards it.

The propagation process of any particular microblog can be expressed as a sequence of gatekeeping output symbols. That is, every time the post is forwarded or commented, a new symbol is generated and appended to the output sequence. The symbol is derived by analyzing the gatekeeper's confidence level and attitude. Specifically, the confidence level is estimated based on some measurable attributes that reflect the credibility of the users and the chance of the users knowing the event or topic discussed in the message. The attitude of gatekeeper is inferred by performing sentiment analysis on the appended comments. We find that the gatekeeping output sequences of truthful information and false information exhibits different patterns. Therefore, we propose a microblog information credibility assessment approach based on gatekeeping behavior modelling. The approach consists of two stages. The first stage trains a Hidden Markov Model (HMM) from a set of truthful microblog posts. In the next stage, the model is used for real-time misinformation detection.

We conduct experiments on a data set collected from Sina Weibo. The experimental results suggest that the proposed approach obtains better accuracy for microblog information credibility assessment in comparison with several existing methods.

The rest of the paper is organized as follows. Section 2 presents a brief review of the microblog information credibility assessment methods proposed in recent studies. In Sect. 3, the gatekeeping behavior analysis and modeling method is described, and a novel misinformation detection scheme is proposed. Section 4 discusses the data set and evaluation methods, along with experimental results and analysis. Finally, we conclude the paper in Sect. 5.

2 Related Work

The problem of information credibility on microblogging platforms has attracted a lot of research interests in recent years. This section presents a brief review of these works.

Al-Khalifa et al. [6] present a prototype system that measures the credibility levels of news content published on Twitter according to the similarity with verified content from external news sources, such as Google News. Suzuki et al. [7] propose a similar approach to assess the credibility of messages in social media based on the content similarity with credible Wikipedia [7] articles. Wikipedia itself is a user generated content website, so the authors develop a method to assess the credibility of Wikipedia articles by using the edit history. Liang et al. [9] propose a microblog misinformation identification framework that involves active human participation. Specifically, they maintain an index of user expertise based on the user generated content. When a suspect rumor message needs to be assessed, help requests are sent to those users whose expertise matches with the given message. In general, this type of methods rely on the availability of similar content from external sources or appropriate experts, which makes them not suitable for assessing real-time data.

Several recent studies have shown that the information credibility on microblogging sites can be assessed by using the signals on the platform itself (without external source of information). Castillo et al. [10] train supervised classifiers to automatically predict whether a tweet on Twitter is newsworthy and credible. In particular, they introduce four types of features, including message-based, user-based, topic-based, and propagation-based attributes. The first three types of features are extracted from the content of tweets or the profile of authors. Propagation-based characteristics consist of the number of initial tweets of the topic and several measurements of the retweet tree, such as the total size, maximum level size, maximum and average depth, and maximum and average degree. Their experimental results show that the classifiers can achieve an accuracy of 89 % for deciding if a tweet is newsworthy, along with an accuracy of 86 % for deciding if the news is credible.

Gupta et al. [11] investigate the credibility of Twitter events, which are collections of tweets and represented by Twitter Trend words. They propose an automatic approach to establish event credibility by analyzing not only the attributes of different entities (i.e., user, tweet and event), but also the inter-entity credibility relationships. Specifically, the features proposed in [9] are adopted, along with a few novel ones, to train a SVM classifier, and then the predictions given by the SVM classifier are used to initialize the credibility of different nodes in a graph of tweets, users and events. PageRank-like credibility propagation and event graph optimization methods are used to obtain the final assessment results. The authors report an accuracy of 86 % for the proposed method, which outperforms the classifier approach (72 %) on their data sets.

Xia et al. [12] study the credibility of emergency events circulating on Twitter. They first propose a sequential K-Means algorithm to detect a sudden burst of related tweets, which is considered as an indicator of emergency situation. When an emergency situation is detected, they use Bayesian Network-based classifier to predict if the tweets related to the situation is credible or not. Four types of features, including author-based, content-based, topic-based, and diffusion-based, are used for the classification.

Yang et al. [13] present one of the earliest studies on information credibility on Sina Weibo, i.e., the leading microblogging service in China. The authors highlight that the difference in language and in the types of trending topics could make some useful features on Twitter not applicable to Weibo. In this regard, they select a set of content-based, account-based, and propagation-based features that are common on both platforms, and they also introduce the unique features available on Weibo, such as the client program and event location. Their experimental result suggests that the new features can increase the accuracy of the SVM classifiers.

In addition, a series of studies [14–17] address the detection of Twitter spam particularly. The approaches proposed in these works share common concepts and mechanisms with information credibility assessment, but they are not directly applicable.

3 Gatekeeping Behavior Analysis

On microblogging sites like Weibo and Twitter, users are not only information consumers but also information gatekeepers. In other words, the users act (e.g., retweet) and response (e.g., reply) so as to express their opinions, feelings, or simply interests on the posts they happen to read on the platform. Their interactions could have effects on further propagation of the message. It can be observed that the gatekeeping behavior sequences of truthful microblogging posts and false rumors exhibit different patterns. In this section, we present a gatekeeping behavior model and described a novel method for detecting misinformation.

3.1 Gatekeeping on Weibo

We define the gatekeepers of a Weibo message as the group of users who are actively involved in the propagation of the particular message. Specifically, the users on Weibo can perform gatekeeping in the following ways:

- Forward: users sharing the message with their followers. On Twitter, this feature is called "retweet". In this case, the original message is reposted and no new information is added.
- Forward and Comment: users adding their own comments as they forward the message. On Twitter, this feature is called "retweet with comment". It allows the original message to be embedded within a new message, so that the followers of the user will see the original message alongside the comments.
- Comment: users posting a comment upon the message. Unlike the "reply" feature implemented on Twitter, Sina Weibo supports the feature of commenting directly on

a message. Therefore, each Weibo message comes with a label that indicates the number of comments towards the message. By clicking this label, the followers can open an expanded view, in which the comments are displayed after the original message.

Typically, a popular message on Weibo will have a large number of gatekeepers, as it is forwarded and commented by the crowd in a short period of time. The gatekeepers are merely the regular users who are interested in the message such that they decide to repost it in their circle or post some comments. Therefore, being a gatekeeper does not necessarily mean that the user has put in the effort to confirm whether the information is true or false. Nevertheless, it is inevitable that the gatekeepers have their own judgement based on their knowledge and background, and their opinion will somehow reflect in their action and comment.

3.2 Gatekeeping Behavior Analysis

In order to take advantage of the judgements and opinions expressed by the gatekeepers, we propose to model their behavior from two perspectives, i.e., who they are and what they think.

Firstly, we describe who they are by defining the confidence of gatekeepers, which reflects their ability of determining the truthfulness of the message. In specific, the confidence level is estimated based on a number of measurable attributes of gatekeepers. On one hand, we include some features that reflect the credibility of the user, such as the number of followers, the number of followings, the number of authored posts, the number of forwarded posts, registration age, and verification status. On the other hand, we include some features that reflect the relationship between the user and the message, so that we can infer whether the user has a better chance to know the event or the topic discussed in the message. Such features are the number of user keywords (including the keywords and hashtags in the user's profile and previous posts) matched in the message and the distance of geolocation between the user and the message whenever available. Based on the features, we can classify the gatekeepers into K groups (for example, we consider $K = 5$ in this work), where each group represents a different confidence level.

Secondly, we estimate what they think by analyzing the actions and comments (when available) of the gatekeepers. Specifically, we consider three types of attitudes (that is, positive, neutral and negative), which can be inferred from the appended comments by performing sentiment analysis. When the gatekeepers forward the message without appending any words, it is difficult to derive their actual thoughts. In this case, we adopt the assumption that forwarding without comment indicates a neutral opinion.

Based on the above definitions, the propagation process of a popular microblog post can be described as a sequence of observations, i.e., $O_1, O_2, \ldots, O_t, \ldots$, in which O_t is the observation on the tth time that this message gets forwarded or commented (see Fig. 1). Moreover, the value of O_t is determined by the confidence level and the attitude of the tth gatekeeper:

$$O_t = \begin{cases} c & \text{if attitude is positive} \\ c + K & \text{if attitude is neutral,} \\ c + 2K & \text{if attitude is negative} \end{cases}$$

where c is the confidence level of tth gatekeeper, i.e., $c \in \{1, 2, \ldots, K\}$.

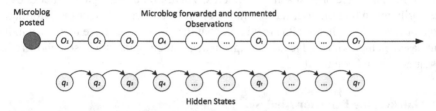

Fig. 1. Gatekeeper behavior sequence

As shown in Fig. 1, we consider that the gatekeeping behavior output is driven by the Hidden Markov Model (HMM) [18]. That is, there are a number of underlying states such that the gatekeeper in each step can be in any of these states and its behavior output is determined by the current state (which is unobservable). The rationale of considering a hidden layer of different states is twofold. Firstly, the gatekeepers can have different purposes (e.g., benign or malicious) when they forward or comment a post. Secondly, a gatekeeper's confidence level and attitude can change over time, especially when they acquire more relevant information.

3.3   Hidden Markov Model

Consider the microblog propagation process that can be described in any step as being in one of a set of N distinct underlying states, $S_1, S_2, \ldots, S_N$, and producing one of a set of M distinct observable output symbols, $v_1, v_2, \ldots, v_M$. We denote the steps as $t = 1, 2, \ldots$, the state in step t as q_t, and the observable symbol in step t as O_t. The underlying state is hidden because it is not observable.

The propagation begins in a random state that is governed by the initial state distribution, $\pi = \{\pi_i\}$, where

$$\pi_i = P[q_1 = S_i], 1 \le i \le N.$$

In each following step, the process undergoes a transition of state (shift back to the same state is possible) according to a set of state transition probabilities, $A = \{a_{ij}\}$, in the form of

$$a_{ij} = P[q_{t+1} = S_j | q_t = S_i], 1 \le i, j \le N,$$

with the coefficients a_{ij} obeying the following standard stochastic constraints $a_{ij} \geq 0$ and $\sum_{j=1}^{N} a_{ij} = 1$. That is, the process of state transition is a Markov chain, where the probability distribution of the next state q_{t+1} depends only on the current state q_t.

Besides, the observation O_t in step t is governed by a probabilistic function of the state, $B = \{b_i(k)\}$, where

$$b_i(k) = P[O_t = v_k | q_t = S_i], 1 \leq i \leq N, 1 \leq k \leq M.$$

In short, with N and M specified, the model can be described by the following parameter set:

$$\lambda = \{A, B, \pi\}.$$

Given an observation sequence $O = O_1, \ldots, O_T$ for training, the forward-backward algorithm [18] can be used to derive λ such that $P(O|\lambda)$ is locally maximized.

Firstly, we define the forward variable as $\alpha_t(i) = P(O_1, O_2, \ldots, O_t, q_t = S_i | \lambda)$ and the backward variable as $\beta_t(i) = P(O_{t+1}, O_{t+2}, \ldots, O_T | q_t = S_i, \lambda)$, which can be derived recursively as

$$\begin{cases} \alpha_1(i) = \pi_i b_i(O_1) \\ \alpha_{t+1}(j) = \left[\sum_{i=1}^{N} \alpha_t(i) a_{ij}\right] b_j(O_{t+1}) \end{cases}$$

and

$$\begin{cases} \beta_T(i) = 1 \\ \beta_t(i) = \sum_{j=1}^{N} a_{ij} b_j(O_{t+1}) \beta_{t+1}(j) \end{cases}.$$

Secondly, given λ and O, we define the probability of being in state S_i at step t and state S_j at the next step as $\xi_t(i,j) = P(q_t = S_i, q_{t+1} = S_j | O, \lambda)$, and the probability of being in state S_i at step t as $\gamma_t(i) = \sum_{j=1}^{N} \xi_t(i,j)$. Therefore, we have:

$$\xi_t(i,j) = \frac{\alpha_t(i) a_{ij} b_j(O_{t+1}) \beta_{t+1}(j)}{P(O|\lambda)}$$

and

$$\gamma_t(i) = \frac{\alpha_t(i) \beta_t(i)}{P(O|\lambda)} = \frac{\alpha_t(i) \beta_t(i)}{\sum_{i=1}^{N} \alpha_t(i) \beta_t(i)}.$$

Based on the above definitions, the maximum likelihood estimate of λ is as follows:

$$\bar{\pi}_i = \gamma_1(i),$$

$$\bar{a}_{ij} = \sum_{t-1}^{T-1} \xi_t(i,j) / \sum_{j=1}^{N} \gamma_t(i),$$

$$\bar{b}_j(k) = \sum_{\substack{t=1 \\ s.t.O_t=v_k}}^{T} \gamma_t(j) / \sum_{t=1}^{T} \gamma_t(j).$$

3.4   Misinformation Detection Using HMM

The proposed method for microblog misinformation detection involves two stages. The first stage is for model training, which takes as input a training data set that consists of truthful microblog posts. An HMM is derived using the algorithm discussed in the last section. The second stage is for real-time detection, where the popular microblog posts are monitored constantly. Every time a post is forwarded or commented, the observation sequence O_{test} will be updated and tested against the trained HMM λ. Specifically, we calculate the log likelihood of $P(O_{test}|\lambda)$, i.e., $Q = \log P(O_{test}|\lambda)$. Recall the definition of the forward variable, Q can be calculated as follows:

$$Q = \log \sum_{i=1}^{N} \alpha_T(i).$$

Finally, if Q is smaller than a predefined threshold, the post will be classified as false information and it will be removed from the monitoring targets. Otherwise, when Q is larger than the threshold, the post is considered as truthful at the moment, and the detection process will be repeated whenever it is forwarded or commented again.

4   Evaluation

4.1   Data Set

In this work, we focus on analyzing popular posts on Sina Weibo (referred to as Weibo in the following for simplicity). The popular posts are defined in terms of being forwarded (i.e., retweeted) by at least 1000 different users.

Due to the law and regulation in China, Weibo comes with official (manual) rumor busting services, which are deeply integrated into the platform. It allows users to raise suspect rumor reports, which will be inspected by the rumor busting team. If a post is confirmed to be misinformation, warning alerts will be appended to the post. Figure 2 shows an example of a confirmed rumor that has already been forwarded over 10 thousand times. The post gives a photo of two women and claims that they are suspected baby traffickers. In addition, Weibo maintains an official Rumor Refuter account that posts some confirmed rumors that are widely spread. This allows us to obtain a data set with accurate ground truth. Specifically, we have collected 1360 popular confirmed rumors with the complete traces of the gatekeepers and their comments.

Fig. 2. An example of widely spread false rumor

Weibo also maintains a real-time trending list of the most popular posts, from which we can collect the samples of true information. Due to the existence of the rumor busting mechanism, most of the trending posts are truthful. Nonetheless, we have carried out extra procedures to establish the ground truth. In specific, we recruit 9 student volunteers to assess the collected trending posts. They are divided into 3 groups, and each group is assigned with a different set of posts. The volunteers are asked to choose from three options (that is, "True", "False", and "Not Sure"). Only the posts that are considered as true by the whole group are included in the data set. In this way, we have obtained 12210 popular truthful posts with complete traces. The data set is summarized in Table 1. The dates of these collected posts are between May 2012 and June 2015.

Table 1. Data set

Weibo posts	Total	Training set	Testing set
True information	12210	8000	4210
False information	1360	–	1360

We have derived the statistics of several typical user features from the data set in terms of the author of true/false information and the gatekeeper of true/false information. In Fig. 3, the proportion of verified and non-verified account in each category is showed. The difference regarding authors is significant. That is, around 70 % of the valid posts are published by verified users, in contrast to about 12 % of those rumor posts. The difference for gatekeepers is minor in this regard. In specific, verified users constitute 11 % and 17 % of the gatekeepers of false rumors and valid posts respectively. In addition, statistics on number of followers, number of followings, registration age, and number of posts/reposts are given in Figs. 4, 5, 6 and 7. We can see that each distribution varies among these four categories.

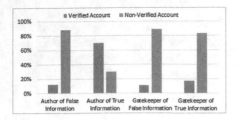

Fig. 3. Statistics on account verification

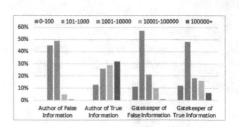

Fig. 4. Statistics on number of followers

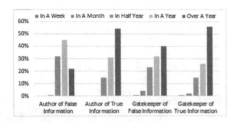

Fig. 5. Statistics on registration age

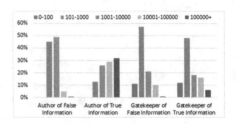

Fig. 6. Statistics on number of followers

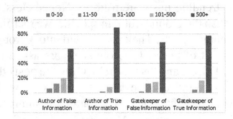

Fig. 7. Statistics on number of posts/reposts

4.2 Gatekeeper Confidence Estimation

From the training data set, we first extract all of the predefined features of gatekeepers and perform K-Means clustering on the data. In particular, the gatekeepers are grouped into five clusters (i.e., $K = 5$). After that, a thousand gatekeepers are randomly selected from each cluster to construct the gatekeeper confidence estimation training set. Based on this, we can train a supervised classifier to predict the confidence level of any given gatekeepers in the real time. For evaluation purpose, we compare a number of popular supervised learning algorithms, including Random Forest (RF), C4.5 decision tree, Naïve Bayes (NB), Support Vector Machine (SVM), and K Nearest Neighbor (KNN).

Figure 8 presents the accuracy results of different learning algorithms, which are obtained by using 10-cross validation. We can see SVM achieves the best accuracy rate at 97 %, followed by Random Forest and C4.5 at 96 % and 95 % respectively. In contrast, the accuracy of Naïve Bayes and KNN is relatively low at around 90 %.

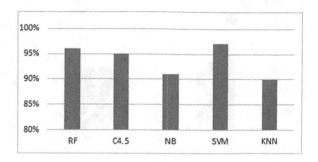

Fig. 8.   Accuracy of gatekeeper confidence analysis

Figure 9 compares different algorithms in terms of training time and testing time in seconds. Note that the result is obtained on a computer with Intel i7 960 CPU and 8 GB RAM. Firstly, C4.5 and Naïve Bayes finish training within 0.2 s, while Random Forest and SVM take around 3 s. Besides, KNN does not require any training. Secondly, Random Forest and C4.5 are the fastest in testing, both finishing within 0.1 s. KNN takes over 5 s, while Naïve Bayes and SVM use around 2 s.

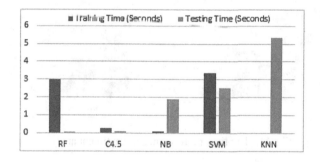

Fig. 9.   Runtime performance of gatekeeper confidence analysis

In summary, Random Forest algorithm is the best option for gatekeeper confidence estimation, as it offers good classification accuracy and fastest classification speed.

4.3   Sentiment Analysis

In order to infer the attitude of gatekeepers from their comments written in Chinese, we modify the sentiment analysis method proposed in [19]. In particular, we train Random Forest models that classify any given Chinese text into three classes, that is, positive, neutral, and negative. For the purpose of evaluation, we construct a data set by manually labeling 3,000 random comments for each class from our Weibo data.

The accuracy result obtained from a 10-cross validation is presented in Fig. 10. In particular, RF represents the Random Forest classifier we use in our work, and SVM stands for the original classifier used in [19]. We can see that the Random Forest model achieves an accuracy rate of 66 % while SVM model yields only 59 % accuracy.

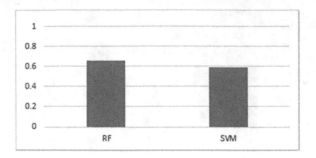

Fig. 10. Accuracy of sentiment analysis

In addition, Fig. 11 illustrates the training time and testing time results in terms of seconds for Random Forest and SVM classifiers. In specific, Random Forest takes less than 2 s to train and finishes classifying the testing data in less than 0.1 s. In contrast, the SVM classifier takes 2.9 s to train and 1.5 s to classify the testing data.

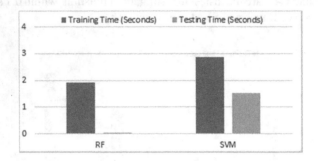

Fig. 11. Runtime performance of sentiment analysis

In short, the proposed sentiment analysis method based on Random Forest classifier outperforms the SVM-based method in terms of both prediction accuracy and runtime performance. Therefore, it is more suitable for opinion mining in real time.

4.4   Misinformation Detection

In this section, we evaluate the effectiveness of the proposed approach for information credibility assessment on microblog sites. As showed in Table 1, we randomly selected 8000 posts out of the 12210 truthful Weibo posts to train the HMM. The rest 4210 posts with true information and 1360 posts with false information are used for testing. Based on the testing data, we can measure the true positives and false positives as well as the precision and recall rates.

Figure 12 presents the ROC (Receiver Operating Characteristic) curve of the resultant HMM. For example, when the threshold is set as –4.76, the false positive rate is 6 % and the true positive rate is around 80 %. In general, the true positive rate can be raised to above 99.9 % at the cost of higher false positive rate at around 14 %.

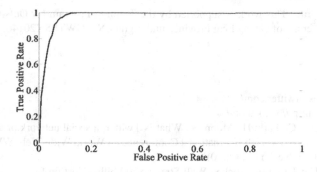

Fig. 12. ROC Curve of the HMM

Figure 13 shows the precision and recall results of the proposed HMM approach, in comparison with three existing methods, including C4.5 [10], Bayesian Network [12], and SVM [13]. The results indicate that HMM achieves the best precision and recall at 92 % and 90 % respectively, followed by C4.5 that yields 85 % precision and 84 % recall. The precision and recall for Bayesian Network is 80 % and 81 % respectively, and that for SVM is 73 % and 72 % respectively.

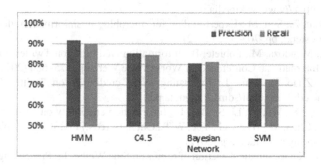

Fig. 13. Comparison with existing approaches

In summary, the experiment results obtained from real world data indicate that the proposed approach is more effective in assessing information credibility for microblog sites.

5 Conclusion

This paper investigates the problem of information credibility assessment in micro-blogging sites. We consider the users who are actively involved in the propagation process of popular microblog messages to be gatekeepers. Based on the concept, we propose to analyze the gatekeeping behavior from the perspectives of 'who they are' and 'what they think'. Accordingly, we train HMMs using the gatekeeping output sequences of truthful microblogs. The experimental results obtained based on Sina Weibo data show that the model can detect misinformation more accurately than existing approaches.

Acknowledgement. This work is supported by the Training Program for Outstanding Young Teachers in University of Guangdong Province under grant No. GWTPSY201403.

References

1. Twitter. https://twitter.com/
2. Sina Weibo. http://weibo.com/
3. Kwak, H., Lee, C., Park, H., Moon, S.: What is Twitter, a social network or a news media? In: Proceedings of the 19th International Conference on World Wide Web, WWW 2010, pp. 591–600. ACM, New York (2010)
4. RT News. The Tweet that rocked Wall Street: $200 billion lost on fake message. 24 April 2013. https://www.rt.com/business/tweet-hackers-wall-street-us-326/
5. Pash, C.: The lure of naked hollywood star photos sent the internet into meltdown in New Zealand. Business Insider, 7 September 2014. http://www.businessinsider.com.au/the-lure-of-naked-hollywood-star-photos-sent-the-internet-into-meltdown-in-new-zealand-2014-9
6. Al-Khalifa, H.S., Al-Eidan, R.M.: An experimental system for measuring the credibility of news content in Twitter. Int. J. Web Inf. Syst. **7**(2), 130–151 (2011)
7. Suzuki, Y., Nadamoto, A.: Credibility assessment using Wikipedia for messages on social network services. In: The Ninth International Conference on Dependable, Autonomic and Secure Computing, pp. 887–894 (2011)
8. Wikipedia. https://www.wikipedia.org/
9. Liang, C., Liu, Z., Sun, M.: Expert finding for microblog misinformation identification. In: COLING (Posters), pp. 703–712 (2012)
10. Castillo, C., Mendoza, M., Poblete, B.: Information credibility on Twitter. In: Proceedings of the 20th International Conference on World Wide Web, pp. 675–684 (2011)
11. Gupta, M., Zhao, P., Han, J.: Evaluating event credibility on Twitter (2012). http://www.cs.uiuc.edu/~hanj/pdf/sdm12_mgupta.pdf
12. Xia, X., Yang, X., Wu, C., Li, S., Bao, L.: Information credibility on Twitter in emergency situation. In: Chau, M., Wang, G., Yue, W.T., Chen, H. (eds.) PAISI 2012. LNCS, vol. 7299, pp. 45–59. Springer, Heidelberg (2012)
13. Yang, F., Yu, X.: Automatic detection of rumor on Sina Weibo. In: Proceedings of the ACM SIGKDD Workshop on Mining Data Semantics, pp. 1–7 (2012)
14. Grier, C., Thomas, K., Paxson, V., Zhang, M.: @spam: the underground on 140 characters or less. In: Proceedings of the 17th ACM Conference on Computer and Communications Security, CCS 10, pp. 27–37. ACM, New York (2010)
15. Thomas, K., Grier, C., Song, D., Paxson, V.: Suspended accounts in retrospect: an analysis of Twitter spam. In: Proceedings of the 2011 ACM SIGCOMM Conference on Internet Measurement Conference, IMC 2011, pp. 243–258. ACM, New York (2011)
16. Lee, S., Kim, J.: Warningbird: a near real-time detection system for suspicious URLs in Twitter stream. IEEE Trans. Dependable Secure Comput. **10**(3), 183–195 (2013)
17. Oliver, J., Pajares, P., Ke, C., Chen, C., Xiang, Y.: An in-depth analysis of abuse on twitter. Technical report, Trend Micro, 225 E. John Carpenter Freeway, Suite 1500 Irving, Texas 75062 U.S.A., September 2014
18. Rabiner, L.R.: A tutorial on hidden Markov models and selected applications in speech recognition. Proc. IEEE **77**(2), 257–286 (1989)
19. Wei, W., Shi-Bin, X.: Sentiment analysis of Chinese microblog based on multi-feature and combined classification. J. Beijing Inf. Sci. Technol. Univ. **28**(4), 39–45 (2013). (in Chinese)

Data Mining for Security Application
(Short Paper)

Finding Anomalies in SCADA Logs Using Rare Sequential Pattern Mining

Anisur Rahman$^{(\boxtimes)}$, Yue Xu, Kenneth Radke, and Ernest Foo

Queensland University of Technology, Brisbane, Australia
anisur.rahman@hdr.qut.edu.au, {yue.xu,k.radke,e.foo}@qut.edu.au

Abstract. Pattern mining is a branch of data mining used to discover hidden patterns or correlations among data. We use rare sequential pattern mining to find anomalies in critical infrastructure control networks such as supervisory control and data acquisition (SCADA) networks. As anomalous events occur rarely in a system and SCADA systems' topology and actions do not change often, we argue that some anomalies can be detected using rare sequential pattern mining. This anomaly detection would be useful for intrusion detection or erroneous behaviour of a system. Although research into rare itemsets mining previously exists, neither research into rare sequential pattern mining nor its applicability to SCADA system anomaly detection has previously been completed. Moreover, since there is no consideration to events order, the applicability to intrusion detection in SCADA is minimal. By ensuring the events' order is maintained, in this paper, we propose a novel Rare Sequential Pattern Mining (RSPM) technique which is a useful anomaly detection system for SCADA. We compared our algorithm with a rare itemset mining algorithm and found anomalous events in SCADA logs.

Keywords: Frequent pattern · Rare pattern · SCADA · Generator pattern

1 Introduction

Anomaly detection is one step of several safeguarding measures applied in critical infrastructure (CI) control networks, such as supervisory control and data acquisition (SCADA). The SCADA system is used to monitor and control the CIs from a remote location. SCADA systems are interlinked with each other, so attacks on SCADA can cause devastating impacts to other dependent infrastructures, environments and even to human lives [1]. Many SCADA systems use conventional IT technology as a backbone to communicate with field devices, so they are prone to be attacked using standard IT network vulnerabilities. Anomaly detection for SCADA systems is important and challenging because of the constant changes in attack patterns. Therefore, it is almost impossible to keep the system protected from increasingly diversified attacks [2].

SCADA are distinguished from traditional IT networks because the normal or regular behaviour of SCADA systems can be predicted using frequent sequential

© Springer International Publishing AG 2016
J. Chen et al. (Eds.): NSS 2016, LNCS 9955, pp. 499–506, 2016.
DOI: 10.1007/978-3-319-46298-1_32

pattern or regular system behaviour. However, rare pattern or irregular behavior of this system which deviates from normal behaviour could be considered as anomalous events. Therefore, in this paper, we assume that rare or infrequent sequence of actions can be considered as an anomalous event, and if analyzed we can find the cause could be either cyber-attacks, system failures, or later inclusion of a benign or novel event. In this paper, we propose a novel Rare Sequential Pattern Mining (RSPM) method for anomaly detection from SCADA logs.

2   Related Work

There has been research in finding anomalies in SCADA systems from diverse perspectives. Some works are at the communication protocol level [3]; however, only a single work uses SCADA logs where Hadžiosmanovič et al. [4] used itemset mining for threat identification. Manganaris et al. [5] show that the absence of frequent events or set of events can be considered as an anomaly. Clifton and Gengo [6] applied a data mining technique to identify the normal behavior of a system based on the frequent occurrence of an alarm event and later filtered them out from suspicious events lists. Barbara et al. [7] defined users normal behavior using data mining association rules from network traffic data to train a model. Later, in their model they looked for any deviation in association rules and considered as an abnormal or anomalous behavior of the system and users.

So, there have been some works in finding rare or infrequent itemset mining. However, these works can not be used to find anomalies in SCADA systems as they do not preserve itemsets' order [4,8]. To the best of our knowledge, until now there has been no work in rare sequential pattern mining for anomaly detection. We are motivated by the work of Szathmary et al. [8] where the authors used minimal frequent itemset generators to find rare patterns. However, their method cannot find correlation among events. We apply a similar idea, but instead of itemsets we use a sequence which preserves the events' order of occurence that results in correlation among the events. Therefore, in this paper, we use rare sequential pattern mining (RSPM) which is a branch of sequential pattern mining first introduced by Agrawal and Srikant [9].

3   Proposed Method

To define our problem, we introduce some related theories from [10] which are applied in our RSPM algorithm, and in other sections of this paper.

Definition 1 (Sequence): *Let $I = \{i_1, i_2, ..., i_l\}$ be a set of all items. An itemset $I_x = \{i_1, i_2, ..., i_m\} \subseteq I$ is a nonempty and unordered set of distinct items. A sequence s is an ordered list of itemsets or events denoted as $\langle I_1, I_2, I_3, ..., I_n \rangle$ such that $I_k \subseteq I$ ($1 \leq k \leq n$).*

Definition 2 (Sequential Database SDB): *A sequential database SDB is a set of sequences, i.e., $SDB = \{s_1, s_2, s_3, ..., s_p\}$, where s_j is a sequence, $1 \leq j \leq p$.* For example, Table 1 shown below is an example of a sequential database SDB containing four sequences. The first sequence SID1 is composed of 5 itemsets. The first itemset is $\{1\}$ which is followed by itemset $\{1, 2, 3\}$. For application domains, the items in one itemset are often considered occur at the same time.

Definition 3 (Sequence containment): *A sequence $S_a = \langle A_1, A_2, ..., A_n \rangle$ is said to be contained in a sequence $S_b = \langle B_1, B_2, ..., B_m \rangle$ if and only if there exist integers $1 \leq i_1 \leq i_2 \leq ... \leq i_n \leq m$, such that, $A_1 \subseteq B_{i1}, A2 \subseteq B_{i2}$, ..., $A_n \subseteq B_{in}$ and this is denoted as $S_a \sqsubseteq S_b$. In this case S_a is considered as a sub-pattern of S_b and S_b is also said to be super-pattern of S_a.*

For example, in Table 1 sequence $\langle \{5\}, \{1, 6\}, \{2\} \rangle$ is contained in sequence SID4.

Definition 4 (Support): *The support of a sequential pattern S_a in a sequential database SDB is determined by the number of sequences $S \in SDB$, such that, $S_a \sqsubseteq S$ and it is denoted by $supSDB(S_a)$.* For example, the pattern $\langle \{1, 2\}, \{6\} \rangle$ is found in 2 sequences in Table 1 and hence the support is 2.

Definition 5 (Frequent Sequential Pattern): *Let minsup be a user-defined threshold and SDB is a sequential database. A sequence S (also called a sequential pattern) is considered frequent if and only if $supSDB (S) \geq minsup$.*

Definition 6 (Sequential Generator): *A sequential pattern S_a is said to be a generator if there is no other sequential pattern S_b such that $S_b \sqsubseteq S_a$ and their supports are equal.* For example, in the sequence database SDB given in Table 1 both $\langle \{5\}, \{2\} \rangle$ and $\langle \{6\}, \{3\} \rangle$ are Generator Sequential Patterns.

Table 1. A sequential database SDB

Sequence ID	Sequences
SID1	$\langle \{1\}, \{1, 2, 3\}, \{1, 3\}, \{4\}, \{3, 6\} \rangle$
SID2	$\langle \{1, 4\}, \{3\}, \{2, 3\}, \{1, 5\} \rangle$
SID3	$\cdot$ $\langle \{5, 6\}, \{1, 2\}, \{4, 6\}, \{3\}, \{2\} \rangle$
SID4	$\langle \{5\}, \{7\}, \{1\ 6\}, \{3\}, \{2\}, \{3\} \rangle$

3.1 Description of RSPM Algorithm

In rare sequential pattern mining, the sequences that fail to meet the *minsup* are known as rare sequences. For example, if the user defined *minsup* is 2 then the sequential patterns $\langle \{7\}, \{1\} \rangle$ and $\langle \{1\}, \{5\} \rangle$ are found to be rare since they fall below the *minsup*. The basic idea is to form a new sequential pattern by combining two minimal generators and the infrequent combinations are considered rare patterns. We are motivated by the work presented in [8] that finds rare itemsets based on minimal generators. However, we propose to find rare sequential patterns based on sequential generators because they are the smallest or minimal patterns of an equivalent class. Usually, shorter patterns are frequent, while by nature, longer patterns are likely to be infrequent or rare and their combination can be even more infrequent. Therefore, it is likely that a combination of two minimal generators would be rare or infrequent, and this rare sequential pattern can be considered interesting and deserves further investigation. Given two sequential patterns, there could exist different ways to combine them to form a new sequential pattern. For example, for the two frequent sequential patterns s_1 = $\langle \{4\}, \{3\}, \{2\} \rangle$ and $s_2 = \langle \{1, 2\}, \{6\} \rangle$ generated from the dataset in Table 1, at the sequence level, we can combine them in two different orders $\langle s_1, s_2 \rangle$ and $\langle s_2, s_1 \rangle$. For example, $\langle \{4\}, \{3\}, \{2\}, \{1, 2\}, \{6\} \rangle$ and $\langle \{1, 2\}, \{6\}, \{4\}, \{3\}, \{2\} \rangle$. In this case, in the resulting sequence, each of the two original sequences is intact. The order of itemsets from one original sequence is preserved. However, if we only want to preserve the original order of itemsets and do not require the integrity of the original sequences, we could have sequences like $\langle \{4\}, \{1, 2\}, \{3\}, \{2\}, \{6\} \rangle$, $\langle \{1, 2\}, \{4\}, \{3\}, \{6\}, \{2\} \rangle$, and much more. So, we preserved both the integrity and itemset order of the original sequence.

The inputs of this algorithm (shown below) are a sequence database SDB and a user defined threshold value as *minsup*. This algorithm will produce a list of minimal rare sequential patterns. At the beginning, minimal sequential generator patterns (mSGP) and frequent sequential patterns are generated from the sequence database SDB in steps 3 and 4. Then for each pair of generators' combinations are checked against the frequent sequential patterns (FSP) as described in step 6 to step 12.

Algorithm 1. Rare Sequential Pattern Mining Algorithm

```
 1: Input:   SDB, minsup // A sequential database and minimum support
 2: Output: RSP // A set of rare sequential patterns
 3: G := ⟨g₁, g₂, ...⟩ // a list of minimal sequential generators
 4: FSP := ⟨s₁, s₂, ...⟩ // a set of frequent sequenial patterns
 5: RSP := { }
 6: for gᵢ in G do
 7:     for gⱼ in G do
 8:         if ⟨gᵢ, gⱼ⟩ ∉ FSP and ∃s ∈ SDB and ⟨gᵢ, gⱼ⟩ ⊑ s then
 9:             RSP := RSP ∪ {⟨gᵢ, gⱼ⟩}
10:         else
11:             if ⟨gⱼ, gᵢ⟩ ∉ FSP and ∃s ∈ SDB and ⟨gⱼ, gᵢ⟩ ⊑ s then
12:                 RSP := RSP ∪ {⟨gⱼ, gᵢ⟩}
13:             end if
14:         end if
15:     end for
16:     Return RSP
17: end for
```

4 Experimental Setup

We assume that attackers cannot alter or delete the SCADA logs that we use as our datasets. We use four real SCADA logs Datasets. First dataset (Dataset-1; shown in Fig. 1) was collected from the logs on an Intelligent Electronic Device that controls an electrical substation while the second, third, and fourth dataset (Dataset-2, Dataset-3, and Dataset-4 respectively) were collected from our three different SCADA laboratory setup. In case of Dataset-1, Log data includes recorded events on that substation which were recorded only when there occurred any system errors.

```
S  3/03/2015 12:28:51:457 PM  INT--WARNING ON
S  3/03/2015 12:28:51:456 PM  INT--TIMESYNCHERROR ON
S  3/03/2015 12:24:08:021 PM  INT--WARNING ON
```

Fig. 1. A partial view of Dataset-1

Dataset-2 comes from a water tank system in our laboratory, which consists of two water tanks and a pump that moves water from a lower tank into the upper tank. Gravity allows water in the upper tank to move back into the lower tank. Dataset-3 is collected from a compressed air pipeline or reactor system. An air compressor pumps air into the pipe system and increases the air pressure. At a given value the air pressure is released. Once the air is released, the compressor starts up again building pressure in the pipe system. Finally, Dataset-4 is a conveyer system that moves objects along a conveyer belt. Dark and light objects are separated into Left and Right directions before returning to the beginning of the system. It is possible to sort objects in opposite directions.

A training session was held in our SCADA lab from 9.30am to 4.00pm. Three system devices (Tank, Reactor, and Conveyer) were switched on and started functioning smoothly. However, the system was compromised in the later half of the day, and all events were recorded.

4.1 Data Preprocessing

In data preprocessing steps, the raw logs from all datasets (Dataset-1 to Dataset-4) have been cleaned and the necessary informative features were selected. It is to be noted that in the log entries of the electrical substation (from where Dataset-1 created), it has been observed that during two minutes time duration the system performs a series of sequential events to bring the system to normal state from erroneous state. Therefore, these sequence of events have been identified as a single sequence which build the sequential database SDB-1 (shown in Fig. 2).

Here, the numbers represent individual events or itemsets of raw logs (Dataset-1) while "−1" indicates ending of events or itemsets and consecutive "−1−2" signals the end of a sequence. However, as in Dataset-2 through Dataset-4, events are recorded in every second, these events are considered as a single item in the sequence which build the databases SDB-2 through SDB-4 respectively.

```
50 4 -1 -2
47 58 25 30 3 18 36 27 49 -1 40 34 31 -1 -2
4 -1 50 -1 -2
```

Fig. 2. A partial view of SDB-1

4.2   Experiment and Results

We performed our experiment with python programming and SPMF [11] tool, which is an open source framework for sequential pattern mining. At first, we generate frequent sequential patterns (FSP) and minimal sequential generator patterns (mSGP). Later, the combination of mSGP are compared with FSP to prune frequent patterns. The remaining rare patterns are once again compared with the sequence database SDB. These patterns are once again found rare and considered anomalous events. However, the rare patterns which are not found in SDB are considered as non-present patterns.

Table 2. A partial view of results for Dataset-3.

Patterns by RSPM	Patterns by rare Itemset
$\langle\{19\}, \{57\}\rangle$	$\{19, 57\}$
$\langle\{58\}, \{19\}\rangle$	$\{19, 58\}$
$\langle\{100\}, \{74\}\rangle$	$\{74, 100\}$

We also applied Szathmary et al.'s rare itemset mining algorithm with the same datasets (Dataset-1 through Dataset-4) used in our RSPM algorithm for comparison. For example, their algorithm has identified rare itemset pattern $\{19, 58\}$ against our RSPM algorithm's rare sequential pattern $\langle\{58\}, \{19\}\rangle$ (shown in Table 2); However, we checked with the original log sequence events and found that the events occurrence order is 58 followed by 19 and not in events' reverse order. We argue that a particular sequential events' order can lead to a particular result and it is very important and significant in our experiment. For example, the following sequential ordered events are a regular system profile for filling a tank reservoir:

1. Turn on pump.
2. Wait for water level to reach 40 %.
3. Turn off pump.

If the system runs with the above events mentioned in the order, then the tank pump turns off after the water level reaches to the 40 % of its capacity label. However, if the above events are performed in a different order as mentioned below:

1. Turn off pump.
2. Wait for water level to reach 40 %.
3. Turn on pump.

then the system floods; therefore, we can say that only the rare patterns cannot be effective in identifying intrusion rather we need rare patterns with ordered events for effective intrusion detection into a system.

5   Discussion

The experimental results for all datasets (Dataset-1 to Dataset-4) show that our RSPM algorithm found not only the rare patterns as identified by Szathmary et al.'s algorithm but also keeps the events occurrence order, which their algorithm did not consider. For example, rare pattern $\langle\{14\}, \{7\}, \{10\}\rangle$ from Dataset-4 has been identified by our algorithm; however, Szathmary et al.'s algorithm identified this pattern as $\{7, 10, 14\}$ even though these are two different patterns considered in sequential pattern domain. Here, the numbers in the pattern $\langle\{14\}, \{7\}, \{10\}\rangle$ represents SCADA log sequence events $\langle\{\text{Conv\_Read\_Conv\_HMI\_Direction}(5)\_0\}, \{\text{Conv\_Read\_Conv\_Present\_PE}(5)\_0\}, \{\text{Conv\_Run\_Status}(5)\_0\}\rangle$ in Dataset-4. We traced this rare pattern in the original log dataset. However, we did not find pattern $\{7, 10, 14\}$ identified by their algorithm in the original log sequence as they did not preserve the sequence order. Different ordered sequential events' can produce different end results. Therefore, our rare sequential pattern can be effective in finding the correlation between consequences and actions.

Moreover, we found the original sequence as a frequent sequence which ends with the event "Conv_Run_Status(5)_-1"; however, in the rare sequence pattern the sequence ends with "Conv_Run_Status(5)_0" which is a deviation from the regular profile of the system. Later, we traced back this deviation in the log file and found that during the events' time period the converyer belt direction was reversed although it was supposed to be moving in other direction. This abnormal incident occured in the second part of the training day when the system was compromised. Therefore, we came to the conclusion that this rare sequence was an anomalous event which happened due to system compromise.

Similarly, we traced back rare sequential patterns $\langle\{19\}, \{57\}\rangle$, $\langle\{58\}, \{19\}\rangle$, and $\langle\{100\}, \{74\}\rangle$ from Dataset-3 and $\langle\{29\}, \{50\}\rangle$ from Dataset-2. In all cases, we found that these rare sequences should not happen in the logs during the specified time period. Therefore, we also believe that these are anomalous events. However, as we do not have a complete labeled test dataset from log files, we cannot find the ratio of false positive and negative. But, to find whether our algorithm can detect anomalous events, we have manually rearranged the order of some sequences with Dataset-1, and our algorithm detects these changes as rare sequences.

6   Conclusion and Future Work

In this paper we have presented RSPM, a novel approach for anomaly detection from SCADA logs using rare sequential pattern mining. However, it may be possible for the adversaries provided that they repeat the malicious events multiple times to evade this technique. In future, we will extend this work to generate all (from minimal to maximal) rare sequential patterns to test which patterns become more effective in detecting intrusion. We will also validate and find computational performances of our methodology with large volume of publicly available labeled SCADA logs. Moreover, we will compare our algorithm with other works as to anomaly detection using non sequential pattern outside SCADA or CIs.

References

1. Pederson, P., Dudenhoeffer, D., Hartley, S., Permann, M.: Critical infrastructure interdependency modeling: a survey of US and international research. Idaho Natl. Lab. **25**, 27 (2006)
2. Cheminod, M., Durante, L., Valenzano, A.: Review of security issues in industrial networks. IEEE Trans. Ind. Inform. **9**(1), 277–293 (2013)
3. Cheung, S., Dutertre, B., Fong, M., Lindqvist, U., Skinner, K., Valdes, A.: Using model-based intrusion detection for SCADA networks. In: Proceedings of the SCADA Security Scientific Symposium, vol. 46, pp. 1–12 (2007)
4. Hadžiosmanovič, D., Bolzoni, D., Hartel, P.H.: A log mining approach for process monitoring in SCADA. Int. J. Inf. Secur. **11**(4), 231–251 (2012)
5. Manganaris, S., Christensen, M., Zerkle, D., Hermiz, K.: A data mining analysis of RTID alarms. Comput. Netw. **34**(4), 571–577 (2000)
6. Clifton, C., Gengo, G.: Developing custom intrusion detection filters using data mining. In: IEEE Proceedings 21st Century Military Communication, vol. 1, pp. 440–443 (2000)
7. Barbara, D., Wu, N., Jajodia, S.: Detecting novel network intrusions using Bayes estimators. In: 1st SIAM Conference on Data Mining, pp. 1–17 (2001)
8. Szathmary, L., Napoli, A., Valtchev, P.: Towards rare itemset mining. In: 19th IEEE International Conference on Tools with Artificial Intelligence (ICTAI 2007), vol. 1, pp. 305–312 (2007)
9. Agrawal, R., Srikant, R.: Mining sequential patterns. In: Proceedings of the 11th International Conference on Data Engineering, pp. 3–14. IEEE (1995)
10. Fournier-Viger, P., Gomariz, A., Šebek, M., Hlosta, M.: VGEN: fast vertical mining of sequential generator patterns. In: Bellatreche, L., Mohania, M.K. (eds.) DaWaK 2014. LNCS, vol. 8646, pp. 476–488. Springer, Heidelberg (2014)
11. Fournier-Viger, P., Gomariz, A., Gueniche, T., Soltani, A., Wu, C., Tseng, V.S.: SPMF: a Java open-source pattern mining library. J. Mach. Learn. Res. (JMLR) **15**, 3389–3393 (2014)

Provable Security (Short Paper)

Improved Security Proof for Modular Exponentiation Bits

Kewei Lv$^{(\boxtimes)}$, Wenjie Qin$^{(\boxtimes)}$, and Ke Wang$^{(\boxtimes)}$

Data Assurance and Communication Security Research Center,
Institute of Information Engineering,
Chinese Academy of Sciences, Beijing 100093, People's Republic of China
kwlu@ucas.ac.cn, {wangke,qinwenjie}@iie.ac.cn

Abstract. For exponentiation function modulo a composite $f_{g,N}(x) = g^x \bmod N$, where $|N| = n$, an elegant algorithm is constructed by Goldreich and Rosen to reprove that the upper and lower half bits of this function are simultaneously hard separately under the factoring intractability assumption. Here we improve their algorithm to reduce the time by a factor $\mathcal{O}(\log n\epsilon^{-1})$. If error probability $\frac{1}{2^{(1-1/2c)m}}$ is tolerated, the reduced factor could be $\mathcal{O}((n\epsilon^{-1})^{1/2c})$ for a constant $c \geq 2$.

Keywords: One-way function · Bit security · Randomization technique · Factoring assumption

1 Introduction

One-way function is easy-to-compute but hard-to-invert as the basis of modern cryptography. An important concept closely linked to one-way function is hard-core bit. For a one-way function $f : \{0,1\}^n \to \{0,1\}^n$, we say that $B : \{0,1\}^n \to \{0,1\}$ is a hard-core bit of f, if, given $y = f(x)$, the success probability for guessing $B(x)$ has only a negligible advantage comparing with $1/2$. If a hard-core bit is in x, we call it individually hard bit. The concept of simultaneously hard bits is a generalization of that of individually hard bit, i.e. for given $y = f(x)$, some bits in x is indistinguishable with a random bit string of the same length. By these concepts, the hardness of retrieving some bits of x and the hardness of retrieving the whole are connected together. With these hard bits, we can construct efficient pseudo-random generators and secure protocols.

In this realm of functions modulo a composite, $f_{g,N}(x) = g^x \bmod N$, since the least significant bit of RSA and Rabin function were proven to be hard by Alexi *et al.* [1] in 1988, many one-way functions have been studied about their hard-core bits: For RSA and Rabin function modulo a composite, Håstad and Nüsland [4] proved that all the bits are individually hard, and for exponentiation modulo a prime all but the last few bits are individuallly hard. In 1993, [5] proved that under the factoring intractability assumption, all the bits are individually

---

This work is partially supported by NSF No. 61272039.

J. Chen et al. (Eds.): NSS 2016, LNCS 9955, pp. 509–516, 2016.
DOI: 10.1007/978-3-319-46298-1_33

hard, and the upper half and lower half bits are simultaneously hard separately. In 2002, by constructing an algorithm, Goldreich and Rosen [2] proved that this function is still pseudo-random when the input was restricted to being half the size. This is an equivalent conclusion with [5] and its reduction algorithm is more elegant. The main idea of this algorithm is to construct a polynomial list of bit strings with the same length and the right plaintext x is made sure to be contained in this list. The list is constructed iteratively, and in each of iteration the strings in it is one bit longer. As the size of the list is growing bigger, "Trimming Rule" algorithm is applied to discard elements which have been proven to be wrong until its size is reduced to polynomial. In the end, we can get the right x by exhaustive search. For simplicity, we call this algorithm "Goldreich-Rosen algorithm" (GR, for brevity). However, efficiency of GR could still be improved as only one element in the list is discard by "Trimming Rule" at once. If we look into the elements of the list more carefully, we could find some consecutive elements may have the same performance in "Trimming Rule". So we could improve the algorithm and discard more elements at once. At the same time we make sure the error probability is still tolerable.

In this paper, we Improve GR algorithm, which reduces time cost of GR by a factor $\mathcal{O}(\log n\epsilon^{-1})$. If we could tolerate higher error probability up to $\frac{1}{2^{(1-\frac{1}{2c})m}}$, the factor could be increased to $\mathcal{O}((n\epsilon^{-1})^{\frac{1}{2c}})$, where $c \geq 2$ is a constant.

Organization. In Sect. 2, we give some preliminaries and introduce Goldreich-Rosen algorithm briefly. Improved GR algorithm is given in Sect. 3 and the improvement tolerating higher error probability is in Sect. 4. Our conclusion is in Sect. 5.

2   Preliminaries

Let $|\cdot|$ denote the length of a binary bit string. For an integer x, $|x| = n$, its binary expansion is denoted by $x_n \cdots x_2 x_1$, where x_i is the ith bit and $x_{i,j}$ are bits from x_j to x_i for $j < i$. $N = pq$ is an integer, where p and q are odd primes with the same length and $|N| = n$. g is an element in $\mathbb{Z}_N^*$ whose order is denoted by $ord(g)$. $P_n = \{\langle N, g \rangle : |N| = n \text{ and } g \in \mathbb{Z}_N^*\}$. $a \xleftarrow{r} S$ means that a is chosen randomly and uniformly from set S. PPT denotes probabilistic polynomial time.

We say $\epsilon(\cdot)$(for brevity, ϵ) is a non-negligible function, if there is a constant $c \geq 2$ such that $\epsilon(n) \geq n^{-c}$. A function $\nu(\cdot)$ (for brevity, ν)is negligible, if for every constant $d \geq 0$, there exists an integer n_d such that $\nu(n) \leq n^{-d}$ for $n \geq n_d$.

Definition 1. *Let* $x = x_n \cdots x_2 x_1$. *We say the* i-*th bit* x_i *of* x *for one-way function* f *is hard, if, for any PPT algorithm* $\mathcal{A}$, *any polynomial* $Q(\cdot)$ *and significantly large* n, *given* $f(x)$, $\Pr[\mathcal{A}(f(x)) = x_i] < 1/2 + 1/Q(n)$ ☐

Definition 2. *Let* $x = x_n \cdots x_2 x_1$. *We say substring* $x_{i,j}(j < i)$ *of* x *for one-way function* f *are simultaneously hard, if for any PPT algorithm* $\mathcal{A}$, *any polynomial* $Q(\cdot)$ *and significantly large* n, *given* $f(x)$, $|\Pr[\mathcal{A}(x_{i,j}, f(x)) = 1] - \Pr[\mathcal{A}(r, f(x)) = 1]| < 1/Q(n)$, *where* r *is chosen uniformly from* $\{0, 1\}^{i-j+1}$. ☐

Factoring Intractability Assumption. Let $H_k = \{N = pq : p, q$ are odd primes and $|p| = |q| = k\}$. Then, for any PPT algorithm $\mathcal{A}$, any polynomial $Q(\cdot)$, and significantly large k, $\Pr[\mathcal{A}(N) = p : p \mid N, p \neq 1, N] < 1/Q(k)$, where the probability is taken over all $n \in H_k$ and coin tosses of $\mathcal{A}$. $\qquad\square$

2.1 Goldreich-Rosen Algorithm

For convenience, we define some probabilistic distributions as follows:
$Full_n = \langle N, g, g^R \mod N \rangle$, $Half_n = \langle N, g, g^r \mod N \rangle$, $H_n^i = \langle N, g, g^x \mod N \rangle$, where $\langle N, g \rangle \in P_n$, $R \xleftarrow{r} [1, ord(g)]$, $r \xleftarrow{r} \{0, 1\}^{\lceil \frac{n}{2} \rceil}$, $x \xleftarrow{r} \{0, 1\}^i$. So $Half_n = H_n^{\lceil \frac{n}{2} \rceil}$.

There are two basic operations about these functions: One is **Left shifting**. That is, for $Y = f_{g,N}(x) = g^x \mod N$, we compute $Y' = Y^2 = g^{2x} \mod N$ to shift all the bits of plaintext to the left by one bit. The other is **Zeroing**. That is, if the jth bit is 1, we compute $Y = f_{g,N}(x) \cdot g^{-2^{j-1}} \mod N$ to zero it.

[2] proved that $f_{g,N}(x)$ is still pseudo-random even when its input is restricted to being half the size, i.e. $Full_n$ and $Half_n$ are computable indistinguishable. By hybrid technique and that $H^{n+\omega(\log n)}$ is statistical close to $Full_n$, distinguishing $Full_n$ and $Half_n$ can be reduced to distinguishing H^i and H^{i+1} for $i \geq \lceil n/2 \rceil$. Then the distinguisher D is used as an oracle of predicting the $i + 1$th bit to construct GR algorithm. In fact, for distinguisher D, let $\beta = \Pr[D(N, g, g^x) = 1 : x \in_R \{0, 1\}^i]$ and $\gamma = \Pr[D(N, g, g^{2^i \mid \omega}) = 1 : x \in_R \{0, 1\}^i]$, then γ(resp.β) is the probability to get correct(resp. wrong) 1-answer from D, and $|\beta - \gamma| \geq 2\epsilon$. Assume $\gamma > \beta$ without loss of generality. Although D might give us erroneous answers, the gap $\gamma - \beta$ can be guaranteed. On the other hand, since we can not tell whether a carry occurs when randomizing our queries to the oracle and get the correct answer, the straightforward way fails.

In GR algorithm, given $f_{g,N}(x)$, where x is a binary string of $i+1$ bit length, we guess the top $m + 1$ bits of x. There are at most 2^{m+1} guesses, which is a polynomial on n. For each guess, we zero these bits one by one. For simplicity, assume x is of length $i - m$, where $m = \lceil \log n\epsilon^{-1} \rceil$. Initially, Let $L_{i-m} = \{0, 1\}$. A list L_l is constructed iteratively from $l = i - m - 1$ to 1 and all values $2u$ and $2u + 1$ are added into it for $u \in L_{l+1}$. But there exists an problem when constructing list L_l, that is, the size of L_l is twice that of L_{l+1}, which leads to the size of L_1 exceeds the polynomial bound. So we must use "Trimming Rule" to throw some out of L_l until its size is proper. Indeed, Since elements in L_l compose a block of consecutive items, we order the list from the largest v_{max}^l to smallest v_{min}^l. If $v_{max}^l - v_{min}^l \geq 2^m$, use Trimming Rule repeatedly until $v_{max}^l - v_{min}^l < 2^m$. Repeating this process until $l = 1$, the size of L_1 is no more than 2^m, which is a polynomial. At last, we check all $v \in L_1$ and see whether $Y = g^v \pmod{N}$. So we can find the right x.

Note that at least one of v_{max}^l and v_{min}^l is not $x_{i-m,l}$. So "Trimming Rule" is used to remove one from list L_l. To do it, a target is defined as $x' = \lceil \frac{2^{2m}}{v_{max}^l - v_{min}^l} \rceil \cdot (x - v_{min}^l \cdot 2^l)$. Let the $l + 2m + 1$st position of x be the **crucial position**(shortly denoted cp) for $l \leq i - m$. So, if v_{min}^l (resp. v_{max}^l)is the correct candidate, i.e., $v_{min}^l = x_{i-m,l}$ (resp. $v_{max}^l = x_{i-m,l}$), then the cp-bit in x' is 0 (resp. 1), and so are m bits to its both right and left. For these two cases, to deduce the value of cp-bit, we try to perform the randomization. We first shift x' to the left by repeated squaring until the cp-bit is placed in the $i + 1$st location, and then multiply the result by g^r for some randomly chosen $r \in \{0, 1\}^i$. An error might occur if a carry to the $i + 1$st location from the addition of r and shifted x' happens. The probability of a carry occurring is less than $1/2^m$. We use a polynomial number of queries to oracle with independently chosen r's and compare the fraction of 1-answers with β and γ to get the value of cp-bit. So we can discard one of v^l_{max} and v^l_{min}. If neither v^l_{max} nor v^l_{min} is correct, a carry may reach the $i + 1$st location since m bits to the right of the cp-bit in x'. Although the frequency of 1-answers is altogether different from β and γ, "Trimming Rule" can discard either one from the list safely. Using Chernoff bound, we can show that the error probability of "Trimming Rule" is exponentially small.

For the right guess of these $m + 1$ bits, procedure "Finding x" output the rest bits correctly with an overwhelming probability. As there is only polynomial guesses, we can get the right plaintext with a non-negligible probability. Once the plaintext of g^N is retrieved, the factorization of N can be obtained, which contradicts with the factoring intractability assumption, while the length of the plaintext $N \mod ord(g)$ of g^N is at most $\lceil n/2 \rceil + 1$. Assume the cost of one query to the oracle is T. The total running time of GR algorithm is $\mathcal{O}(Tn^7\epsilon^{-4})$.

3   Improved Goldreich-Rosen Algorithm

In "Trimming Rule", one element v^l_{max} or v^l_{min} is discarded each time. When we observe the construction from list L_{l+1} to list L_l in GR, $l + 1 \leq i - 2m$, we know that elements of list L_{l+1} form a block of 2^{i-m-l} consecutive strings. If either v^l_{max} or v^l_{min} is not $x_{i-m,l}$, then each in a small block neighbouring it is not correct either since these elements may share the same performance under "Trimming Rule". In the small block, term less than $2^{\mathcal{O}(\lceil \log m \rceil)-1} - 1$ must be not correct. Note that at least one of v^l_{max} and v^l_{min} is not correct (i.e., not $x_{i-m,l}$), so we discard the small block of size $2^{\mathcal{O}(\lceil \log m \rceil)}$ in the list once instead of one such that efficiency can be improved. Thus we get "improved Trimming Rule" and the improved Goldreich-Rosen algorithm (shortly by IGR) for given $f_{g,N}(x)$ in Fig. 1. To complete this improvement, we define a new target

$$x' = e \cdot (x - v^l_{min} \cdot 2^l) + 2^{m+l+\mathcal{O}(\lceil \log m \rceil)+1}, \text{ where } e = \lceil \frac{2^{2m}}{v^l_{max} - v^l_{min}} \rceil.$$

Fact 1. *If $v_{min} + j$ is the correct $x_{i-m,l}$ for some $j \in [0, 2^{\mathcal{O}(\lceil \log m \rceil)} - 1]$, then the cp-bit in x' is 0, and at least $m - \mathcal{O}(\lceil \log m \rceil) - 1$ bits to its right are all 0.*

Proof. Assume one of $v_{min}+j$ for $0 \leq j \leq 2^{\mathcal{O}(\lceil \log m \rceil)}-1$ is the correct $i-m-l+1$ top bits of x'. When we trim L_l, $2^{m+1} \geq v^l_{max} - v^l_{min} \geq 2^m$. Then

$$x' = e \cdot (v^l_{min} \cdot 2^l + j \cdot 2^l + x_{l,1} - v^l_{min} \cdot 2^l) + 2^{m+l+\mathcal{O}(\lceil \log m \rceil)+1}$$

$$\leq 2^m \cdot x_{l,1} + j \cdot 2^{l+m} + 2^{m+l+\mathcal{O}(\lceil \log m \rceil)+1}$$

$$\leq 2^{cp-m-1} + 2^{cp-(m-\mathcal{O}(\lceil \log m \rceil))-1} + 2^{cp-(m-\mathcal{O}(\lceil \log m \rceil)-1)-1}.$$

Finding x: input $\langle N, g \rangle \in P_n$, index i and $Y = g^x \pmod{N}$, where $|x| = i - m$

1. Let $L_{i-m} = \{0, 1\}$
2. For $l = i - m - 1$ to 1, do the following:
   (a) Let $L_l = \{2u, 2u + 1 : u \in L_{l+1}\}$, order the list from the largest v^l_{max} to smallest v^l_{min}.
   (b) If $v^l_{max} - v^l_{min} \geq 2^m$, use **Improved Trimming Rule** repeatedly until $v^l_{max} - v^l_{min} < 2^m$.
3. Check all $v \in L_1$, and see whether $Y = g^v \pmod{N}$. If yes, that is the right x.

Improved Trimming Rule(for current L_l, v^l_{max} and v^l_{min}):

1. Compute $Y' = g^{x'} = \left(Y \cdot g^{-v^l_{min} \cdot 2^l} \right)^e \cdot g^{2m+l+\mathcal{O}(\lceil \log m \rceil)+1}$, where $Y = g^x$ and
   $e = \lceil \frac{2^{2m}}{v^l_{max} - v^l_{min}} \rceil$.
2. Shift x' to the left by $i + 1 - cp$ bits by computing $Y'' = (Y')^{2^{i+1-cp}}$.
3. Choose $t(n) = n^4/\varepsilon^2$ elements $r_1, \cdots, r_{t(n)} \in \{0,1\}^i$ randomly.
4. For each $1 \leq k \leq t(n)$, query the oracle for $Y'' \cdot g^{r_k} \pmod{N}$. Let b_k denote its answer(i.e. $b_k = D(g^{x' \cdot 2^{i+1-cp}+r_k})$) and set $M = \sum_{k=1}^{t(n)} b_k / t(n)$.
5. If $M \leq (\beta + \frac{\gamma - \beta}{2})$, discard $v^l_{max} - j$, $0 \leq j \leq 2^{\mathcal{O}(\lceil \log m \rceil)} - 1$ from L_l. Otherwise (i.e. $M > (\beta + \frac{\gamma - \beta}{2})$) discard $v^l_{min} + j$, $0 \leq j \leq 2^{\mathcal{O}(\lceil \log m \rceil)} - 1$.

Fig. 1. Improved Goldreich-Rosen algorithm

So for each $v_{min} + j$, the cp-bit in x' is 0, and the $m - \mathcal{O}(\lceil \log m \rceil) - 1$ bits to its right are all 0. □

All $v_{min} + j$ would share the same success probability in the randomization technique, as they share the same error probability $\frac{1}{2^{m-\mathcal{O}(\lceil \log m \rceil)+1}}$ from a carry into the $(i + 1)$st location for the addition of r and the shifted x'.

Fact 2. If one of $v_{max} - j$ for $j \in [0, 2^{\mathcal{O}(\lceil \log m \rceil)} - 1]$ is the correct $x_{i-m,l}$, then the cp-bit in x' is 1, and at least $m - \mathcal{O}(\lceil \log m \rceil) - 2$ bits to its right are all 0.

Proof. Assume one of $v_{max} - j$ for $0 \leq j \leq 2^{\mathcal{O}(\lceil \log m \rceil)} - 1$ is the correct $i - m - l + 1$ top bits of x'. Then

$$x' = e \cdot (v^l_{max} \cdot 2^l - j \cdot 2^l + x_{l,1} - v^l_{min} \cdot 2^l) + 2^{m+l+\mathcal{O}(\lceil \log m \rceil)+1}$$
$$= 2^{2m+l} + \delta \cdot (v^l_{max} - v^l_{min}) \cdot 2^l + e \cdot x_{l,1} - e \cdot j \cdot 2^l$$
$$+ 2^{m+l+\mathcal{O}(\lceil \log m \rceil)+1} \leq 2^{2m+l} + 2^{m+l+\mathcal{O}(\lceil \log m \rceil)+1},$$

where $\delta = e - \frac{2^{2m}}{v^l_{max} - v^l_{min}}$. Note that $2^{m+1} \geq v^l_{max} - v^l_{min} \geq 2^m$. Since $\delta \cdot (v^l_{max} - v^l_{min}) \cdot 2^l \leq 2^{cp-m}$, $e \cdot x_{l,1} \leq 2^{cp-m-1}$ and $0 \leq 2^{m+l+\mathcal{O}(\log m)+1} - e \cdot j \cdot 2^l \leq 2^{cp-m+\mathcal{O}(\lceil \log m \rceil)}$, for each $v_{max} - j$, $0 \leq j \leq 2^{\mathcal{O}(\lceil \log m \rceil)} - 1$, the cp-bit in x' is 1, and the $m - \mathcal{O}(\lceil \log m \rceil) - 2$ bits to its right are all 0. □

As to the case the correct $x_{i-m,l}$ is not in the intervals above, we do not care about it, because whatever the algorithm discards, the correct $x_{i-m,l}$ is still in the list. In order to prove that it is reasonable to discard $2^{\mathcal{O}(\lceil \log m \rceil)}$ elements at once, we only need to make sure "Improved Trimming Rule" is right for every involved element. For this purpose, we need to study the success probability for some particular element.

Lemma 1 (Chernoff bound). *Let $X_1, X_2, \cdots, X_n$ be mutually independent random variables over $\{0,1\}$ and let $\mu = \sum_{i=1}^{n} E[X_i]$. Then for any $c > 0$,*

$$\Pr\left[\left|\sum_{i=1}^{n} X_i - \mu\right| \geq c\mu\right] \leq 2^{-c^2 n/2}.$$

We define **event 1** to be that the correct item is discarded in a block, that is, a correct element is discarded, and **event 2** to be that the correct item is in a block and the block is discarded by "Improved Trimming Rule". Then the probability of **event 1** is estimated in Lemma 2 and that of **event 2** is estimated in Theorem 1 which involves ranging over all possible cases of the difference j between v_{min} (or v_{max}) and the correct item.

Lemma 2. *The probability of* **event 1** *is exponentially small.*

Proof. Since only one of v_{min} and v_{max} is correct, without loss of generality, we assume that for some j, $0 \leq j \leq 2^{\mathcal{O}(\lceil \log m \rceil)} - 1$, $v_{min} + j$ is the correct $i - m - l + 1$ top bits of x'. Let δ denote the shifted x' by $i + 1 - cp$ to its left, i.e. $\delta = x' \cdot 2^{i+1-cp}$. By Fact 1 we know $\delta \leq 2^{i-m+\mathcal{O}(\lceil \log m \rceil)+1}$. Each time we query oracle distinguisher D, the expectation of oracle answer b_k on $g^{\delta + r_k}$ is

$$E(b_k) = \Pr[D(g^{\delta + r_k}) = 1 | 0 \leq r_k \leq 2^i - 1 - \delta] \cdot \Pr[0 \leq r_k \leq 2^i - 1 - \delta]$$
$$+ \Pr[D(g^{\delta + r_k}) = 1 | 2^i - 1 - \delta \leq r_k \leq 2^i - 1] \cdot \Pr[2^i - 1 - \delta \leq r_k \leq 2^i - 1]$$
$$\leq \frac{\beta \cdot 2^i}{2^i - \delta} \cdot \frac{2^i - \delta}{2^i} + 1 \cdot \frac{\delta}{2^i} = \beta + \frac{\delta}{2^i}.$$

$$\Pr[\textbf{event 1} \text{ on } v_{min} + j] = \Pr\left[\sum_{k=1}^{t(n)} b_k > (\beta + \frac{\gamma - \beta}{2}) \cdot t(n)\right]$$
$$\leq \Pr\left[\left|\sum_{k=1}^{t(n)} b_k - E(\sum_{k=1}^{t(n)} b_k)\right| > (\beta + \frac{\gamma - \beta}{2}) \cdot t(n) - E(\sum_{k=1}^{t(n)} b_k)\right]$$
$$= \Pr\left[\left|\sum_{k=1}^{t(n)} b_k - E(\sum_{k=1}^{t(n)} b_k)\right| > \lambda \cdot E(\sum_{k=1}^{t(n)} b_k)\right],$$

where $\lambda = \frac{(\beta + \frac{\gamma-\beta}{2}) \cdot t(n) - E(\sum_{k=1}^{t(n)} b_k)}{E(\sum_{k=1}^{t(n)} b_k)}$. As $\lambda \geq \frac{\epsilon}{4}$ for significantly large n, by Lemma 1, $\Pr[\text{discard } v_{min} + j] \leq 2^{-\frac{\lambda^2 \cdot t(n)}{2}} \leq 2^{-\frac{n^4}{32}} \leq 2^{-\mathcal{O}(n^3)}$. $\square$

Theorem 1. *The success probability of retrieving x in IGR is exponentially close to 1.*

Proof. By Lemma 1, for a particular element, the success probability for "Improved Trimming Rule" is greater than $1 - 2^{\mathcal{O}(-n^3)}$. Discarding more elements at once, the success probability is at least $1 - \Pr[\textbf{event 2} \text{occurs}]$. When **event 2** occurs, discarding one of involved elements are wrong. So $\Pr[\textbf{event 2} \text{occurs}] \leq 1 - \prod_j(1 - \Pr[\textbf{event 1} \text{on } v_{min} + j])$. The success probability is at least $(1 - 2^{\mathcal{O}(-n^3)})2^{\mathcal{O}(\lceil \log m \rceil)} > 1 - \mathcal{O}(\frac{\log n\epsilon^{-1}}{2^{n^3}})$, which is negligible close to 1.

During the construction from L_{j+1} to L_j, we use "Improved Trimming Rule" for $\frac{2^m}{2^{\mathcal{O}(\lceil \log m \rceil)}}$ times at most, which is still a polynomial about n. At the same time, we need to run "Improved Trimming Rule" for $i - 2m = \mathcal{O}(n)$ list at most. So for the right guess of the top $m + 1$ bits, we can retrieve the rest bits of x with probability negligible close to 1. After checking all the guesses, we can retrieve the right plaintext with a probability exponentially close to 1. The proof is complete.

Theorem 1 shows it is reasonably to discard $2^{\mathcal{O}(\lceil \log m \rceil)}$ at once. All $v_{min}+j$ (or $v_{max}-j$) have the same success probability in the randomization technique, since they share the same error probability less than $\frac{1}{2^{m-\mathcal{O}(\lceil \log m \rceil)}}$ from a carry into the $i+1$st location with the addition of r and the shifted x'. Running "Improved Trimming Rule", we discard $2^{\mathcal{O}(\lceil \log m \rceil)}$ consecutive elements at once, so running time of IGR is $2^{m+1} \cdot T \cdot (i - 2m) \cdot \frac{2^m}{2^{\mathcal{O}(\lceil \log m \rceil)}} \cdot n^4/\epsilon^2 = \mathcal{O}(Tn^7\epsilon^{-4}/\log n\epsilon^{-1})$. Comparing with GR algorithm, we reduce it by a factor $\mathcal{O}(\log n\epsilon^{-1})$.

4   The Improvement Tolerating Higher Error Probability

In Sect. 3, we tolerate probability $\frac{1}{2^{m-\mathcal{O}(\lceil \log m \rceil)-2}}$ to have a carry. It is just slightly larger than that of GR. If we could tolerate higher probability than GR, more bits could be discard at once.

If we take $\frac{1}{2^{(1-\frac{1}{2c})m}}$ as tolerable error probability, we construct algorithm IGR', similar to IGR except for $x' = e \cdot (x - v_{min}^l \cdot 2^l) + 2^{m+\frac{m}{2c}+l+1}$. We discard $2^{\frac{m}{2c}}$ elements in "Improved Trimming Rule" at once. Similar to the analysis in Sect. 3, we have

Fact 3. *If $v_{min} + j$, $j \in [0, 2^{\frac{m}{2c}} - 1]$ is the correct $x_{i-m,l}$, then the cp-bit in x' is 0, and $m - \frac{m}{2c} - 2$ bits to its right are all 0.*

Fact 4. *If $v_{min} + j$, $j \in [0, 2^{\frac{m}{2c}} - 1]$ is the correct $x_{i-m,l}$, then the cp-bit in x' is 1, and $m - \frac{m}{2c} - 2$ bits to its right are all 0.*

Theorem 2. *The error probability of retrieving x with IGR' is negligible.*

Proof. the proof is almost identical to Theorem 1, except for $\delta \leq 2^{i-m+\frac{m}{2c}+1}$, and $\lambda \geq \dfrac{\epsilon - \frac{1}{2^{m-\frac{m}{2c}-2}}}{2} \geq \dfrac{\epsilon - \frac{4}{n^{1-1/2c}\epsilon^{1/2c}} \cdot \epsilon}{2} \geq \dfrac{\epsilon - \frac{4}{n^{1/4}} \cdot \epsilon}{2} \geq \dfrac{\epsilon - \frac{4\epsilon}{5}}{2} \geq \dfrac{\epsilon}{10}$.

Similar to the analysis in Sect. 3, we discard $2^{\frac{m}{2c}}$ consecutive elements at once, and the running time of IGR' algorithm is $2^{m+1} \cdot T \cdot (i - 2m) \cdot \frac{2^m}{2^{\frac{m}{2c}}} \cdot n^4/\epsilon^2 = \mathcal{O}(Tn^7\epsilon^{-4}/(n\epsilon^{-1})^{\frac{1}{2c}})$. We reduce it by a factor $\mathcal{O}((n\epsilon^{-1})^{\frac{1}{2c}})$ comparing with GR algorithm.

5   Further Remarks

We improve Goldreich and Rosen's algorithm on bit security of exponentiation function modulo a composite. The Improved algorithm reduces the running time of Goldreich and Rosen's algorithm by a factor $\mathcal{O}(\log n\epsilon^{-1})$. If we could tolerate error probability $\frac{1}{2^{(1-\frac{1}{2c})m}}$, the factor would be $\mathcal{O}((n\epsilon^{-1})^{\frac{1}{2c}})$. Our improvement could be also applied to all the algorithms using the "Trimming Rule" to better their efficiency, such as in [5–8] and therein.

References

1. Alexi, W., Chor, B., Goldreich, O., Schnorr, C.: RSA and rabin functions: certain parts are as hard as the whole. SIAM J. Comput. **17**(2), 194–209 (1988)
2. Goldreich, O., Rosen, V.: On the security of modular exponentiation with application to the construction of pseudorandom generators. J. Cryptology **16**, 71–93 (2003)
3. Goldreich, O., Rosen, V.: On the security of modular exponentiation with application to the construction of pseudorandom generators. ECCC, TR02-049 (2002)
4. Håstad, J., Nüsland, M.: The security of all RSA and discrete log bits. J. ACM **51**(2), 187–230 (2004)
5. Håstad, J., Schrift, A.W., Shamir, A.: The discrete logarithm modulo a composite hides $O(n)$ bits. J. Comput. Syst. Sci. **47**, 376–404 (1993)
6. Su, D., Lv, K.: A new hard-core predicate of Paillier's trapdoor function. In: Roy, B., Sendrier, N. (eds.) INDOCRYPT 2009. LNCS, vol. 5922, pp. 263–271. Springer, Heidelberg (2009)
7. Su, D., Lv, K.: Pailliers trapdoor function hides $\Theta(n)$ bits. Sci. China Inform. Sci. **54**(9), 1827–1836 (2011)
8. Su, D., Wang, K., Lv, K.: The bit security of two variants of Pailliers trapdoor function. Chinese J. Comput. **6**, 1050–1059 (2010)

Security Protocol (Short Paper)

Secure Outsourced Bilinear Pairings Computation for Mobile Devices

Tomasz Hyla$^{(\boxtimes)}$ and Jerzy Pejaś

Faculty of Computer Science and Information Technology,
West Pomeranian University of Technology, Szczecin, Poland
{thyla,jpejas}@zut.edu.pl

Abstract. The cloud can be used to outsource data storage or data computation. Data computation outsourcing enables to move computationally expensive operations outside a mobile device. Many pairing-based cryptographic schemes are designed to enable documents' encryption while fulfilling some defined security requirements. In practice, client applications should be implemented for mobile devices. Their computational capabilities are significantly lower than standard computers. Thus, advanced cryptographic calculations, like bilinear pairing calculation, might take too much time for a good user experience. In this paper, we analyse the possibilities to securely outsource bilinear pairings computation from a mobile device to possibly dishonest servers. Several test scenarios were implemented. Also, we have modified one of the pairing-based schemes that allows to encrypt and decrypt documents and we have created its secure outsourced version. Next, we have tested execution times of encryption and decryption algorithms of the original scheme and its outsourced version. The tests were conducted using different outsourcing models. The execution times showing time spent on the mobile device and the server are presented and discussed. The tests have shown that in certain conditions outsourcing bilinear pairing calculation can speed up overall computation time. Also, it simplifies implementation on different mobile operating systems.

Keywords: Secure outsourcing · Secure delegation protocol · Bilinear pairing · Encryption · Mobile device

1 Introduction

The cloud is often used in mobile applications to outsource data storage or computation. Difficulty of implementation and code maintenance together with slower mobile processors cause that moving complex and computationally intensive parts of the code to external servers are often used to simplify mobile application.

The cloud can be used to outsource data storage or data computation. In recent years, many cloud drive' services became available. Some of them provide client-side encryption (e.g., in a web browser) to ensure privacy, but privacy of most of the drives is based on the assumption that the cloud servers are honest or trusted. Also, many techniques have been proposed to better secure data. S. Foresti in [1] described a comprehensive solution for protecting sensitive information when it is stored on third parties system

© Springer International Publishing AG 2016
J. Chen et al. (Eds.): NSS 2016, LNCS 9955, pp. 519–529, 2016.
DOI: 10.1007/978-3-319-46298-1_34

outside owner's sole control. An access control solution for data storage in outsourcing scenarios using a re-encryption execution model was presented by [2]. The solution that guarantee assured file deletion was proposed by [3] and the schema that allows unauthorized modifications detection by [4]. M. Sujithra et al. [5] described how mobile data can be securely stored in the remote cloud using cryptographic techniques with minimal performance degradation.

Data computation outsourcing enables to move computationally expensive operations outside a mobile device. When outsourcing computation to third party servers, one must consider two questions. Firstly, is it required that data sent to be computed to remain secret? Secondly, is it required to have a tool enabling results' verification? Several techniques that enable verifying outsourced computation results done by untrusted servers have been proposed in the literature (e.g., [6]). More difficult is to process data in such a way, that an untrusted server will not have possibility to see original data and still it will be able to perform requested computation. It usually requires to do some pre- and post-processing in a mobile device.

In new cryptographic schemes based on bilinear pairings, e.g., schemes that enable document encryption, the number of computationally intensive operations (bilinear pairing calculation, point multiplication or exponentiation on elliptic curves) can cause that total decryption and encryption times will be too long for a good user experience.

1.1 Our Contribution

Many pairing-based cryptography schemes are designed to enable encryption or signing of documents while fulfilling some defined security requirements. In practice, client application should be implemented also for mobile devices. Their computational capabilities are significantly lower than standard computers.

In this paper, we show how computations can be outsourced from a mobile device to a server using different outsourcing models and we discuss required infrastructure. The possibilities to securely outsource bilinear pairings computation from a mobile device to possibly dishonest servers were analysed. Several test scenarios were implemented using Miracl library [7]. Three algorithms for secure outsourced bilinear pairing computation were tested. Also, we have modified one of the pairing-based schemes, i.e., IE-CBE scheme [8] (the scheme allows to encrypt and decrypt documents using implicit and explicit certificates) and create its outsourced version called SO-IE-CBE. We have tested speed of encryption and decryption algorithms of the original scheme and its outsourced version. The tests were conducted using different outsourcing models. The execution times showing time spent on the mobile device and the server are presented and discussed.

Our main goal was to find a way to speed up our Implicit end Explicit Certificates-Based Encryption (IE-CBE) scheme that was implemented and tested in our previous research project. In the paper, we modify that scheme and show how in different outsourcing scenarios calculations can be accelerated.

1.2 Paper Organisation

The remainder of this paper is organized as follows. Section 2 contains short descriptions of algorithms used further in tests, i.e., the algorithms for secure pairing outsourcing and the implicit and explicit certificate-based encryption scheme. In Sect. 3, different possibilities for secure outsourcing of bilinear pairings are mentioned. Next, the secure outsourced version of IE-CBE is introduced and discussed. The tests' results for different outsourcing scenarios are presented in Sect. 4. The paper ends with conclusions about outsourcing bilinear pairings from a mobiles devices.

2 Delegation of Pairing Computation

In pairing-based cryptography, computation of a bilinear pairing is one of the most time-consuming operation. Definition, notations and details about bilinear pairings can be found in [9].

Delegation of pairing calculation must be performed in such a way that an untrusted helper (an outsourced server) does not have possibility to find the values A, B from $\hat{e}(A, B)$ and outsourcer (a device with limited capabilities) can verify correctness of a pairing value. Formal security definitions, models and notations for secure outsourcing of cryptographic computations can be found in [10].

One of the secure paring delegation algorithms was presented by Chevallier-Mames et al. [11, 12] (*Alg. CM_1* further in the paper). The algorithm achieves unconditional security (security is not based on any computational assumption). The algorithm takes as an input two random points $A, B \in G_1$, and the result is $\hat{e}(A, B)$. The algorithm assumes also that a computationally limited device (outsourcer T) and a server U receive the generators $P, Q \in G_1$, while additionally receives the value of $\hat{e}(P, Q)$. The main drawback of the algorithm is that it requires to perform some computationally expensive operations like point multiplication and exponentiations.

We can use simpler approach, when we resign from the possibility to verify the correctness of a pairing calculated by U. For example, when pairing calculation is delegated to U in some function performed by T and the received value is verified later in the function. In that situation, we can use a simple, not secure pairing delegation algorithm mentioned by Chevallier-Mames et al. [11] (*Alg. CM_2* further in the paper).

Another *algorithm Pair* [12] requires less expensive calculations than *Alg. CM_1* and provides the similar level of security. However, it is secure in *one-malicious version of two untrusted program model* [10]. In that model, we have U_1 and U_2 from which one is honest. This model has an assumption that U_1 and U_2 communicate only trough T, which might be difficult to achieve in real world scenarios. Also, in *Alg. Pair T* calls subroutine *Rand* which returns a tuple of six values, including the result of the pairing. The tuples can be pre-calculated, probably by some kind of a trusted server.

Computationally intensive operations in pairing-based cryptography are also point multiplications and modular exponentiations. Time required to calculate point multiplication in some cases is similar to time required to calculate Tate pairing [13]. Algorithms for outsource-secure modular exponentiations was presented in [10].

We have proposed IE-CBE encryption scheme in 2014 [8]. The scheme has been built on a new paradigm called Implicit and Explicit Certificates-Based Public Key Cryptography (IEC-PKC). The idea of this paradigm is an extension of PKC paradigm [14] and combines a strong authentication of the user's identity, its public key and relationship between these two elements. Moreover, any encryption scheme with this mechanism should be immune to the DoD attack [15]. The IE-CBE scheme is IND-CCA and DoD-Free secure in the random oracle model, relative to the hardness of the standard k-CAA hard problem [8].

3   Secure Outsourced Implicit and Explicit Certificate-Based Encryption Scheme

In this section, different possibilities of secure outsourcing of bilinear pairings are mentioned. Next, the secure outsourced version of IE-CBE is introduced and discussed.

3.1   Outsourcing Models

The pairing computation can be outsourced from mobile devices because of three basic reasons: implementation difficulty, computation speed and power efficiency.

The implementation of IE-CBE scheme requires to use a library for pairing calculations. In case of mobile devices, current API of three most popular mobile operating systems (i.e., Android, iOS, Windows Phone) does not support pairing computation. It is possible to call C libraries like Miracl [7], but its integration might be difficult. The most important reason for computation outsourcing is speed, which is expected to be significantly lower on mobile devices.

The computation of pairing $\alpha = \hat{e}(A,\ B)$ can be outsourced from a mobile device T to a server U using the following models:

- **Model 0 – No Outsourcing:** calculations are done solely on a mobile device;
- **Model 1 – Semi-Secure Outsourcing:** U does not know A and B. If U is dishonest, no mechanism exist that enables T to verify if α is correct.
- **Model 2 – Secure Outsourcing:** U does not know A and B. T can verify if α is correct. U can be dishonest.
- **Model 3 – Full Outsourcing:** a mobile device is only a thin client (provides only an interface), requires a fully trusted and honest U. A and B are send to U in an overt form.

3.2   Outsourced Encryption Schemes

The SO-IE-CBE scheme is a modified version of the IE-CBE scheme that is using secure outsource algorithm for pairing calculation (Model 2). The IE-CBE scheme, involves three entities: a trusted authority TA, an encrypter S, a decrypter R. The S and R entities use four algorithms from the IE-CBE scheme: two from setup phase (*Create-User, Set-Private-Key*) – executed only once per entity and two algorithms (*Encrypt, Decrypt*) that can be used many times. However, algorithm *Create-User* does not involve pairing calculations.

Two outsourced versions of IE-CBE scheme are proposed:

– **SO-IE-CBE:** SO-IE-CBE is IE-CBE scheme with three modified algorithms (*SO-Set-Private-Key, SO-Encrypt, SO-Decrypt*). The scheme uses a secure outsourcing algorithm **SO-PAR** for pairing calculation. The **SO-PAR** algorithm is a secure outsourcing algorithm for a symmetric pairing calculation, that takes as an input A, $B \in G_1$ and returns $\hat{e}(A, B) \in G_2$.

– **O-IE-CBE:** O-IE-CBE is IE-CBE scheme with three modified algorithms (*O-Set-Private-Key, O-Encrypt, O-Decrypt*). The scheme uses a semi-secure outsourcing algorithm **O-PAR** for pairing calculation. The **O-PAR** algorithm is a semi-secure outsourcing algorithm for a symmetric pairing calculation, that takes as an input A, $B \in G_1$ and returns $\hat{e}(A, B) \in G_2$.

SO-IE-CBE and O-IE-CBE schemes are similar. They use different algorithm for outsourced pairing calculation. Also, the *O-Encrypt* algorithm has an additional step (f), which is optional in *SO-Encrypt* (see below). The O-IE-CBE scheme is able to detect potentials pairing error. However, the error can be indistinguishable for other possible errors like a wrong secret key error. The SO-IE-CBE algorithms are as follows:

SO-Set-Private-Key. An entity R calculates a full private key Sk_{ID_R}:

(a) R calculates the values A_1, B_1, A_2, B_2:

$$A_1 = Sk'_{ID_R}$$
$$B_1 = Y_{ID_R} + q_{ID_R} X_{ID_R} + \bar{q}_{ID_R} \left(\bar{P}_0 + q_{ID_R} P \right) \tag{1}$$
$$A_2 = P; B_2 = s_{1_{ID_R}} s_{2_{ID_R}} \bar{P}_0$$

(b) R runs **SO-PAR** algorithm twice:

$$eAB_1 = \mathbf{SO} - \mathbf{PAR}(A_1, B_1); eAB_2 = \mathbf{SO} - \mathbf{PAR}(A_2, B_2) \tag{2}$$

(c) R verifies correctness of Sk'_{ID_R}:

$$eAB_1 = eAB_2 \tag{3}$$

(d) R calculates a second part of the private key:

$$\overline{Sk}_{ID_R} = s_{1_{ID_R}}^{-1} \left(s_{2_{ID_R}} + \bar{q}_{ID_R} \right) Sk'_{ID_R} = \frac{1}{s_{TA} + q_{ID_R}} Y_{ID_R} \tag{4}$$

(e) R formulates a private key for entity R in the form: $Sk_{ID_R} = \left(s_{2_{ID_R}}, \overline{Sk}_{ID_R} \right)$.

SO-Encrypt. To encrypt the message $m \in \{0, 1\}^n$, the sender S:

(a) S calculates $q_{ID_R} = H_1(CI_{ID_R})$;

(b) S calculates the values B_1 and B_6:

$$B_1 = q_{ID_R}Y_{ID_R} + Z_{ID_R}; B_6 = r(q_{ID_R}Y_{ID_R} + Z_{ID_R}) \tag{5}$$

(c) S runs a **SO-PAR** algorithm six times:

$$eAB_1 = \mathbf{SO} - \mathbf{PAR}(Cert_{ID_R}, B_1); eAB_2 = \mathbf{SO} - \mathbf{PAR}(P, Y_{ID_R}) \tag{6}$$

$$eAB_3 = \mathbf{SO} - \mathbf{PAR}(X_{ID_R}, \tilde{P}_0); eAB_4 = \mathbf{SO} - \mathbf{PAR}(Y_{ID_R}, \bar{P}_0) \tag{7}$$

$$eAB_5 = \mathbf{SO} - \mathbf{PAR}(Z_{ID_R}, P); eAB_6 = \mathbf{SO} - \mathbf{PAR}(Cert_{ID_R}, B_6) \tag{8}$$

(d) S verifies the authenticity of the certificate $Cert_{ID_R}$:

$$eAB_1 = eAB_2 \tag{9}$$

$$eAB_3 = eAB_4 = eAB_5 \tag{10}$$

Remark. When Eqs. (9) and (10) are true, then components of public key Pk_{ID_R} are authentic, which implies that a public key Pk_{ID_R} belonging to the entity with an identity ID_R is authentic.

(e) if the verification result from the previous step is positive, then S chooses a random number $v \in \{0, 1\}^n$ and calculates:

$$r = H_2(v, m, ID_R, Pk_{ID_R}) \tag{11}$$

$$U = r(\bar{P}_0 + q_{ID_R}P) \tag{12}$$

$$k = H_3(U, eAB_6, r(Y_{ID_R} + q_{ID_R}X_{ID_R})) \tag{13}$$

$$V = v \oplus k, W = m \oplus H_4(v) \tag{14}$$

(f) Optional step (obligatory in O-IE-CBE scheme). S verify if the value eAB_6 was calculated properly:

$$eAB_1 = (eAB_6)^r \tag{15}$$

(g) S creates the ciphertext $C = (U, V, W)$ and sends it to a recipient R.

SO-Decrypt. A decryption entity R reconstruct message m using the ciphertext C.

(a) R runs a **SO-PAR** algorithm:

$$eAB_1 = \mathbf{SO - PAR}\left(\overline{Sk}_{ID_R}, U\right);$$ (16)

(b) R calculates:

$$k' = H_3\left(U, eAB_1, s_{2_{ID_R}} U\right)$$ (17)

$$v' = V \oplus k'$$ (18)

$$m' = W \oplus H_4\left(v'\right)$$ (19)

$$r' = H_2\left(v', m', ID_R, Pk_{ID_R}\right)$$ (20)

(c) if $U \neq r'\left(H_1\left(CI_{ID_R}\right)P + \bar{P}_0\right)$, then decryption process is incorrect, otherwise m' is a correct plain text corresponding to the ciphertext $C = (U, V, W)$.

The basic IE-CBE scheme is proven IND-CCA and DoD-Free secure [8] in the random oracle model, relative to the hardness of the standard k-CAA hard problem. The only difference between the SO-IE-CBE scheme (using secure outsourcing) and basic scheme is a secure outsourcing algorithm for pairing calculations. The algorithm is unconditionally secure (security is not based on any computational assumption, e.g., [11, 12]). Hence, usage of such algorithm does not change the security of the basic IE-CBE scheme, as it provides the same security properties as a paring calculation algorithm from a local resources.

The O-IE-CBE scheme uses semi-secure outsourcing algorithm for pairing calculation. In this version of the scheme, the outsourcing algorithm is not proven to return correct results. However, the O-IE-CBE has a few steps (Set-Private-Key: step (c); Encrypt: steps (d) and (f); Decrypt step (c)) that allow to verify the results of pairing calculation. In these steps incorrect results from the outsourcing algorithms will be detected, because of that the O-IE-CBE has the same level of security as basic scheme. Proof of that is trivial and will be omitted here.

4   Performance Tests

The pairing calculation is the most time consuming operation in the pairing-based cryptographic schemes. The IE-CBE scheme and its outsourced versions (O-IE-CBE, SO-IE-CBE) were implemented to test their performance using different pairing outsourcing models. O-IE-CBE uses outsourcing algorithm *Alg. CM_1*. SO-IE-CBE v1 and SO-IE-CBE v2 use algorithm *Alg. CM_1* and algorithm *Alg. Pair*, respectively.

The schemes were implemented using MIRACL library [7]. The test environment consisted of a server (Intel Core i7-4700MQ processor - 7752 points in cpubenchmark.net benchmark, 32 GB RAM, 256 GB SSD drive, Windows 10 Pro 64 bit) and a tablet (Intel Atom Z3745 processor - 1118 points in cpubenchmark.net benchmark, 2 GB RAM, 16 GB SSD drive, Windows 10). The server U and the tablet T were both connected to a separated Wi-Fi network. In test, Type 1 symmetric pairing built on GF(p) curve were used (in MIRACL library: MR_PAIRING_SSP, AES-128 security GF(p)). Time was measured using C++ *chrono* library. All results are the average of 1,000 repetitions. All test programs are using a single thread.

The pairing calculation time is around 4 times longer on the tablet (Table 1). In the test environment, the pairing time using algorithm *Alg. CM_2* is comparable to calculation time on the tablet. However, on the market is easy to find a server processor that should be 2–3 faster on single core operations (based on performance tests from www.cpu-benchmark.net benchmark). In that case, the *Alg. CM_2* would be faster. The *Alg. CM_1* have a big overhead, and even with better ratio of server to tablet CPU speed, it would be difficult to achieve faster speed than pairing calculation on the tablet. The outsourced pairing calculation time includes 9 ms of time used to transfer data from T to U and from U to T.

Table 1. The pairing calculation time

No.	Operation	Time [ms]
1	Server U - pairing	54,7
2	Tablet T - pairing	237,3
3	Outsourced pairing $T + U$ (Alg. CM_1)	874,2
4	Outsourced pairing $T + U$ (Alg. CM_2)	237,9
5	Outsourced pairing $T + U$ (Alg. Pair)	233,7

It should be noted that algorithms *Alg. CM_1* and *Alg. Pair* internally require to calculate 4 pairings. The pairings can be calculated simultaneously. In such case overall time would significantly shorter (around 70 ms for *Alg. Pair*).

The comparison of encryption and decryption time of AES secret key (32 bytes) using different version of IE-CBE schemes is presented on the Fig. 1.

The IE-CBE Encryption algorithm requires to calculate 6 bilinear pairings. Because of that, the SO-IE-CBE Encryption algorithm (using secure outsourcing *Alg. CM_1*) execution time is more than 5 s, which is in practice unacceptable. The O-IE-CBE and SO-IE-CBE v2 encryption algorithms are a little bit faster with comparison to not outsourced version of the algorithm. Decryption algorithm contains only one pairing operation, but the speed ratios of different version of the algorithms are similar as that in Encryption algorithms. In the test scenario, the average data transfer time between T and U was 9 ms and is almost invisible on the Fig. 1. In scenarios involving communication over the Internet, data transfer time would be in usually between 50 and 200 ms.

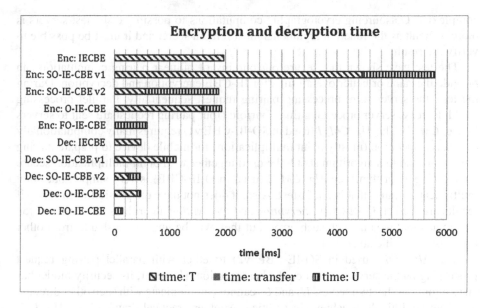

Fig. 1. Comparison of encryption and decryption time

5 Conclusions

Mobile devices like tablets and smartphones are very popular and in practice every system that manages any kind of documents must include a mobile application. Three types of infrastructure can be used to deploy the application using pairing-based cryptographic schemes to a mobile device. Two boundary cases can be called *mobile only* and *thin client*. In *mobile only* infrastructure, all cryptographic calculations are done on a mobile device. The test have shown that in case of IE-CBE scheme it is possible, though the encryption time below 2 s is on the threshold time accepted by users. The time could be shortened using parallel pairings' processing, but it would increase the complexity of application. In our opinion, the complexity of implementation (and later maintenance) of pairing based cryptographic schemes for three major mobile operating systems is the major reason to move the most complicated operations outside a mobile.

In a *thin client* type infrastructure (FO-IE-CBE version of IE-CBE scheme) the mobile application is only an interface (it can be a web application). This is the fastest option as servers are several time faster. Also, the implementation is simpler and must be done only for one operating system. The main drawback of such solution is the necessity to have a fully trusted, honest server for outsourcing all computations. This could be acceptable in enterprise-wide applications, but in other cases, it would be extremely difficult to setup such server that would be acceptable by millions of users.

The intermediate approach (i.e., outsourcing only the most computation expensive operation without compromising the security and without the need for an additional trusted server) enables to increase the mobile application speed and lower the code complexity. Outsourcing cryptographic computations to possibly dishonest servers is more difficult as the function arguments must remain secret and it must be possible to verify the result.

The test have shown that secure outsourcing of bilinear pairing computation can provide the same or better overall time for IE-CBE encryption and decryption. During the test, the server were processing pairing request sequentially. Parallel processing could decrease server processing time fourfold (four pairing request are sent to servers in *Alg. CM_1*). The *Alg. CM_1* (used in SO-IE-CBE v1) requires many computationally expensive operation (mostly point multiplication) for mobile device to prepare pairing arguments and this algorithm should be used together with point multiplication secure outsourcing algorithm. The *Alg. CM_2* (used in O-IE-CBE) is very simple, but point multiplication cause that is not fastest. Also, it does not have the possibility to verify if results are correct. O-IE-CBE *Encryption* and *Decryption* algorithms have verification statements that would catch such error, but they will be undistinguishable from other errors (e.g., certificate errors).

The *Alg. Pair* (used in SO-IE-CBE v2) together with parallel pairing request processing on the servers would be the best solution. However, its security model has an assumptions that two servers U_1 and U_2 cannot communicate with each other directly. This can be difficult to achieve in practice. Another practical drawback of *Alg. Pair* algorithm is the need for pre-calculated tuple of values (including a pairing result). If we assume that a mobile application does not have possibility to calculate pairing, then an additional secure, honest server is required.

References

1. Foresti, S.: Preserving Privacy in Data Outsourcing. Advances in Information Security, vol. 51. Springer, Heidelberg (2011)
2. Zhang, Y., Chen, J.-L.: Efficient access control of sensitive data service in outsourcing scenarios. IACR Cryptology ePrint Archive 2010. 242 (2010)
3. Patil, P.D., Badre, R.R.: Access control and file deletion as a service in cloud computing. Int. J. Comput. Technol. Appl. **5**, 1057–1060 (2014)
4. Al-Sakran, H.O.: Accessing secured data in cloud computing environment. Int. J. Netw. Secur. Appl. **7**(1), 19–28 (2015)
5. Sujithra, M., Padmavathi, G., Narayanan, S.: Mobile device data security: a cryptographic approach by outsourcing mobile data to cloud. Procedia Comput. Sci. **47**, 480–485 (2015)
6. Gennaro, R., Gentry, C., Parno, B.: Non-interactive verifiable computing: outsourcing computation to untrusted workers. In: Rabin, T. (ed.) CRYPTO 2010. LNCS, vol. 6223, pp. 465–482. Springer, Heidelberg (2010)
7. CertiVox/MIRACL, https://github.com/CertiVox/MIRACL. Accessed 20 Feb 2016
8. Hyla, T., Maćków, W., Pejaś, J.: Implicit and explicit certificates-based encryption scheme. In: Saeed, K., Snášel, V. (eds.) CISIM 2014. LNCS, vol. 8838, pp. 651–666. Springer, Heidelberg (2014)
9. Al-Riyami, S.S., Paterson, K.G.: Certificateless public key cryptography. In: Laih, C.-S. (ed.) ASIACRYPT 2003. LNCS, vol. 2894, pp. 452–473. Springer, Heidelberg (2003)
10. Hohenberger, S., Lysyanskaya, A.: How to securely outsource cryptographic computations. In: Kilian, J. (ed.) TCC 2005. LNCS, vol. 3378, pp. 264–282. Springer, Heidelberg (2005)

11. Chevallier-Mames, B., Coron, J.-S., McCullagh, N., Naccache, D., Scott, M.: Secure delegation of elliptic-curve pairing. In: Gollmann, D., Lanet, J.-L., Iguchi-Cartigny, J. (eds.) CARDIS 2010. LNCS, vol. 6035, pp. 24–35. Springer, Heidelberg (2010)
12. Chen, X., Susilo, W., Li, J., Wong, D.S., Ma, J., Tang, S., Tang, Q.: Efficient algorithms for secure outsourcing of bilinear pairings. Theor. Comput. Sci. **562**, 112–121 (2015)
13. Galbraith, S.D., Paterson, K.G., Smart, N.P.: Pairings for cryptographers. Discrete Appl. Math. **156**, 3113–3121 (2008)
14. Lu, Y., Li, J., Xiao, J.: Constructing efficient certificate-based encryption with paring. J. Comput. **4**(1), 19–26 (2009)
15. Lai, J., Kou, W.: Self-generated-certificate public key encryption without pairing. In: Okamoto, T., Wang, X. (eds.) PKC 2007. LNCS, vol. 4450, pp. 476–489. Springer, Heidelberg (2007)

The Design and Implementation
of Multi-dimensional Bloom Filter
Storage Matrix

Fei Xu[1,2], Pinxin Liu[1(✉)], Jianfeng Yang[1], and Jing Xu[1]

[1] Law School, Renmin University of China, Beijing, China
xufei@iie.ac.cn, liupinxin@263.net,
yangjianfengchina@126.com, tourist215512@163.com
[2] Institute of Information Engineering,
Chinese Academy of Sciences, Beijing, China

Abstract. Bloom filter is a bit array (a one-dimensional storage structure) that provides a compact representation for a set of data, which can be used to answer the membership query in an efficient manner with possible false positives. It has a lot of applications in many areas. In this paper, we further improve Bloom filter by proposing the use of multi-dimensional matrix to replace the one-dimensional structure. Based on our N-dimensional matrix structure, we propose four kinds of filter implementation, namely OFFF, ZFFF, WOFF, FFF (we refer it as Feng Filter). We prove that the false positive rate of our method is lower than the traditional one-dimensional Bloom filter. We also present the detailed implementation of our proposed filter. The traditional Bloom filter can be regarded as a special case of the Feng Filter.

Keywords: Bloom filter · Multi-dimensional · Storage metrix

1   Introduction

Information representation and query processing are two core problems of many computer applications, and are often associated with each other. Representation means organizing information according to some formats and mechanisms, and making information operable by the corresponding method. Query processing means making a decision about whether an element with a given set of attribute values belongs to a given set. For this purpose, Bloom filter (BF) can be an appropriate candidate.

Bloom filter, conceived by Burton Howard Bloom in 1970, is a simple space-efficient randomized data structure for representing a set in order to support membership queries [1]. BFs may yield a small number of false positives in answering membership queries; that is, an element might be incorrectly recognized as a member of the set. Although Bloom filters allow false positives, for many applications, the

---

This work is supported by Beijing Natural Science Foundation (4164089).

J. Chen et al. (Eds.): NSS 2016, LNCS 9955, pp. 530–538, 2016.
DOI: 10.1007/978-3-319-46298-1_35

savings in space and efficient searching time (constant time) outweigh this drawback when the probability of false positives can be made sufficiently small.

Initially, BF was applied to database applications, spell checkers and file operations. In recent years, BFs have received a lot of attention in networking applications, such as peer-to-peer applications, resource routing, security, and web caching [5, 6]. A survey on the applications of Bloom filters in distributed systems can be found in [7]. BFs are also being used in practice. For instance, Google Chrome uses a Bloom filter to represent a blacklist of dangerous URLs.

The idea of a standard BF is to allocate a vector A of m bits, initially all set to 0, for representing a set S = {x_1, x_2, ..., x_n} of n elements. The BF uses k independent hash functions h_1, h_2, ..., h_k, each with range of {0, ..., m − 1}. A BF is constructed as follows. Each element x in S is hashed by k independent hash functions. All bits at positions hi(x) in A are set to 1. A particular position in the vector A may be set to 1 multiple times, but only the first time has an effect, i.e., it is set to 1. In the querying phase, to query for an element y, we check the bits at position hi(y) for all i = 1, 2, ..., k. If any of these bits are 0, the element is definitely not in the set. Otherwise, either the element is in the set, or the bits have by chance been set to 1 during the insertion of other elements, resulting in a false positive.

The contributions of this paper can be summarized as follows:

Multi-dimensional Storage Filter: we proposed a multi-dimensional Storage filter, which is an improvement of the traditional one-dimensional Bloom filter in terms of both the accuracy and also the efficiency.

Four Different Mappings: Based of the different mapping methods, we proposed four different kinds of Feng Filter: One First Feng Filter (OFFF), Zero First Feng Filter (ZFFF), Whole One Feng Filter (WOFF), and Function Feng Filter (FFF). Users can choose one of the four filters based on the application(s).

False Positive rate Analysis: We formally analyzed the false positive rate of Feng Filter and showed that Feng Filter has much lower false positive rate in some cases.

System Design of Feng Filter: We provide the design and details of the implementation of the proposed Feng Filter.

Section 2 presents the basic idea, operation and design of Feng filter. Section 3 describes four different implementation of Feng filter while Sect. 4 analyzes the positive rate of Feng filter. Section 5 concludes this paper and provides some possible future works for Feng Filter.

2 Feng Filter

In this section, we introduce the basic idea of Feng Filter. We first will discuss the basic idea of multi-dimensional filter and the preconditions. Then, we will provide the details of the basic operations.

2.1   Basic Idea

Feng filter storage architecture is a multi-dimensional storage matrix, which is a combination of different levels of storage space. One dimension of the storage matrix represents the bit vector array. Assume that we have n elements in the data set. In Feng filter, using k hash functions, the n elements are mapped to a storage matrix M with N dimensions of size of m bits. The mapping is based on the followings: k hash functions, N dimensional storage matrix, a perfect hash location adjust function L and the given mapping relation. There are four different mapping methods, which we will discuss in the next section of this paper. In each dimension, the row being selected is based on the perfect hash location adjust function L, and the k hash functions. When there is a position in M that meets the required mapping function, then this position will be set to 1 from 0. Nothing will be done otherwise. Figure 1 shows the basic idea of Feng Filter.

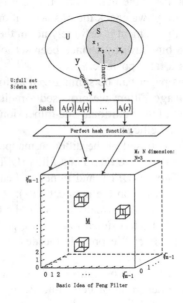

Fig. 1. Basic idea of Feng filter

There are several requirements that we need to make clear about the relation between original data set and the data in set S.

1. The relation between original data set and the data in set S.

Elements are given based on the true situation, there is no similarity between any two elements. Elements in the set can be equal to each other or otherwise it will not affect the outcome of the filter.

2. Independence of the k hash functions.

One hash function on an element will not affect the other hash function. That is to say, for a given hash function k, there is no certain mapping relationship, in which function f represents the hash mapping relation. All hash functions have the same extract range.

3. Bits in multi-dimensional storage matrix M can be set to 0 or 1:

0 represents that after one mapping relation, this bit is not selected while 1 represents that after a hash function, this bit is occupied. The bit in the matrix can only be set to 0 or 1. At first, all the bits in matrix M are set to 0. With the operation of the hash function and mapping, some bits will be set to 1.

4. Multi-dimensional storage matrix M.

In real implementation, one can choose to use two-dimensional matrix, then matrix M is two-dimensional. If they need to use three-dimensional matrix, then matrix M is three-dimensional. For simplicity, we suggest to choose a fixed dimensional for M. and each dimension of matrix M is equal to the other dimensions.

5. Perfect hash location adjust function L.

For each k input position, the position needs to be divided into N group without any changes to the k hash function results. For each group, there are k/N elements. The range of the results of function L is restricted to $[0, m)]$. We designed the prefect hash location adjust function; the range is from $[0, m - 1]$. We organize the k hash results based on their values, and then divide them into N groups. The smallest is allocated to the first group, which represents the first position in the first dimension. The second smallest is allocated to the second dimension... the n smallest is allocated to the n dimension. Then the $n + 1$ smallest will then be allocated to the second place in the first dimension again, and so on. Totally there will be k/N elements in each group. This is how we get all the bits in the matrix.

6. The mapping to matrix M is a strong relation.

Strong relation means that in a multi-dimensional storage matrix, there is a one to one mapping relationship between the chosen place and the k hash functions, where n represents the n dimensions, i represents the i-th position in dimension n which is chosen. In OFFF, WOFF and FFF, as we will discuss later, there is a strong relation needed. There can be exceptions too. For example, in ZFFF, weak relation is also allowed. We will discuss the detailed mapping relation in the following sections. We introduced a strong relation, to avoid the collision caused by mapping. But weak relation may better make use of the space in the matrix.

7. Basic relations required.

The dimension N, hash function number k, storage matrix M space m, and original dataset S and element number should follow the basic requirements. (1) N, k, m, n are all positive integers; (2) k is a multiple of N.

2.2   Basic Operations

There are two basic operations in Feng Filter: Insert and Query. When you need to insert element x into the storage matrix M of Feng Filter, we follow the steps below:

- Apply k hash functions on x, and get k hash results.
- For the k hash results, use the perfect hash location adjust function L to get k locations, and then divide the k locations into N groups, and each group will be mapped to the first dimension, second dimension, and so on. There are k/N elements in each group, which means k/N positions in each dimension.
- Put k/N positions of the N dimensions as input, and based on the mapping function, we obtain the positions in the N dimensions.
- Set each bit position of matrix M into 1 based on the results of the related function.

Query is to decide if a given element y is in the original data set or not. We can do that by checking if y is in the Feng Filter storage. The basic process of element query is as follows:

- Apply k hash functions on y to get k hash results.
- For the k hash results, use the perfect hash location adjust function L to get k locations, and then divide the k locations into N groups, and each group will be mapped to the first dimension, second dimension, and so on. There are k/N elements in each group, which means k/N positions in each dimension.
- Put k/N positions of the N dimensions as input, and based on the mapping function, we will get the positions of the N dimensions.
- Check the related position in the matrix M to see if all bits in these positions are 1, if the answer is no, that means element y is definitely not in the original dataset S. If the answer if yes, that means under the reasonable false positive rate, this element is in original dataset S.

After the discussing of the basic idea and basic operations of Feng Filter, the following two pictures show the detailed design and the UML class diagram of Feng Filter (Fig. 2).

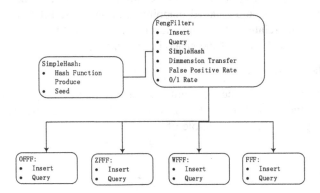

Fig. 2. Design of Feng filter

3 Mapping Relation of Feng Filter

Element x after applying k hash functions, and the operation of perfect hash location adjust function L, will be divided into different groups,

$$\left\{ \left\{ L_{11}, L_{12}, \cdots, L_{1\frac{k}{N}} \right\}, \left\{ L_{21}, L_{22}, \cdots, L_{2\frac{k}{N}} \right\}, \cdots, \left\{ L_{N1}, L_{N2}, \cdots, L_{N\frac{k}{N}} \right\} \right\}$$

which correspond to the N dimensional matrix. In which L_{ij} represents the j-th position in the dimension. The input of mapping relation is the positions of these N groups. Feng Filter has four different implementations based on the four different mapping algorithms, which will be described below.

3.1 One First Feng Filter, OFFF

For the positions of N group mapping values, starting with the smallest L_{i1}, and set all the related positions of $M(L_{11}, L_{21}, \cdots, L_{N1})$ as 1, after that, the second round will start with L_{i2}, and set all $M(L_{12}, L_{22}, \cdots, L_{N2})$ as 1, the third round will start with L_{i3}, ..., and so on, until all the numbers are being set. In the process of setting some positions of the N dimensional storage matrix M as 0 or 1, the mapping relation is based on the ascending order of the mapping relation, and not every position will be set to 1. So we name this type as One First Feng Filter, OFFF.

3.2 Zero First Feng Filter, ZFFF

For the positions of N group mapping values, starting with the smallest L_{i1}, consider all the related positions of $M(L_{11}, L_{21}, \cdots, L_{N1})$, check if the position is 0, if yes, set this bit into 1, after that, the second round will start with L_{i2}, and set all $M(L_{12}, L_{22}, \cdots, L_{N2})$ into 1, the third round will start with L_{i3}, ..., and so on, until all the numbers are being set accordingly. In the process of setting the N dimensional storage matrix M as 0 or 1, the mapping relation is based on the ascending order of the mapping relation, and we will check if it is 0 or not. So we name this type of Feng Filter as Zero First Feng Filter (ZFFF).

3.3 Whole One Feng Filter, WOFF

For the positions of N group mapping values, set the entire bits in the cross position as 1, that is to say, to set all the following positions into 1.

$$M(L_{11}, L_{21}, \cdots, L_{N1}), M(L_{12}, L_{21}, \cdots, L_{N1}), \ldots, M(L_{1N}, L_{21}, \cdots, L_{N1})$$
$$M(L_{11}, L_{22}, \cdots, L_{N1}), M(L_{12}, L_{22}, \cdots, L_{N1}), \ldots, M(L_{1N}, L_{22}, \cdots, L_{N1})$$
$$\cdots$$
$$M(L_{11}, L_{2N}, \cdots, L_{NN}), M(L_{12}, L_{2N}, \cdots, L_{NN}), \ldots, M(L_{1N}, L_{2N}, \cdots, L_{NN})$$

In this mapping relation, because during the process of setting the N dimensional storage matrix M as 0 or 1, the mapping relation is based on setting $(k/N)^N$ as 1, So we name this type of Feng Filter as Whole One Feng Filter (WOFF).

3.4   Function Feng Filter, FFF

The mapping relation of Function Feng Filter is based on the specific function. All the three Feng Filters we discussed above can be regarded as a specific case of FFF. We recommend the mapping relation of FFF to be a strong relation. In this mapping relation, Because during the setting process of setting the N dimensional storage matrix M as 0 or 1, the mapping relation is based on the specific function, So we name this type of Feng Filter as Function Feng Filter (FFF).

4   False Positive Rate

In this section we will discuss the false positive rate of the proposed Feng Filter. Take One First Feng Filter (OFFF) as an example, we will present the calculation of False Positive Rate. And we will give out the results of the other three Feng Filter directly.

4.1   OFFF

In one operation, the possibility of one bit in the N dimensional storage matrix M to be set to 1 is $1/m$, and for one bit, the probability of it being set to 0 is $1-1/m$, there are n elements in the original dataset S, and for OFFF, each element in this filter will k/N times operations, to sum up to a total of nk/N, we use p to represent the possibility of one bit still is 0 in the two dimensional storage matrix M after nk/N times operation, then:

$$p = \left(1 - \frac{1}{m}\right)^{\left(\frac{nk}{N}\right)}$$

As we can see, the possibility of this bit to be 1 is $1 - p$.

For a given query element y, to decide if y belongs to Feng Filter, the condition is that after applying k hash functions on y, all the relation k/N is 1, so the false positive function of y in the original dataset is:

$$f_{OFFF} = (1 - p)^{\frac{k}{N}}$$

Put this into the function, we will get the following results.

$$f_{OFFF}(m, n, k, N) = \left(1 - \left(1 - \frac{1}{m}\right)^{\frac{nk}{N}}\right)^{\frac{k}{N}}$$

4.2 ZFFF

$$f_{ZFFF}(m, n, k, N) = \left(1 - \left(1 - \frac{1}{m} \right)^{\frac{nk}{N}} \right)^{\frac{k}{N}}$$

4.3 WFFF

$$f_{WFFF}(m, n, k, N) = \left(1 - \left(1 - \frac{1}{m} \right)^{\left(n\left(\frac{k}{N}\right)^N \right)} \right)^{\left(\frac{k}{N}\right)^N}$$

4.4 FFF

$$f_{FFF}(m, n, k, N) - \left(1 \quad \left(1 - \frac{1}{m} \right)^{nt} \right)^{t}$$

5 Conclusions

In this paper, based on the basic idea of Bloom, we further improve Bloom filter and propose the use of multi-dimensional matrix storage structure as the store structure of the filter. Our method extends the Bloom filter from one-dimensional vector storage into N-dimensional matrix storage. To distinguish them clearly, we further put forward the Feng Filter. From the perspective of the storage structure, the Bloom Filter can be regarded as a special case of the Feng Filter in one-dimensional storage. Our paper gives the definitions and detailed operation algorithms of multi-dimensional filter. Depending on the mapping relationship, we propose four kinds of implementation for Feng filter, namely OFFF, ZFFF, WOFF, FFF. The False Positive Rate of our method is proved to be lower than that of the traditional Bloom Filter.

References

1. Mullin, J.K.: Optimal semijoins for distributed database systems. IEEE Trans. Softw. Eng. **16**(5), 558–560 (1990)
2. Mellroy, M.: Development of a spelling list. IEEE Trans. Software Commun. **30**(1), 91–99 (1982)

3. Mullin, J.K.: Estimating the size of a relational join. Informa. Syst. **18**(3), 189–196 (1993)
4. Manber, U., Wu, S.: An algorithm for approximate membership checking with application to password security. Inform. Process. Lett. **50**(44), 191–197 (1994)
5. Gremilion, L.L.: Designing a Bloom filter for differential file access. Communications of ACM. **25**(9), 600–604 (1982)
6. Bonomi, F., Mitzenmacher, M., Panigraphy, R., et al.: Beyond Bloom filters: from approximate membership checks to approximate state machines. In: Proceedings of ACM SIGCOMM 2006, pp. 315–326. ACM Press, Pisa (2006)
7. Broder, A., Mitzenmacher, M.: Network applications of Bloom filters: a survey. Internet Math. **1**(4), 485–509 (2005)
8. Li, J., Taylor, J., Serban, L., et al.: Self-organization in peer-to-peer system. In: Proceedings of the 10th European SIGOPS Workshop (2002)
9. Cuena-Acuna, F.M., Peery, C., Martin, R.P., et al.: PlantP: using gossiping to build content addressable peer-to-peer information sharing communities. In: Proceedings of 12th IEEE International Symposium on High Performance Distributed Computing, pp. 236–246. IEEE Computer Society (2003)
10. Rhea, S.C., Kubiatowicz, J.: Probabilistic location and routing. In: Proceedings of INFOCOM 2002, pp. 1248–1257. IEEE Computer Society, New York (2002)

Author Index

Printed in the United States
By Bookmasters